Lecture Notes in Computer Science

Lecture Notes in Artificial Intelligence   16094

Founding Editor

Jörg Siekmann

Series Editors

Randy Goebel, *University of Alberta, Edmonton, AB, Canada*
Wolfgang Wahlster, *DFKI, Berlin, Germany*
Zhi-Hua Zhou, *Nanjing University, Nanjing, China*

The series Lecture Notes in Artificial Intelligence (LNAI) was established in 1988 as a topical subseries of LNCS devoted to artificial intelligence.

The series publishes state-of-the-art research results at a high level. As with the LNCS mother series, the mission of the series is to serve the international R & D community by providing an invaluable service, mainly focused on the publication of conference and workshop proceedings and postproceedings.

Giovanni Casini · Besik Dundua · Temur Kutsia
Editors

Logics in Artificial Intelligence

19th European Conference, JELIA 2025
Kutaisi, Georgia, September 1–4, 2025
Proceedings, Part II

Editors
Giovanni Casini ⓘ
CNR - ISTI
Pisa, Italy

Besik Dundua ⓘ
Kutaisi International University
Kutaisi, Georgia

Temur Kutsia ⓘ
Johannes Kepler University Linz
Linz, Austria

ISSN 0302-9743   ISSN 1611-3349 (electronic)
Lecture Notes in Artificial Intelligence
ISBN 978-3-032-04589-8   ISBN 978-3-032-04590-4 (eBook)
https://doi.org/10.1007/978-3-032-04590-4

LNCS Sublibrary: SL7 – Artificial Intelligence

Preface

These two volumes contain the proceedings of the 19th European Conference on Logics in Artificial Intelligence (JELIA 2025), held at Kutaisi International University, Kutaisi, Georgia from September 1 to 4, 2025.

The European Conference on Logics in Artificial Intelligence — Journées Européennes sur la Logique en Intelligence Artificielle (JELIA) — was first held in 1988 as a workshop, in response to the need for a European forum to discuss emerging research in this field. Since then, JELIA has been organized biennially, with its proceedings published in the Springer Lecture Notes in Artificial Intelligence (LNAI) series. Previous editions were hosted in Roscoff, France (1988); Amsterdam, The Netherlands (1990); Berlin, Germany (1992); York, UK (1994); Évora, Portugal (1996); Dagstuhl, Germany (1998); Málaga, Spain (2000); Cosenza, Italy (2002); Lisbon, Portugal (2004); Liverpool, UK (2006); Dresden, Germany (2008); Helsinki, Finland (2010); Toulouse, France (2012); Madeira, Portugal (2014); Larnaca, Cyprus (2016); Rende, Italy (2019); Klagenfurt, Austria (2021, held online due to the COVID-19 pandemic); and Dresden, Germany (2023).

The aim of JELIA is to bring together active researchers interested in all aspects of the use of logics in artificial intelligence, providing a forum to discuss current research, results, challenges, and applications of both a theoretical and practical nature. JELIA seeks to foster connections and encourage the cross-fertilization of ideas among researchers from diverse disciplines, between academia and industry, and between theoreticians and practitioners. Over the years, the conference has attracted growing interest from the scientific community, including increasing participation from researchers outside Europe. Combined with the consistently high technical quality of the contributions, JELIA has evolved into a major biennial forum and a key reference point for the discussion of logic-based approaches to artificial intelligence.

JELIA 2025 received a total of 108 submissions in two formats: 94 long and 14 short papers. Each submission was single-blindly reviewed by three members of the Program Committee. Of the 108 submissions, 44 were accepted - 39 as long papers and 5 as short papers. Among the 41 submissions declared to have a student as the lead author, 17 were accepted for inclusion in the program. All accepted papers were allocated a slot for oral presentation at the conference. This year's conference featured a Special Track on Logics for Explainable and Trustworthy AI, which focused on logic-based approaches to enhancing AI transparency, safety, and trustworthiness. Of the 108 submissions, 19 were submitted to this special track; they underwent the same rigorous review process, resulting in 4 papers being accepted and presented in a dedicated session. The conference program also included three invited talks by Natasha Alechina, Claudia d'Amato, and Andreas Herzig. The abstracts of their talks are included in these proceedings.

JELIA 2025 recognized two outstanding contributions with awards: the Best Paper Award and the Best Student Paper Award, both selected by the Program Committee for their exceptional quality. Each award was accompanied by a prize of 500 euros, generously sponsored by Springer.

We would like to express our sincere gratitude to the members of the Program Committee and the additional reviewers for their efforts in providing fair, thorough, and constructive evaluations of the submitted papers, which is essential for a successful scientific conference. Our thanks also go to all authors who submitted their work, including those whose papers were not accepted: the large number of high-quality submissions on important and timely topics made the selection process particularly competitive. We are grateful to the invited speakers for accepting our invitation and for delivering exceptional talks that greatly enriched the program. Our heartfelt thanks also go to the local organizing committee for their commitment and effort in ensuring that JELIA 2025 was a well-organized and memorable event. Finally, we wish to acknowledge the team behind EasyChair, whose conference management system was invaluable throughout the review process.

July 2025

Giovanni Casini
Besik Dundua
Temur Kutsia

Organization

General Chair

Besik Dundua
Kutaisi International University/Tbilisi State University, Georgia

Program Committee Chairs

Giovanni Casini
CNR - ISTI, Italy

Temur Kutsia
Johannes Kepler University Linz, Austria

Program Committee

Sergio Abriola
Universidad de Buenos Aires, Argentina

Jose Julio Alferes
Universidade NOVA de Lisboa, Portugal

Mario Alviano
University of Calabria, Italy

Leila Amgoud
IRIT - CNRS, France

Grigoris Antoniou
Leeds Beckett University, UK

Carlos Areces
Universidad Nacional de Córdoba, Argentina

Ofer Arieli
Academic College of Tel Aviv-Yaffo, Israel

Dörthe Arndt
TU Dresden, Germany

Franz Baader
TU Dresden, Germany

Alexander Baumgartner
Universidad de O'Higgins, Chile

Peter Baumgartner
CSIRO, Australia

Salem Benferhat
CRIL - CNRS, Université d'Artois, France

Leopoldo Bertossi
SKEMA Business School Canada inc., Canada

Armin Biere
University of Freiburg, Germany

Alexander Bochman
Holon Institute of Technology, Israel

Bart Bogaerts
KU Leuven, Belgium

Richard Booth
Cardiff University, UK

Pedro Cabalar
University of Corunna, Spain

Francesco Calimeri
University of Calabria, Italy

Diego Calvanese
Free University of Bozen-Bolzano, Italy

Franco Alberto Cardillo
CNR - Institute for Computational Linguistics, Italy

David Cerna   Dynatrace Research, Austria / Czech Academy of
                                       Sciences - Institute of Computer Science,
                                       Czechia
Joe Collenette   University of Chester, UK
Silvano Colombo Tosatto   CSIRO, Australia
Mehdi Dastani   Utrecht University, The Netherlands
Marc Denecker   KU Leuven, Belgium
Martín Diéguez   University of Angers, France
Martin Diller   TU Dresden, Germany
Dragan Doder   Utrecht University, The Netherlands
Didier Dubois   IRIT-CNRS, France
Besik Dundua   Kutaisi International University/Tbilisi State
                                       University, Georgia
Wolfgang Dvořák   TU Wien, Austria
Thomas Eiter   TU Wien, Austria
Stefan Ellmauthaler   Echo Intelligence GmbH, Austria
Esra Erdem   Sabanci University, Turkey
Santiago Escobar   Universitat Politècnica de València, Spain
Wolfgang Faber   University of Klagenfurt, Austria
Eduardo Fermé   Universidade da Madeira, Portugal
Masood Feyzbakhsh Rankooh   University of Helsinki, Finland
Johannes K. Fichte   Linköping University, Sweden
Michael Fisher   University of Manchester, UK
Tommaso Flaminio   Artificial Intelligence Research Institute, IIIA -
                                       CSIC, Spain
Gerhard Friedrich   University of Klagenfurt, Austria
Maurice Funk   Universität Leipzig, Germany
Sarah Alice Gaggl   TU Dresden, Germany
Marco Garapa   Universidade da Madeira, Portugal
Tobias Geibinger   Vienna University of Technology, Austria
Alessandro Gianola   INESC-ID/Instituto Superior Técnico,
                                       Universidade de Lisboa, Portugal
Laura Giordano   Università del Piemonte Orientale, Italy
Marianna Girlando   University of Amsterdam, The Netherlands
Lluis Godo   Artificial Intelligence Research Institute, IIIA -
                                       CSIC, Spain
Lucía Gómez Álvarez   Inria, France
Ricardo Gonçalves   Universidade NOVA de Lisboa, Portugal
Jonas Philipp Haldimann   TU Wien, Austria; University of Cape Town and
                                       CAIR, South Africa
Markus Hecher   French National Centre for Scientific Research
                                       (CNRS), UMR 8188, Université d'Artois
                                       (CRIL), France

Luisa Herrmann	TU Dresden, Germany
Jesse Heyninck	Open Universiteit, The Netherlands
Aaron Hunter	British Columbia Institute of Technology, Canada
Anthony Hunter	University College London, UK
Souhila Kaci	LIRMM, University of Montpellier, France
Antonis Kakas	University of Cyprus, Cyprus
Cezary Kaliszyk	University of Melbourne, Australia
Gabriele Kern-Isberner	Technische Universität Dortmund, Germany
Hiroyuki Kido	Cardiff University, UK
Matthias Knorr	Universidade NOVA de Lisboa, Portugal
Jedrzej Kołodziejski	TU Dortmund, Germany
Boris Konev	University of Liverpool, UK
Sébastien Konieczny	CRIL - CNRS, France
Roman Kontchakov	Birkbeck, University of London, UK
Markus Krötzsch	TU Dresden, Germany
Davide Lanti	Free University of Bozen-Bolzano, Italy
Joao Leite	Universidade NOVA de Lisboa, Portugal
Vladimir Lifschitz	University of Texas at Austin, USA
Anela Lolic	TU Wien, Austria
Emiliano Lorini	IRIT, France
Sanja Lukumbuzya	TU Wien, Austria
Quentin Manière	Universität Leipzig, Germany
Marco Maratea	University of Genova, Italy
Pierre Marquis	Université d'Artois, CNRS, CRIL - Institut Universitaire de France, France
Maria Vanina Martinez	Artificial Intelligence Research Institute (IIIA - CSIC), Spain
Andrea Mazzullo	Free University of Bozen-Bolzano, Italy
Arne Meier	Leibniz Universität Hannover, Germany
Thomas Meyer	University of Cape Town and CAIR, South Africa
Loizos Michael	Open University of Cyprus, Cyprus
Angelo Montanari	University of Udine, Italy
Michael Morak	University of Klagenfurt, Austria
Johannes Oetsch	Jönköping University, Sweden
Manuel Ojeda-Aciego	University of Málaga, Spain
Cem Okulmus	Paderborn University, Germany
Nicola Olivetti	LSIS, Aix-Marseille University, France
Juri Opitz	University of Zurich, Switzerland
Magdalena Ortiz	Vienna University of Technology, Austria
Stipe Pandzic	University of Milan, Italy
Nina Pardal	University of Huddersfield, UK
Pere Pardo	University of Luxembourg, Luxembourg

Xavier Parent	TU Wien, Austria
Francesco Parisi	University of Calabria, Italy
David Pearce	Universidad Politécnica de Madrid, Spain
Rafael Peñaloza	University of Milano-Bicocca, Italy
Luís Moniz Pereira	Universidade NOVA de Lisboa, Portugal
Laurent Perrussel	IRIT - Université de Toulouse, France
Ramon Pino Perez	Université d'Artois, France
Nico Potyka	Cardiff University, UK
Carlo Proietti	National Research Council of Italy (CNR) - Institute for Computational Linguistics (ILC), Italy
Antonio Rago	Imperial College London, UK
Anna Rapberger	Imperial College London, UK
Maurício Reis	Universidade da Madeira, Portugal
Francesco Ricca	University of Calabria, Italy
Aldo Ricioppo	University of Cyprus, Cyprus
Tjitze Rienstra	Maastricht University, The Netherlands
Giuliano Rosella	University of Turin, Italy
Sebastian Rudolph	TU Dresden, Germany
Mikheil Rukhaia	Tbilisi State University, Georgia
Irene Russo	CNR - Institute of Computational Linguistics, Italy
Chiaki Sakama	Wakayama University, Japan
Uli Sattler	University of Manchester, UK
Kai Sauerwald	FernUniversität in Hagen, Germany
Andrea Schaerf	University of Udine, Italy
Wolfgang Schreiner	Johannes Kepler University Linz, Austria
François Schwarzentruber	École normale supérieure de Lyon, France
Gerardo Simari	Universidad Nacional del Sur and CONICET, Argentina
Guillermo R. Simari	Universidad del Sur, Argentina
Mantas Šimkus	TU Vienna, Austria
Marija Slavkovik	University of Bergen, Norway
Umberto Straccia	CNR - ISTI, Italy
Hannes Strass	TU Dresden, Germany
Michael Thielscher	University of New South Wales, Australia
Matthias Thimm	FernUniversität in Hagen, Germany
David Toman	University of Waterloo, Canada
Anni-Yasmin Turhan	Paderborn University, Germany
Sara Ugolini	Artificial Intelligence Research Institute, IIIA - CSIC, Spain
Mauro Vallati	University of Huddersfield, UK

Leon van der Torre	University of Luxembourg, Luxembourg
Ivan Varzinczak	Université Sorbonne Paris Nord, France
Joost Vennekens	Vrije Universiteit Brussel, Belgium
Srdjan Vesic	CRIL, CNRS – Université d'Artois, France
Carlos Viegas Damásio	Universidade NOVA de Lisboa, Portugal
Miikka Vilander	Tampere University, Finland
Mateu Villaret	Universitat de Girona, Spain
Johannes P. Wallner	TU Graz, Austria
Frank Wolter	University of Liverpool, UK
Stefan Woltran	TU Wien, Austria

Organization Chair

| Mikheil Rukhaia | Tbilisi State University, Georgia |

Technical Chair

| Nika Gagua | Kutaisi International University, Georgia |

Organization Committee

Matthias Baaz	TU Wien, Austria
Mariam Gamsakhurdia	TU Wien, Austria
Revaz Grigolia	Tbilisi State University, Georgia
Lia Kurtanidze	Georgian National University, Georgia
Aleksandre Maskharashvili	University of Illinois Urbana-Champaign, USA
Konstantine Pkhakadze	GTU Research Institute for Cultural Protection and Technological Development of Georgian State Languages, Georgia
Levan Uridia	Tbilisi State University, Georgia

Additional Reviewers

Iosif Apostolakis	Pietro Galliani
Lars Bengel	Didier Galmiche
Aysu Bogatarkan	Lukas Gerlach
Cristhian Ariel David Deagustini	Maksim Gladyshev
Francesco Di Cosmo	Miika Hannula

Djordje Markovic
Oliviero Nardi
Iliana Petrova
Davide Emilio Quadrellaro
Luis Angel Rodriguez Reiners

Francisco Simoes
Daniele Theseider Dupre
Dieter Vandesande
Giovanni Varricchione
Baturay Yılmaz

Logic for Safe Reinforcement Learning

Natasha Alechina

Open University Netherlands and Flanders/Utrecht University, the Netherlands
n.a.alechina@uu.nl

Abstract. Reinforcement learning is famously about learning by trial and error, the agent getting feedback from the environment in the form of rewards. However, it is often quite difficult to specify a reward function to ensure that the learned behaviour is what the designer intended. It is also difficult to ensure that the agent's behaviour is always safe, especially when training is on- rather than offline. I will talk about using logic to provide declarative specification of desired/safe behaviours and ensuring that the learned behaviour conforms to those specifications. In particular, I will talk about how to block unsafe actions both during training and after deployment of the agent.

Tackling Semantics-Aware Machine Learning and Explanations for Knowledge Graph Refinement

Claudia d'Amato

University of Bari, Italy
claudia.damato@uniba.it

Abstract. Knowledge Graphs (KGs) are receiving increasing attention from both academia and industry, as they represent a source of graph-based structured knowledge of unprecedented dimension, to be exploited in a multitude of application domains and research fields. Despite their wide usage, it is well known that KGs suffer from incompleteness and noise, being the result of a complex building process. Significant research efforts are currently devoted to improve the coverage and quality of existing KGs via adopting numeric-based Machine Learning (ML) solutions that have proved to scale on very large KGs. They are usually grounded on the graph structure and they generally consist of series of numbers without any obvious human interpretation, thus possibly affecting the interpretability, the explainability and sometimes the trustworthiness of the results. Nevertheless, KGs may rely on expressive representation languages, e.g. RDFS and OWL (ultimately grounded on Description Logics) that are also endowed with deductive reasoning capabilities, but both expressiveness and reasoning are most of the time disregarded by the majority of the numeric methods that have been developed so far. In this talk, the role and the added value that the semantics may have for ML solutions, which include symbolic approaches, will be argued. Additionally, the importance of taking into account semantics when computing explanations for tasks such as link prediction will be addressed. Hence, the research directions on empowering ML and explanation solutions by injecting background knowledge will be presented jointly with the analysis of the most urgent issues that need to be solved.

It is Possible! Distance Semantics for Modal Belief Revision

Andreas Herzig

IRIT, CNRS, Université de Toulouse, France
herzig@irit.fr

Abstract. The belief revision literature only contains a few approaches with a modal logic basis. This talk discusses how the Alchourron-Gärdenfors-Makinson (AGM) approach to belief revision can be extended from propositional logic to modal logic S5. We propose three new rationality postulates involving the modal operator of possibility $\diamond$:

(M1) If $\varphi \wedge \diamond\mu$ is consistent, then $\varphi * \mu \vdash \diamond\varphi$.

(M2) If $\psi \wedge \diamond\mu$ is consistent, then $\varphi \vdash \psi$ implies $\varphi * \diamond\mu \vdash \psi$, for propositional μ.

(M3) If $\psi \wedge \diamond\mu$ is consistent, then $\varphi \vdash \diamond\psi$ implies $\varphi * \mu \vdash \diamond\psi$, for propositional μ.

The associated distance semantics is in terms of a lexicographic ordering that lifts the Hamming distance from a distance between valuations to a distance between pointed S5 models. Based on this account, we revisit a consequence of the AGM approach that has been much debated in knowledge representation, namely that the revisions of $p \wedge q$ and $p \wedge (p \rightarrow q)$ should be identical. We show that the problem disappears if one replaces material implication $\varphi \rightarrow \psi$ by strict implication $\varphi \succ \psi$. The latter can be expressed in modal logic as the necessity of material implication, that is, as $\Box(\varphi \rightarrow \psi)$.

The talk is based on joint work with Carlos Aguilera-Ventura and Jonathan Ben-Naim and is based on our paper "Minimal Change in Modal Logic S5" (Proc. AAAI 2025) and ongoing work.

Contents – Part II

Temporal Reasoning

Theorem Proving

Contents – Part I

Deontic Reasoning

Description Logics and Ontological Reasoning

Higher-order and Non-classical Logics

Logic Programming and Answer Set Programming

Non-monotonic Reasoning and Belief Change

Comparing Dialectical Systems: Contradiction and Counterexample in Belief Change

Uri Andrews[1]($\boxtimes$)(iD) and Luca San Mauro[2](iD)

[1] University of Wisconsin–Madison, Madison, WI 53706, USA
andrews@math.wisc.edu
[2] University of Bari, Bari, Italy
luca.sanmauro@gmail.com,lucafrancesco.sanmauro@uniba.it
http://math.wisc.edu/~andrews , https://www.lucasanmauro.com/

Abstract. Dialectical systems are a mathematical formalism for modeling an agent updating a knowledge base seeking consistency. Introduced in the 1970s by Roberto Magari, they were originally conceived to capture how a working mathematician or a research community refines beliefs in the pursuit of truth. Dialectical systems also serve as natural models for the belief change of an automated agent, offering a unifying, computable framework for dynamic belief management. The literature distinguishes three main models of dialectical systems: (d-)dialectical systems based on revising beliefs when they are seen to be inconsistent, p-dialectical systems based on revising beliefs based on finding a counterexample, and q-dialectical systems which can do both.

We answer an open problem in the literature by proving that q-dialectical systems are strictly more powerful than p-dialectical systems, which are themselves known to be strictly stronger than (d-)dialectical systems. This result highlights the complementary roles of counterexample and contradiction in automated belief revision, and thus also in the reasoning processes of mathematicians and research communities.

Keywords: Belief change · Dialectical systems · Limiting belief sets

1 Introduction

The question of how a rational agent updates their beliefs in response to new information is fundamental to artificial intelligence research and central to the field of belief revision. Belief revision, surveyed e.g. in [8], systematically investigates the logical and epistemological principles guiding changes in an agent's beliefs.

Modern belief revision is primarily characterized by the AGM framework, introduced by Alchourrón, Gärdenfors, and Makinson [1]. Within AGM, an agent's beliefs are represented as sentences forming a deductively closed *belief set*. *Revision* becomes necessary when a new sentence contradicts the existing

© The Author(s), under exclusive license to Springer Nature Switzerland AG 2026
G. Casini et al. (Eds.): JELIA 2025, LNAI 16094, pp. 3–18, 2026.
https://doi.org/10.1007/978-3-032-04590-4_1

belief set. To preserve consistency, AGM incorporates an initial step known as *contraction*. Central to this step is the concept of a *remainder*, defined as the family of inclusion-maximal subsets of a given belief set that are consistent with the new sentence which the agent aims to incorporate. Further refinement is achieved through *epistemic entrenchment*, a partial ordering reflecting the epistemic values the agent assigns to the elements of the belief set, thus determining which beliefs the agent is more willing to abandon, if needed. AGM's principal innovation, *partial meet contraction*, leverages epistemic entrenchment to select among maximal consistent subsets, ensuring minimal informational loss.

Despite its theoretical elegance, the AGM model presupposes idealized agents endowed with unrealistic cognitive abilities. Specifically, for sufficiently expressive logical languages—including those susceptible to Gödelian incompleteness phenomena—determining whether a belief set is consistent with a given sentence is generally undecidable. Consequently, the computation of remainders becomes intractable, yet classical AGM-based revision procedures assume these operations to be executable in a single step. Recognizing these limitations has spurred interest in alternative frameworks better aligned with realistic computational constraints (see, e.g., [7, 10, 11, 15–17, 23]).

In this paper, we investigate a distinctive class of frameworks known as *dialectical systems*—along with their natural variants—which are well-suited to model the *internal* processes by which an agent arrives at a consistent belief state, in contrast to the *external* revision operations characteristic of AGM-style approaches. These systems avoid reliance on unrealistic assumptions and provide a computational perspective on belief formation. Dialectical systems also offer algorithmic models for a range of problems in artificial intelligence, such as extracting a consistent subset from an inconsistent knowledge base, or capturing a single step of belief revision in the AGM tradition. These and related applications are discussed in detail in Sect. 3.

Dialectical systems, originating from the work of Roberto Magari and his school in the 1970s [6, 12, 19, 20] (alongside the conceptually related Jeroslow's experimental logics [14, 18]), were initially proposed to model the evolution of real mathematical theories and the process of discovery by a working mathematician or an entire mathematical community. These systems explicitly employ trial-and-error methodologies, where *arguments* (or *axioms*, following Magari's terminology) are provisionally accepted and subsequently revised in response to emerging inconsistencies—events which are inherently unpredictable by computational means. Recently revived through the lens of computability theory [2–4], dialectical systems have re-emerged as fertile ground for contemporary investigation.

In this paper, we address an open problem concerning the comparative expressive power of natural variants of dialectical systems, elucidating connections between two complimentary forms of performing belief change. To contextualize this, we briefly describe dialectical systems, reserving formal definitions for Sect. 2.

In essence, a dialectical system operates via a consequence operator which acts, stage by stage, upon a collection of provisionally accepted arguments. At each stage, such a collection of arguments expands by incorporating new arguments drawn from a computable stream. Upon encountering *contradictions*, a contraction procedure, guided by a naturally defined epistemic entrenchment ordering, restores consistency by selectively removing problematic arguments. The expressive strength of the system is determined by the set of arguments eventually accepted, which constitutes the system's limiting belief set.

The p-dialectical and the q-dialectical systems, introduced and thoroughly investigated in [2–4], enhance basic dialectical systems by incorporating an argument replacement mechanism triggered by the emergence of *counterexamples*. Unlike contradictions, which lead solely to the removal of problematic arguments, counterexamples make it possible to retain part of the informational content of a discarded argument by *replacing* it with an alternative. For instance, if the argument a asserts that "all prime numbers are odd", the counterexample triggered by the prime number 2 prompts a replacement such as "all prime numbers greater than 2 are odd".

In p-dialectical systems, the consequence operator produces only counterexamples, so replacement is always required when contraction occurs. In contrast, q-dialectical systems may produce both counterexamples and contradictions, with replacement occurring in the former case and simple removal in the latter.

Prior work [4] established that both p- and q-dialectical systems surpass basic dialectical systems in expressive power but left open (see [2, Problem 2.3]) the relative expressiveness between the two variants. In Sect. 4, we solve this problem by showing that q-dialectical systems possess strictly greater expressive power than p-dialectical systems. This suggests that the ability to perform contractions both with and without replacement enhances the capabilities of rational agents. Our proof employs techniques from computability theory, specifically the finite injury priority method. Finally, Sect. 5 elaborates on implications of these findings for broader discussions in the belief revision literature.

2   Background

For any set X, we denote by $P(X)$ the *power set* of X: i.e., the collection of all subsets of X. By $P^{\text{fin}}(X)$, we denote the collection of finite subsets of X. A function f is acyclic if $f^n(x) \neq x$ for every $n \geq 1$ and x. Here $f^n(x)$ represents the nth iterate of f applied to x.

A *string* is a finite sequence of elements from a given set. For a string σ, $|\sigma|$ denotes its length; $\sigma(n)$ denotes its nth element; and $\sigma \upharpoonright_k$ denotes the string formed by taking the k initial elements of σ. If a string τ coincides with $\sigma \upharpoonright_k$, for some k, we write $\tau \preceq \sigma$ and say that τ is a *prefix* of σ. Finally, the string $\sigma^\frown \tau$ denotes the string formed by concatenating σ and τ.

We often make reference to (partial) *computable functions*. These are the (partial) functions computed by a Turing machine. We use a standard indexing where φ_e is the partial computable function whose instruction-set is encoded by the number e. The *computably enumerable* (c.e. sets) are the ranges of partial computable functions.

2.1   Consequence and Approximated Consequence Operators

Our agents will revise their beliefs in response to seeing either a contradiction or counterexample arise from the set of arguments that they currently accept. In aiming to model realistic reasoning, we do *not* assume that it is immediately evident whether a given set of arguments is contradictory or admits a counterexample. As shown by Gödel's incompleteness theorems [13,22], even in highly idealized or extremely simple settings, determining the inconsistency of a set of statements is as hard as solving the Halting Problem. It is therefore completely unrealistic to expect either an automated reasoner or a working mathematician to reliably determine whether a belief set is consistent. Instead, we adopt the notion of an approximated consequence operator, whereby a reasoner observes, over time, an increasing sequence of consequences derived from their arguments. If the arguments are inconsistent, a contradiction will eventually be revealed at some finite stage (corresponding to a halting computation); however, no finite stage can ever certify consistency, as this would amount to verifying that a contradiction never arises (which corresponds to proving that a computation never halts).

Our consequence operators include two additional logical symbols: $\bot$, representing a contradiction, and $\lozenge$, representing a counterexample. In many logical systems—arithmetic being a standard example—the statement $0 = 1$ is conventionally used to denote falsity, thereby playing the role of $\bot$. To maintain full generality in our framework, we introduce distinct symbols for contradiction and counterexample, without presupposing any specific properties of the set of arguments $\mathcal{A}$.

Definition 1. *Let $\mathcal{A}$ be a non-empty set. A* Tarskian consequence operator *on $\mathcal{A}$ is a function H^∞ from $P(\mathcal{A})$ to $P(\mathcal{A} \cup \{\bot, \lozenge\})$ satisfying the following conditions, for all $F, G \in P(\mathcal{A})$,*

- *(Monotony) $F \subseteq G$ implies $H^\infty(F) \subseteq H^\infty(G)$;*
- *(Inclusion) $F \subseteq H^\infty(F)$;*
- *(Iteration) $H^\infty(H^\infty(F) \cap \mathcal{A}) = H^\infty(F)$.*

An approximated consequence operator *on $\mathcal{A}$ is a computable function H from $\mathbb{N} \times P^{fin}(\mathcal{A})$ to $P^{fin}(\mathcal{A} \cup \{\bot, \lozenge\})$ satisfying the following, for all $n \in \mathbb{N}$ and $F, G \in P^{fin}(\mathcal{A})$,*

- *$F \subseteq G$ implies $H(n, F) \subseteq H(n, G)$;*
- *$F \subseteq H(n, F) \subseteq H(n + 1, F)$;*
- *letting $H^\infty(Y) := \bigcup_{n \in \mathbb{N}, F \subseteq Y} H(n, F)$, we have that H^∞ is a Tarskian consequence operator on $\mathcal{A}$.*

2.2   Representing Current Beliefs and Operations of Revision

In a dialectical system, our agent forms beliefs about a countably infinite set of arguments $\mathcal{A}$. At each stage s the agent's current belief state is represented by a string σ_s of elements from $\mathcal{A} \cup \{*\}$. In each position, the string σ_s either contains an argument from $\mathcal{A}$ or will contain the placeholder symbol $*$. The presence of $*$ at a given position indicates that the agent has encountered a reason to reject the corresponding argument, whereas the presence of the argument itself indicates continued belief in its truth.

For a string σ from $\mathcal{A} \cup \{*\}$, we let $\mathrm{ran}(\sigma)$ be the elements in $\mathcal{A}$ which appear in σ.

Definition 2. *Let $\mathcal{A} := \{a_i : i \in \mathbb{N}\}$ be a set of arguments. We define four operations on strings to model how our agents revise their beliefs about the elements of $\mathcal{A}$:*

- **Contraction:** Given a string σ and a number $k < |\sigma|$, this operation replaces σ with its prefix $\sigma \upharpoonright_k$;
- **Expansion:** Given a string σ, this operation replaces σ with $\sigma^\frown a_{|\sigma|}$;
- **Replacement:** Given a string $\sigma = \tau^\frown a_i$, this operation replaces σ with $\tau^\frown a_j$, for some $j \neq i$;
- **Excision:** Given a string $\sigma = \tau^\frown a_i$, this operation replaces σ by $\tau^\frown *$.

These operations incorporate our two methods for revising the set of arguments in response to either a contradiction or a counterexample. When a contradiction is detected, we apply **Contraction** followed by **Excision** to remove and mark the offending argument as contradictory. In the case of a counterexample, we instead apply **Contraction** followed by **Replacement**, allowing the original argument to be refined rather than discarded outright.

2.3   Dialectical Systems

We begin by formally defining a q-dialectical system. We note that we offer a re-design of the formal exposition of these systems, while ensuring that our definitions remain equivalent to the original ones; see Appendix A of the extended version [5] for a proof of such equivalence. Dialectical systems and p-dialectical systems will then be introduced as special cases of q-dialectical systems[1]. In a nutshell, a q-dialectical system is a framework for iterated belief revision that accommodates both primary sources of revision: contradictions and counterexamples.

Definition 3. *A q-dialectical system Γ is a triple $(\mathcal{A}, H, r)$ where $\mathcal{A}$ is some computable sequence $\{a_i : i \in \mathbb{N}\}$ of arguments, H is an approximated consequence operator on $\mathcal{A}$, and r is a computable acyclic function from $\mathcal{A}$ to $\mathcal{A}$.*

---

[1] This ordering does not reflect the historical development of these notions—dialectical systems were introduced first, followed by q-dialectical and then p-dialectical systems—but we adopt this presentation for greater clarity.

The computable listing of the elements in $\mathcal{A}$ serves to impose an epistemic entrenchment ordering on the arguments, which guides the choice of which remainder to retain (either via excision or replacement) during successive belief revision steps.

Restricting the system to respond to only one type of revision—either contradictions or counterexamples—yields the following variants:

Definition 4. A p-*dialectical system* is a q-*dialectical system in which contradiction are never produced: i.e.,* $\bot \notin H^\infty(\mathcal{A})$. A *dialectical system (in the literature, also called a d-dialectical system) is a q-dialectical system in which counterexamples are never produced: i.e.,* $\lozenge \notin H^\infty(\mathcal{A})$.

The following definition specifies how our systems operate:

Definition 5. Let Γ be a q-dialectical system. A run of Γ is an infinite sequence of strings σ_i^Γ from $\mathcal{A} \cup \{*\}$, defined recursively as follows:
σ_0^Γ is the empty string. Given σ_s^Γ, we define σ_{s+1}^Γ by case distinction:

- Case 1: $\bot$ or $\lozenge$ is in $H(s, \mathrm{ran}(\sigma_s^\Gamma))$. Let k be least so that $\bot$ or $\lozenge$ is in $H(s, \mathrm{ran}(\sigma_s^\Gamma \restriction k))$.
  - If $\bot \in H(s, \mathrm{ran}(\sigma_s^\Gamma \restriction k))$, then $\sigma_{s+1}^\Gamma = (\sigma_s^\Gamma \restriction_{k-1})^\frown *$.
  - Otherwise, $\sigma_{s+1}^\Gamma = (\sigma_s^\Gamma \restriction_{k-1})^\frown r(\sigma_s^\Gamma(k-1))$.
- Case 2: Not case 1. We apply expansion. Let $\sigma_{s+1}^\Gamma = (\sigma_s^\Gamma)^\frown a_{|\sigma_s^\Gamma|}$.

2.4   Limiting Belief Sets

Definition 6. Let Γ be a q-dialectical system, and let $n \in \mathbb{N}$. If there exists some argument $a \in \mathcal{A}$ so that $\sigma_t^\Gamma(n) = a$ for all sufficiently large t, then we write $\lim_s \sigma_s^\Gamma(n)$ for a. If $\lim_s \sigma_s^\Gamma(n)$ exists for every n, then we call Γ loopless.

Note that the determine if a given q-dialectical system is loopless is not a decidable property.

Definition 7. For Γ a q-dialectical system, the limiting belief set of Γ is

$$B_\Gamma = \{a \in \mathcal{A} : \exists n(a = \lim_s \sigma_s^\Gamma(n))\} = \mathrm{ran}(\lim_s \sigma_s^\Gamma).$$

Thus, the limiting belief set of a system Γ comprises the arguments that are ultimately accepted (hence, believed) by the system.

2.5   Related Work

We briefly summarize the most pertinent results from the literature: Firstly, the limiting belief sets are deductively closed.

Theorem 1. ([3, **Lemma 3.14**]). If Γ is a loopless q-dialectical system, then $B_\Gamma = H^\infty(B_\Gamma)$.

Next, dialectical systems, p-dialectical systems, and q-dialectical systems each have limiting belief sets in exactly the c.e. Turing degrees.

Theorem 2. ([4, **Theorem 3.2**]). *For any q-dialectical system Γ, the Turing degree of B_Γ is the Turing degree of a c.e. set. Conversely, if C is a c.e. set, then there is a dialectical system Γ, and a p-dialectical system Γ' so that B_Γ and $B_{\Gamma'}$ are in the same Turing degree as C.*

Despite the complexity of their limiting belief sets being the same, p-dialectical systems are strictly stronger than dialectical systems.

Theorem 3. ([2, **Theorem 2.1 and Corollary 6.11**]). *If Γ is a dialectical system, then B_Γ is the limiting belief set of some p-dialectical system Γ'.*

However, there are p-dialectical systems Γ so that B_Γ is not the limiting belief set of any dialectical system.

In [2], the following question was posed regarding the relative strength of q-dialectical and p-dialectical systems:

Question 1. *([2, Problem 2.3]). Is there a q-dialectical system Γ such that B_Γ is not the limiting belief set of any p-dialectical system?*

In other words, does an iterated belief revision agent *require* the notion of contradiction (i.e., the operation of excision), or is the concept of counterexample (i.e., the operation of replacement) alone sufficient?

In the next section, we resolve this question by proving that q-dialectical systems are strictly more expressive than p-dialectical systems.

3 Applications of Dialectical Systems

We describe natural applications of dialectical systems to problems arising in artificial intelligence, particularly in the management and evolution of knowledge under conditions of inconsistency and change.

Repairing an Inconsistent Knowledge Base: A fundamental application is to the case of an agent equipped with a knowledge base K that may be internally inconsistent. Suppose further that K is equipped with an entrenchment ordering reflecting the relative importance or reliability of its elements. As the agent draws inferences, contradictions or counterexamples may arise. In response, the agent applies excision or revision operations as specified by a corresponding (q-)dialectical system Γ. In many classical models, inconsistency is handled purely syntactically and does not accommodate the notion of counterexamples. In such cases, Γ may be taken as a d-dialectical system. Thus, the dialectical framework provides a theoretical model for an algorithmic procedure to manage and repair inconsistent knowledge bases.

Belief Revision: In belief revision, a consistent knowledge base K must be updated to incorporate a new belief b given a Tarskian consequence operator

H^∞ and an entrenchment order on K, yielding a revised set K' that includes b and retains as much of K as possible while preserving consistency. This is the central concern of the AGM framework. We model this phenomenon within the dialectical model, by defining a dialectical system Γ whose collection of arguments is K with the given entrenchment ordering. We then define H by setting $H(n, F) = H'(n, F \cup \{b\}) \cap (K \cup \{\bot\})$ where H' is an approximated consequence operator limiting to H^∞. The limiting belief set of Γ is a set K' so that K' preserves a subset of K which is consistent with b.

In this setting, we consider a single new argument b which we accept as externally given truth and we revise K accordingly. Essentially the same method allows us to accept a computable sequence of externally given truths (b_i). We simply define $H(n, F) = H'(n, F \cup \{b_i \mid i \le n\}) \cap (K \cup \{\bot\})$.

In each of these applications, dialectical systems offer *a unifying, computable framework for dynamic belief management*. They support the reconciliation of inconsistency, enable rational belief revision, and handle iterative updates in a principled and theoretically grounded manner.

4   The Main Theorem

We construct a q-dialectical system Γ with the aim of ensuring, via diagonalization, that $B_\Gamma \ne B_\Lambda$ for every p-dialectical system Λ. To achieve this, we require a computable enumeration of all p-dialectical systems:

Definition 8. *We fix a computable collection* $\mathcal{A} = \{a_n : n \in \mathbb{N}\}$ *of arguments, and a computable bijection* π *between the natural numbers and the elements of* $P^{fin}(\mathcal{A} \cup \{\emptyset\})$.

Next, for $i_0, i_1, i_2 \in \mathbb{N}$, *we define a partial p-dialectical system* $(\mathcal{A}', H, r)$ *for* (i_0, i_1, i_2) *as follows:*

- $\mathcal{A}' = \{g_n \mid n \in \mathbb{N}\}$, *where* $g_n = a_{\varphi_{i_0}(n)}$;
- $H(s, X) = \bigcup_{t \le s} \pi(\varphi_{i_1}(t, \pi^{-1}(X)))$;
- $r(g_n) = g_{\varphi_{i_2}(n)}$.

For any $m \in \mathbb{N}$ *where* $m = 2^{i_0} 3^{i_1} 5^{i_2} \cdot k$ *where* $2, 3, 5$ *do not divide* k, *we let* Λ_m *be the above partial p-dialectical system for* (i_0, i_1, i_2).

Note that for $j \le 2$, the functions φ_{i_j} may be partial, and the resulting operator H^∞ may fail to satisfy the axioms of a Tarskian consequence operator. Consequently, Λ_m does not represent a valid p-dialectical system for every m. However, every p-dialectical system is represented by some Λ_m for an appropriate $m \in \mathbb{N}$.

Theorem 4. *There is a loopless q-dialectical system* Γ *such that* B_Γ *is not the limiting belief set of any p-dialectical system.*

Proof. We fix $\mathcal{A} = \{a_i \mid i \in \mathbb{N}\}$ and aim to define a q-dialectical system $\Gamma = (\mathcal{A}, H, r)$ by specifying computable functions H and r. In the "construction" phase of the proof, we explicitly describe the algorithms for computing these functions. At each stage s, an instruction to "put a into $H(s, F)$" means that we set $H(s, F) := H(s - 1, F) \cup \{a\}$.

The core idea of the proof is to diagonalize against the possibility that $B_\Gamma = B_{\Lambda_i}$ for any partial p-dialectical system Λ_i. To this end, we introduce an infinite collection of strategies $Strat_i$, one for each $i \in \mathbb{N}$. Each strategy $Strat_i$ will act as a module executed by the algorithm constructing Γ, with the specific goal of ensuring that $B_\Gamma \neq B_{\Lambda_i}$.

To clarify the overall construction, we begin by informally describing how we might construct a q-dialectical system to satisfy a single strategy, $Strat_0$, whose task is to guarantee that $B_\Gamma \neq B_{\Lambda_0}$. For simplicity, in the next subsection, we let $\Lambda := \Lambda_0$.

An informal description of one strategy to ensure $B_\Gamma \neq B_\Lambda$.

This strategy consists of two parts. **Part 1** identifies pair of arguments a_i, a_j and stage s so that a_i, a_j appear in opposite orders in σ_s^Γ and σ_s^Λ. **Part 2** then exploits this mismatch to ensure that $B_\Gamma \cap \{a_i, a_j\} \neq B_\Lambda \cap \{a_i, a_j\}$.

Part 1: We fix the arguments a_0, a_1, a_2 to be used by this strategy and define $r(a_0) = a_2$. Then we wait for a stage at which we find $l < m < n$ such that $\{g_l, g_m, g_n\} = \{a_0, a_1, a_2\}$ and σ_s^Λ has length greater than $> n$. We also wait until $r^\Lambda(g_l)$ is obtained. Note that we are currently building $B_\Gamma = \mathcal{A}$: i.e., our approximated consequence operator does not produce any contradictions or counterexamples. If, during this waiting period, Λ produces any counterexample, then some argument will leave B_Λ while remaining in B_Γ, and this will give us a trivial victory for ensuring $B_\Lambda \neq B_\Gamma$.

Assuming such a stage is reached, we now distinguish cases. If the order of a_0, a_1, a_2 in σ_s^Λ is different than the order in σ_s^Γ, then we are already done with Part 1. Thus, we may assume $g_l = a_0$, $g_m = a_1$, and $g_n = a_2$. Our action now depends on the value of $r^\Lambda(g_l)$.

– *Case 1:* $r^\Lambda(g_l) = a_1$
  We put $\lozenge$ into $H(s, \{a_0\})$. This triggers replacement of a_0 with a_2 in σ_{s+1}^Γ, placing a_2 before a_1. In σ_t^Λ for $t > s$, to let $a_0 \notin B_\Lambda$, the system must replace a_0 with a_1, thus putting a_1 before a_2. Hence, the ordering of a_1 and a_2 will differ between σ_t^Λ and σ_t^Γ at some stage $t > s$.
– *Case 2:* $r^\Lambda(g_l) = a_2$
  We put $\bot$ into $H(s, \{a_0\})$. This excises a_0 in σ_{s+1}^Γ, leaving a_1 before a_2 in σ_t^Γ for each $t > s$. In σ_t^Λ for $t > s$, to let $a_0 \notin B_\Lambda$, the system must replace it with a_2, yielding a_2 before a_1—again, a mismatch.
– *Case 3:* $r^\Lambda(g_l) = g_i$, for some $g_i \notin \{a_1, a_2\}$
  We ensure that g_i remains in B_Λ, so that this argument will not be replaced in σ_t^Λ for any $t > s$. Then, we put $\lozenge$ into $H(s, \{a_0\})$, replacing a_0 with a_2 in

σ_{s+1}^Γ. This puts a_2 before a_1 in σ_t^Γ for each $t > s$, while in σ_t^Λ, a_1 will precede a_2—again, a mismatch.

At this point, we have transitioned from building $B_\Gamma = \mathcal{A}$ to $B_\Gamma = \mathcal{A} \smallsetminus \{a_0\}$. Thus, for B_Λ to equal B_Γ, Λ can only derive $\lozenge$ in a way that removes a_0. Any additional replacement will necessarily cause $B_\Lambda \neq B_\Gamma$. In this way, we ensure that once σ_t^Λ grows large enough, we will see the intended order difference. (Note: We will have to be more careful when we discuss the full construction with many simultaneously running modules, each working towards different strategies).

Part 2: Now that we have identified a pair of arguments a_i and a_j that appear in opposite orders in σ_t^Λ and σ_t^Γ, we force a difference in the corresponding limiting belief sets.

Suppose that a_i appears first in σ_t^Λ and a_j appears first in σ_t^Γ. We add $\perp$ to $H(t + 1, \{a_i, a_j\})$. This causes a_i to leave the range of σ_{t+1}^Γ.

If $B_\Lambda = B_\Gamma$ were to hold, then at some later stage, Λ must derive $\lozenge$ on a_i, i.e., insert $\lozenge$ into $H(t', \sigma_t^\Lambda \restriction_{(k+1)})$ where $\sigma_t^\Lambda(k) = a_i$. If this happens, we will finally put $\perp$ into $H(x + 1, \{a_j\})$ ensuring that a_j will not be in B_Γ. After this action, a_i re-enters σ_y^Γ, since its only conflict was with a_j, and a_j has been removed. However, a_i cannot re-enter σ_y^Λ without Λ removing some other argument that still belongs to B_Γ, again guaranteeing $B_\Gamma \neq B_\Lambda$.

We now discuss how to fit together multiple strategies, and then give a more formal algorithm for each strategy.

Fitting multiple strategies together.

A central feature of our strategy for ensuring $B_\Gamma \neq B_\Lambda$ is maintaining B_Γ sufficiently large so that few arguments in σ_s^Λ are candidates for replacement. In particular, we must prevent any element $\sigma_s^\Lambda(j)$ for $j \in [0, m]$ from being replaced by a_2, which would otherwise reverse the intended order of a_1 and a_2 in σ_t^Λ. We accomplish this by ensuring that all arguments in $\mathrm{ran}(\sigma_s^\Lambda \restriction_{(n+1)}) \smallsetminus \{a_0\}$ remain in B_Γ.

When multiple strategies $Strat_i$ run in parallel, no single strategy can simply assume that $B_\Gamma = \mathcal{A}$ unless it chooses to add a contradiction or counterexample to H. We can also not wait for $Strat_0$ to finish before beginning $Strat_1$, since $Strat_0$ might remain indefinitely waiting for Λ_0 to exhibit some specific behavior. Despite this, other strategies $Strat_j$ for $j > 0$ must still be able to proceed and succeed. That means they must be allowed to introduce their own consequences into H—involving contradictions or counterexamples—without interfering with the goals of $Strat_0$. Ensuring this kind of mutual coherence between strategies is essential to the success of the overall construction.

To manage these interactions, we employ a classical method from computability theory: the *finite-injury priority method*, introduced independently by Friedberg [9] and Muchnik [21]. The core idea is to resolve conflicts between strategies by prioritizing the needs of $Strat_i$ over the needs of $Strat_j$ when $i < j$. This ensures that each strategy $Strat_i$, being only *injured* (i.e., reset) by the finitely many higher-priority strategies $Strat_j$ for $j < i$, eventually will be allowed to stabilize and succeed.

In a typical finite-injury construction, whenever a strategy $Strat_i$ acts, all lower-priority strategies, i.e., $Strat_j$ with $j > i$, are deactivated. These lower-priority strategies must then restart from scratch. Since each $Strat_i$ acts only finitely often, every lower-priority strategy will eventually face no further interference and will complete its task.

A fundamental principle of the priority method is that lower-priority strategies must never cause any harm to higher-priority ones. Accordingly, when defining our strategies in the next subsection, we will carefully design each one so that its actions are harmless to those of higher priority.

Concretely, suppose strategy $Strat_i$ intends to put, say, $\Diamond$ into $H(t, F)$, for some finite set of arguments F. To avoid harming higher-priority strategies, it will ensure that F contains any set X that a higher-priority strategy might later use to derive a contradiction or a counterexample. This guarantees that, should the higher-priority strategy act, the counterexample based on F becomes moot, and no conflict arises.

We now explicitly describe the algorithm performed by each strategy $Strat_i$.

Part 1 of $Strat_i$:

Step 1: We fix three fresh arguments a_N, a_{N+1}, a_{N+2} such that N is larger than any number ever mentioned in the construction before. We define the parameter $Z_i = \emptyset$. Let S be the set of all arguments a_k with $k < N$ which are not currently in $\bigcup_{j<i} Z_j$.

Comment: If a higher-priority strategy (for Λ_k with $k < i$) has found his g_l, g_m, g_n and considered $\sigma_s^{\Lambda_k}$, then N is larger than any m so that $a_m \in \text{ran}(\sigma_s^{\Lambda_k})$. By choosing this N large, the strategy for Λ_i is making an effort to ensure that its actions will not affect any higher-priority strategy. As N is larger than the index of any mentioned argument, we have that for every finite set F, $H(s, F) = H(s, F \cup \{a_N, a_{N+1}, a_{N+2}\})$. The parameter Z_i keeps track of which elements this strategy wants to remove from B_Γ. Thus, the set S includes all arguments which a higher-priority strategy may, in the future, remove from $\text{ran}(\sigma_s^\Gamma)$. As described above, S will be included in all of our derivations of contradictions or counterexamples.

Step 2: Wait to see a stage s at which we find $l < m < n$ with $\{g_l, g_m, g_n\} = \{a_N, a_{N+1}, a_{N+2}\}$ and for $\sigma_s^{\Lambda_i}$ to have length $> n$. Also, wait for $r^{\Lambda_i}(g_l)$ to be defined.

Step 3: We now act based on cases.

- If $g_l \neq a_N$, then we have already ensured success in **Part 1**. Go to **Part 2** and deactivate all lower-priority requirements;
- If instead $g_l = a_N$, call the module $\texttt{PredictOrder}(\Lambda_i, s, a_N, a_{N+1}, a_{N+2})$.

Comment: The goal here is to apply either excision or replacement to a_N in order to force a specific order between a_{N+1} and a_{N+2} in σ_t^Γ that diverges from the order in $\sigma_t^{\Lambda_i}$. However, a subtlety arises. Even if a_{N+1} appears before a_{N+2} in

$\sigma_s^{\Lambda_i}$, this order may change in future stages due to interactions with other arguments. For example, suppose an argument c, positioned between a_N and a_{N+2} in $\sigma_s^{\Lambda_i}$, was replaced by a_{N+1} as a result of a counterexample derived from the set $\{a_N, c\}$. If a_N is later removed (through replacement or excision), then c may reappear, and the original derivation of $\lozenge$ from a_N, c will no longer apply. As a result, a_{N+1} may not re-enter the string in place of c. Consequently, the eventual ordering of a_{N+1} and a_{N+2} in some future stage $\sigma_t^{\Lambda_i}$ may differ from their ordering in $\sigma_s^{\Lambda_i}$. To address this, the module $\texttt{PredictOrder}(\Lambda_i, s, a_N, a_{N+1}, a_{N+2})$, described below, returns a string ρ representing a sufficiently long initial segment of $\sigma_t^{\Lambda_i}$, computed at a suitably late stage t. The purpose of ρ is to determine which of a_{N+1} or a_{N+2} appears first at this later stage: that is, if the last entry of ρ is a_K ($K \in \{N+1, N+2\}$), we will know that a_K will come first in $\sigma_t^{\Lambda_i}$.

Step 4: We perform the following action depending on the last entry of $\rho :=$ $\texttt{PredictOrder}(\Lambda_i, s, a_N, a_{N+1}, a_{N+2})$:

- *Case 1: ρ ends in a_{N+1}*
  We put $\lozenge$ into $H(s, S \cup \{a_N\})$ and let $Z_i = \{a_N\}$.
- *Case 2: ρ ends in a_{N+2}.*
  We put $\perp$ into $H(s, S \cup \{a_N\})$ and let $Z_i = \{a_N\}$.

Comment: These actions enforce a specific ordering in σ_t^{Γ}: either replacement (putting a_{N+2} before a_{N+1}) or excision (leaving a_{N+1} before a_{N+2}). In Lemma 3, we will prove that either the strategy succeeds or the ordering predicted by ρ will persist in $\sigma_t^{\Lambda_i}$ at some future stage t.

After performing the appropriate action, deactivate all lower-priority strategies and proceed to **Part 2**.

Part 2 of $Strat_i$:

Step 5: Wait for a stage t so that $\rho \preceq \sigma_t^{\Lambda_i}$.

Comment: We will show in Lemma 3 below that if no such stage t exists, then $Strat_i$ still succeeds. This may occur because, e.g., Λ_i removes too many arguments to match B_Γ, or because Λ_i is not a valid p-dialectical system.

Step 6: Let $\{a_I, a_J\} = \{a_{N+1}, a_{N+2}\}$ be so that the last entry of ρ is a_I. We add $\perp$ to $H(t, S \cup \{a_I, a_J\})$ and update $Z_i := \{a_N, a_I\}$.

Comment: This action triggers excision in the run of Γ, removing a_I from σ_t^{Γ}. All lower-priority strategies are deactivated. As we will show in Lemma 1, this ensures that (assuming no further interference from an higher-priority strategy) the limiting belief set satisfies $\{a_I, a_J\} \cap B_\Gamma = \{a_J\}$. Thus, either $B_\Gamma \neq B_{\Lambda_i}$ holds already, or a future stage t' will witness the derivation $\lozenge \in H^{\Lambda_i}(t', \rho)$.

Step 7: Wait for a t' where $\lozenge \in H^{\Lambda_i}(t', \rho)$.

Step 8: Put $\perp$ into $H(x, S \cup \{a_J\})$, where x is the current stage, and update $Z_i := \{a_N, a_J\}$. Deactivate all lower-priority requirements, and declare $Strat_i$ complete.

Comment: This final step ensures that $\{a_I, a_J\} \cap B_\Gamma = \{a_I\}$. At the same time, the fact that $\lozenge \in H^{\Lambda_i}(t', \rho)$ ensured that $a_I \notin B_\Lambda$. Hence, $B_\Gamma \neq B_{\Lambda_i}$, completing the diagonalization.

The PredictOrder Module: Step PO1: Define E to be $\{a_N\} \cup \bigcup_{j<i} Z_j$. **Step PO2:** WAIT for a stage t where we see, for each $j < n$, enough convergences of r^{Λ_i} iterated on g_j enough times that $(r^{\Lambda_i})^e(g_j) \notin E$.

Comment: Recall that if Λ_i is in fact a p-dialectical system, then r^{Λ_i} is an acyclic recursive function, so at some stage we should see each of these required convergences.

Step PO3: Let τ be the string so $\tau(j) = (r^{\Lambda_i})^{e_j}(g_j)$ where e_j is least so that $(r^{\Lambda_i})^{e_j}(g_j) \notin E$. Return the smallest prefix ρ of τ containing either a_{N+1} or a_{N+2}.

Comment: Note that $a_{N+1}, a_{N+2} \notin E$, so $\tau(m) = g_m \in \{a_{N+1}, a_{N+2}\}$, thus ρ is well-defined as has length no more than m.

Overarching program running each strategy: At stage 0 of the construction, all strategies are deactivated.

At any given stage $s > 0$, there may be some activated strategies and some deactivated strategies. If any of the activated strategies want to act (i.e., some Wait condition has been satisfied), we let the highest-priority strategy act according to the description of the strategies above. This deactivates all lower-priority strategies.

If none of the active strategies want to act, then we let Λ_k be the highest-priority strategy which is not yet activated, and we activate it. This means that it performs its first step of choosing new numbers a_N, a_{N+1}, a_{N+2} and sets its Wait condition determining if it will later want to act again.

We also take the least k so that $r(a_k)$ is not yet defined and let it equal a_{k+1}.

Comment: We note that we only ever put $\lozenge$ into $H(t, F)$ for any $t \in \mathbb{N}$ and $F \in P^{\text{fin}}(\mathcal{A})$ in Step 4 of some $Strat_j$. In this case, we use $r(a_N)$, which is defined in Step 1 of the same $Strat_j$ (recall N was new, so $r(a_N)$ was not already defined when a_N was chosen). Thus, we include this definition for r in the construction in order that r be a total function, but we will never perform replacement based on any of these values of r.

This completes the description of the construction of the q-dialectical system Γ. We now shift to verifying the result that $B_\Gamma \neq B_{\Lambda_i}$ for every i.

Verification: We proceed with a series of Lemmas which ensure that our construction does in fact produce a q-dialectical system Γ so that $B_\Gamma \neq B_{\Lambda_i}$ for each p-dialectical system Λ_i.

Note that a strategy that is never deactivated after stage s must have one of five possible outcomes: It could forever wait in Steps 2, 5, 7, PO2, or it may successfully get to Step 8 and complete the strategy. The following Lemmas, whose proofs appear in Appendix B of the extended version [5], follow via a careful analysis of the outcomes in each of these cases, along with a careful induction on the parameters of the strategies.

Lemma 1. *Suppose a strategy $Strat_i$ is activated at stage s and is never deactivated after stage s. Let N be the parameter chosen by $Strat_i$. Then $B_\Gamma \cap \{a_i \mid i < N\} = \{a_i \mid i < N\} \setminus \bigcup_{j<i} Z_j$. (Note that the value of Z_j cannot change after stage s since the higher-priority strategies do not act after stage s.)*

Lemma 2. *Suppose a module* `PredictOrder`$(\Lambda_i, s, a_N, a_{N+1}, a_{N+2})$ *returns a value* ρ *at stage* s. *Let* E *be the set* E *in the computation of* `PredictOrder`$(\Lambda_i, s, a_N, a_{N+1}, a_{N+2})$. *Let* M *be the largest number mentioned in the construction by stage* s. *Then either a higher-priority strategy than* $Strat_i$ *acts or* $B_\Gamma \cap (\{a_j \mid j \le M\} \smallsetminus \{a_{N+1}, a_{N+2}\}) = \{a_j \mid j \le M\} \smallsetminus (\{a_{N+1}, a_{N+2}\} \cup E)$.

Lemma 3. *Suppose that a strategy* $Strat_i$ *is not deactivated after stage* s, *and that* `PredictOrder`$(\Lambda_i, s, a_N, a_{N+1}, a_{N+2})$ *returns a value* ρ. *Then either* $B_\Gamma \ne B_{\Lambda_i}$ *or at some stage* t, *we have* $\rho \preceq \sigma_t^{\Lambda_i}$.
Also, either $B_\Gamma \ne B_{\Lambda_i}$ *or at all large enough stages, we have* $\rho \upharpoonright_{|\rho|-1} \preceq \sigma_t^{\Lambda_i}$.

Lemma 4. *Each strategy is deactivated at only finitely many stages.*

Lemma 5. *For each* i, $B_\Gamma \ne B_{\Lambda_i}$.

This completes the proof of Theorem 4.   □

5   Discussion

This work demonstrates that q-dialectical systems—those that revise beliefs in response to both contradictions and counterexamples—are strictly more powerful than p-dialectical systems, which rely solely on counterexamples. This result clarifies an important theoretical distinction: Reasoning with both contradictions and counterexamples and responding accordingly introduces a form of reasoning that cannot be replicated by counterexamples alone.

In terms of belief dynamics, this distinction maps naturally onto two different operations: excision, the removal of beliefs that lead to contradictions, and replacement, the refinement of beliefs in light of counterexamples. Our results thus highlight that both operations are essential for a fully expressive and robust model of rational belief change. Considering the two connections from Sect. 3, we raise the question of how q-dialectical or p-dialectical systems can be used in the two settings of repairing inconsistent knowledge bases, and belief revision.

These findings deepen our theoretical understanding of how mathematicians or research communities evolve their beliefs. The practice of mathematical inquiry does not rely exclusively on refining conjectures in response to failed examples; it also depends crucially on recognizing when a contradiction signals the need for more fundamental revision. By modeling both forms of reasoning, q-dialectical systems more accurately reflect the dual mechanisms driving knowledge development in such domains.

From an artificial intelligence perspective, the implications are similarly significant. An adaptive agent that relies only on counterexample-driven revision may miss critical inconsistencies in its belief state, while one that responds only to contradictions may fail to adjust to new, refining evidence. Our results support the view that both counterexample-based and contradiction-based reasoning are necessary components of intelligent belief management. The integration of both mechanisms, as formalized in q-dialectical systems, provides a pathway toward more general and effective approaches to automated reasoning.

Acknowledgments. This work was supported by the the National Science Foundation under Grant DMS-2348792. San Mauro is a member of INDAM-GNSAGA.

Disclosure of Interests. The authors have no competing interests to declare that are relevant to the content of this article.

References

1. Alchourrón, C.E., Gärdenfors, P., Makinson, D.: On the logic of theory change: partial meet contraction and revision functions. J. Symbolic Logic **50**(2), 510–530 (1985). https://doi.org/10.2307/2274239
2. Amidei, J., Andrews, U., Pianigiani, D., San Mauro, L., Sorbi, A.: Trial and error mathematics: dialectical systems and completions of theories. J. Logic Comput. **29**(1), 157–184 (2019). https://doi.org/10.1093/logcom/exy033
3. Amidei, J., Pianigiani, D., San Mauro, L., Simi, G., Sorbi, A.: Trial and error mathematics i: Dialectical and quasidialectical systems. Rev. Symb. Log. **9**(2), 299–324 (2016). https://doi.org/10.1017/S1755020315000404
4. Amidei, J., Pianigiani, D., San Mauro, L., Sorbi, A.: Trial and error mathematics II: Dialectical sets and quasidialectical sets, their degrees, and their distribution within the class of limit sets. Rev. Symb. Log. **9**(4), 810–835 (2016). https://doi.org/10.1017/S1755020316000253
5. Andrews, U., San Mauro, L.: Comparing dialectical systems: contradiction and counterexample in belief change (extended version) (2025). https://arxiv.org/abs/2507.06798
6. Bernardi, C.: Aspetti ricorsivi degli insiemi dialettici. Bollettino della Unione Matematica Italiana. Series IV **9**, 51–61 (1974)
7. Dalal, M.: Investigations into a theory of knowledge base revision: preliminary report. In: Proceedings of the Seventh AAAI National Conference on Artificial Intelligence, pp. 475–479 (1988)
8. Fermé, E., Hansson, S.O.: Belief change: introduction and overview. Springer (2018)
9. Friedberg, R.M.: Two recursively enumerable sets of incomparable degrees of unsolvability (solution of post's problem, 1944). Proc. Natl. Acad. Sci. **43**(2), 236–238 (1957)
10. Garapa, M.P.F.: Advances on belief base dynamics. Ph.D. thesis, Universidade da Madeira (Portugal) (2017)
11. Gärdenfors, P.: The dynamics of belief systems: Foundations vs. coherence theories. Revue internationale de philosophie, pp. 24–46 (1990)
12. Gnani, G.: Insiemi dialettici generalizzati. Matematiche **29**(2), 1–11 (1974)
13. Gödel, K.: Über formal unentscheidbare sätze der principia mathematica und verwandter systeme i. Monatshefte für Mathematik und Physik **38**(1), 173–198 (1931). https://doi.org/10.1007/BF01700692
14. Hájek, P.: Experimental logics and $\pi30$ theories1. J. Symbolic Logic **42**(4), 515–522 (1977)
15. Hansson, S.O.: In defense of base contraction. Synthese **91**, 239–245 (1992)
16. Hansson, S.O.: Kernel contraction. J. Symbolic Logic **59**(3), 845–859 (1994)
17. Harman, G.: Change in view: principles of reasoning. The MIT Press (1986)
18. Jeroslow, R.G.: Experimental logics and Δ_2^0-theories. J. Philos. Logic **4**(3), 253–267 (1975). https://doi.org/10.1007/BF00262039

19. Magari, R.: Su certe teorie non enumerabili. Annali di Matematica **98**(1), 119–152 (1974). https://doi.org/10.1007/BF02414017
20. Montagna, F., Simi, G., Sorbi, A.: Logic and probabilistic systems. Arch. Math. Logic **35**, 225–261 (1996)
21. Muchnik, A.A.: Negative answer to the problem of reducibility of the theory of algorithms. Dokl. Akad. Nauk SSSR **108**(2), 194–197 (1956)
22. Shoenfield, J.R.: Mathematical Logic. Mass, Addison-Wesley, Reading (1967)
23. Wassermann, R.: Resource bounded belief revision. Erkenntnis **50**(2), 429–446 (1999)

The InfOCF Library for Reasoning With Conditional Belief Bases

Christoph Beierle[1]([⊠])[iD], Jonas Haldimann[2,3][iD], Arthur Sanin[1], Aron Spang[1][iD],
Lars-Phillip Spiegel[1][iD], and Martin von Berg[1][iD]

[1] Knowledge-Based Systems, Faculty of Mathematics and Computer Science, FernUniversität
in Hagen, 58084 Hagen, Germany
christoph.beierle@fernuni-hagen.de
[2] Institute of Logic and Computation, TU Wien, 1040 Vienna, Austria
[3] University of Cape Town and CAIR, Cape Town 7700, South Africa

Abstract. This paper presents an overview of the Python library InfOCF that
provides powerful tools for working with conditional belief bases consisting of
defeasible rules of the form "*If A, then usually B*". Because many operations on
belief bases, like checking their consistency or performing nonmonotonic reasoning for answering queries, require solving propositional satisfiability problems and generalizations thereof, InfOCF builds upon the power of current SMT
and MaxSAT solvers. For achieving solver independence, established interfaces
like PySMT are used, allowing the user to select from different solvers. Multiple
queries can be run in parallel for speeding up the answering process. Besides its
rigorous focus on modularity and extensibility, further notable features of InfOCF
include comprehensive methods for caching program states enabling the reuse of
intermediate results across different queries to the same belief base. Successful
applications realized with, and now available in, InfOCF cover state-of-the-art
implementations of nonmonotonic reasoning with p-entailment, system Z, lexicographic inference, c-inference, and system W; each of these implementations
scales up and outperforms all previous implementations of the corresponding
inference operator by an order of magnitude.

Keywords: Conditional · Belief base · Nonmonotonic reasoning ·
p-Entailment · System Z · Lexicographic inference · c-Inference · system W ·
Implementations · Python library · SMT solver · Partial MaxSAT solver

1 Introduction

The theoretical foundations of belief bases containing conditionals of the form "*If A,
then usually B*" have been studied extensively for a long time, e.g., in [1,13,33,34].
Less attention has been paid to the practical side of actually implementing systems for
answering the question what a belief bases entails. The Python-based library InfOCF
provides sophisticated and powerful tools for realizing nonmonotonic reasoning from
conditional belief bases. It employs the power of current SMT and Partial MaxSAT
Solvers, e.g., Z3 [17] and RC2 [24], for answering queries with respect to a belief base
and an inference method. InfOCF supports inference according to different established

G. Casini et al. (Eds.): JELIA 2025, LNAI 16094, pp. 19–27, 2026.
https://doi.org/10.1007/978-3-032-04590-4_2

inductive inference operators [27] that complete the beliefs given explicitly in a belief base to a full inference relation. The implemented inference operators include the seminal p-entailment [21] which coincides with inference according to system P [18,33], system Z [34] which coincides with rational closure [33], Lehmann's lexicographic inference [32], c-inference [5,6] taking all all c-representations [25,26] into account, and system W [28,29].

In this short paper, we present a brief introduction to InfOCF. Section 2 gives on overview of InfOCF, describes its main functionalities, lists some of its notable features, and provides small examples for using it. Section 3 addresses applications realized with InfOCF and their evaluation, demonstrating impressively how InfOCF scales up reasoning with conditional belief bases. In Sect. 4, we conclude and point out future work.

2   Overview of InfOCF

The complete library InfOCF is publically available and can be found on GitHub[1]

2.1   Main Functionalities of InfOCF

The main purpose of InfOCF is to provide a toolbox for working and reasoning with conditional belief bases, leading to the following core functionalities:

- Reading and parsing belief bases and queries in the .cl-format used in the CLKR repository [9];
- Computation of the *tolerance partition* [34] of a belief base Δ that plays an important role in consistency checking and in inference operators like system Z, and system W;
- Checking the consistency of a belief base, both for (strong) consistency in the sense of [21] and for weak consistency [23];
- Computing the conditional structure induced by a belief base Δ, comprising verifying and falsifying worlds for the conditionals in Δ [25]
- Answering queries with respect to a belief base Δ according to an inductive inference operator; currently, p-entailment [21], system Z [34], lexicographic inference [32], c-inference [5], and system W [29] are covered.

2.2   Description of the Library

A conditional "*If A, then usually B*", formally denoted by $(B|A)$, consists of the antecedent A and the consequent B, where A, B are propositional formulas. To represent propositional formulas, InfOCF uses the corresponding functionality from PySMT [20], a library that gives us easy access to a range of SAT/SMT solvers. Building upon this, InfOCF provides a class `Conditionals` for representing conditionals and a class `BeliefBase` for representing belief bases. A special class `Queries` extends

---

[1] https://github.com/jonasphilipp/InfOCF.

`BeliefBase` and is used to represent a set of conditionals that are to be interpreted as queries, because in the context of a given belief base Δ, believing that A entails B corresponds to accepting the conditional $(B|A)$.

Support functions to read belief bases and queries from files using the `.cl`-format [9] are found in `parser/Wrappers.py`. Methods for common tasks like checking a belief base for consistency or finding its tolerance partition are found in `consistency_sat.py`.

The core of InfOCF are the implementations of inferences from conditional belief bases. The individual inference operators are each implemented in a class that extends the abstract class `Inference`; thus providing uniform access to all inferences. To draw inferences, an instance of the corresponding `Inference`-subclass is created for the given belief base; then single queries or batches of multiple queries can be answered by calls to the instances methods.

For p-entailment, it is known that A entails B in the context of a belief base Δ if and only if $\Delta \cup (\neg B|A)$ is inconsistent [21]. The implementation of p-entailment, available in the class `PEntailment`, is based on this property and the consistency check for belief bases. System Z is implemented in the class `SystemZ` and uses an algorithm relying on a solver for SAT problems [12]. Lexicographic inference is implemented in the class `LexInf` and also requires solving SAT and MaxSAT problems. While system Z and lexicographic inference can be both characterized by a total preorder on possible worlds, system W is based on the preferred structure on worlds [29] which is a strict partial order. In addition to solvers for SAT problems, the implementation of the algorithm for system W given in [11], available in the class `SystemW`, also employs a solver for Partial MaxSAT problems.

Among the models of a belief base Δ, c-representations are special ranking models obtained by assigning individual integer impacts to the conditionals in Δ [25,26]. For realizing c-inference taking all c-representations of a belief base Δ into account [6], showing the unsolvability of a complex constraint satisfaction problem (CSP) is required [4,5]. The implementation of c-inference, available in the class `CInference`, uses an encoding of this CSP involving the belief base and the query into an SMT problem with linear arithmetic [19] developed in [3,14]. This SMT problem is then reduced and simplified via transformation and compilations steps [10,16] by employing a Partial MaxSAT solver.

Observe that these inference operators cover a large variety of semantic structures. While p-entailment takes all ranking models of a belief base Δ into account, system Z is defined in terms of a single ranking function, the unique minimal ranking model of Δ. Similarly, lexicographic is defined by a single total preorder (TPO) on worlds. c-Inference is based on the (possibly infinite) subset of ranking functions that are c-representations of Δ, and system W is induced by a strict partial order (SPO) on the possible worlds.

Typical inference operators require some preprocessing on the belief base before the first query can be answered, e.g., for system Z this includes the computation of the tolerance partition. To store the results of this preprocessing for later use, every instance of an `Inference` has a variable called *epistemic state*. To be compatible with a wide range of inference operators requiring different types of variables, the epistemic state is a Python-dictionary which can be used to store different types of information: these can be tolerance partitions, encodings of the belief base as constraints, or other types of intermediate results. The epistemic state also contains the belief base and possibly other external parameters and is given to the instance during initialization. The epistemic state can furthermore be used to keep track of queries, results, timings, and other data.

To make creating Inference-classes easier, the wrapper class InferenceOperator can be used to take care of creating the epistemic state dictionary and initializing the inference class. It also provides additional functionality beyond the bare inference: It allows keeping track of the runtimes for different operations in detail which is useful for benchmarks and testing purposes, and it supports fine-grained control over timeouts for the operations. For example, timeouts for preprocessing and inference can be set independently if desired. Furthermore, it provides results, timings, and other data in Pandas DataFrames[2] which makes the further processing or storing of results easy.

An example for the usage of InfOCF is shown in the listing below: the program loads a belief base from the file birds.cl and checks if it p-entails the queries $p \rightsquigarrow f$ and $b \rightsquigarrow f$.

```
from parser.Wrappers import parse_belief_base, parse_queries
from inference.inference_operator import InferenceOperator

belief_base = parse_belief_base("birds.cl")
queries = parse_queries("(f|p),(!f|p)")

pent = InferenceOperator(belief_base,
            inference_system="p-entailment")
results = pent.inference(queries)
```

```
print(results)
```

Additional parameters to the initialization of InferenceOperator can be used to select specific solvers. Optional parameters to the inference method set timeouts, or enable parallel solving of queries in multiple threads.

```
sysw = InferenceOperator(belief_base,
            inference_system="system-w",
            smt_solver="z3", pmaxsat_solver="rc2_g4")
results = sysw.inference(queries, total_timeout=300,
            multi_inference=True)
```

```
print(results)
```

This code answers for the belief base belief_base the queries given in queries for system W using Z3 as SMT solver and RC2 with the internal solver g4 (Glucose 4) for MaxSAT problems. It sets a timeout of 300 s for preprocessing and reasoning combined, and allows both queries to be processed in parallel after the preprocessing is completed.

---

[2] https://pandas.pydata.org/.

2.3   Use of SMT and Partial MaxSAT Solvers

The implementations of the inference operators feature algorithms that heavily rely on solving SAT, SMT and MaxSAT problems. For this, InfOCF uses external solvers. One of the key features of InfOCF is its solver independence. By simply changing a parameter during initialization of the inference, the user can choose from a range of different solvers.

For solving SAT problems, any of the solvers compatible with PySMT [20] can be used. This includes the solvers already included in PySMT, like Z3, cvc5, or yices. Furthermore, any solver compliant with SMT-Lib 2 [2] can be easily added via PySMT's SMT-Lib wrapper. For MaxSAT, either of the solvers Z3 or RC2 can be selected, and for RC2, the user can then again choose from a range of internal solvers implemented within RC2.

2.4   Further Notable Features

By using state-of-the-art algorithms in combination with modern solvers, the implementations in InfOCF are at least an order of magnitude faster than older implementations of the inference operators. To further speed up inference, the library supports parallelization of query answering across multiple CPU cores, and tries to reuse intermediate results as much as possible by storing them in the inference objects epistemic state.

Special care was taken to keep the library modular and easily extensible. In addition to the solver independence described above, the classes implementing specific inferences are clearly separated from other functions like the parser, profiling, and convenience methods for easy usage of the library. To implement an additional inference operator it suffices to add a new class inheriting from `Inference`.

Finally, to simplify the installation of the library on UNIX-like environments, InfOCF comes with a `flake.nix` file that specifies the required dependencies and allows reproducing the development environment.

3   Applications and Evaluation

The Python library InfOCF described above and its Java-based predecessor [30] have been used to implement increasingly powerful versions of the online reasoning platform InfOCF-Web[3] [7,8,31]. The most recent version InfOCF-Web 2.0 [8], covering implementations of the inductive inference operators p-entailment, system Z, c-inference, and system W, is based on the Python library InfOCF presented in this paper. For an extensive evaluation of InfOCF, belief bases and queries were constructed by a randomized scheme taking a signature Σ as input [15]. In the evaluation, belief bases with signature sizes $|\Sigma|$ and number of conditionals $|\Delta|$ both ranging from 60 to 120 were considered, incremented in steps of 20. For each of the 16 $(|\Sigma|, |\Delta|)$-combinations in the evaluation, 100 belief bases were created along with 10 queries for each belief base, resulting in 1600 belief bases and 16000 queries; the problem set CLKR-PS003

---

[3] InfOCF-Web is available at https://www.fernuni-hagen.de/wbs/research/infocf-web/.

Table 1. Excerpt of evaluation results [8] of InfOCF-Web 2.0 implementations of system **P**, system **Z**, c-inference (**C**) and system **W**; belief bases are over signatures with size $|\Sigma|$ and contain $|\Delta|$ conditionals. For each $(|\Sigma|, |\Delta|)$-combination, 10 different queries for 100 different belief bases had to be answered. %**S**: Percentage of belief bases where all queries were answered without a timeout. **T**: Mean time (in milliseconds) required for answering a single query if all 1000 queries were answered without a timeout; timeout was set to 5 min for query-independent preprocessing plus 5 min for inference.
Evaluation environment: Mobile workstation equipped with an i9-11950H OctaCore processor, 128 DDR4-3200 working memory and a PCIe-x4 SSD hard drive. Windows 11 running Ubuntu 22.04.04 in a Windows Subsystem for Linux 2 environment.

$\vdash$	$|\Sigma|$	$|\Delta|$	%S	T	$|\Sigma|$	$|\Delta|$	%S	T	$|\Sigma|$	$|\Delta|$	%S	T	$|\Sigma|$	$|\Delta|$	%S	T
P			100	54			100	29			100	37			100	37
Z	60	60	100	57	80	60	100	59	100	80	100	76	120	80	100	78
C			98	–			100	340			100	700			100	531
W			100	115			100	97			100	152			100	144
P			100	40			100	36			100	44			100	51
Z	60	80	100	74	80	80	100	72	100	100	100	84	120	120	100	94
C			96	–			98	–			94	–			89	–
W			100	338			100	193			100	329			100	810

obtained thereby is available at the CLKR repository [9]. The evaluation times for each $(|\Sigma|, |\Delta|)$-combination were calculated as means over the corresponding 1000 queries. Table 1 shows a small excerpt of the detailed empirical evaluation of InfOCF-Web 2.0 given in [8]. Note that except for c-inference, all queries underlying the evaluation results shown in Table 1 were answered without running into a timeout. This relates to the situation that the implementation of c-inference is more intricate than the implementations of the other inference methods because it requires to show the unsolvability of a large constraint satisfaction problem [3,5,15,16]. In full compliance with these evaluations results, another evaluation of the system Z and system W implementations available in InfOCF-Web 2.0 demonstrates that they can also easily handle belief bases with up to 200 conditionals [12].

The smallest problem size in the comprehensive evaluation in [8] involves belief bases with $|\Sigma| = 60$, and to the best of our knowledge, apart from the implementations now available in InfOCF, there is no other implementation of an inference operator for conditional belief bases (e.g., [7,35–37]) for which such problem sizes are feasible. Therefore, all other implementation approaches would run into timeout consistently for all problem sizes examined in Table 1 or in [8]. The implementation of system P in [35] can handle a signature size of at most 50 and 100 conditionals, but it achieves only approximate results within hours for a belief base of this size, whereas the approach using our Python library InfOCF delivers exact results within less than 100 milliseconds. In summary, the evaluation results for the realized inductive inference operators, covering belief bases of 60 to 120 conditionals over 2^{60} to 2^{120} possible worlds, clearly demonstrate that InfOCF provides a key for scaling up nonmonotonic reasoning from conditional belief bases to a new dimension.

4   Conclusions and Future Work

We have presented an overview of the library InfOCF whose core functionalities provide implementations of established inductive inference operators like p-entailment and system Z. By using algorithms specifically tailored for employing the power of current SMT and MaxSAT solvers, the implementations in InfOCF outperform previous implementations of these and all other inference operators considered in this paper.

Our current and future work includes extending the inference operators available in InfOCF to cover also belief bases that are only weakly consistent [22, 23], to include additional inference operators, e.g., c-core inference [38], and to further exploit the evolving capabilities of SMT and MaxSAT solvers.

Acknowledgments. We are grateful to Steven Kutsch for his work in the development of the first version of the InfOCF library in Java that lead to the Python-based version presented in this paper, and to all who contributed to the previous Java versions InfOCF. This work was supported by the Deutsche Forschungsgemeinschaft (DFG, German Research Foundation) - 512363537, grant BE 1700/12-1 awarded to Christoph Beierle.

References

1. Adams, E.: The logic of conditionals. Inquiry **8**(1–4), 166–197 (1965)
2. Barrett, C., Stump, A., Tinelli, C.: The SMT-LIB standard: version 2.0. In: Gupta, A., Kroening, D. (eds.) Proceedings of the 8th International Workshop on Satisfiability Modulo Theories, Edinburgh, UK (2010)
3. Beierle, C., von Berg, M., Sanin, A.: Realization of C-inference as a SAT problem. In: Keshtkar, F., Franklin, M. (eds.) Proceedings of the Thirty-Fifth International Florida Artificial Intelligence Research Society Conference (FLAIRS), Hutchinson Island, Florida, USA, 15–18 May 2022 (2022). https://doi.org/10.32473/flairs.v35i.130663
4. Beierle, C., Eichhorn, C., Kern-Isberner, G.: Skeptical inference based on C-representations and its characterization as a constraint satisfaction problem. In: Gyssens, M., Simari, G. (eds.) FoIKS 2016. LNCS, vol. 9616, pp. 65–82. Springer, Cham (2016). https://doi.org/10.1007/978-3-319-30024-5_4
5. Beierle, C., Eichhorn, C., Kern-Isberner, G., Kutsch, S.: Properties of skeptical C-inference for conditional knowledge bases and its realization as a constraint satisfaction problem. Ann. Math. Artif. Intell. **83**(3-4), 247–275 (2018). https://doi.org/10.1007/s10472-017-9571-9
6. Beierle, C., Eichhorn, C., Kern-Isberner, G., Kutsch, S.: Properties and interrelationships of skeptical, weakly skeptical, and credulous inference induced by classes of minimal models. Artif. Intell. **297**, 103489 (2021). https://doi.org/10.1016/j.artint.2021.103489
7. Beierle, C., Haldimann, J., Kollar, D., Sauerwald, K., Schwarzer, L.: An implementation of nonmonotonic reasoning with system W. In: Bergmann, R., Malburg, L., Rodermund, S.C., Timm, I.J. (eds.) KI 2022. LNCS, vol. 13404, pp. 1–8. Springer, Cham (2022). https://doi.org/10.1007/978-3-031-15791-2_1

8. Beierle, C., et al.: Scaling up reasoning from conditional belief bases. In: Destercke, S., Martinez, M.V., Sanfilippo, G. (eds.) SUM 2024. LNCS, vol. 15350, pp. 29–44. Springer, Cham (2024). https://doi.org/10.1007/978-3-031-76235-2_3

9. Beierle, C., Haldimann, J., Schwarzer, L.: CLKR – conditional logic and knowledge representation. KI – Künstliche Intell. **38**, 61–67 (2024). https://doi.org/10.1007/s13218-024-00842-z

10. Beierle, C., Kutsch, S., Sauerwald, K.: Compilation of static and evolving conditional knowledge bases for computing induced nonmonotonic inference relations. Ann. Math. Artif. Intell. **87**(1-2), 5–41 (2019). https://doi.org/10.1007/s10472-019-09653-7

11. Beierle, C., Spang, A., Haldimann, J.: A Partial MaxSAT approach to nonmonotonic reasoning with system W. In: Proceedings of the 37th International Florida Artificial Intelligence Research Society Conference (2024). https://doi.org/10.32473/FLAIRS.37.1.135330

12. Beierle, C., Spang, A., Haldimann, J.: Using SAT and Partial MaxSAT for reasoning with system Z and system W. In: Gierasimczuk, N., Heyninck, J. (eds.) Proceedings of the 22nd International Workshop on Nonmonotonic Reasoning (NMR 2024). CEUR Workshop Proceedings, vol. 3835, pp. 132–141. CEUR-WS.org (2024). https://ceur-ws.org/Vol-3835/paper14.pdf

13. Benferhat, S., Dubois, D., Prade, H.: Possibilistic and standard probabilistic semantics of conditional knowledge bases. J. Log. Comput. **9**(6), 873–895 (1999)

14. von Berg, M., Sanin, A., Beierle, C.: Representing nonmonotonic inference based on C-representations as an SMT problem. In: Bouraoui, Z., Jabbour, S., Vesic, S. (eds.) ECSQARU 2023. LNCS, vol. 14249, pp. 210–223. Springer, Cham (2023). https://doi.org/10.1007/978-3-031-45608-4_17

15. von Berg, M., Sanin, A., Beierle, C.: An implementation of nonmonotonic reasoning with C-representations using an SMT solver. Int. J. Approx. Reason. **175**, 109285 (2024). https://doi.org/10.1016/j.ijar.2024.109285

16. von Berg, M., Sanin, A., Beierle, C.: Scaling up nonmonotonic C-inference via partial MaxSAT problems. In: Meier, A., Ortiz, M. (eds.) FoIKS 2024. LNCS, vol. 14589, pp. 182–200. Springer, Cham (2024). https://doi.org/10.1007/978-3-031-56940-1_10

17. Bjørner, N., de Moura, L., Nachmanson, L., Wintersteiger, C.M.: Programming Z3. In: Bowen, J., Liu, Z., Zhang, Z. (eds.) Engineering Trustworthy Software Systems. SETSS 2018. Lecture Notes in Computer Science, vol. 11430, pp. 148–201. Springer, Cham (2019). https://doi.org/10.1007/978-3-030-17601-3_4

18. Dubois, D., Prade, H.: Conditional objects as nonmonotonic consequence relationships. Spec. Issue Conditional Event Algebra IEEE Trans. Syst. Man Cybern. **24**(12), 1724–1740 (1994)

19. Dutertre, B., de Moura, L.: A fast linear-arithmetic solver for DPLL(T). In: Ball, T., Jones, R.B. (eds.) CAV 2006. LNCS, vol. 4144, pp. 81–94. Springer, Heidelberg (2006). https://doi.org/10.1007/11817963_11

20. Gario, M., Micheli, A.: PySMT: a solver-agnostic library for fast prototyping of SMT-based algorithms. In: SMT Workshop 2015 (2015)

21. Goldszmidt, M., Pearl, J.: Qualitative probabilities for default reasoning, belief revision, and causal modeling. Artif. Intell. **84**(1–2), 57–112 (1996)

22. Haldimann, J., Beierle, C., Kern-Isberner, G.: Syntax splitting and reasoning from weakly consistent conditional belief bases with c-inference. In: Meier, A., Ortiz, M. (eds.) FoIKS 2024. LNCS, vol. 14589, pp. 85–103. Springer, Cham (2024). https://doi.org/10.1007/978-3-031-56940-1_5

23. Haldimann, J., Beierle, C., Kern-Isberner, G., Meyer, T.: Conditionals, infeasible worlds, and reasoning with system W. In: The International FLAIRS Conference Proceedings, vol. 36, no. 1 (2023). https://doi.org/10.32473/flairs.36.133268

24. Ignatiev, A., Morgado, A., Marques-Silva, J.: RC2: an efficient MaxSAT solver. J. Satisf. Boolean Model. Comput. **11**(1), 53–64 (2019). https://doi.org/10.3233/SAT190116
25. Kern-Isberner, G.: Conditionals in Nonmonotonic Reasoning and Belief Revision. LNAI, vol. 2087. Springer, Heidelberg (2001). https://doi.org/10.1007/3-540-44600-1
26. Kern-Isberner, G.: A thorough axiomatization of a principle of conditional preservation in belief revision. Ann. Math. Artif. Intell. **40**(1–2), 127–164 (2004)
27. Kern-Isberner, G., Beierle, C., Brewka, G.: Syntax splitting = relevance + independence: new postulates for nonmonotonic reasoning from conditional belief bases. In: Calvanese, D., Erdem, E., Thielscher, M. (eds.) Principles of Knowledge Representation and Reasoning: Proceedings of the 17th International Conference, KR 2020, pp. 560–571. IJCAI Organization (2020). https://doi.org/10.24963/kr.2020/56
28. Komo, C., Beierle, C.: Nonmonotonic inferences with qualitative conditionals based on preferred structures on worlds. In: Schmid, U., Klügl, F., Wolter, D. (eds.) KI 2020. LNCS (LNAI), vol. 12325, pp. 102–115. Springer, Cham (2020). https://doi.org/10.1007/978-3-030-58285-2_8
29. Komo, C., Beierle, C.: Nonmonotonic reasoning from conditional knowledge bases with system W. Ann. Math. Artif. Intell. **90**(1), 107–144 (2022). https://doi.org/10.1007/s10472-021-09777-9
30. Kutsch, S.: InfOCF-Lib: A Java library for OCF-based conditional inference. In: Proceedings of the DKB/KIK-2019. CEUR Workshop Proceedings, vol. 2445, pp. 47–58. CEUR-WS.org (2019)
31. Kutsch, S., Beierle, C.: InfOCF-Web: An online tool for nonmonotonic reasoning with conditionals and ranking functions. In: Zhou, Z. (ed.) Proceedings of the Thirtieth International Joint Conference on Artificial Intelligence, IJCAI 2021, pp. 4996–4999. ijcai.org (2021).https://doi.org/10.24963/ijcai.2021/711
32. Lehmann, D.: Another perspective on default reasoning. Ann. Math. Artif. Intell. **15**(1), 61–82 (1995)
33. Lehmann, D.J., Magidor, M.: What does a conditional knowledge base entail? Artif. Intell. **55**(1), 1–60 (1992)
34. Pearl, J.: System Z: A natural ordering of defaults with tractable applications to nonmonotonic reasoning. In: Parikh, R. (ed.) Proceedings of the 3rd conference on Theoretical aspects of reasoning about knowledge (TARK1990). pp. 121–135. Morgan Kaufmann Publishers Inc., San Francisco (1990)
35. Stojanovic, T., Ikodinovic, N., Davidovic, T., Ognjanovic, Z.: Automated non-monotonic reasoning in system P. Ann. Math. Artif. Intell. **89**(5–6), 471–509 (2021)
36. Thimm, M.: Tweety: A comprehensive collection of Java libraries for logical aspects of artificial intelligence and knowledge representation. In: KR 2014, pp. 528–537. AAAI Press (2014)
37. Tönnies, D.: Implementierung und empirische Untersuchung lexikographischer Inferenz für das nichtmonotone Schließen. Bachelor thesis, FernUniversität in Hagen, Germany (2022). (in German)
38. Wilhelm, M., Kern-Isberner, G., Beierle, C.: Core C-representations and C-core closure for conditional belief bases. In: Meier, A., Ortiz, M. (eds.) FoIKS 2024. LNCS, vol. 14589, pp. 104–122. Springer, Cham (2024). https://doi.org/10.1007/978-3-031-56940-1_6

On Lockean Beliefs that are Deductively Closed and Minimal Change

Tommaso Flaminio[1(✉)], Lluis Godo[1], Ramón Pino Pérez[2], and Lluis Subirana[3]

[1] Artificial Intelligence Research Institute (IIIA - CSIC), Campus de la UAB,
Bellaterra, Spain
{tommaso,godo}@iiia.csic.es
[2] Centre de Recherche en Informatique de Lens (CRIL), Université d'Artois,
UMR 8188, Lens, France
pinoperez@cril.fr
[3] Department of Mathematics, University of Barcelona (UB), Barcelona, Spain
lsubirana@yahoo.com

Abstract. Within the formal setting of the Lockean thesis, an agent belief set is defined in terms of degrees of confidence and these are described in probabilistic terms. This approach is of established interest, notwithstanding some limitations that make its use troublesome in some contexts, like, for instance, in belief change theory. Precisely, Lockean belief sets are not generally closed under (classical) logical deduction. The aim of the present paper is twofold: on one side we provide two characterizations of those belief sets that are closed under classical logic deduction, and on the other we propose an approach to probabilistic update that allows us for a minimal revision of those beliefs, i.e., a revision obtained by making the fewest possible changes to the existing belief set while still accommodating the new information. In particular, we show how we can deductively close a belief set via a minimal revision.

Keywords: Lockean thesis · Deductive closure · Belief change · Minimal revision

1 Introduction

In [10] Foley introduces what he calls the *Lockean thesis*, a philosophical principle suggesting that *beliefs* can be defined in terms of *confidence*, the latter being formulated within the (subjective) probabilistic setting. More concretely, given the language $\mathcal{L}$ of classical propositional logic over finitely many variables, Foley claims that it is rational for an agent to believe in a statement, written φ in $\mathcal{L}$, provided that the agent's subjective probability of φ overcomes a certain threshold.

Lockean thesis: For any $\varphi \in \mathcal{L}$, it is rational to believe in φ provided that its probability $P(\varphi)$ overcomes a certain threshold λ.

G. Casini et al. (Eds.): JELIA 2025, LNAI 16094, pp. 28–42, 2026.
https://doi.org/10.1007/978-3-032-04590-4_3

Given a threshold λ and a probability function P, one can hence define a *Lockean belief set*, as:

$$\mathscr{B}_{\lambda,P} = \{\varphi \in \mathcal{L} : P(\varphi) \geq \lambda\}. \tag{1}$$

Lockean belief sets represent the epistemic states of rational agents, and they have been considered as a basis for theories of probabilistic belief change. The idea of grounding belief change on Lockean belief sets is in fact not new and it has been proposed and already explored and investigated by others. Among them, it is worth recalling the following ones, whose ideas inspired the present paper: [23] by Shear and Fitelson; [12,13] both by Hannson; [18] by Leitgeb and [5] by Cantwell and Rott who, similarly to what we also propose in the present paper, adopt (a variation of) Jeffrey conditionalization to deal with the belief revision process.

The elementary observation that if a rational agent believes φ then it is reasonable to assume that she does not believe its negation $\neg\varphi$ forces the threshold λ to be strictly above $1/2$. This requirement immediately implies that belief sets defined as in (1) do not contain pairs of contradictory formulas, in the sense that it is not the case that, for any formula φ, φ and its negation $\neg\varphi$ both belong to a Lockean belief set $\mathscr{B}_{\lambda,P}$.

Although they are not contradictory in the above sense, Lockean belief sets lack some properties that are usually required in the classical approaches to belief change as developed by Alchourrón, Gärdenfors, and Makinson [1]; Katsuno and Mendelzon [16] etc. One of them is *deductive closure*. Denoting by $\vdash$ the consequence relation of classical propositional logic, this principle reads as follows.

Deductive closure: For any belief set $\mathscr{B}$, if $\mathscr{B} \vdash \varphi$, then $\varphi \in \mathscr{B}$.

As we will see in a while, the deductive closure for a Lockean belief set is equivalent to the apparently weaker principle of *conjunctive closure*.

Conjunctive closure: For any belief set $\mathscr{B}$, if $\varphi_1 \in \mathscr{B}, \ldots, \varphi_n \in \mathscr{B}$, then $\varphi_1 \wedge \ldots \wedge \varphi_n \in \mathscr{B}$.

The above principle of conjunctive closure has been studied in the literature (see [4] and [2]) and it is involved in the discussions concerning some paradoxical situations, the best known being Kyburg's lottery paradox [17] and Makinson's preface paradox [19].

Our current research line aims at understanding how probabilistic belief change theory can be approached in a way that is alternative to those mentioned above and precisely by employing variants of Jeffrey's conditionalization that allow a principle of minimal change. These ideas will be discussed in Sect. 5, while the core of this article is to present results that tell us under which conditions the key property of deductive closure can be safely assumed to hold for Lockean belief sets.

More precisely, we will present two main results, both of which give a characterization for those probability functions P ensuring the existence of suitable thresholds λ for which $\mathscr{B}_{\lambda,P}$ is closed under logical deduction. These are the main results of Sect. 3 and Sect. 4, respectively. Then, in Sect. 5 we discuss how to revise a Lockean belief coherently with an intuitive principle of minimal change. Interestingly, our minimal change desiderata are met by a method that revises a prior probability that is closely related to Jeffrey conditionalization. In the same Sect. 5 we will show that, indeed, this revision method is *minimal* in a sense that will be made clear there. Also in that section we characterize the conditions under which a (non necessarily deductively closed) Lockean belief set becomes deductively closed once revised by a suitable formula. Related works will be discussed in Sect. 6. We end this paper with some remarks and suggestions for future work that will be presented in Sect. 7. In Sect. 2 we recall basic logical and algebraic notion and we fix our notation.

2 Preliminaries

The ground of our investigation is classical propositional logic (CPL) and our language $\mathcal{L}$, up to redundancy, is built from a finite set of propositional variables, say $x_1, \ldots, x_n$, connectives $\wedge, \vee, \neg$ for *conjunction*, *disjunction*, and *negation* respectively, and constants $\top, \bot$ for *true* and *false*. Formulas in that language will be denoted by lower case Greek letters $\varphi, \psi, \ldots$ with possible subscripts. The connective of *implication* is defined as $\varphi \to \psi = \neg\varphi \vee \psi$, and *double implication* is $\varphi \leftrightarrow \psi = (\varphi \to \psi) \wedge (\psi \to \varphi)$.

The consequence relation of CPL is denoted by $\vdash$ and hence $\vdash \varphi$ means that φ is a *theorem*. If $\mathscr{T}$ is a set of formulas and φ a formula, $\mathscr{T} \vdash \varphi$ means that φ is provable from $\mathscr{T}$ within CPL. A set $\mathscr{T}$ of formulas of $\mathcal{L}$ is said to be *deductively closed* (or a *theory* in some textbooks), provided that $\varphi \in \mathscr{T}$ iff $\mathscr{T} \vdash \varphi$. Two formulas φ_1 and φ_2 are said to be *logically equivalent* or *equal up to logical equivalence* whenever $\vdash \varphi_1 \leftrightarrow \varphi_2$.

From the semantic point of view, every formula φ can be identified with the set $[\![\varphi]\!]$ of its models, i.e., those logical valuations $\omega : \mathcal{L} \to \{0,1\}$ such that $\omega(\varphi) = 1$, also written $\omega \models \varphi$. If we denote by $\Omega_{\mathcal{L}}$ the set of logical valuations for $\mathcal{L}$ (or simply Ω when the language $\mathcal{L}$ is clear by the context), the basic algebraic structure that is needed to interpret formulas in the above sense is the finite Boolean algebra of subsets of Ω, $\mathbf{2}^{\Omega} = (2^{\Omega}, \cap, \cup, ^c, \emptyset, \Omega)$ with the usual set-theoretic operations of intersection, union and complementation, respectively. For any pair of formulas φ and ψ, we write $[\![\varphi]\!] \subseteq [\![\psi]\!]$ to denote that the models of φ are included into those of ψ. Notice that φ and ψ are logically equivalent if and only if $[\![\varphi]\!] = [\![\psi]\!]$. A formula φ is consistent if $[\![\varphi]\!] eq \emptyset$. The set of consistent formulas will be denoted by $\mathcal{L}^*$.

Although the results we are going to recall below hold in general for finite Boolean algebras, that we assume the reader to be familiar with, we will henceforth only state them for the case of $\mathbf{2}^{\Omega}$.

Let us start by recalling that a non-empty proper subset F of $\mathbf{2}^{\Omega}$ is a *filter* if (i) $[\![\varphi]\!], [\![\psi]\!] \in F$ implies $[\![\varphi]\!] \cap [\![\psi]\!] \in F$ (conjunctive closure), and (ii) $[\![\varphi]\!] \in F$ and $[\![\varphi]\!] \subseteq [\![\psi]\!]$, implies that $[\![\psi]\!] \in F$ (upward closure). Notice that (ii) implies that $[\![\top]\!] \in F$ for every filter F, since filters are non-empty. The fact that F is a proper subset of 2^{Ω} implies that $[\![\bot]\!] \notin F$.

Filters of 2^{Ω} and deductively closed sets of formulas (theories) from $\mathcal{L}$ are tightly linked. Actually, one can define filters on $\mathcal{L}$ in the following way: a subset $\mathscr{F}$ of $\mathcal{L}$ is an $\mathcal{L}$-filter if $F = \{[\![\varphi]\!] \mid \varphi \in \mathscr{F}\}$ is a filter on 2^{Ω}.

It is easy to see that $\mathcal{L}$-filters $\mathscr{F}$ correspond to consistent theories, that is, subsets of formulas of $\mathcal{L}$ which are logically closed and consistent. Thus, an $\mathcal{L}$-filter $\mathscr{F}$ can be characterized syntactically by: (i) if $\varphi, \psi \in \mathscr{F}$ then $(\varphi \wedge \psi) \in \mathscr{F}$; (ii) $\varphi \in \mathscr{F}$ and $\vdash (\varphi \to \psi)$ then $\psi \in \mathscr{F}$; and (iii) $\bot \notin \mathscr{F}$. That is to say, an $\mathcal{L}$-filter $\mathscr{F}$ is a consistent and deductively closed theory.

Moreover, let F be a filter of 2^{Ω} and consider the set $\mathscr{F} = \{\varphi \in \mathcal{L} \mid [\![\varphi]\!] \in F\}$. Then $\mathscr{F}$ is deductively closed and consistent. Conversely, let $\mathscr{T}$ be a consistent theory (a consistent deductively closed set of formulas) of $\mathcal{L}$ and consider $F = \{[\![\varphi]\!] \in 2^{\Omega} \mid \varphi \in \mathscr{T}\}$. As we already observed above, F is a filter of 2^{Ω}. Note that by this correspondence, we identify $\mathcal{L}$-filters (consistent theories) with filters of 2^{Ω}.

For a later use, let us recall the following.

Fact 1. *For every filter F of 2^{Ω}, there exists a unique (up to logical equivalence) $\psi \in \mathcal{L}$ such that $F = \{[\![\varphi]\!] \in 2^{\Omega} \mid [\![\psi]\!] \subseteq [\![\varphi]\!]\}$.*

In such a case, we say that F is *principally generated* by $[\![\psi]\!]$ or that $[\![\psi]\!]$ *generates* F, and we will write $F = \uparrow[\![\psi]\!]$.

A theory $\mathscr{T}$ is *maximally consistent* if for all $\varphi \in \mathcal{L}$ either $\varphi \in \mathscr{T}$ or $\neg\varphi \in \mathscr{T}$. *Ultrafilters* are filters that are maximal with respect to the usual set-theoretic inclusion. It is well known that maximally consistent theories and ultrafilters are in correspondence [6]. For a later use, let us recall that if U is an ultrafilter of 2^{Ω} then there exists a unique valuation $\omega \in \Omega$ such that $U = \{[\![\varphi]\!] \in 2^{\Omega} \mid \omega \in [\![\varphi]\!])\}$.

To close this section, and following [20], let us recall that a probability distribution on Ω is a mapping $P : \Omega \to [0,1]$ such that $\sum_{\omega \in \Omega} P(\omega) = 1$, and extends to subsets of Ω by additivity, i.e. by letting $P(S) = \sum_{\omega \in S} P(\omega)$ for all non-empty $S \subseteq \Omega$ and $P(\emptyset) = 0$. A probability distribution is said to be *positive* if $P(\omega) > 0$ for all $\omega \in \Omega$. For every formula $\varphi \in \mathcal{L}$, we will hence write $P(\varphi)$ for $\sum_{\omega \in [\![\varphi]\!]} P(\omega)$. We henceforth assume probability functions to be positive.

3   Lockean Belief Sets that Are Deductively Closed

In this section we will present a first characterization for Lockean belief sets that are deductively closed in terms of suitable probability functions. The main result will be given by selecting those probability functions P for which there exists a parameter $\lambda > 1/2$ such that $\mathscr{B}_{\lambda,P}$ is deductively closed. Due to the identification between theories of $\mathcal{L}$ and filters of 2^{Ω} we mentioned in the above section, we will consider Lockean belief sets as subsets of 2^{Ω} and we will equivalently say that $\mathscr{B}_{\lambda,P}$ is deductively closed or that $\mathscr{B}_{\lambda,P}$ is a filter without risk of ambiguity.

Remark 1. Let us notice that the monotonicity of probability functions implies that every Lockean belief set is upward closed. Indeed, if $\psi \in \mathscr{B}_{\lambda,P}$ and $\llbracket \psi \rrbracket \subseteq \llbracket \varphi \rrbracket$, then $P(\varphi) \geq P(\psi) \geq \lambda$, whence $\varphi \in \mathscr{B}_{\lambda,P}$. Therefore, in order for $\mathscr{B}_{\lambda,P}$ to be deductively closed, it is enough that it satisfies conjunctive closure.

The first result introduces a notational convention that will be often used throughout the paper.

Lemma 1. *For a positive probability P on $\mathbf{2}^{\Omega}$ and $\lambda > 1/2$, there exist a minimal λ_m and a maximal λ_M such that: $\lambda_M = P(\psi)$ for some $\psi \in \mathbf{2}^{\Omega}$, $\lambda_m < \lambda \leq \lambda_M$, and $\mathscr{B}_{\lambda',P} = \mathscr{B}_{\lambda,P}$ for every $\lambda' \in (\lambda_m, \lambda_M]$.*

Proof. Since $\mathcal{L}$ is finite, $\mathbf{2}^{\Omega}$ is finite as well and the image of every probability P on $\mathbf{2}^{\Omega}$ is a finite subset of $[0,1]$ of increasing values, say $\{q_0 = 0, q_1, q_2, \ldots, q_{t-1}, q_t = 1\}$. Thus, for every $\lambda > 1/2$, let $0 \leq i \leq t-1$ such that $q_i < \lambda \leq q_{i+1}$ and call $\lambda_m = \max\{1/2, q_i\}$ and $\lambda_M = q_{i+1}$. Then, $\psi \in \mathscr{B}_{\lambda,P}$ iff $P(\psi) \geq \lambda$ iff $P(\psi) \geq \lambda'$ for every $\lambda' \in (\lambda_m, \lambda_M]$. In other words, $\mathscr{B}_{\lambda',P} = \mathscr{B}_{\lambda,P}$ for every $\lambda' \in (\lambda_m, \lambda_M]$ and the claim is settled. $\qquad\square$

We say that a belief set $\mathscr{B}_{\lambda,P}$ is *trivial* when $\mathscr{B}_{\lambda,P} = {\uparrow}\llbracket \top \rrbracket$. Note that if P is a positive probability and $\mathscr{B}_{\lambda,P}$ is non-trivial, then $\lambda_M < 1$. An immediate consequence of the above lemma is the following easy remark.

Remark 2. Let P and λ be such that $\mathscr{B}_{\lambda,P}$ is deductively closed, i.e. $\mathscr{B}_{\lambda,P}$ is a filter of $\mathbf{2}^{\Omega}$. Let ψ be such that $\mathscr{B}_{\lambda,P} = {\uparrow}\llbracket \psi \rrbracket$. Then, although we cannot ensure that $P(\psi) = \lambda$, we know that $P(\psi) = \lambda_M$, and by the above lemma, $\mathscr{B}_{\lambda,P} = \mathscr{B}_{\lambda_M,P}$.

Next we establish a result useful in the sequel.

Lemma 2. *If $\mathscr{B}_{\lambda,P}$ is a filter and $P(\psi) = \lambda$ then $\mathscr{B}_{\lambda,P} = {\uparrow}\llbracket \psi \rrbracket$.*

Proof. Let φ be such that $\llbracket \varphi \rrbracket$ is a generator of the filter $\mathscr{B}_{\lambda,P}$. Since $P(\psi) = \lambda$, $\psi \in \mathscr{B}_{\lambda,P}$. Thus, $\varphi \vdash \psi$, i.e., $\llbracket \varphi \rrbracket \subseteq \llbracket \psi \rrbracket$. We claim that $\llbracket \psi \rrbracket \subseteq \llbracket \varphi \rrbracket$ as well. If not, there exists ω such that $\omega \in \llbracket \psi \rrbracket$ and $\omega \notin \llbracket \varphi \rrbracket$. Thus, $P(\psi) \geq P(\varphi) + P(\omega) > \lambda$, a contradiction.[1] Then we have $\llbracket \psi \rrbracket = \llbracket \varphi \rrbracket$. Therefore, $\mathscr{B}_{\lambda,P} = {\uparrow}\llbracket \psi \rrbracket$. $\qquad\square$

Let us start our analysis with a first result that collects some basic, yet quite interesting, facts about probabilities and deductively closed sets of formulas (see [9] for a proof).

Proposition 1. *The following conditions hold:*

(1) Let P and λ be such that $\mathscr{B}_{\lambda,P}$ is a filter of $\mathbf{2}^{\Omega}$. If P is a homomorphism of $\mathbf{2}^{\Omega}$ to $\{0,1\}$, then $\mathscr{B}_{\lambda,P}$ is maximal (and in that case $\lambda_M = 1$).
(2) $\mathscr{B}_{\lambda,P}$ is a maximal filter iff there is $\omega \in \Omega$ such that $P(\omega) \geq \lambda$.
(3) For a positive probability P, $\mathscr{B}_{\lambda,P} = {\uparrow}\llbracket \top \rrbracket$ iff $\mathscr{B}_{\lambda,P} = \{\varphi \mid P(\varphi) = 1\}$.

---

[1] Since P is positive by our general assumption.

The above result then highlights the following elementary facts:

1. If P is a homomorphism of 2^Ω to $\{0,1\}$ then $\mathscr{B}_{\lambda,P}$ is a maximal filter of 2^Ω and $\lambda = 1$, necessarily. Thus, from what we pointed out in Sect. 2, $\mathscr{B}_{\lambda,P}$ corresponds to a maximally consistent theory. Moreover, all maximally consistent theories are described in this way.
2. If P is positive and $\lambda = 1$, then again $\mathscr{B}_{\lambda,P}$ is deductively closed, but it corresponds to the trivial theory containing only logical theorems.

It now remains to study the general situation in which $\mathscr{B}_{\lambda,P}$ is a proper filter of 2^Ω that is neither maximal, nor a singleton.

Given what we recalled in the above section, for P and λ as above, $\mathscr{B}_{\lambda,P}$ is deductively closed if and only if $\mathscr{B}_{\lambda,P}$ is a filter of 2^Ω and hence, by Fact 1, there exists a unique $\psi \in \mathcal{L}$ such that $\mathscr{B}_{\lambda,P} = \uparrow[\![\psi]\!]$.

In general, we can prove the following result that provides a first characterization of those Lockean belief sets that are deductively closed. In the statement of the next result, and henceforth, we will adopt the notation of Lemma 1.

Theorem 1. *For a positive probability $P : 2^\Omega \to [0,1]$ and $\lambda > 1/2$, $\mathscr{B}_{\lambda,P}$ is deductively closed iff there exists $\psi \in \mathscr{B}_{\lambda,P}$ such that $P(\psi) = \lambda_M$ and $1 - \lambda_M < \min\{P(\omega) \mid \omega \in [\![\psi]\!]\}$ and, in such a case, $\mathscr{B}_{\lambda,P} = \uparrow[\![\psi]\!]$.*

Proof. By Lemma 1, $\mathscr{B}_{\lambda,P} = \mathscr{B}_{\lambda_M,P}$, and hence we will prove the theorem considering $\mathscr{B}_{\lambda_M,P}$ without loss of generality.

Let us assume that $\mathscr{B}_{\lambda_M,P}$ is deductively closed, and hence a filter of 2^Ω, and let $[\![\psi]\!]$ be its generator, i.e., $\mathscr{B}_{\lambda_M,P} = \uparrow[\![\psi]\!]$. Towards a contradiction, assume there exists $\omega \in [\![\psi]\!]$ such that $P(\omega) \leq 1 - \lambda_M$. Then, take γ such that $[\![\gamma]\!] = \Omega \setminus \{\omega\}$. Clearly $[\![\gamma]\!] \not\supseteq [\![\psi]\!]$ whence γ does not belong to $\mathscr{B}_{\lambda_M,P} = \uparrow[\![\psi]\!]$, while

$$P(\gamma) \geq 1 - (1 - \lambda_M) = \lambda_M,$$

contradicting the fact that filters are upward closed.

Conversely, assume that $P(\psi) = \lambda_M$ and $1 - \lambda_M < \min\{P(\omega) \mid \omega \in [\![\psi]\!]\}$. The latter implies that for all δ, γ such that $[\![\delta]\!] \subseteq [\![\psi]\!]^c$ and $[\![\gamma]\!] \subseteq [\![\psi]\!]$,

$$P(\delta) \leq 1 - \lambda_M < \min\{P(\omega) \mid \omega \in [\![\psi]\!]\} \leq P(\gamma). \tag{2}$$

Therefore, if $[\![\tau]\!] \not\supseteq [\![\psi]\!]$, one has $P(\tau) = P((\tau \wedge \neg\psi) \vee (\tau \wedge \psi)) = P(\tau \wedge \neg\psi) + P(\tau \wedge \psi) < P(\psi \wedge \neg\tau) + P(\tau \wedge \psi)$ by (2) because $[\![\tau \wedge \neg\psi]\!] \subseteq [\![\psi]\!]^c$, while $[\![\psi \wedge \neg\tau]\!] \subseteq [\![\psi]\!]$. Now, $P(\psi \wedge \neg\tau) + P(\tau \wedge \psi) = P(\psi) = \lambda_M$ and hence $\tau \notin \mathscr{B}_{\lambda_M,P}$. Equivalently, for all ρ, if $\rho \in \mathscr{B}_{\lambda_M,P}$ then $[\![\rho]\!] \supseteq [\![\psi]\!]$, i.e., $\mathscr{B}_{\lambda_M,P} = \uparrow[\![\psi]\!]$, and hence it is a filter. $\square$

Corollary 1. *If $\lambda > 1/2$ and $\mathscr{B}_{\lambda,P} = \uparrow[\![\psi]\!]$, and hence deductively closed, with $|[\![\psi]\!]| = n$, then $\lambda_M > n/(n+1)$. Hence $P(\psi) > n/(n+1)$ and $P(\neg\psi) < 1/n$.*

Proof. By the above theorem, $P(\psi) = \sum_{\omega \in [\![\psi]\!]} P(\omega) > n(1 - \lambda_M)$, hence $1 = P([\![\psi]\!]) + P([\![\psi]\!]^c) > n(1 - \lambda_M) + (1 - \lambda_M) = (n+1)(1 - \lambda_M)$, and it follows that $\lambda_M > n/(n+1)$. $\square$

The intuition behind the previous results is that, for a positive probability P and a threshold λ to define a deductively closed set of formulas $\mathscr{B}_{\lambda,P}$ one has to ensure:

- the existence of a formula ψ such that $P(\psi) = \lambda$ (or $P(\psi)$ is greater than, yet sufficiently close to λ);
- that ψ is unique and this property can be ensured by requiring that the probability distribution that gives $P(\psi) = \lambda$ is sufficiently low on $\neg\psi$ as required in the hypothesis of Proposition 1;
- as a consequence, for instance, if P is the counting measure on $\mathbf{2}^{\Omega}$ (i.e., it comes from the uniform distribution on Ω), then for no λ one has that $\mathscr{B}_{\lambda,P}$ is deductively closed, unless $\lambda > \frac{n-1}{n}$, where n is the cardinal of $\mathbf{2}^{\Omega}$.

So, examples of probability distributions that, on the other hand, ensure that $\mathscr{B}_{\lambda,P}$ is deductively closed are those P for which there exists $\omega \in \Omega$ such that $P(\omega) > \sum_{\omega' \neq \omega} P(\omega')$. In this case if $P(\omega) > 1/2$ then $\mathscr{B}_{\lambda,P}$ is a maximal filter for $\lambda = P(\omega)$.

4   Step Probabilities: A Second Characterization Result

The characterization provided in Theorem 1 will be made more clear in the following Theorem 2. Let us begin by defining a class of probability functions that will play a central role in what follows.

Definition 1. *Let P be a probability function on $\mathbf{2}^{\Omega}$ and let $\omega \in \Omega$. Then P is said to have an ω-step (or to have a step at ω), provided that it satisfies*

$$(\omega S) \quad P(\omega) > \sum_{\omega':P(\omega')<P(\omega)} P(\omega') > 0.$$

A probability P is said to be a step probability *if it has an ω-step for some $\omega \in \Omega$.*[2]

A probability function might have more than one step as the following example shows.

Example 1. Consider P defined on $\Omega = \{\omega_1, \omega_2, \omega_3, \omega_4\}$ such that $P(\omega_1) = P(\omega_4) = 0.05$, $P(\omega_2) = 0.3$ and $P(\omega_3) = 0.6$. The probability P has the following steps:

- A step at ω_3 because $0.6 = P(\omega_3) > P(\omega_1) + P(\omega_2) + P(\omega_4) = 0.4$;
- A step at ω_2 because $0.3 = P(\omega_2) > P(\omega_1) + P(\omega_4) = 0.1$.   □

Let P be a probability that has a step at ω. Call Φ_ω a formula such that

$$[\![\Phi_\omega]\!] = \{\omega' \in \Omega \mid P(\omega') \geq P(\omega)\}. \tag{3}$$

Continuing the above Example 1, we have that

---

[2] The name "step probability" is inspired by *big-stepped probabilities* introduced in [3] and also considered in [18]; these ideas will be briefly recalled in Sect. 6 below.

- $[\![\Phi_{\omega_3}]\!] = \{\omega_3\}$;
- $[\![\Phi_{\omega_2}]\!] = \{\omega_2, \omega_3\}$.

Proposition 2. *If P has an ω-step, then $1 > P(\Phi_\omega) > 1/2$.*

Proof. By the very definition of ω-step and Φ_ω, one has that

$$P(\Phi_\omega) \geq P(\omega) > P(\omega) > \sum_{\omega' \notin [\![\Phi_\omega]\!]} P(\omega') = \sum_{\omega' \notin [\![\Phi_\omega]\!]} P(\omega') = P(\neg\Phi_\omega).$$

It follows that $P(\Phi_\omega) > P(\neg\Phi_\omega)$, therefore $P(\Phi_\omega) > 1/2$. Moreover, P having an step at ω also implies $0 < \sum_{P(\omega')<P(\omega)} P(\omega') = P(\neg\Phi_\omega)$, from where it also follows that $P(\Phi_\omega) < 1$. $\square$

Notice that, if P has an ω-step, then $P(\omega)$ necessarily coincides with the minimum value among the $P(\omega')$'s for $\omega' \in [\![\Phi_\omega]\!]$. Such an ω for which $P(\omega)$ reaches that minimum is not supposed to be unique; in any case the next result holds.

Lemma 3. *If P has an ω-step then $P(\omega) = \min\{P(\omega') \mid \omega' \in [\![\Phi_\omega]\!]\}$.*

We can now prove the following characterization result.

Theorem 2. *For every positive probability P, there exists $1 > \lambda > 1/2$ such that $\mathscr{B}_{\lambda,P}$ is deductively closed non-trivial iff P has an ω-step.*

Proof. Let us begin by showing the "if" part. Assume that P has an ω-step. Then, by Proposition 2, $1 > P(\Phi_\omega) > 1/2$. Take $\lambda = P(\Phi_\omega)$. By Lemma 3 and the definition of ω-step one has

$$\min\{P(\omega') \mid \omega' \in [\![\Phi_\omega]\!]\} = P(\omega) > \sum_{P(\omega')<P(\omega)} P(\omega') = P(\neg\Phi_\omega) = 1 - \lambda.$$

Therefore, since $\lambda = P(\Phi_\omega)$, by Lemma 1, $\lambda = \lambda_M$ and hence $\mathscr{B}_{\lambda,P} = \mathscr{B}_{\lambda_M,P}$. By Theorem 1, we have $\mathscr{B}_{\lambda,P} = \uparrow[\![\Phi_\omega]\!]$. And so, clearly $\mathscr{B}_{\lambda,P}$ is deductively closed and not trivial.

Conversely, let $1 > \lambda > 1/2$ and assume that $\mathscr{B}_{\lambda,P}$ is deductively closed and non-trivial. By Theorem 1 and the assumption of non-triviality of $\mathscr{B}_{\lambda,P}$, there exists ψ such that $P(\psi) = \lambda_M < 1$ and $\tau = \min\{P(\omega) \mid \omega \in [\![\psi]\!]\} > 1 - \lambda_M = P(\neg\psi)$. Then let ω in Ω be where P attains the value τ.

Claim. $[\![\psi]\!] = [\![\Phi_\omega]\!]$.

Proof. (of the Claim) By definition $[\![\Phi_\omega]\!] = \{\omega' : P(\omega') \geq P(\omega) = \tau\}$ and hence $[\![\psi]\!] \subseteq [\![\Phi_\omega]\!]$ because, if $\omega' \in [\![\psi]\!]$, then $P(\omega') \geq \tau$. Towards a contradiction, assume that $[\![\Phi_\omega]\!] \not\subseteq [\![\psi]\!]$. Then there exists ω' such that $\omega' \in [\![\Phi_\omega]\!]$ and $\omega' \notin [\![\psi]\!]$. But since $\omega' \in [\![\Phi_\omega]\!]$ then $P(\omega') \geq \tau > 1 - \lambda_M$, and since $\omega' \notin [\![\psi]\!]$ then $P(\omega') \leq P(\neg\psi) = 1 - \lambda_M$, contradiction. Hence, the claim is settled. $\square$

Now we go back to the proof of Theorem 2 and we prove that P has a step at ω. Indeed, by the above claim, $P(\psi) = P(\Phi_\omega) = \lambda_M < 1$ and hence,

$$P(\omega) = \tau > 1 - \lambda_M = P(\neg\psi) = P(\neg\Phi_\omega) = \sum_{P(\omega') < P(\omega)} P(\omega') > 0.$$

Thus, P has a step at ω and this settles the claim. $\square$

The proof of the above theorem shows that a probability function P with a step at ω determines the deductively closed set

$$\mathscr{B}_{P(\Phi_\omega),P} = \{\varphi \mid P(\varphi) \geq P(\Phi_\omega)\}$$

for $\lambda = P(\Phi_\omega)$, where Φ_ω is defined as in (3). Indeed, a probability P determines as many deductively closed sets as steps it has.

Example 2. Let us consider again the probability P from Example 1. The two steps at ω_3 and ω_2 determine the deductively closed sets:

- $\mathscr{B}_{0.6,P} = \{\varphi \mid P(\varphi) \geq P(\omega_3) = 0.6\} = \{\varphi \mid \omega_3 \in [\![\varphi]\!]\}$;
- $\mathscr{B}_{0.9,P} = \{\varphi \mid P(\varphi) \geq P(\{\omega_2,\omega_3\}) = 0.9\} = \{\varphi \mid \{\omega_2,\omega_3\} \subset [\![\varphi]\!]\}$.

Notice that $\mathscr{B}_{0.6,P}$ is maximally consistent, while $\mathscr{B}_{0.9,P}$ is not and in fact $\mathscr{B}_{0.9,P}$ is strictly contained in $\mathscr{B}_{0.6,P}$.

5   Minimal Change of Lockean Belief Sets

Now that we have established under which precise conditions a probability P ensures that a Lockean belief set $\mathscr{B}_{\lambda,P}$ is deductively closed we can put forward a first preliminary analysis on revising $\mathscr{B}_{\lambda,P}$ by a formula ψ.

Given the probabilistic setting of our approach, a natural way to revise a Lockean belief set $\mathscr{B}_{\lambda,P}$ by a formula ψ (and hence getting $\mathscr{B}_{\lambda,P} * \psi$) is relying on the conditional probability $P(\cdot \mid \psi) = P_\psi(\cdot)$, and hence defining $\mathscr{B}_{\lambda,P} * \psi = \{\varphi \in \mathcal{L} \mid P_\psi(\varphi) \geq \lambda\}$. This method, which has been already considered by several authors, and notably in [11], does not generally fit with a basic, yet only informally expressible principle of *minimal change* stipulating that, when revising beliefs, one should make the fewest possible changes to the existing belief set while still accommodating the new information. Our goal is hence to revise a generic Lockean belief set $\mathscr{B}_{\lambda,P}$ by a formula ψ, in such a way that the obtained set $\mathscr{B}_{\lambda,P} * \psi$ meets the following desiderata:

1. If $\psi \in \mathscr{B}_{\lambda,P}$ then $\mathscr{B}_{\lambda,P} * \psi = \mathscr{B}_{\lambda,P}$, that is to say, no revision is produced by those formulas that are already believed.
2. If $\psi \notin \mathscr{B}_{\lambda,P}$, then we include ψ in $\mathscr{B}_{\lambda,P}$ by minimally changing its probability; in other words, if a priori $P(\psi) < \lambda$, then a posteriori $P_\psi(\psi) = \lambda$.

In order to fulfill the above requests, we will define the following.

Definition 2. *Given a positive probability P on Ω and $\psi \in \mathcal{L}$ and $\lambda > 1/2$, the revised probability of P by ψ and λ is the function R_ψ^λ defined on Ω by putting:*

$$R_\psi^\lambda(\omega) = \begin{cases} P(\omega) \cdot \max\left\{1, \frac{\lambda}{P(\psi)}\right\} & \text{if } \omega \in [\![\psi]\!] \\ P(\omega) \cdot \min\left\{1, \frac{1-\lambda}{P(\neg\psi)}\right\} & \text{if } \omega \notin [\![\psi]\!] \end{cases}. \tag{4}$$

Notice that the above definition accommodates the above desideratum 1 because, if $\psi \in \mathscr{B}_{\lambda,P}$, then $P(\psi) \geq \lambda$ and hence $\lambda/P(\psi) \leq 1$. Thus $R_\psi^\lambda(\omega) = P(\omega)$ for all $\omega \in [\![\psi]\!]$ and hence $R_\psi^\lambda(\psi) = P(\psi) \geq \lambda$. It also satisfies desideratum 2 because, if $P(\psi) < \lambda$, $R_\psi^\lambda(\psi) = \lambda$ as required.

Also, regardless whether $P(\psi) < \lambda$ or $P(\psi) \geq \lambda$, one can easily check that $\sum_{\omega \in \Omega} R_\psi^\lambda(\omega) = 1$. For instance, when $P(\psi) < \lambda$, $R_\psi^\lambda(\omega) = P(\omega) \cdot \frac{\lambda}{P(\psi)}$ for $\omega \in [\![\psi]\!]$ and $R_\psi^\lambda(\omega) = P(\omega) \cdot \frac{1-\lambda}{P(\neg\psi)}$ for $\omega \notin [\![\psi]\!]$. Thus, $\sum_{\omega \in \Omega} R_\psi^\lambda(\omega) = \sum_{\omega \in [\![\psi]\!]} R_\psi^\lambda(\omega) + \sum_{\omega \in [\![\neg\psi]\!]} R_\psi^\lambda(\omega) = \sum_{\omega \in [\![\psi]\!]} P(\omega) \cdot \frac{\lambda}{P(\psi)} + \sum_{\omega \in [\![\neg\psi]\!]} P(\omega) \cdot \frac{1-\lambda}{P(\neg\psi)} = P(\psi) \cdot \frac{\lambda}{P(\psi)} + P(\neg\psi) \cdot \frac{1-\lambda}{P(\neg\psi)} = \lambda + 1 - \lambda = 1$. It follows that R_ψ^λ is a probability distribution on Ω that extends to a probability function on $\mathcal{L}$ which we will indicate by the same symbol. Interestingly, we can prove the following result that connects our revised probability function R_ψ^λ with the well-known *Jeffrey conditionalization*, see [15] (see also [5] for an application to belief revision): for every positive probability P on $\mathcal{L}$, for every $\varphi, \psi \in \mathcal{L}$ with $0 < P(\psi) < 1$, and for every $\lambda \in [0, 1]$, the Jeffrey conditionalization of φ given ψ is defined as

$$P_\psi^\lambda(\varphi) = \lambda P(\varphi \mid \psi) + (1-\lambda)P(\varphi \mid \neg\psi) = \lambda \frac{P(\varphi \wedge \psi)}{P(\psi)} + (1-\lambda)\frac{P(\varphi \wedge \neg\psi)}{P(\neg\psi)}.$$

Observe that, when $\lambda = 1$ the above expression recovers the usual definition of conditional probability. That is to say, $P_\psi^1(\varphi) = P(\varphi \mid \psi)$.

Proposition 3. *For every probability P, $\lambda > 1/2$ and ψ such that $P(\psi) > 0$, we have for all $\varphi \in \mathcal{L}$,*

$$R_\psi^\lambda(\varphi) = \begin{cases} P_\psi^\lambda(\varphi), & \text{if } P(\psi) \leq \lambda \\ P(\varphi), & \text{otherwise} \end{cases}.$$

Thus, when $P(\psi) \leq \lambda$, R_ψ^λ is the Jeffrey conditionalization of P by ψ.

Proof. We begin by assuming that $P(\psi) \leq \lambda$, so that $\max\{1, \frac{\lambda}{P(\psi)}\} = \frac{\lambda}{P(\psi)}$ and $\min\{1, \frac{1-\lambda}{P(\neg\psi)}\} = \frac{1-\lambda}{P(\neg\psi)}$. Then we have $R_\psi^\lambda(\varphi) = R_\psi^\lambda(\varphi \wedge \psi) + R_\psi^\lambda(\varphi \wedge \neg\psi) = P(\varphi \wedge \psi) \cdot \frac{\lambda}{P(\psi)} + P(\varphi \wedge \neg\psi) \cdot \frac{1-\lambda}{P(\neg\psi)} = \lambda P(\varphi \mid \psi) + (1-\lambda)P(\varphi \mid \neg\psi)$.

Conversely, if $P(\psi) > \lambda$, $\max\{1, \frac{\lambda}{P(\psi)}\} = \min\{1, \frac{1-\lambda}{P(\neg\psi)}\} = 1$. Then, $R_\psi^\lambda(\varphi) = R_\psi^\lambda(\varphi \wedge \psi) + R_\psi^\lambda(\varphi \wedge \neg\psi) = P(\varphi \wedge \psi) \cdot 1 + P(\varphi \wedge \neg\psi) \cdot 1 = P(\varphi)$. $\qquad\square$

Using the revised probability R_ψ^λ, we now formally introduce our revision operator for Lockean belief sets.

Actually, the present setting may be read within the framework introduced in [22] by defining an epistemic space as $\mathcal{E}_\lambda = (\mathscr{P}, B_\lambda)$ where $\frac{1}{2} < \lambda < 1$, $\mathscr{P}$ are the positive probabilities on 2^Ω and for every $P \in \mathscr{P}$ we put $B_\lambda(P) = \mathscr{B}_{\lambda,P}$. Then, on this epistemic space, we define an operator $\circ : \mathscr{P} \times \mathcal{L}^* \to \mathscr{P}$ by putting $P \circ \psi = R_\psi^\lambda$. This operator induces a revision operator $*_{ml}$ at the level of beliefs. More precisely we have the following definition:

Definition 3. *Given a Lockean belief set $\mathscr{B}_{\lambda,P}$, and a proposition ψ, the* mini- *mal Lockean* revision *of $\mathscr{B}_{\lambda,P}$ by ψ is defined as:*

$$\mathscr{B}_{\lambda,P} *_{ml} \psi = \{\varphi \mid R_\psi^\lambda(\varphi) \geq \lambda\} = \mathscr{B}_{\lambda,R_\psi^\lambda}.$$

Note that $\mathscr{B}_{\lambda,P} *_{ml} \psi = B_\lambda(P \circ \psi)$.

We are now ready to put together the notions and results provided so far to characterize under which conditions we can revise a Lockean belief set $\mathscr{B}_{\lambda,P}$ in such a way that the obtained $\mathscr{B}_{\lambda,P} *_{ml} \psi$ is deductively closed. Next result fully describes the situations in which $\mathscr{B}_{\lambda,P} *_{ml} \psi$ is deductively closed.

Theorem 3. *Let $\mathscr{B}_{\lambda,P}$ be a Lockean belief set, ψ a consistent proposition and $\tau = \min\{P(\omega) \mid \omega \in [\![\psi]\!]\}$. Then:*

(i) $\mathscr{B}_{\lambda,P} *_{ml} \psi$ is deductively closed whenever $P(\psi) < \frac{\tau\lambda}{1-\lambda}$. Moreover, in that case, $\mathscr{B}_{\lambda,P} *_{ml} \psi = {\uparrow}[\![\psi]\!]$
(ii) Conversely, assuming $\psi \notin \mathscr{B}_{\lambda,P}$, if $\mathscr{B}_{\lambda,P} *_{ml} \psi$ is deductively closed then $P(\psi) < \frac{\tau\lambda}{1-\lambda}$.

Proof. (i) According to Theorem 1, in order to show that $\mathscr{B}_{\lambda,R_\psi^\lambda} = \mathscr{B}_{\lambda,P} *_{ml} \psi$ is deductively closed, it is enough to find $\chi \in \mathcal{L}$ such that $R_\psi^\lambda(\chi) = \lambda$ and that $1 - \lambda < R_\psi^\lambda(\omega)$ for all $\omega \in [\![\chi]\!]$. Notice that in that case $\lambda = \lambda_M$ relative to the probability R_ψ^λ.

Let us take $\chi = \psi$ itself. Then $R_\psi^\lambda(\psi) = \lambda$ holds by definition, so it remains to check that $1 - \lambda < R_\psi^\lambda(\omega)$ for all $\omega \in [\![\psi]\!]$. But, again by the definition of R_ψ^λ, if $\omega \in [\![\psi]\!]$ then $R_\psi^\lambda(\omega) = \lambda P(\omega)/P(\psi)$. Hence, $R_\psi^\lambda(\omega) = \lambda P(\omega)/P(\psi) > 1 - \lambda$ iff $P(\psi) < \frac{P(\omega)\lambda}{1-\lambda}$ for all $\omega \in [\![\psi]\!]$ and hence iff $P(\psi) < \frac{\tau\lambda}{1-\lambda}$.

(ii) If $\psi \notin \mathscr{B}_{\lambda,P}$ we have $P(\psi) < \lambda$ and $R_\psi^\lambda(\psi) = \lambda$. Since $\mathscr{B}_{\lambda,P} *_{ml} \psi$ is deductively closed, by Lemma 2, $[\![\psi]\!]$ generates $\mathscr{B}_{\lambda,P} *_{ml} \psi$ and by Theorem 1, $1 - \lambda < \tau$. Thus $\frac{\tau}{1-\lambda} > 1$ and hence $P(\psi) < \lambda < \frac{\tau}{1-\lambda} \cdot \lambda$. □

Let us observe that in (ii) above, the condition $\psi \notin \mathscr{B}_{\lambda,P}$ is in fact necessary as the following simple example shows. Take $\Omega = \{\omega_1, \ldots, \omega_4\}$ and define P by $P(\omega_1) = P(\omega_2) = 0.35$, $P(\omega_3) = P(\omega_4) = 0.15$. Put $\lambda = 0.7$. It is easy to see that $\mathscr{B}_{\lambda,P}$ is closed. Let ψ be a formula such that $[\![\psi]\!] = \{\omega_1, \omega_2, \omega_3\}$, i.e., with $P(\psi) = 0.85$. Thus, $\mathscr{B}_{\lambda,P} *_{ml} \psi = \mathscr{B}_{\lambda,P}$ is closed but $P(\omega_3) < P(\psi)\frac{1-\lambda}{\lambda}$.

Now we briefly examine which of AGM basic postulates for revision ($\text{K}*_{ml}1$-$\text{K}*_{ml}6$) from [1] are satisfied in our framework. More detailed proofs can be found in [9].

K*1 (Closure): $\mathscr{B}_{\lambda,P} * \psi$ *is logically closed.* This is not generally satisfied. However, it is satisfied if either $\psi \in \mathscr{B}_{\lambda,P}$ and $\mathscr{B}_{\lambda,P}$ is closed or $\psi \notin \mathscr{B}_{\lambda,P}$ and ψ satisfies the condition (i) of Theorem 3.

K*2 (Success): $\psi \in \mathscr{B}_{\lambda,P} * \psi$. This holds by definition of R_ψ^λ.

K*3 (Inclusion): $\mathscr{B}_{\lambda,P}*\psi \subseteq Cn(\mathscr{B}_{\lambda,P}\cup\{\psi\})$. This postulate holds. Essentially, this is due to the fact that if $\varphi \in \mathscr{B}_{\lambda,P} * \psi$ then $(\psi \to \varphi) \in \mathscr{B}_{\lambda,P}$ (see details in [9]).

K*4 (Preservation): *If* $\mathscr{B}_{\lambda,P} \nvdash \neg\psi$ *then* $\mathscr{B}_{\lambda,P} \subseteq \mathscr{B}_{\lambda,P} * \psi$. This postulate is not satisfied in general (see [9] for a counterexample).

K*5 (Consistency): *If* ψ *is consistent then* $\mathscr{B}_{\lambda,P} * \psi$ *is consistent.* This postulate is not satisfied in general (see [9] for a counterexample). However, if ψ satisfies the conditions of Theorem 3.(i), the postulate holds.

K*6 (Extensionality): *If* $\vdash \psi \leftrightarrow \varphi$ *then* $\mathscr{B}_{\lambda,P} * \psi = \mathscr{B}_{\lambda,P} * \varphi$. This postulate clearly holds because the revision is defined semantically.

Finally, let us observe that the function R_ψ^λ, used for our revision is somehow minimal in the sense that R_ψ^λ changes less drastically the a priori P than the usual conditioning by ψ when $\lambda < 1$ and $P(\psi) < \lambda$.

One of the most basic distances d between probabilities is defined by

$$d(P, P') = \sum_{\omega \in \Omega} |P(\omega) - P'(\omega)|. \tag{5}$$

The following, whose proof appears detailed in [9], holds.

Fact 2. *According to the above distance function* d, R_ψ^λ *is closer to* P *than* $P(\cdot \mid \psi)$, *the simple conditioning.*

It should be noted that the distance d is too rough to distinguish R_ψ^λ among the set of those distributions satisfying that the probability of ψ is equal to λ. However, there exists a measure of divergence (which is not a distance) for which R_ψ^λ is minimal with respect to distributions satisfying that the probability of ψ is equal to λ. This is the *Kullback-Leibler divergence* [14,21] (also called relative entropy), defined as follows:

$$D_{K,L}(P', P) = \sum_{\omega \in \Omega} P'(\omega) \log(P'(\omega)/P(\omega)).$$

Using the Lagrange multipliers method, one can easily prove the next fact, whose proof is again detailed in [9].

Proposition 4. R_ψ^λ *minimizes the Kullback-Leibler divergence among the distributions* P' *such that* $P'(\psi) = \lambda$.

6   Related Work

There are several definitively relevant works in the literature which are related to the approach proposed in this paper in the sense of using standard (non-infinitesimal) probabilistic semantics to model the notion of belief.

In the context of conditional knowledge bases and the non-monotonic reasoning System P, the authors in [3] look for some standard probabilistic semantics for defaults "generally, if φ then ψ" of the kind $P(\psi \mid \varphi) > 1/2$, or equivalently $P(\psi \mid \varphi) > P(\neg\psi \mid \varphi)$. Since this general semantics does not satisfy the OR postulate of System P and the corresponding sets of (conditional) beliefs $\{\psi \mid P(\psi \mid \varphi) > 1/2\}$ are not deductively closed, they consider a particular subclass of probability distributions, namely Snow's *atomic bound systems* [24], also called big-stepped probabilities by these authors. More precisely, a big-stepped probability on a (finite) algebra set $\mathbf{A} = 2^{\Omega}$ is a probability function $P : \mathbf{A} \to [0, 1]$ such that (i) $P(\omega) > 0$ for all $\omega \in \Omega$, (ii) it induces a linear ordering $>$ on Ω, whereby $\omega > \omega'$ if and only if $P(\omega) > P(\omega')$, and (iii) for each interpretation ω, $P(\omega) > \sum_{\omega':\omega>\omega'} P(\omega')$. From this definition it is clear that a big-stepped probability is a stronger notion than an ω-step probability.

Big-stepped probabilities are closely related to probabilities which are *acceptance functions*. According to [8], an acceptance function is a mapping $g : 2^{\Omega} \to [0, 1])$ satisfying:

(AC1) if $g(\varphi) > g(\neg\varphi)$ and $\varphi \models \psi$ then $g(\psi) > g(\neg\psi)$, and
(AC2) if $g(\varphi) > g(\neg\varphi)$ and $g(\psi) > g(\neg\psi)$ then $g(\varphi \wedge \psi) > g(\neg(\varphi \wedge \psi))$.

Then φ is an accepted belief when $g(\varphi) > g(\neg\varphi)$. Indeed, if g is an acceptance function, then $\{\varphi \mid g(\varphi) > g(\neg\varphi)\}$ is a belief set that is deductively closed. The authors show in [8] that the only (positive) probabilities P that are acceptance functions are those that satisfy either:

(i) $P(\omega) > 1/2$ for some $\omega \in \Omega$, or
(ii) there exist $\omega, \omega' \in \Omega$ such that $P(\omega) = P(\omega') = 1/2$.

It is clear that big-stepped probabilities are both ω-step probabilities (for some ω) and (probability) acceptance functions, but the converse does not hold (one has to require that P induces a linear order on Ω). On the other hand, it is easy to check that non-trivial[3] probability acceptance functions are exactly those ω-step probability functions for which there exists $\lambda > 1/2$ such that $\mathscr{B}_{\lambda,P}$ is (deductively closed and) a maximal filter.

Another closely related work is that of Leitgeb [18], where the author considers a weakened version of the Lockean thesis, namely, given a probability P and a threshold λ, the corresponding beliefs should necessarily have a probability higher than λ, but this is not a sufficient condition to become a belief. The corner notion at work in his proposal is the concept of P-stable$^{\lambda}$ set. Adapted to our framework, a proposition ψ is P-stable$^{\lambda}$ if for any proposition φ such that $\psi \wedge \varphi \not\models \bot$ and $P(\varphi) > 0$, it holds that $P(\psi \mid \varphi) > \lambda$.[4] What P-stability$^{\lambda}$ requires is that if some proposition is consistent with all the other beliefs, then conditionalizing on such a proposition should not decrease the probability of

---

[3] A probability acceptance function P is called *trivial* when $P(\varphi) > 1/2$ iff $\models \varphi$.
[4] The author shows that this condition is equivalent to require that, for any model ω of ψ, it holds that $P(\omega) > \frac{\lambda}{1-\lambda}P(\neg\psi)$.

any believed proposition below the threshold λ. But, as the author notices, not every believed proposition has to be P-stable$^\lambda$. In fact, it is shown in [18] that the set of rationality postulates which he proposes a set of beliefs should satisfy (one of them being to be closed under deduction) entails that P-stability$^\lambda$ is only required for the strongest believed proposition, which is the conjunction of all believed propositions. Obviously, P-stable$^\lambda$ sets are a stronger notion than closed Lockean belief sets. Indeed, using the condition expressed in Footnote 4, one can check that if $\mathscr{B}_{\lambda,P}$ is closed and ψ is its strongest belief, then $P(\neg\psi) = 1 - \lambda$, while ψ is P-stable$^\lambda$ only when $P(\neg\psi) < (1 - \lambda).\frac{\tau}{\lambda} \leq 1 - \lambda$, where $\tau = \min\{P(\omega) \mid \omega \in [\![\psi]\!]\}$.

7 Conclusions and Future Work

In the first part of the paper we have provided two characterizations of those probability functions P on formulas ensuring the existence of suitable thresholds λ for which the corresponding Lockean set of beliefs $\mathscr{B}_{\lambda,P}$ is closed under logical deduction. Then, in the second part, we have discussed how to revise a Lockean belief set in a way that is compatible with an intuitive principle of minimal change. We have shown that this principle univocally leads to a revision procedure of an a priori given probability by a formula that, in fact, is closely related (but not equal) to Jeffrey conditionalization. Finally, we have characterized under which condition a (non necessarily deductively closed) Lockean belief set becomes deductively closed once revised by a suitable formula.

Regarding our revision operator for Lockean belief sets $*_{ml}$, an interesting line for future work is to investigate the fulfillment of Darwiche-Pearl postulates for iterated revision [7], and to find which postulates fully characterize $*_{ml}$ for a given probability and a given threshold. Also we plan to study in more detail the links of our approach with that of Leitgeb based on P-stable$^\lambda$ sets [18].

Acknowledgments. The authors thank the reviewers for their valuable and helpful comments as well as Vanina M. Martinez and Ricardo O. Rodriguez for initial interesting discussions on the topic of the paper. Tommaso Flaminio acknowledges partial support from the Spanish project SHORE (PID2022-141529NB-C22) funded by the MCIN/AEI/10.13039/501100011033. Lluis Godo acknowledges support by the Spanish project LINEXSYS (PID2022-139835NB-C21). Flaminio and Godo also acknowledge partial support from the H2020-MSCA-RISE-2020 project MOSAIC (Grant Agreement number 101007627). Ramón Pino Pérez has benefited from the support of the AI Chair BE4musIA of the French National Research Agency (ANR-20-CHIA-0028) and the support of I. Bloch's chair in AI (Sorbonne Université and SCAI).

References

1. Alchourrón, C.E., Gärdenfors, P., Makinson, D.: On the logic of theory change: partial meet contraction and revision functions. J. Symb. Log. **50**, 510–530 (1985)

2. Benci, V., Horsten, L., Wenmackers, S.: Infinitesimal probabilities. Br. J. Philos. Sci. **69**(2), 509–552 (2016)
3. Benferhat, S., Dubois, D., Prade, H.: Possibilistic and standard probabilistic semantics of conditional knowledge bases. J. Log. Comput. **9**(6), 873–895 (1999)
4. Bonzio, S., Cevolani, G., Flaminio, T.: How to believe long conjunctions of beliefs: probability, quasi-dogmatism and contextualism. Erkenntnis **88**(3), 965–990 (2023)
5. Cantwell, J., Rott, H.: Probability, coherent belief and coherent belief change. Ann. Math. Artif. Intell. **87**, 259–291 (2019)
6. Cori, R., Lascar, D.: Mathematical Logic: A Course with Exercises. Oxford University Press, New York (2000)
7. Darwiche, A., Pearl, J.: On the logic of iterated belief revision. Artif. Intell. **89**(1), 1–29 (1997)
8. Dubois, D., Prade, H.: Numerical representation of acceptance. In: Proceedings of the 11th Conference on Uncertainty in Artificial Intelligence (UAI 1995), Montreal, pp. 149–156 (1995)
9. Flaminio, T., Godo, L., Pino Pérez, R., Subirana, L.: On Lockean beliefs that are deductively closed and minimal change (2025). http://arxiv.org/abs/2507.06042
10. Foley, R.: Working Without a Net. Oxford University Press, Oxford (1992)
11. Gärdenfors, P.: The dynamic of belief: contractions and revisions of probability functions. Topoi **5**, 29–37 (1986)
12. Hansson, S.O.: Revising probabilities and full beliefs. J. Philos. Log. **49**, 1005–1039 (2020)
13. Hansson, S.O.: A basis for AGM in Bayesian probability revision. J. Philos. Log. **52**, 1535–1559 (2023)
14. Jacobs, B.: Learning from what's right and learning from what's wrong. In: Electronic Proceedings in Theoretical Computer Science, vol. 351, pp. 116–133 (2021)
15. Jeffrey, R.C.: The Logic of Decision, 2nd edn. University of Chicago Press, Chicago (1983)
16. Katsuno, H., Mendelzon, A.O.: Propositional knowledge base revision and minimal change. Artif. Intell. **52**, 263–294 (1991)
17. Kyburg, H.: Probability and the Logic of Rational Belief. Wesleyan University Press, Middletown (1967)
18. Leitgeb, H.: Reducing belief simpliciter to degrees of belief. Ann. Pure Appl. Logic **164**, 1338–1389 (2013)
19. Makinson, D.: The paradox of the preface. Analysis **25**(6), 205–207 (1965)
20. Paris, J.B.: The Uncertain Reasoner's Companion. A Mathematical Perspective. Cambridge University Press (1994)
21. Pinzón, C., Palamidessi, C.: Jeffrey's update rule as a minimizer of Kullback-Leibler divergence (2025). https://arxiv.org/abs/2502.15504
22. Schwind, N., Konieczny, S., Pino Pérez, R.: On the representation of Darwiche and Pearl's epistemic states for iterated belief revision. In: Proceedings of the 19th International Conference on Principles of Knowledge Representation and Reasoning (KR 2022) (2022)
23. Shear, T., Fitelson, B.: Two approaches to belief revision. Erkenntnis **84**, 487–518 (2019)
24. Snow, P.: Diverse confidence levels in a probabilistic semantics for conditional logics. Artif. Intell. **113**, 269–279 (1999)

Extending Defeasibility for Propositional Standpoint Logics

Nicholas Leisegang[1]($\boxtimes$)(iD), Thomas Meyer[1](iD), and Ivan Varzinczak[1,2](iD)

[1] University of Cape Town and CAIR, Cape Town, South Africa
lsgnic001@myuct.ac.za, tommie.meyer@uct.ac.za
[2] Université Sorbonne Paris Nord, Inserm, Sorbonne Université, Limics, 93017 Bobigny, France
ivan.varzinczak@sorbonne-paris-nord.fr

Abstract. In this paper, we introduce a new defeasible version of propositional standpoint logic by integrating Kraus et al.'s defeasible conditionals, Britz and Varzinczak's notions of defeasible necessity and distinct possibility, along with Leisegang et al.'s approach to defeasibility into the standpoint logics of Gómez Álvarez and Rudolph. The resulting logical framework allows for the expression of defeasibility on the level of implications, standpoint modal operators, and standpoint-sharpening statements. We provide a preferential semantics for this extended language and propose a tableaux calculus, which is shown to be sound and complete with respect to preferential entailment. We also establish the computational complexity of the tableaux procedure to be in PSPACE.

1 Introduction

Standpoint logics are a recently introduced family of agent-centred knowledge representation formalisms [7]. Their main feature is to allow the integration of the viewpoints of two or more agents into a single knowledge base, especially when the agents have conflicting takes on a given matter. Standpoint logics are tightly related to various systems of epistemic and doxastic logics since they build on modalities for expressing viewpoints and also assume a Kripke-style possible-worlds semantics. Sentences with standpoint-indexed modal operators such as $\Box_s\alpha$ and $\Diamond_s\alpha$ read, respectively, "from the s standpoint, it is unequivocal that α," and "from the s standpoint, it is possible that α". With standpoint-sharpening statements of the form $s \leq t$ (which, in modal-logic terms, is an abbreviation for an axiom schema establishing the interaction between two modalities), one expresses that one standpoint is at least as specific as another, which is a way to say both standpoints agree to some extent.

In spite of allowing for the opinions upheld by agents to be in conflict without causing the knowledge base to be inconsistent, classical standpoint logics do not allow for each agent to handle exceptional cases *within* their respective standpoints. This has been partially remedied by Leisegang et al. [18], who have extended standpoint logics with both defeasible conditionals in the scope of modalities and a non-monotonic form of entailment. The resulting framework, defeasible restricted standpoint logic (DRSL), allows agents to reason about exceptions relative to their own beliefs and for defeasible

G. Casini et al. (Eds.): JELIA 2025, LNAI 16094, pp. 43–57, 2026.
https://doi.org/10.1007/978-3-032-04590-4_4

consequences of a knowledge base to be derived. Nevertheless, DRSL still leaves open the question of a more general approach to defeasibility.

As pointed out by Britz and Varzinczak [3], logical languages with modalities make room for exploring defeasibility elsewhere than in conditionals: we can talk of *defeasible necessity* and *distinct possibility*, represented, respectively, by the modal operators $\mathbin{\reflectbox{$\sim$}}$ and $\diamondsuit$. These enrich modal systems with defeasibility at the object level and meet a variety of applications in reasoning about defeasible knowledge, defeasible action effects, defeasible obligations, and others. It seems only natural that defeasible modalities can be fruitful in providing a formal account of the defeasible standpoints motivated above.

The goal of the present paper is to introduce Propositional Defeasible Standpoint Logic (PDSL), a new defeasible version of standpoint logic enriched with defeasibility aspects on various levels. First, we allow for a defeasible form of implication which is different from the restricted one by Leisegang et al. [18]. Second, drawing on the work of Britz and Varzinczak [3], we define defeasible versions of the standpoint modal operators found in classical standpoint logic. Finally, we extend classical standpoint logic further by allowing for the possibility of defeasible standpoint-sharpening statements.

The example below gives an idea of the level of expressivity available in PDSL.

Example 1. We consider the standpoints of vegetarians, vegans, pacifists, and environmentalists. From a vegetarian's *usual* standpoint, egg and cheese, although animal-based, are not considered unethical animal products to consume. In PDSL, this can be expressed with the sentence $\mathbin{\reflectbox{$\sim$}}_{\mathsf{Vegetarian}}((\mathsf{egg} \lor \mathsf{cheese}) \to \lnot \mathsf{animal})$, which should not conflict with $\diamondsuit_{\mathsf{Vegetarian}}(\mathsf{egg} \land \mathsf{animal})$, an exception compatible with the vegetarian standpoint which formalises that it is possible (although unusual) to consider an egg an unethical animal product. From the vegan standpoint, though, egg and cheese are unethical animal products. This is formalised with $\square_{\mathsf{Vegan}}((\mathsf{egg} \lor \mathsf{cheese}) \to \mathsf{animal})$, and is in line with the intuition that the vegan standpoint is a more specific version of the vegetarian one. This is captured by the sharpening sentence $\mathsf{Vegan} \leq \mathsf{Vegetarian}$. The intuition that *usually*, the vegetarian standpoint is a more specific version of the pacifist one, but allows for exceptions, e.g. those who do not eat meat only for health reasons, can be formalised as the defeasible sharpening $\mathsf{Vegetarian} \precsim \mathsf{Pacifist}$. Among the consequences of the above, we may expect that there exists a vegan who is a typical representative of the vegan standpoint, who believes that eggs are an unethical animal product and conclude $\diamondsuit_{\mathsf{Vegan}}(\mathsf{egg} \to \mathsf{animal})$. Moreover, while we may expect that typical environmentalists are vegetarians and so $\mathsf{Environmentalist} \precsim \mathsf{Vegetarian}$ holds, we would not expect that typical environmentalists are necessarily pacifists, and so would expect that $\mathsf{Environmentalist} \precsim \mathsf{Pacifist}$ does not hold, even though $\mathsf{Vegetarian} \precsim \mathsf{Pacifist}$ holds.

The plan of the paper is as follows: Sect. 2 recalls the background and notation for the upcoming sections. Following that, and inspired by the work of Britz and Varzinczak [3] and Leisegang et al. [18], Sect. 3 introduces Propositional Defeasible Standpoint Logic (PDSL). In particular, we show that a preferential semantics *à la* KLM is suitable for interpreting defeasibility in PDSL and also enables us to define *preferential entailment* [17] from PDSL knowledge bases. In Sect. 4, we provide a tableaux-based algorithm for computing preferential entailment for PDSL, we prove its soundness and completeness, and show that its complexity is in PSPACE. Section 5 is a brief discussion on related work. Section 6 closes the paper and considers future work.

2 Preliminaries

In this section we briefly introduce the basics of classical propositional standpoint logic, as well as defeasible modalities and defeasible reasoning in modal logic, which form the basis for the logic PDSL introduced in this paper. Standpoint logic was introduced by Gómez Álvarez and Rudolph [7] for the propositional case. Given a vocabulary $\mathcal{V} = (\mathcal{P}, \mathcal{S})$, where $\mathcal{P}$ is a set of propositional atoms and $\mathcal{S}$ a finite set of standpoints including the universal standpoint $*$, the language $\mathcal{L}_\mathbb{S}$ over $\mathcal{V}$ is defined by:

$$\phi ::= s \leq t \mid p \mid \neg \phi \mid \phi \wedge \phi \mid \Box_s \phi$$

where $s, t \in \mathcal{S}$ and $p \in \mathcal{P}$. Statements of the form $s \leq t$ are referred to as *standpoint sharpening statements*. The Boolean connectives $\vee$, $\rightarrow$, $\leftrightarrow$ are defined via $\neg$ and $\wedge$ in their usual manner, and for each standpoint $s \in \mathcal{S}$, we define $\Diamond_s$ as $\neg \Box_s \neg$.

A *standpoint structure* is a triple $M = (\Pi, \sigma, \gamma)$ where Π is a non-empty set of precisifications; $\sigma : \mathcal{S} \to 2^\Pi$ is a function such that $\sigma(*) = \Pi$ and $\sigma(s) \neq \emptyset$ for all $s \in \mathcal{S}$; $\gamma : \Pi \to 2^\mathcal{P}$ is a function which assigns each precisification a set of atoms. Intuitively, the mapping σ allows one to allocate to a standpoint s the set of all "reasonable ways to make s's beliefs correct", and γ assigns a set of basic propositions which are 'true' in that precisification. For a standpoint structure M and a precisification $\pi \in \Pi$, we define the satisfaction relation $\Vdash$ as follows (where $\phi, \phi_1, \phi_2 \in \mathcal{L}_\mathbb{S}$, $s, t \in \mathcal{S}$, and $p \in \mathcal{P}$): $M, \pi \Vdash p$ iff $p \in \gamma(\pi)$; $M, \pi \Vdash \neg \phi$ iff $M, \pi \nVdash \phi$; $M, \pi \Vdash \phi_1 \wedge \phi_2$ iff $M, \pi \Vdash \phi_1$ and $M, \pi \Vdash \phi_2$; $M, \pi \Vdash \Box_s \phi$ iff $M, \pi' \Vdash \phi$ for all $\pi' \in \sigma(s)$; $M, \pi \Vdash s \leq t$ iff $\sigma(s) \subseteq \sigma(t)$, and $M \Vdash \phi$ iff $M, \pi \Vdash \phi$ for all $\pi \in \Pi$.

Defeasible reasoning in modal logic is largely based off of similar methods in the propositional case derived from the notion of preferential consequence relations introduced by Kraus et al. [14], and rational consequence relations introduced by Lehmann and Magidor [17]. Named after the aforementioned authors, this is often called the KLM approach to defeasibility. Preferential consequence relations were considered in the modal case by Britz et al. [1,2] and extended to include KLM-style defeasibility within modal operators themselves by Britz and Varzinczak [3]. In our paper, we build upon the defeasible multi-modal language $\mathcal{L}^\approx$ [3]. For a set of propositional atoms $\mathcal{P}$, the language is $\mathcal{L}^\approx$ defined by:

$$\phi ::= p \mid \neg \phi \mid \phi \wedge \phi \mid \Box_i \phi \mid \mathbin{\rotatebox[origin=c]{180}{$\approx$}}_i \phi \mid \phi \rightsquigarrow \phi$$

where $p \in \mathcal{P}$, and $1 \leq i \leq n$, for some $n \in \mathbb{N}$. The other connectives, $\vee$, $\rightarrow$, and $\leftrightarrow$, are defined as usual. The modality $\Diamond_i$ is defined as $\neg \Box_i \neg$, and $\mathbin{\rotatebox[origin=c]{45}{$\Diamond$}}_i$ is (analogously) defined as $\neg \mathbin{\rotatebox[origin=c]{180}{$\approx$}}_i \neg$. Intuitively, $\Box_i$ indicates necessity and $\Diamond_i$ possibility (both with respect to i). Regarding the three new operators, $\mathbin{\rotatebox[origin=c]{180}{$\approx$}}_i$ is intended to indicate "usual necessity" (with respect to i), while $\mathbin{\rotatebox[origin=c]{45}{$\Diamond$}}_i$ is intended to convey "distinct" or "strong" possibility (with respect to i), and $\rightsquigarrow$ is a (possibly nested) defeasible conditional.

A preferential Kripke model is a quadruple $P = (W, R, V, \prec)$, where W is a non-empty set of worlds, $R := < R_1, \ldots, R_n >$, where each $R_i \subseteq W \times W$ is an accessibility relation on W, $V : W \longrightarrow 2^{\mathcal{P}}$ is a valuation function which maps each world to a set of propositional atoms, and $\prec$ is a strict partial order on W that is well-founded (for every $W' \subseteq W$ and every $v \in W'$, either v is $\prec$-minimal in W', or there is a $u \in W'$ that is $\prec$-minimal in W' and $u \prec v$). Satisfaction with respect to P and a world $w \in W$ is defined as follows: For $p \in \mathcal{P}$, $P, w \Vdash p$ iff $p \in V(w)$; $P, w \Vdash \neg\phi$ iff $P, w \nVdash \phi$; $P, w \Vdash \phi_1 \land \phi_2$ iff $P, w \Vdash \phi$ and $P, w \Vdash \phi_2$; $P, w \Vdash \Box_i\phi$ iff $P, v \Vdash \phi$ for every $v \in W$ such that $(w, v) \in R_i$; $P, w \Vdash \widetilde{\boxdot}_i \phi$ iff $P, v \Vdash \phi$ for every $v \in W$ such that $v \in \min_{\prec} R_i(w)$ (where $R_i(w) = \{w' \mid (w, w') \in R_i\}$); $P, w \Vdash \phi_1 \rightsquigarrow \phi_2$ whenever $w \notin \min_{\prec}[\![\phi_1]\!]^P$ or $w \in [\![\phi_2]\!]^P$ (where $[\![\phi_1]\!]^P$ refers to those elements v of W for which $P, v \Vdash \phi_1$, and similarly for $[\![\phi_2]\!]^P$). Finally, $P \Vdash \phi$ iff $P, w \Vdash \phi$ for every $w \in W$.

Classical multi-modal statements are interpreted in the standard way. Statements of the form $\widetilde{\boxdot}_i\phi$ are true with respect to P and w whenever ϕ is true with respect to P and all the most typical worlds accessible from w, while statements of the form $\widetilde{\diamondsuit}_i\phi$ are true with respect to P and w whenever ϕ is true with respect to P and at least one most typical world accessible from w. Statements of the form $\phi_1 \rightsquigarrow \phi_2$ are true in the model P when ϕ_2 is true in the most typical ϕ_1-worlds.

Britz and Varzinczak present a tableaux method for checking whether or not a statement in $\mathcal{L}^{\boxdot}$ is satisfiable in some preferential Kripke model. They prove soundness and completeness for their tableaux method, and show that it is PSPACE-complete.

3   Propositional Defeasible Standpoint Logic (PDSL)

Having dispensed with the necessary preliminaries, we now proceed to introduce Propositional Defeasible Standpoint Logic, or PDSL.

Definition 1. *Given a vocabulary* $\mathcal{V} = (\mathcal{P}, \mathcal{S})$ *where* $\mathcal{P}$ *is a set of propositional atoms and* $\mathcal{S}$ *is a set of standpoints, we define the set of standpoint expressions* $\mathcal{E}$ *over* $\mathcal{S}$ *as*

$$e ::= * \mid s \mid -e \mid e \cap e$$

where $s \in \mathcal{S}$. *We define* $\widetilde{\mathcal{L}}_{\mathbb{S}}$ *over* $\mathcal{V}$ *(where* $p \in \mathcal{P}$ *and* $e, d \in \mathcal{E}$*) as follows:*

$$\alpha ::= \top \mid p \mid e \lesssim d \mid \neg\alpha \mid \alpha \land \alpha \mid \Box_e\alpha \mid \widetilde{\boxdot}_e\alpha \mid \alpha \rightsquigarrow \alpha$$

From this, we can define statements of the form $\alpha \lor \beta$, $\alpha \rightarrow \beta$ and $\alpha \leftrightarrow \beta$ in the usual way. We can also define dual symbols for both classical and defeasible standpoint modalities. That is, we define $\diamondsuit_e\alpha := \neg\Box_e\neg\alpha$ and $\widetilde{\diamondsuit}_e\alpha := \neg\widetilde{\boxdot}_e\neg\alpha$. Intuitively, $\diamondsuit_e\alpha$ reads "it is possible to e that α" and $\widetilde{\diamondsuit}_e\alpha$ represents the stronger notion that "*in the most typical understandings of* e's *viewpoint, it is possible that* α *holds*". We can also define new standpoint symbols $e \cup d$ and $e \setminus d$ by as $e \cup d := -(-e \cap -d)$ and $e \setminus d := e \cap -d$, for all $e, d \in \mathcal{E}$. We are also able to define classical standpoint sharpening statements as $e \leq d := \Box_{e \setminus d}\bot$. Note that $e \leq d$ intuitively denotes that "standpoint e

is a more specific version of standpoint d". That is, every precisification associated with e's standpoint can also be associated with d's standpoint. The sentence $e \precsim d$ can then be thought of as the defeasible version of this sentence, which reads that the *most typical* precisifications associated with standpoint e are also associated with standpoint d.

The semantic structure used for defeasible standpoint modalities takes the conventions of the semantics for standpoint propositional logics [7], as well as complex standpoint expressions introduced in first-order standpoint logic [8], and adds an ordering to precisifications, where, intuitively, lower precisifications should be considered as "more typical" or more preferred states. This again follows the convention for the defeasible modalities introduced for more generalised multimodal logics [3].

Definition 2. *A **state-preferential** standpoint structure (SPSS) is a quadruple $M = (\Pi, \sigma, \gamma, \prec)$ where,*

- *Π is a set of precisifications.*
- *$\sigma : \mathcal{E} \to 2^{\Pi}$ is a function such that $\sigma(*) = \Pi$, $\sigma(e \cap d) = \sigma(e) \cap \sigma(d)$, and $\sigma(-e) = \Pi \setminus \sigma(e)$. Moreover, we require that $\sigma(s) \neq \emptyset$ for all $s \in \mathcal{S}$.*
- *$\gamma : \Pi \to 2^{\mathcal{P}}$ is a map which assigns a classical valuation to each precisification.*
- *$\prec$ is a strict partial order on Π such that for every subset X of Π, and every $\pi \in X$, either π is a $\prec$-minimal element of X, or there is a $\pi' \in X$ such that π' is a $\prec$-minimal element of X, and $\pi' \prec \pi$ (well-foundedness).*

Example 2. (Example 1 continued). Assume $\mathcal{P} = \{\mathsf{animal}, \mathsf{cheese}, \mathsf{egg}\}$ and $\mathcal{S} = \{\mathsf{Environmentalist}, \mathsf{Pacifist}, \mathsf{Vegan}, \mathsf{Vegetarian}\}$. Figure 1 depicts an example of a state preferential standpoint structure for the given vocabulary.

We then define satisfaction for a given SPSS.

Definition 3. *For an SPSS M and a precisification $\pi \in \Pi$, we define the satisfaction relation $\Vdash$ inductively as follows (where $\alpha, \alpha_1, \alpha_2 \in \mathcal{L}_\mathbb{S}$, $s, s_1, s_2 \in \mathcal{S}$ and $p \in \mathcal{P}$):*

- *$M, \pi \Vdash \top$.*
- *$M, \pi \Vdash p$ iff $p \in \gamma(\pi)$.*
- *$M, \pi \Vdash e \precsim d$ iff $\min_{\prec}(\sigma(e)) \subseteq \sigma(d)$.*
- *$M, \pi \Vdash \neg \alpha$ iff $M, \pi \nVdash \alpha$.*
- *$M, \pi \Vdash \alpha_1 \wedge \alpha_2$ iff $M, \pi \Vdash \alpha_1$ and $M, \pi \Vdash \alpha_2$.*
- *$M, \pi \Vdash \square_s \alpha$ iff $M, \pi' \Vdash \alpha$ for all $\pi' \in \sigma(s)$.*
- *$M, \pi \Vdash \diagdown_s \alpha$ iff $M, \pi' \Vdash \alpha$ for all $\pi' \in \min_{\prec}(\sigma(s))$.*
- *$M, \pi \Vdash \alpha_1 \rightsquigarrow \alpha_2$ iff $\pi \notin \min_{\prec} [\![\alpha_1]\!]$ or $\pi \in [\![\alpha_2]\!]$.*
- *$M \Vdash \alpha$ iff $M, \pi \Vdash \alpha$ for all $\pi \in \Pi$.*

We also note here several rules which the semantics introduced above satisfies in general. However, it should be noted that this list is not exhaustive by any means. Firstly, it should be clear that, since both the language and the semantics introduce notions of defeasibility on top of the existing propositional standpoint logic $\mathcal{L}_\mathbb{S}$, any sentences in $\mathcal{L}_\mathbb{S}$ which are tautologous in the original logic (as discussed by Gómez Álvarez and Rudolph [7]) are still tautologies in our case. We therefore will only discuss the defeasible parts of the logic explicitly here. We first compare the defeasible statements to their non-defeasible counterparts.

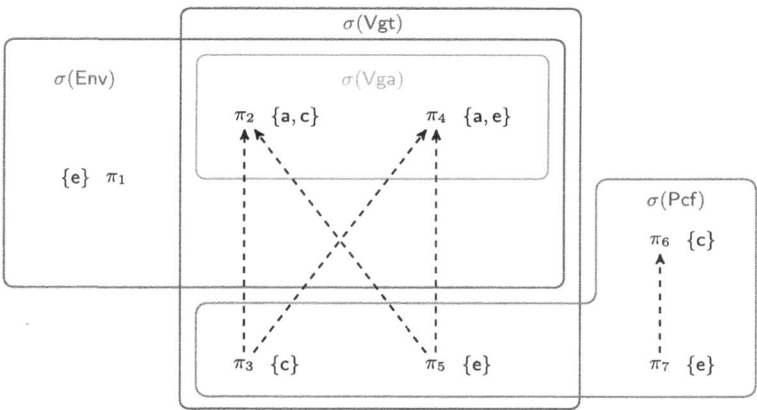

Fig. 1. A state preferential standpoint structure for $\mathcal{P} = \{animal, cheese, egg\}$ and $\mathcal{S} = \{Environmentalist, Pacifist, Vegan, Vegetarian\}$, where $\Pi = \{\pi_i \mid 1 \leq i \leq 7\}$, $\sigma(Environmentalist) = \{\pi_1, \pi_2, \pi_4\}$, $\sigma(Pacifist) = \{\pi_6, \pi_7\}$, $\sigma(Vegan) = \{\pi_2, \pi_4\}$, and $\sigma(Vegetarian) = \{\pi_2, \pi_3, \pi_4, \pi_5\}$. Moreover, $\gamma(\pi_1) = \{egg\}$, $\gamma(\pi_2) = \{animal, cheese\}$, $\gamma(\pi_3) = \{cheese\}$, $\gamma(\pi_4) = \{animal, egg\}$, $\gamma(\pi_5) = \{egg\}$, $\gamma(\pi_6) = \{cheese\}$, and $\gamma(\pi_7) = \{egg\}$. (Standpoints and atomic propositions are abbreviated for conciseness.) The strict partial order on Π is given by $\prec = \{(\pi_3, \pi_2), (\pi_3, \pi_4), (\pi_5, \pi_2), (\pi_5, \pi_4), (\pi_7, \pi_6)\}$.

Proposition 1. (Supra-classicality). *For any SPSS M, and any $\pi \in \Pi$:*

1. $M, \pi \Vdash \Box_e \alpha \implies M, \pi \Vdash \mathbin{\reflectbox{$\boxtimes$}}_e \alpha.$ *3.* $M, \pi \Vdash e \leq d \implies M, \pi \Vdash e \lesssim d.$

2. $M, \pi \Vdash \Diamond_e \alpha \implies M, \pi \Vdash \diamondsuit_e \alpha.$ *4.* $M, \pi \Vdash \alpha \to \beta \implies M, \pi \Vdash \alpha \rightsquigarrow \beta.$

And in general none of the converses hold.

This tells us that $\mathbin{\reflectbox{$\boxtimes$}}$, $\lesssim$ and $\rightsquigarrow$ are strictly weaker notions than their classical counterparts, while $\diamondsuit$ is a stronger notion. We can also note how defeasible modalities affect the unions and intersections of standpoint symbols.

Proposition 2. *For an SPSS M and $\pi \in \Pi$, we have $M, \pi \Vdash \mathbin{\reflectbox{$\boxtimes$}}_e \alpha \wedge \mathbin{\reflectbox{$\boxtimes$}}_d \alpha \implies M, \pi \Vdash \mathbin{\reflectbox{$\boxtimes$}}_{e \cup d} \alpha$ and $M, \pi \Vdash \diamondsuit_{e \cup d}\alpha \implies M, \pi \Vdash \diamondsuit_e \alpha \vee \diamondsuit_d \alpha$. In general, the converses do not hold.*

This shows the relationship that defeasible modalities have when combining them with more "compound" standpoint symbols. It is also worth noting that this relationship is different to the case for classical standpoint modalities. For example $M \Vdash \Box_e \alpha \wedge \Box_d \alpha$ and $M \Vdash \Box_{e \cup d}\alpha$ are equivalent, while this is not the case for defeasible modalities.

Our semantics also gives us a clearer understanding of $\lesssim$. The statement $e \leq d$ can be written as a modal sharpening $\Box_{e \setminus d} \bot$, which refers to the semantic condition on a standpoint structure M where $\sigma(e) \subseteq \sigma(d)$ [8]. In the defeasible case, it is clear that an analogous translation does not occur. Consider the SPSS M in Fig. 1. Clearly, $M \Vdash Vegetarian \lesssim Pacifist$, while $M \not\Vdash \Box_{Vegetarian \setminus Pacifist} \bot$ and

$M \not\Vdash \Join_{\mathsf{Vegetarian} \setminus \mathsf{Pacifist}} \perp$, since $\pi_2 \in \min_{\prec} \sigma(\mathsf{Vegetarian} \setminus \mathsf{Pacifist})$. In fact, the interpretation of the defeasible sharpening $\precsim$ behaves as a defeasible consequence relation on the standpoint hierarchy, since $s \precsim t$ can be interpreted semantically as stating "precisifications in s are *typically* included in t". In order to motivate this, we note that $\precsim$ satisfies a version of the KLM rationality postulates [14].

Proposition 3. *For $e, d, g \in \mathcal{E}$, an SPSS M, and $\pi \in \Pi$ we have:*

- $M, \pi \not\Vdash * \precsim e \cap -e$ *(Consistency)*
- $M, \pi \Vdash e \precsim e$ *(Reflexivity)*
- *If $M, \pi \Vdash (e \leq d) \wedge (d \leq e)$ and $M, \pi \Vdash e \precsim g$ then $M, \pi \Vdash d \precsim g$*   *(LLE)*
- *If $M, \pi \Vdash e \precsim d$, and $M, \pi \Vdash d \leq g$ then $M, \pi \Vdash e \precsim g$*   *(RW)*
- *If $M, \pi \Vdash e \precsim d$, and $M, \pi \Vdash e \precsim g$ then $M, \pi \Vdash e \precsim d \cap g$*   *(And)*
- *If $M, \pi \Vdash e \precsim d$, and $M, \pi \Vdash g \precsim d$ then $M, \pi \Vdash e \cup g \precsim d$*   *(Or)*
- *If $M, \pi \Vdash e \precsim d$, and $M, \pi \Vdash e \precsim g$ then $M, \pi \Vdash e \cap g \precsim d$*   *(CM)*

We can also see that defeasible sharpenings satisfy an adapted version of the classical standpoint axiom **(P)** [7], given by $(e \leq d) \to (\square_d \phi \to \square_e \phi)$, and thus behaves as a natural extension of the classical sharpening statements.

Proposition 4. *For $e, d \in \mathcal{E}$, $\phi \in \widetilde{\mathcal{L}}_{\mathbb{S}}$, an SPSS $M = (\Pi, \sigma, \gamma, \prec)$, and any $\pi \in \Pi$, we have that $M, \pi \Vdash (e \precsim d) \to (\square_d \phi \to \Join_e \phi)$.*

However, other variants of **(P)** which incorporate defeasible symbols, such as $(e \precsim d) \to (\Join_d \phi \to \square_e \phi)$ or $(e \leq d) \to (\Join_d \phi \to \Join_e \phi)$, are not satisfied by every SPSS.

It is shown in the more general modal logic $\mathcal{L}^{\Join}$, introduced by Britz and Varzinczak [3], that the defeasible implication operator $\rightsquigarrow$ satisfies a similar set of KLM postulates. This gives us a notion of defeasible implication between Boolean formulas in the logic. However, it is worth noting that, while $\rightsquigarrow$ gives us the original KLM-style consequence for Boolean formulas in our language, this intuition does not follow when we combine it with standpoint modalities in our language. In particular, when we bound a defeasible implication $p \rightsquigarrow q$ with some defeasible or non-defeasible standpoint modality, we may expect this to tell us something about a standpoints defeasible beliefs. For example, we may expect $\square_s(p \rightsquigarrow q)$ to tell us that "*from s's standpoint, the most typical instances of p are instances of q*". The following example shows us that this is not the case.

Example 3. Consider an SPSS $M = (\Pi, \sigma, \gamma, \prec)$ over propositional atoms p and q and a single standpoint s defined as follows: $\Pi = \{\pi_1, \pi_2\}$, $\sigma(s) = \{\pi_2\}$, $\gamma(\pi_1) = \{p, q\}$, $\gamma(\pi_2) = \{p\}$, and $\pi_1 \prec \pi_2 \prec \pi_3$. Then note $M \Vdash \square_s(p \rightsquigarrow q)$ iff $M, \pi \Vdash p \rightsquigarrow q$ for all $\pi \in \sigma(s)$. That is, $\pi \in \sigma(s)$ implies $\pi \notin \min_{\prec}[\![p]\!]$ or $\pi \in [\![q]\!]$. Since in the above model $\sigma(s) \cap \min_{\prec}[\![p]\!] = \emptyset$, we have $M \Vdash \square_s(p \rightsquigarrow q)$, even though the only precisification in $\sigma(s)$ (and therefore the minimal one) violates $p \to q$, and so s's standpoint intuitively does not believe that the most typical instances of p are instances of q.

Thus, defeasible implication $\widetilde{\mathcal{L}}_{\mathbb{S}}$ does not serve to represent standpoints holding defeasible beliefs, and a separate semantics is introduced for this problem in [18]. We also note that $\rightsquigarrow$ does not provide an intuitive account of defeasible consequences for modal statements. For example, $M \Vdash \Box_e \alpha \rightsquigarrow \beta$ if and only every $\pi \in \min_{\prec} [\![\Box_e \alpha]\!] \subseteq [\![\beta]\!]$. However, it is clear that by definition, either $[\![\Box_e \alpha]\!] = \emptyset$ or $[\![\Box_e \alpha]\!] = \Pi$. In the first case, $M \Vdash \Box_e \alpha \rightsquigarrow \beta$ trivially; in the second, $M \Vdash \Box_e \alpha \rightsquigarrow \beta$ iff $M, \pi \Vdash \beta$ for every $\pi \in \min_{\prec} \Pi$, which is equivalent to $M \Vdash_{\approx_*} \beta$. We therefore treat $\rightsquigarrow$ as a part of the language which is useful for describing defeasible implication between Boolean statements, but not as an intuitively meaningful statement outside of these bounds.

4 Satisfiability Checking and Preferential Entailment

In this section we address the notion of preferential satisfiability and preferential entailment in the semantics for $\widetilde{\mathcal{L}}_{\mathbb{S}}$. We differentiate between local and global satisfaction, as is defined below.

Definition 4. *Let α be a sentence in $\widetilde{\mathcal{L}}_{\mathbb{S}}$. We say that α is **locally satisfiable** if there exists an SPSS $M = (\Pi, \sigma, \gamma, \prec)$ for which there is some precisification $\pi \in \Pi$ such that $M, \pi \Vdash \alpha$. We say that α is **globally satisfiable** if there exists an SPSS M such that $M \Vdash \alpha$. For any finite set $A \subseteq \widetilde{\mathcal{L}}_{\mathbb{S}}$, we say that A is locally (resp. globally) satisfiable if $\bigwedge A$ is locally (resp. globally) satisfiable.*

Closely related to this is the notion of preferential entailment, which extends the notion of preferential entailment found in the propositional case by Kraus et al. [14], and in the case for defeasible modalities in logic **K** by Britz et al. [1].

Definition 5. *Consider a finite knowledge base $\mathcal{K} \subseteq \widetilde{\mathcal{L}}_{\mathbb{S}}$, and a sentence $\alpha \in \widetilde{\mathcal{L}}_{\mathbb{S}}$. We say that $\mathcal{K}$ **preferentially entails** α or write $\mathcal{K} \models_P \alpha$ if, for every SPSS M such that $M \Vdash \phi$ for all $\phi \in \mathcal{K}$, we have $M \Vdash \alpha$.*

It is noted by Britz et al. [2] that preferential entailment defined this way induces a monotonic consequence operator. Therefore while the defeasible symbols we introduce are non-monotonic on the object-level, the entailment-level reasoning remains monotonic. The following propositions show that both global satisfiability and preferential entailment can be expressed in terms of local satisfiability.

Proposition 5. *Consider a globally satisfiable knowledge base $\mathcal{K} \subseteq \widetilde{\mathcal{L}}_{\mathbb{S}}$ and a sentence $\alpha \in \widetilde{\mathcal{L}}_{\mathbb{S}}$. Then α is globally satisfiable iff $\Box_* \alpha$ is locally satisfiable. Furthermore, $\mathcal{K} \models_P \alpha$ iff $\Box_* (\bigwedge \mathcal{K}) \wedge \neg \alpha$ is not locally satisfiable.*

Our first method for checking preferential satisfiability is via translating our logic into classical propositional standpoint logic as described by Gómez Álvarez and Rudolph [7], including complex standpoint expressions.

Definition 6. *Let $M = (\Pi, \sigma, \gamma, \prec)$ be a state preferential standpoint structure over the vocabulary $\mathcal{V} = (\mathcal{P}, \mathcal{S})$. Then the translation $T(M) = (\Pi, \sigma', \gamma)$ of M is a standpoint structure over the vocabulary $\mathcal{V} = (\mathcal{P}, \mathcal{S} \cup \widetilde{\mathcal{E}})$ where: Π and γ are the same in each structure, $\widetilde{\mathcal{E}} = \{\widetilde{e} \mid e \in \mathcal{E}\}$, and σ' is defined by $\sigma'(s) = \sigma(s)$ for $s \in \mathcal{S}$ and $\sigma'(\widetilde{e}) = \min_{\prec} \sigma(e)$ for $\widetilde{e} \in \widetilde{\mathcal{E}}$. The value of σ' is extended to complex standpoint expressions inductively, as is done in the literature [8].*

We can then express the satisfiability of defeasible modalities and sharpenings in terms of classical standpoint logic.

Proposition 6. *For any SPSS M, and any sentence α in classical standpoint logic, we have that $M \Vdash \widetilde{\boxtimes}_e \alpha$ iff $T(M) \Vdash \Box_{\tilde{e}}\alpha$, and $M \Vdash e \precsim d$ iff $T(M) \Vdash \tilde{e} \leq d$.*

This can then give us a means to determine satisfiability, using existing methods in standpoint logics [7,8].

Corollary 1. *For any sentence $\alpha \in \widetilde{\mathcal{L}}_{\mathbb{S}}$ not containing the symbol "$\rightsquigarrow$", we have that α is locally satisfiable iff $T(\alpha)$ is satisfiable in classical standpoint semantics, where $T(\alpha)$ is the sentence formed by replacing every instance of $\widetilde{\boxtimes}_e$ occurring in α with $\Box_{\tilde{e}}$ and every subsentence of the form $e \precsim d$ with $\tilde{e} \leq d$.*

This approach however, has two weaknesses. Firstly, it does not provide a method for determining the satisfiability of sentences in $\widetilde{\mathcal{L}}_{\mathbb{S}}$ containing "$\rightsquigarrow$". Secondly, the set $\tilde{\mathcal{E}}$ as given in Definition 6 is infinite. Since $\mathcal{E}$ behaves as a Boolean algebra of subsets, we could clearly reduce the size of $\tilde{\mathcal{E}}$ to account for equivalences between Boolean formulas. However, for any complex standpoint expression e, we cannot in general express $\tilde{e}$ in terms of other, smaller standpoint symbols in $\tilde{\mathcal{E}}$. For example, we cannot express $\widetilde{e \cap d}$ in terms of $\tilde{e}$ and $\tilde{d}$. This means that if $|\mathcal{S}| = n$, then the size of $\tilde{\mathcal{E}}$ (once reduced to account for Boolean equivalences) may still be as big as 2^{2^n}, since we need to consider a new standpoint for every non-equivalent Boolean combination of the original standpoints. This potential double exponential blow-up means that the given translation is not an effective means for determining satisfiability in $\widetilde{\mathcal{L}}_{\mathbb{S}}$. However, in the restricted case where we only allow sentences with atomic standpoint indexes (i.e., where we restrict $\mathcal{E}$ to the set $\mathcal{S} \cup \{*\}$), the size of $\tilde{\mathcal{E}}$ is only $2n + 2$. Therefore, since satisfiability for propositional standpoint logic is NP-complete [7], the translation above provides an NP-complete means for checking satisfiability in the setting where only atomic standpoint indexes occur in α.

However, in the general case for determining satisfiability and preferential entailments, we need to turn to other methods in order to avoid a double exponential blow-up in standpoint symbols. We therefore propose a tableau algorithm for computing whether a given statement in $\widetilde{\mathcal{L}}_{\mathbb{S}}$ is locally satisfiable. Our tableau is semantic in nature, and follows closely conventions for semantic tableau in related modal logics [3,4,12]. To this end, we introduce a normal form for sentences in $\widetilde{\mathcal{L}}_{\mathbb{S}}$.

Definition 7. *If a standpoint expression $c \in \mathcal{E}$ is of the form $c = s_1 \cap s_2 \cap ... \cap s_k \cap -s_{k+1} \cap ... \cap -s_l$ where $s_1, ..., s_l \in \mathcal{S}$ we call it a **standpoint conjunct**. If $k = 0$, for the sake of the tableau we add $*$ to the conjunct so that $c = * \cap -(s_{k+1} \cup ... \cup s_m)$.*

*For any $e \in \mathcal{E}$, we say that e is in **disjunctive normal form** (DNF) if it is of the form $e = c_1 \cup ... \cup c_m$ where $c_1, ..., c_m$ are all standpoint conjuncts. We then say a formula $\alpha \in \widetilde{\mathcal{L}}_{\mathbb{S}}$ is in **index normal form** (INF) if every standpoint expression which appears in ϕ is in disjunctive normal form.*

Since the logic of standpoint expressions operates as a Boolean algebra of subsets, the well-known result that each standpoint expression has an equivalent expression in

DNF holds. Therefore, when we check for satisfiability using the following tableau method, we first assume each formula is in INF. In general, in the tableau, an indexed lowercase letter c will denote a standpoint-literal conjunction, while an indexed letter s will denote an atomic standpoint. e and d refer to any standpoint in DNF. This allows us to describe our tableau system.

Definition 8. ([3]). *If $n \in \mathbb{N}$ and $\alpha \in \tilde{\mathcal{L}}_{\mathbb{S}}$, then $n :: \alpha$ is a **labelled sentence**.*

Intuitively, the labelled sentence $n :: \alpha$ indicates semantically that there is a precisification n in the model such that α holds at n.

Definition 9. *A **skeleton** is a function $\Sigma : \mathcal{E} \to 2^{\mathbb{N}}$. A **preference** relation $\prec$ is a binary relation on $\mathbb{N}$.*

A skeleton intuitively assigns each standpoint a set of precisifications, while the preference relation in the tableau acts to construct the preference ordering in an SPSS. Both Σ and $\prec$ are built cumulatively, and so at the beginning of the tableau we assume $\prec = \emptyset$ and $\Sigma(e) = \emptyset$ for all $e \in \mathcal{E}$.

Definition 10. ([3]). *A **branch** is a tuple $(\mathcal{B}, \Sigma, \prec)$ where $\mathcal{B}$ is a set of labelled sentences, Σ is a skeleton and $\prec$ is a preference relation.*

Definition 11. ([3]). *A **tableau rule** is of the form*

$$(\rho) \frac{\mathcal{N} : \Gamma}{\mathcal{D}_1; \Gamma_1 | ... | \mathcal{D}_k; \Gamma_k}$$

*where $\mathcal{N} : \Gamma$ is the **numerator** and $\mathcal{D}_\infty; \Gamma_1 | ... | \mathcal{D}_\infty; \Gamma_1$ is the **denominator**.*

As in [3], $\mathcal{N}$ is a set of labelled sentences called the *main sentences* of ρ, while Γ specifies a set of conditions on Σ and $\prec$. each $\mathcal{D}_i$ is a set of labelled sentences, while each Γ_i is a set of conditions that have to be added cumulatively to Σ and $\prec$ after the rule is applied. The symbol "|" indicates where the branch splits. That is, an instance where a non-deterministic choice of possible outcomes has to be explored.

A rule ρ is *applicable* to a branch $(\mathcal{B}, \Sigma, \prec)$ iff $\mathcal{S}$ contains the main sentences of ρ and the conditions of Γ are satisfied. The rule (**non-empty** $\mathcal{S}$) given below has the additional condition that it is only applied when no other rules are applicable.

We also require that *applicable rules* have not already been satisfied. That is, that the denominators have not occurred in the branch before, and in the case of "fresh" labels in the denominator, that there are no existing labels $n \in \mathbb{N}$ which satisfy all the conditions of the denominator. We write $n \in W_e$ to denote $n \in \Sigma(e)$ and define $W_{\mathcal{B}}^{\phi} := \{n \in \mathbb{N} \mid n :: \phi \in \mathcal{B}\}$, where $\mathcal{B}$ is a branch in the tableau. $n \in \min_{\prec} X$ denotes that n is a minimal element of the set X. That is, $n' \in X$ implies $n' \not\prec n$. We also use $n^{\star}$ to denote the addition of a "fresh" label which has not been used before in the tableau. Our tableau rules are defined in Fig. 2.

1. Classical Rules:

$$(\bot)\ \frac{n :: \alpha,\ n :: \neg\alpha}{n :: \bot} \qquad (\neg)\ \frac{n :: \neg\neg\alpha}{n :: \alpha} \qquad (\wedge)\ \frac{n :: \alpha \wedge \beta}{n :: \alpha,\ n :: \beta} \qquad (\vee)\ \frac{n :: \neg(\alpha \wedge \beta)}{n :: \neg\alpha \mid n :: \neg\beta}$$

2. Standpoint Hierarchy and Modality Rules:

$$(\cap)\ \frac{n \in W_{e\cap d}}{n \in W_e,\ n \in W_d} \qquad (\cup)\ \frac{n \in W_{e\cup d}}{n \in W_e \mid n \in W_d} \qquad (\bot-)\ \frac{n \in W_e,\ n \in W_{-e}}{n :: \bot}$$

$$(*_1)\ \frac{n :: \alpha}{n \in W_*} \qquad (*_2)\ \frac{n \in W_e}{n \in W_*} \qquad (\Diamond_e)\ \frac{n :: \neg\Box_e\alpha}{n^\star :: \neg\alpha;\ n^\star \in W_e}$$

$$(\Box_{e\cup d})\ \frac{n :: \Box_{e\cup d}\alpha}{n :: \Box_e\alpha,\ n :: \Box_d\alpha} \qquad (\Box_c)\ \frac{n :: \Box_{s_1\cap s_2...\cap s_k\cap -s_{k+1}\cap...\cap -s_m}\alpha;\ n' \in \Gamma^c}{n' \in W_{s_{k+1}\cup...\cup s_m} \mid n' :: \alpha}$$

$$(\Box_{c+})\ \frac{n :: \Box_{s_1\cap s_2...\cap s_k}\alpha;\ n' \in \Gamma^c}{n' :: \alpha} \quad \text{where } \Gamma^c = \{n' \in \mathbb{N} \mid n' \in W_{s_1}, ..., n' \in W_{s_k}\}.$$

3. Defeasibility and Minimality Rules:

$$(\widetilde{\Diamond}_e)\ \frac{n :: \neg\, \widetilde{\boxtimes}_e\, \alpha}{n^\star :: \neg\alpha;\ n^\star \in \min_\prec W_e} \qquad (\rightsquigarrow)\ \frac{n :: \alpha \rightsquigarrow \beta}{n :: \neg\alpha \mid n^\star :: \alpha;\ n^\star \prec n \mid n :: \beta}$$

$$(\not\rightsquigarrow)\ \frac{n :: \neg(\alpha \rightsquigarrow \beta)}{n :: \alpha,\ n :: \neg\beta;\ n \in \min_\prec W^\alpha_\mathcal{B}}$$

$$(\bot_\prec)\ \frac{n \in \min_\prec W,\ n' \prec n,\ n' \in W}{n :: \bot} \qquad (\lesssim)\ \frac{n :: c_1 \cup ... \cup c_m \lesssim d;\ n' \in \Gamma}{n' \in W_{s_{k+1}\cup...\cup s_l} \mid n' \in W_d \mid n^\star \in W_d,\ \Gamma^\star}$$

$$(\lesssim^+)\ \frac{n :: c_1 \cup ... \cup c_m \lesssim d;\ n' \in \Gamma^+}{n' \in W_d \mid n^\star \in W_d,\ \Gamma^\star} \qquad (\lnsim)\ \frac{n :: \neg(e \lesssim d)}{n^\star \in \min_\prec W_e,\ n^\star \in W_{-d}}$$

$$(\widetilde{\boxtimes})\ \frac{n :: \widetilde{\boxtimes}_{c_1\cup...\cup c_m}\, \alpha;\ n' \in \Gamma}{n' :: \alpha \mid n' \in W_{s_{k+1}\cup...\cup s_l} \mid n^\star :: \alpha;\ \Gamma^\star} \qquad (\widetilde{\boxtimes}^+)\ \frac{n :: \widetilde{\boxtimes}_{c_1\cup...\cup c_m}\, \alpha;\ n' \in \Gamma^+}{n' :: \alpha \mid n^\star :: \alpha;\ \Gamma^\star}.$$

where $\Gamma^+ = \{n' \in \mathbb{N} \mid n' \in W_{s_1}, ..., n' \in W_{s_k},\ c_i = s_1 \cap ... \cap s_k$ for some $1 \le i \le m\}$,
$\Gamma^\star = \{n^\star \prec n',\ n^\star \in W_{c_1\cup...\cup c_m}\}$, and
$\Gamma = \{n' \in \mathbb{N} \mid n' \in W_{s_1}, ..., n' \in W_{s_k},\ c_i = s_1\cap...\cap s_k\cap -s_{k+1}\cap...\cap -s_l$ where $1 \le i \le m\}$

(non-empty $\mathcal{S}$):
If, after all other applicable rules are applied to a branch $(\mathcal{B}, \Sigma, \prec)$, there is some $s \in \mathcal{S}$ such that $n \in W_s$ does not appear for any $n \in \mathbb{N}$, then add $n^\star \in W_s$ to Σ.

Fig. 2. Tableau Rules for Local Satisfiability in $\widetilde{\mathcal{L}}_S$

Many of the rules are straightforward, or have been discussed in the literature [3], but we provide an explanation for some of the rules which are specific to our case. In Sect. 2. of Fig. 2, the rules $(\cap)$ and $(\cup)$ allocate every label n within a complex standpoint into the possible set of standpoint literals associated with this complex standpoint literals. This is important to ensure termination, and in order for the modal rules to be applied to each label correctly, since the conditions in the numerators of modal rules are written specifically in terms of atomic standpoints. Rules $(*_1)$ and $(*_2)$ make sure every label is associated to the universal standpoint. Rule $(\bot_-)$ accounts for the semantic contradiction which occurs when a label is allocated to both a standpoint and its negation. Rules $(\Box_c)$ and $(\Box_c^+)$ deal with sentences bound by strict modalities with conjuncts as indexes, and the conditions are phrased so that the applicability of the rule applies to labels which fulfil the required atomic standpoints. $(\Box_c^+)$ deals with conjuncts with no negative literals, while $(\Box_c)$ deals with conjuncts with negative literals. The first branch in the denominator of $(\Box_c)$ intuitively accounts for the case where a label n satisfies the positive literals in the conjunct but is not in one of the negative conjuncts, and so the sentence $n :: \alpha$ need not appear. Rule $(\Box_{e \cup d})$ deals with indexes which have unions of multiple conjuncts. Section 3. describes the behaviour of defeasible parts of the logic. Rules $(\approxeq_e)$, $(\rightsquigarrow)$, $(\not\rightsquigarrow)$ and $(\bot_\prec)$ follow similar intuitions to those appearing in tableau construted by Britz and Varzinczak [3]. Rules $(\lesssim)$ and $(\lesssim^+)$ allocates necessary labels to a new standpoint when a defeasible sharpening occurs. The conditions are again referred to in terms of atomic standpoints, and rules $(\lesssim)$ and $(\lesssim^+)$ differ in the same manner that $(\Box_c)$ and $(\Box_c^+)$ do. Both rules also have a branch which expresses that when $n :: e \lesssim d$ occurs, it is possible that a label in W_e is not allocated to W_d on the account of it being non-minimal. Rule $(\not\lesssim)$ deals with negated defeasible sharpenings. Lastly, rules $(\approxeq)$ and $(\approxeq^+)$ deal with sentences bound by $\approxeq$ with a similar differentiation between conjuncts with literals and without. It is worth noting that by Proposition 2, we cannot break unions of conjuncts down into their parts as is done in classical modalities, and so have to treat the general case of sentences in INF.

Definition 12. *[3] A **tableau** $\mathcal{T}$ for $\alpha \in \widetilde{\mathcal{L}}_{\mathbb{S}}$ is the limit of a sequence $\mathcal{T}^0, ..., \mathcal{T}^k, ...$ of sets of branches where the initial $\mathcal{T}^0 := \{(\{0 :: \alpha\}, \emptyset, \emptyset)\}$ and every $\mathcal{T}^{i+1}$ is obtained by the application of one of the applicable rules in Fig. 2 to some branch in $\mathcal{T}^i$. Such a limit is denoted $\mathcal{T}^\infty$.*

We assume here that the limit is only found once every applicable rule is applied. We say a tableau is *saturated* if no rule is applicable to any of its branches.

Definition 13. *A branch $(\mathcal{B}, \Sigma, \prec)$ is **closed** iff $n :: \bot \in \mathcal{B}$ for some n. A saturated tableau $\mathcal{T}$ for $\alpha \in \widetilde{\mathcal{L}}_{\mathbb{S}}$ is closed iff all its branches are closed. If a saturated tableau $\mathcal{T}$ is not closed, we say that it is **open**.*

We then can describe the *tableau algorithm* for local satisfaction checking as follows: If we are given a sentence $\alpha \in \widetilde{\mathcal{L}}_{\mathbb{S}}$ and want to check if it is locally satisfiable, then we construct a saturated tableau for α as in Definition 12. If the resulting tableau is closed, then we conclude that α *is not* locally satisfiable, and if the tableau is open, we conclude that α *is* locally satisfiable. However, in order for this algorithm to be useful, we need the proposed tableau calculus to be sound, complete and to terminate. We therefore present the following two theorems, which are the main results of our paper:

Theorem 1. (Complexity). *The tableau algorithm runs in* PSPACE.

This tells us that our tableau calculus terminates and that it is in the same complexity class as the tableau algorithms for modal logic $\mathbf{K}_n$ with defeasible modalities [2], as well as for the classical normal modal logics $\mathbf{K}$ and $\mathbf{K}_n$ [13,15].

Theorem 2. (Soundness and Completeness.). *The tableau algorithm is sound and complete with respect to local satisfiability in SPSS semantics.*

Moreover, by Theorem 2 and Proposition 5, we can easily adapt our tableau algorithm in order to obtain algorithms for global satisfiability and for preferential entailment which are sound, complete and computable in PSPACE. Lastly, it is worth noting that the rules in Sects. 1 and 2 provide a tableau calculus for an extension of Gómez Álvarez and Rudolph's [7] classical propositional standpoint logic, in which full complex standpoint expressions are permitted. This is on its own a novel contribution to the field of standpoint logics.

5 Related Work

The most closely related work to this paper is that of Leisegang et al. [18] who also consider combining defeasibility and standpoint logics. However, their paper aims at representing situations where standpoints *hold* defeasible beliefs, while this paper considers defeasibility and typicality relations between the precisifications themselves. In particular, the language DRSL is given in the form $\phi ::= \psi \mid \phi \wedge \phi \mid \Box_s \psi \mid \Diamond_s \psi,$[1] where ψ is a boolean formula or a defeasible implication $\alpha \rightsquigarrow \beta$ where α and β are Boolean. The semantics is given by *ranked standpoint structures*, which consist of a triple $M = (\Pi, \sigma, \gamma)$ where Π and σ are as in classical standpoint structures. However, γ maps each precisification not to a classical valuation, but a *ranked interpretation* as defined by Lehmann and Magidor [17]. That is, each $\gamma(\pi)$ is a ranking function $\gamma(\pi) : 2^{\mathcal{P}} \rightarrow \mathbb{N} \cup \{\infty\}$. Such a ranking function intuitively expresses how "typical" or preferred a state of the world is, with lower rankings signifying more typical states. This in turn induces a preference ordering for each precisification where $v \prec_\pi u$ iff $\gamma(\pi)(v) < \gamma(\pi)(u)$. Then if α and β are Boolean formulae, $M, \pi \Vdash \alpha$ iff $\gamma(v) \neq \infty$ implies $v \Vdash \alpha$ $M, \pi \Vdash \alpha \rightsquigarrow \beta$ iff $\min_{\prec_\pi} [\![\alpha]\!] \subseteq [\![\beta]\!]$. The satisfaction standpoint modalities and conjunctions are defined inductively on top of this as in the classical case (for example, $M, \pi \Vdash \Box_s \phi$ iff $M, \pi' \Vdash \phi$ for all $\phi \in \sigma(s)$). These semantics for DRSL therefore utilize preference orderings, but such orderings are internal to the underlying valuation of each precisification, while the ordering in PDSL occurs on the set of precisifications itself. Another distinction in the work of Leisegang et al. [18] is that it focuses on extending *rational closure*, a non-monotonic form of reasoning introduced by Lehman and Magidor [17], into the DRSL case, while our work focusses on an extension of preferential entailment.

---

[1] As well as classical sharpening statements.

Besides this work, defeasibility has been considered for basic normal modal logics by Britz et al. [1,2] and Britz and Varzinczak [3], and in the case of Linear Temporal Logic by Chafik et al. [5]. Standpoint modalities have been considered in the propositional case by Gómez Álvarez and Rudolph [7], in first-order logic and its decidable fragments by Gómez Álvarez et al. [8–10] and in the case of linear temporal logic by Gigante et al. [6], who also use semantic tableau methods. Other forms of non-monotonic reasoning in standpoint logics have been considered by Gorczyca and Straß [11].

6 Conclusion

In this paper, we propose an extension to both defeasible modalities, and standpoint logics by considering a logic of defeasible standpoint modalities. We define the language $\tilde{\mathcal{L}}_\mathbb{S}$ which extends propositional standpoint logic with defeasible modalities of the form $\mathbin{\rlap{\sim}\square}_e$ and $\mathbin{\rlap{\sim}\lozenge}_e$, as well as defeasible standpoint sharpenings and implications. The main contribution of the paper is to provide a semantics for the logical language in Sect. 3, and provide a sound, complete and terminating method to check satisfiability with respect to these semantics. In particular, in Sect. 4 we consider a translation to plain standpoint logic which allows for an NP-complete satisfiability checking in a restricted setting, and go on to provide a tableau algorithm for the unrestricted case which is computable in PSPACE.

For future work, we believe investigating other forms of non-monotonic entailment for defeasible reasoning in the propositional case [16,17] in the language $\tilde{\mathcal{L}}_\mathbb{S}$ would expand the given logic's ability to reason prototypically about information. Moreover, it would be worth investigating whether defeasible standpoint modalities can be added to more expressive logics, such as lightweight description logics, where classical standpoint modalities have been investigated [9,10]. Lastly, it would be worth investigating a deeper comparison and fusion of the logic proposed in our paper with the related approach to defeasibility in standpoint logics given by Leisegang et al. [18].

Acknowledgements. This work is based on the research supported in part by the National Research Foundation of South Africa (REFERENCE NO: SAI240823262612). This work has been partially supported by the Programme Hubert Curien Campus France Protea 48957ZC "Symbolic Artificial Intelligence for Cyber Security". Nicholas Leisegang is supported by the University of Cape Town Science Faculty PhD Fellowship, and the South African Media, Information and Communication Technologies Sector Education and Training Authority (MICT-SETA) Bursary.

References

1. Britz, K., Meyer, T., Varzinczak, I.: Preferential reasoning for modal logics. Electron. Notes Theor. Comput. Sci. **278**, 55–69 (2011). In: Proceedings of the 7th Workshop on Methods for Modalities (M4M'2011) and the 4th Workshop on Logical Aspects of Multi-Agent Systems (LAMAS'2011)

2. Britz, K., Meyer, T., Varzinczak, I.: Normal modal preferential consequence. In: Proceedings of the 25th Australasian Joint Conference in Artificial Intelligence, pp. 505–516. Springer, Heidelberg (2012)
3. Britz, K., Varzinczak, I.: From KLM-style conditionals to defeasible modalities, and back. J. Appl. Non-Classical Logics 28(1), 92–121 (2018)
4. Castilho, M.A., Gasquet, O., Herzig, A.: Formalizing action and change in modal logic i: the frame problem. J. Logic Comput. 9, 701–735 (1999). https://api.semanticscholar.org/CorpusID:9882199
5. Chafik, A., Cheikh-Alili, F., Condotta, J.F., Varzinczak, I.: Defeasible linear temporal logic. J. Appl. Non-Classical Logics 33(1), 1–51 (2023)
6. Gigante, N., Gómez Álvarez, L., Lyon, T.S.: Standpoint linear temporal logic. In: Proceedings of the 20th International Conference on Principles of Knowledge Representation and Reasoning, KR 2023, Rhodes, Greece, September 2–8, 2023, pp. 311–321 (2023)
7. Gómez Álvarez, L., Rudolph, S.: Standpoint logic: Multi-perspective knowledge representation. In: Proceedings of the 12th International Conference (FOIS 2021) Frontiers in Artificial Intelligence and Applications. Frontiers in Artificial Intelligence and Applications, vol. 3344, pp. 3 – 17. IOS Press (2021)
8. Gómez Álvarez, L., Rudolph, S., Straß, H.: How to agree to disagree: Managing ontological perspectives using standpoint logic. In: Proceedings of the 21st International Semantic Web Conference (ISWC 22). Lecture Notes in Computer Science, vol. 13489. Springer (2022)
9. Gómez Álvarez, L., Rudolph, S., Straß, H.: Pushing the boundaries of tractable multiperspective reasoning: A deduction calculus for standpoint EL+. In: Proceedings of the 20th International Conference on Principles of Knowledge Representation and Reasoning, KR 2023, Rhodes, Greece, September 2–8, 2023, pp. 333–343 (2023)
10. Gómez Álvarez, L., Rudolph, S., Straß, H.: Tractable diversity: Scalable multiperspective ontology management via standpoint EL. In: Elkind, E. (ed.) Proceedings of the Thirty-Second International Joint Conference on Artificial Intelligence, IJCAI-23, pp. 3258–3267. International Joint Conferences on Artificial Intelligence Organization (2023)
11. Gorczyca, P., Straß, H.: Adding standpoint modalities to non-monotonic S4F: preliminary results. In: Gierasimczuk, N., Heyninck, J. (eds.) Proceedings of the 22nd International Workshop on Non-Monotonic Reasoning (2024)
12. Goré, R.: Tableau methods for modal and temporal logics, pp. 297–396. Springer Netherlands (1999)
13. Halpern, J.Y., Moses, Y.: A guide to completeness and complexity for modal logics of knowledge and belief. Artif. Intell. 54(3), 319–379 (1992). https://doi.org/10.1016/0004-3702(92)90049-4
14. Kraus, S., Lehmann, D., Magidor, M.: Nonmonotonic reasoning, preferential models and cumulative logics. Artif. Intell. 44(1–2), 167–207 (1990)
15. Ladner, R.E.: The computational complexity of provability in systems of modal propositional logic. SIAM J. Comput. 6(3), 467–480 (1977)
16. Lehmann, D.: Another perspective on default reasoning. Ann. Math. Artif. Intell. 15, 61–82 (1995)
17. Lehmann, D., Magidor, M.: What does a conditional knowledge base entail? Artif. Intell. 55(1), 1–60 (1992)
18. Leisegang, N., Meyer, T., Rudolph, S.: Towards propositional KLM-Style defeasible standpoint logics. In: Gerber, A., Maritz, J., Pillay, A.W. (eds.) Proceedings of the 5th Southern African Conference on AI Research (SACAIR 2024). CCIS, vol. 2326, pp. 459–475. Springer (2024)

Axiomatics of Restricted Choices by Linear Orders of Sets with Minimum as Fallback

Kai Sauerwald[1]([⊠]), Kenneth Skiba[1], Eduardo Fermé[2], and Thomas Meyer[3]

[1] University of Hagen, Hagen, Germany
kai.sauerwald@fernuni-hagen.de
[2] University of Madeira and NOVA-LINCS, Funchal, Portugal
[3] University of Cape Town and CAIR, Cape Town, South Africa

Abstract. We study how linear orders can be employed to realise choice functions for which the set of potential choices is restricted, i.e., the possible choice is not possible among the full powerset of all alternatives. In such restricted settings, constructing a choice function via a relation on the alternatives is not always possible. However, we show that one can always construct a choice function via a linear order on sets of alternatives, even when a fallback value is encoded as the minimal element in the linear order. The axiomatics of such choice functions are presented for the general case and the case of union-closed input restrictions. Restricted choice structures have applications in knowledge representation and reasoning, and here we discuss their applications for theory change and abstract argumentation.

Keywords: choice functions · theory change · argumentation

1 Introduction

A (classical) choice structure $\langle A, \mathbb{S} \rangle$ consists of a set of alternatives A and a set of subsets $\mathbb{S} \subseteq \mathcal{P}(A)$ of A. A (classical) choice function $O : \mathbb{S} \to \mathcal{P}(A)$ for $\langle A, \mathbb{S} \rangle$ maps each set $S \in \mathbb{S}$ to a subset of S. Some authors also demand that $O(S)$ is non-empty if and only if S is non-empty and in some communities, choice functions are required to output a singleton whenever S is non-empty.

Example 1.1. We are planning to buy snacks in a supermarket for the evening. From experience, one knows that the typical snacks that are available in a supermarket are $A = \{\texttt{chocolate}, \texttt{nachos}, \texttt{pretzels}, \texttt{dips}, \texttt{chillies}\}$. We determine that we want to buy only salty snacks $S = \{\texttt{nachos}, \texttt{pretzels}, \texttt{dips}\}$. Because one does not want to buy all available options, one might decide to choose from one of the available options $O(S) = \{\texttt{pretzels}, \texttt{nachos}\}$. ∎

Work on choices has applications in, e.g., social choice theory and economics [33], mathematics and logic [37], and knowledge representation (KR) [18,27]. Here,

G. Casini et al. (Eds.): JELIA 2025, LNAI 16094, pp. 58–74, 2026.
https://doi.org/10.1007/978-3-032-04590-4_5

we are aiming at its impact on KR, where approaches to choice are connected to nonmonotonic reasoning, belief change, update, and conditionals [26]. Research in semantics of, e.g., belief revision, shows that revisions satisfy desired properties exactly when the result of revision is chosen by employing an underlying preference structure [20]. However, as observed, the connection between known axiomatizations and choice developed, which hold, e.g., for propositional logic, does not carry over to certain settings. Examples are preferential team-based logics, where the axiomatization turns out to be difficult [30], Horn logic [9, 10], or belief change in epistemic spaces, where belief change operators are not realizable in certain circumstances [28, 32]. The rationale why classical connections do not carry over to these settings is that the output of potential choices is restricted in these settings. The choice function cannot simply output an element of the full powerset over the alternatives, i.e., $O(S)$ "should" be a certain set, but $O(S)$ is not expressible, e.g. in Horn logic. The following Example 1.2 illustrates that one is often more restricted in choice on the output side than the original setting of choice permits, i.e., the codomain of a choice $O(S)$ is not the full powerset of all alternatives.

Example 1.2 (Continued from Example 1.1). Originally, in Example 1.1, we decided to buy `pretzels` and `nachos`, but nothing else. However, the supermarket we are visiting offers `nachos`, `dips` and `chillies` only in a bundle together. This means that the choice $O(S) = \{\texttt{pretzels}, \texttt{nachos}\}$ given in Example 1.1 is not valid in this setting, because the supermarket has no such offer in their stock. ∎

Existence and non-existence of choice functions in the classical setting of choice has been studied extensively [8]. The existence of any choice functions is not guaranteed when considering arbitrary sets within the Zermelo-Fraenkel (ZF) set theory [19]. This can be resolved by adding the Axiom of Choice (ZFC), which enforces the existence of choice functions (that output only singletons):

(Axiom of Choice) For each set of non-empty sets $\mathbb{S}$, there exists a function
$$f : \mathbb{S} \to \bigcup_{S \in \mathbb{S}} S \text{ with } f(S) \in S \text{ for every } S \in \mathbb{S}.$$

From social choice theory [21], it is well-known that already mild assumptions about the representation of choice functions lead to the non-existence of choice functions, even when one assumes ZFC. An often considered case is the construction of choice functions via a relation. This is done by considering a preference relation $\leq \, \subseteq A \times A$ on the alternatives A. A choice function O is then defined by letting $O(S)$ be the most preferred elements within S according to $\leq$, which we write as $O(S) = \min(S, \leq)$.[1] Many authors follow the suggestion from Sen's seminal work [33] to consider unrestricted inputs, i.e., having $\mathbb{S} = \mathcal{P}(A)$.

---

[1] We follow here the convention that being smaller in $\leq$ corresponds to being more preferred, which is in line with the typical reading of orders in belief revision and nonmonotonic reasoning. Technically, one could also consider everything from a dual perspective, where the larger elements are the more preferred elements.

Effectively, many theoretical results for choice functions are given under this condition.

In this paper, we study in a general manner the setting where choices are limited to a set of choices $\mathbb{E} \subseteq \mathcal{P}(A)$ (which we call the realizable choices) and where the sets to choose from are limited to $\mathbb{S} \subseteq \mathcal{P}(A)$. A *restricted choice function* is a function $C : \mathbb{S} \to \mathbb{E}$ where $C(S) \subseteq S$ holds, whenever possible. Formally, the setting of restricted choice functions enables us to model the situation from Example 1.2 easily.

Example 1.3 (Continued from Example 1.2). We are only permitting choices where nachos, dips and chillies appear together, i.e., by setting $\mathbb{E}$ to

$$\mathbb{E} = \{X \subseteq A \mid (\{\texttt{nachos}, \texttt{dips}, \texttt{chillies}\} \cap X \neq \emptyset)$$
$$\text{implies } \{\texttt{nachos}, \texttt{dips}, \texttt{chillies}\} \subseteq X\}$$
$$= \{\{\texttt{pretzels}\}, \{\texttt{chocolate}\}, \{\texttt{pretzels}, \texttt{chocolate}\},$$
$$\{\texttt{nachos}, \texttt{dips}, \texttt{chillies}\}, \{\texttt{pretzels}, \texttt{nachos}, \texttt{dips}, \texttt{chillies}\},$$
$$\{\texttt{chocolate}, \texttt{nachos}, \texttt{dips}, \texttt{chillies}\}, A\} \ .$$

Consequently, the only valid output $C(S)$ for $S = \{\texttt{pretzels}, \texttt{nachos}, \texttt{dips}\}$ from Example 1.1 is $C(S) = \{\texttt{pretzels}\}$ because we decided beforehand not to buy chillies, i.e., $\texttt{chillies} \notin S$. Moreover, we have thought carefully about snacks and come to the conclusion that we only want nachos when we can also get dips. One can model such personal restrictions on the input side, e.g., by considering restricted choice functions for $\mathbb{S} = \{S \subseteq X \mid \texttt{nachos} \in S \Rightarrow \texttt{dips} \in S\}$. ∎

The setting of restricted choice is a powerful generalization of the classical setting that permits specification of restrictions on the output side. Two basic conceptual problems arise, which we resolve in this paper:

– Unrealisable choices
– Existence and representation of restricted choice functions

The latter is because the axiom of choice does not immediately guarantee the existence of a restricted choice function. Specifically, it is not clear how a choice function for restricted choice structures can be represented or constructed via orders. Here, we show that an efficient way is to employ a linear order on sets of alternatives. The problem of unrealisable choices arises, because there are situations where it is impossible to yield a choice for a set $S \in \mathbb{S}$ because there is no $E \in \mathbb{E}$ in the co-domain of C such that $E \subseteq S$. However, as C is a function, there has to be an output for $C(S)$.

Example 1.4. Consider again the situation discussed in Example 1.3 where nachos are bundled with dips and chillies. For example, for $S' = \{\texttt{nachos}, \texttt{dips}\}$ there is no $E \in \mathbb{E}$ such that $E \subseteq S'$.

Here, we solve the problem of unrealisable choices by output a fallback value. For that, we encode the fallback value as the minimal element in a linear order.

We demonstrate how restricted choice functions can be employed in theory change and abstract argumentation. Specifically, we show that our representation theorem for linear choice functions carries over to theory change and abstract argumentation. We see that linear choice functions lead to a natural general approach to theory change operators. In abstract argumentation, we show that employing choice functions leads to a new approach to argumentation semantics, which has not been explored and generalizes extension selection [7, 22, 34].

In summary, the main content of the paper is the following, which we also consider as the main contributions of this paper[2]:

- [Restricted Choice Structures and their Choice Functions] We introduce the concepts of restricted choice structures and (restricted) choice functions for restricted choice structures. Restricted choice structures provide a more expressive setting than the original choice setting that permits taking unrealisable choices into account.
- [Linear Choice Functions] We present a uniform way of constructing restricted choice functions by employing a linear order on the available outcomes. We show that this construction provides a restricted choice function for any restricted choice structure, a feature that typical construction methods via orders on alternatives do not guarantee. Moreover, the full axiomatization of linear order-based choice functions is provided for both union-closed restricted choice structures and arbitrary restricted choice structures.
- [Applications in KR] We discuss the application of restricted choice structures and their choice functions in knowledge representation and reasoning (KR). We discuss the application in theory revision and argumentation.

In the next section, we start by presenting the background of order theory. In Sect. 3 we formally introduce restricted choice structures and their choice functions. Linear choice functions are introduced in Sect. 4. The axiomatics of linear choice functions is given in Sect. 5. Section 6 is dedicated to explore applications of the restricted choice structures and linear choice functions in knowledge representation and reasoning; namely theory change (Sect. 6.1) and argumentation (Sect. 6.2). The conclusion of this paper is given in Sect. 7.

2   Background on Relations and Order Theory

We use $\mathbb{N}$ for the natural numbers including 0, and $\mathbb{N}^+$ for the natural numbers excluding 0. The powerset of a set X is denoted by $\mathcal{P}(X)$. In the following, we present the background on basic notions of relations and order theory. Moreover, we present some basic background in extensions of relations to orders.

Relations and Orders. A (binary) relation on a set X is a subset of $X \times X$. We will often use order symbols for relations and write them infix, e.g., $x \preceq y$ means the same as $(x, y) \in \preceq$ for a relation $\preceq$. With $\prec$ we denote the strict part of a relation $\preceq$ on X and with $\simeq$ we denote the equivalent part of $\preceq$, i.e.,

---

[2] The full proofs are given in the supplement of the arXiv version of this paper [31].

$\simeq \ = \ \preceq \cap \left\{ (x_2, x_1) \in X \times X \mid x_1 \preceq x_2 \right\}$ and $\prec \ = \ \preceq \setminus \simeq$. The following properties of a relation $\preceq \ \subseteq X \times X$ are considered in this article:

(reflexive) $x \preceq x$

(total) $x_1 \preceq x_2$

(antisymmetric) $x_1 \preceq x_2$ and $x_2 \preceq x_1$ imply $x_1 = x_2$

(transitive) $x_1 \preceq x_2$ and $x_2 \preceq x_3$ imply $x_1 \preceq x_3$

(consistent) $x_0 \preceq x_1, \ ..., \ x_{n-1} \preceq x_n$ implies $x_n \not\prec x_0$

A *preorder* $\preceq$ on a set X is a relation $\preceq \ \subseteq X \times X$ such that $\preceq$ is reflexive and transitive. We also consider *total preorders*, i.e., preorders that also satisfy totality. A *linear order* on a set X is a total preorder on X that is additionally antisymmetric. The consistency property is due to Suzumura and has a central place in order theory, as it guarantees the existence of an order-extension [35]. A subtle aspect of the consistency property is that one demands $x_n \not\prec x_0$ instead of $x_n \not\preceq x_0$. This ensures that the consistency property does not apply when $x_n \simeq x_0$ holds. If $\preceq$ is transitive, then $\preceq$ is also consistent, and if $\preceq$ is total, then $\preceq$ is also reflexive.

Minimal Elements. We define two types of minimal elements for $\preceq \ \subseteq X \times X$, the (globally) minimal elements $\min(\preceq)$, and the minimal elements $\min(M, \preceq)$ with respect to a set M, which are given by:

$$\min(\preceq) = \left\{ \ x \in X \qquad \mid x' \preceq x \text{ implies } x \preceq x' \text{ for all } x' \in X \right\}$$
$$\min(M, \preceq) = \left\{ \ x \in M \cap X \mid x' \preceq x \text{ implies } x \preceq x' \text{ for all } x' \in M \right\}$$

Note that for arbitrary relations (even on a finite set) there might be no minimal elements, i.e., $\min(\preceq)$ and $\min(M, \preceq)$ might be empty sets. However, if $\preceq$ is a total preorder on a finite (non-empty) set, then $\min(\preceq)$ is always non-empty, and $\min(M, \preceq)$ is only empty if M is empty. We say that $\preceq \ \subseteq X \times X$ is *well-founded* if for each $M \subseteq X$ holds $\min(M, \preceq) \neq \emptyset$.

We deal in this paper with relations on sets of sets $\mathcal{E} \subseteq \mathcal{P}(A)$ over some base-set A. For such a relation $\leq \ \subseteq \mathcal{E} \times \mathcal{E}$, we overload the notion of $\min(\cdot, \cdot)$ by extending it to elements from $\mathcal{P}(A)$. When $S \in \mathcal{P}(A)$ is an element from $\mathcal{P}(A)$, then we let $\min(S, \leq) = \min(\left\{ E \in \mathcal{E} \mid E \subseteq S \right\}, \leq)$. That is, $\min(S, \leq)$ is the set of $\leq$-minimal elements among all elements from $\mathcal{E}$ that are also subsets of S.

3   Restricted Choice Structures

We define restricted choice structures and their corresponding choice functions.

Definition 3.1. *A (normal) restricted choice structure is a tuple $\mathcal{R} = \langle A, \mathbb{S}, \mathbb{E} \rangle$ where*

- *A is a set (the set of alternatives),*
- *$\mathbb{S} \subseteq \mathcal{P}(A)$ is a non-empty set of subsets of A (the domain), and*
- *$\mathbb{E} \subseteq \mathcal{P}(A)$ is a non-empty subset of $\mathbb{S}$ (the realizable choices) with $\mathbb{E} \subseteq \mathbb{S}$.*

We call $\mathcal{R}$ (input) union-closed if $S_1 \cup S_2 \in \mathbb{S}$ holds for all $S_1, S_2 \in \mathbb{S}$.

Next, we define the notion of choice functions for restricted choice structures.

Definition 3.2. *Let $\mathcal{R} = \langle A, \mathbb{S}, \mathbb{E} \rangle$ be a restricted choice structure. A function $C : \mathbb{S} \to \mathbb{E}$ is called a* choice function *for $\mathcal{R}$ if for each $S \in \mathbb{S}$ holds $C(S) = E \in \mathbb{E}$ with $E \subseteq S$, if such an $E \in \mathbb{E}$ exists. If $C(S) = K$ for all $S \in \mathbb{S}$ for which no $E \in \mathbb{E}$ with $E \subseteq S$ exists, we say that K is the* fallback (value) *of C.*

Note that a (unrestricted) choice structure $\langle A, \mathbb{S} \rangle$ can **not** be simply reconstructed by taking $\langle A, \mathbb{S}, \mathcal{P}(\mathcal{P}(A)) \rangle$, as the latter violates $\mathbb{E} \subseteq \mathbb{S}$ and thus is not a (normal) restricted choice structures. Instead, the restricted choice structure $\langle A, \mathbb{S}, \mathbb{E} \rangle$ with $\mathbb{E} = \bigcup_{S \in \mathbb{S}} \mathcal{P}(S)$ reconstructs $\langle A, \mathbb{S} \rangle$ in the following sense:

(a) for every choice function $O : \mathbb{S} \to \mathcal{P}(A)$ for $\langle A, \mathbb{S} \rangle$, there is a choice function $C : \mathbb{S} \to \mathbb{E}$ for $\langle A, \mathbb{S}, \mathbb{E} \rangle$, such that $O(S) = C(S)$ for all $S \in \mathbb{S}$.
(b) for every choice function $C : \mathbb{S} \to \mathbb{E}$ for $\langle A, \mathbb{S}, \mathbb{E} \rangle$, there is a choice function $O : \mathbb{S} \to \mathcal{P}(A)$ for $\langle A, \mathbb{S} \rangle$, such that $O(S) = C(S)$ for all $S \in \mathbb{S}$.

One might get the impression that the last condition of $\mathbb{E} \subseteq \mathbb{S}$ in Definition 3.1 is too restrictive, as one may imagine settings of restricted choice, where the condition $\mathbb{E} \subseteq \mathbb{S}$ does not hold. However, without $\mathbb{E} \subseteq \mathbb{S}$, we have to deal with (potentially) unwanted consequences for choice functions C. Examples are:

- $\mathbb{E}$ contains elements that are not in the image of any choice function at all;
- choice might be not chainable, e.g., $C(C(S))$ is undefined;
- $C(K)$ is undefined, while K is the fallback of C.

Because of that, we call a restricted choice structure without $\mathbb{E} \subseteq \mathbb{S}$ *non-normal*. In this paper, we refrain from considering non-normal restricted choice structures and assume normality for the remainder of the paper. However, non-normal restricted choice structures might be of interest in future work.

4   Linear Choice Functions

In this section, we show how to construct a choice function for a restricted choice structure by employing a linear order on the sets of realizable choice sets. Not all linear orders are suitable for the approach. The property we require is the existence of minima for all cases in which one wants to make choices. We call this property *smoothness*. Fallbacks will be encoded as the globally minimal element.

Definition 4.1 ($\mathcal{R}$-smoothness, K-minimal). *Let $\mathcal{R} = \langle A, \mathbb{S}, \mathbb{E} \rangle$ be a restricted choice structure, let $K \in \mathbb{E}$ and let $\leq \subseteq \mathcal{E} \times \mathcal{E}$ be a relation on a set $\mathcal{E} \subseteq \mathbb{E}$. We say that $\leq$ is $\mathcal{R}$-smooth if for each $S \in \mathbb{S}$ holds $\min(S, \leq) \neq \emptyset$ whenever there is some $E \in \mathcal{E}$ such that $E \subseteq S$. We say that $\leq$ is K-minimal if $\min(\leq) = \{K\}$.*

One might compare the notion of smoothness with the notion of a well-founded relation. The difference is that one demands the existence of minimal elements only for certain elements of interest, which is a more liberal requirement. The closest related notion is the notion of smoothness by Kraus, Lehmann and Magidor [24], for which it has been shown that one cannot replace smooth relations with well-founded relations [25]. K-minimality means that K is the (globally unique) minimal element of $\leq$.

For a $\mathcal{R}$-smooth relation, we define a corresponding choice function for $\mathcal{R}$ and some K, which will act as a fallback value. Linear choice functions for $\mathcal{R}$ are then such choice functions for $\mathcal{R}$ given by a $\mathcal{R}$-smooth relation that is a linear order on $\mathbb{E}$. If the relation is also K-minimal, we say that it is a K-minimal linear choice function for $\mathcal{R}$, i.e., when the fallback value K is encoded as the (globally) minimal element.

Definition 4.2 (linear choice function). *Let $\mathcal{R} = \langle A, \mathbb{S}, \mathbb{E} \rangle$ be a restricted choice structure and let $K \in \mathbb{E}$. For each $\mathcal{R}$-smooth linear order $\ll \subseteq \mathbb{E} \times \mathbb{E}$ on $\mathbb{E}$, we define the function $\triangledown^K_{\ll} : \mathbb{S} \to \mathbb{E}$ as:*

$$\triangledown^K_{\ll}(S) = \begin{cases} E & \text{if } \min(S, \ll) = \{E\} \\ K & \text{otherwise} \end{cases} \tag{$\star$}$$

A function $\triangledown : \mathbb{S} \to \mathbb{E}$ is a linear choice function *for $\mathcal{R}$ if $\triangledown = \triangledown^K_{\ll}$ for some $\mathcal{R}$-smooth linear order $\ll$. Additionally, we say that $\triangledown^K_{\ll}$ is K-minimal if $\ll$ is also K-minimal.*

Note that $\ll$ in Definition 4.2 is a linear order on the full set $\mathbb{E}$. In contrast, the relation $\leq$ in Definition 4.1 is a relation on any subset of $\mathbb{E}$. The additional flexibility in the latter case is required for the proofs of theorems in Sect. 5.

The following proposition witnesses that linear choice functions for a restricted choice structure $\mathcal{R}$ are indeed choice functions for $\mathcal{R}$. Moreover, when one assumes the Axiom of Choice, it is guaranteed that there exists some K-minimal linear choice function $\mathcal{R}$.

Proposition 4.3. *Let $\mathcal{R} = \langle A, \mathbb{S}, \mathbb{E} \rangle$ be a restricted choice structure and let $K \in \mathbb{E}$. The following statements hold:*

(a) $\triangledown^K_{\ll} : \mathbb{S} \to \mathbb{E}$ is a choice function for $\mathcal{R}$ with fallback K for any $\mathcal{R}$-smooth linear order $\ll \subseteq \mathbb{E} \times \mathbb{E}$.

(b) Assume the Axiom of Choice. There exists a K-minimal linear choice function for $\mathcal{R}$.

Proof. We start by showing Statement (a). If some $E \in \mathbb{E}$ with $E \subseteq S$ exists, then $\min(S, \ll) = \{E'\}$ is non-empty and thus, according to $(\star)$, we have $\triangledown_{\ll}^K(S) = E'$. This implies that we have $\triangledown_{\ll}^K(S) \subseteq S$. We obtain that $\triangledown_{\ll}^K$ is a choice function for $\mathcal{R}$. Moreover, if no $E \in \mathbb{E}$ with $E \subseteq S$ exists, then we have $\triangledown_{\ll}^K(S) = K$ due to $(\star)$. Consequently, K is the fallback of $\triangledown_{\ll}^K$.

For Statement (b), assume the Axiom of Choice. It is known that the Axiom of Choice is equivalent to the well-ordering theorem [19], which states that on every set S there is a linear order $\leq \subseteq S \times S$ that is well-founded. Let $\ll' \subseteq \mathbb{E} \times \mathbb{E}$ be such a well-founded linear order on $\mathbb{E}$. Because $\ll'$ is a well-founded linear order and $\mathbb{E}$ is non-empty, there exist some unique minimal singleton set $\{K'\} = \min(\mathbb{E}, \ll')$. Now, let $\ll \subseteq \mathbb{E} \times \mathbb{E}$ be the linear order, in which K and K' are mutually substituted. This is the relation:

$$\begin{aligned}
\ll = {} & (\ll' \setminus \{(K, S), (S, K), (K', S), (S, K') \mid S \in \mathbb{E}\}) \cup \{(K, K), (K', K')\} \\
& \cup \{(K', S) \mid K \ll' S \text{ and } S \neq K\} \cup \{(S, K') \mid S \ll' K \text{ and } S \neq K\} \\
& \cup \{(K, S) \mid K' \ll' S \text{ and } S \neq K'\} \cup \{(S, K) \mid S \ll' K' \text{ and } S \neq K'\} \\
& \cup \{(K', K) \mid K' \ll' K\} \cup \{(K, K') \mid K \ll' K'\}
\end{aligned}$$

One can show that the relation $\ll$ is a well-founded linear order on $\mathbb{E}$. Clearly, we have $\min(\mathbb{E}, \ll) = \{K\}$ and thus, $\ll$ is K-minimal, and because $\ll$ is well-wounded, $\ll$ is $\mathcal{R}$-smooth. Statement (b) follows by employing the latter observation and Statement (a). □

Example 4.4 (Continued from Example 1.3). We consider the restricted choice structure $\mathcal{R} = \langle A, \mathbb{S}, \mathbb{E} \rangle$, where A, $\mathbb{S}$ and $\mathbb{E}$ are from Examples 1.1–1.3, and let $K = \{\texttt{pretzels}, \texttt{nachos}, \texttt{dips}, \texttt{chillies}\}$. We let $\ll \subseteq \mathbb{E} \times \mathbb{E}$ be the following linear order on $\mathbb{E}$:

$$K \ll \{\texttt{nachos}, \texttt{dips}, \texttt{chillies}\} \ll \{\texttt{pretzels}, \texttt{chocolate}\} \ll \{\texttt{pretzels}\}$$
$$\ll \{\texttt{chocolate}\} \ll \{\texttt{chocolate}, \texttt{nachos}, \texttt{dips}, \texttt{chillies}\} \ll A$$

One can see that $\ll$ is K-minimal and $\mathcal{R}$-smooth. By employing $\ll$, we obtain the function $\triangledown_{\mathrm{Ex}} = \triangledown_{\ll}^K$. According to Proposition 4.3, $\triangledown_{\mathrm{Ex}}$ is a K-minimal linear choice function for $\mathcal{R}$. For $S = \{\texttt{nachos}, \texttt{pretzels}, \texttt{dips}\}$ from Example 1.1 we obtain $\triangledown_{\mathrm{Ex}}(S) = \{\texttt{pretzels}\}$; and for $S' = \{\texttt{nachos}, \texttt{dips}\}$ from Example 4.4, we obtain the fallback value $\triangledown_{\mathrm{Ex}}(S') = K$. ■

Proposition 4.3 guarantees existence of K-minimal linear choice function for every restricted choice structure $\mathcal{R}$. In the following section, we will axiomatize such choice functions.

5   Axiomatics of K-Minimal Linear Choice Functions

We axiomatise K-minimal linear choice functions for union-closed and arbitrary restricted choice structures. Given a restricted choice structure $\mathcal{R} = \langle A, \mathbb{S}, \mathbb{E} \rangle$, we make use of the following postulates for some fixed $K \in \mathbb{E}$:

(SS0) If $\mathbb{E} \cap \mathcal{P}(S) \neq \emptyset$, then $\triangledown(S) \subseteq S$.

(SS1) If $\triangledown(S) \not\subseteq S$, then $\triangledown(S) = K$.

(SS2) If $K \subseteq S$, then $\triangledown(S) = K$.

(SS3) If $\triangledown(S_1) \subseteq S_2$ and $\triangledown(S_2) \subseteq S_1$, then $\triangledown(S_1) = \triangledown(S_2)$.

(SS4) If $\triangledown(S_1) \subseteq S_1$ and $S_1 \subseteq S_2$, then $\triangledown(S_2) \subseteq S_2$.

(SS5) If $\triangledown(S_i \cup S_{i+1}) = S_i$ for $0 \leq i \leq n$, then $S_0 \neq S_n$ implies $\triangledown(S_0 \cup S_n) \neq S_n$.

(SS6) If $\triangledown(S_1 \cup S_2) = S_3$, then $\triangledown(S_1 \cup S_3) = S_3$.

By (SS0), we ensure that a choice is made among the elements of S whenever $\mathbb{E}$ permits this. The postulate (SS1) describes that either a choice is made among S or the function falls back to K. With (SS2), we express that when K is a subset of S, we must choose exactly K. The postulate (SS3) demands that if S_1 and S_2 are mutually supersets of the choices among them, then choosing among S_1 or S_2 leads to the same result. With (SS4) we obtain that choosing among elements of S is inherited to all super-sets of S. With (SS5) one prevents cyclic situations among the potential choices. The postulate (SS6) describes that when chooses S_3 from S, then for each subset $S' \subseteq S$, we have that S_3 is chosen from $S' \cup S_3$, i.e., the elements of S_3 are prevalent against the other elements of S.

The first main theorem of this paper is that (SS0)–(SS6) exactly characterizes K-minimal linear choice functions for union-closed restricted choice structures. Because of the limited space, we present an outline of the proof of the following Theorem 5.1. The full proof is given in the supplemental material (see footnote 2).

Theorem 5.1. *Assume the Axiom of Choice. Let $\mathcal{R} = \langle A, \mathbb{S}, \mathbb{E} \rangle$ be a union-closed restricted choice structure and let $K \in \mathbb{E}$. A function $\triangledown : \mathbb{S} \to \mathbb{E}$ is a K-minimal linear choice function for $\mathcal{R}$ if and only if the axioms (SS0)–(SS6) are satisfied* [3].

Proof (Outline). ["⇒"] The left-to-right direction amounts to checking the satisfaction of the postulates point-by-point. ["⇐"] The right-to-left direction consists of three steps. In *Step 1*, one constructs a relation $\trianglelefteq$ on an appropriate subset $\mathcal{E} \subseteq \mathbb{E}$ by the following encoding scheme [33]: $A_1 \trianglelefteq A_2$ if $\triangledown(A_1 \cup A_2) = A_1$ The relation $\trianglelefteq$ is reflexive, antisymmetric, consistent and $\mathcal{R}$-smooth on $\mathcal{E}$. However, $\trianglelefteq$ is not a linear order on $\mathbb{E}$. In *Step 2*, Suzumuras theorem [35] yields an extension of the relation $\trianglelefteq$ to a $\mathcal{R}$-smooth linear order $\lll$ on $\mathcal{E}$. *Step 3* consists of expanding $\lll$ to a linear order $\ll$ on $\mathbb{E}$ such that $\triangledown = \triangledown_{\ll}^{K}$. □

The second main result is an axiomatization of K-minimal linear choice functions for arbitrary restricted choice structure, by axioms that follow the same ideas as (SS1)–(SS6).

---

[3] As usual, satisfaction of (SS0)–(SS6) (by $\triangledown$) means that the properties described by (SS0)–(SS6) hold for all $S, S_0, S_1, \ldots \in \mathbb{S}$ for the specifically considered $\triangledown$. Note that K and $\mathbb{E}$ in (SS0)–(SS6) are externally given, and thus, are not all-quantified.

Theorem 5.2 (Representation Theorem). *Assume the Axiom of Choice. Let* $\mathcal{R} = \langle A, \mathbb{S}, \mathbb{E} \rangle$ *be a restricted choice structure and let* $K \in \mathbb{E}$. *A function* $\triangledown : \mathbb{S} \to \mathbb{E}$ *is a* K*-minimal linear choice function for* $\mathcal{R}$ *if and only if the axioms* (SS0)–(SS4) *and the following axioms are satisfied:*

(SS5E) If $S_i \cup S_{i+1} \subseteq S_{i,i+1}$ *and* $\triangledown(S_{i,i+1}) = S_i$ *for* $0 \leq i \leq n$,
        then $S_n \cup S_0 \subseteq S_{n,0}$ *and* $S_n \neq S_0$ *imply* $\triangledown(S_{n,0}) \neq S_n$.

(SS6E) If $S_{1,2} = S_1 \cup S_2$ *and* $S_{1,3} = S_1 \cup S_3$ *and* $\triangledown(S_{1,2}) = S_3$,
        then $\triangledown(S_{1,3}) = S_3$.

The proof of Theorem 5.2 is given in the supplemental material (see footnote 2). The postulates (SS5E) and (SS6E) are variations of (SS5) and (SS6) that take into account that the union of elements of $\mathbb{S}$ might not be in $\mathbb{S}$. Note that one demands $S_i \cup S_{i+1} \subseteq S_{i,i+1}$ in (SS5E) and not $S_i \cup S_{i+1} = S_{i,i+1}$.

6   Applications in Knowledge Representation

In this section, we discuss instantiations of union-closed restricted choice structures and the respective interpretation of linear choice functions and Theorem 5.1 in the context of these applications.

6.1   Linear Choice in Theory Change

In theory change, one asks how to change a knowledge base K according to new information S. Specifically for revision, one wants that S holds after revising K. Notably, in the framework by Katsuno and Mendelzon [20] a change operator is a function $\mathcal{L} \times \mathcal{L} \to \mathcal{L}$, where $\mathcal{L}$ is a language of propositional logic. We adapt the notion of a change operator to the setting here. When $\mathbb{S} \subseteq \mathcal{P}(A)$ is a system of subsets of some set A, we define a change operator as a function $\varoslash : \mathbb{S} \times \mathbb{S} \to \mathbb{S}$. The following definition defines a change operator that is based on a choice function.

Definition 6.1. *A change operator* $\varoslash : \mathbb{S} \times \mathbb{S} \to \mathbb{S}$ *for* $\mathbb{S}$ *(over* A*) is called* choice-based *if for each* $K \in \mathbb{S}$ *there is a choice function* C_K *for some restricted choice structure* $\mathcal{R}_K = \langle A, \mathbb{S}, \mathbb{E}_K \rangle$ *with* $K \in \mathbb{E}_K$ *such that:*

$$K \varoslash S = C_K(S)$$

We say $\varoslash$ *fits the* $\mathbb{S}$*-indexed family of restricted choice structure* $\{\langle A, \mathbb{S}, \mathbb{E}_K \rangle\}_{K \in \mathbb{S}}$. *If each* C_K *is a* K*-minimal linear choice function for* $\mathcal{R}$, *we say that* $\varoslash$ *is* linear.

Choice functions have already been employed to define change operators [18,27]. The novelty here is the restriction on the output side; leading to a model of change operators for agents that are *not able* to conduct certain changes. In such a setting AGM revision operators are not realizable in general [32] or learnable [3]. In the following theorem, we employ Theorem 5.1 to give an axiomatization for linear choice-based change operators.

Theorem 6.2. *Assume the Axiom of Choice and let $\oslash : \mathbb{S} \times \mathbb{S} \to \mathbb{S}$ be a change operator for a union-closed set of sets $\mathbb{S} \subseteq \mathcal{P}(A)$. The operator $\oslash$ is linear choice-based if and only if the following postulates are satisfied:*

(LCR1) $K \oslash S \subseteq S$ or $K \oslash S = K$.

(LCR2) If $K \subseteq S$, then $K \oslash S = K$.

(LCR3) If $K \oslash S_1 \subseteq S_2$ and $K \oslash S_2 \subseteq S_1$, then $K \oslash S_1 = K \oslash S_2$.

(LCR4) If $K \oslash S_1 \subseteq S_1$ and $S_1 \subseteq S_2$, then $K \oslash S_2 \subseteq S_2$.

(LCR5) If $K \oslash (S_i \cup S_{i+1}) = S_i$ for $0 \leq i \leq n$,
$$\text{then } S_0 \neq S_n \text{ implies } K \oslash (S_0 \cup S_n) \neq S_n.$$

(LCR6) If $K \oslash (S_1 \cup S_2) = S_3$, then $K \oslash (S_1 \cup S_3) = S_3$.

Proof (sketch). We show each direction independently. ["$\Rightarrow$"] Let $\oslash$ be a linear choice-based change operator. Inspecting Definition 6.1 reveals that for every K there is a K-minimal linear choice function C_K for $\mathcal{R}_K$ such that $K \oslash S = C_K(S)$. By employing Theorem 5.1 we obtain that C_K satisfies (SS0)–(SS6) for each K. From the latter, one obtains easily that (LCR1)–(LCR6) are satisfied, by substituting $\triangledown(S)$ by "$K \oslash S$". ["$\Leftarrow$"] Assume that $\oslash$ satisfies (LCR1)–(LCR6). For each fixed K, define a function $C_K : \mathbb{S} \to \mathbb{E}_K$ with $K \oslash S = C_K(S)$ and $\mathbb{E}_K = \bigcup_{S \in \mathbb{S}} \{K \oslash S\}$. One can see easily that each C_k satisfies (SS1)–(SS6) by replacing "$K \oslash S$" in every postulate (LCR1)–(LCR6) by "$C_K(S)$". The postulates (SS0) is satisfied because (SS1) is satisfied and because $\mathbb{E}_K$ contains only elements that in the image of $K \oslash S$. By employing Theorem 5.1 we obtain that each C_K is a K-minimal linear choice function and, hence, that $\oslash$ is linear. □

The postulates (LCR1)–(LCR6) are reformulations of the postulates (SS1)–(SS6). Note that there is no counterpart of (SS0); inspecting Theorem 6.2 reveals that the definition of linear change operator is made in a way that the integrated choice function satisfies already (SS0). Note that Proposition 4.3 guarantees that linear choice-based change operators always exist.

Corollary 6.3. *Assume the Axiom of Choice and let $\mathbb{S} \subseteq \mathcal{P}(A)$ be a set of sets. For any $\mathbb{S}$-indexed family of restricted choice structure $\{\langle A, \mathbb{S}, \mathbb{E}_K \rangle\}_{K \in \mathbb{S}}$ with $K \in \mathbb{E}_K$ for every $K \in \mathbb{S}$ there is a linear choice-based operator that fits that family.*

We consider the postulates (LCR1)–(LCR6). In theory change the postulates (LCR1)–(LCR4) are known[4] as (Relative Success), (Idempotence), (Right-Reciprocity), and (Successs Monotonicity). (LCR1) is especially known from non-prioritized revision [16]. In non-prioritized revision, one provides change operators for agents that are not willing to accept every new information unquestioned and fully [13,17,23,29]. However, the kind of changes we are drafting here differ from non-prioritized change conceptually. It is not that an agent is not willing to accept some new information, but she cannot because of the restricted

---

[4] When one reads $\subseteq$ as some kind of entailment.

outputs. Technically speaking, in non-prioritized change, the restriction is on how to deal with the inputs within the language. Restricted choice is about restrictions on the meta-level (especially on the outputs). Thus, (LCR1) seems to be a postulate that is not exclusive to non-prioritized change; it is more of an expression of dealing with restrictions through a fallback value. The following example reinterprets our running example in the context of change, demonstrating both cases (LCR1) describes.

Example 6.4 (Continued from Example 4.4). We consider $K = \{\texttt{pretzels},$ $\texttt{nachos}, \texttt{dips}, \texttt{chillies}\}$ from Example 4.4. In the context of change, K stands for the initial information. The linear order $\ll$ from Example 4.4 gives rise to $\triangledown_{\text{Ex}}$, which we employ for changing K, by setting $K \oslash S = \triangledown_{\text{Ex}}(S)$. We obtain, e.g., $K \oslash \{\texttt{nachos}, \texttt{pretzels}, \texttt{dips}\} = \{\texttt{pretzels}\}$ and $K \oslash \{\texttt{nachos}, \texttt{dips}\} = K$. ∎

The postulate (LCR2) describes that when the initial information K is a suitable choice, the operator $\oslash$ has to output K. This conforms with the special role the initial beliefs have in many belief change approaches [12]. In a certain way, (LCR2) is a basic form of "minimal change". Note that, minimal change in AGM [1,15] involves that when $K \cap S \neq \emptyset$, then $K \oslash S = K \cap S$. However, in the restricted choice setting this is not always possible, as $K \cap S \notin \mathbb{E}$ might hold. The remaining postulates (LCR3)–(LCR6) deal with the nature of linear orders over sets. Note that the postulates (LCR5) and (LCR6) seem to be novel for the change context; they are different from those for linear orders on alternatives [6].

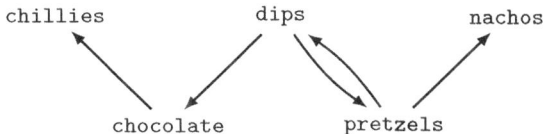

Fig. 1. Illustration of the abstract argumentation framework from Example 6.7.

6.2   Linear Choice in Argumentation

Formal argumentation [2] deals with conflicting pieces of information, where conflicting information is modelled as *arguments* in a discussion. Dung [11] proposed *abstract argumentation frameworks* (AFs) as a directed graph, where arguments are vertices and an *attack* between two arguments is a directed edge. Formally, given a (possible infinite) set of arguments $\mathcal{U}$, an *abstract argumentation framework* (AF) for $\mathcal{U}$ is a directed graph $F = \langle A, R \rangle$, where $A \subseteq \mathcal{U}$ is a (often finite) non-empty set of arguments and R is an *attack relation* $R \subseteq A \times A$. With $\mathsf{AF}[\mathcal{U}]$ we denote the set of all abstract argumentation frameworks for $\mathcal{U}$.

There are different approaches to the semantics of abstract argumentation frameworks [4]. Most prominently, extension-based semantics assign to each AF $F = \langle A, R \rangle$ a set of sets of arguments $\sigma(F) \subseteq \mathcal{P}(A)$ (called the σ-extensions of F). The intended meaning is that $\sigma(F)$ represents the viable solutions of the conflict resolution between the arguments in F. A generalization of extension-based semantics are extension-ranking semantics, which additionally equip the extensions with an ordering [34], i.e., functions τ that map each AF to an ordering $\leq_F^\tau$ over some subsets of $\mathcal{P}(A)$. Extension-ranking semantics provide much more structure to the solutions given by extension-based semantics, i.e., that some extensions are "better" than others. We define a semantics for AFs that is based on choice functions.

Definition 6.5. *A* choice-based extension semantics *for $\mathcal{U}$ is a function Π that maps each AF $F = \langle A, R \rangle$ for $\mathcal{U}$ to a choice function $\Pi_F : \mathcal{P}(A) \to \mathbb{E}_F$ for some choice structure $\mathcal{R}_F = \langle A, \mathcal{P}(A), \mathbb{E}_F \rangle$ where $\mathbb{E}_F$ is non-empty. We say that Π is* linear, *if every Π_F is a K_F-minimal linear choice function for some $K_F \in \mathbb{E}_F$.*

Choice-based extension semantics provide for every argumentation framework F a restricted choice function Π_F over the arguments of F. A instantiation for $\mathbb{E}_F$ could be the extensions of F (with respect to some extension-based semantics). Given that, one can interpret a choice $\Pi_F(E)$ for some $E \subseteq A$ as answer to the question of "which arguments in E (if any) are conflict free?". Some AFs can have a big number of arguments, hence it is of interest to only look at a selection of extensions that only concern these arguments. This is also known extension selection [7, 22, 34].

Next, we consider the axiomatic linear choice-based extension semantics provided by Theorem 5.1.

Theorem 6.6. *Assume the Axiom of Choice and let Π be a choice-based extension semantics for $\mathcal{U}$. The semantics Π is linear if and only if the following postulates are satisfied (for a suitable K_F for each $F \in \mathsf{AF}[\mathcal{U}]$):*

(LCA1) $\Pi_F(E) \subseteq E$ or $\Pi_F(E) = K_F$.

(LCA2) If $K_F \subseteq \Pi_F(E)$, then $\Pi_F(E) = K_F$.

(LCA3) If $\Pi_F(E_1) \subseteq E_2$ and $\Pi_F(E_2) \subseteq E_1$, then $\Pi_F(E_1) = \Pi_F(E_2)$.

(LCA4) If $\Pi_F(E_1) \subseteq E_1$ and $E_1 \subseteq E_2$, then $\Pi_F(E_2) \subseteq E_2$.

(LCA5) If $\Pi_F(E_i \cup E_{i+1}) = E_i$ for $0 \leq i \leq n$,
        then $E_0 \neq E_n$ implies $\Pi_F(E_0 \cup E_n) \neq E_n$.

(LCA6) If $\Pi_F(E_1 \cup E_2) = E_3$, then $\Pi_F(E_1 \cup E_3) = E_3$.

Proof. We show each direction independently. ["⇒".] Let Π be a linear choice-based extension semantics. Then for every $F \in \mathsf{AF}[\mathcal{U}]$ there is a K_F-minimal linear choice function Π_F for $\mathcal{R}_F$. By employing Theorem 5.1, we obtain that Π_F satisfies (SS1)–(SS6) for each K_F, which yields the satisfaction of (LCA1)–(LCA6). ["⇐".] Assume that Π satisfies (LCA1)–(LCA6). This implies that every function Π_F satisfies (SS1)–(SS6). Now define $\mathbb{E}_F = \bigcup_{E \in \mathcal{P}(A)} \{\Pi_F(E)\}$. Then, the satisfaction of (SS0) by Π_F is guaranteed by satisfaction of (SS1) and by the definition of $\mathbb{E}_F$. Because Π_F satisfies (SS0)–(SS6), we obtain that Π_F is a K_F-minimal linear choice function from Theorem 5.1, and thus, that Π is linear. $\qquad\square$

A direct connection to principles for abstract argumentation semantics [5, 36] is not obvious. This is because, from the perspective of argumentation, much of the quality of the results $\Pi_F(E)$ depends on the internally chosen set $\mathbb{E}_F$. However, for the discussion here, we just assume that each element in $\mathbb{E}_F$ is well-behaving, e.g., conflict free, i.e., for $E \in \mathbb{E}_F$ we have $a, b \in E$ implies that $(a, b) \notin R$ [11]. Hence, under this assumption, our restriction of $\Pi_F(E)$ to $\mathbb{E}_F$ guarantees well-behaving outputs.

Example 6.7 (Continued from Example 6.4). We interpret Examples 1.1–4.4 in the context of argumentation. Here, the elements of A are understood as arguments and the elements of $\mathbb{E}$ are meant to be the "feasible" subset of arguments. The linear order $\ll$ provides an ordering on $\mathbb{E}$, where the smaller elements are more "feasible". An argumentation framework that suits this scenario is the framework $F = \langle A, R \rangle$ with $R = \{(\texttt{pretzels}, \texttt{nachos}), (\texttt{pretzels}, \texttt{dips}), (\texttt{dips}, \texttt{pretzels}), (\texttt{dips}, \texttt{chocolate}), (\texttt{chocolate}, \texttt{chillies})\}$. For an illustration, see Fig. 1. Example of outputs of the choice-based extension semantics Π are $\Pi_F(\{\texttt{nachos}, \texttt{pretzels}, \texttt{dips}\}) = \{\texttt{pretzels}\}$ and $\Pi_F(\{\texttt{nachos}, \texttt{dips}\}) = K$. ∎

Choice-based extension semantics seem to be an interesting novel type of abstract argumentation semantics. However, how linear choice-based extension semantics handles fallback values does not seem appropriate. In Example 6.7, we observe the behaviour of $\Pi_F(\{\texttt{nachos}, \texttt{dips}\}) = K$ in Example 6.7. This is because the fallback value is the minimal element of the respective linear order. Thus, one might not want the fallback value to be the minimal element in abstract argumentation. For instance, for some semantics, the empty extension $\emptyset$ would be a suitable fallback value. However, when $K_F = \emptyset$ is the minimal element, then $\Pi_F(E) = \emptyset$ holds for all $E \in \mathbb{S}$.

7   Conclusion

In this paper, we considered the novel setting of restricted choices. A full axiomatization (Theorem 5.2) is given for K-minimal linear choice functions, i.e., those choice functions that can be represented by a linear order over sets of sets where a fallback value is encoded as the minimal element. As given by Proposition 4.3, such choice functions always exist regardless of which restrictions on choices are given. We showed that Theorem 5.2 can be simplified to Theorem 5.1 for choice structures where the input is closed under union, i.e., in this setting, (SS1)–(SS6) fully characterise K-minimal linear choice functions. We give a first hint on the applications of linear choice function in theory change and argumentation.

In future work, we will transfer the approach of this paper to the area of non-monotonic reasoning, especially preferential reasoning [24]. It turns out that transferring preferential reasoning to other domains is axiomatically challenging [30]. As non-monotonic reasoning and belief change are known to be connected [14], we are optimistic that our approach here might have applications in the axiomatization of non-monotonic reasoning approaches. Furthermore, for the area of argumentation, the idea of choice-based semantics sketched here is a promising and interesting area to explore.

Another avenue of future work is further exploration of the framework itself. We will consider alternative fallback behaviours for choice functions and explore their conceptual relevance. For that, identifying natural fallback behaviours for different applications in knowledge representation and beyond will be very helpful.

Acknowledgments. We thank the reviewers of this paper for their valuable and constructive feedback, which significantly helped us to improve the paper. The research reported here is partially funded by the Deutsche Forschungsgemeinschaft (DFG, German Research Foundation) – project 506604007 (Algorithms for Inconsistency Measurement) and project 465447331 (Explainable Belief Merging). Kenneth Skibka was supported by project 506604007 and Kai Sauerwald was supported by project 465447331. Eduardo Fermé was partially supported by UID/04516/NOVA Laboratory for Computer Science and Informatics (NOVA LINCS) with the financial support of FCT.IP. This work is based on t he research supported in part by the National Research Foundation of South Africa (REFERENCE NO: SAI240823262612).

References

1. Alchourrón, C.E., Gärdenfors, P., Makinson, D.: On the logic of theory change: Partial meet contraction and revision functions. J. Symb. Log. **50**(2), 510–530 (1985)
2. Atkinson, K., et al.: Towards artificial argumentation. AI Mag. **38**(3), 25–36 (2017). https://doi.org/10.1609/AIMAG.V38I3.2704
3. Baltag, A., Gierasimczuk, N., Smets, S.: Truth-tracking by belief revision. Stud. Log. **107**(5), 917–947 (2018). https://doi.org/10.1007/s11225-018-9812-x
4. Baroni, P., Gabbay, D., Giacomin, M., Van der Torre, L.: Handbook of formal argumentation (2018)
5. Baroni, P., Giacomin, M.: On principle-based evaluation of extension-based argumentation semantics. Artif. Intell. **171**(10–15), 675–700 (2007). https://doi.org/10.1016/J.ARTINT.2007.04.004
6. Belahcène, K., Gaigne, J., Lagrue, S.: On decisive revision operators and totally ordered information. In: Destercke, S., Martinez, M.V., Sanfilippo, G. (eds.) SUM 2024. LNCS, vol. 15350, pp. 45–52. Springer, Cham (2024). https://doi.org/10.1007/978-3-031-76235-2_4
7. Bonzon, E., Delobelle, J., Konieczny, S., Maudet, N.: Combining extension-based semantics and ranking-based semantics for abstract argumentation. In: Thielscher, M., Toni, F., Wolter, F. (eds.) Proceedings of the 16th International Conference, Principles of Knowledge Representation and Reasoning (KR 2018), pp. 118–127. AAAI Press (2018)

8. Bossert, W., Suzumura, K.: Consistency, Choice, and rationality. Harvard University Press (2010)
9. Creignou, N., Papini, O., Pichler, R., Woltran, S.: Belief revision within fragments of propositional logic. J. Comput. Syst. Sci. **80**(2), 427–449 (2014). https://doi.org/10.1016/J.JCSS.2013.08.002
10. Delgrande, J.P., Peppas, P.: Belief revision in Horn theories. Artif. Intell. **218**, 1–22 (2015). https://doi.org/10.1016/j.artint.2014.08.006
11. Dung, P.M.: On the acceptability of arguments and its fundamental role in nonmonotonic reasoning, logic programming and n-person games. Artif. Intell. **77**(2), 321–358 (1995). https://doi.org/10.1016/0004-3702(94)00041-X
12. Fermé, E.L., Hansson, S.O.: Belief Change - Introduction and Overview. Springer Briefs in Intelligent Systems. Springer (2018). https://doi.org/10.1007/978-3-319-60535-7
13. Fermé, E.L., Hansson, S.O.: Selective revision. Stud. Log. **63**(3), 331–342 (1999). https://doi.org/10.1023/A:1005294718935
14. Gärdenfors, P., Makinson, D.: Nonmonotonic inference based on expectations. Artif. Intell. **65**(2), 197–245 (1994). https://doi.org/10.1016/0004-3702(94)90017-5
15. Gärdenfors, P.: Knowledge in Flux: Modeling the Dynamics of Epistemic States. MIT Press, Cambridge (1988)
16. Hansson, S.O.: A survey of non-prioritized belief revision. Erkenntnis **50**(2), 413–427 (1999). https://doi.org/10.1023/A:1005534223776
17. Hansson, S.O., Fermé, E.L., Cantwell, J., Falappa, M.A.: Credibility limited revision. J. Symb. Log. **66**(4), 1581–1596 (2001)
18. Haret, A.: Choosing what to believe: belief change through the lens of rational choice (2020). https://doi.org/10.34726/hss.2020.42785
19. Jech, T.J.: Set Theory. Springer Monographs in Mathematics, 3 edn. Springer, Berlin (2002). https://doi.org/10.1007/3-540-44761-X
20. Katsuno, H., Mendelzon, A.O.: Propositional knowledge base revision and minimal change. Artif. Intell. **52**(3), 263–294 (1991). https://doi.org/10.1016/0004-3702(91)90069-V
21. Kelly, J.S.: Social Choice Theory: An Introduction. Springer (2013)
22. Konieczny, S., Marquis, P., Vesic, S.: On supported inference and extension selection in abstract argumentation frameworks. In: Destercke, S., Denoeux, T. (eds.) ECSQARU 2015. LNCS (LNAI), vol. 9161, pp. 49–59. Springer, Cham (2015). https://doi.org/10.1007/978-3-319-20807-7_5
23. Konieczny, S., Pino Pérez, R.: Improvement operators. In: Brewka, G., Lang, J. (eds.) Proceedings of the 11th International Conference on Principles of Knowledge Representation and Reasoning (KR 2008), pp. 177–187. AAAI Press (2008)
24. Kraus, S., Lehmann, D., Magidor, M.: Nonmonotonic reasoning, preferential models and cumulative logics. Artif. Intell. **44**(1–2), 167–207 (1990). https://doi.org/10.1016/0004-3702(90)90101-5
25. Lehmann, D., Magidor, M.: What does a conditional knowledge base entail? Artif. Intell. **55**(1), 1–60 (1992). https://doi.org/10.1016/0004-3702(92)90041-U
26. Makinson, D.: Five faces of minimality. Stud. Log. **52**(3), 339–379 (1993). https://doi.org/10.1007/BF01057652
27. Rott, H.: Change, Choice and Inference: A Study of Belief Revision and Nonmonotonic Reasoning. Oxford University Press, New York (2001)
28. Sauerwald, K.: Credibility-limited revision for epistemic spaces. In: Sanfilippo, G., Destercke, S., Martinez, V. (eds.) Proceedings of the 16th International Confer-

ence on Scalable Uncertainty Management (SUM 2024) (2024). https://doi.org/10.24963/kr.2022/42

29. Sauerwald, K., Beierle, C.: Decrement operators in belief change. In: Kern-Isberner, G., Ognjanović, Z. (eds.) ECSQARU 2019. LNCS (LNAI), vol. 11726, pp. 251–262. Springer, Cham (2019). https://doi.org/10.1007/978-3-030-29765-7_21

30. Sauerwald, K., Kontinen, J.: A first peek into preferential logics with team semantics. In: Gierasimczuk, N., Heyninck, J. (eds.) Proceedings of the 22nd International Workshop on Nonmonotonic Reasoning (NMR 2024) Co-located with 21st International Conference on Principles of Knowledge Representation and Reasoning (KR 2024), Hanoi, Vietnam, 2–4 November 2024. CEUR Workshop Proceedings, vol. 3835, pp. 94–100. CEUR-WS.org (2024)

31. Sauerwald, K., Skiba, K., Fermé, E., Meyer, T.: Axiomatics of restricted choices by linear orders of sets with minimum as fallback. CoRR abs/2506.03315 (2025). https://doi.org/10.48550/ARXIV.2506.03315

32. Sauerwald, K., Thimm, M.: The realizability of revision and contraction operators in epistemic spaces. In: Marquis, P., Ortiz, M., Pagnucco, M. (eds.) Proceedings of the 21st International Conference on Principles of Knowledge Representation and Reasoning (KR 2024), pp. 665–670 (2024). https://doi.org/10.24963/KR.2024/62

33. Sen, A.K.: Choice functions and revealed preference. Rev. Econ. Stud. **38**(3), 307–317 (1971). https://doi.org/10.2307/2296384

34. Skiba, K., Rienstra, T., Thimm, M., Heyninck, J., Kern-Isberner, G.: Ranking extensions in abstract argumentation. In: Zhou, Z. (ed.) Proceedings of the 30th International Joint Conference on Artificial Intelligence (IJCAI 2021), pp. 2047–2053. ijcai.org (2021). https://doi.org/10.24963/IJCAI.2021/282

35. Suzumura, K.: Remarks on the theory of collective choice. Economica **43**(172), 381–390 (1976). https://doi.org/10.2307/2553273

36. van der Torre, L., Vesic, S.: The principle-based approach to abstract argumentation semantics. J. Log. Their Appl. **4**(8), 2735–2778 (2017)

37. Zermelo, E.: Beweis, daß jede menge wohlgeordnet werden kann. Math. Ann. **59**(4), 514–516 (1904). https://doi.org/10.1007/BF01445300

Propositional Reasoning, QBF, and Satisfiability Problems

AxSAT – Bringing Axioms to SAT Planning

Gregor Behnke[1]([⊠])(iD), David Speck[2](iD), and Daniel Gnad[3,4](iD)

[1] ILLC, Universiteit van Amsterdam, Amsterdam, The Netherlands
g.behnke@uva.nl
[2] University of Basel, Basel, Switzerland
davidjakob.speck@unibas.ch
[3] Heidelberg University, Heidelberg, Germany
daniel.gnad@uni-heidelberg.de
[4] Linköping University, Linköping, Sweden

Abstract. Planning as SAT is, in addition to explicit and symbolic search, one of the main approaches for solving planning problems. Such planners proved very successful, especially in combinatorially complex domains. SAT-based planning has to date focused on the core formalisms of planning. Notably, there is no SAT-based planner that supports axioms and derived predicates. In this paper, we present our new planner AxSAT that supports axioms as well as conditional effects. Furthermore, we show how to allow for action parallelism using the ∃-step encoding in the presence of axioms. Our empirical evaluation shows that AxSAT performs favorably compared to state-of-the-art approaches for satisficing classical planning with axioms, and provides complementary capabilities.

1 Introduction

A central aspect of intelligent decision-making is reasoning before acting, which involves determining a sequence of actions to transform the current state into a desired one. Such reasoning problems are typically described as classical planning tasks in dedicated modeling languages such as PDDL [26]. While PDDL is rich in modeling features allowing for concise encoding of planning tasks, many of them are not supported by modern planners. One such feature is the use of axioms, which provide a means to specify a background theory to derive certain facts about the world in the current state, and thus often allow for natural, elegant and efficient modeling and problem specification [16,22,27,41,44]. Importantly, axioms enable the modeling of complex action preconditions and goal conditions. Despite the fact that axioms are an essential modeling feature, i.e., they cannot simply be compiled away [44], their expressive power poses a challenge to support them. This is especially true for planners based on the heuristic-search paradigm. It is challenging to design heuristics (goal-distance estimators) that are both informative and fast, while taking into account the background theory [43]. In particular, admissible heuristics used in optimal planning are complex to adapt [22], but for inadmissible heuristics such as the FF heuristic [19] it poses a

G. Casini et al. (Eds.): JELIA 2025, LNAI 16094, pp. 77–93, 2026.
https://doi.org/10.1007/978-3-032-04590-4_6

challenge, too. Thus, axioms are often treated naively, making the incorporation of heuristic estimates difficult.

In this paper, we focus on planning as satisfiability [24, 33]. We show how planning tasks with axioms can be encoded as a propositional satisfiability (SAT) problem with a fixed (parallel) plan length bound. Our approach generalizes existing SAT planning encodings, such as the sequential encoding, $\forall$-step encodings [25], and the $\exists$-step encoding [11, 33].

While our approach is the first to model planning axioms as boolean satisfiability, there have been related approaches. Bofill et al. [7] considered a domain-specific SAT implementation of axioms for a puzzle game, which is not easily generalizable to domain-independent planning. Other works have introduced axiom support for compilations of planning to integer programming and answer-set programming [10, 27]. None of the approaches supports parallelism, the encodings are purely sequential. Speck et al. [40, 43] showed how to support axioms in symbolic search. Their dominant approach is to precompute the formulas under which derived facts become true, in order to replace those facts in the conditions with the computed formula. While this approach is similar to ours, there are critical differences. On the theoretical side, based on our encodings, SAT solvers can infer the same formulas, but it is done lazily, only when necessary to show satisfiability instead of a precomputation. On the practical side, symbolic search is mainly used for optimal planning, while SAT-based planning has its merits mainly in satisficing planning. As we will show empirically, these two approaches complement each other well: the symbolic search approach of Speck et al. [40, 43] is strong in finding optimal plans, while our SAT-based approach, AxSAT, shows strong performance in satisficing planning. Overall, AxSAT compares favorably to state-of-the-art approaches for satisficing planning with axioms such as the well-known heuristic search planner LAMA [30].

2   Preliminaries

In this section, we provide the necessary background for our work by introducing classical planning with axioms and planning as satisfiability.

2.1   FDR Planning

We consider planning problems with conditional effects given in Finite Domain Representation (FDR) [18], of which we describe the base formalism first. States are described via a set of state variables $\mathcal{V}$, each $v \in \mathcal{V}$ having its own finite domain D_v. A partial state s is any partial function from variables $\mathcal{V}$ to values. We write $V(s)$ to denote the set of variables for which s is defined. A state is a function mapping each variable v to a value D_v, i.e., $s : \mathcal{V} \mapsto D_v$. An action is a pair $a = \langle p, e \rangle$, where p is a partial state and e is a set of expressions $l \triangleright r$ where l is a partial state and r is a fact of the form $v = o$ for a variable $v \in \mathcal{V}$ and a value $o \in D_v$. Given an action a, we write $pre(a)$ to refer to its precondition p and $eff(a)$ for its effects e. An action a is applicable in a state

s, if s agrees with p for every variable for which p is defined, i.e., if $p \subseteq s$. Let e be a set of conditional effects. The firing conditional effects $f(e, s)$ in a state s are defined as $f(e, s) = \{v = o \mid l \triangleright v = o \in e, l \subseteq s\}$. We write $V(f(e, s))$ for the variables mentioned in the firing conditional effects. The set of all effects of conditional effects $\alpha(e)$ is defined as $\alpha(e) = \{v = o \mid l \triangleright v = o \in e\}$. Applying a set of conditional effects e to a state s leads to the state $\gamma(s, e) = \{(v, s(v)) \mid v \notin V(f(e, s))\} \cup f(e, s)$. Technically, this definition can lead to conflicts if two firing conditional effects set the same variable to different values. We assume by definition that this is not possible. Applying a in s leads to a successor state $\gamma(s, a) = \gamma(s, e)$ if applicable, otherwise to $\bot$. For a sequence of actions $\pi = (a_1, \ldots, a_n)$, we define its application to a state s inductively as $\gamma(s, (a_1)) = \gamma(s, a_1)$ and $\gamma(s, (a_1, a_2, \ldots, a_n)) = \gamma(\gamma(s, a_1), (a_2, \ldots, a_n))$. An FDR planning problem Π is then specified by its variables $\mathcal{V}$, actions $\mathcal{A}$, initial state s_I, and its goal s_G, which is a partial state. A plan that solves this FDR problem is any sequence of actions π such that $s_G \subseteq \gamma(s_I, \pi)$.

2.2 Derived Predicates and Axioms

In this paper, we use an extension to pure FDR planning: derived predicates [18, 44]. Derived predicates are logical atoms and thus can only have two values: true and false. To keep our notation clean, we make an explicit distinction between the original finite domain variables and the derived predicates. To represent them, we denote the set of derived predicates as $\mathcal{D}$. A partial state s is now a pair $\langle F, \delta \rangle$, where F is a partial function from the FDR variables $\mathcal{V}$ to values and $\delta \subseteq \mathcal{D}$ is a set of derived predicates that is true in s. States are partial states for which F is a total function $F : \mathcal{V} \mapsto D_v$. The truth value of derived predicates is instead determined using a logic-program-style set of rules, called axioms. An axiom for the derived predicate $d \in \mathcal{D}$ is a formula of the form $\bigwedge_i (v_i = o_i) \wedge \bigwedge_j d_j \wedge \bigwedge_k \neg d_k \rightarrow d$. It is an implication whose left-hand side can contain positive conditions on the FDR variables (negation is not allowed here), and both positive and negative condition on derived predicates. The right-hand side is a single positive derived predicate d which is defined to be true whenever the left-hand conditions are satisfied. For an axiom ax, we will write $\ell(ax)$ to denote the set of literals on its left-hand side and $r(ax)$ for the derived predicate on its right-hand side. Furthermore, we write $\ell^f(ax)$ to denote the set of conditions on FDR variable on the left-hand side and $\ell^+(ax)$ and $\ell^-(ax)$ for the positively and negatively occurring derived predicates respectively. Thus, an axiom can be written as $\bigwedge_{(v_i = o_i) \in \ell^f(ax)} (v_i = o_i) \wedge \bigwedge_{d_j \in \ell^+(ax)} d_j \wedge \bigwedge_{d_k \in \ell^-(ax)} \neg d_k \rightarrow r(ax)$. An axiom ax is applicable in a state $\langle F, \delta \rangle$ iff (1) $\forall v = o \in \ell(ax) : F(v) = o$, (2) $\forall d \in \ell(ax) : d \in \delta$, and (3) $\forall \neg d \in \ell(ax) : d \notin \delta$. Applying an axiom ax in a state $\langle F, \delta \rangle$ yields the state $\langle F, \delta \cup \{r(ax)\} \rangle$. Let A be the set of all axioms of an FDR problem. Given a pure FDR state $F : \mathcal{V} \mapsto D_v$, we define the saturated state $sat(F)$ of F under A as a set-inclusion-minimal fixpoint $\langle F, \delta \rangle$ of applying all axioms $ax \in A$. Intuitively, this means starting with the state $\langle F, \emptyset \rangle$, applying all axioms until no further new axiom is applicable. This definition causes issues if $\ell(ax)$ contains negative literals, as the fixpoint might not be unique. We restrict the set of allowed axioms to Stratified Axiom Programs, for which the fixpoint is unique [34]. As a tool for this definition and our later work, we define the truth dependency graph (TDG) of the derived predicates as follows: $G = (\mathcal{D}, E)$, where $\mathcal{D}$ is the set of derived predicates, and we have an edge $(d_i, d_j) \in E$ if there is an axiom $ax \in A$ where $d_i \in \ell(ax)$ or $\neg d_i \in \ell(ax)$ and $d_j = r(ax)$. Next, we consider the strongly connected components (SCCs) of the TDG. If there is an axiom ax where $\neg d_i \in \ell(ax)$ and $d_j = r(ax)$ while d_i and d_j are in the same SCC, then evaluating axioms might have non-unique fixpoints. If there is no such axiom, then the set of axioms is a Stratified Axiom Program. In this paper, we only consider such planning problems – notably all domains of the International Planning Competition[1] containing axioms are of this type.

Lastly, we define the application of actions in this setting. An action o comprises four elements $\langle p, p_{\mathcal{D}}^+, p_{\mathcal{D}}^-, e \rangle$ where p is a partial pure FDR state, $p_{\mathcal{D}}^+, p_{\mathcal{D}}^- \subseteq \mathcal{D}$, and e is a set of conditional effects $(l, l_{\mathcal{D}}^+, l_{\mathcal{D}}^-) \rhd (v = o)$ where l is a partial pure FDR state and $l_{\mathcal{D}}^+, l_{\mathcal{D}}^- \subseteq \mathcal{D}$. An action $\langle p, p_{\mathcal{D}}^+, p_{\mathcal{D}}^-, e \rangle$ is applicable in a state $\langle F, \delta \rangle$ iff $p \subseteq F$, $p_{\mathcal{D}}^+ \subseteq \delta$, and $p_{\mathcal{D}}^- \cap \delta = \emptyset$. The firing conditional effects $f(e, s)$ in a state $\langle F, \delta \rangle$ are defined as $f(e, s) = \{v = o \mid l, l_{\mathcal{D}}^+, l_{\mathcal{D}}^- \rhd v = o \in e, l \subseteq F, l_{\mathcal{D}}^+ \subseteq \delta, l_{\mathcal{D}}^- \cap \delta = \emptyset\}$. Applying a set of conditional effects e to a state $s = \langle F, \delta \rangle$ leads to the state $\gamma(s, e) = sat(\{(v, F(v)) \mid v \notin V(f(e, s))\} \cup f(e, s))$, i.e., we apply all FDR effects and then saturate the axioms. Note that thereby the planner is *forced* to evaluate all axioms in every state. Application of sequences of actions is again defined inductively. The initial state is given as a pure FDR state for which the axioms need to be saturated. The goal comprises $p, p_{\mathcal{D}}^+, p_{\mathcal{D}}^-$ mirroring the preconditions of actions. The task is again to find a sequence of actions that, if applied in the initial state, leads to a goal state. Such a plan is optimal if there is no shorter sequence of actions that also solve the problem.

2.3 SAT Planning

One means to solve planning problems is via reduction to Boolean satisfiability (SAT). Given a length bound N, we generate a propositional formula ϕ_N that is satisfiable iff there is a plan of at most N actions. This SAT formula ϕ_N represents the plan as a sequence of N time steps. To obtain a complete SAT-based planner, we then iterate over the length bound N until a solution has been found[2]. The basic encoding has been proposed by Kautz and Selman [24] – but is formulated for STRIPS planning only. There is a dedicated encoding of FDR planning into SAT [20], but its size is cubic in the size of variable domains. We instead opted to adapting the STRIPS-style encoding to FDR planning directly. Here, we present the encoding for FDR planning without derived predicates. The SAT formula comprises two types of variables $(v = o)@t$ indicating that variable v has value o at time t and $a@t$ indicating that action a is executed at time t. Whenever the time step is clear from context, typically if the encoding is repeated for every time step, we will omit the $@t$ to improve readability. For every

---

[1] see https://www.icaps-conference.org/competitions/.
[2] There are more intelligent options than pure iteration, which we discuss in Sect. 6.

variable $v \in \mathcal{V}$, we assert that exactly one of its values is true – which can be split into at least and at most one value. The at-least-one constraint is a simple disjunction $\bigvee_{o \in D_v} (v = o)$. For encoding the at-most-one constraint $amo(X)$ for a set of decision variables X, multiple formulae have been proposed [12,39]. We use the binomial encoding if $|X| \leq 256$ and the binary encoding otherwise. Preconditions and effects of actions are asserted by implications: $\forall (v = o) \in pre(a) : a@n \rightarrow (v = o)@n$ and

$$a@n \wedge \bigwedge_{v' = o' \in l} (v' = o')@n \rightarrow (v = o)@(n + 1) \quad \forall l \rhd (v = o) \in \mathit{eff}(a)$$

To ensure that the truth value of unchanged variables remains the same, we introduce the following frame axiom:

$$\neg(v = o)@n \wedge (v = o)@(n + 1) \rightarrow \bigvee_{\substack{a \in \mathcal{A} \\ l \rhd v = o \in \mathit{eff}(a)}} (a@n \wedge \bigwedge_{v' = o' \in l} (v' = o')@n)$$

In case of conditional effects with non-empty condition, additional decision variables via Tseitin encoding [45] are introduced to compactly encode the right-hand side of the implication. Furthermore, we need to assert that the initial state and goal are met via $(v = o)@1$ for $s_I(v) = o$ and $(v = o)@(N + 1)$ for $s_G(v) = o$. Lastly, for the base encoding, we have to assert that at most one action is performed at every time, i.e., $amo(\{a@n \mid a \in \mathcal{A}\})$.

Some extensions of SAT-encodings to more expressive planning formalisms have been proposed in the past. These include lifted planning [21] and hierarchical planning [3–5,28,36]. Similarly, extensions of SAT solving have been used to solve problems in more expressive planning formalisms, notably quantified boolean formulae solving (QBF) for lifted planning [38] and SAT modulo theory solving for temporal and numeric planning [8,9,32,35].

2.4   Parallelism in SAT Planning

On its own, the presented base encoding is not competitive with the state of the art in search-based planning. To achieve this, action parallelism has been added to the encoding. Instead of restricting to a single action to be executed at every time step, one allows for multiple actions – as long as their execution does not interfere. The most common definition of "execution non-interference" is the $\exists$-step semantics. There are more relaxed versions (the relaxed-$\exists$-step [46] and relaxed-relaxed-$\exists$-step semantics [2]), which we do not consider in this paper.

Definition 1 (Based on Rintanen [33]). *Let $E \subseteq \mathcal{A}$ be a set of actions. We call this set $\exists$-step executable in the state s, if there is a total ordering $\langle a_1, \ldots, a_n \rangle$ of the actions in E such that $(a_1, \ldots, a_n)$ is applicable in s.*

Determining for such a set E whether it is $\exists$-step executable is NP-complete [33, Thm. 2.22]. As such, SAT encodings assert and check only a more relaxed version of this ∃-step criterion. The main idea is that we fix a total order of all actions $\mathcal{A}$, i.e., $\vec{\mathcal{A}} = \langle a_1, \ldots, a_n \rangle$ and assert that if a set of actions E is executed, then it is executed precisely in this order. This then makes testing for restricted ∃-step parallelism trivial, as we solely have to check the executability of subsequences $\vec{\mathcal{A}}|_E$. This restriction is however not enough to ensure that encoding the executability of the sequence is easy. The ∃-step encoding further asserts:

Definition 2 (Based on Rintanen [33]). *Let $\pi = \langle a_1, \ldots, a_n \rangle$ be a sequence of actions. We call π ∃-step encodable in s, iff (1) all a_i are applicable in s, (2) $\forall i < j \forall v \in V(pre(a_j)) \cap V(\alpha(\textit{eff}(a_i))) : \alpha(\textit{eff}(a_i))(v) = pre(a_j)(v)$, i.e., no action deletes something needed by a later action, and (3) $\forall i < j \forall l \triangleright (v' = o') \in \textit{eff}(a_j) \forall v \in V(l) \cap V(\alpha(\textit{eff}(a_i))) : \alpha(\textit{eff}(a_i))(v) = l(v)$, i.e., no action deletes the condition of a later effect.*

To simplify the SAT encoding, conditions (2) and (3) are independent of the actual state. By construction if $\langle a_1, \ldots, a_n \rangle$ is ∃-step encodable, it is ∃-step executable.

We say that an action a_i disables an action a_j iff the order $\langle a_i, a_j \rangle$ would violate either condition (2) or (3). Operationally, disabling of actions can equivalently be determined using the sets of deleted and needed facts for each action. For each fact $v = o$, the set of actions needing this fact – where $v = o$ is either a precondition or a condition of a conditional effect – is defined as $nee(v = o) := \{a \in \mathcal{A} \mid v = o \in pre(a)\} \cup \{a \in \mathcal{A} \mid l \triangleright r \in \textit{eff}(a), v = o \in l\}$. The set of deleting actions is defined as $del(v = o) := \{a \in \mathcal{A} \mid l \triangleright v = o' \in \textit{eff}(a), o \neq o'\}$. Then, an action a_i disables a_j iff there is a fact $v = o$ such that $a_i \in del(v = o)$ and $a_j \in nee(v = o)$. The disabling graph (DG) encodes the disabling relation between actions. The DG's nodes are the actions and there is an edge from a_i to a_j iff (i) both are potentially executable in the same state and (ii) a_i disables a_j. Determining condition (i) is PSPACE-complete. To approximate, two actions a_i and a_j are presumed to be executable in the same state if there is no $v \in \mathcal{V}$ such that $pre(a_i)(v) \neq pre(a_j)(v)$ while both are defined. To encode the ∃-step semantics into a SAT formula, we select an ordering of the actions $\vec{\mathcal{A}}$. If there is an edge (a_i, a_j) in the DG, we prefer to have a_j before a_i in $\vec{\mathcal{A}}$, in which case the constraints of Definition 2 are automatically satisfied. If this is not possible due to cyclic dependencies, we choose any order of the actions involved in the cycle. Formally, we select $\vec{\mathcal{A}}$ as the reverse topological order of the condensation[3] of the DG. For every strongly connected component of the DG, we need to encode the constraints of Definition 2 in the SAT formula. This is done using so-called *chains* [33]. One chain is generated for every fact $(v = o)$ ensuring that after a deleting action $a \in del(v = o)$ no needing action $a' \in nee(v = o)$ in $\vec{\mathcal{A}}$ is executed. We omit details of the encoding and refer the reader to Rintanen [33, Sec. 3.2.2.].

---

[3] To condensate a graph, we replace each of its strongly connected components with a single node.

3   Evaluating Axioms in SAT

Our objective is to extend the capabilities of SAT-based planning to being able to handle derived predicates and axioms efficiently. This comprises two challenges: firstly, we need to be able to evaluate axioms correctly and efficiently inside the SAT formula; secondly, we need to integrate axioms into the reasoning of the $\exists$-step encoding. In this section, we start by addressing the first challenge.

3.1   Using the Truth Dependency Graph

To obtain a compact encoding, we utilize the structural information contained in the TDG. We observe that if there is no path from d_i to d_j in the TDG, then determining the truth value of d_j is independent of the truth value of d_i. Consequently, we consider the strongly connected components (SCCs) and their dependency structure. Notably, we determine a topological ordering of the TDG's SCCs as $\vec{S} = \langle S_1, \ldots, S_n \rangle$ where the S_i are sets of derived predicates inside an SCC and $i < j$ implies that there is no path in the TDG from a predicate in S_j to a predicate in S_i. For this ordering, the evaluation of the truth value of any $d \in S_i$ depends only on the truth value of derived predicates $d' \in S_j$ with $j \leq i$. Since by the same argument, the truth value of d' does not depend on d iff $j < i$, we can evaluate the truth values of the derived predicates in each SCC one after another. Notably the truth of $d \in S_i$ depends only the finally determined truth values of all $d' \in S_j$ with $j < i$ and not on any intermediate value. As such we can introduce decision variables $d^*@n$ representing the value of the derived predicate d at time n. The encoding of an SCC S_i will only refer to variables $d^*@n$ for $d \in S_j$ with $j < i$ or additional variables internal to the SCC. Actions a at time n with a precondition on d are similarly encoded with the implication $a@n \rightarrow d^*@n$. To evaluate the derived predicates, we can now handle the SCCs of the TDG independently of each other.

3.2   Base Encoding

Consider a SCC S of the TDG. In an naive attempt, one could try to simply convert each axiom into one clause of the SAT formula per time step. This leads to problems due to self-supporting cycles in the axioms, i.e., we might not find the smallest fixpoint of axiom evaluation. As an example, suppose there are only two axioms: $d_1 \rightarrow d_2$ and $d_2 \rightarrow d_1$. In any state, none of these axioms fire, so both d_1 and d_2 are false. If we directly add the two axioms as clauses into a SAT formula, there are two valuation that satisfy them: one where both d_1 and d_2 are false and one where both are true.

To only allow the first valuation, we need to disallow such self-supporting cycles. There are multiple methods of doing so. We opted for the conceptually simplest one: to evaluate the axioms in steps or layers, where derived predicates in layer ℓ can only become true based on the truth values in layer $\ell - 1$. Such an encoding avoids cycles by construction, but can have substantial size for large SCCs S. Several other methods for breaking cycles have been proposed in the literature (e.g. [13,14,29]). We did not experiment with these more complex encodings so far, as the simpler layer-based encoding was sufficient for the benchmarks we considered. We consider this to be future work.

Given the number of layers L, we introduce SAT variables $d_i^\ell @ n$ for $0 \le \ell \le L$ that indicate that $d_i \in S$ is true in layer ℓ for every time step n. Since the encoding of axioms is identical for every time step, we omit the indication of the time step from now on. For layer 0, we statically assert all derived predicates to false (i.e. $\neg d_i^0$). For every layer, we need to force the derived predicate d_i to true if the conditions of an axiom ax that has d_i as a consequent are met. Consider an axiom ax of the form $\bigwedge_{(v_i = o_i) \in \ell^f(ax)} (v_i = o_i) \wedge \bigwedge_{d_j \in \ell^+(ax)} d_j \wedge \bigwedge_{d_k \in \ell^-(ax)} \neg d_k \rightarrow d$. The left-hand side of ax contains two types of derived predicates: those that are in the current SCC S and those that are part of earlier SCCs. For the latter, we can use the decision variables d_j containing their already determined value. Only for the variable in the same SCC, we need to consider the layering structure. We thus introduce the following clause $\bigwedge_{(v_i = o_i) \in \ell^f(ax)} (v_i = o_i) \wedge \bigwedge_{d_j \in \ell^+(ax) \cap S} d_j^{\ell-1} \wedge \bigwedge_{d_k \in \ell^-(ax) \cap S} \neg d_k^{\ell-1} \wedge \bigwedge_{d_j \in \ell^+(ax) \backslash S} d_j^* \wedge \bigwedge_{d_k \in \ell^-(ax) \backslash S} \neg d_k^* \rightarrow d_j^\ell$. Next, we need to ensure that the derived predicate is true only if there is an axiom that makes it true. So we need to add a clause of the form $d_j^\ell \rightarrow \bigvee_{ax} \big(\bigwedge_{(v_i = o_i) \in \ell^f(ax)} (v_i = o_i) \wedge \bigwedge_{d_j \in \ell^+(ax) \cap S} d_j^{\ell-1} \wedge \bigwedge_{d_k \in \ell^-(ax) \cap S} \neg d_k^{\ell-1} \wedge \bigwedge_{d_j \in \ell^+(ax) \backslash S} d_j^* \wedge \bigwedge_{d_k \in \ell^-(ax) \backslash S} \neg d_k^* \big)$. Since this formula is not in CNF, we introduce intermediate Tseitin variables [45] for the right-hand side of the disjunction, as we do for conditional effects in the base encoding. We do not have to encode a reason for the axiom to stay false – as we force it to be true if one of the axioms fire and axioms cannot force a derived predicate to become false.

Next, we need to determine how many layers to use. Theoretically, it is sufficient to choose the longest simple path inside the SCC S. However, computing it is NP-complete, and even the approximation is hard within a constant factor [23]. Thus, we simply use the size of S as an upper approximation. This however leads to an encoding with at least $\mathcal{O}(|S|^2)$ many clauses. Lastly, we identify d_i^L with the decision variables d_i^* containing the value determined for d_i.

3.3   Efficient Handling Special SCCs Structures

In practice, that is, in our experiments detailed in Sect. 6, we often find that some SCCs of the TDG have a special structure. The presented base encoding for axioms does not take advantage of these structures. Therefore, we propose two cases for which axioms can be encoded more efficiently.

Implicational SCCs. Some domains have derived predicates that express a notion of reachability, e.g., the fact of x being above y, directly or indirectly. The axioms related to these derived predicates have a very simple form: $d_i \rightarrow d_j$ – denoting that if d_i is true, then d_j must be true. Formally, we distinguish two types of axioms: axioms ax are external for the SCC S iff $\ell(ax) \cap S = \emptyset$, i.e., if no derived predicate of the SCC occurs as an antecedent in ax. Otherwise, they are internal. An SCC S is implicational, if all internal axioms ax are of the form $d_i \rightarrow d_j$.

For implicational SCCs the truth of the derived predicates depends solely on the initial values of the derived predicates as set by external axioms. The key insight is that external axioms need only to be evaluated once – as the truth of their antecedents is fixed and cannot change if the SCCs are processed in topological order. Next, due to the SCC being implicational, a derived predicate d_j is true in the final layer if and only if there is a chain of internal axioms $d_i \rightarrow d_{i'} \rightarrow \cdots \rightarrow d_j$ such that d_i is set to true by an external axiom.

We can exploit this to reduce the number of layers required to fully evaluate the axioms to two. For the first layer, we generate the clauses determining the truth of the d_i^1 variables restricting only the external axioms using the same encoding as in the general case above. Next, we will determine for every $d_i \in S$ the set of derived predicates that will turn true if d_i is true. This can be done by depth-first search over the internal axioms and results in the set $R(d_i)$. Similarly, we compute $R^{-1}(d_i) = \{d_j \mid d_i \in R(d_j)\}$ – the set of all derived predicates d_j that if true force d_i to be true. Given an implicational SCC S, we add the following clauses, evaluating the axioms deriving predicates in S in layer two: $\forall d_i \in S \forall d_j \in R(d_i) : d_i^1 \rightarrow d_j^2$ and $\forall d_i \in S : d_i^2 \rightarrow \bigvee_{d_j \in R^{-1}(d_i)} d_j^1$. As before we identify d_i^2 with the final value d_i^*.

One Variable Dependent SCC. Implicational SCCs do occur in planning problems, but are relatively restrictive. We can extend the same idea to a slightly more complex type of SCCs. In these SCCs, we allow for one additional literal on the left-hand side of axioms. That is, we consider SCCs S in which all internal axioms are of the form $v_k = o_k \wedge d_i \rightarrow d_j$, with $v_k \in \mathcal{V}$, $o_k \in D_{v_k}$ and $d_i, d_j \in S$.

We use a core property of the FDR formalism: a variable $v \in \mathcal{V}$ can have only a single value in each state. For this, we require that the additional literal in all internal axioms of the SCC refers to the same variable v, i.e., that the axioms are of the form $v = o_k \wedge d_i \rightarrow d_j$.[4] We can now split the axioms into sets A_{o_k} – depending on the variables value. If in the current state $v = o_\ell$, we know that all axioms A_{o_k} for $k \neq \ell$ will never fire as their antecedents are false, while the axioms in A_{o_ℓ} effectively turn into implicational axioms. We can use a similar encoding as for the implicational SCCs while adding a guard for the value of the variable. For this, we compute $R_{o_k}(d_i)$ as the set of all derived predicates reachable from d_i using only axioms in A_{o_k} and $R_{o_k}^{-1}(d_i) = \{d_j \mid d_i \in R_{o_k}(d_j)\}$. Given a one variable dependent SCC S, we add $\forall d_i \in S \forall o_k \in D_v \forall d_j \in R_{o_k}(d_i)$ the clause $v = o_k \wedge d_i^1 \rightarrow d_j^2$ and $\forall d_i \in S \forall o_k \in D_v$ the frame axiom: $d_i^2 \wedge v = o_k \rightarrow \bigvee_{d_j \in R_{o_k}^{-1}(d_i)} d_j^1$. This frame axiom is sufficient as we know that the variable v will have exactly one value.

---

[4] We also allow for purely implicational axioms as well as dependency on a single other derived predicate from a different SCC. They can be viewed as a set of axioms $v = o \wedge d_i \rightarrow d_j$ for all values $o \in D_v$.

4   Parallelism and Axioms

The encoding of axioms described in the previous section solely extends SAT planning to allow for evaluating axioms after **one** action has been executed. However, a critical element of efficiency for modern SAT-based planners is the ability to find parallel plans, i.e., plans in which at every time step multiple actions can be executed in parallel.

For adapting the ∃-step encoding to axioms, we need to change (1) the construction of the DG and (2) potentially adapt the *chain* clauses. To construct the DG, we need to determine, for every fact f (either an FDR fact or a derived predicate literal), the set $nee(f) \subseteq \mathcal{A}$ of actions that need f, and the set $del(f) \subseteq \mathcal{A}$ of actions that delete it. For $nee(f)$ nothing changes – an action a needs a derived predicate d or its negation $\neg d$ iff it occurs in its precondition or a conditional effect condition.

For $del(f)$, the effects of an action can, via axioms, have an indirect effect on derived predicates. We need to determine which derived predicates could be made true or false by an action. Determining this exactly is NP-complete, as we can use FDR variables not mentioned by a to choose a valuation and the axioms to evaluate a SAT formula. Thus, we approximate. We maintain four sets T_{def}^a, T_{pos}^a, F_{def}^a, and F_{pos}^a – sets of facts that the action a could **pos**sibly (T_{pos}^a, F_{pos}^a) or **def**initively (T_{def}^a, F_{def}^a) make **T**rue or **F**alse, respectively. Whenever we add a derived predicate d to any of these sets, we add $\neg d$ to the respective negated set. We first compute definitive effects. For FDR variables, we add for every effect $v = o_i$ of action a, $v = o_i$ to T_{def}^a and $v = o_j$ for $o_i \neq o_j$ to F_{def}^a. Next we handle definitive effects on derived predicates. For every axiom ax, where $\ell(ax) \subseteq T_{\text{def}}^a$, we add $r(ax)$ to T_{def}^a. For every derived predicate d for which all axioms ax that derive d, i.e., all axioms with $d = r(ax)$ have $\ell(ax) \cap F_{\text{def}}^a \neq \emptyset$, we add d to F_{def}^a. We repeat this until convergence.

We proceed to compute possible effects by tracing possible changes through the axioms. Initially, we set $T_{\text{pos}}^a := T_{\text{def}}^a$ and $F_{\text{pos}}^a := F_{\text{def}}^a$. If there is an axiom ax so that $T_{\text{pos}}^a \cap \ell(ax) \neq \emptyset$ and $F_{\text{def}}^a \cap \ell(ax) = \emptyset$ – that is at least one of its conditions can possibly turn true, but none of the conditions definitely turns false – the axiom might be newly applicable and might turn $r(ax)$ true. We thus add $r(ax)$ to T_{pos}^a. We cannot take into account whether any condition is actually false in a given state as we need to derive $del(\cdot)$ state independently. It cannot be the case that $r(ax) \in F_{\text{def}}^a$ as it can only be added if $F_{\text{def}}^a \cap \ell(ax) \neq \emptyset$. Similarly, if there is an axiom ax so that $F_{\text{pos}}^a \cap \ell(ax) \neq \emptyset$ and $r(ax) \notin T_{\text{def}}^a$, i.e., for which one condition might turn false and the right-hand-side is not known to definitely turn true via another axiom, we add $r(ax)$ to F_{pos}^a.

Given these sets, we can approximate that an action a potentially makes all literals in F_{pos}^a false, i.e., we add a to all $del(d)$ for $d \in F_{\text{pos}}^a$. From this point on, we use the standard definition of the DG, i.e., an action a_i disables a_j if they have non-contradictory preconditions (here we don't consider axioms at all) and if $\exists v = o : a_i \in del(v = o) \wedge a_j \in nee(v = o)$. The generation of the ∃-step's chain constraints then proceeds as normal – treating derived predicates d as if they were regular facts using the updated definition of $del()$. As F_{pos}^a

over-approximates which literals over derived predicates can become false, the conditions (2) and (3) of Definition 2 are satisfied with respect to the derived predicates. This ensures correctness of the encoding.

5   Handling Large Disabling Graphs

This section describes how we handle large DGs in practice.

In some domains, the sets $del(f)$ and $nee(f)$ can be large for some facts f (more than 1.000 actions, mostly for derived predicates). Here, the DG can contain up to $|del(f)| \cdot |nee(f)|$ edges, which can exhaust the planner's memory. In these cases, often at most one of the affected actions can be executed at any time anyway, as all actions disable each other, making any explicit reasoning about them in the DG useless. Hence, we commit to executing at most one of these actions and will always execute it as the last action of a time step. Then, we accumulate these actions in a set $\mathfrak{L}$ of last actions.

We use a threshold T[5] to determine when the disabling edges for a single fact should not be generated. If $|del(f)| \cdot |nee(f)| > T$, we add all actions in $del(f)$ to the set of last actions $\mathfrak{L}$ and do not generate any edges for them. When computing the action ordering $\vec{\mathcal{A}}$ for the $\exists$-step encoding, we ignore actions in $\mathfrak{L}$ and place them last in the ordering. For the $\exists$-step semantics, we do not generate any chain for f and add an at-most-one constraint over all action variables $a@n \in \mathfrak{L}$ for all time steps n.

To prove soundness, consider a case in which a set of actions is selected that is not executable. This set must contain exactly one action a^* out of $\mathfrak{L}$, otherwise it is executable by virtue of the correctness of the $\exists$-step encoding. Of this set, a^* will be executed last. So this sequence can only be non-executable if a^*'s preconditions are not met. This would only be the case, if there is an action deleting a fact that a^* has as precondition. If this is a fact for which a chain was generated, a^* cannot be selected to be executed. Else, all deleters of this fact are part of $\mathfrak{L}$. As a^* was selected, no other $a \in \mathfrak{L}$ can be chosen for execution, and thus a^*'s precondition could not have been deleted. For completeness, note that it is possible to select only a single action $a \in \mathfrak{L}$ and no action $a \in \mathcal{A} \setminus \mathfrak{L}$ and vice versa.

6   Empirical Evaluation

We implemented our planner AxSAT, using the described encoding, on top of Fast Downward (FD) in version 23.06 [17]. Our experiments were conducted on a cluster of Intel Xeon Gold 6130 CPUs using Downward Lab 8.2 [37], with runtime/memory limits of 30 min/3.5 GiB. We use the benchmark set collected by Speck et al. [43], which contains 1269 problem instances with axioms. As a backend solver for SAT formulas, we use Kissat[6]. AxSAT's code[7] and the empirical results are publicly available [6].

---

[5] In our experiments (Sect. 6), this value is set to $5 \cdot 10^6$.
[6] https://github.com/arminbiere/kissat.
[7] https://github.com/galvusdamor/decoupling-transformer-sat.

Table 1. Coverage results (number of instances solved) and action parallelism on the axiom benchmark set. See text for a detailed discussion.

Domain	#	Coverage							Action Parallelism	
		blind	SymK	Iterative		Parallel		LAMA	Iterative	Parallel
				Seq	∃	Seq	∃		∃	∃
airport-adl	50	19	19	11	21	28	**49**	40	2.24	1.98
appn-adl	33	11	23	16	**33**	**33**	**33**	**33**	8.41	8.08
assembly	30	0	11	2	16	17	**30**	**30**	4.7	4.34
blocker	7	**7**	6	**7**	6	**7**	6	4	1	0.87
blocks-axioms	35	18	30	**35**	**35**	**35**	**35**	**35**	1	0.94
cats-horndl	20	**20**	**20**	11	**20**	**20**	**20**	**20**	13.1	2.62
drones-horndl	24	**23**	16	**23**	**23**	**23**	**23**	**23**	2.17	2.25
fridge	30	0	1	0	**30**	21	**30**	**30**	26.6	26.6
ged1-ds2nd	12	**12**	8	**12**	**12**	**12**	**12**	**12**	1	0.5
ghosh-cc2	27	9	0	14	18	18	**20**	**20**	1.63	1.45
grid-axioms	5	1	3	4	3	4	4	**5**	1.33	1.08
miconic-axioms	150	60	**150**	35	**150**	**150**	**150**	**150**	15.5	6.2
miconic-fulladl	150	78	111	59	72	130	**139**	**139**	1.88	1.8
openstacks	30	7	16	5	7	20	22	**30**	1.66	1.35
openstacks-opt08-adl	30	8	**30**	3	6	**30**	**30**	**30**	1.38	1.25
openstacks-sat08-adl	25	4	12	2	3	12	14	**25**	1.37	1.33
optical-telegraphs	48	2	3	1	**48**	6	**48**	4	32.45	25.5
philosophers	48	5	12	3	**48**	12	**48**	46	25.5	22.95
psr-large	50	14	25	22	25	25	28	**44**	5.84	3.27
psr-middle	36	26	**36**	35	**36**	**36**	**36**	**36**	6.43	3.88
queens-horndl	30	23	10	**30**	**30**	**30**	**30**	**30**	3.93	2.07
robot-horndl	56	45	42	37	37	53	52	**56**	1	0.94
robotConj-horndl	56	45	43	41	41	**56**	**56**	**56**	1	0.93
snowman-basic	41	**30**	29	13	12	16	17	22	1.06	0.97
snowman-cheating	41	33	32	33	**36**	**36**	**36**	23	2.28	2.19
snowman-reach	41	**27**	25	19	17	20	18	23	1.07	0.9
sokoban-axioms	30	24	25	12	12	13	13	**28**	1	0.81
taskassign-horndl	20	**20**	12	**20**	**20**	**20**	**20**	**20**	11.95	5.51
tpsa-horndl	15	4	6	10	9	12	12	**15**	1.17	1
trucks	30	8	9	5	19	13	**25**	15	2.7	2.44
vta-horndl	15	**15**	4	13	13	**15**	**15**	**15**	1	1
vta-roles-horndl	15	**15**	0	13	13	**15**	**15**	**15**	1	1
others	39	37	37	37	37	37	37	37	2.15	2.01
Σ	1269	650	806	583	908	975	**1123**	1111	5.06	3.92

We run AxSAT in two different search configurations, an **iterative mode**, working on one formula at a time, and a **parallel mode**, which handles multiple formulas in parallel. The iterative mode constructs formulas for increasing plan-length bounds, incrementing it by 1 in each iteration, and runs the SAT solver until it terminates, i.e., shows the formula (un)satisfiable, or runs out of time/memory. Rintanen [33] proposed a parallel mode, in which solving multiple bounds is interleaved in a round-robin fashion on a single core. We use a simpler variant that in our experiments performed better: we run the formulas for different bounds sequentially, but limit each to 5min. If Kissat runs into our time or memory limit, we proceed to the next bound. This "parallel mode" increases the plan-length exponentially, i.e., iteration i runs with limit $5 \cdot (\sqrt{2})^i$, like Madagascar [31]. On the encoding side, we distinguish between the **sequential** (Seq), with one action per time step, and the **∃-step encoding** (∃).

As baselines, we compare our approach against FD's **blind** search, the symbolic search of **SymK** [42], and the first iteration of **LAMA** [30]. Note that we cannot compare ourselves against other SAT-based planner as these do not

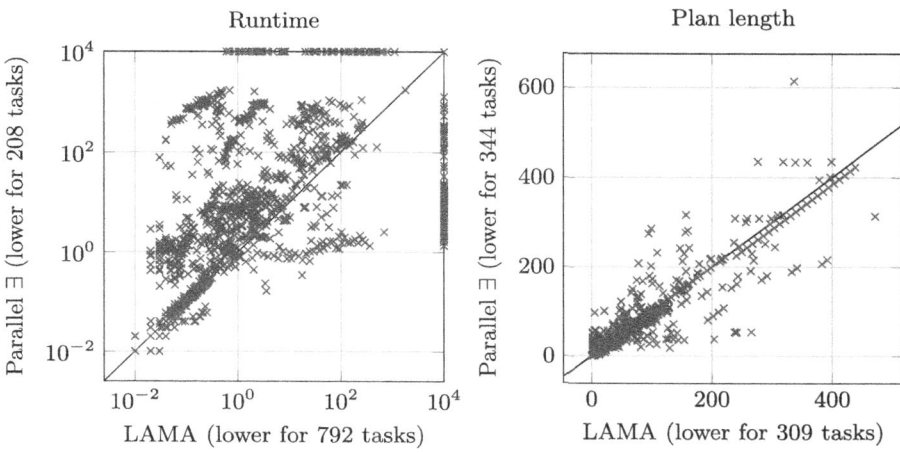

Fig. 1. Per-instance comparison of runtime (left) and plan length (right) for LAMA and our parallel ∃-step planner on the axiom benchmarks.

support axioms in the problem descriptions. There do exist methods based on answer-set programming and integer linear programming that support axioms, implemented in ASPlan and IPlan [27], respectively Plasp [10]. Unfortunately, neither ASPlan nor IPlan are publicly available. The axiom support for Plasp is very limited, only allowing for axioms that result from compiling away complex action preconditions and effects, but derived predicates are not supported. This means that Plasp is applicable only to a small fraction of our benchmarks, so we omit it in our evaluation.

The left of Table 1 shows coverage results (number of solved instances). Overall, the iterative sequential algorithm is not competitive, but it outperforms blind search and SymK significantly on a few domains (blocks, gosh, queens, tpsa). Our iterative ∃ variant outperforms both of these baselines overall, where the approaches have their strengths in different domains. Our parallel search variants improve by a lot over the iterative ones. With ∃-step encoding, our planner is overall better than LAMA, which is the state-of-the-art planner in satisficing classical planning with axioms. Taking a closer look at the two best-performing configurations, we observe that both solve all instances across many domains. On the remaining domains, they clearly have complementary strengths. Our SAT-based planner does very well in airport, optical-telegraphs, snowman-cheating, and trucks, whereas LAMA shines in openstacks, psr, snowman basic and reach, as well as sokoban. The scatter plot in Fig. 1 (left) sheds further light at this comparison. It clearly confirms the complementary strengths of the two approaches, with both techniques obtaining speed-ups of several orders of magnitude over the other in different domains. Overall, our SAT-based approach shows state-of-the-art performance on domains with axioms.

In the right of Table 1 we show the action parallelism in the plans found by iterative ∃ and parallel ∃ on instances commonly solved by these two configurations. We compute the parallelism as the ratio between plan length and the number of steps encoded in the SAT formula. Hence, the sequential encoding always obtains a parallelism of at most 1.0 (there can be steps in which no action is applied). We have two main observations: (1) in domains with high parallelism, ∃ significantly improves of Seq, and (2) in the same domains parallel ∃ is very competitive with LAMA. Another observation is that parallel ∃ typically achieves lower parallelism than the iterative variant, which is due to the greedy behavior of increasing the bound without waiting for the SAT solver to prove the respective formula to be unsatisfiable.

We compare the solution quality of LAMA and the parallel ∃ configuration in Fig. 1 (right). There is no clear advantage for either of the methods. Overall, the parallel ∃ configuration finds shorter solutions in 344 instances (mostly in appn-adl, assembly, and robotConj-horndl) than LAMA, and longer solutions in 309 instances (mostly in airport-adl, blocks-axioms, philosophers).

We also analyzed the structure of the TDG in the benchmark instances. A substantial amount of SCCs of the TDGs has size one, which are by definition implicational as they lack internal axioms. In most domains, all derived variables are in size-1 SCCs. Exceptions are psr (only 44%, respectively 51% of SCCs are size-1), snowman-reach (46%), social-planning (86%) and sokoban (85%). These are, with the exception of social-planning, the domains in which our approach falls behind LAMA.

7   Conclusion

We introduce the first encoding for axioms and derived predicates for SAT-based planning. This closes a significant gap, as other common planning paradigms, such as heuristic explicit-state search or symbolic search, have previously supported planning with axioms. We show a sequential encoding as well as an exists-step encoding tailored to axioms, which is the standard in modern SAT-based planners. Our planner AxSAT, based on this encoding, is competitive with the state of the art in satisficing planning with axioms and performs favorably overall compared to the well-known LAMA planner.

For future work, we plan to investigate encodings specifically designed for more specialized forms of stratified axiom programs. A particularly interesting direction is to study the recent decoupled task transformation [41], which embodies decoupled search [15] and relies heavily on axioms. This includes examining the relationship between decoupled search and action parallelism (∃-step encoding). Further, we will consider encodings of parallelism in planning that admit more parallelism, notably the relaxed ∃-step [46] and relaxed-relaxed ∃-step encodings [2]. Both are challenging to incorporate as they require reasoning about when and importantly how the truth values of derived predicates changes during the execution of actions *inside* of the SAT formula – in contrast to our encoding which is based on a cautious precomputed estimate.

Acknowledgments. This publication is part of the project "Exploiting Problem Structures in SAT-based Planning" of the research programme Open Competition which is financed under the grant OCENW.M.22.050 by the Dutch Research Council (NWO). David Speck was funded by the Swiss National Science Foundation (SNSF) as part of the project "Unifying the Theory and Algorithms of Factored State-Space Search" (UTA). This work was partially supported by the Wallenberg AI, Autonomous Systems and Software Program (WASP) funded by the Knut and Alice Wallenberg Foundation, and by TAILOR, a project funded by the EU Horizon 2020 research and innovation programme under grant agreement no. 952215. The computations were enabled by resources provided by the National Academic Infrastructure for Supercomputing in Sweden (NAISS), partially funded by the Swedish Research Council through grant agreement no. 2022-06725.

References

1. Proceedings of the ICAPS 2024 (2024)
2. Balyo, T.: Relaxing the relaxed exist-step parallel planning semantics. In: 25th International Conference on Tools with Artificial Intelligence (ICTAI 2013), pp. 865–871. IEEE Computer Society (2013)
3. Behnke, G.: Block compression and invariant pruning for SAT-based totally-ordered HTN planning. In: ICAPS 2021, pp. 25–35. AAAI Press (2021). https://doi.org/10.1609/icaps.v31i1.15943
4. Behnke, G., Höller, D., Biundo, S.: totSAT – totally-ordered hierarchical planning through SAT. In: AAAI 2018, pp. 6110–6118. AAAI Press (2018)
5. Behnke, G., Höller, D., Biundo, S.: Bringing order to chaos – a compact representation of partial order in SAT-based HTN planning. In: AAAI 2019, pp. 7520–7529. AAAI Press (2019). https://doi.org/10.1609/aaai.v33i01.33017520
6. Behnke, G., Speck, D., Gnad, D.: AxSAT – bringing axioms to sat planning (2025). https://doi.org/10.5281/zenodo.15848556
7. Bofill, M., Borralleras, C., Espasa, J., Martín, G., Patow, G., Villaret, M.: A good snowman is hard to plan. arXiv:2310.01471 [cs.AI] (2023)
8. Bofill, M., Espasa, J., Villaret, M.: The RANTANPLAN planner: system description. Knowl. Eng. Rev. **31**(5), 452–464 (2016)
9. Bryce, D., Gao, S., Musliner, D.J., Goldman, R.P.: SMT-based nonlinear PDDL+ planning. In: Proceedings of the AAAI 2015, pp. 3247–3253 (2015)
10. Dimopoulos, Y., Gebser, M., Lühne, P., Romero, J., Schaub, T.: plasp 3: towards effective ASP planning. Theory Pract. Log. Program. **19**(3), 477–504 (2019)
11. Dimopoulos, Y., Nebel, B., Koehler, J.: Encoding planning problems in nonmonotonic logic programs. In: Proceedings of the ECAI 1997, pp. 169–181 (1997)
12. Frisch, A.M., Giannaros, P.A.: SAT encodings of the at-most-k constraint: some old, some new, some fast, some slow (2010). Manuscript
13. Gebser, M., Janhunen, T., Rintanen, J.: ASP encodings of acyclicity properties. In: Proceedings of the KR 2014, pp. 634–637 (2014)
14. Gebser, M., Janhunen, T., Rintanen, J.: Declarative encodings of acyclicity properties. J. Log. Comput. **30**(4), 923–952 (2020)
15. Gnad, D., Hoffmann, J.: Star-topology decoupled state space search. AIJ **257**, 24–60 (2018)
16. Grundke, C., Röger, G., Helmert, M.: Formal representations of classical planning domains. In: Proceedings of the ICAPS 2024 [1], pp. 239–248 (2024)

17. Helmert, M.: The Fast Downward planning system. JAIR **26**, 191–246 (2006)
18. Helmert, M.: Concise finite-domain representations for PDDL planning tasks. AIJ **173**, 503–535 (2009)
19. Hoffmann, J., Nebel, B.: The FF planning system: fast plan generation through heuristic search. JAIR **14**, 253–302 (2001)
20. Huang, R., Chen, Y., Zhang, W.: SAS$^+$ planning as satisfiability. JAIR **43**, 293–328 (2012)
21. Höller, D., Behnke, G.: Encoding lifted classical planning in propositional logic. In: ICAPS 2022, pp. 137–144. AAAI Press (2022). https://doi.org/10.1609/icaps. v32i1.19794
22. Ivankovic, F., Haslum, P.: Optimal planning with axioms. In: Proceedings of the IJCAI 2015, pp. 1580–1586 (2015)
23. Karger, D.R., Motwani, R., Ramkumar, G.D.S.: On approximating the longest path in a graph. Algorithmica **18**(1), 82–98 (1997)
24. Kautz, H., Selman, B.: Planning as satisfiability. In: Proceedings of the ECAI 1992, pp. 359–363 (1992)
25. Kautz, H., Selman, B.: Pushing the envelope: planning, propositional logic, and stochastic search. In: Proceedings of the AAAI 1996, pp. 1194–1201 (1996)
26. McDermott, D.: The 1998 AI planning systems competition. AI Mag. **21**(2), 35–55 (2000)
27. Miura, S., Fukunaga, A.: Automatic extraction of axioms for planning. In: Proceedings of the ICAPS 2017, pp. 218–227 (2017)
28. Quenard, G., Pellier, D., Fiorino, H.: SibylSat: using sat as an oracle to perform a greedy search on TOHTN planning. In: ECAI 2024, pp. 4157–4164. IOS Press (2024)
29. Rankooh, M.F., Rintanen, J.: Propositional encodings of acyclicity and reachability by using vertex elimination. In: Proceedings of the AAAI 2022, pp. 5861–5868 (2022)
30. Richter, S., Westphal, M.: The LAMA planner: guiding cost-based anytime planning with landmarks. JAIR **39**, 127–177 (2010)
31. Rintanen, J.: Madagascar: scalable planning with SAT. In: IPC-8 Planner Abstracts, pp. 66–70 (2014)
32. Rintanen, J.: Temporal planning with clock-based SMT encodings. In: Proceedings of the IJCAI 2017, pp. 743–749 (2017)
33. Rintanen, J., Heljanko, K., Niemelä, I.: Planning as satisfiability: parallel plans and algorithms for plan search. Artif. Intell. **170**(12–13), 1031–1080 (2006)
34. Röger, G., Grundke, C.: Negated occurrences of predicates in PDDL axiom bodies. In: Proceedings of the KI-2024 Workshop on Planning, Scheduling, Design and Configuration (PuK 2024) (2024)
35. Scala, E., Ramirez, M., Haslum, P., Thiébaux, S.: Numeric planning with disjunctive global constraints via SMT. In: ICAPS 2016, pp. 276–284 (2016)
36. Schreiber, D.: Lilotane: a lifted SAT-based approach to hierarchical planning. JAIR **70**, 1117–1181 (2021)
37. Seipp, J., Pommerening, F., Sievers, S., Helmert, M.: Downward lab (2017). https://doi.org/10.5281/zenodo.790461
38. Shaik, I., van de Pol, J.: Classical planning as QBF without grounding. In: Proceedings of the ICAPS 2022, pp. 329–337 (2022)
39. Sinz, C.: Towards an optimal CNF encoding of Boolean cardinality constraints. In: van Beek, P. (ed.) CP 2005. LNCS, vol. 3709, pp. 827–831. Springer, Heidelberg (2005). https://doi.org/10.1007/11564751_73

40. Speck, D., Geißer, F., Mattmüller, R., Torralba, Á.: Symbolic planning with axioms. In: Proceedings of the ICAPS 2019, pp. 464–472 (2019)
41. Speck, D., Gnad, D.: Decoupled search for the masses: a novel task transformation for classical planning. In: Proceedings of the ICAPS 2024 [1], pp. 546–554 (2024)
42. Speck, D., Mattmüller, R., Nebel, B.: Symbolic top-k planning. In: Proceedings of the AAAI 2020, pp. 9967–9974 (2020)
43. Speck, D., Seipp, J., Torralba, Á.: Symbolic search for cost-optimal planning with expressive model extensions. JAIR **82**, 1349–1405 (2025)
44. Thiébaux, S., Hoffmann, J., Nebel, B.: In defense of PDDL axioms. AIJ **168**(1–2), 38–69 (2005)
45. Tseitin, G.: On the complexity of derivation in the propositional calculus. In: Studies in Constructive Mathematics and Mathematical Logic, Part II, pp. 115–125. Consultants Bureau, New York (1968). English Translation
46. Wehrle, M., Rintanen, J.: Planning as satisfiability with relaxed ∃-step plans. In: Proceedings of the AJCAI 2007, pp. 244–253 (2007)

On Extracting Legal Arguments

Noah Collinet[1]([✉]), Yakoub Salhi[2] [ID], and Souhila Kaci[1] [ID]

[1] LIRMM UMR 5506, University of Montpellier, CNRS, Montpellier, France
noah.collinet@lirmm.fr
[2] CRIL UMR 8188, University of Artois, CNRS, Arras, France

Abstract. Building on the principles of case-based reasoning, we investigate the extraction of arguments from legal case databases. An argument is modeled as a set of factors that frequently support one party (plaintiff or defendant) over the other. The relevance of an argument is assessed by the number of cases that confirm it versus those that contradict it. Following established practices in data mining, we introduce a condensed representation of arguments called closed arguments, which capture the strongest form of support given the factors they contain. We develop propositional SAT-based encodings to enable the extraction of both arguments and closed arguments using SAT solvers. Additionally, we define a more compact condensed representation called maximal arguments, which eliminates redundancy by retaining only the most informative arguments with respect to given thresholds. We propose a level-wise algorithm that builds on our SAT-based approach for argument extraction. Preliminary experiments demonstrate the feasibility of our SAT-based mining methods.

Keywords: Cased-based reasoning · Legal case databases · Argumentation extraction · Problem Modeling · Propositional Satisfiability

1 Introduction

Case-based reasoning is a fundamental mode of human reasoning [16]. It consists of drawing analogies from past situations to solve new problems. In the common law systems, decisions are guided by the rule of precedent [8, 19, 25, 28], particularly the so-called *ratio decidendi* rules. These rules are used as jurisprudence for new judicial decisions based on one or more previous cases, called precedents. The law therefore also evolves with each new decision. This dynamic helps to frame the power of courts: their rulings influence the law [8, 17], even though they do not hold legislative authority. Such rules form a dynamic doctrine. The addition of new cases can refine, extend, or even create exceptions to existing legal principles [25, 28]. This doctrine is a way to start analysing new legal situations. We could say that legal reasoning in common law evolves to match society's values. In legal reasoning, decisions are not just based on facts themselves. However, although this doctrine provides a structured framework,

© The Author(s), under exclusive license to Springer Nature Switzerland AG 2026
G. Casini et al. (Eds.): JELIA 2025, LNAI 16094, pp. 94–108, 2026.
https://doi.org/10.1007/978-3-032-04590-4_7

identifying relevant legal data from a large database of precedents remains a difficult task. Another contributing factor is the way these facts are structured into arguments supporting one party over another party. However, the growing volume of data and factors in cases makes it difficult to identify relevant patterns. Although there are already systems for textual features, there is a gap in the literature about tools for formalizing and systematically extracting and evaluating legal arguments in cases. Thus, it raises the need for formal approaches capable of modeling such argumentative patterns, assessing their strength, and extracting them in a compact way.

To address this challenge, we draw inspiration from data mining and knowledge representation. Data mining consists of exploring large collections of data to discover the information it contains. It is the application of efficient algorithms [9] using breadth-first search [1] or depth-first-search [12,22,30,33] to identify meaningful patterns [29], associations [18] and regularities [32,35] in a database such that this information can help decision-making. This process is iterative and interactive and it uncovers information that is new, valid, useful and understandable from a large volume of data. However, such patterns can be numerous and redundant. This motivates the use of condensed representations of these patterns that preserve essential information while reducing the overlaping.

We present in this work a modeling for a legal argument as a set of factors systematically supporting one of the parties. Then, we are able to evaluate the relevance of such arguments by comparing their frequency of confirmation vs. contradiction across cases. Our objective is firstly to extract *strong arguments*, defined as patterns appearing in favor of either side with threshold values, and secondly to identify *condensed* forms of arguments such as maximal and closed to reduce redundancy. With this goal in mind, we develop algorithms to extract those arguments, and we present experiments run with our algorithms which show the feasibility of our approaches. By comparing databases of precedent cases favoring different sides (e.g., plaintiff vs. defendant), we aim to extract legal arguments that support decision-making.

We adopt a SAT-based (Boolean satisfiability) encoding to represent constraints over legal factors and their occurrences across cases. There are two main reasons for this choice. First, the structure of legal reasoning imposes constraints on argument formulation, such as consistency and minimality. Representing arguments in propositional logic permits to clearly identify such constraints and the relationships between factors. This logic-based formalism facilitates the introduction of new knowledge during the extraction process—such as domain-specific constraints or normative rules—making it particularly suitable for modeling evolving legal doctrines. Second, modern SAT solvers [6,13] provide highly optimised engines for exploring large combinatorial spaces efficiently.

We present experimental results based on artificially generated legal case data. These experiments show the feasibility of our approaches and illustrate the interpretability of the extracted arguments. In particular, they highlight the potential of strong, closed and maximal arguments to bring out important factors in legal disputes.

2 Background

This work sits at the intersection of legal reasoning, pattern mining, and formal logic-based representation. Previous studies in AI and Law have investigated the extraction of arguments from case texts. They generally made use of natural language processing and machine learning techniques. In contrast, our approach adopts a symbolic perspective, operating on structured representations of factors and cases.

The present paper is mainly concerned with two subjects, namely the argumentation mining problem and the SAT problem. In the following we provide the necessary background.

We consider propositional logic variables denoted $p, q, r, \ldots$. The symbols $\vee, \wedge, \neg$ respectively denote n-ary disjunction, n-ary conjunction and unary negation. $\rightarrow$ denotes the classical implication. $\phi \leftrightarrow \psi$ stands for $\phi \rightarrow \psi \wedge \psi \rightarrow \phi$. A literal is a positive (p) or negated $(\neg p)$ propositional variable. The literals p and $\neg p$ are called complementary. A clause is a disjunction of literals. Classical logic formulas are denoted $\phi, \psi, \ldots$. A Conjunctive Normal Form (CNF) formula ϕ is a conjunction of clauses. $\vdash$ denotes the entailment of a formula. Any propositional formula can be written in CNF, thanks to Tseitin's linear encoding [27]. In the remainder of this paper, we suppose that propositional logic formulas are CNF. A boolean interpretation $\mathcal{I}$ of a formula ϕ is a function which associates to each variable in ϕ a boolean value. An interpretation that satisfies a formula, denoted $\mathcal{I}(\phi) = 1$ (true), is called a model of the fomula. Given a formula, the SAT problem refers here to decide whether this formula admits a model or not.

The integration of formal constraints through propositional logic also aligns with work in logic-based reasoning systems, offering a flexible framework to encode evolving legal doctrines. This places our contribution within a broader movement toward explainable and interpretable AI in legal contexts, while providing a new formal tool for structured legal case analysis.

3 Strong Argument Mining

We follow the formalism defined in [5] to represent legal factors and cases. We thus define Ω as a finite set of *factors* that are legally relevant to a specific issue. Let Ω^p and Ω^d respectively represent the factors favoring the plaintiff and the factors favoring the defendant. We suppose that $\Omega = \Omega^p \cup \Omega^d$ and $\Omega^p \cap \Omega^d = \emptyset$. If s denotes one side, either p (plaintiff) or d (defendant), $\bar{s}$ denotes the opposite side.

A *legal case* is defined as a tuple $\langle X, R, s \rangle$, where $X \subseteq \Omega$, R is a subset of either $X \cap \Omega^p$ or $X \cap \Omega^d$. The side s is set to p if $R \subseteq X \cap \Omega^p$, and to d otherwise. X represents the set of the available factors, and R represents the reason leading to the victory of side s.

Given a legal case $C = \langle X, R, s \rangle$, $\rho(C)$ denotes the reason R in favor of the decision s taken in C, and $F(C)$ denotes the set of factors X of C.

A *case database* is defined as a finite set of ordered pairs (id, C), where id is a unique case identifier, and C is a legal case. We define the set $\mathcal{D}_{|s}$ as all the cases favoring the side s, and $\mathcal{D}_{|\bar{s}}$ as the set of cases favoring the opposite side. For any case database $\mathcal{D}$, we observe that $\mathcal{D}_{|s} \cup \mathcal{D}_{|\bar{s}} = \mathcal{D}$ and $\mathcal{D}_{|s} \cap \mathcal{D}_{|\bar{s}} = \emptyset$.

A *precedent argument*, or simply an argument, is a tuple $(R_s, R_{\bar{s}})$ written as an expression of the form $R_s \succ R_{\bar{s}}$ where $s \in \{p, d\}$, $R_s \subseteq \Omega^s$ and $R_{\bar{s}} \subseteq \Omega^{\bar{s}}$. It expresses that the reason R_s favoring s is stronger than the reason $R_{\bar{s}}$ favoring the opposite side $\bar{s}$. Let $\mathtt{Arg}(\Omega, s)$ denote the set of all possible precedent arguments in favor of a side s.

We say that a legal case $C = \langle X, R, s' \rangle$ *supports* a precedent argument $A = R_s \succ R_{\bar{s}}$, written $C \models A$, if: $s' = s$, $R \subseteq R_s$, and $R_{\bar{s}} \subseteq X$. Additionally, we say that C *contradicts* A, written $C \models \tilde{A}$, if C supports $R_{\bar{s}} \succ R_s$.

The *cover* of a precedent argument A in a case database $\mathcal{D}$, denoted $\mathtt{cover}(A, \mathcal{D})$, is defined as: $\mathtt{cover}(A, \mathcal{D}) = \{id \mid (id, C) \in \mathcal{D}, C \models A\}$.

The *support* of A in $\mathcal{D}$, denoted $\mathtt{support}(A, \mathcal{D})$, is defined as the cardinality of the cover. Namely, $\mathtt{support}(A, \mathcal{D}) = |\mathtt{cover}(A, \mathcal{D})|$.

The *countercover* of A in $\mathcal{D}$, represented by $\mathtt{countercover}(A, \mathcal{D})$, is defined as the following set: $\mathtt{countercover}(A, \mathcal{D}) = \{id \mid (id, C) \in \mathcal{D}, C \models \tilde{A}\}$.

The *countersupport* of A in $\mathcal{D}$, denoted $\mathtt{countersupport}(A, \mathcal{D})$, is the cardinality of the countercover: $\mathtt{countersupport}(A, \mathcal{D}) = |\mathtt{countercover}(A, \mathcal{D})|$.

In the context of the common law, laws continually adapt over time to reflect the evolving values, ethics and cultural norms. Arguments used to justify a given decision are based on ethics, values and cultural norms, which are bound to evolve over time. That is why arguments or reasoning steps that were previously considered as valid may no longer be compatible with modern principles. To formalize the rejection of such arguments, we employ propositional formulas to encode the disqualification of certain reasoning patterns. These formulas serve as systematic tools to identify and invalidate argument forms that no longer align with current legal frameworks, ethical standards, or that are simply considered unworthy of further consideration.

Some examples of these formulas include:

- Let S be a set of factors favoring a side s. To express that any argument in favor of s must include at least one factor of S, we use $\bigvee_{a \in S} a$.
- To express that the set S is insufficient for s, we use $\bigvee_{f \in \Omega^s \setminus S} f$.
- Let a, b be two factors and R be a reason. To express that a and b must either both belong to the reason or be excluded, R has to satisfy $a \leftrightarrow b$.
- Let X be a set of factors including factors favoring one side and factors favoring the opposite side. To express that the reason for a side s must have a greater size than the reason for the opposite side, we can use the constraint $|\{a \in \Omega^s \cap X\}| - |\{b \in \Omega^{\bar{s}} \cap X\}| \geq 1$.

Thus, we associate to our argument task a propositional formula ϕ_s using factors as propositional variables. This formula requires constraints on arguments favoring the plaintiff and the defendant.

An argument $A = R_s \succ R_{\bar{s}}$ is said to be inconsistent with a formula ϕ, written $A \vdash \neg\phi$ if the following formula is inconsistent:

$$\left(\bigwedge_{a \in R_s \cup R_{\bar{s}}} a \right) \wedge \left(\bigwedge_{b \in \Omega \setminus R_s \cup R_{\bar{s}}} \neg b \right) \wedge \phi.$$

If this formula is consistent, we denotes this by $A \nvdash \neg\phi$.

We define the *strong argument mining* problem as follows.

Definition 1 (Strong Arguments). *Given a case database $\mathcal{D}$, a formula ϕ_s, a minimum support threshold σ, a minimum countersupport threshold κ and a side s, the objective is to compute the following set:*

$$\mathcal{SA}(\mathcal{D}, \phi_s, \sigma, \kappa, s) = \{A \in \texttt{Arg}(\Omega, s) \mid A \nvdash \neg\phi_s, \texttt{support}(A, \mathcal{D}) \geq \sigma,$$
$$\texttt{countersupport}(A, \mathcal{D}) \leq \kappa\}.$$

In simpler terms, an argument $A = R_s \succ R_{\bar{s}}$ is extracted if it is frequently supported in $\mathcal{D}_{|s}$ and rarely contradicted in $\mathcal{D}_{|\bar{s}}$.

The following proposition states that if an argument is considered strong, then strengthening the supporting reason or weakening the opposing reason will not change the argument's strength. Indeed, if an argument A is strong, it means that the factors included in R_s are more often winners when confronted to the factors of $R_{\bar{s}}$. What does happen when we add more factors favoring the side s? This side is still winning. Moreover, when we remove factors favoring the opposite side there is no reason to let that side win.

Proposition 1. *Let $A = R_s \succ R_{\bar{s}}$ be an argument in $\mathcal{SA}(\mathcal{D}, \phi_s, \sigma, \kappa, s)$. Then for any $R'_s \subseteq \Omega^s$ with $R_s \subseteq R'_s$ and any $R'_{\bar{s}} \subseteq R_{\bar{s}}$, if $A' = R'_s \succ R'_{\bar{s}}$ is consistent with ϕ_s, then A' also belongs to $\mathcal{SA}(\mathcal{D}, \phi_s, \sigma, \kappa, s)$.*

Proposition 2. *Let $A = R_s \succ R_{\bar{s}}$ be an argument in $\mathcal{SA}(\mathcal{D}, \phi_s, \sigma, \kappa, s)$. For all σ', κ' such that $\sigma' \leq \sigma$ and $\kappa' \geq \kappa$, A belongs to $\mathcal{SA}(\mathcal{D}, \phi_s, \sigma', \kappa', s)$.*

This proposition is directly implied by the monotonicity of the support of argument. We have then that the property of being strong for an argument is monotonic for σ anti-monotonic for κ. Let us now introduce a condensed representation of a set of arguments that is analogous to closed itemsets [2, 20, 21, 30, 31, 34].

Definition 2 (Closed Arguments).
An argument $A = R_s \succ R_{\bar{s}}$ is said to be closed in a case database $\mathcal{D}$ with respect to the constraint ϕ_s if it satisfies the two following conditions:
For any factor $a \in R_s$, either one of the following holds for the argument $A' = R_s \setminus \{a\} \succ R_{\bar{s}}$:

- $A' \vdash \neg\phi_s$,
- $\texttt{support}(A, \mathcal{D}) > \texttt{support}(A', \mathcal{D})$,
- $\texttt{countersupport}(A, \mathcal{D}) < \texttt{countersupport}(A', \mathcal{D})$.

For any factor $a \in \Omega^{\bar{s}} \setminus R_{\bar{s}}$, either one of the following holds for the argument $A' = R_s \succ R_{\bar{s}} \cup \{a\}$:

- $A' \vdash \neg\phi_s$,
- $\texttt{support}(A, \mathcal{D}) > \texttt{support}(A', \mathcal{D})$,
- $\texttt{countersupport}(A, \mathcal{D}) < \texttt{countersupport}(A', \mathcal{D})$.

Alternatively stated, a closed argument is an argument that cannot remain as strong when removing factors from the supporting side or adding factors to the opposing side. Indeed, any such modification would be of rejected form, reduce its support or increase its countersupport. By applying Proposition 1, we conclude that the closed elements in $\mathcal{SA}(\mathcal{D}, \phi_s, \sigma, \kappa, s)$ are sufficient to derive all the arguments in this set without requiring any scan of the case database.

4 Example

Example 1. Consider an issue about whether the termination of contract was justified of not. This falls under the employment law spectrum. We assume that the plaintiff (p) is the employee and the defendant (d) is the employer.

A first factor in favor of the employee can be a positive review shortly before the termination. A factor in favor of the employer can be an accusation of policy violation. Another factor in favor of the employee can be an absence of a report of following the disciplinary procedure after a violation. The two factors in favor of the plaintiff are denoted respectively f_r (for the positive review) and f_{ndp} (for no disciplinary procedure). The factor in favor of the defendant is denoted f_{pv} (for policy violation). Let us now consider three situations:

- The employee had recently received a good performance review but was also accused of a policy violation. The court then decided to favor the plaintiff, suggesting that the review was done after the accusation of policy violation, thus undermined the seriousness of the said violation. The fact in favor of the plaintiff is $\{f_r\}$. The fact in favor of the defendant is then $\{f_{pv}\}$. The rule used by the judge to decide is: $\{f_r \rightarrow \mathrm{p}\}$. Thus we can model the case as $C_1 = \langle \{f_r, f_{pv}\}, \{f_r\}, p \rangle$.
- The employer skipped required disciplinary steps before firing the employee, even though there was a policy violation. Based on these facts, the court again sided with the employee, emphasizing procedural fairness. Case 2 is modeled by: $C_2 = \langle \{f_{ndp}, f_{pv}\}, \{f_{ndp}\}, p \rangle$.
- The firing is done after a policy violation from the employee. With no favorable facts for the employee, the court ruled in favor of the employer. Case 3 is modeled by: $C_3 = \langle \{f_{pv}\}, \emptyset, d \rangle$.

We want to extract the strong arguments for the side p in the database formed by these three cases, with a support threshold and a countersupport threshold both equal to 1. The extracted strong arguments are the following: $\{\{f_r\} \succ \emptyset, \{f_{ndp}\} \succ \emptyset, \{f_r\} \succ \{f_{pv}\}, \{f_{ndp}\} \succ \{f_{pv}\}, \{f_r, f_{ndp}\} \succ \emptyset, \{f_r, f_{ndp}\} \succ \{f_{pv}\}\}$.

The set of closed arguments is a subset of the set of strong arguments. We remove the arguments with $\emptyset$ as the opposite reason because we can find at least one argument with a larger (in terms of size) opposite reason with the same support and countersupport. We keep the argument $\{f_r, f_{ndp}\} \succ \{f_{pv}\}$ because its support is different. The closed strong arguments extracted are the following: $\{\{f_r\} \succ \{f_{pv}\}, \{f_{ndp}\} \succ \{f_{pv}\}, \{f_r, f_{ndp}\} \succ \{f_{pv}\}\}$.

Such a factor-based model does not capture certain subtleties of legal reasoning. As illustrated in the example, a policy violation may be insufficient to justify termination when countered by procedural irregularities or a recent positive review. In our proposed framework, all factors are equally treated. It does not take into account their relative importance nor their contextual strength. Addressing this limitation would require a richer representation of arguments that incorporates notions of argument strength. This issue falls in the context of preference-based argumentation frameworks, left to future work.

5   A SAT-Based Encoding of Arguments Extraction

In this section, we propose a SAT-based encoding for extracting arguments and closed strong arguments. Several contributions addressed other data mining problems using either constraint programming (CP) [11,24] or propositional satisfiability (SAT) [14,15]. Let $\mathcal{D} = \{(1, C_1), \ldots, (n, C_n)\}$ be a case database, s be a side, ϕ_s be a propositional formula expressing constraints on factors, σ be a minimum support threshold and κ be a maximum countersupport threshold.

5.1   Encoding Strong Arguments

We first propose a SAT-based encoding for extracting all strong arguments in a case database $\mathcal{D}$. Given a decision s, we define the encoding $\texttt{SAT-SA}(\mathcal{D}, \phi_s, \sigma, \kappa, s)$ which allows the extraction of strong arguments in favor of s.

To construct the encoding, in addition to the propositional variables corresponding to the elements of Ω, we introduce the following variables: for each legal case C_i in $\mathcal{D}$, we associate a propositional variable q_i.

The encoding $\texttt{SAT-SA}(\mathcal{D}, \phi_s, \sigma, \kappa, s)$ is defined as the conjunction of the following components:

– We represent the consistency with the formula ϕ_s as a formula expressing the presence of factors in favor of s and the absence of factors in favor of $\bar{s}$:

$$(\bigvee_{a \in \phi_s \cap \Omega^s} a) \wedge \neg (\bigvee_{b \in \phi_s \cap \Omega^{\bar{s}}} b) \tag{1}$$

– For each legal case $C_i = \langle X, R, s \rangle \in \mathcal{D}_{|s}$, we add a formula which ensures that if q_i is true, then the case C supports the extracted argument:

$$q_i \rightarrow (\bigwedge_{a \in R} a) \wedge (\bigwedge_{b \in \Omega^{\bar{s}} \setminus X} \neg b) \tag{2}$$

– We add the cardinality constraint that ensures that the support of the argument meets the threshold σ.

$$\sum_{C \in \mathcal{D}_{|s}} q_i \geq \sigma \tag{3}$$

- For each legal case $C = \langle X, R, \bar{s} \rangle \in \mathcal{D}_{|\bar{s}}$, we add a formula which ensures that if C contradicts the extracted argument, then q_i is false:

$$(\bigwedge_{b \in R} b) \wedge (\bigwedge_{a \in \Omega^s \setminus X} \neg a) \rightarrow \neg q_i \tag{4}$$

- We finally add the cardinality constraint that enforces that the countersupport of the argument does not exceed κ.

$$\sum_{C \in \mathcal{D}_{|\bar{s}}} q_i \leq \kappa \tag{5}$$

A cardinality constraint is a linear inequality of the form $\sum_{i=1}^{m} p_i \geq n$ (or $\leq n$). We refer to the constraints $AtLeast\sigma$ and $AtMost\kappa$ to encode our cardinality constraints in CNF [3,4,10,23] for Eqs. 3 and 5 respectively.

Since σ captures frequent argument while κ captures rare arguments, this mining task makes more sense when $\kappa < \sigma$. We will also keep arguments extracted with $R_s = \emptyset$ or $R_{\bar{s}} = \emptyset$. This is interesting for real-life applications, as sometimes a decision is assumed and chosen without a sufficient set of opposite factors. For example, in some legal systems, everyone is considered innocent when accused without any solid proof of culpability. Thus, an argument of the form $A = \emptyset \succ R_{\bar{s}}$ captures the idea that the set $R_{\bar{s}}$ is not sufficient to make the default decision s change.

5.2 Encoding Closed Strong Arguments

In this subsection, we describe the encoding for extracting all closed strong arguments. For this purpose, we assume that for any decision s, ϕ_s is given in a conjunctive normal form (CNF) expressed as $c_1 \wedge c_2 \wedge \ldots \wedge c_k$, where each c_i is a clause. We associate a distinct propositional variable r_i for each clause c_i in ϕ_s. We denote this encoding by $\texttt{SAT-CSA}(\mathcal{D}, \phi_s, \sigma, \kappa, s)$ for the extraction of all closed arguments. It is the conjunction of the following components:

- The encoding $\texttt{SAT-SA}(\mathcal{D}, \phi_s, \sigma, \kappa, s)$ with the implications ($\rightarrow$) replaced in equivalences ($\leftrightarrow$). This modification ensures that the variables q_i capture both the cover and the countercover of the arguments. Thus, we replace Formula 2 with:

$$q_i \leftrightarrow (\bigwedge_{a \in R} a) \wedge (\bigwedge_{b \in \Omega^{\bar{s}} \setminus X} \neg b) \tag{6}$$

And we replace Formula 4 with:

$$(\bigwedge_{b \in R} b) \wedge (\bigwedge_{a \in \Omega^s \setminus X} \neg a) \leftrightarrow \neg q_i \tag{7}$$

- To associate the truth of a propositional variable r_i with the existence of at least two true literals in the clause c_i of ϕ_s, we add:

$$\bigwedge_{c_i \in \phi_s} (r_i \rightarrow \bigvee_{l,l' \in c_i, l \neq l'} l \wedge l') \tag{8}$$

We use this formula to express that if the clause c_i, which is a disjunction, contains at least two true literals, then by switching one literal to false, ϕ_s remains true. This is going to be necessary to express the closure of arguments.

- To satisfy the first property of the definition of closed arguments (Definition 2), we use the following formula:

$$\bigwedge_{a \in \Omega^s} ((\bigwedge_{C_i \in \mathcal{D}_{|s}, a \notin \rho(C_i)} \neg q_i) \wedge (\bigwedge_{C_i \in \mathcal{D}_{|\bar{s}}, a \notin F(C_i)} \neg q_i) \wedge (\bigwedge_{c_i \in \phi_s, a \in c_i} r_i) \to \neg a) \quad (9)$$

This formula ensures that for any factor appearing in the favoring side, we can remove it if ϕ is still satisfied and neither the support or countersupport conditions will be violated.

- To satisfy the second property of the definition of closed arguments (Definition 2), we use the following formula:

$$\bigwedge_{b \in \Omega^{\bar{s}}} ((\bigwedge_{C_i \in \mathcal{D}_{|s}, b \notin F(C_i)} \neg q_i) \wedge (\bigwedge_{C_i \in \mathcal{D}_{|\bar{s}}, b \notin \rho(C_i)} \neg q_i) \wedge (\bigwedge_{c_i \in \phi_s, \neg b \in c_i} r_i) \to b) \quad (10)$$

This formula ensures that the addition of any factor favoring the opposite side leaves the conditions satisfied, which are ϕ_s, the support and the countersupport conditions. Together, these two formulas ensure that the argument is closed. That is, only the necessary factors are included, and no factor from the favoring side can me removed and no factor from the opposite side can me removed.

Example 2. (continuation from Example 1)
The encoding for strong arguments with support threshold and countersupport threshold values equal to 1 is the following: $\{q_1 \to f_r, q_2 \to f_{ndp}, q_1 + q_2 \geq 1, f_{pv} \wedge \neg f_r \wedge \neg f_{ndp} \to \neg q_3, q_3 \leq 1\}$.
　　　Consider now $\phi_s = (f_r \wedge f_{ndp}) \vee \neg f_{pv}$. The encoding of closed strong arguments with the same threshold values for consists of ϕ_s and the following:
$\{q_1 \leftrightarrow f_r, q_2 \leftrightarrow f_{ndp}, \neg q_3 \leftrightarrow f_{pv} \wedge \neg f_{ndp} \wedge \neg f_r, r_1 \to f_r \wedge f_{ndp},$
$\neg q_2 \wedge \neg q_3 \wedge r_1 \to \neg f_r, \neg q_1 \wedge \neg q_3 \wedge r_1 \to \neg f_{ndp}, r_1 \to f_{pv}, q_1 + q_2 \geq 1, q_3 \leq 1\}$.

6　Maximal Arguments

In this section, we introduce another compact representation of arguments analogous to the notion of maximal itemsets [30]. Maximal arguments provide a condensed and meaningful summary of strong arguments in a case database.

Definition 3 (Maximal Arguments).
An argument $A = R_s \succ R_{\bar{s}}$ is said to be maximal in a case database $\mathcal{D}$ with respect to the propositional constraint ϕ_s, the minimum support threshold σ and the maximum countersupport threshold κ if the following conditions are satisfied:

- $\mathtt{support}(A, \mathcal{D}) \geq \sigma$ *and* $\mathtt{countersupport}(A, \mathcal{D}) \leq \kappa$

- For any factor $a \in R_s$, either one of the following holds for the argument $A' = R_s \setminus \{a\} \succ R_{\bar{s}}$:
  - $A' \vdash \neg\phi_s$,
  - $\mathrm{support}(A', \mathcal{D}) < \sigma$,
  - $\mathrm{countersupport}(A', \mathcal{D}) > \kappa$.
- For any factor $a \in \Omega^{\bar{s}} \setminus R_{\bar{s}}$, either one of the following holds for the argument $A' = R_s \succ R_{\bar{s}} \cup \{a\}$:
  - $A' \vdash \neg\phi_s$,
  - $\mathrm{support}(A', \mathcal{D}) < \sigma$,
  - $\mathrm{countersupport}(A', \mathcal{D}) > \kappa$.

A maximal argument is an argument that meets the required thresholds for support and countersupport. Moreover, it cannot be strengthened by removing any factor from the supporting side or adding any factor to the opposing side without being of a rejected form or falling below the support threshold or exceeding the countersupport threshold. Maximal itemsets serves the same utility in the context of itemset mining. They present a condensed representation of the strong arguments without loss of information: we can deduce the set of all strong arguments from the set of maximal arguments.

Algorithm 1. Algorithm for Computing All Maximal Arguments

Require: A case database $\mathcal{D}$, a side $s \in \{p, d\}$, a propositional constraint ϕ_s, a minimal support threshold σ, and a maximal countersupport κ
Ensure: A set Res of all maximal arguments for s
1: Res $\leftarrow \emptyset$
2: $\Psi \leftarrow$ SAT-SA$(\mathcal{D}, \phi_s, \sigma, \kappa, s)$
3: **for** $i = 0$ to $|\Omega^s|$ **do**
4:     **for** $j = |\Omega^{\bar{s}}|$ to 0 **do**
5:         $\Psi \leftarrow \Psi \wedge \left(\sum_{a \in \Omega^s} a = i \wedge \sum_{b \in \Omega^{\bar{s}}} b = j \right)$
6:         **while** SAT(Ψ) **do**
7:             $R_s \leftarrow \{a \in \Omega^s \mid \omega(a) = 1\}$ ▷ ω is a model of Ψ
8:             $R_{\bar{s}} \leftarrow \{b \in \Omega^{\bar{s}} \mid \omega(b) = 1\}$
9:             Res $\leftarrow$ Res $\cup \{R_s \succ R_{\bar{s}}\}$
10:            $\Psi \leftarrow \Psi \wedge \bigvee_{a \in R_s \cup R_{\bar{s}}} \neg a$
11:        **end while**
12:    **end for**
13: **end for**
14: **return** Res

Algorithm 1 provides a systematic method for incrementally extracting all maximal arguments. It works as follows. For each argument enumerated with an increasing size for R_s (line 3) and a decreasing size for $R_{\bar{s}}$ (line 4), we add a size constraint. As long as the constraints are satisfied (line 6), we extract that argument and iteratively block (line 10) subsets of previously found models.

Proposition 3 (Soundness of Algorithm 1). *Let $\mathcal{D}$ be a case database, $s \in \{p, d\}$ a side, σ a minimal support threshold, κ a maximal countersupport threshold, and ϕ_s a propositional constraint. Every argument $A = R_s \succ R_{\bar{s}}$ extracted by Algorithm 1 is a maximal argument with respect to Definition 3.*

7   Experiments

We conducted experimentations of the SAT encoding of strong arguments (SAT-SA encoding) and closed strong arguments (SAT-CSA encoding). We also implemented Algorithm 1. We used an Intel CPU i7-13850HX with 16 GB of RAM, and the Ubuntu 24.04.2 LTS OS. The code was written and run with Python 3.12.3 using the solver Glucose3.

7.1   Data and Setup

We consider a set of randomly generated instances for the benchmark of these algorithms with 4 variables: the database size (number of cases), the number of factors, a support and a countersupport threshold. The factors are numbered constants grouped in two sets (for each party they are in favor of), not representing real-life events. We generated instances with any combination of size 5 to 50 (with a step of 5) with a number of factors from 5 to 25 (also with a step of 5). We keep the instances simple as we aim to show the feasibility of our approach, not its scalability. Each instance is tested with each combination of σ and κ from 1 to half the size of the database. Indeed, we consider instances with half the database size cases favoring each decision. We keep $\phi_s = \emptyset$, meaning that we only look at precedents datatabases. For each instance, we measured the execution time of our three algorithms. It corresponds to the time to model the problem, solve and extract the arguments.

7.2   Results

Table 1 presents the size of the sets of arguments depending on the number of factors and the argument type: Strong Arguments (SA), Maximal -strong- Arguments (MSA), and Closed -strong- Arguments (CSA). The size grows exponentially with the number of factors, as expected. The set of strong arguments is always the biggest, while the set of closed arguments is around 10 times smaller. The set of maximal strong arguments is exponentially smaller than the set of strong arguments and always smaller than the set of closed arguments.

Table 1. Average size of sets extracted by algorithms by number of factors

Number of factors	SA	CSA	MSA
5	7.09	1.78	1.10
10	104.05	15.68	4.53
15	1350.44	152.54	12.60
20	21392.14	2851.42	31.96

Figure 1 presents the logarithmic-scale average computation times (in milliseconds) for the SAT encodings of our three argumentation procedures as a function of the number of factors. The x-axis denotes the cardinality of the factor set, while the log-scaled y-axis represents the average time required to compute the desired arguments. We observe a clear and expectable growth in computation time for all procedures as the number of factors increases. With a smaller database, the maximal arguments are the longest to compute but after increasing the number of factors to 20, it becomes much faster than the other two encodings. This is expected due to the combinatorial nature of argument generation.

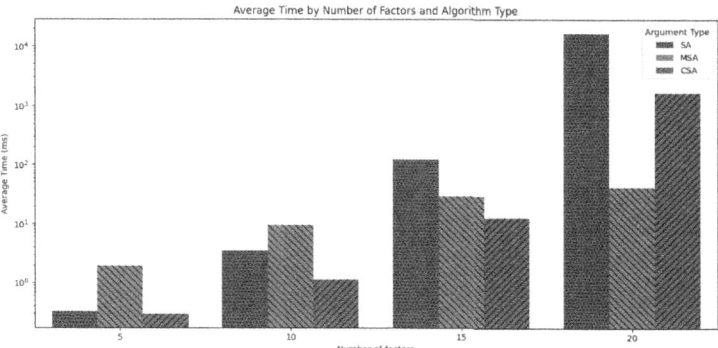

Fig. 1. Average time by number of factors and algorithm type on generated instances

Figures 2 presents the influence of the values of σ and κ on the average computing time for Algorithm 1 with a fixed number of factors. We selected the computation time of the maximal arguments with the highest number of factors to illustrate the following. The two horizontal axis denotes κ and σ values. We observe that the smaller σ is and the higher κ is, the more time it takes to compute the results, with a greater influence from σ. This can be intuitively deduced, as the constraints are much less restrictive (implying significantly more models).

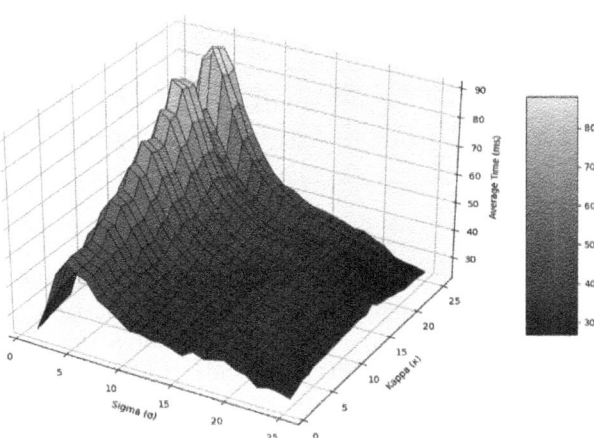

Fig. 2. Average Algorithm 1 computing time with varying κ and σ for 20 factors.

8   Conclusion and Perspectives

We introduced the problem of extracting strong arguments from a database of legal cases, where arguments are viewed as sets of factors supporting one side over another. We first formalized the notion of a strong argument, grounded in case-based reasoning, and proposed a characterization based on support asymmetry across opposing cases. We refined the basic notion of strong arguments by defining two extensions—maximal strong arguments and closed strong arguments. We developed propositional SAT encodings for the computation of all three argument types, enabling the use of SAT solvers for argument extraction. We implemented our encodings and conducted a series of experiments to evaluate the computational performance of our methods with respect to varying numbers of factors and parameter values. This work opens several avenues for future research. First, we aim to define a partial order over arguments based on their strength, potentially supporting preference-based reasoning [26]. Second, we plan to quantify the strength of arguments, thereby enabling more fine-grained comparisons in decision-making contexts. Finally, we envision extending our framework toward abstract argumentation in Dung's style [7], where extracted arguments are related with attack and defense relations.

References

1. Agrawal, R., Srikant, R.: Fast algorithms for mining association rules in large databases. In: VLDB, pp. 487–499. Morgan Kaufmann (1994)
2. Aliberti, G., Colantonio, A., Pietro, R.D., Mariani, R.: EXPEDITE: express closed itemset enumeration. Expert Syst. Appl. **42**(8), 3933–3944 (2015)

3. Bailleux, O., Boufkhad, Y.: Efficient CNF encoding of Boolean cardinality constraints. In: Rossi, F. (ed.) CP 2003. LNCS, vol. 2833, pp. 108–122. Springer, Heidelberg (2003). https://doi.org/10.1007/978-3-540-45193-8_8

4. Bailleux, O., Boufkhad, Y.: Full CNF encoding: the counting constraints case. In: SAT 2004 - The Seventh International Conference on Theory and Applications of Satisfiability Testing, 10–13 May 2004, Vancouver, BC, Canada, Online Proceedings (2004)

5. Canavotto, I.: Reasoning with inconsistent precedents. Artif. Intell. Law **33**(1), 137–166 (2025)

6. Davis, M., Logemann, G., Loveland, D.W.: A machine program for theorem-proving. Commun. ACM **5**(7), 394–397 (1962)

7. Dung, P.M.: On the acceptability of arguments and its fundamental role in non-monotonic reasoning, logic programming and n-person games. Artif. Intell. **77**(2), 321–358 (1995)

8. Eisenberg, M.A.: The nature of the common law. Revue internationale de droit compare **42**(3), 1036–1038 (1990)

9. Fournier-Viger, P., Lin, J.C., Vo, B., Truong, T.C., Zhang, J., Le, H.B.: A survey of itemset mining. WIREs Data Min. Knowl. Discov. **7**(4) (2017)

10. Gent, I.P.: Arc consistency in SAT. In: ECAI, pp. 121–125. IOS Press (2002)

11. Guns, T., Nijssen, S., Raedt, L.D.: Itemset mining: a constraint programming perspective. Artif. Intell. **175**(12–13), 1951–1983 (2011)

12. Han, J., Pei, J., Yin, Y., Mao, R.: Mining frequent patterns without candidate generation: a frequent-pattern tree approach. Data Min. Knowl. Discov. **8**(1), 53–87 (2004)

13. Ignatiev, A., Tan, Z.L., Karamanos, C.: Towards universally accessible SAT technology. In: SAT. LIPIcs, vol. 305, pp. 16:1–16:11. Schloss Dagstuhl - Leibniz-Zentrum für Informatik (2024)

14. Jabbour, S., Sais, L., Salhi, Y.: The Top-k frequent closed itemset mining using top-k SAT problem. In: Blockeel, H., Kersting, K., Nijssen, S., Železný, F. (eds.) ECML PKDD 2013. LNCS (LNAI), vol. 8190, pp. 403–418. Springer, Heidelberg (2013). https://doi.org/10.1007/978-3-642-40994-3_26

15. Jabbour, S., Sais, L., Salhi, Y.: On SAT models enumeration in itemset mining (2015)

16. Kolodner, J.L.: An introduction to case-based reasoning. Artif. Intell. Rev. **6**(1), 3–34 (1992). https://doi.org/10.1007/BF00155578

17. Lamond, G.: Do precedents create rules? Leg. Theory **11**(1), 1–26 (2005). https://doi.org/10.1017/S1352325205050019

18. Lenca, P., Vaillant, B., Meyer, P., Lallich, S.: Association rule interestingness measures: experimental and theoretical studies. In: Guillet, F.J., Hamilton, H.J. (eds) Quality Measures in Data Mining. Studies in Computational Intelligence, vol. 43, pp. 51–76. Springer, Heidelberg (2007). https://doi.org/10.1007/978-3-540-44918-8_3

19. Levi, E.H.: An introduction to legal reasoning. Univ. Chicago Law Rev. **15**(3), 501–574 (1948)

20. Lucchese, C., Orlando, S., Perego, R.: Fast and memory efficient mining of frequent closed itemsets. IEEE Trans. Knowl. Data Eng. **18**(1), 21–36 (2006)

21. Papadimitriou, C.H.: Novel computational approaches to information retrieval and data mining. In: Beeri, C., Buneman, P. (eds.) ICDT 1999. LNCS, vol. 1540, pp. 31–31. Springer, Heidelberg (1999). https://doi.org/10.1007/3-540-49257-7_25

22. Pei, J., Han, J., Lu, H., Nishio, S., Tang, S., Yang, D.: H-mine: hyper-structure mining of frequent patterns in large databases. In: Cercone, N., Lin, T.Y., Wu, X. (eds.) Proceedings of the 2001 IEEE International Conference on Data Mining, 29 November–2 December 2001, San Jose, California, USA, pp. 441–448. IEEE Computer Society (2001). https://doi.org/10.1109/ICDM.2001.989550
23. Prestwich, S.D.: CNF encodings. Handb. Satis. **185**, 75–97 (2009)
24. Raedt, L.D., Guns, T., Nijssen, S.: Constraint programming for itemset mining. In: KDD, pp. 204–212. ACM (2008)
25. Raz, J.: The Authority of Law: Essays on Law and Morality. Oxford University Press (1979). https://doi.org/10.1093/acprof:oso/9780198253457.001.0001
26. Roversi, C. (ed.): Preference-Based Reasoning: Rules, pp. 1181–1205. Springer, Dordrecht (2005). https://doi.org/10.1007/1-4020-3505-5_46
27. S., T.G.: On the complexity of derivation in propositional calculus. Struct. Construct. Math. Math. Log. 115–125 (1968)
28. Simpson, A.: The Ratio Decidendi of a Case and the Doctrine of Binding Precedent. Oxford University Press (1960)
29. Tanbeer, S.K., Ahmed, C.F., Jeong, B.-S., Lee, Y.-K.: Discovering periodic-frequent patterns in transactional databases. In: Theeramunkong, T., Kijsirikul, B., Cercone, N., Ho, T.-B. (eds.) PAKDD 2009. LNCS (LNAI), vol. 5476, pp. 242–253. Springer, Heidelberg (2009). https://doi.org/10.1007/978-3-642-01307-2_24
30. Uno, T., Kiyomi, M., Arimura, H.: Lcm ver. 2: efficient mining algorithms for frequent/closed/maximal itemsets. In: Workshop on Frequent Itemset Mining Implementations (FIMI). CEUR-WS.org (2004)
31. Vo, B., Hong, T., Le, B.: DBV-miner: a dynamic bit-vector approach for fast mining frequent closed itemsets. Expert Syst. Appl. **39**(8), 7196–7206 (2012). https://doi.org/10.1016/J.ESWA.2012.01.062
32. Yan, X., Han, J.: gSpan: graph-based substructure pattern mining. In: ICDM, pp. 721–724. IEEE Computer Society (2002)
33. Zaki, M.J.: Scalable algorithms for association mining. IEEE Trans. Knowl. Data Eng. **12**(3), 372–390 (2000)
34. Zaki, M.J., Hsiao, C.: CHARM: an efficient algorithm for closed itemset mining. In: Grossman, R.L., Han, J., Kumar, V., Mannila, H., Motwani, R. (eds.) Proceedings of the Second SIAM International Conference on Data Mining, Arlington, VA, USA, 11–13 April 2002, pp. 457–473. SIAM (2002). https://doi.org/10.1137/1.9781611972726.27
35. Zimmermann, A.: Understanding episode mining techniques: benchmarking on diverse, realistic, artificial data. Intell. Data Anal. **18**(5), 761–791 (2014)

Inclusion with Repetitions and Boolean Constants – Implication Problems Revisited

Matilda Häggblom[(✉)] [ID]

University of Helsinki, Helsinki, Finland
matilda.haggblom@helsinki.fi

Abstract. Inclusion dependencies form one of the most widely used classes of database dependencies. We expand existing results on the axiomatization and computational complexity of their implication problem to two extended variants. First, we present an alternative completeness proof for standard inclusion dependencies and generalize it to inclusion dependencies with repetitions that can express equalities between attributes. The proof uses only two values, enabling us to work within the Boolean setting. Furthermore, we study inclusion dependencies with Boolean constants, provide a complete axiomatization, and show that no such axiomatization is k-ary. We also establish that the decision problems for both extended versions remain PSPACE-complete. The extended inclusion dependencies are common in team semantics, which serves as the formal framework for the results.

Keywords: Inclusion dependency · Boolean inclusion · Implication problem · Axiomatization · Team semantics · Computational complexity

1 Introduction

Inclusion dependencies have been extensively studied in database theory due to their widespread use. A fundamental question for dependencies is the *implication problem*: Does a set of dependencies imply a given dependency? The axiomatization and computational complexity of the implication problem for standard inclusion dependencies were established in [2]. In this work, we identify and address gaps in the literature concerning the implication problem for natural variants of inclusion dependencies, namely inclusion in the Boolean setting, inclusion with repetitions, and inclusion with Boolean constants.

The extended variants of the inclusion dependencies are common in team semantics, making it a convenient setting for presenting the results. Team semantics was introduced in [11,12] and further developed in [15] to form *dependence logic*. In team semantics, formulas are evaluated under a set of assignments, called a *team*. Teams enable the evaluation of relationships between variables in a meaningful way, which is often not possible under single assignments. Since

© The Author(s), under exclusive license to Springer Nature Switzerland AG 2026
G. Casini et al. (Eds.): JELIA 2025, LNAI 16094, pp. 109–124, 2026.
https://doi.org/10.1007/978-3-032-04590-4_8

teams correspond to uni-relational databases, variables to attributes, and atoms to dependencies, the results of this paper are immediately transferable between the database and team semantic setting.

Inclusion dependencies were adapted into the team semantic setting in [6] as *inclusion atoms* of the form $x \subseteq y$, where x and y are finite sequences of variables of equal length. The inclusion atom $x \subseteq y$ is satisfied in a team if the values of x are among those of y. More formally, a team T satisfies $x \subseteq y$, written $T \models x \subseteq y$, if and only if for all assignments $s \in T$ there is some $s' \in T$ such that $s(x) = s'(y)$. In database theory, it is common to prohibit repetitions of variables within the sequences x and y. Removing this restriction, as often done in team semantics, enables inclusion atoms to express the semantic equality between x and y via $xy \subseteq xx$, since such an inclusion atom being satisfied in a team implies that for each assignment in the team, the values of x and y are identical. Examining this class of atoms is thus a natural consideration.

Furthermore, we generalize the syntax in the Boolean setting, where variables take only the values 0 and 1, by allowing the constants $\bot$ and $\top$ within the sequences. This allows us to specify the inclusion of specific values. For instance, $T \models \top \subseteq p$ expresses that the proposition p must be made true by some assignment in the team T. Additionally, contradictions like $\top \subseteq \bot$ can be expressed, which is not possible with standard inclusion atoms.

To illustrate the difference in expressive power between the three classes of inclusion atoms, we provide simple natural language examples in the Boolean setting. Consider the team $T := \{s_{2021}, s_{2022}, s_{2023}\}$, and let $\{p_a, p_b\}$ be a set of two propositional symbols, for which $s_{2021}(p_a) = 1$ if student a passed their exams in 2021, and $s_{2021}(p_a) = 0$ if student a failed their exams in 2021, etc.

Without repetitions: $T \models p_a \subseteq p_b$ expresses that during the three years, student a failing one year means that also student b failed at least once. Similarly, if student a passed one year, then student b must have passed at least once.

With repetitions: $T \models p_a p_b \subseteq p_a p_a$ expresses that each year, student b passed their exams if and only if student a did. Note that this is not implied by $T \models p_a \subseteq p_b$ and $T \models p_b \subseteq p_a$, since the students' similar results can be witnessed at different years.

With Boolean constants: $T \models p_a \bot \subseteq \top p_b$ expresses that student a passed their exams every year, while student b failed at least once.

Although the inclusion atoms we consider have been studied within the larger language of *propositional inclusion logic* [17], which further contains atomic formulas p and connectives $(\neg, \vee, \wedge)$, their axiomatization from [2] has previously not been confirmed complete in the Boolean setting. We address this gap in the literature by providing an alternative completeness proof for the system within the language of repetition-free inclusion atoms using only two values, which is not in general possible using the chase-like construction from [2]. Indeed, the system for repetition-free inclusion atoms remains complete, something that can not be taken for granted, since any complete system for *exclusion atoms* in the Boolean setting necessarily extends their usual system from [3], as noted in [8].

Inclusion with repetitions has been considered in [13] together with functional dependencies. We extract the inclusion rules from their system and prove completeness in the Boolean setting, which their completeness proof does not entail since it relies on having more than two available values. Furthermore, we confirm that the decision problem for finite sets of atoms with repetitions is PSPACE-complete, as in the repetition-free case [2]. Still, some basic semantic properties differ: Without a restriction on the number of possible values, inclusion atoms have *Armstrong relations* [5], i.e., for any set of inclusion atoms, there exists a team that satisfies exactly the atoms entailed by the set. We prove that this is not the case in the Boolean setting.

Team-based propositional logic can be extended with dependence atoms to form *propositional dependence logic*. Dependence atoms, which capture functional dependencies, are *downward-closed*, meaning that if a team satisfies such an atom, all its subteams do as well. When these atoms are added to propositional logic, the resulting system becomes expressively complete for all downward-closed team properties that contain the empty team [18]. In contrast, inclusion atoms are *union-closed*, meaning that if multiple teams satisfy an inclusion atom, so does their union. Merely adding inclusion atoms to propositional logic does not yield an expressively complete logic for all union-closed team properties with the empty team, as noted in [17]: Over a single variable, the atom $p \subseteq p$ is a tautology and does not extend the expressivity. To achieve expressive completeness, we require inclusion atoms with Boolean constants such as $\top \subseteq p$. The axiomatization presented in [17] does not explicitly provide rules for inclusion atoms with Boolean constants simpliciter, as their system relies on the connectives of the language.

To fill this gap in the literature, we introduce a complete axiomatization of inclusion atoms with Boolean constants. Furthermore, we show that no such system can be k-ary, i.e., there exists no bound k on the number of assumptions in the rules. This result contrasts with the complete systems for the other inclusion atoms considered, which are 2-ary. Still, for this extended class, the decision problem for finite sets of atoms is PSPACE-complete.

The paper is organized as follows. We recall the basic definitions and results of inclusion atoms in Sect. 2, and their repetition-free version in Sect. 3. We examine the implication problem for (Boolean) inclusion atoms with repetitions in Sect. 4, and establish corresponding results for inclusion atoms with Boolean constants in Sect. 5. We conclude with a summary and directions for future research in Sect. 6.

2   Preliminaries

We recall the basic definitions for teams and inclusion atoms, see, e.g., [6].

A team T is a set of assignments $s : \mathcal{V} \longrightarrow M$, where $\mathcal{V}$ is a set of variables and M is any set whose members we call values. We write $x_i, y_i, \ldots$ for individual variables and $x, y, \ldots$ for finite (possibly empty) sequences of variables. Given a sequence x, we denote its i:th variable by x_i. Let $x := x_1 \ldots x_n$ and $y := y_1 \ldots y_m$.

We write $s(x)$ as shorthand for the tuple $s(x_1) \ldots s(x_n)$. The concatenation xy is the sequence $x_1 \ldots x_n y_1 \ldots y_m$. The sequences x and y are equal if and only if they are of the same length, denoted $|x| = |y|$, and $x_1 = y_1, \ldots, x_n = y_n$. We let $V(x)$ denote the set of variables appearing in the sequence x.

Inclusion atoms are of the form $x \subseteq y$, where $|x| = |y|$ is the arity of the atom. We often refer to the variables in x as the variables on the left-hand side, etc. We recall the semantics of inclusion atoms,

$$T \models x \subseteq y \text{ if and only if for all } s \in T \text{ there exists } s' \in T \text{ with } s(x) = s'(y).$$

Let $T[x] := \{s(x) \mid s \in T\}$. The definition of $T \models x \subseteq y$ expresses that any value of x in T is a value of y in T, giving us the equivalent semantic clause:

$$T \models x \subseteq y \text{ if and only if } T[x] \subseteq T[y].$$

Inclusion atoms are union-closed: If $T_i \models x \subseteq y$ for each i in a nonempty index set I, then $\bigcup_{I \in I} T_i \models x \subseteq y$. They also have the empty team property: All inclusion atoms are satisfied by the empty team. We call inclusion atoms of the form $x \subseteq x$ *trivial*, since they are satisfied in all teams.

We write $\Sigma \models u \subseteq v$ if for all teams T, $T \models u \subseteq v$ whenever $T \models x \subseteq y$ for all $x \subseteq y \in \Sigma$. If it is not the case that $\Sigma \models u \subseteq v$, we write $\Sigma \not\models u \subseteq v$. For a singleton $\Sigma := \{x \subseteq y\}$, we drop the brackets and write $x \subseteq y \models u \subseteq v$.

For inclusion atoms in the Boolean setting, we denote variable sequences by $p, q, \ldots$ and restrict the values of individual variables $p_i, q_i, \ldots$ to 0 and 1. The semantic clause for $T \models p \subseteq q$ and the above-mentioned union closure and empty team properties are as in the general case.

3   Repetition-Free Inclusion

We say that an inclusion atom $x \subseteq y$ is *repetition-free* if there are no repeated variables within the sequences x and y, respectively. A repetition-free inclusion atom is $x_1 \subseteq x_1$, while $x_1 x_1 \subseteq y_1 y_2$ is not. In the database literature, inclusion dependencies are often defined to be repetition-free.

We call a set of rules a *system*, and recall the sound and complete system for repetition-free inclusion atoms.

Definition 1 ([2]).   *The system* $\mathbf{R}_0$ *for repetition-free inclusion atoms consists of rules $I1$–$I4$.*

(I1) $x \subseteq x$.
(I2) If $x \subseteq z$ and $z \subseteq y$, then $x \subseteq y$.
(I3) If $xyz \subseteq uvw$, then $xzy \subseteq uwv$, provided that $|x| = |u|$ and $|y| = |v|$.
(I4) If $xy \subseteq uv$, then $x \subseteq u$.

For a set of atoms Σ and a set of rules $\mathbf{R}$, we write $\Sigma \vdash_{\mathbf{R}} x \subseteq y$ when the rules we apply in the derivation are restricted to the ones in $\mathbf{R}$, and $\Sigma \not\vdash_{\mathbf{R}} x \subseteq y$ if such a derivation is not possible. If Σ is a singleton, we drop the brackets, and we write $\vdash_{\mathbf{R}} x \subseteq y$ for $\emptyset \vdash_{\mathbf{R}} x \subseteq y$. If $\mathbf{R}$ is a singleton, we also omit the brackets, and if $\mathbf{R} := \mathbf{R}_0$, we sometimes write $\Sigma \vdash x \subseteq y$. We follow this convention for all types of inclusion atoms and their respective proof systems.

Theorem 1 (Soundness and completeness [2]). *Let $\Sigma \cup \{x \subseteq y\}$ be a set of repetition-free inclusion atoms. Then $\Sigma \models x \subseteq y$ if and only if $\Sigma \vdash_{\mathbf{R}_0} x \subseteq y$.*

The completeness proof of Theorem 1 in [2] uses a chase-like argument that requires the use of $|x| + 1$ many values. We extend this completeness result to the Boolean setting by providing an alternative argument using only two values in the proof of Theorem 3 below.

4   Inclusion with Repetitions

We remove the restriction on repetition of variables and consider *inclusion atoms*, common in the team semantics literature. They are syntactically and semantically extended versions of their repetition-free counterparts.

The rules for inclusion atoms are presented in [13] as part of a larger system for inclusion and functional dependencies. We extract the rules for inclusion atoms and show that the system is complete also in the Boolean setting.

Definition 2 ([13]). *The system $\mathbf{R}_1$ for inclusion atoms extends the system $\mathbf{R}_0$ in Definition 1 with rules I5 and I6.*

(I5) If $xy \subseteq uv$, then $xyy \subseteq uvv$.
(I6) If $x_1x_2 \subseteq y_1y_1$ and $z \subseteq vx_1$, then $z \subseteq vx_2$.

Theorem 2 (Soundness [13]). *The rules in $\mathbf{R}_1$ are sound.*

For a set Σ of inclusion atoms, we define the *derivable equality* relation $\equiv_\Sigma$ by taking $x_i \equiv_\Sigma y_j$ whenever $\Sigma \vdash x_iy_j \subseteq u_lu_l$ for some variable u_l. Note that the members of the relation are pairs of single variables. If $x_i \equiv_\Sigma y_j$ is not a derivable equality, we write $x_i \not\equiv_\Sigma y_j$. To avoid any ambiguity, we only write $x = y$ for *actual* equalities where the variable sequences x and y denote the same sequence. We note that in the case of an actual equality $x_1 = x_2$, we derive $\vdash_{I1} x_1x_1 \subseteq x_1x_1$, hence $x_1 \equiv_\emptyset x_1$ and by $x_1 = x_2$, $x_1 \equiv_\emptyset x_2$. Moreover, we can consider the semantic equality atom $x_1 \approx y_1$ defined by $T \models x_1 \approx y_1$ if for all $s, s' \in T$, $s(x_1) = s'(y_1)$. It is not difficult to see that the language of inclusion atoms with repetitions and the language of repetition-free inclusion atoms and semantic equality atoms are expressively equivalent.

The system in [13] has a more general substitution rule than I6, allowing substitution of derivable equalities on both sides. We show that the more general substitution rule is derivable in $\mathbf{R}_1$, and that either substitution rule, together with rules I1 and I2, derives the other. Moreover, given a set of derivable equalities, we can reduce any inclusion atom to a provably equivalent one without repetitions on the right-hand side. We write $x \subseteq y \dashv\vdash_{\mathbf{R}} \Gamma$ for a set of inclusion atoms Γ whenever $\Gamma \vdash_{\mathbf{R}} x \subseteq y$ and $x \subseteq y \vdash_{\mathbf{R}} \gamma$ for all $\gamma \in \Gamma$.

Lemma 1. *Consider the right and left-hand substitution rules:*

$$\text{If } x_1x_2 \subseteq y_1y_1 \text{ and } z \subseteq vx_1, \text{ then } z \subseteq vx_2. \qquad (I6)$$

$$\text{If } x_1x_2 \subseteq y_1y_1 \text{ and } zx_1 \subseteq v, \text{ then } zx_2 \subseteq v. \qquad (I6_l)$$

(i) *Substitution on the left-hand side ($I6_l$) is derivable using rules $I1$–$I3$ and $I6$.*

(ii) *Substitution on the right-hand side ($I6$) is derivable using rules $I1$–$I3$ and $I6_l$.*

(iii) *Let $\Sigma := \{u \subseteq v\}$ and let Γ be the set of all inclusion atoms in the derivable equality relation $\equiv_\Sigma$. Then there is an inclusion atom $x \subseteq y$ with distinct variables on the right-hand side such that $u \subseteq v \dashv\vdash_{\mathbf{R}_1} \{x \subseteq y, \Gamma\}$. In particular, $u_1u_2u_3 \subseteq y_1y_1v_3 \dashv\vdash_{\mathbf{R}_1} \{u_1u_3 \subseteq y_1v_3, u_1u_2 \subseteq y_1y_1\}$.*

Proof. (i) We have $\vdash_{I1} zx_2 \subseteq zx_2$ and $x_1x_2 \subseteq y_1y_1 \vdash_{I3} x_2x_1 \subseteq y_1y_1$. Now $x_2x_1 \subseteq y_1y_1, zx_2 \subseteq zx_2 \vdash_{I6} zx_2 \subseteq zx_1$. We conclude $zx_2 \subseteq zx_1, zx_1 \subseteq v \vdash_{I2} zx_1 \subseteq v$.

(ii) Similar to item (i).

(iii) W.l.o.g., consider the inclusion atom $u \subseteq v$ of the form $u_1u_2u' \subseteq y_1y_1v'$. We have that $u_1u_2u' \subseteq y_1y_1v'$ derives both $u_1u' \subseteq y_1v'$ and Γ by $I4$. For the other direction, clearly $u_1u_2 \subseteq y_1y_1 \in \Gamma$, and $u_1u' \subseteq y_1v' \vdash u_1u_1u' \subseteq y_1y_1v'$ by $I3$ and $I5$. Putting these together, $u_1u_2 \subseteq y_1y_1, u_1u_1u' \subseteq y_1y_1v' \vdash u_1u_2u' \subseteq y_1y_1v'$ by item (i) and $I3$. Hence $u_1u_2u' \subseteq y_1y_1v' \dashv\vdash_{\mathbf{R}_1} \{u_1u' \subseteq y_1v', \Gamma\}$. Iterate this process with the atom $u_1u' \subseteq y_1v'$ and the set Γ until there are no more repeated variables in the atom's right-hand side. □

We are now ready to provide an alternative completeness proof to the ones in the literature [2,13]. The main difference is that this alternative proof uses only two values; thus, the completeness result in the Boolean setting follows immediately. For any set Σ of inclusion atoms, its *generic team* consists of all assignments $s : \mathcal{V} \longrightarrow \{0,1\}$ that respect the derivable equalities, and therefore satisfy all atoms in Σ. In case Σ contains infinitely many variables, its generic team is infinite. We modify the generic teams slightly to obtain the counterexample teams, with Table 1 and Table 2 providing two examples. Denote by 0^n the n-tuple $00\ldots0$.

Theorem 3 (Completeness). *Let $\Sigma \cup \{x \subseteq y\}$ be a set of inclusion atoms. If $\Sigma \models x \subseteq y$, then $\Sigma \vdash_{\mathbf{R}_1} x \subseteq y$.*

Proof. Let $n := |x|$. If $x_i \equiv_\Sigma y_i$ for all $i \in \{1,\ldots,n\}$, we have that $\vdash_{I1} y \subseteq y$ and use $I3$ and $I6$ repeatedly to derive $\Sigma \vdash x \subseteq y$. The previous argument also covers the case when x and y denote the same sequence. Assume now that $x_i \not\equiv_\Sigma y_i$ for some $i \in \{1,\ldots,n\}$, and that $\Sigma \not\vdash x \subseteq y$. We define the counterexample team T by $s \in T$ if and only if the following conditions are satisfied.

(1) $s : \mathcal{V} \longrightarrow \{0,1\}$,

(2) If $u_i \equiv_\Sigma u_j$, then $s(u_i) = s(u_j)$.

If there are indices j, k such that $y_j \equiv_\Sigma y_k$ and $x_j \not\equiv_\Sigma x_k$, then we stop here. Otherwise, demand also:

(3) For w such that $\Sigma \vdash w \subseteq y$: $s(w) \neq 0^n$.

The decision to choose 0^n specifically in condition (3) is motivated by sequences like 0^n never being at risk of removal by condition (2), ensuring that $0^n \in T[x]$. Now condition (3) implies that $T \not\models x \subseteq y$.

Let $u \subseteq v \in \Sigma$, we show that $T \models u \subseteq v$. Note that $T[v]$ is missing 01-combinations only in the cases when the sequence contains a pair of variables in the relation $\equiv_\Sigma$, or when there is some w such that $\Sigma \vdash w \subseteq y$ and $V(w) \subseteq V(v)$.

First, consider the cases where the team is constructed without condition (3), or when $V(w) \not\subseteq V(v)$ for all w such that $\Sigma \vdash w \subseteq y$. If v does not contain variables affected by condition (2), then all 01-combinations are in $T[v]$ and $T \models u \subseteq v$ follows. If there are variables in v such that $v_i \equiv_\Sigma v_j$, by construction of the team, there is some z_k such that $\Sigma \vdash v_i v_j \subseteq z_k z_k$. By $I3$ and $I4$, $u \subseteq v \vdash u_i u_j \subseteq v_i v_j$. Now $u_i u_j \subseteq z_k z_k$ follows by $I2$, thus $s(u_i) = s(u_j)$ for all $s \in T$. Now any value missing from $T[v]$ is also missing from $T[u]$, hence $T \models u \subseteq v$.

Else, for each w, $V(w) \subseteq V(v)$, such that $\Sigma \vdash w \subseteq y$, we have $0^n \notin T[w]$ by condition (3). We derive $u \subseteq v \vdash u' \subseteq w$ by $I3$, $I4$ and $I5$, where $V(u') \subseteq V(u)$. By $I2$, $\Sigma \vdash u' \subseteq y$. Since $\Sigma \not\vdash x \subseteq y$, we have that $u' \neq x$ also after substituting derivable equalities using $I6$ and Lemma 1 item (i). Therefore, by condition (3), $0^n \notin T[u']$. The effect of condition (2) is like in the previous case, hence we conclude $T \models u \subseteq v$. $\qquad\square$

Table 1. Illustrated in the four tables are all possible assignments to the values 0 and 1 over the variables in $\{x_1, x_2, y_1, y_2, z_1\}$. The counterexample team, according to the proof of Theorem 3, for the consequence $x_1 x_2 \subseteq y_1 y_2$ and assumption set $\Sigma := \{y_1 y_2 \subseteq z_1 z_1, x_1 z_1 \subseteq z_1 z_1\}$ consists of all non-crossed out lines. Since $y_1 \equiv_\Sigma y_2$ while $x_1 \not\equiv_\Sigma x_2$, condition (3) is not used in the construction of the team.

x_1	x_2	y_1	y_2	z_1		x_1	x_2	y_1	y_2	z_1		x_1	x_2	y_1	y_2	z_1		x_1	x_2	y_1	y_2	z_1
1	1	1	1	1		1	1	1	0	1		1	1	0	1	1		1	1	0	0	1
1	0	1	1	1		1	0	1	0	1		1	0	0	1	1		1	0	0	0	1
0	1	1	1	1		0	1	1	0	1		0	1	0	1	1		0	1	0	0	1
0	0	1	1	1		0	0	1	0	1		0	0	0	1	1		0	0	0	0	1
1	1	1	1	0		1	1	1	0	0		1	1	0	1	0		1	1	0	0	0
1	0	1	1	0		1	0	1	0	0		1	0	0	1	0		1	0	0	0	0
0	1	1	1	0		0	1	1	0	0		0	1	0	1	0		0	1	0	0	0
0	0	1	1	0		0	0	1	0	0		0	0	0	1	0		0	0	0	0	0

For repetition-free inclusion atoms, the completeness proof of Theorem 3 without condition (2) suffices for the repetition-free system $\mathbf{R}_0$.

Similarly to the decision problem for repetition-free inclusion atoms [2], the decision problem for inclusion atoms is PSPACE-complete.

Theorem 4 (Complexity). *Let $\Sigma \cup \{x \subseteq y\}$ be a finite set of inclusion atoms. Deciding whether $\Sigma \vdash_{\mathbf{R}_1} x \subseteq y$ is PSPACE-complete.*

Table 2. The counterexample team in the proof of Theorem 3 for the consequence $x_1 x_2 \subseteq y_1 y_2$ and assumption set $\Sigma := \{y_2 z_1 \subseteq z_1 z_1, x_1 z_1 \subseteq y_1 y_2\}$ consists of all non-crossed out lines from the four subteams illustrated below.

x_1	x_2	y_1	y_2	z_1
1	1	1	1	1
1	0	1	1	1
0	1	1	1	1
0	0	1	1	1
1	1	1	1	0
1	0	1	1	0
0	1	1	1	0
0	0	1	1	0

x_1	x_2	y_1	y_2	z_1
1	1	1	0	1
1	0	1	0	1
0	1	1	0	1
0	0	1	0	1
1	1	1	0	0
1	0	1	0	0
0	1	1	0	0
0	0	1	0	0

x_1	x_2	y_1	y_2	z_1
1	1	0	1	1
1	0	0	1	1
0	1	0	1	1
0	0	0	1	1
1	1	0	1	0
1	0	0	1	0
0	1	0	1	0
0	0	0	1	0

x_1	x_2	y_1	y_2	z_1
1	1	0	0	1
1	0	0	0	1
0	1	0	0	1
0	0	0	0	1
1	1	0	0	0
1	0	0	0	0
0	1	0	0	0
0	0	0	0	0

Proof. PSPACE-hardness is immediate by the corresponding result for repetition-free inclusion in [2]. We sketch the proof for PSPACE membership.

First, identify the derivable equalities by scanning all of Σ for repeated variables on the right-hand side of the atoms. Collect these into a list of pairs, e.g., (x_2, x_2), (z_1, z_1). Scan Σ again, and if the variables from some pair on the list both appear on the right-hand side of an atom, add the pair of corresponding variables on the left-hand side to the list, e.g. if $z_2 y u_3 \subseteq x_2 y x_2 \in \Sigma$ then we add (z_2, u_3) (motivated by rules $I2$-$I4$). Iterate this process until no more pairs can be added to the list. Since Σ is finite, the procedure necessarily terminates in at most $|\mathcal{V}|^2$ steps, where each step is in linear time.

With the list of derivable equalities, construct Σ^* by replacing all equal variables in Σ with exactly one of them, and modify the atoms further such that no variable is repeated on the right-hand side of the atoms, as outlined in Lemma 1 item (iii). Rewrite also $x \subseteq y$ in the same way, and denote it by $x \subseteq y^*$. Now, Σ^* together with the list of derivable equalities is equivalent to Σ, and similarly for $x \subseteq y^*$. Since Σ^* contains no repetitions of variables on its atoms' right-hand sides, no more derivable equalities follow from Σ^*. Thus, it suffices to determine whether Σ^* entails $x \subseteq y^*$. Since the complete system for inclusion atoms has no rule specific to repetitions on the left-hand side, we use the usual PSPACE algorithm from [2] to check the entailment. $\square$

We end this section by showing that, unlike inclusion atoms in the first-order setting [5], not even unary inclusion atoms have Armstrong relations in the Boolean setting. We say that a set of dependencies Σ has Armstrong relations if for all $\Sigma' \subseteq \Sigma$, there is a team such that only the atoms entailed by Σ' are satisfied.

Theorem 5 (Nonexistence of Armstrong relations). *There is a set Σ' of propositional inclusion atoms such that no team satisfies exactly the propositional inclusion atoms that Σ' semantically entails.*

Proof. Let $Prop := \{p_1, p_2, p_3\}$ and $\Sigma' := \{p_1 \subseteq p_2\}$. We show that any team satisfying Σ' must satisfy either $p_3 \subseteq p_2$ or $p_2 \subseteq p_1$, neither of which is entailed by Σ'. If $T \models p_3 \subseteq p_2$, we are done. So suppose that $T \models \Sigma'$ and $T \not\models p_3 \subseteq p_2$. Then there is a value $a \in \{0, 1\}$ such that $a \in T[p_3] \setminus T[p_2]$. W.l.o.g. let $a = 0$. Now by $T \models p_1 \subseteq p_2$, we have that $T[p_1] \subseteq T[p_2] = \{1\}$. Thus, $T \models p_2 \subseteq p_1$. $\square$

5   Inclusion with Boolean Constants

We remain in the Boolean setting and consider inclusion atoms with Boolean constants of the form $p_1 \ldots p_n \subseteq q_1 \ldots q_n$, where $p_1 \ldots p_n, q_1 \ldots q_n$ are either propositional variables or the constants $\top$ and $\bot$. We introduce a complete system, show that the decision problem is PSPACE-complete, and conclude that there is no complete k-ary system for inclusion atoms with Boolean constants.

We extend the scope of assignments to the constants $\top$ and $\bot$ as follows: For any assignment $s : \mathcal{V} \cup \{\top, \bot\} \longrightarrow \{0, 1\}$, we have that $s(\top) = 1$ and $s(\bot) = 0$ always hold. The semantic clause for inclusion atoms with Boolean constants is then as before. In this setting, in addition to trivial atoms, we also have *contradictory* atoms that are only satisfied in the empty team, e.g., $\bot \subseteq \top$. We cannot express contradictions with the usual propositional inclusion atoms, making the inclusion atoms with Boolean constants strictly more expressive.

We define the system for inclusion atoms with Boolean constants by extending the system in Definition 2. Hereforth we exclusively use $x := x_1 \ldots x_n$ to denote a sequence of constants $\top$ and $\bot$. Otherwise, we do not exclude the constants $\top$ and $\bot$ from the sequences p, q, r, or any other variable sequence, unless explicitly mentioned.

We say that $x_1 \ldots x_n \subseteq r_1 \ldots r_n$ is *consistent* if for all $i, j \in \{1, \ldots, n\}$, $r_i \in \{\top, \bot\}$ implies $r_i = x_i$, and additionally, if $r_i = r_j$, then $x_i = x_j$. Now $\top\bot \subseteq \top p_2$ and $\top\top \subseteq p_2 p_2$ are consistent, while $\top\bot \subseteq \bot p_2$ and $\top\bot \subseteq p_2 p_2$ are not.

Definition 3. *The system for inclusion atoms with Boolean constants $\mathbf{R}_2$ extend the system $\mathbf{R}_1$ in Definition 2 with rules B1, B2 and schema B3.*

(B1) *If $\top \subseteq \bot$, then $q \subseteq r$.*
(B2) *If $p \subseteq q$, then $p\top \subseteq q\top$ and $p\bot \subseteq q\bot$.*

(B3) *Let $n := |p|$ and $A \subseteq \{r \subseteq q \mid r_i \in \{p_i, \top, \bot\}, 1 \leq i \leq n\}$ be a minimal set such that for any $\times$ with consistent $\times \subseteq p$, there is some $r \subseteq q \in A$ such that $\times \subseteq r$ is consistent. If A, then $p \subseteq q$.*

Rule $B1$ allows us to derive any atom from $\top \subseteq \bot$, since it is only satisfied by the empty team. We also derive any atom from the assumption $\bot \subseteq \top$, since we have $\vdash_{I1} \top \subseteq \top$, and $\bot \subseteq \top \vdash \top\bot \subseteq \top\top$ by $I3$ and $B2$, thus $\top \subseteq \bot$ follows by $I6$. Rule $B2$ is from the larger system for propositional inclusion logic in [17], and allows us to add constants to both sides of any inclusion atom. Note that in general $p \subseteq q \not\models pr \subseteq qr$.

The schema $B3$ has many instances, and we will closely examine one of the more involved ones in Theorem 9. A simple application of the schema is if all $\top\bot$-combinations are included in q, then any sequence is included in q. Another example is that $p \subseteq q$ follows from $\top p_2 \ldots p_n \subseteq q_1 \ldots q_n$ and $\bot p_2 \ldots p_n \subseteq q_1 \ldots q_n$.

Theorem 6 (Soundness). *The rules in $\mathbf{R}_2$ are sound.*

Proof. Proving soundness of $B1$ and $B2$ is straightforward. We show the claim for $B3$. Let A be as in the statement of the rule, and assume that $T \models r \subseteq q$, for all $r \subseteq q \in A$. Let $s \in T$, and consider the sequence $\times$ for which $s(p) = s(\times)$. By the definition of A, there is some $r \subseteq q \in A$ such that $\times \subseteq r$ is consistent. Thus we find some $s' \in T$, for which $s(p) = s(\times) = s'(r) \subseteq T[q]$. Hence, $T \models p \subseteq q$. $\square$

We generalize the completeness proof of Theorem 3 to inclusion atoms with Boolean constants. Table 3 shows an instance of the counterexample team.

Theorem 7 (Completeness). *Let $\Sigma \cup \{p \subseteq q\}$ be a set of inclusion atoms with Boolean constants. If $\Sigma \models p \subseteq q$, then $\Sigma \vdash_{\mathbf{R}_2} p \subseteq q$.*

Proof. Suppose that $\Sigma \not\vdash p \subseteq q$. We can assume that $\Sigma \not\vdash \top \subseteq \bot$, since otherwise we could derive $\Sigma \vdash_{B1} p \subseteq q$. Furthermore, if $p_i \equiv_\Sigma q_i$ for all $i \in \{1, \ldots, n\}$, we derive $\Sigma \vdash p \subseteq q$ by $I1$, $I3$ and $I6$, so assume that $x_i \not\equiv_\Sigma y_i$ for some $i \in \{1, \ldots, n\}$.

We first show that under the assumption $\Sigma \not\vdash p \subseteq q$, there is a sequence $\times$ such that $\Sigma \not\vdash \times \subseteq q$ and $\times \subseteq p$ is consistent. Let $n := |p|$ and consider sequences r such that $r_i \in \{p_i, \top, \bot\}$, $1 \leq i \leq n$. If there is no r such that $\Sigma \vdash r \subseteq q$, then let $c := s(\times)$ be a tuple for some $\times$ for which $\times \subseteq p$ is consistent, where s is any assignment. Otherwise, lest we derive $\Sigma \vdash p \subseteq q$ by $B3$, there is some n-sequence $\times$ such that $\times \subseteq p$ is consistent but $\times \subseteq r$ is not consistent for any r with $\Sigma \vdash r \subseteq q$. In particular, $\Sigma \not\vdash \times \subseteq q$, so we set $c := s(\times)$, where again s is any assignment.

Build the team T by letting $s \in T$ if the following three conditions are met.

(1) $s : \mathcal{V} \cup \{\top, \bot\} \longrightarrow \{0, 1\}$,
(2) If $u_i \equiv_\Sigma u_j$, then $s(u_i) = s(u_j)$.

If there are indices j, k such that $q_j \equiv_\Sigma q_k$ and $p_j \not\equiv_\Sigma p_k$, then we stop here. Otherwise, demand also:

(3) For w such that $\Sigma \vdash w \subseteq q$: $s(w) \neq c$.

Condition (2) handles derivable equalities not only between variables, but also between variables and constants, since, e.g., $\Sigma \vdash u_i \subseteq \top \vdash_{B2} u_i \top \subseteq \top\top$.

The intuition as to why the counterexample team works is the same as in the case of Theorem 3: It is as close to the generic team as possible, i.e., it satisfies conditions (1) and (2), with a minimal intervention by condition (3) ensuring that $T \not\models p \subseteq q$. Thus, showing that $T \models u \subseteq v$ for all $u \subseteq v \in \Sigma$ is analogous to the proof of Theorem 3. □

Next, we examine schema $B3$ from a computational complexity standpoint.

Lemma 2. *Deciding whether* $A \vdash_{B3} p \subseteq q$ *is co-NP-complete.*

Table 3. The counterexample team in the proof of Theorem 7 for the consequence $p_1 p_2 \subseteq q_1 q_2$ and assumption set $\Sigma := \{\perp\perp \subseteq q_1 q_2, \top\top \subseteq q_1 q_2, \perp\top \subseteq q_1 q_2\}$ consists of all the non-crossed out lines. Here, condition (3) is applied with $c := 10$.

p_1	p_2	q_1	q_2	r_1	p_1	p_2	q_1	q_2	r_1	p_1	p_2	q_1	q_2	r_1	p_1	p_2	q_1	q_2	r_1
1	1	1	1	1	1	1	1	0	1	1	1	0	1	1	1	1	0	0	1
1	0	1	1	1	1	0	1	0	1	1	0	0	1	1	1	0	0	0	1
0	1	1	1	1	0	1	1	0	1	0	1	0	1	1	0	1	0	0	1
0	0	1	1	1	0	0	1	0	1	0	0	0	1	1	0	0	0	0	1
1	1	1	1	0	1	1	1	0	0	1	1	0	1	0	1	1	0	0	0
1	0	1	1	0	1	0	1	0	0	1	0	0	1	0	1	0	0	0	0
0	1	1	1	0	0	1	1	0	0	0	1	0	1	0	0	1	0	0	0
0	0	1	1	0	0	0	1	0	0	0	0	0	1	0	0	0	0	0	0

Proof. Let A be an assumption set as stated in the schema $B3$, and let $n := |p|$.

For co-NP-hardness, we reduce the co-NP-complete [4] complement of the 3-SAT problem. Let $\phi := (a_1 \lor a_2 \lor a_3) \land (a_4 \lor a_5 \lor a_6) \land \cdots \land (a_{n-2} \lor a_{n-1} \lor a_n)$ be a conjunction of Boolean disjunctive clauses with three disjuncts, where $a_i \in \{p_i, \neg p_i\}$, $1 \leq i \leq n$. Note that we allow $p := p_1 \ldots p_n$ to have repeated variables.

To determine whether $\phi \notin$ 3-SAT, associate assignments s over the variables in p to sequences x in the obvious way: $x_i = \top$ iff $s(p_i) = 1$. For $1 \leq i \leq n$, define

$$\bar{a}_i = \begin{cases} \perp & \text{if } a_i = p_i, \\ \top & \text{if } a_i = \neg p_i. \end{cases}$$

Let r be an n-sequence of fresh propositional symbols. The reduction is completed through the equivalences between the following statements.

- $(a_1 \lor a_2 \lor a_3) \land (a_4 \lor a_5 \lor a_6) \land \cdots \land (a_{n-2} \lor a_{n-1} \lor a_n) \notin$ 3-SAT.

- For all sequences x corresponding to an assignment s, there is some $i \in \{1, 4, \ldots, n-2\}$ such that $\mathsf{x}_i\mathsf{x}_{i+1}\mathsf{x}_{i+2} = \overline{a_i}\overline{a_{i+1}}\overline{a_{i+2}}$.
- For all x where $\mathsf{x} \subseteq p$ is consistent, there is some $i \in \{1, 4, \ldots, n-2\}$ such that $\mathsf{x}_i\mathsf{x}_{i+1}\mathsf{x}_{i+2} = \overline{a_i}\overline{a_{i+1}}\overline{a_{i+2}}$.
- $A \vdash_{B3} p \subseteq r$, where

$$A := \left\{ b \subseteq r \; \middle| \; \begin{array}{l} \text{there is exactly one } i \in \{1, 4, \ldots, n-2\} \text{ such that} \\ b_ib_{i+1}b_{i+2} = \overline{a_i}\overline{a_{i+1}}\overline{a_{i+2}} \text{ and } b_j = p_j \text{ when } j \notin \{i, i+1, i+2\} \end{array} \right\}.$$

For co-NP-membership, it suffices to show that $A \nvdash_{B3} p \subseteq q$ is in NP. We sketch the proof. Guess a sequence x for which $x \subseteq p$ is consistent. Check whether there is some u appearing as the left-hand side of some atom in A such that $\mathsf{x} \subseteq u$ is consistent. If no, the algorithm accepts x as the witness, and we can find a certificate for $A \nvdash_{B3} p \subseteq q$ in polynomial time. □

We conclude this section by showing that the decision problem for inclusion atoms with Boolean constants is PSPACE-complete.

Theorem 8 (Complexity). *Let $\Sigma \cup \{p \subseteq q\}$ be a finite set of inclusion atoms with Boolean constants. Deciding whether $\Sigma \models p \subseteq q$ is PSPACE-complete.*

Proof. PSPACE-hardness follows from the corresponding result for inclusion atoms in [2]. We give a sketch of PSPACE-membership. Extend the procedure in the proof of Theorem 4 to also list derivable equalities between variables and constants, by adding, e.g., $(p_1, \top)$ to the list if there is an atom with p_1 on the left-hand side in the same relative position as $\top$ on the right-hand side. We again modify Σ to Σ^*, such that no atom in Σ^* has repeated variables or constants on its right-hand side. By Lemma 1 item (iii) and $B2$, the set Σ is equivalent to Σ^* together with the list of derivable equalities. We also modify $p \subseteq q$ in the same way and denote it by $p \subseteq q^*$.

Now it suffices to check whether $\Sigma^* \models p \subseteq q^*$, hence we only need to extend the PSPACE algorithm in [2] to entailments with constants on the left-hand side in the atoms, i.e., entailments corresponding to $B3$, which by Lemma 2 do not exceed PSPACE. □

5.1 No k-Ary Axiomatization

The complete proof system defined in Definition 3 is large, due to schema $B3$ not having an upper bound on the number of assumptions its instances can require. We show that this is necessary, i.e., no complete k-ary proof system exists for inclusion atoms with Boolean constants.

Let p and q be n-sequences of distinct propositional variables. Define B by

$$B := \left\{ r \subseteq q \; \middle| \; \begin{array}{l} r = \bot^n, \text{ or there is exactly one } i \in \{1, \ldots, n\} \\ \text{such that } r_i = \top \text{ and } r_j = p_j \text{ when } j \neq i \end{array} \right\}.$$

We consider the following instances of the schema $B3$:

$$\text{If } B, \text{ then } p \subseteq q. \tag{B3*}$$

The number of assumptions, i.e., the arity, of rule B3* is $n + 1$ for atoms of arity n, and we show that it cannot be reduced. It follows that the arity of the system grows with the arity of the atoms considered.

We show the claim by following the proof strategy in [14], and prove that no assumption can be derived from the others and that no nontrivial atom can be concluded from the assumption set, except for the conclusion of the rule. This is a general strategy to show the absence of k-ary axiomatizations, as per [2]. We end the section by sketching the proof.

Theorem 9. *There is no k-ary axiomatization of inclusion atoms with Boolean constants.*

Proof sketch. Consider the n-ary atom $p \subseteq q$, and let B be as in the statement of the rule B3*. Then $B \vdash p \subseteq q$. We show that any complete proof system necessarily includes a rule for this derivation with $n + 1$ assumptions. It suffices to prove the following two claims:

(1) No assumption is derived from the others.
(2) The only nontrivial atom derivable from the assumption set B is the conclusion $p \subseteq q$.

We easily build teams witnessing (1). For (2), we reduce the set of nontrivial atoms we need to consider to ones of the form $u \subseteq q$ where $u \neq p$ due to the following arguments. By the complete proof system in Definition 3, any nontrivial transformation of the assumptions would have to involve either $I2$ or $B3$. Rule $I2$ is not applicable, and using $B3$ on a strict subset of the assumption set results in atoms of the form $p' \subseteq q'$, with p', q' being proper subsequences of p, q, and such a collection would be strictly less expressive than the original assumption set. Therefore, it suffices to show that for all $u \subseteq q$, we can build teams that satisfy the assumptions in the rule B3* but not $u \subseteq q$.

There are many distinct cases based on the configuration of the variables and constants appearing in u. Still, two types of teams can be used (with some modification) in all cases. The first team is $T_1 := \{s_1, s_2\}$ with $s_1(pq) = 1^{2n}$ and $s_2(pq) = 1^n 0^n$. The second team $T_2 := \{s_1, \ldots s_{n+1}\}$ is defined by $T_2 = \{s \mid s(p) = 0^n$ and there is at most one $1 \leq i \leq n$ such that $s(q_i) = 1\}$. The team T_1 covers the cases when there are i, j such that $u_i = \bot$ and $u_j \neq \bot$, and T_2 the cases when there are different i, j such that $u_i = u_j = \top$. Both teams are illustrated in Table 4. We note that variants of these teams can also cover cases when u contains some fresh variable r_j that does not appear in the sequences p and q, thus even the introduction of fresh variables cannot help reduce the arity of the rule. □

Table 4. The teams T_1 and T_2 from the proof of Theorem 9.

$T_2:$	p_1	p_2	$\cdots$	p_n	q_1	q_2	$\cdots$	q_n
	0	0	$\cdots$	0	1	0	$\cdots$	0
	0	0	$\cdots$	0	0	1	$\cdots$	0
			$\ddots$				$\ddots$	
	0	0	$\cdots$	0	0	0	$\cdots$	1
	0	0	$\cdots$	0	0	0	$\cdots$	0

$T_1:$	p_1	p_2	$\cdots$	p_n	q_1	q_2	$\cdots$	q_n
	1	1	$\cdots$	1	1	1	$\cdots$	1
	1	1	$\cdots$	1	0	0	$\cdots$	0

6   Conclusion and Future Work

We list the paper's key contributions regarding the implication problem for inclusion with repetitions and Boolean constants and subsequently suggest directions for future work.

- Providing an alternative completeness proof for standard inclusion dependencies for the usual system [2], using only two values, thereby demonstrating completeness also in the Boolean setting.
- Extending the alternative completeness proof to inclusion atoms with repetitions for a system extracted from [13].
- Introducing a complete proof system for inclusion atoms with Boolean constants and confirming that no such system is k-ary.
- Demonstrating that the decision problems for both extended inclusion atoms remain PSPACE-complete.

The completeness proofs for the systems of functional dependence [7], non-conditional independence [7], and now also inclusion, only use two values, making the systems complete when restricted to the Boolean setting. This is not always the case; there are semantic entailments valid only in the Boolean setting for anonymity and exclusion atoms (see [16] and [8] for their definitions). For anonymity and exclusion, the following entailments serve as examples that are only sound in the Boolean setting: $q \Upsilon p, p \Upsilon r_1 \models r_1 \Upsilon p$ and $p_1 p_2 | p_2 p_1 \models p_1 | p_2$. Extending the systems in [8,16] to complete systems in the Boolean setting for anonymity and exclusion atoms remains as future work.

Another use of our alternative completeness proof is in the axiomatization of quantity approximate inclusion atoms of the form $x \subseteq_n y$ in [9], allowing n values of x to be missing from y. The alternative counterexample teams are advantageous compared to the existing ones when the degree to which they should not satisfy the assumed non-derivable atom needs to be carefully controlled.

Inclusion atoms with repetitions can express semantic equalities between variables, making this a natural dependency class to consider. Similarly, for exclusion atoms, allowing repetitions increases the expressivity, and the rules for repetition-free exclusion in [3] must be extended to obtain the complete system provided in [8]. We could thus consider extending the system for the combined implication problem for repetition-free inclusion and exclusion in [3] to deal with repetitions. Additionally, the language of team-based propositional logic augmented with inclusion atoms is axiomatized in [17], creating a direction of future study: The axiomatization of propositional inclusion-exclusion logic.

In propositional inclusion logic [17], inclusion atoms with Boolean constants suffice to achieve the desired expressive completeness result. The modal logic setting presents a similar situation, where standard inclusion atoms alone are insufficient for the desired expressivity (see [1, 10]). Even more extended inclusion atoms are needed, which allow modal logic formulas to function as 'variables' within the atom, such as $p \subseteq \Diamond q$. A natural extension of this work would be to axiomatize and determine the computational complexity of the implication problems for more subclasses of these extended inclusion atoms.

Acknowledgments. This work was in part supported by the Vilho, Yrjö and Kalle Väisälä Foundation. The author wants to thank the anonymous reviewers for their detailed comments and the helpful suggestions from Åsa Hirvonen, Fan Yang, Miika Hannula and Juha Kontinen. The connection between schema $B3$ and the complexity class co-NP was Miika Hannula's observation.

Disclosure of Interests. The author has no competing interests to declare that are relevant to the content of this article.

References

1. Anttila, A., Häggblom, M., Yang, F.: Axiomatizing modal inclusion logic and its variants. Arch. Math. Logic **64**(5), 755–793 (2025). https://doi.org/10.1007/s00153-024-00957-y
2. Casanova, M.A., Fagin, R., Papadimitriou, C.H.: Inclusion dependencies and their interaction with functional dependencies. J. Comput. Syst. Sci. **28**(1), 29–59 (1984). https://doi.org/10.1016/0022-0000(84)90075-8
3. Casanova, M.A., Vidal, V.M.P.: Towards a sound view integration methodology. In: ACM SIGACT-SIGMOD-SIGART Symposium on Principles of Database Systems (1983). https://doi.org/10.1145/588058.588065
4. Cook, S.A.: The complexity of theorem-proving procedures. In: Proceedings of the Third Annual ACM Symposium on Theory of Computing, STOC 1971, New York, NY, USA, pp. 151–158 (1971). https://doi.org/10.1145/800157.805047
5. Fagin, R.: Horn clauses and database dependencies. J. ACM **29**(4), 952–985 (1982). https://doi.org/10.1145/322344.322347
6. Galliani, P.: Inclusion and exclusion dependencies in team semantics – on some logics of imperfect information. Ann. Pure Appl. Logic **163**(1), 68–84 (2012). https://doi.org/10.1016/j.apal.2011.08.005
7. Galliani, P., Väänänen, J.: On dependence logic. In: Baltag, A., Smets, S. (eds.) Johan van Benthem on Logic and Information Dynamics. OCL, vol. 5, pp. 101–119. Springer, Cham (2014). https://doi.org/10.1007/978-3-319-06025-5_4
8. Häggblom, M.: Axiomatization of approximate exclusion. In: Proceedings of the 21st International Conference on Principles of Knowledge Representation and Reasoning, pp. 405–409 (2024). https://doi.org/10.24963/kr.2024/38

9. Häggblom, M.: Axiomatizing approximate inclusion (2025). https://arxiv.org/abs/2505.19834
10. Hella, L., Stumpf, J.: The expressive power of modal logic with inclusion atoms. Electron. Proc. Theor. Comput. Sci. **193**, 129–143 (2015). https://doi.org/10.4204/EPTCS.193.10
11. Hodges, W.: Compositional semantics for a language of imperfect information. Log. J. IGPL **5**(4), 539–563 (1997). https://doi.org/10.1093/jigpal/5.4.539
12. Hodges, W.: Some strange quantifiers. In: Mycielski, J., Rozenberg, G., Salomaa, A. (eds.) Structures in Logic and Computer Science. LNCS, vol. 1261, pp. 51–65. Springer, Heidelberg (1997). https://doi.org/10.1007/3-540-63246-8_4
13. Mitchell, J.C.: Inference rules for functional and inclusion dependencies. In: Proceedings of the 2nd ACM SIGACT-SIGMOD Symposium on Principles of Database Systems, PODS 1983, New York, NY, USA, pp. 58–69 (1983). https://doi.org/10.1145/588058.588067
14. Parker, D.S., Parsaye-Ghomi, K.: Inferences involving embedded multivalued dependencies and transitive dependencies. In: Proceedings of the 1980 ACM SIGMOD International Conference on Management of Data, SIGMOD 1980, New York, NY, USA, pp. 52–57 (1980). https://doi.org/10.1145/582250.582259
15. Väänänen, J.: Dependence Logic: A New Approach to Independence Friendly Logic. London Mathematical Society Student Texts. Cambridge University Press, Cambridge (2007). https://doi.org/10.1017/CBO9780511611193
16. Väänänen, J.: An atom's worth of anonymity. Log. J. IGPL **31**(6), 1078–1083 (2022). https://doi.org/10.1093/jigpal/jzac074
17. Yang, F.: Propositional union closed team logics. Ann. Pure Appl. Log. **173**(6), 103102 (2022). https://doi.org/10.1016/j.apal.2022.103102
18. Yang, F., Väänänen, J.: Propositional logics of dependence. Ann. Pure Appl. Log. **167**(7), 557–589 (2016). https://doi.org/10.1016/j.apal.2016.03.003

Enhancing Query Efficiency for D-DNNF Representations Through Preprocessing

Jean Marie Lagniez$^{(\boxtimes)}$ (ID) and Emmanuel Lonca$^{(\boxtimes)}$ (ID)

CRIL, U. Artois & CNRS, 62300 Lens, France
`{lagniez,lonca}@cril.fr`

Abstract. In this paper, we investigate preprocessing techniques aimed at improving the efficiency of accessing models of propositional formulas represented in conjunctive normal form (CNF). We focus on three fundamental tasks: uniform sampling, direct model access, and model enumeration. Our analysis reveals that most state-of-the-art preprocessors, when they do not preserve formula equivalence, are generally unsuitable for these tasks. In contrast, we demonstrate that preprocessors which preserve model counts can be effectively leveraged, provided relevant preprocessing information is maintained. To validate our approach, we perform extensive experiments on a diverse suite of benchmarks from multiple domains. The experimental results show that our preprocessing methods are both efficient and robust, yielding significant performance improvements for model access queries when CNF formulas are compiled into d-DNNF representations.

Keywords: Preprocessing techniques · Uniform sampling · Direct access · Model enumeration · Decision-DNNF

1 Introduction

Propositional logic forms the backbone of a wide array of fields, including databases [1], automated planning [11], and explainable artificial intelligence [9], among others. When problems from these domains are encoded as propositional formulas, efficiently querying these formulas becomes essential for extracting meaningful insights and solving practical tasks. Crucial queries in this context include *model counting*, *direct access*, *uniform sampling*, and *model enumeration*. However, the computational complexity of these queries, often #P-complete, poses significant challenges, making the choice of suitable formula representations highly influential to overall performance. In this work, we focus specifically on formulas expressed in *conjunctive normal form* (CNF), the predominant representation in many practical settings due to its compatibility with modern SAT solvers and widespread use in real-world applications.

To overcome the inherent computational difficulties associated with these queries on CNF formulas, *preprocessing* has emerged as a vital strategy. Preprocessing involves transforming a CNF formula into an equivalent (or, under certain relaxations, satisfiability-equivalent) CNF representation that is better suited for efficient query evaluation. Such transformations are valuable if they facilitate downstream tasks, even after

© The Author(s), under exclusive license to Springer Nature Switzerland AG 2026
G. Casini et al. (Eds.): JELIA 2025, LNAI 16094, pp. 125–140, 2026.
https://doi.org/10.1007/978-3-032-04590-4_9

accounting for the preprocessing cost itself. Indeed, preprocessing has proven effective across a variety of reasoning tasks, such as SAT solving [3], model counting [22,29], and almost-uniform sampling [28], often yielding significant runtime improvements.

This paper provides a comprehensive analysis of elementary preprocessing techniques, with a particular focus on their impact and suitability for direct access, uniform sampling, and model enumeration tasks. The techniques considered include *vivification*, *occurrence reduction*, *backbone identification*, *variable elimination*, *blocked clause elimination*, and the removal of *implicitly* and *explicitly defined variables* [19,22]. Notably, the first three techniques preserve full logical equivalence, making them broadly applicable regardless of the specific query. In contrast, variable elimination and blocked clause elimination only preserve satisfiability, limiting their utility for our target queries. Finally, under certain conditions, eliminating implicitly or explicitly defined variables (while preserving the model count) can enable more efficient solutions for direct access, uniform sampling, and model enumeration.

To empirically evaluate the practical benefits of preprocessing techniques, we adopt a pipeline centered on compiling propositional formulas into d-DNNF. Specifically, we first apply preprocessing to the CNF formula, then compile the resulting CNF into a d-DNNF representation, upon which queries are subsequently answered. This workflow reflects the common strategy for tackling the considered queries, as many inference and enumeration tasks can be performed efficiently on d-DNNF representations. Our experiments leverage a diverse suite of benchmarks, utilizing the state-of-the-art d-DNNF compiler **d4** [21] in conjunction with preprocessing capabilities from **B+E** [23]. We systematically assess the impact of different preprocessing strategies, ranging from no preprocessing to advanced techniques that remove explicitly defined variables, on overall query runtime and efficiency. Through this study, we aim to provide practitioners with clearer insight into the trade-offs between preprocessing overhead and query performance, and to illustrate how effective preprocessing can substantially enhance the practical utility of logical reasoning tools for challenging inference and enumeration tasks.

The remainder of this paper is organized as follows. Section 2 presents the necessary formal preliminaries. Section 3 introduces and analyzes the considered preprocessing techniques, focusing on their applicability to direct access, uniform sampling, and model enumeration. Section 4 reports our experimental results and evaluates the effectiveness of these techniques. Finally, Sect. 5 concludes the paper and outlines promising directions for future work.

2 Formal Preliminaries

We consider a propositional language $PROP_{PS}$ in the standard manner, derived from a finite set PS of propositional symbols and the standard logical connectives ($\land$, $\lor$, $\leftarrow$, $\leftrightarrow$, $\neg$). $PROP_{PS}$ is interpreted classically. For any formula Σ in $PROP_{PS}$, $Var(\Sigma)$ denotes the set of propositional variables present in Σ. Given a finite set of variables X, $\{0,1\}^X$ represents the set of all possible Boolean assignments to the variables in X. Each propositional formula Σ in $PROP_{PS}$ defines a Boolean function over $Var(\Sigma)$, mapping Σ from $\{0,1\}^{|Var(\Sigma)|}$ to $\{0,1\}$. Assignments to $Var(\Sigma)$ that evaluate to 1 under Σ are termed *satisfying assignments* or *models* of Σ. $Mod(\Sigma)$ represents the set of all models of Σ. Two formulas Σ_1 and Σ_2 are considered equivalent if their sets of models are identical, that is, if $Mod(\Sigma_1) = Mod(\Sigma_2)$. This equivalence is denoted as $\Sigma_1 \equiv \Sigma_2$. Σ_1 implies Σ_2, denoted as $\Sigma_1 \models \Sigma_2$, if $Mod(\Sigma_1) = Mod(\Sigma_2)$. $\bot$ represents the formula which is always falsified and $\top$ the formula which is always satisfied.

A *literal* is defined as either a Boolean variable or its negation. For any literal ℓ, $Var(\ell)$ represents the variable x of ℓ ($Var(x) = x$ and $Var(\neg x) = x$), and $\sim\ell$ denotes the complementary literal of ℓ. In other words, for every variable x, $\sim x = \neg x$ and $\sim\neg x = x$. The conditioning of a formula Σ by a literal $\ell = x$ (resp. $\ell = \neg x$) results in the formula $\Sigma[\ell]$, where each occurrence of x (resp. $\neg x$) in Σ is replaced by $\top$, and each occurrence of $\neg x$ (resp. x) is replaced by $\bot$. After such replacement, simplification is carried out using the semantics of the logical connectors (e.g., $\top \vee \Gamma = \top$, $\top \wedge \Gamma = \Gamma$, etc.) until a fixed point is reached. This notion can be extended to set of literals $S = \{\ell_1, \ldots, \ell_m\}$ in the following way $\Sigma[S] = ((\Sigma[\ell_1])\ldots)[\ell_m]$. Each assignment μ is conceptualized as a (conjunctively interpreted) set of literals. We differentiate between total assignments and partial assignments based on whether all variables are assigned truth values or not, respectively.

A CNF formula Σ is a conjunction of clauses, where a clause is a disjunction of literals. Every CNF is viewed as a set of clauses, and every clause is viewed as a set of literals.

Example 1. Let $\Psi = \{a \vee b, \neg a \vee \neg b, c \vee d \vee a, c \vee d \vee b\}$ a CNF formula and $Var(\Psi) = \{a, b, c, d\}$.

2.1 Knowledge Compilation and D-DNNF Representation

A d-DNNF formula, which stands for Deterministic Decomposable Negation Normal Form, is a Boolean circuit with a single output, serving as its root. It can be conceptualized as a rooted Directed Acyclic Graph (DAG), denoted as $\langle V, E \rangle$, where each input is either a literal or a Boolean constant ($\bot$ or $\top$), and each internal gate is either a decomposable $\wedge$ gate or a deterministic $\vee$ gate. In a decomposable gate $N = \wedge(N_1, \ldots, N_k)$, no common variable is shared between the sub-circuits rooted at N_i and N_j for all $i \neq j$. In a deterministic gate $N = \vee(N_1, \ldots, N_k)$, the sub-circuits rooted at N_i and N_j are jointly inconsistent for all $i \neq j$. The size of a d-DNNF $\Sigma = \langle V, E \rangle$, denoted by $|\Sigma|$ is its number of edges $|E|$. d-DNNF is universal, as it can accommodate every propositional theory [7].

Knowledge compilers such as **C2D** [8], **Dsharp** [24], **d4** [21], and **SharpSAT-TD** [16] are not able to produce d-DNNF but they are able of producing a sub-class of d-DNNF which is decision-DNNF (decision Decomposable Negation Normal Form) representations. decision-DNNF is defined similarly, but with decision gates of the form $N = ite(x, N_1, N_2)$ replacing deterministic $\vee$ gates. Here, x is the decision variable at gate N, absent in the sub-circuits N_1 or N_2, and *ite* is a ternary connective denoting "if ... then ... else ...". decision-DNNF representations, also termed decomposable decision graphs [10], can be converted into specific d-DNNF representations in linear time. By replacing a decision node of the form $N = ite(x, N_1, N_2)$ in a decision-DNNF representation with $N = (\neg x \wedge N_1) \vee (x \wedge N_2)$, the resulting d-DNNF representation maintains decomposable $\wedge$ nodes (as x appears neither in N_1 nor in N_2) and a deterministic $\vee$ node (since $(\neg x \wedge N_1) \wedge (x \wedge N_2)$ is inconsistent). For simplicity of exposition, we will use the term d-DNNF throughout the remainder of this paper, although our experiments are carried out using decision-DNNF representations. Importantly, all our results apply equally to both d-DNNF and decision-DNNF formats.

Example 2 (Example 1 cont'ed). Consider the CNF formula Ψ given in Example 1, the d-DNNF $\Sigma = ((\neg a \wedge b) \vee (a \wedge \neg b)) \wedge (c \vee (\neg c \wedge d))$ is equivalent to Ψ.

d-DNNF serves as a compelling language of representation due to its ability to efficiently handle various queries and transformations, such as satisfiability and conditioning in polynomial time. Notably, queries involving direct access [4,5], uniform sampling [26] and model enumeration [7], which we will discuss in the next section, can be answered efficiently when the formula is represented as a d-DNNF. Although our experimental methodology is based on compiling CNF formulas into d-DNNF, the applicability of our findings regarding suitable preprocessing techniques extends beyond this specific approach. Indeed, these results hold for any query-strategy, as preprocessing can be applied prior to query evaluation, and the answers obtained for the simplified formula can subsequently be mapped back to the original CNF in polynomial time. This generality underscores the practical value of our recommended preprocessing techniques, regardless of the downstream reasoning or enumeration strategy.

2.2   Model Enumeration, Direct Access and Uniform Sampling Queries

The enumeration problem involves listing the set of models of a propositional formula without redundancies, commonly referred to as the disjoint AllSAT problem. Models can be enumerated in two forms: *complete* or *partial*. A *complete model* assigns a value to every propositional variable in the formula. However, due to the often vast number of complete models associated with a formula, compact representations are desirable in certain applications. A *partial model* provides such a compact representation by allowing some variables to remain unassigned. For a partial model to be valid, it must ensure that assigning any truth value to the unassigned variables does not alter the satisfiability of the model. Consequently, a partial model with m assigned variables represents 2^{n-m} complete models, where n is the total number of variables.

As we will demonstrate in the next section, the preprocessing techniques applicable to these two enumeration tasks behave differently and require distinct considerations.

Example 3 (Example 1 cont'ed). For the CNF formula Φ provided in Example 1, the complete models of $Mod(\Psi)$ are: $\{a, \neg b, c, d\}$, $\{\neg a, b, c, d\}$, $\{a, \neg b, c, \neg d\}$ $\{\neg a, b, c, \neg d\}$, $\{a, \neg b, \neg c, d\}$, $\{\neg a, b, \neg c, d\}$.

A possible compact representation of Φ can be expressed using the following partial models: $\{a, \neg b, c\}$, $\{\neg a, b, c\}$, $\{a, \neg b, \neg c, d\}$, $\{\neg a, b, \neg c, d\}$.

The direct access task, first introduced in the database context by [2], consists of, given an input k and an order $\prec_{lex}$ over the assignments, returning the k-th model of a propositional formula Φ with respect to $\prec_{lex}$ if $k \leq |Mod(\Phi)|$ and failing otherwise. In the case of propositional logic, $\prec_{lex}$ involves fixing an order τ on the Boolean variables and then considering each assignment as a word constructed from $\{0, 1\}^{|Var(\Phi)|}$. We will denote $\prec_{lex}^{\tau}$ when $\prec_{lex}$ depends on the order τ. We will use the notation $<_{\tau}$ to specify that a variable x precedes a variable y according to τ, i.e., $x <_{\tau} y$.

Example 4 (Example 1 cont'ed). Given the CNF formula Φ in Example 1, if $\tau = (a, b, c, d)$, then the first model of Φ is $\{\neg a, b, \neg c, d\}$ (corresponding to the word (0101)) and the third model is $\{\neg a, b, c, d\}$ (corresponding to the word (0111)). If instead we use the variable ordering $\tau = (d, c, b, a)$, the first model becomes $\{a, \neg b, c, \neg d\}$ (bitstring (0101)), and the last model is $\{\neg a, b, c, d\}$ (bitstring (1110)).

The direct access query can serve as a building block for many other important tasks, such as counting, enumerating, and sampling without repetition [26]. However, answering this query is generally hard (#P-difficult) for propositional logic. Nevertheless, since d-DNNF supports both conditioning and model counting in polynomial time, this query can be answered in polynomial time. Specifically, if $|Mod(\Phi)| \leq k$, an error is returned. Otherwise, starting with an empty term σ and an interval $I = [0, |Mod(\Phi)|]$, the algorithm iteratively picks the next variable x in order. If $I.min + |Mod(\Phi[\sigma][\neg x])| \geq k$, then $\sigma = \sigma \cup \{\neg x\}$ and I is updated to $[I.min, I.min + |Mod(\Phi[\sigma][\neg x])|]$. Otherwise, $\sigma = \sigma \cup \{x\}$ and I is updated to $[I.min + |Mod(\Phi[\sigma][\neg x])| + 1, I.max]$, where $I.min$ is the lower endpoint and $I.max$ is the upper endpoint.

Example 5 (Example 4 cont'ed). Let us consider the previous example when we seek the third model. The algorithm starts with $\sigma = \emptyset$ and $I = [0, 6]$. As we can see, $|Mod(\Phi[\neg a])| = 3$, which means $\neg a$ is added to σ and I is updated to $[0, 3]$. Next, b is considered, and $|Mod(\Phi[\{\neg a, \neg b\}])|$ is computed to be 0. Since $0 + 0 < 3$, b is added to σ and I remains $[0, 3]$. Then, c is selected and $|Mod(\Phi[\{\neg a, b, \neg c\}])|$ is computed to be 1. As $0 + 1 < 3$, c is added to σ and I becomes $[1, 3]$. Finally, d is picked, and since $|Mod(\Phi[\{\neg a, b, c, \neg d\}])| = 1$ and $1 + 1 < 3$, σ is ultimately equal to $\{\neg a, b, c, d\}$, which is the expected result of I.

The concept of uniform sampling involves generating samples $\mathcal{R}_{\Phi}$ from the set of models of Φ using a generator $\mathcal{G}$ that ensures $\forall \mu \in \mathcal{R}_{\Phi}, Pr[\mathcal{G}(\Phi) = \mu] = 1/|Mod(\Phi)|$. A technique for uniform sampling involves these steps: first, count the total number of models, c. Then, generate k integers uniformly within the range $\{1, \ldots, c\}$ and use direct access to identify the corresponding models.

Example 6 (Example 1 cont'ed). Given the CNF formula Φ in Example 1, we first compute its total number of models, which is 6, before selecting 2 random models. Next, we randomly choose a set of two integers from the set $\{1, \ldots, 6\}$; for example, $\{1, 4\}$. Finally, if the order considered for the direct access query is the lexicographical order of the variables in Φ, then the set of models $\{\{\neg a, b, \neg c, d\}, \{a, \neg b, \neg c, d\}\}$ is returned.

In [14], the authors observed a deep relationship between model counting and uniform sampling. They showed that given access to an exact model counter, it is possible to design a uniform generator that requires only polynomially many queries to the exact model counter. Specifically, since d-DNNF supports model counting queries in polynomial time, it is evident that this language is well-suited for sampling a set of models.

In [26], the authors propose an approach that tags the d-DNNF circuit to efficiently compute uniform sampling. This approach leverages recent advances in knowledge compilation, which can be harnessed to design a scalable uniform sampler.

It is important to note that the approach proposed in [26] does not impose any order on the models, meaning that the uniform sampling generated cannot be controlled by a seed. More specifically, the set of models produced depends on the d-DNNF formula generated by the compiler, and in general, compilers do not allow for control over the compilation process. In the following, we will show that the selection of preprocessing techniques may vary depending on whether or not we require the ability to control the set of models through a seed.

3   Preprocessing for Direct Access, Uniform Sampling, and Model Enumeration

Preprocessing a propositional formula transforms it while preserving properties like satisfiability and model count. This process is beneficial because the problem at hand (e.g., satisfiability) can often be solved more efficiently after the input formula has been preprocessed, accounting for the preprocessing time in the overall solving time. Various preprocessing techniques are now recognized as valuable for SAT solving, QBF solving, and model counting [3, 12, 19, 21, 28]. These techniques can be categorized based on the type of equivalence they maintain with the input formula: satisfiability, model counting, or logical equivalence.

First, let us examine the preprocessing techniques that produce a formula equivalent to the input formula, such as vivification, backbone detection, and occurrence elimination [20, 25]. The backbone of a CNF formula Φ is the set of all literals implied by Φ when Φ is satisfiable; if Φ is unsatisfiable, the backbone is the empty set. The purpose of backbone identification is to explicitly identify the backbone of the input CNF formula Φ and conjoin it to Φ. Vivification [25] is a preprocessing technique aimed at reducing a given CNF formula Φ by removing some clauses and literals while preserving equivalence. Given a clause $\alpha = \ell_1 \vee \ldots \vee \ell_k$ in Φ, two rules are used to determine whether α can be removed from Φ or simply shortened. On one hand, if for any $j \in \{1, \ldots, k\}$, a Boolean Constraint Propagator (BCP) [31] can prove that $\Phi \setminus \{\alpha\} \models \ell_1 \vee \ldots \vee \ell_j$, then α is entailed by $\Phi \setminus \{\alpha\}$ and can be removed from Φ. On the other hand, if BCP can prove that $\Phi \setminus \{\alpha\} \models \ell_1 \vee \ldots \vee \ell_j \vee \sim\ell_{j+1}$, then ℓ_{j+1} can be removed from α without affecting equivalence. Occurrence elimination considers only the second rule, focusing on the elimination of literals instead of clauses.

Example 7 (Example 1 cont'ed). Let us consider again the CNF formula Φ given in Example 1. When we observe the models, we see that the variables can take all possible values, indicating that the backbone of Φ is empty. Upon employing occurrence elimination, the third clause can be simplified to $c \vee d$, as $\Phi \setminus \{c \vee d \vee a\} \models c \vee d \vee \neg a$, provable via BCP. Φ is now equal to $\{a \vee b, \neg a \vee \neg b, c \vee d, c \vee d \vee b\}$. Now, we can see that the fourth clause can be removed using the vivification rule since $\Phi \setminus \{c \vee d \vee b\}$ can infer $c \vee d$ by BCP.

Preprocessing techniques that ensure equivalence can be applied to a variety of queries, such as direct access, uniform sampling, and both complete and partial model enumeration. However, not all techniques share this versatility. Prominent SAT-solving preprocessing methods [18,20] are unsuitable for model counting as they may alter the number of models in equisatisfiable formulas. Now, let us explore the effects of preprocessing techniques solely maintaining satisfiability, like blocked clause elimination and variable elimination [13,30], on the queries under consideration.

The resolution rule asserts that, given two clauses $\alpha_1 = \{\ell, a_1, \ldots, a_n\}$ and $\alpha_2 = \{\sim\ell, b_1, \ldots, b_m\}$, the resulting clause $\alpha = \{a_1, \ldots, a_n, b_1, \ldots, b_m\}$ is the *resolvent* of α_1 and α_2 on the literal ℓ. Variable elimination of x in Φ is performed by removing from Φ all clauses containing the variable x (either as a positive or negative literal) and adding into Φ all possible resolvents between the removed clauses. It is equivalent to existentially quantify x in Φ. This rule is applied effectively only when it does not increase the number of clauses in Φ [30]. The simplification technique known as *blocked clause elimination* [13] targets the removal of specific clauses, termed *blocked clauses*, from CNF formulas. A literal ℓ within a clause α is termed a *blocking literal* if it blocks α with respect to Φ. This occurs when, for every clause α' in Φ containing $\sim\ell$, the resulting resolvent on ℓ is a tautology. Essentially, a clause is considered blocked if it contains a literal that can effectively block it. Applying blocked clause elimination to Φ involves removing every clause containing a blocking literal and repeating the process iteratively until no blocked literals remain.

Proposition 1. *Let Φ be a CNF formula. Variable elimination and blocked clause elimination cannot be applied when the objective is to answer direct access, uniform sampling and model enumeration queries.*

Proof. Consider the CNF formula $\Phi = \{a \vee b\}$ over the variable set $X = \{a, b\}$. It is evident that both preprocessing techniques produce the formula $\Phi' = \top$. From Φ' it is impossible to retrieve the models of Φ. Thus, these preprocessing techniques are unsuitable for the queries considered.

These findings echo conclusions drawn from the model counting domain, revealing the inadequacy of these preprocessing methods for addressing such problems. This underscores the interrelationship between model counting, direct access, and uniform sampling queries. To delve deeper into this relationship, let us investigate preprocessing techniques tailored to the model counting task, like eliminating defined variables [18,20]. Defined variables $\mathcal{O}$ of Φ are variables whose valuation depends on other variables from $Var(\Phi) \setminus \mathcal{O}$. In propositional logic, definability can manifest in two equivalent forms: implicit and explicit. More precisely, the formula Φ *implicitly defines* the variable y in terms of $X \subset Var(\Phi)$ if and only if for assignment γ_X over X, we have $\gamma_X \wedge \Phi \models y$ or $\gamma_X \wedge \Phi \models \neg y$. The formula Φ *explicitly defines* the variable y in terms of X if and only if there exists a formula $\Psi_X \in PROP_X$ such that $\Phi \models (\Psi_X \leftrightarrow y)$. In such a case, Ψ_X is called a *definition (or gate) of y on X in Φ*, y is the *output variable* of the gate, and X are its *input variables*. In [18], the authors demonstrate that defined variables can be eliminated while keeping the number of models unchanged.

Example 8 (Example 1 cont'ed). Let Φ the CNF formula given in Example 1. As we can see, $a \leftrightarrow \neg b$, meaning that Φ defines the variable a in terms of $\{b\}$. After eliminating a, the resulting formula is $\Phi' = \{c \vee d \vee \neg b, c \vee d \vee b\} \equiv \{c \vee d\}$, defined over the Boolean variables $\{b, c, d\}$. The list of models of Φ' is $\{\{\neg b, c, d\}, \{b, c, d\}, \{\neg b, c, \neg d\}, \{b, c, \neg d\}, \{\neg b, \neg c, d\}, \{b, \neg c, d\}\}$. As we can see, the model count of Φ', which is 6, is the same as that of Φ.

While preserving the number of models, as stated in Proposition 2, such preprocessing techniques cannot be applied directly when the targeted queries are direct access, uniform sampling and model enumeration.

Proposition 2. *Let Φ be a CNF formula and x a variable such that Φ defines x in terms of $Var(\Phi) \setminus \{x\}$. The formula obtained after eliminating x from Φ cannot be used solely to answer either direct access, uniform sampling or model enumeration queries.*

Proof. Consider the CNF formula $\Phi = (\neg x \vee y_1 \vee \ldots \vee y_k) \wedge (\bigwedge_{i=1}^{k}(x \vee \neg y_i))$, which represents the Boolean function $x \leftrightarrow y_1 \vee \ldots \vee y_k$. Clearly, Φ defines x in terms of $\{y_1, \ldots, y_k\}$. Eliminating the variable x produces the CNF formula $\Phi' = \top$ over the variables $\{y_1, \ldots, y_k\}$. Although Φ and Φ' have the same number of models, the models of Φ cannot be obtained from Φ' alone.

Proposition 2 demonstrates that, in the general case, it is impossible to answer direct access or uniform sampling queries on the preprocessed formula Φ' to obtain the results for the original formula Φ. However, as demonstrated in Proposition 3, this preprocessing can be utilized for uniform sampling and complete model enumeration queries, provided that the values of the eliminated variables can be determined from the variables in Φ'. But first, let us introduce the concept of a compatible evaluation function.

Definition 1 (Compatible Evaluation Function). *Let Φ be a CNF formula, and let $\mathcal{O} \subseteq Var(\Phi)$ be a set of variables that Φ defines in terms of $\mathcal{I} = Var(\Phi) \setminus \mathcal{O}$. f is called a compatible evaluation function, if given any $o \in \mathcal{O}$ and $\gamma \in \{0,1\}^{\mathcal{I}}$, it computes the literal associated with o given γ regarding Φ (which is o if Φ forces o to be true given γ, and $\neg o$ otherwise).*

Proposition 3. *Let Φ be a CNF formula, let $\mathcal{O} \subseteq Var(\Phi)$ be a set of variables defined by Φ in terms of $\mathcal{I} = Var(\Phi) \setminus \mathcal{O}$, and let f be the associated compatible evaluation function. Let Φ' be the formula obtained by eliminating the variables in $\mathcal{O}$ from Φ. The following results hold:*

1. *If $\mathcal{R}_{\Phi'}$ is a uniform sample of Φ', then $\mathcal{R}_{\Phi} = \{\omega \cup \bigcup_{o \in \mathcal{O}} f(o, \omega) \mid \omega \in \mathcal{R}_{\Phi'}\}$ is a uniform sample of Φ;*
2. *$Mod(\Phi) = \{\omega \cup \bigcup_{o \in \mathcal{O}} f(o, \omega) \mid \omega \in Mod(\Phi')\}$.*

Proof. Proposition 1 in [19] establishes that $|Mod(\Phi)| = |Mod(\Phi')|$. The proof relies on showing that if $\omega \in Mod(\Phi')$, then $\omega \cup \bigcup_{o \in \mathcal{O}} f(o, \omega) \in Mod(\Phi)$. This implies that f defines a bijection between $Mod(\Phi')$ and $Mod(\Phi)$. Given that f is bijective, the results follow directly:

1. Since $\mathcal{R}_{\Phi'}$ is a uniform sample of Φ', applying f preserves uniformity. Thus, $\mathcal{R}_{\Phi} = \{\omega \cup \bigcup_{o \in \mathcal{O}} f(o, \omega) \mid \omega \in \mathcal{R}_{\Phi'}\}$ is a uniform sample of Φ.
2. The bijection guarantees that every model of Φ' is transformed into a unique model of Φ, ensuring $Mod(\Phi) = \{\omega \cup \bigcup_{o \in \mathcal{O}} f(o, \omega) \mid \omega \in Mod(\Phi')\}$.

Observe that if f can be computed in polynomial time, it facilitates the polynomial-time construction of both uniform samples and the complete models of Φ from Φ'. This is particularly applicable when the eliminated variables are explicitly defined by Boolean functions, such as equivalence gates, AND-gates, OR-gates, or XOR-gates.

Now, let us consider the scenario where the direct access query is the focus. As demonstrated in the following example, merely knowing the function f is insufficient for effectively answering this query.

Example 9 (Example 1 cont'ed). Let us revisit the CNF formula Φ' computed in Example 8, which is derived from the original CNF formula Φ introduced in Example 1. Considering the natural order, the first model of Φ', $\{\neg b, \neg c, d\}$, is augmented using the information from f, resulting in $\{a, \neg b, \neg c, d\}$ (due to $a \leftrightarrow \neg b$). However, this differs from the first model of Φ, which is $\{\neg a, b, \neg c, d\}$.

The problem arises because variable valuation can depend on variables that come later in the order τ specified by $\prec_{lex}^{\tau}$ for the direct access task. To overcome this, we define a *compatible order* as follows:

Definition 2 (Compatible order). *Let Φ be a CNF formula, and let $\mathcal{O} \subseteq Var(\Phi)$ be a set of variables defined by Φ in terms of $\mathcal{I} = Var(\Phi) \setminus \mathcal{O}$. An order τ over $\langle \Phi, \mathcal{I}, \mathcal{O} \rangle$ is a compatible order if and only if τ is an order over $Var(\Phi)$, $(\mathcal{I}, \mathcal{O})$ is a bi-partition over $Var(\Phi)$, and for every $o \in \mathcal{O}$, $x <_\tau o$ for all $x \in \mathcal{I}_o$, where Φ defines o in terms of $\mathcal{I}_o$.*

Two strategies can be applied regarding the control the user has regarding the choice of τ. The first strategy involves adjusting the order to comply with the preprocessing step, meaning all eliminated variables must be placed at the end of τ. For example, in the previous case, $\tau = (b, c, d, a)$ is a compatible order. The second strategy involves constraining the preprocessing method to only eliminate a variable o if Φ defines o in terms of $\mathcal{I}$, such that for all $x \in \mathcal{I}$, $x <_\tau o$. For example, in the previous case, $\tau = (b, a, c, d)$ is a compatible order.

We can observe that the first strategy allows for the elimination of more variables during the preprocessing step but restricts the operator $\prec_{lex}^{\tau}$ by partially fixing it. Conversely, the second strategy may reduce the number of eliminated variables, but it grants the user complete freedom in choosing $\prec_{lex}^{\tau}$. Regardless of the chosen strategy, Proposition 4 demonstrates that it is possible to leverage preprocessing methods that eliminate defined variables to construct a CNF formula Φ' from the input CNF formula Φ, while still maintaining the ability to reason about Φ' to answer the direct access query on Φ.

Proposition 4. *Let Φ be a CNF formula, let $\mathcal{O} \subseteq Var(\Phi)$ be a set of variables such that Φ defines $\mathcal{O}$ in terms of $\mathcal{I} = Var(\Phi) \setminus \mathcal{O}$, and f the associated compatible evaluation function. Let $\Phi' = \exists \mathcal{O}.\Phi$ and τ is a compatible order over $\langle \Phi, \mathcal{I}, \mathcal{O} \rangle$. If ω' is the k-th model of Φ' with respect to $\prec_{lex}^{\tau'}$ (where τ' is the projection of τ onto $Var(\Phi')$), then $\omega = \omega' \cup \bigcup_{o \in \mathcal{O}} f(\mathcal{I}_o, o)$ will be the k-th model of Φ.*

Proof. First, since the preprocessing technique preserves the number of models, if $k > |Mod(\Phi')|$, then $k > |Mod(\Phi)|$. Therefore, the answer to the direct access query remains the same whether it is applied to Φ' or Φ, meaning that it will fail for both formulas as expected. Now let us suppose that $k \leq |Mod(\Phi')|$.

First, let us demonstrate that if $\omega_1, \omega_2 \in Mod(\Phi)$ such that $\omega_1 \prec_{lex}^{\tau} \omega_2$, then $\omega_1' \prec_{lex}^{\tau'} \omega_2'$. As $\Phi' = \exists \mathcal{O}.\Phi$, we directly deduce that ω_1' and ω_2' are models of Φ'. Now, let us argue by contradiction. Suppose $\omega_2' \prec_{lex}^{\tau'} \omega_1'$. By the definition of $\prec_{lex}^{\tau'}$, this implies that there exists $\neg x \in \omega_2'$ such that $x \in \omega_1'$, and $\forall \ell \in \omega_2'$ with $Var(\ell) <_{\tau'} x$, we have $\ell \in \omega_1'$. Since ω_1' and ω_2' are projections of ω_1 and ω_2 onto $Var(\Phi')$, it follows that $\neg x \in \omega_2$ and $x \in \omega_1$. Moreover, for all literals $\ell \in \omega_1$ with $Var(\ell) <_{\tau} x$, we have $\ell \in \omega_2$. This is because if $Var(\ell) \in \mathcal{I}$, then ℓ is trivially in ω_2. Otherwise, since τ is a compatible order, all variables in $\mathcal{O}$ will be fixed with respect to f in both ω_1 and ω_2. Since $\neg x \in \omega_2$ and $x \in \omega_1$, this implies $\omega_2 \prec_{lex}^{\tau} \omega_1$, contradicting the initial assumption that $\omega_1 \prec_{lex}^{\tau} \omega_2$.

Then, let us demonstrate that if $\omega_1', \omega_2' \in Mod(\Phi')$ such that $\omega_1' \prec_{lex}^{\tau'} \omega_2'$, then $\omega_1 \prec_{lex}^{\tau} \omega_2$ with $\omega_1 = \omega_1' \cup \bigcup_{o \in \mathcal{O}} f(o, \omega_1')$ and $\omega_2 = \omega_2' \cup \bigcup_{o \in \mathcal{O}} f(o, \omega_2')$. The proof is straightforward and follows from the fact that τ is a compatible order.

To conclude this proof, let us demonstrate that if ω' is the k-th model of Φ' with respect to $\prec_{lex}^{\tau'}$, then $\omega = \omega' \cup \bigcup_{o \in \mathcal{O}} f(o, \omega')$, will be the k-th model of Φ. We will argue by contradiction and assume that ω is not the k-th model of Φ. This means ω is the j-th model of Φ where $j < k$ or $j > k$. First, consider the case where $j < k$. Let $\Omega' \subseteq Mod(\Phi')$ be the first k models of Φ'. By construction, all models in Ω' are disjoint, and by the definition of definability, each corresponds to exactly one model of Φ. Since $\omega_1' \prec_{lex}^{\tau'} \omega_2'$ implies $\omega_1 \prec_{lex}^{\tau} \omega_2$, the k-th model of Φ' cannot be associated with the j-th model of Φ where $j < k$, otherwise $|\Omega'| < k$. Now, consider the case where $j > k$. Let $\Omega \subseteq Mod(\Phi)$ be the first $j - 1$ models of Φ with respect to τ. Since τ is a compatible order, particularly Φ defines $\mathcal{O}$ in terms of $\mathcal{I}$, for all $\omega_1, \omega_2 \in \Omega$, the projected models ω_1' and ω_2' of ω_1 and ω_2 over $Var(\Phi')$ are such that $\omega_1' \neq \omega_2'$. Since $\omega_1 \prec_{lex}^{\tau} \omega_2$ implies $\omega_1' \prec_{lex}^{\tau'} \omega_2'$, there exist at least k models Ω'' of Φ' such that $\omega'' \prec_{lex} \omega'$ with $\omega'' \in \Omega''$. This contradicts the fact that ω' is the k-th model of Φ'.

It is important to note that, by leveraging the previous proposition, it is also possible to design a pseudo-uniform sampler that incorporates a seed as part of its operation. This capability is particularly valuable when determinism is required, as the seed allows the sampling process to be reproducible and consistent across different runs. Such a pseudo-uniform sampler can be employed in scenarios where repeatability is essential, such as debugging, benchmarking, or ensuring fairness in randomized processes.

In conclusion, when enumerating partial models, it is important to note that eliminating defined variables during preprocessing can create an exponential gap between the number of partial models in the original and simplified formulas. This is demonstrated in the following example, where the preprocessing step significantly reduces the formula but at the cost of losing information critical for partial model enumeration.

Example 10. Consider the CNF formula Φ representing the Boolean function $x \leftrightarrow \bigoplus_{i=1}^{n} y_i$. In this function, the variable x is fully determined by the parity of the variables $\{y_1, \ldots, y_n\}$. As such, during the preprocessing phase, x can be safely eliminated,

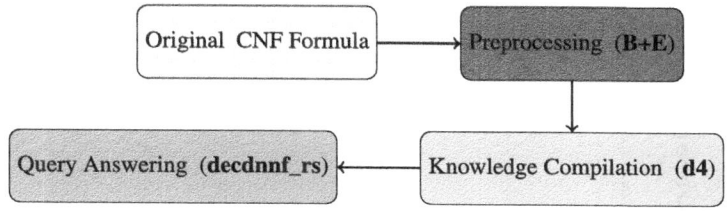

Fig. 1. Experimental pipeline for preprocessing, compilation, and query answering.

resulting in the simplified formula $\Phi' = \exists x.\Phi = \top$. A compact representation of Φ' is $\{\top\}$. However, this representation no longer encodes any partial models of the original formula Φ. Moreover, it is well known that the parity function $\neg x \oplus \bigoplus_{i=1}^{n} y_i$ does not admit a compact representation. Thus, there is an exponential gap between the number of partial models of Φ and those of Φ'.

4 Experimentation

To systematically evaluate the impact of the preprocessing methods outlined above on the efficiency of answering direct access, uniform sampling, and model enumeration queries, we conducted a series of experiments focused on runtime performance and scalability. The knowledge compiler **d4** (https://github.com/crillab/d4v2) served as the backbone for the d-DNNF compilation process, while preprocessing strategies were inspired and implemented based on features available in the **B+E** framework (https://github.com/crillab/b-plus-e. Our work also introduced new preprocessing techniques that emphasize fixed variable orderings, extending the capabilities of existing tools.

Implementation Pipeline. Our experimental pipeline, presented in Fig. 1, comprises the following stages:

- **Preprocessing:** The **B+E** [23] preprocessor is used to apply a suite of simplifications, including variable elimination and redundancy detection. Depending on the experimental setting, **B+E** is configured to operate in equivalence-preserving or model count-preserving modes, optionally enforcing a fixed variable ordering.
- **Knowledge Compilation:** The simplified CNF formula is compiled into a decision-DNNF using the **d4** [21] compiler. As previously discussed, our results apply to both decision-DNNF and general d-DNNF representations.
- **Query Answering:** For each compiled circuit, we answer direct access, uniform sampling, and model enumeration queries using the **decdnnf_rs** tool (https://crates.io/crates/decdnnf_rs, building on customized enumeration modules.

Preprocessing Strategies. We evaluated the following preprocessing configurations in our experiments:

- no: **d4** is run directly on the original formula, without preprocessing.

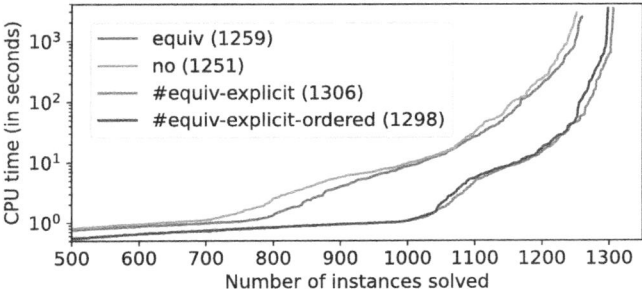

Fig. 2. Cactus plot showing the running time of **d4** with various preprocessing methods. Each line represents a different preprocessing method, with the number of instances solved indicated in parentheses in the legend. The plot displays the number of instances completed within a given CPU time limit, measured in seconds.

- equiv: The formula is preprocessed using vivification, backbone detection, and occurrence elimination.
- #equiv-explicit: In addition to the equiv preprocessing, explicitly defined variables are eliminated.
- #equiv-explicit-ordered: Builds on #equiv-explicit but enforces a compatible variable ordering τ; for our experiments, we select the natural order.

These strategies extend and customize the core functionalities of **B+E** to suit the requirements of our workflow.

Experimental Setup. All experiments were conducted on a cluster with dual quad-core Intel Xeon E5-2637 v4 CPUs (3.50 GHz)., 128 GiB RAM, and running CentOS 8 (kernel 4.18.0-301.1.el8.x86_64). Hyperthreading was disabled and no cache sharing between cores was permitted. Each run was constrained to 3,600 s of CPU time and 32GiB of memory. Compilation was performed with g++ version 13.2.0. We evaluated 1,425 benchmark instances from previous uniform sampling studies [26], available at https://github.com/meelgroup/KUS. All experimental logs and materials needed for reproducibility are provided at https://zenodo.org/records/15837216.

Results. Figure 2 presents a cactus plot that illustrates the impact of each preprocessing method on the performance of **d4**. This plot also shows the number of instances solved for each preprocessing method used. As observed, the preprocessing method that preserves equivalence, #equiv, is not particularly effective, as it provides only a marginal improvement in the performance of **d4**. Specifically, it enables the solver to handle only 8 additional instances compared to the version without preprocessing.

#equiv-explicit-ordered substantially enhances the performance of **d4**, enabling it to handle 47 more instances than the compiler without preprocessing. One of the key advantages of this method is that it supports answering direct access queries. Next, let us examine the preprocessing method #equiv-explicit. Notably, this method is able to solve 8 more instances than #equiv-explicit-ordered, demonstrating its enhanced effectiveness. Its flexibility lies in the fact that it does not

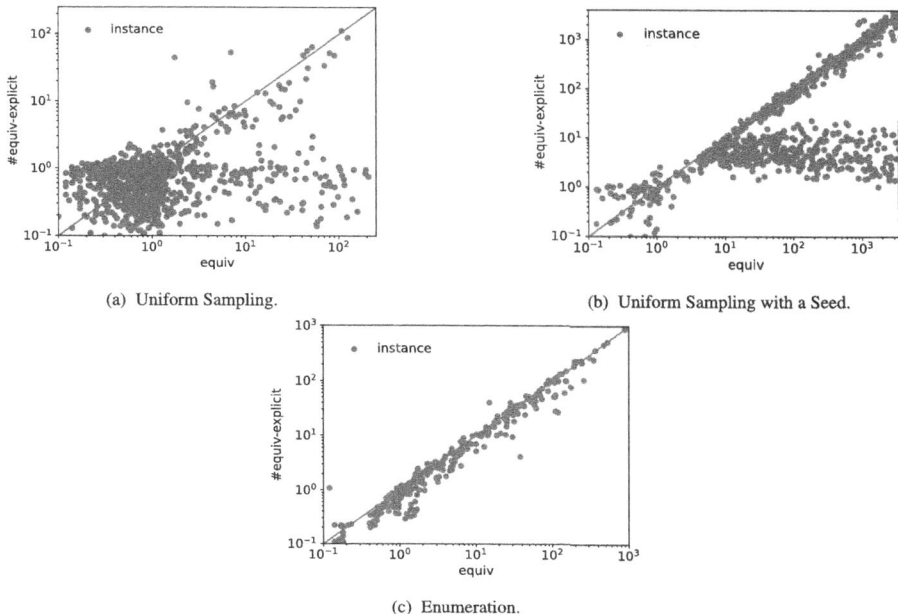

(a) Uniform Sampling.   (b) Uniform Sampling with a Seed.

(c) Enumeration.

Fig. 3. Comparison of CPU time for the tasks under consideration: uniform sampling, uniform sampling with a seed, and model enumeration. The d-DNNF representations analyzed were obtained using the preprocessing methods `equiv` and `#equiv-explicit` for uniform sampling and enumeration, and `equiv` and `#equiv-explicit-ordered` for uniform sampling with a seed.

require constraints on the ordering of variable assignments, making it particularly suitable for tasks such as model enumeration and uniform sampling.

Now, let us analyze the impact of preprocessing on the efficiency of answering the targeted queries. For uniform sampling and model enumeration queries, we focus the d-DNNF representations produced after applying the preprocessing methods `equiv` and `#equiv-explicit`. To assess the direct access query, we consider uniform sampling with a seed, which leverages the direct access query. For each instance and each query, a timeout of 3600 s and a memory limit of 32 GiB were imposed. It is important to note that this runtime does not include the compilation time.

Figure 3 displays three scatter plots comparing the running times of various d-DNNF representations across the three queries. Each data point corresponds to an instance, with the x-axis showing the time (in seconds) required to solve it using the d-DNNF formula obtained after applying the `equiv` preprocessing, and the y-axis showing the time needed when using the d-DNNF derived from preprocessings that eliminate defined variables. The experimental results clearly demonstrate that queries can be answered more efficiently using d-DNNF representations generated from formulas preprocessed with the `#equiv-explicit` based methods. Furthermore, the figures highlight instances where the `#equiv-explicit` based preprocessings achieve speeds up to an order of magnitude faster than the equiv preprocessing, irrespective of the query type.

We evaluate the impact of #equiv-explicit over equiv on uniform sampling runtimes (size 10,000). Figure 3a illustrates this analysis, which includes 1,255 instances from the 1,425 assessed in the previous experiment. Instances excluded are 51 that failed to compile with equiv, 4 with #equiv-explicit, and 115 where neither preprocessing method succeeded. As shown in the figure, #equiv-explicit generally outperforms equiv except for instances solvable in under 2 s. Most points lie above the diagonal, indicating faster uniform sampling queries when using #equiv-explicit. Moreover, memory limits were reached in 15 instances with equiv, compared to only 1 instance with #equiv-explicit, primarily due to the larger size of the d-DNNF generated under equiv.

For model enumeration queries, we consider instances with at least 10^4 models but fewer than 10^9 models, resulting in 367 instances solved by both approaches. Figure 3c highlights the benefits of using #equiv-explicit, which generally provides faster enumeration. However, the performance gains are less pronounced than for uniform sampling queries, as enumeration still requires generating all models, even when the d-DNNF simplifies to $\top$.

To conclude, we examine the deterministic uniform sampling query (size 10,000) results in Fig. 3b. This analysis considers 1,254 out of the 1,425 instances from the previous experiment. Instances excluded include 44 that failed to compile with equiv, 4 with #equiv-explicit-ordered, and 122 where neither method was successful. The d-DNNF produced by #equiv-explicit-ordered improves the manageability of uniform sampling with a seed, solving more instances and often one order of magnitude faster. Furthermore, #equiv-explicit-ordered significantly reduces timeouts, with only 173 compared to 391 for equiv.

5   Conclusion and Perspectives

We have investigated the potential of using preprocessing methods to enhance the efficiency of direct access, uniform sampling, and model enumeration queries. We show that, except for the preprocessing method that maintains equivalence, current state-of-the-art preprocessing techniques are unsuitable for these queries as they lead to incorrect results. However, we demonstrate that preprocessing techniques preserving the number of models can be effectively employed if information about the eliminated variables is retained. Our experimental evaluations clearly show that employing such preprocessing methods in practice is advantageous.

As a future direction, we intend to assess the preprocessing methods discussed in this paper on other advanced sampling techniques [6,15,27]. Since these approaches do not necessarily depend on model counting, different types of preprocessing methods might be leveraged. Another area for improvement involves exploring alternative kinds of explicit definitions. In this paper, we concentrated on explicit definitions expressed as equivalences, AND-gates, OR-gates, and XOR-gates, but it may be beneficial to explore other types of definitions, such as NOR and NAND gates.

Acknowledgments. We thank the reviewers for their insightful comments and constructive suggestions, which helped improve the quality of this paper. This work has benefited from the support of the AI Chair EXPEKCTATION (ANR-19-CHIA-0005-01) of the French National Research Agency (ANR).

References

1. Abiteboul, S., Hull, R., Vianu, V.: Foundations of Databases. Addison-Wesley (1995)
2. Bagan, G., Durand, A., Grandjean, E., Olive, F.: Computing the jth solution of a first-order query. RAIRO Theor. Inform. Appl. **42**(1), 147–164 (2008)
3. Biere, A., Järvisalo, M., Kiesl, B.: Preprocessing in SAT solving. In: Handbook of Satisfiability - Second Edition, vol. 336, pp. 391–435. IOS Press (2021)
4. Bringmann, K., Carmeli, N., Mengel, S.: Tight fine-grained bounds for direct access on join queries. In: Proceedings of PODS 2022, pp. 427–436 (2022)
5. Carmeli, N., Tziavelis, N., Gatterbauer, W., Kimelfeld, B., Riedewald, M.: Tractable orders for direct access to ranked answers of conjunctive queries. ACM Trans. Database Syst. **48**(1), 1:1–1:45 (2023)
6. Chakraborty, S., Meel, K.S., Vardi, M.Y.: A scalable and nearly uniform generator of SAT witnesses. In: Proceedings of CAV 2013, pp. 608–623 (2013)
7. Darwiche, A.: A compiler for deterministic, decomposable negation normal form. In: Proceedings of AAAI 2002, pp. 627–634 (2002)
8. Darwiche, A.: New advances in compiling CNF into decomposable negation normal form. In: Proceedings of ECAI 2004, pp. 328–332 (2004)
9. Darwiche, A.: Logic for explainable AI. In: LICS 2023, pp. 1–11 (2023)
10. Fargier, H., Marquis, P.: On the use of partially ordered decision graphs in knowledge compilation and quantified Boolean formulae. In: Proceedings of AAAI 2006, pp. 42–47 (2006)
11. Fikes, R., Nilsson, N.J.: STRIPS: a new approach to the application of theorem proving to problem solving. Artif. Intell. 189–208 (1971)
12. Heule, M.J.H., Seidl, M., Biere, A.: Solution validation and extraction for QBF preprocessing. J. Autom. Reason. **58**(1), 97–125 (2017)
13. Järvisalo, M., Biere, A., Heule, M.: Blocked clause elimination. In: Esparza, J., Majumdar, R. (eds.) TACAS 2010. LNCS, vol. 6015, pp. 129–144. Springer, Heidelberg (2010). https://doi.org/10.1007/978-3-642-12002-2_10
14. Jerrum, M., Valiant, L.G., Vazirani, V.V.: Random generation of combinatorial structures from a uniform distribution. Theor. Comput. Sci. **43**, 169–188 (1986)
15. Jordan, M.I., Ghahramani, Z., Jaakkola, T.S., Saul, L.K.: An introduction to variational methods for graphical models. Mach. Learn. **37**(2), 183–233 (1999)
16. Kiesel, R., Eiter, T.: Knowledge compilation and more with sharpSAT-TD. In: Proceedings of KR 2023, pp. 406–416 (2023)
17. Lagniez, J., Lonca, E.: Leveraging decision-dnnf compilation for enumerating disjoint partial models. In: KR 2024 (2024)
18. Lagniez, J., Lonca, E., Marquis, P.: Improving model counting by leveraging definability. In: Proceedings of IJCAI 2016, pp. 751–757 (2016)
19. Lagniez, J., Lonca, E., Marquis, P.: Definability for model counting. Artif. Intell. **281**, 103229 (2020)
20. Lagniez, J., Marquis, P.: Preprocessing for propositional model counting. In: Proceedings of AAAI 2014, pp. 2688–2694 (2014)
21. Lagniez, J., Marquis, P.: An improved decision-DNNF compiler. In: Proceedings of IJCAI 2017, pp. 667–673 (2017)

22. Lagniez, J., Marquis, P.: On preprocessing techniques and their impact on propositional model counting. J. Autom. Reason. **58**(4), 413–481 (2017)
23. Lagniez, J., Marquis, P.: Boosting definability bipartition computation using SAT witnesses. In: Proceedings of JELIA 2023, pp. 697–711 (2023)
24. Muise, C., McIlraith, S.A., Beck, J.C., Hsu, E.I.: DSHARP: fast d-DNNF compilation with sharpSAT. In: Kosseim, L., Inkpen, D. (eds.) AI 2012. LNCS (LNAI), vol. 7310, pp. 356–361. Springer, Heidelberg (2012). https://doi.org/10.1007/978-3-642-30353-1_36
25. Piette, C., Hamadi, Y., Sais, L.: Vivifying propositional clausal formulae. In: Proceedings of ECAI 2008, pp. 525–529 (2008)
26. Sharma, S., Gupta, R., Roy, S., Meel, K.S.: Knowledge compilation meets uniform sampling. In: Proceedings of LPAR 2022, vol. 57, pp. 620–636 (2018)
27. Sinclair, A., Jerrum, M.: Approximate counting, uniform generation and rapidly mixing Markov chains. Inf. Comput. **82**(1), 93–133 (1989)
28. Soos, M., Meel, K.S.: Arjun: an efficient independent support computation technique and its applications to counting and sampling. In: Proceedings of ICCAD 2022, pp. 71:1–71:9 (2022)
29. Soos, M., Meel, K.S.: Engineering an efficient preprocessor for model counting. In: DAC 2024, pp. 108:1–108:6 (2024)
30. Subbarayan, S., Pradhan, D.K.: NiVER: non increasing variable elimination resolution for preprocessing SAT instances. In: Proceedings of SAT 2004 (2004)
31. Zhang, L., Madigan, C.F., Moskewicz, M.W., Malik, S.: Efficient conflict driven learning in Boolean satisfiability solver. In: Proceedings of ICCAD 2001, pp. 279–285 (2001)

Explanations of Unsatisfiability Beyond Minimal Subsets

Pablo Martínez-Naredo[1] , Raúl Mencía[1] , Joao Marques-Silva[2] ,
and Carlos Mencía[1](✉)

[1] University of Oviedo, Gijón, Spain
{martineznpablo,menciaraul,menciacarlos}@uniovi.es
[2] ICREA and University of Lleida, Lleida, Spain
jpms@icrea.cat

Abstract. The analysis of unsatisfiable propositional formulas is crucial across a wide range of application domains. While minimal unsatisfiable subsets (MUSes) are standard explanations in this setting, gaining a clear understanding of the underlying reasons for unsatisfiability is often difficult when relying solely on them. As an alternative form of explanation, this paper investigates the practical application of power indices to measure the importance of clauses and variables in the inconsistency of a formula. Power indices were originally proposed in game theory to quantify the relative importance of voters in weighted voting games, and their use has been proposed in a variety of areas, including explainability and as measures of inconsistency for knowledge bases. To enable practical computation, this paper introduces a SAT-based approach to approximate the Shapley-Shubik power index. Our approach leverages a probabilistic algorithm with theoretical guarantees and incorporates optimization techniques to significantly improve performance. Experimental results demonstrate the suitability of the proposed algorithm.

Keywords: unsatisfiability analysis · measures of importance

1 Introduction

The analysis of inconsistency has been the subject of research since at least the early 1980s [21, 27, 30, 77], with contributions ever since [14, 20].

In this context, two central tasks arise [58]: explaining the reasons for the observed inconsistency and correcting it. These tasks have been widely studied, especially in the case of unsatisfiable propositional formulas in conjunctive normal form (CNF). In this scenario, explanations are typically given as *minimal unsatisfiable subsets* (MUSes), whereas corrections correspond to *minimal correction subsets* (MCSes). Consequently, a wealth of algorithms have been proposed for MUS extraction [2,3,5,8,16,21,33,40,56,64], MCS extraction [1,4,32,54,61,63,66], MCS enumeration [10,31,54,65,70] and MUS enumeration [4,9,50–52,68]. Beyond these core tasks, related topics include MUS membership [39], variable-MUSes [7], smallest MUSes [38], union of MUSes [41,46,62] or counting MUSes and MCSes [11–13], among others [47,48,55–57,60].

G. Casini et al. (Eds.): JELIA 2025, LNAI 16094, pp. 141–158, 2026.
https://doi.org/10.1007/978-3-032-04590-4_10

Another related topic is analyzing the degree of the inconsistency of knowledge bases by means of so-called *inconsistency measures* [28,29,34,43–46], some of which are based on MUSes/MCSes.

A well-known downside of enumerating MUSes is their worst-case exponential number, which often hinders a clear understanding of the reasons for inconsistency. As an alternative form of explanation, this paper explores assigning a *measure of importance* to each component of an unsatisfiable formula. The primary objective is, therefore, to quantify the individual influence of each formula component on its global unsatisfiability. Specifically, the paper studies the application of *power indices* [26], such as the Shapley-Shubik index, among others, to quantify the relative importance of clauses and variables in the unsatisfiability of a CNF formula. Originating in weighted voting games, these indices provide an aggregated, quantitative view of influence. While the use of Shapley values for quantifying inconsistency has been explored, albeit mostly theoretically, in prior work on inconsistency measures [35,36] and related frameworks [71], our focus is on developing practical algorithms.

To achieve this, we introduce a SAT-based approach that rigorously approximates the Shapley-Shubik index. Our method leverages the sampling-based CGT algorithm [17], which offers strong theoretical guarantees on the approximation quality. The proposed method incorporates several optimization techniques to significantly improve performance. Moreover, we broaden the practical utility of this approach to aggregate the information provided by a collection of MUSes. This is valuable in scenarios where direct approximation of the Shapley-Shubik index is infeasible, but partial MUS enumeration can still be performed.

The paper is organized as follows. Section 2 introduces the notation and necessary background. Section 3 describes how game theory can be applied in the analysis of unsatisfiable CNF formulas. Section 4 presents the proposed SAT-based approach for estimating the Shapley-Shubik index in this setting. Section 5 discusses the aggregation of a set of MUSes. Section 6 presents preliminary experimental results. The paper concludes in Sect. 7.

2   Preliminaries

2.1   Boolean Satisfiability

We consider propositional formulas in Conjunctive Normal Form (CNF), defined over a set of variables $\text{var}(\mathcal{F}) = \{x_1, ..., x_n\}$ as a conjunction (or set) of clauses $\mathcal{F} = \{c_1, ..., c_m\}$, where a clause is a disjunction (or set) of literals, and a literal is a variable x or its negation $\neg x$. Also, $\text{var}(c_i)$ is the set of variables in c_i.

A truth assignment, or interpretation, is a mapping $\mu : \text{var}(\mathcal{F}) \to \{0, 1\}$. We say μ is a model of $\mathcal{F}$ if it satisfies $\mathcal{F}$, denoted $\mu \models \mathcal{F}$. The formula $\mathcal{F}$ entails $\mathcal{G}$, written $\mathcal{F} \models \mathcal{G}$, if and only if all the models of $\mathcal{F}$ are models of $\mathcal{G}$. A formula $\mathcal{F}$ is satisfiable if it has at least one model, i.e. $\mathcal{F} \not\models \bot$, and it is unsatisfiable otherwise, i.e., $\mathcal{F} \models \bot$. The Boolean Satisfiability (SAT) problem consists in determining whether a given formula is satisfiable or not. SAT is NP-complete [22].

We focus on unsatisfiable formulas, where the following notion applies:

Definition 1 (MUS). $\mathcal{M} \subseteq \mathcal{F}$ *is a* minimal unsatisfiable subset *(MUS) if and only if* $\mathcal{M} \models \bot$ *and for all* $\mathcal{M}' \subsetneq \mathcal{M}$, $\mathcal{M}' \nvDash \bot$.

An MUS $\mathcal{M}$ provides an explanation for the unsatisfiability of $\mathcal{F}$. A related concept is that of *minimal correction subset* (MCS). An MCS is a minimal subset of the clauses whose removal renders the formula satisfiable. Every MUS is a minimal hitting set of the set of MCSes and vice versa [15,72]. In addition, there can be a worst-case exponential number of MUSes and MCSes [53][1].

A clause $c \in \mathcal{F}$ is said *relevant*, or *potentially necessary* [47], if and only if it belongs to some MUS $\mathcal{M} \subseteq \mathcal{F}$. Determining if a given clause is relevant is a Σ_2^P-complete problem [49]. The union of MUSes, $\texttt{UMU}(\mathcal{F})$, is the set of all relevant clauses, and it represents a concise summary of all the causes of inconsistency.

The *lean kernel* of $\mathcal{F}$ is a closely related concept [42]. The lean kernel is the set of clauses that are used in some resolution refutation of $\mathcal{F}$, and it contains the union of MUSes. Consequently, any clause outside the lean kernel is irrelevant for the unsatisfiability of the formula. The lean kernel can be alternatively defined in terms of autarkies. An *autarky* is a set of variables $A \subseteq \texttt{var}(\mathcal{F})$ for which there exists a truth assignment that satisfies all the clauses in $\mathcal{F}$ containing literals in the variables of A. There exists a unique largest autarky, and it can be computed using a polynomial number of invocations to an NP oracle w.r.t. the number of variables [48,55]. Then, the lean kernel is computed by removing from $\mathcal{F}$ all the clauses containing some literal in the variables of the largest autarky.

The definitions above can be reformulated in terms of the variables of the formula, instead of its clauses. To this aim, $\mathcal{F}|_V$ denotes the formula induced by set of variables $V \subseteq \texttt{var}(\mathcal{F})$. This formula is obtained by removing from $\mathcal{F}$ all the clauses that contain a literal in a variable not included in the set V. Then, explanations are defined in terms of variables as follows [7,19]:

Definition 2 (VMUS). $V_M \subseteq \textit{var}(\mathcal{F})$ *is a* variable-MUS *(VMUS) if and only if* $\mathcal{F}|_{V_M} \models \bot$ *and for all* $V_M' \subsetneq V_M$, $\mathcal{F}|_{V_M'} \nvDash \bot$.

Example 1. Consider $\mathcal{F}_{ex} = \{c_1 \colon (x_1), c_2 \colon (\neg x_1), c_3 \colon (\neg x_1 \vee x_2), c_4 \colon (\neg x_2), c_5 \colon (x_2 \vee x_3), c_6 \colon (\neg x_3), c_7 \colon (\neg x_3 \vee \neg x_2), c_8 \colon (\neg x_4 \vee \neg x_1)\}$. The largest autarky is $A = \{x_4\}$, and so the lean kernel of $\mathcal{F}_{ex}$ is $\{c_1, ..., c_7\}$. There are 3 MUSes: $\mathcal{M}_1 = \{c_1, c_2\}$, $\mathcal{M}_2 = \{c_1, c_3, c_4\}$ and $\mathcal{M}_3 = \{c_4, c_5, c_6\}$. Their union is $\texttt{UMU}(\mathcal{F}_{ex}) = \{c_1, ..., c_6\}$. Finally, $\mathcal{F}_{ex}$ has 2 VMUSes: $V_1 = \{x_1\}$ and $V_2 = \{x_2, x_3\}$.

---

[1] The results in this paper can be generalized to cases where formulas are partitioned as $\mathcal{F} = (\mathcal{B}, \mathcal{S})$, where $\mathcal{B}$ represents *background* knowledge, i.e., *hard* clauses that must be satisfied, and $\mathcal{S}$ is a set of *soft* clauses. In such setting, MUSes and MCSes are subsets of $\mathcal{S}$. For simplicity of presentation, we consider *plain* formulas, where all the clauses are soft.

2.2   Cooperative Games and Power Indices

In cooperative game theory, players form coalitions to achieve a common goal.

A cooperative game is defined by a pair (N, v), where N is a set of players and $v : 2^N \to \mathbb{R}$ is its characteristic function. This function assigns a value to every subset (coalition) $S \subseteq N$ of players, representing its worth [18].

We will focus on simple games, where the characteristic function is defined as $v : 2^N \to \{0, 1\}$ and it must satisfy three properties: $v(\emptyset) = 0$, $v(N) = 1$, and for all $W \subseteq S \subseteq N$, $v(W) \leq v(S)$ (known as monotonicity). If $v(S) = 1$, S is a winning coalition; otherwise, S is a losing coalition. Furthermore, a minimal winning coalition is a winning coalition such that all its proper subsets are losing coalitions. Throughout, $\mathbb{M}$ denotes the set of all minimal winning coalitions, and $\mathbb{M}_i$, the set of minimal winning coalitions containing player i.

A common example is a weighted voting game (WVG). In this context, N is a set of voters. Each voter $i \in N$ has a non-negative value $w_i \in \mathbb{R}$. Besides, there is a quota q with $q \leq \sum_{i \in N} w_i$. A winning coalition $S \subseteq N$ is such that $\sum_{i \in S} w_i \geq q$. Thus, the characteristic function for a WVG is defined as $v(S) := \text{ITE}(\text{WinC}(S), 1, 0)$, where ITE is the IF-THEN-ELSE operator, and WinC is a predicate that holds true if and only if S is a winning coalition.

Example 2. The notation $[7; 5, 5, 2, 1]$ summarizes a WVG, with a quota of 7, and four voters, each having respectively 5, 5, 2, and 1 votes. The subset $\{1, 3, 4\}$ is a winning coalition, whereas $\{1, 3\}$ is a minimal winning coalition. In contrast, $\{1, 4\}$ is a losing coalition.

Since the 1940s [67], researchers have been interested in measures of relative importance of voters in weighted voting games. These measures are known as *power indices* [26]. Prominent examples include the Shapley-Shubik [74], Banzhaf [6] and Deegan-Packel [23] indices.

For a voter $i \in N$ and a coalition $S \subseteq N$, the marginal contribution of voter i is $\Delta_i(S) := v(S) - v(S \setminus \{i\})$. Generally, a power index, $\text{Im}(i)$, is defined as a weighted sum of these marginal contributions across all coalitions $S \subseteq N$:

$$\text{Im}(i) \quad := \quad \sum_{S \subseteq N} \varsigma(S) \times \Delta_i(S) \tag{1}$$

The specific definition of ς depends on the power index considered.

3   Unsatisfiability Games

We aim to determine the importance of clauses or variables in the unsatisfiability of a propositional formula. To do this, we will first define two simple games where either clauses or variables form coalitions seeking unsatisfiability. We will then apply measures of importance based on power indices within these settings.

Clauses. For clauses, we define $N = \mathcal{F}$ (the set of all clauses in the formula) and the characteristic function:

$$v_{cls}(S) \quad := \quad \text{ITE}(\neg\text{SAT}(S), 1, 0) \tag{2}$$

This function is based on the predicate $\neg\text{SAT}(S)$, which is true if and only if the clause set $S \subseteq N$ is unsatisfiable. This predicate is monotonically increasing, as any superset of an unsatisfiable set of clauses is also unsatisfiable. Furthermore, the minimal sets over this predicate (which correspond to the minimal winning coalitions in this game) are precisely the set of MUSes of $\mathcal{F}$ [57].

Variables. We define $N = \text{var}(\mathcal{F})$, and the caracteristic function:

$$v_{var}(S) \quad := \quad \text{ITE}(\neg\text{SAT}(\mathcal{F}|_S), 1, 0) \tag{3}$$

Here, the predicate $\neg\text{SAT}(\mathcal{F}|_S)$ is true if and only if the formula induced by the set of variables $S \subseteq N$ is unsatisfiable. This predicate is also monotone: if a set of variables induces an unsatisfiable formula, any superset of those variables will also induce an unsatisfiable formula, since the latter formula contains the former. The minimal winning coalitions in this game are the VMUSes of $\mathcal{F}$.

3.1   Measures of Importance for Unsatisfiability

Power indices can be generalized to settings where the characteristic function is defined by a monotonically increasing predicate P. This led to the introduction of *Uninstantiated Measures of Importance* (UMIs) [59].

In this context, the characteristic function is $v(S) := \text{ITE}(P(S), 1, 0)$, with $S \subseteq N$. Since P is monotone, (N, v) forms a simple game. The marginal contribution $\Delta_i(S)$ is always 0 or 1. Specifically, $\Delta_i(S) = 1$ if and only if both $v(S) = 1$ and $v(S \setminus \{i\}) = 0$.

An element $i \in N$ is critical for a set $S \subseteq N$ if the condition $P(S) \wedge \neg P(S \setminus \{i\})$ holds. This condition is captured by the predicate $\text{Crit}_s(i, S)$. It is clear that $\Delta_i(S) = 1$ if and only if i is critical for S.

An (uninstantiated) measure of importance (UMI), denoted as $\text{Im} : N \to \mathbb{R}$, maps elements to real values, quantifying their importance. We consider three specific UMIs: Shapley-Shubik (Im_S) [74], Banzhaf (Im_B) [6], and Deegan-Packel (Im_D) [23]. They are defined as follows:

$$\text{Im}_S(i) := \sum\nolimits_{S \subseteq N \wedge \text{Crit}_s(i,S)} \left(1 / \left(|N| \times \binom{|N| - 1}{|S| - 1} \right) \right)$$

$$\text{Im}_B(i) := \sum\nolimits_{S \subseteq N \wedge \text{Crit}_s(i,S)} \left(1/2^{|N|-1} \right)$$

$$\text{Im}_D(i) := \sum\nolimits_{S \in \mathbb{M}_i} \left(1/(|S| \times |\mathbb{M}|) \right)$$

While Im_S and Im_D naturally sum to 1, Im_B can optionally be normalized [24] to achieve this property. This normalized version is denoted Im_{Bn}.

The Shapley-Shubik index for $i \in N$ is the proportion of permutations of N where i is *pivotal*. An element is pivotal if it is the first element that together with the preceeding ones in the permutation causes the predicate to hold. The Banzhaf UMI quantifies the importance of $i \in N$ by the fraction of times it is critical across all subsets containing a critical element. In contrast, the Deegan-Packel index focuses on the minimal winning coalitions that contain i.

Table 1. Measures of importance for clauses in Example 1

	Clauses							
	c_1	c_2	c_3	c_4	c_5	c_6	c_7	c_8
$\mathsf{Im}_S(i)$	0.35	0.22	0.05	0.18	0.10	0.10	0.00	0.00
$\mathsf{Im}_B(i)$	0.74	0.48	0.13	0.39	0.22	0.22	0.00	0.00
$\mathsf{Im}_{Bn}(i)$	0.34	0.22	0.06	0.18	0.10	0.10	0.00	0.00
$\mathsf{Im}_D(i)$	0.28	0.17	0.11	0.22	0.11	0.11	0.00	0.00

These measures can be applied to the two simple games defined earlier in this section, thus quantifying the importance of clauses or variables for the unsatisfiability of a given formula.

Example 3. Table 1 shows the measures of importance for clauses in $\mathcal{F}_{ex}$ (Example 1), rounded to two decimal places. Recall that $\mathcal{F}_{ex}$ has three MUSes: $\mathcal{M}_1 = \{c_1, c_2\}$, $\mathcal{M}_2 = \{c_1, c_3, c_4\}$ and $\mathcal{M}_3 = \{c_4, c_5, c_6\}$. Both Shapley-Shubik and Banzhaf yield the same ranking: c_1, c_2, c_4 in the top three positions. Clauses c_5 and c_6 follow with equal importance, then c_3, and finally c_7 and c_8 with an index of 0, indicating their irrelevance. Deegan-Packel, however, assigns more importance to clause c_4 than to c_2. Additionally, c_3 is assigned the same importance as c_5 and c_6.

In this paper, we focus on the Shapley-Shubik power index. This power index results from the application of the Shapley value [73] to weighted voting games, and it is unique in satisfying the following four axioms: Efficiency, symmetry, null player and linearity. First, efficiency means that the sum of all power indices across players equals 1. Symmetry, also known as *equal treatment of equals*, states that players with identical contributions to all winning coalitions have the same power index. The null player axiom dictates that the power index of a player that is not necessary for any winning coalition is 0. Finally, linearity ensures that if two games are combined, the power index of each player in the combined game is the sum of its power indices in the original games.

4   Estimating Shapley-Shubik for Unsatisfiability

The Shapley-Shubik power index exhibits a number of desirable theoretical properties. However, computing exact Shapley values is generally $\#P$-hard, even

---

Algorithm 1: The CGT algorithm ([17])

Input: N, v, α, ϵ
Output: $\hat{\mathsf{lm}}_S$

1   Determine *nsamples* from α and ϵ;
2    $iter \leftarrow 0$; $\hat{\mathsf{lm}}_S(i) \leftarrow 0$ for all $i \in N$;
3   **while** $iter < nsamples$ **do**
4   Select $\tau \in \pi(N)$ with probability $1/|N|!$;
5   **foreach** $i \in N$ **do**
6          $\Delta_i(\tau) \leftarrow v(\texttt{Pre}^i(\tau) \cup \{i\}) - v(\texttt{Pre}^i(\tau))$;
7          $\hat{\mathsf{lm}}_S(i) \leftarrow \hat{\mathsf{lm}}_S(i) + \Delta_i(\tau)$;
8       $iter \leftarrow iter + 1$;
9    $\hat{\mathsf{lm}}_S(i) \leftarrow \hat{\mathsf{lm}}_S(i)/nsamples$ for all $i \in N$;
10   **return** $\hat{\mathsf{lm}}_S$;

---

when evaluating the characteristic function is easy. Therefore, approximation methods are usually the only feasible option.

A well-known approach for this purpose is `ApproShapley` [17], an algorithm designed to estimate Shapley values, which we refer to as CGT (after its authors). In our context of simple games, this algorithm estimates the Shapley-Shubik index. This algorithm is based on sampling, and it provides reliable estimations in polynomial time, provided that the characteristic function can be evaluated efficiently. In the analysis of unsatisfiability, evaluations are expensive, so a careful adaptation is necessary for practical efficiency.

4.1 The CGT Algorithm

Given a game (N, v) and parameters $\alpha, \epsilon \in (0, 1)$, CGT computes an estimation of $\mathsf{lm}_S = (\mathsf{lm}_S(1), ..., \mathsf{lm}_S(n))$, referred to as $\hat{\mathsf{lm}}_S = (\hat{\mathsf{lm}}_S(1), ..., \hat{\mathsf{lm}}_S(n))$.

Its pseudocode is shown in Algorithm 1. The algorithm guarantees that the absolute error is bounded by ϵ with a probability of at least $1 - \alpha$, i.e., $P(|\hat{\mathsf{lm}}_S(i) - \mathsf{lm}_S(i)| \leq \epsilon) \geq 1 - \alpha$. It iteratively samples random permutations of N. For every sampled permutation $\tau \in \pi(N)$, it calculates the marginal contribution $\Delta_i(\tau)^2$ of each element $i \in N$ relative to its precedessors in the sequence, denoted $\texttt{Pre}^i(\tau)$. This value is then accumulated in $\hat{\mathsf{lm}}_S(i)$. Finally, the accumulated values are divided by the number of samples, providing the final estimation.

The number of samples must satisfy $nsamples \geq Z_{\alpha/2}^2 \sigma^2 \epsilon$, where $Z_{\alpha/2}^2$ is the value such that $P(Z \geq Z_{\alpha/2}^2) = \alpha/2$ for a standard normal random variable $Z \sim \mathcal{N}(0, 1)$. As the variance σ^2 is not known, the upper bound $(\max_{S \subseteq N} v(S) - \min_{S \subseteq N} v(S))/4$ is used instead. In simple games, the upper bound is $1/4$, since $v(S)$ is either 0 or 1 for any $S \subseteq N$. The resulting sample size grows polynomially as α and ϵ decrease, and it does not depend on $|N|$.

---

[2] We use $\Delta_i(\tau)$ as a shorthand for $\Delta_i(\texttt{Pre}^i(\tau) \cup \{i\})$.

4.2 SAT-Based Approach

CGT can be instantiated to measure the importance of clauses and variables in the unsatisfiability of a formula, by defining N and υ appropriately.

As discussed earlier, in both cases the characteristic function is monotonically increasing. Consequently, for any given permutation τ, all the marginal contributions $\Delta_i(\tau)$ will be 0, except for exactly one element $p \in N$, for which $\Delta_p(\tau) = 1$. This element p is the pivotal element (given τ), and it is such that $\upsilon(\texttt{Pre}^p(\tau)) = 0$ and $\upsilon(\texttt{Pre}^p(\tau) \cup \{p\}) = 1$. That is, adding p to its predecessors makes the set to be a winning coalition. This property enables replacing the inner loop of Algorithm 1 (lines 5–7) with a search for the pivotal element in the given permutation, potentially reducing the number of characteristic function evaluations. In addition, these evaluations require the use of a SAT solver.

Characteristic Function Evaluations. To optimize performance, our approach makes extensive use of incremental SAT solving [25] in the evaluation of the characteristic functions. Concretely, a single instance of a SAT solver is used across different invocations. Initially, the SAT solver is provided with a formula, denoted as $\mathcal{F}_{inc}$, that depends on whether we are considering the case of clauses or variables. Then, in each invocation, different subsets of clauses or variables are selected using assumption literals associated with the elements of N.

Clauses. From the formula $\mathcal{F}$ we build $\mathcal{F}_{inc}$ as follows: For each clause $c_i \in \mathcal{F}$, we add the clause $sc_i \rightarrow c_i$ to $\mathcal{F}_{inc}$, where sc_i is a selector variable associated with c_i. To test the satisfiability of a formula $\mathcal{G} \subseteq \mathcal{F}$, the SAT solver is invoked on $\mathcal{F}_{inc}$ with the assumption literals $\{sc_i \mid c_i \in \mathcal{G}\}$.

Variables. Given the formula $\mathcal{F}$, we introduce a selector variable sx_i associated to each variable $x_i \in \texttt{var}(\mathcal{F})$. Then, for every $c_i \in \mathcal{F}$ we add the clause $(\bigwedge_{x_i \in \texttt{var}(c_i)} sx_i) \rightarrow c_i$ to $\mathcal{F}_{inc}$. For any set $V \subseteq \texttt{var}(\mathcal{F})$, the satisfiability of $\mathcal{F}|_V$ is determined by setting the assumptions $\{sx_i \mid x_i \in V\}$.

Searching for Pivotal Elements. Our approach searches for the pivotal element within each sampled permutation τ of N. We instantiate three general strategies for this purpose: insertion [76], deletion [21] and binary search [33]. We also incorporate optimizations to improve performance.

Throughout, υ represents the characteristic function for either clauses (υ_{cls}) or variables (υ_{var}). Additionaly, τ_i denotes the i-th element of the permutation, and $T_i = \{\tau_1, ..., \tau_i\}$ is the set of elements up to τ_i. Furthermore $\mathcal{F}(S)$ denotes the formula determined by the set of elements $S \subseteq N$, which means S itself if S is a set of clauses, or $\mathcal{F}|_S$ if S is a set of variables.

Search Strategies.   The `Insertion` approach traverses τ from left to right. At step i, if $\upsilon(T_i) = 0$ (i.e., $\mathcal{F}(T_i)$ is satisfiable), it continues to the next element. Otherwise, τ_i is identified as the pivotal element.

In contrast, `Deletion` iteratively discards elements from the right of τ. It continues as long as $\upsilon(T_{|N|-i}) = 1$ (that is, $\mathcal{F}(T_{|N|-i})$ is unsatisfiable). When $\upsilon(T_{|N|-i}) = 0$, then τ_{i+1} is determined to be the pivotal element.

While both approaches require worst case $|N| - 1$ evaluations of the characteristic function, the `BinarySearch` strategy significatly reduces this to $\mathcal{O}(\log(|N|))$. This algorithm maintains the indices l and r, such that $v(T_l) = 0$ and $v(T_r) = 1$. Initially $(l, r) = (0, |N|)$. In each iteration, it checks the middle position $m = \lfloor (l + r)/2 \rfloor$. If $v(T_m) = 0$, l is set to m. Otherwise, r becomes m. The algorithm terminates when $l = r - 1$, returning τ_r as the pivotal element.

Optimization Techniques. The algorithms above only consider whether $v(T_i)$ is 0 or 1, that is, if $\mathcal{F}(T_i)$ is satisfiable or not. However, modern SAT solvers provide additional information that can significantly reduce the number of evaluations.

The first technique exploits models returned by the SAT solver for satisfiable formulas and can be used to speed up `Insertion` and `BinarySearch`. If $\mathcal{F}(T_i)$ is satisfiable, the solver returns a model μ. This model might also satisfy subsequent formulas $\mathcal{F}(T_{i+1})$, $\mathcal{F}(T_{i+2})$, etc. We can then efficiently check if μ satisfies those formulas. The first $\mathcal{F}(T_k)$ not satisfied by μ points to a tighter lower bound for the pivotal element, i.e., τ_k, potentially skipping multiple SAT solver calls.

The second technique involves the use of unsatisfiable cores, and it can be integrated into `Deletion` and `BinarySearch`. If $\mathcal{F}(T_i)$ is unsatisfiable, the SAT solver returns an unsatisfiable core, which is a subset $U \subseteq T_i$ such that $\mathcal{F}(U)$ is unsatisfiable as well. Let τ_k be the last element in τ that is contained in U. Then, it holds that $\mathcal{F}(T_k)$ is unsatisfiable as well, since $U \subseteq T_k$ and U is unsatisfiable. This implies that the pivotal element must be at or before τ_k, providing a tighter upper bound for its position.

Exploiting the Lean Kernel. Our final enhancement consists in computing the lean kernel of the formula $\mathcal{F}$ and using this simplified formula instead. This brings two potential advantages: it reduces the number of SAT solver calls for finding pivotal elements, and it simplifies each invocation due to its smaller size.

Beyond efficiency, the lean kernel provides a significant theoretical benefit. Any clause or variable not included in the lean kernel can be definitely declared irrelevant, i.e., its Shapley value is exactly zero. This mitigates a limitation of CGT, in which an approximation of zero does not confirm irrelevance. Importantly, the Shapley values for elements within the lean kernel remain identical to those in the original formula.

To compute the lean kernel we use an approach from [55]. We first find the largest autarky of $\mathcal{F}$ by computing the unique maximal model of the encoding Γ_3, using a linear search approach [4,54]. The lean kernel is then computed by removing all clauses containing a variable in the largest autarky.

5 Partial Explanations from Sets of (V)MUSes

Although polynomial, the number of samples required by CGT can quickly become practically infeasible. For instance, guaranteeing $\alpha = 0.05$ and $\epsilon = 0.001$ requires almost one million samples, which may be out of reach when dealing with computationally hard formulas.

Nevertheless, current technology allows for partial enumeration of MUSes, or even their full enumeration if their total number is not excessively large, e.g., [9,50–52,68]. In these situations, understanding the underlying causes of unsatisfiability by inspecting these sets may not be a trivial task.

We propose using measures of importance to synthesize the information provided by a set of MUSes. A set of MUSes represents an approximation of the unsatisfiability of the formula. This approximation operates as follows: if a set of clauses contains an MUS included in the given set, it is unsatisfiable; if it does not, we treat the set as satisfiable, even though we cannot affirm it unless the entire set of MUSes is available. Notably, checking if a set of clauses contains an MUS out of a given set can be done in time polynomial in the number of MUSes provided in the set.

This applies to VMUSes as well. For a unified presentation, we consider a simple game (N, v), where N and v are appropriately defined for each case. Accordingly, $\mathbb{M}$ will represent the set of all minimal winning coalitions (either all MUSes or all VMUSes), and $\mathbb{X} \subseteq \mathbb{M}$ a subset of $\mathbb{M}$. Consider the following characteristic function (notice it is parameterized by the set $\mathbb{X}$), where $S \subseteq N$:

$$v_{\mathbb{X}}(S) \quad := \quad \text{ITE}(\exists M \in \mathbb{X} : M \subseteq S), 1, 0) \tag{4}$$

Measures of importance, like the Shapley-Shubik index, can be computed using the function $v_{\mathbb{X}}$, providing users an aggregated view of the minimal sets they have. While the accuracy of these measures in approximating the true values for the formula depends on the specific set $\mathbb{X}$, the following is guaranteed.

Proposition 1. *Let $S \subseteq N$. If $v_{\mathbb{X}}(S) = 1$, then $v(S) = 1$.*

Proof. By definition, if $v_{\mathbb{X}}(S) = 1$ there exist a minimal winning coalition contained in S. Thus, S is a winning coalition and $v(S) = 1$.

As a consequence, no irrelevant element will be assigned an importance greater than 0. Furthermore, if the entire set $\mathbb{M}$ is available, $v_{\mathbb{M}}(S) = v(S)$ for all $S \subseteq N$, ensuring the characteristic function fully reflects the original.

The function $v_{\mathbb{X}}$ can be evaluated by using a SAT solver on the formula $\mathcal{F}_{\mathbb{X}}$. In this formula, variables correspond to the elements of N. Each set $M \in \mathbb{X}$ yields the clause $\bigvee_{m_i \in M} \neg m_i$. This formula is monotone (all its literals are pure), which ensures its satisfiability is tested in polynomial time under any set of assumption literals. To evaluate a set $S \subseteq N$, the formula $\mathcal{F}_{\mathbb{X}}$ is solved under the assumptions $\{s_i \mid s_i \in S\}$. An unsatisfiable outcome indicates that a clause was falsified by the assumptions, proving that at least one MUS is contained in S. This technique was used in [69] in the context of MCS enumeration.

In addition, we apply the CGT algorithm for approximating Shapley-Shubik values in this context. The previously discussed strategies and optimizations remain applicable.

6   Experimental Results

To assess the performance of the proposed methods, we built a propotype in Python, interfacing the SAT solver MiniSat 2.2 [25] via PySAT [37].

We performed experiments over 360 instances, including automotive product configuration [75], circuit diagnosis benchmarks, as well as instances with up to 10000 clauses from the MUS track of the SAT competition 2011. These benchmarks were used in previous works on MUS and MCS enumeration [51,61,63], inconsistency measures [78], smallest MUS [38] or the union of MUSes [62].

The experiments were run on a Linux machine (AMD 7985WX 3.2GHz, 125GByte), with a time limit of 1 h for each execution.

Table 2. Summary of results (clauses)

	$\alpha = 0.05$			$\alpha = 0.01$		
ϵ	0.0025	0.0015	0.001	0.0025	0.0015	0.001
Ins	3	2	1	2	2	1
EIns	185	107	73	130	80	42
Del	201	89	62	113	73	30
EDel	**331**	**326**	**183**	**329**	**242**	**97**
Bin	325	98	18	192	24	10
EBin	326	171	89	275	111	70

6.1   Strategies and Optimizations

We first evaluate the CGT algorithm using different strategies to find the pivotal element, and the effect of the optimization techniques. To this end, we consider the basic versions of insertion, deletion and binary search (Ins, Del and Bin), and their enhanced versions (EIns, EDel and EBin) including all the optimizations, i.e., exploting models and unsatisfiable cores, and computing the lean kernel.

These configurations were run for both the cases of clauses and variables, recording the time taken to reach different error goals.

The error goals are given by different combinations of α and ϵ, which result in different numbers of iterations (samples) of the CGT algorithm that are necessary. Concretely, the goals are those given by the combinations with $\alpha \in \{0.05, 0.01\}$ and $\epsilon \in \{0.0025, 0.0015, 0.001\}$.

Table 2 shows the number of instances where each goal was achieved within the time limit. In all cases, the enhanced versions of the algorithms significantly outperform their basic counterparts. The difference is notable in most scenarios. As can be observed, the best performing algorithms are those based on Deletion, followed by those based on BinarySearch. Table 3 shows the results for the

Table 3. Summary of results (variables)

ϵ	$\alpha = 0.05$			$\alpha = 0.01$		
	0.0025	0.0015	0.001	0.0025	0.0015	0.001
Ins	5	3	3	4	3	2
EIns	334	189	114	286	129	99
Del	**341**	315	138	332	227	97
EDel	**341**	**338**	**334**	**338**	**334**	**330**
Bin	337	327	133	333	164	58
EBin	338	331	184	333	249	115

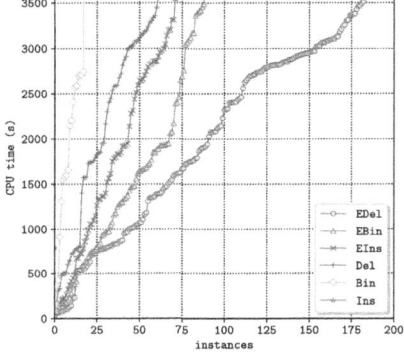

Fig. 1. Clauses

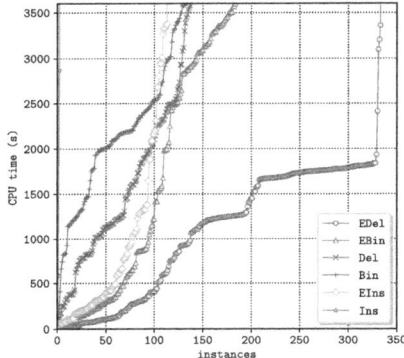

Fig. 2. Variables

case of variables. Similar conclusions can be drawn in this case, although the algorithms are even more effective. Notably, EDel achieves the most challenging goal for 330 out of the 360 instances.

Figures 1 and 2 show cactus plots comparing the methods for clauses and variables respectively, trying to achieve the error goal of $\alpha = 0.05$ and $\epsilon = 0.001$ within the time limit. These figures further illustrate the points mentioned earlier, especially the effectiveness of the optimizations in practice.

We conducted further experiments to measure the contribution of each optimization technique, considering the error goal of $\alpha = 0.05$ and $\epsilon = 0.001$.

To evaluate the impact of exploiting unsatisfiable cores, we ran a version of Deletion that uses this feature, but without calculating the lean kernel. Comparing its performance to both Del and EDel, we found that exploiting cores allowed the algorithm to complete 1.58 times more iterations. Using the lean kernel, in addition, led to completing 1.79 times more iterations.

Similarly, to measure the contribution of exploiting models, we compared a new version of Insertion (which uses models but not the lean kernel) against Ins and EIns. The results revealed that exploiting models enabled the algorithms

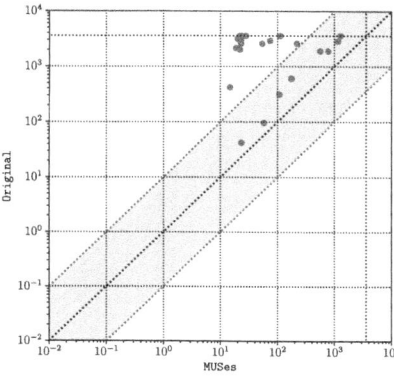

Fig. 3. Clauses

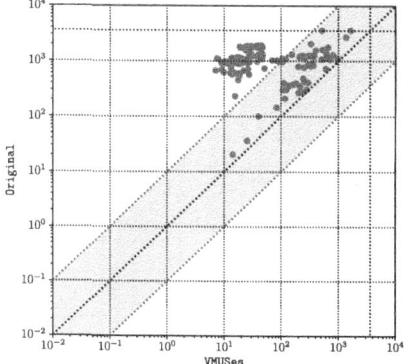

Fig. 4. Variables

to complete an impressive 22.58 times more iterations, while computing the lean kernel contributed 2.84 times more iterations.

These results clearly show that exploiting unsatisfiable cores and models significantly improves performance. The gains from exploiting models were more substantial, but it should be noted that the base `Ins` algorithm performed considerably worse than `Del`. Also, computing the lean kernel clearly contributes to improving performance. Calculating the lean kernel took 0.39 s on average across all the instances.

6.2   Explanations from Sets of (V)MUSes

This section evaluates the performance of approximating the Shapley-Shubik index from a set of MUSes or VMUSes, depending on whether clauses or variables are considered. For this purpose, we developed an approach that first enumerates (V)MUSes for 300 s using the MARCO algorithm [51]. Then, we compute the measures of importance from these obtained sets, as indicated in Sect. 5.

The number of MUSes enumerated by 300 s ranged from 1 to 14383, with an average value of 1093.64, and a median of 224.5. Full enumeration of MUSes was achieved for 28 of the 360 instances. On the other hand, the number of VMUSes was significantly lower, from 1 to 3446, with an average value of 90.38, and a median of 2.0. Notably, full enumeration was achieved for 296 instances.

Approximating the Shapley-Shubik index from these sets proved efficient. Particularly, the goal of $\alpha = 0.05$ and $\epsilon = 0.001$ was achieved by a time limit of 1 h for 336 instances in the case of clauses and 356 instances in the case variables, often in very short times. Notice that, in this case, the goal is to aggregate the information provided by the obtained sets of (V)MUSes.

Figures 3 and 4 present scatter plots comparing the running times of `EDel` when applied to the original formula versus using the enumerated sets of MUSes and VMUSes, respectively. These plots include the (V)MUS enumeration time and only consider instances where full enumeration was completed. Since the characteristic functions are equivalent when full enumeration is achieved, this comparison is highly meaningful. As the figures clearly show, working with the sets of (V)MUSes is considerably faster.

These results highlight areas for further research beyond the scope of this paper. We aim to assess how partial (V)MUS enumeration impacts the approximation quality of the unsatisfiability of the original formula. Furthermore, investigating different (V)MUS enumeration approaches in this context represents a promising research direction.

7   Conclusions

This paper introduces novel practical algorithms for the analysis of inconsistent formulas. Instead of targeting the extraction and enumeration of MUSes, the paper studies instead measures of importance of individual clauses and variables. Concretely, the paper studies the well-known Shapley-Shubik, Banzhaf and Deegan-Packel power indices, adapted to the case of unsatisfiable formulas.

The paper develops a SAT-based approach that rigorously estimates the Shapley-Shubik power index in this setting. This approach incorporates techniques that lead to substantial performance improvements in practice. Furthermore, we show how to aggregate the information provided by a set of MUSes, broadening the practical applicability of these measures to complex scenarios.

Despite the inherent complexity of the problem, the experimental results show significant promise and open novel lines of future research.

Acknowledgments. We are grateful to the anonymous reviewers for their comments and suggestions. This work is partially supported by the Spanish Government under grants PID2023-152814OB-I00, PID2022-141746OB-I00 and TED2021-131938B-I00, and by the Principality of Asturias under grant SEK-25-GRU-GIC-24-018.

Disclosure of Interests. The authors have no competing interests to declare that are relevant to the content of this article.

References

1. Bacchus, F., Davies, J., Tsimpoukelli, M., Katsirelos, G.: Relaxation search: a simple way of managing optional clauses. In: AAAI, pp. 835–841 (2014)
2. Bacchus, F., Katsirelos, G.: Using minimal correction sets to more efficiently compute minimal unsatisfiable sets. In: CAV, pp. 70–86 (2015). https://doi.org/10.1007/978-3-319-21668-3_5
3. Bacchus, F., Katsirelos, G.: Finding a collection of MUSes incrementally. In: CPAIOR, pp. 35–44 (2016). https://doi.org/10.1007/978-3-319-33954-2_3
4. Bailey, J., Stuckey, P.J.: Discovery of minimal unsatisfiable subsets of constraints using hitting set dualization. In: PADL, pp. 174–186 (2005). https://doi.org/10.1007/978-3-540-30557-6_14
5. Bakker, R.R., Dikker, F., Tempelman, F., Wognum, P.M.: Diagnosing and solving over-determined constraint satisfaction problems. In: IJCAI, pp. 276–281 (1993)

6. Banzhaf, J.F., III.: Weighted voting doesn't work: a mathematical analysis. Rutgers L. Rev. **19**, 317 (1965)
7. Belov, A., Ivrii, A., Matsliah, A., Marques-Silva, J.: On efficient computation of variable MUSes. In: SAT, pp. 298–311 (2012). https://doi.org/10.1007/978-3-642-31612-8_23
8. Belov, A., Lynce, I., Marques-Silva, J.: Towards efficient MUS extraction. AI Commun. **25**(2), 97–116 (2012). https://doi.org/10.3233/AIC-2012-0523
9. Bendík, J., Cerná, I.: Replication-guided enumeration of minimal unsatisfiable subsets. In: CP, pp. 37–54 (2020). https://doi.org/10.1007/978-3-030-58475-7_3
10. Bendík, J., Cerna, I.: Rotation based MSS/MCS enumeration. In: LPAR, pp. 120–137 (2020). https://doi.org/10.29007/8BTB
11. Bendík, J., Meel, K.S.: Counting maximal satisfiable subsets. In: AAAI, pp. 3651–3660 (2021). https://doi.org/10.1609/AAAI.V35I5.16481
12. Bendík, J., Meel, K.S.: Counting minimal unsatisfiable subsets. In: Silva, A., Leino, K.R.M. (eds.) CAV, pp. 313–336 (2021). https://doi.org/10.1007/978-3-030-81688-9_15
13. Bendík, J., Meel, K.S.: Hashing-based approximate counting of minimal unsatisfiable subsets. Formal Methods Syst. Des. **63**(1), 5–39 (2024). https://doi.org/10.1007/S10703-023-00419-W
14. Bertossi, L.E., Hunter, A., Schaub, T. (eds.): Inconsistency Tolerance [result from a Dagstuhl seminar], Lecture Notes in Computer Science, vol. 3300. Springer (2005). https://doi.org/10.1007/B104925
15. Birnbaum, E., Lozinskii, E.L.: Consistent subsets of inconsistent systems: structure and behaviour. J. Exp. Theor. Artif. Intell. **15**(1), 25–46 (2003). https://doi.org/10.1080/0952813021000026795
16. Bleukx, I., Verhaeghe, H., Bogaerts, B., Guns, T.: Exploiting symmetries in MUS computation. In: AAAI, pp. 11122–11130 (2025). https://doi.org/10.1609/AAAI.V39I11.33209
17. Castro, J., Gómez, D., Tejada, J.: Polynomial calculation of the Shapley value based on sampling. Comput. Oper. Res. **36**(5), 1726–1730 (2009). https://doi.org/10.1016/J.COR.2008.04.004
18. Chalkiadakis, G., Elkind, E., Wooldridge, M.J.: Computational Aspects of Cooperative Game Theory. Morgan & Claypool Publishers (2012). https://doi.org/10.2200/S00355ED1V01Y201107AIM016
19. Chen, Z., Ding, D.: Variable minimal unsatisfiability. In: TACM. Lecture Notes in Computer Science, vol. 3959, pp. 262–273. Springer (2006). https://doi.org/10.1007/11750321_25
20. Chinneck, J.W.: Feasibility and Infeasibility in Optimization:: Algorithms and Computational Methods, vol. 118. Springer Science & Business Media (2007)
21. Chinneck, J.W., Dravnieks, E.W.: Locating minimal infeasible constraint sets in linear programs. INFORMS J. Comput. **3**(2), 157–168 (1991). https://doi.org/10.1287/IJOC.3.2.157
22. Cook, S.A.: The complexity of theorem-proving procedures. In: STOC, pp. 151–158 (1971). https://doi.org/10.1145/800157.805047
23. Deegan, J., Packel, E.W.: A new index of power for simple n-person games. Internat. J. Game Theory **7**, 113–123 (1978)
24. Dubey, P., Shapley, L.S.: Mathematical properties of the Banzhaf power index. Math. Oper. Res. **4**(2), 99–131 (1979)
25. Eén, N., Sörensson, N.: An extensible SAT-solver. In: SAT, pp. 502–518 (2003). https://doi.org/10.1007/978-3-540-24605-3_37

26. Felsenthal, D.S., Machover, M.: The Measurement of Voting Power. Edward Elgar Publishing (1998)
27. Gleeson, J., Ryan, J.: Identifying minimally infeasible subsystems of inequalities. INFORMS J. Comput. **2**(1), 61–63 (1990). https://doi.org/10.1287/IJOC.2.1.61
28. Grant, J.: Classifications for inconsistent theories. Notre Dame J. Formal Log. **19**(3), 435–444 (1978). https://doi.org/10.1305/NDJFL/1093888404
29. Grant, J., Hunter, A.: Measuring inconsistency in knowledgebases. J. Intell. Inf. Syst. **27**(2), 159–184 (2006). https://doi.org/10.1007/S10844-006-2974-4
30. Greenberg, H.J., Murphy, F.H.: Approaches to diagnosing infeasible linear programs. INFORMS J. Comput. **3**(3), 253–261 (1991). https://doi.org/10.1287/IJOC.3.3.253
31. Grégoire, É., Izza, Y., Lagniez, J.: Boosting MCSes enumeration. In: IJCAI, pp. 1309–1315 (2018). https://doi.org/10.24963/ijcai.2018/182
32. Grégoire, É., Lagniez, J., Mazure, B.: An experimentally efficient method for (MSS, CoMSS) partitioning. In: AAAI, pp. 2666–2673 (2014)
33. Hemery, F., Lecoutre, C., Sais, L., Boussemart, F.: Extracting MUCs from constraint networks. In: ECAI, pp. 113–117 (2006)
34. Hunter, A.: Logical comparison of inconsistent perspectives using scoring functions. Knowl. Inf. Syst. **6**(5), 528–543 (2004). https://doi.org/10.1007/S10115-003-0125-6
35. Hunter, A., Konieczny, S.: Shapley inconsistency values. In: KR, pp. 249–259 (2006)
36. Hunter, A., Konieczny, S.: On the measure of conflicts: Shapley inconsistency values. Artif. Intell. **174**(14), 1007–1026 (2010). https://doi.org/10.1016/J.ARTINT.2010.06.001
37. Ignatiev, A., Morgado, A., Marques-Silva, J.: PySAT: a python toolkit for prototyping with SAT oracles. In: SAT, pp. 428–437 (2018). https://doi.org/10.1007/978-3-319-94144-8_26
38. Ignatiev, A., Previti, A., Liffiton, M.H., Marques-Silva, J.: Smallest MUS extraction with minimal hitting set dualization. In: CP, pp. 173–182 (2015). https://doi.org/10.1007/978-3-319-23219-5_13
39. Janota, M., Marques-Silva, J.: On deciding MUS membership with QBF. In: CP, pp. 414–428 (2011). https://doi.org/10.1007/978-3-642-23786-7_32
40. Junker, U.: QUICKXPLAIN: preferred explanations and relaxations for overconstrained problems. In: AAAI, pp. 167–172 (2004)
41. Kleine Büning, H.: Classes of propositional UMU formulas and their extensions to minimal unsatisfiable formulas. Theor. Comput. Sci. **998**, 114538 (2024). https://doi.org/10.1016/J.TCS.2024.114538
42. Kleine Büning, H., Kullmann, O.: Minimal unsatisfiability and autarkies. In: Biere, A., Heule, M., van Maaren, H., Walsh, T. (eds.) Handbook of Satisfiability, Frontiers in Artificial Intelligence and Applications, vol. 185, pp. 339–401. IOS Press (2009). https://doi.org/10.3233/978-1-58603-929-5-339
43. Knight, K.: Measuring inconsistency. J. Philos. Log. **31**(1), 77–98 (2002). https://doi.org/10.1023/A:1015015709557
44. Konieczny, S., Lang, J., Marquis, P.: Quantifying information and contradiction in propositional logic through test actions. In: IJCAI, pp. 106–111 (2003)
45. Kuhlmann, I., Gessler, A., Laszlo, V., Thimm, M.: Comparison of SAT-based and ASP-based algorithms for inconsistency measurement. J. Artif. Intell. Res. **82**, 563–685 (2025). https://doi.org/10.1613/JAIR.1.16888
46. Kuhlmann, I., Niskanen, A., Järvisalo, M.: Computing MUS-based inconsistency measures. In: JELIA, pp. 745–755 (2023). https://doi.org/10.1007/978-3-031-43619-2_50

47. Kullmann, O., Lynce, I., Marques-Silva, J.: Categorisation of clauses in conjunctive normal forms: minimally unsatisfiable sub-clause-sets and the lean kernel. In: SAT, pp. 22–35 (2006). https://doi.org/10.1007/11814948_4
48. Kullmann, O., Marques-Silva, J.: Computing maximal autarkies with few and simple oracle queries. In: SAT, pp. 138–155 (2015). https://doi.org/10.1007/978-3-319-24318-4_11
49. Liberatore, P.: Redundancy in logic I: CNF propositional formulae. Artif. Intell. **163**(2), 203–232 (2005). https://doi.org/10.1016/j.artint.2004.11.002
50. Liffiton, M.H., Malik, A.: Enumerating infeasibility: finding multiple muses quickly. In: CPAIOR, pp. 160–175 (2013). https://doi.org/10.1007/978-3-642-38171-3_11
51. Liffiton, M.H., Previti, A., Malik, A., Marques-Silva, J.: Fast, flexible MUS enumeration. Constraints **21**(2), 223–250 (2015). https://doi.org/10.1007/s10601-015-9183-0
52. Liffiton, M.H., Sakallah, K.A.: Algorithms for computing minimal unsatisfiable subsets of constraints. J. Autom. Reasoning **40**(1), 1–33 (2008). https://doi.org/10.1007/s10817-007-9084-z
53. Liffiton, M.H., Sakallah, K.A.: Searching for autarkies to trim unsatisfiable clause sets. In: SAT, pp. 182–195 (2008). https://doi.org/10.1007/978-3-540-79719-7_18
54. Marques-Silva, J., Heras, F., Janota, M., Previti, A., Belov, A.: On computing minimal correction subsets. In: IJCAI, pp. 615–622 (2013)
55. Marques-Silva, J., Ignatiev, A., Morgado, A., Manquinho, V.M., Lynce, I.: Efficient autarkies. In: ECAI, pp. 603–608 (2014). https://doi.org/10.3233/978-1-61499-419-0-603
56. Marques-Silva, J., Janota, M., Belov, A.: Minimal sets over monotone predicates in boolean formulae. In: CAV, pp. 592–607 (2013). https://doi.org/10.1007/978-3-642-39799-8_39
57. Marques-Silva, J., Janota, M., Mencía, C.: Minimal sets on propositional formulae. problems and reductions. Artif. Intell. **252**, 22–50 (2017). https://doi.org/10.1016/J.ARTINT.2017.07.005
58. Marques-Silva, J., Mencía, C.: Reasoning about inconsistent formulas. In: IJCAI, pp. 4899–4906 (2020). https://doi.org/10.24963/IJCAI.2020/682
59. Marques-Silva, J., Mencía, C., Mencía, R.: The sets of power. CoRR **abs/2410.07867** (2024). https://doi.org/10.48550/ARXIV.2410.07867
60. Marques-Silva, J., Previti, A.: On computing preferred MUSes and MCSes. In: SAT, pp. 58–74 (2014). https://doi.org/10.1007/978-3-319-09284-3_6
61. Mencía, C., Ignatiev, A., Previti, A., Marques-Silva, J.: MCS extraction with sublinear oracle queries. In: SAT, pp. 342–360 (2016). https://doi.org/10.1007/978-3-319-40970-2_21
62. Mencía, C., Kullmann, O., Ignatiev, A., Marques-Silva, J.: On computing the union of MUSes. In: SAT, pp. 211–221 (2019). https://doi.org/10.1007/978-3-030-24258-9_15
63. Mencía, C., Previti, A., Marques-Silva, J.: Literal-based MCS extraction. In: IJCAI, pp. 1973–1979 (2015)
64. Nadel, A.: Boosting minimal unsatisfiable core extraction. In: FMCAD, pp. 221–229 (2010)
65. Narodytska, N., Bjørner, N., Marinescu, M., Sagiv, M.: Core-guided minimal correction set and core enumeration. In: IJCAI, pp. 1353–1361 (2018). https://doi.org/10.24963/ijcai.2018/188
66. Nöhrer, A., Biere, A., Egyed, A.: Managing SAT inconsistencies with HUMUS. In: VaMoS, pp. 83–91 (2012). https://doi.org/10.1145/2110147.2110157

67. Penrose, L.S.: The elementary statistics of majority voting. J. Roy. Stat. Soc. **109**(1), 53–57 (1946)
68. Previti, A., Marques-Silva, J.: Partial MUS enumeration. In: AAAI, pp. 818–825 (2013). https://doi.org/10.1609/AAAI.V27I1.8657
69. Previti, A., Mencía, C., Järvisalo, M., Marques-Silva, J.: Improving MCS enumeration via caching. In: SAT, pp. 184–194 (2017). https://doi.org/10.1007/978-3-319-66263-3_12
70. Previti, A., Mencía, C., Järvisalo, M., Marques-Silva, J.: Premise set caching for enumerating minimal correction subsets. In: AAAI, pp. 6633–6640 (2018)
71. Raddaoui, B., Straßer, C., Jabbour, S.: Towards a principle-based framework for assessing the contribution of formulas on the conflicts of knowledge bases. In: IJCAI, pp. 3541–3548 (2024)
72. Reiter, R.: A theory of diagnosis from first principles. Artif. Intell. **32**(1), 57–95 (1987). https://doi.org/10.1016/0004-3702(87)90062-2
73. Shapley, L.S.: A value for n-person games. Contrib. Theory Games **2**(28), 307–317 (1953)
74. Shapley, L.S., Shubik, M.: A method for evaluating the distribution of power in a committee system. Am. Polit. Sci. Rev. **48**(3), 787–792 (1954)
75. Sinz, C., Kaiser, A., Küchlin, W.: Formal methods for the validation of automotive product configuration data. AI EDAM **17**(1), 75–97 (2003). https://doi.org/10.1017/S0890060403171065
76. de Siqueira N., J.L., Puget, J.: Explanation-based generalisation of failures. In: ECAI, pp. 339–344 (1988)
77. Van Loon, J.: Irreducibly inconsistent systems of linear inequalities. Eur. J. Oper. Res. **8**(3), 283–288 (1981)
78. Xiao, G., Ma, Y.: Inconsistency measurement based on variables in minimal unsatisfiable subsets. In: ECAI, pp. 864–869 (2012). https://doi.org/10.3233/978-1-61499-098-7-864

Refined Notions of QBF Equivalences

Peter Pfeiffer[1,2](✉) ⓘ, Daniel Große[2] ⓘ, and Martina Seidl[1] ⓘ

[1] Institute for Symbolic Artificial Intelligence, JKU Linz, Linz, Austria
martina.seidl@jku.at
[2] Institute for Complex Systems, JKU Linz, Linz, Austria
{peter.pfeiffer,daniel.grosse}@jku.at

Abstract. Usually, two quantified Boolean formulas (QBFs) are said to be equivalent if they have the same truth value for every assignment to the free variables. This notion of equivalence is very coarse-grained in the sense that it considers only assignments to the free variables, but it does not take the models or counter-models of the two QBFs into account. In this paper, we investigate refined notions of equivalences on the solution level to obtain a more fine-grained comparison of two formulas. We show that the problem of checking solution equivalence is PSPACE complete.

Keywords: QBF · QBF Solutions · Equivalence Checking

1 Introduction

Quantified Boolean formulas (QBFs) [1,3] extend propositional logic by quantifiers, enabling the compact representation of PSPACE-hard problems, which have numerous practical applications [7]. In such applications not only the truth values of the QBFs but also their solutions are of interest. These solutions encode the found plans in planning, error traces in formal verification, or a winning strategy in a two-player game. Solutions of QBFs are represented either as trees of a certain structure or, in practical solving, usually more compactly as Skolem functions for true QBFs and, dually, as Herbrand functions for false QBFs.

Classically, two QBFs are said to be equivalent if they evaluate to the same truth value for every assignment to their free variables, i.e., variables that are not bound by a quantifier [4]. Notably, this notion of equivalence neither requires the two QBFs to be defined over the same set of quantified variables nor takes the quantifier structure into account. When developing and optimizing QBF encodings, however, it is more useful to compare not only the truth values of different formulas but also their solutions. The notion of equivalence models presented in [5] ultimately focus on the free variables as well while considering one specific solution only. Shaik et al. [6] presented a debugging tool that allows for user-guided exploration of whether two QBFs have matching solutions w.r.t.

Supported by the LIT AI Lab and the LIT Secure and Correct Systems Lab funded by the state of Upper Austria and by the Austrian Science Fund (FWF) [10.55776/COE12].

G. Casini et al. (Eds.): JELIA 2025, LNAI 16094, pp. 159–165, 2026.
https://doi.org/10.1007/978-3-032-04590-4_11

their quantified variables. This approach generates solutions for one encoding and checks if they are solutions for the other encoding as well.

In this paper, we investigate the notion of *solution equivalence* for checking if two given QBFs with the same quantifier prefix have the same set of models/counter-models. To this end, we first focus on true formulas and introduce the notion of *Skolem entailment* that allows to define the notion of *Skolem equivalence*. For Skolem entailment checking, we present a compact QBF encoding that can be directly employed for solution equivalence checking. Finally, we show that solution equivalence checking is PSPACE complete.

2   Preliminaries

We consider *Boolean formulas* built from a given set of variables V, truth constants $\top$ (true) and $\bot$ (false), and the logical connectives $\{\neg, \wedge, \vee, \rightarrow, \leftrightarrow\}$. By $var(\phi)$ we denote the set of variables occuring in a formula ϕ. An *assignment* $\sigma : V' \rightarrow \{\top, \bot\}$ is a function that maps propositional variables $V' \subseteq V$ to $\top$ and $\bot$. By $[\phi]_\sigma$ we denote the formula obtained when the variables in ϕ are replaced according to σ and the resulting formula is simplified under standard semantics. If $[\phi]_\sigma = \top$, then σ is a *model* of ϕ, if $[\phi]_\sigma = \bot$, then σ is a *counter-model*.

A *quantified Boolean formula* (QBF) $\Phi = P.\phi$ consists of a *quantifier prefix* $P = Q_1 v_1 \ldots Q_n v_n$ ($Q_i \in \{\forall, \exists\}$, $v_i \in V$, $v_i \neq v_j$ for $i \neq j$) and a Boolean formula ϕ, which is also called *matrix*. With $var(P) = \{v_i \mid Q_i v_i$ occurs in $P\}$ we denote the set of variables bound in prefix P. *Free variables* $free(\Phi) = var(\phi) \setminus var(P)$ are not bound by a quantifier. If $free(\Phi) = \emptyset$ then Φ is a *closed formula*. We sometimes write successive quantifiers $Qx_1 \ldots Qx_n$ of the same type more compactly as QX where $X = \{x_1, \ldots, x_n\}$. If the variables in X do not occur in a prefix P, $QX : P$ denotes the prefix obtained by prepending QX to P. For a QBF $\Phi = P.\phi$, the negation $\neg\Phi$ is the QBF $P'.(\neg\phi)$ where P' is obtained from P by flipping the quantifiers. The semantics of QBFs is follows: A QBF $\forall v P.\phi$ is true iff $(P.[\phi]_{\{v=\top\}})$ and $(P.[\phi]_{\{v=\bot\}})$ are true. Dually, a QBF $\exists v P.\phi$ is true iff $(P.[\phi]_{\{v=\top\}})$ or $(P.[\phi]_{\{v=\bot\}})$ is true. A QBF $\Phi = P.\phi$ with free variables V' is true iff there exists an assignment $\sigma : V' \rightarrow \{\top, \bot\}$ such that the closed QBF $[\Phi]_\sigma = P.[\phi]_\sigma$ is true. Models and counter-models of closed QBFs are expressed in terms of binary trees of a certain structure. Consider a true QBF $\Phi = Q_1 v_1 \ldots Q_n v_n.\phi$ with n variables. Then a model S of Φ is a tree of height $n + 1$ such that each leaf node is labeled with $\top$ and each node at level i of the tree corresponds to variable v_i of Φ. Each node at level i has two children if $\mathcal{Q}_i = \forall$ and one child otherwise. One edge from a node with a universal variable is labeled with $\bot$, the other edge is labeled with $\top$. For existential nodes, the label on the edge to the child has to be set in such a manner that the full variable assignment on each path from the root to a leaf over the respective edge satisfies ϕ. We write $\sigma \in S$, if there is a path in S that corresponds to assignment σ. The set of all models of a closed QBF Φ is denoted by $\mathbb{S}_\exists(\Phi)$. Obviously, if Φ is false, then $\mathbb{S}_\exists(\Phi) = \emptyset$. Counter-models of false QBFs $\Phi = Q_1 v_1 \ldots Q_n v_n.\phi$ are defined dually: nodes with existential variables have two children, nodes with universal variables have one child, and the leaves of the tree contain $\bot$. Each full assignment on a path from the root to a leaf is a counter-model of ϕ. The set of all counter-models of a closed QBF Φ is denoted by $\mathbb{S}_\forall(\Phi)$. Obviously, if Φ is true, then $\mathbb{S}_\forall(\Phi) = \emptyset$. Given a closed QBF Φ, by $\mathbb{S}(\Phi)$ we denote the set of all models and counter-models, i.e., $\mathbb{S}(\Phi) = \mathbb{S}_\exists(\Phi) \cup \mathbb{S}_\forall(\Phi)$. QBF models can also be represented as Skolem functions and QBF counter-models can be represented as Herbrand functions, but for this work the tree-representation is more convenient.

3   Notions of Equivalences

In propositional logic, two Boolean formulas ϕ and ψ which are defined over the same variables are said to be *equivalent* (written as $\phi \Leftrightarrow \psi$) if for every assignment $\sigma : V \to \{\top, \bot\}$ it holds that $[\phi]_\sigma = [\psi]_\sigma$. The more relaxed notion of *satisfiability equivalence* only requires that both formulas are satisfiable or that both formulas are unsatisfiable. For many purposes like efficient normal form transformation [8] or formula simplification through preprocessing [2], preserving satisfiability equivalence is sufficient. The notions of (satisfiability) equivalence have also been transfered to QBFs with free variables [4,5].

Definition 1. *Let Φ and Ψ be QBFs with free variables V'. Then Φ and Ψ are equivalent (resp. satisfiability equivalent) iff $[\Phi]_\sigma$ and $[\Psi]_\sigma$ have the same truth values for all assignments (resp. for some assignment) $\sigma : V' \to \{\top, \bot\}$.*

In this definition, equivalence and satisfiability equivalence have the free variables as discriminator. Quantified variables are not considered at all, hence equivalence and satisfiability equivalence are the same for closed QBFs.

Example 1. The two quantifier-free formulas $\phi_1 = (((a \leftrightarrow b) \vee c) \wedge d)$ and $\phi_2 = (((a \leftrightarrow b) \vee \neg c) \wedge d)$ are not equivalent, but satisfiability equivalent. The closed QBFs $\Phi_1 = P.\phi_1$ and $\Phi_2 = P.\phi_2$ with prefix $P = \forall a \exists b \forall c \exists d$ are equivalent in the sense of Definition 1 and so are Φ_1 and $\Phi_3 = P.d$, but $P.\phi_1$ and $P.(\phi_1 \wedge c)$ are not, because the former formula is true and the latter is false.

In the example above, the equivalent QBFs Φ_1 and Φ_2 even have the same solutions, i.e., $\mathbb{S}(\Phi_1) = \mathbb{S}(\Phi_2)$. Note that their matrices ϕ_1 and ϕ_2 are not equivalent. In contrast, Φ_1 and Φ_3 have different solutions, i.e., $\mathbb{S}(\Phi_1) \neq \mathbb{S}(\Phi_3)$ despite being equivalent according to Definition 1: any assignment in which variable d is set to $\top$ satisfies the matrix of Φ_3. However, setting d to $\top$ is not enough for satisfying the matrix of Φ_1. In the following, we present a more fine-grained notion of QBF equivalence that also takes the solutions of the formulas into account. As indicated by the example above, requiring that the matrices of the two QBFs are equivalent is not a necessary criterion. For simplicity, we consider only closed QBFs, but the introduced notions naturally extend to QBFs with free variables. To relate two QBFs, we first start with the notion of Skolem entailment.

Definition 2 (Skolem Entailment). *Let $\Phi = P.\phi$ and $\Psi = P.\psi$ be two closed QBFs. Then Φ Skolem entails Ψ (written as $\Phi \models_{\mathsf{Sk}} \Psi$) iff $\mathbb{S}_\exists(\Phi) \subseteq \mathbb{S}_\exists(\Psi)$.*

In the definition of Skolem entailment, not only the truth values of the given QBFs are considered, but also their models. The definition requires that the two QBFs have the same quantifier prefix to ensure that the tree models have the same structure. A false formula trivially Skolem entails every formula, while a false formula is only Skolem entailed by a false formula. This is consistent with the definition of entailment as commonly found in the literature (e.g., [4]).

Example 2. Consider the QBFs $\Phi_1 = P.(((a \leftrightarrow b) \vee c) \wedge d)$, $\Phi_2 = P.(((a \leftrightarrow b) \vee \neg c) \wedge d)$, and $\Phi_3 = P.d$ with prefix $P = \forall a \exists b \forall c \exists d$ from the previous example. It holds that $\Phi_1 \models_{\mathsf{Sk}} \Phi_2$ and $\Phi_2 \models_{\mathsf{Sk}} \Phi_1$. Further, $\Phi_1 \models_{\mathsf{Sk}} \Phi_3$, but $\Phi_3 \not\models_{\mathsf{Sk}} \Phi_1$.

Next, we use Skolem entailment to define the notion of Skolem equivalence which holds if two formulas with the same prefix have the same set of models.

Definition 3 (Skolem Equivalence). *Two closed QBFs Φ and Ψ are Skolem equivalent (written as $\Phi \Leftrightarrow_{\mathsf{Sk}} \Psi$) iff $\Phi \models_{\mathsf{Sk}} \Psi$ and $\Psi \models_{\mathsf{Sk}} \Phi$, i.e., $\mathbb{S}_\exists(\Phi) = \mathbb{S}_\exists(\Psi)$.*

Example 3. The QBFs Φ_1 and Φ_2 from the previous example are Skolem equivalent ($\Phi_1 \Leftrightarrow_{\mathsf{Sk}} \Phi_2$), but Φ_1 and Φ_3 are not ($\Phi_1 \not\Leftrightarrow_{\mathsf{Sk}} \Phi_3$).

Two false formulas Φ and Ψ with the same prefix are always Skolem equivalent, because $\mathbb{S}_\exists(\Phi) = \mathbb{S}_\exists(\Psi) = \emptyset$. To consider counter-models as well, we introduce the notion of *solution equivalence* as follows.

Definition 4 (Solution Equivalence). *Two closed QBFs Φ and Ψ are solution equivalent (written as $\Phi \Leftrightarrow_{\mathsf{Sol}} \Psi$) iff $\mathbb{S}(\Phi) = \mathbb{S}(\Psi)$.*

Obviously, a true QBF Φ and a false QBF Ψ can never be solution equivalent, because $\mathbb{S}_\forall(\Phi) = \emptyset$, $\mathbb{S}_\exists(\Psi) = \emptyset$, and the intersection of the non-empty sets $\mathbb{S}_\exists(\Phi)$ and $\mathbb{S}_\forall(\Psi)$ is empty. Since the models of a true QBF Φ are the counter-models of the false QBF $\neg\Phi$ and, dually, since the counter-models of a false QBF Ψ are the models of the true QBF $\neg\Psi$, solution equivalence can be expressed in terms of Skolem equivalence.

Lemma 1. *Two closed QBFs Φ and Ψ which have the same prefix are solution equivalent ($\Phi \Leftrightarrow_{\mathsf{Sol}} \Psi$) iff $\Phi \Leftrightarrow_{\mathsf{Sk}} \Psi$ and $\neg\Phi \Leftrightarrow_{\mathsf{Sk}} \neg\Psi$.*

This lemma allows us to express solution equivalence checking in terms of Skolem equivalence checking, which, in turn, can be expressed in terms of Skolem entailment checking. Next, we present a QBF encoding for this reasoning task.

4   Equivalence Checking

Two propositional formulas ϕ and ψ over variables V are equivalent if the QBF $\forall V.(\phi \leftrightarrow \psi)$ is true. In the previous section, an example showed that the equivalence of their propositional matrices is not a criterion for solution equivalence of QBFs. To obtain a QBF encoding for solution equivalence checking, we first introduce a QBF $\Delta(\Phi, \Psi)$ which has the same prefix as Φ and Ψ plus some prepended existential variables and is false iff $\Phi \models_{\mathsf{Sk}} \Psi$.

Theorem 1. *Let $\Phi = P.\phi$ and $\Psi = P.\psi$ be two true closed QBFs with the same prefix P. Then $\Phi \models_{\mathsf{Sk}} \Psi$ iff the QBF*

$$\Delta(\Phi, \Psi) = \exists X' : P.(\phi \wedge ((X' \leftrightarrow X) \rightarrow \neg \psi))$$

is false where $X' = \{u_x \mid \forall x \text{ occurs in } P\}$ and $(X' \leftrightarrow X) := \bigwedge_{u_x \in X'} (u_x \leftrightarrow x)$.

Proof. $\Rightarrow$: Assume that $\Phi \models_{\mathsf{Sk}} \Psi$. By definition, every model $S \in \mathbb{S}(\Phi)$ is also a model of Ψ. Further assume that $\Delta(\Phi, \Psi)$ is true. As the QBFs Φ and $[\Delta(\Phi, \Psi)]_\sigma$ have the same prefix P, and as the matrix of $\Delta(\Phi, \Psi)$ strengthens the matrix ϕ of Φ, it holds that $\mathbb{S}([\Delta(\Phi, \Psi)]_\sigma) \subseteq \mathbb{S}(\Phi)$ for any assignment $\sigma : X' \rightarrow \{\top, \bot\}$.

Let $\tau_1 : X' \rightarrow \{\top, \bot\}$ be an assignment such that $[\Delta(\Phi, \Psi)]_{\tau_1} = \top$ and let $S \in \mathbb{S}([\Delta(\Phi, \Psi)]_{\tau_1})$. Now we pick a path from the root to a leaf in S such that for the corresponding variable assignment $\tau_2 \in S$ it holds that $\tau_2(x) = \tau_1(u_x)$ for all $u_x \in X', x \in X$. Let $\tau = \tau_1 \cup \tau_2$. Then $[\phi]_\tau = \top$ and $[X \leftrightarrow X']_\tau = \top$. Because of $\Phi \models_{\mathsf{Sk}} \Psi$, $[\neg \psi]_\tau = \bot$, hence $[\delta]_\tau = \bot$ where δ is the matrix of $\Delta(\Phi, \Psi)$. This contradicts the assumption that S is a model of $[\Delta(\Phi, \Psi)]_{\tau_1}$.

$\Leftarrow$: Assume that $\Delta(\Phi, \Psi)$ is false, but $\Phi \models_{\mathsf{Sk}} \Psi$ does not hold, i.e., there is a model $S \in \mathbb{S}(\Phi)$ of Φ that is not a model of Ψ, i.e., $S \notin \mathbb{S}(\Psi)$. Hence, there is an assignment $\sigma \in S$ with $[\phi]_\sigma = \top$, but $[\psi]_\sigma = \bot$. Let $\tau : X' \rightarrow \{\top, \bot\}$ be an assignment such that $\tau(u_x) = \sigma(x)$ for all $u_x \in X', x \in X$. For all assignments $\tau' \in S$ with $\tau' \neq \sigma$, (1) $[\phi]_{\tau'} = \top$, because S is a model of ϕ and (2) $[(X' \leftrightarrow X) \rightarrow \neg \psi]_{\tau \cup \tau'} = \top$. The latter holds, because $\tau(u_X) \neq \tau'(x)$ for some $u_x \in X', x \in X$ and the left-hand side of the implication is false. But also $[(X' \leftrightarrow X) \rightarrow \neg \psi]_{\tau \cup \sigma} = \top$, because $\tau(x') = \sigma(x)$ for all $x' \in X', x \in X$ and $[\neg \psi]_\sigma = \top$. Hence, S is a model for $P.[\delta]\tau$ with δ being the matrix of $\Delta(\Phi, \Psi)$. This means that $\Delta(\Phi, \Psi)$ has a model, contradicting the assumption that $\Delta(\Phi, \Psi)$ is false. It follows that $\Phi \models_{\mathsf{Sk}} \Psi$.

$\square$

The Δ formula introduces a set of existentially quantified variables X' at the beginning of its prefix such that X' contains one variable for each universal variable of P. Then Δ is true if there is an assignment to the universal variables such that there is an assignment to the existential variables satisfying matrix ϕ, but falsifying matrix ψ. This is illustrated in the following example.

Example 4. Consider the QBFs $\Phi_3 = P.d$ and $\Phi_2 = P.(((a \leftrightarrow b) \vee \neg c) \wedge d)$ with $P = \forall a \exists b \forall c \exists d$ from the previous examples. Then

$$\Delta(\Phi_3, \Phi_2) = \exists a' \exists c' \forall a \exists b \forall c \exists d : d \wedge (((a' \leftrightarrow a) \wedge (c' \leftrightarrow c)) \rightarrow \neg(((a \leftrightarrow b) \vee \neg c) \wedge d))$$

is true if a' is set to $\bot$ and c' is set to $\top$. The reason can be seen in the assignment tree shown in Fig. 1. The yellow subtree is a model of Φ_3, but not of Φ_2, because of the assignment on the red path on which a and c have the same values as a' and c' that make $\Delta(\Phi_3, \Phi_2)$ true.

Since Skolem entailment can be reduced to a QBF, Skolem equivalence checking can also be reduced to a QBF. Consequently, by Lemma 1, solution equivalence checking can be reduced to a QBF as well. It follows that all three problems

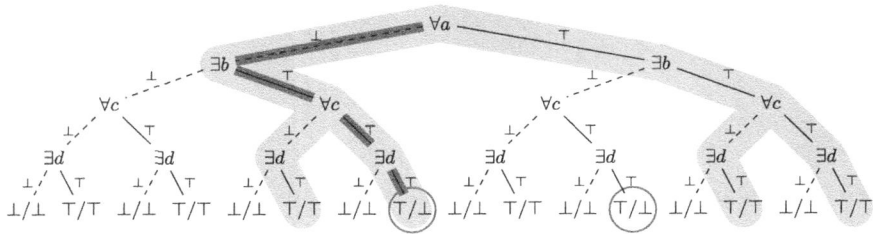

Fig. 1. Full assignment tree for QBFs Φ_3/Φ_2 from Example 4. The leaves contain truth values of ϕ_3/ϕ_2 under the assignment on the path to the root (different results are in red circles). The yellow subtree is a model of Φ_3, but not of Φ_2 because of the red path.

lie in PSPACE. Furthermore, PSPACE-hardness is derived from the following lemma.

Lemma 2. *A closed QBF Φ is true iff $\Phi \models_{\mathsf{Sk}} \bot$ does not hold.*

Proof. On the one hand, if Φ is true, then $\mathbb{S}_\exists(\Phi) \neq \emptyset$, but $\mathbb{S}_\exists(\bot) = \emptyset$. Hence, $\mathbb{S}_\exists(\Phi) \not\subseteq \mathbb{S}_\exists(\top)$ and $\Phi \models_{\mathsf{Sk}} \bot$ cannot hold. On the other hand, if $\Phi \models_{\mathsf{Sk}} \bot$ does not hold, then $\mathbb{S}_\exists(\Phi) \neq \emptyset$. Hence, Φ is true. □

Proposition 1. *The problems of Skolem entailment checking, Skolem equivalence checking, and solution equivalence checking are PSPACE complete.*

The notions and the results discussed above can be directly extended to formulas with free variables. For example, solution equivalence checking with free variables is defined as follows.

Definition 5. *Let Φ and Ψ be QBFs with free variables V'. Then Φ and Ψ are solution equivalent iff $[\Phi]_\sigma \Leftrightarrow_{\mathsf{Sol}} [\Psi]_\sigma$ for all assignments $\sigma : V' \to \{\top, \bot\}$.*

It follows that solution equivalence checking for QBFs with free variables is PSPACE complete as well.

5   Conclusion

In this work, we introduced the notion of solution equivalences for QBFs. Solution equivalence does not consider only truth values and assignments of free variables to compare two formulas, but models and counter-models. We showed that solution equivalence checking is PSPACE complete.

The QBF encoding we presented in this paper has the potential for practical applications in future work. On the basis of this encoding, a QBF solver can be used to check solution equivalence of two formulas. The current approach is limited to compare QBFs with the same prefix. In the future, we plan to explore more general notions of equivance that are more relaxed with respect to prefix structures.

References

1. Beyersdorff, O., Janota, M., Lonsing, F., Seidl, M.: Quantified Boolean formulas. In: Handbook of Satisfiability - Second Edition, Frontiers in Artificial Intelligence and Applications, vol. 336, pp. 1177–1221. IOS Press (2021)
2. Heule, M., Järvisalo, M., Lonsing, F., Seidl, M., Biere, A.: Clause elimination for SAT and QSAT. J. Artif. Intell. Res. **53**, 127–168 (2015)
3. Kleine Büning, H., Bubeck, U.: Theory of quantified Boolean formulas. In: Handbook of Satisfiability - Second Edition, Frontiers in Artificial Intelligence and Applications, vol. 336, pp. 1131–1156. IOS Press (2021)
4. Kleine Büning, H., Lettmann, T.: Aussagenlogik – Deduktion und Algorithmen. Teubner (1994)
5. Kleine Büning, H., Zhao, X.: Equivalence models for quantified Boolean formulas. In: Proc. of the 7th Int. Conf. on Theory and Applications of Satisfiability Testing (SAT). Lecture Notes in Computer Science, vol. 3542, pp. 224–234. Springer (2004)
6. Shaik, I., Heisinger, M., Seidl, M., van de Pol, J.: Validation of QBF encodings with winning strategies. In: Proc. of the 26th Int. Conf. on Theory and Applications of Satisfiability Testing (SAT). Leibniz International Proceedings in Informatics (LIPIcs), vol. 271, pp. 1–10. Schloss Dagstuhl – Leibniz-Zentrum für Informatik (2023)
7. Shukla, A., Biere, A., Pulina, L., Seidl, M.: A Survey on Applications of Quantified Boolean Formulas. In: Proc. of the 2019 IEEE 31st Int. Conf. on Tools with Artificial Intelligence (ICTAI), pp. 78–84. IEEE (2019)
8. Tseitin, G.S.: On the Complexity of Derivation in Propositional Calculus, pp. 466–483. Springer Berlin Heidelberg, Berlin (1983)

Refinement-Based Enumeration of QBF Solutions

Andreas Plank[(✉)][ID], Clemens Hofstadler[ID], Maximilian Heisinger[ID], and Martina Seidl[ID]

Institute for Symbolic Artificial Intelligence, Johannes Kepler University, Linz, Austria
{andreas.plank,clemens.hofstadler,maximilian.heisinger, martina.seidl}@jku.at

Abstract. Counting the number of solutions of true and false quantified Boolean formulas (QBFs) has received increased interest in recent years. However, the explicit enumeration of all solutions for a QBF is almost unexplored so far. For QBF solution counting, it has been shown that enumeration-based counting as employed in SAT is not complete for QBF. Solution enumeration runs into the same problem.

We propose a refinement-based approach to enumerate (all) solutions of true and false QBFs. To this end, we develop a novel framework to characterize the enumeration problem at quantifier level two and present a complete enumeration algorithm that can be interrupted at any time as soon as enough solutions are found. We evaluated our implementation called QEnum in three different case studies.

1 Introduction

Encoding and solving problems using quantified Boolean formulas (QBFs) offers a uniform method to address challenges across various application fields such as formal verification or artificial intelligence (see [19] for a survey). The QBF decision problem is the archetypical PSPACE-complete problem that has been well investigated over the last decades [3]. For QBF encodings of application problems it is important to know not only their truth value but also their solutions. The problem of finding all solutions of a QBF with free variables was already introduced in [2]. There, an approach was presented to find assignments to the free variables (variables which are not bound by a quantifier) such that the resulting QBF is true. In this work, we also consider the task of enumerating all solutions but in a more general setting. Let's consider a true QBF of the form $\Phi = \forall X \exists Y.\phi$. A model F of this formula is a set of propositional formulas such that for each $y \in Y$, there is a formula $f_y \in F$ over X and the propositional formula ϕ' obtained by replacing each y_i by its f_{y_i} is valid. Dually, let $\Psi = \exists X \forall Y.\phi$ be a false QBF. A counter-model G of Ψ is a set of propositional formulas over the variables X. Then there is a formula $g_y \in G$ for each $y \in Y$ such that the propositional formula ψ', which is obtained by replacing each y by g_y, is unsatisfiable. We are interested in enumerating all models of a true QBF and all counter-models of a false QBF.

G. Casini et al. (Eds.): JELIA 2025, LNAI 16094, pp. 166–181, 2026.
https://doi.org/10.1007/978-3-032-04590-4_12

A problem closely related to solution enumeration is the problem of solution counting also known as #QBF [10]. Contrary to #SAT [6] (counting models for propositional formulas), which has been a prominent research area in many different fields such as analysis of software vulnerability [4,20], verification of neural networks [1,13] and probabilistic reasoning [5,16], the first practical solution counters for QBFs have been presented only in recent years [11,15,18]. An enumerative method for counting (counter-)models was introduced in [15]: Given a QBF Φ, a QBF solver is called to compute a solution F_1. Next, a new QBF Φ_1 is constructed from Φ such that F_1 is no longer a solution. Then, a solution F_2 of Φ_1 is computed. In QBF Φ_2, F_1 and F_2 are both excluded from the solution space. More solutions are enumerated and excluded until finally Φ_n does not have the same truth value as Φ anymore. While, in propositional logic, the exact model count is obtained in this way, this approach is not complete for QBFs. To compute the full model count of a true QBF, a SAT solver as well as a propositional model counter is used in [15]. While conceptually dual, this approach does not work for counting all solutions of false QBFs.

We present a novel approach that enumerates solutions at the second quantifier level. In contrast to previous work [15], the new procedure (1) works for true and false QBFs in a dual manner and (2) can be interrupted at any time as soon as enough solutions are found. The approach is implemented in the tool QEnum and evaluated in three case studies.

2   Preliminaries

Let $X_1, \ldots, X_n$ be pairwise disjoint non-empty sets of propositional variables. We consider *quantified Boolean formulas (QBFs)* of the form $\Phi = \Pi.\phi$, which consist of a *quantifier prefix* $\Pi = Q_1 X_1 \ldots Q_n X_n$ with *quantifiers* $Q_1, \ldots, Q_n \in \{\exists, \forall\}$, $Q_i \neq Q_{i+1}$ for $1 \leq i < n$ and of a (propositional) *matrix* ϕ. The matrix ϕ is a propositional formula over the variables $X_1 \cup \cdots \cup X_n$, the truth constants $\top$ (true) and $\bot$ (false), and the standard Boolean connectives. A variable $x \in X_i$ is called *existential* in Φ if $Q_i = \exists$ and *universal* otherwise.

We only consider *closed* formulas in this work, i.e., all variables occurring in the propositional matrix ϕ also occur in the quantifier prefix Π. A QBF $\Pi.\phi$ is in *prenex conjunctive normal form (PCNF)* if ϕ is a conjunction of clauses, where a clause is a disjunction of literals and a literal is a variable or its negation. An *assignment* σ is a function $\sigma \colon X \to \{\top, \bot\}$ that maps a subset of the variables $X \subseteq X_1 \cup \cdots \cup X_n$ to truth values. It is called a *partial (X-)assignment* if X is a strict subset of $X_1 \cup \cdots \cup X_n$ and a *full* assignment otherwise.

For a propositional formula ϕ and an assignment σ, we denote by $\phi(\sigma)$ the formula obtained from ϕ by setting all variables in the domain of σ to their truth values as specified by σ. We call $\phi(\sigma)$ the *evaluation* of ϕ under σ. Thus, for example, if $\sigma = \{x \mapsto \top, y \mapsto \bot\}$, then $\phi(\sigma)$ denotes the propositional formula obtained from ϕ by setting the variable x to $\top$ and y to $\bot$. If $\phi(\sigma)$ simplifies to $\top$ (using the classical equivalences of Boolean algebra), we say that ϕ is *true* (or *satisfiable*) and that σ is a *model* (or a *satisfying assignment*) for ϕ.

The semantics of QBF is defined as follows: a QBF $\forall x \Pi.\phi$ is *true* if and only if both $\Pi.\phi(\{x \mapsto \top\})$ and $\Pi.\phi(\{x \mapsto \bot\})$ are true, and $\exists x \Pi.\phi$ is *true* if and only if $\Pi.\phi(\{x \mapsto \top\})$ or $\Pi.\phi(\{x \mapsto \bot\})$ is true. A QBF that is not true is *false*. For example, the QBF $\forall x \exists y.(x \leftrightarrow y)$ is true, while $\exists x \forall y.(x \leftrightarrow y)$ is false.

The notion of a model for a true QBF lifts the notion of a satisfying assignment to the quantified setting. Instead of mapping variables to truth constants, existential variables are now mapped to propositional formulas in (some of) the universal variables. Formally, a *model* for a true QBF $\Pi.\phi$ containing existential variables $y_1, \ldots, y_k$ is a set $F = \{f_{y_1}, \ldots, f_{y_k}\}$, where each f_{y_i} is a propositional formula in the universal variables that appear to the left of y_i in the prefix Π, such that the propositional formula obtained from ϕ by replacing each y_i by f_{y_i} simplifies to $\top$. For example, the set $F = \{f_y = x\}$ is a model for the true QBF $\forall x \exists y.(x \leftrightarrow y)$, because replacing y by $f_y = x$ yields $x \leftrightarrow x \equiv \top$. A model F for a true QBF is also called a *Skolem set* and the elements of F are called *Skolem functions*. Counter-models for false QBFs are defined dually: a set $H = \{h_{x_1}, \ldots, h_{x_l}\}$ of propositional formulas is a *counter-model* for a false QBF $\Pi.\phi$ with universal variables $x_1, \ldots, x_l$ if the propositional formula obtained from ϕ by replacing each x_i with h_{x_i} simplifies to $\bot$. Here, each h_{x_i} is a formula in the existential variables that appear to the left of x_i in the prefix Π. Counter-models are also called *Herbrand sets* and their elements are *Herbrand functions*.

Models and counter-models can be visualized as trees. Let $m = |X_1 \cup \cdots \cup X_n|$. Then a model F for a true QBF $\Phi = \Pi.\phi$ can be considered as a tree of height $m + 1$, where the nodes in the k-th level ($k \in \{1, \ldots, m\}$) correspond to the k-th variable x_k in the quantifier prefix Π (from left to right; assuming an arbitrary but fixed order of the variables within each set X_i). Each node on level k has two children if x_k universal in Φ and exactly one child if it is existential. In the former case, the two edges are labeled by $\bot$ and $\top$, respectively. In the latter case, the label of the single edge is given by the evaluation of the Skolem function $f_{x_k} \in F$ under the partial assignment induced by the unique path from the root to the considered edge. Since f_{x_k} only depends on the universal variables that appear to the left of x_k in Π, this evaluation yields either $\top$ or $\bot$. Any path from the root to a leaf of this tree corresponds to a full assignment σ such that $\phi(\sigma)$ simplifies to $\top$. For counter-models, the roles of the quantifiers are exchanged, i.e., now each node on level k has two children if x_k is existential and only one child if it is universal. In the latter case, the label of the single edge is given by the evaluation of the Herbrand function h_{x_k}. A path from the root to a leaf corresponds to an assignment σ such that $\phi(\sigma)$ simplifies to $\bot$.

3   Introductory Example

In the following example, we demonstrate our enumerative approach with a simple 4×4 Tic-Tac-Toe game. Enumerative approaches exclude already identified solutions. As models for QBFs are represented as sets of propositional formulas, models for quantified formulas are excluded from the search space by appending *blocking sets* to the formula. All concepts will be formally introduced below.

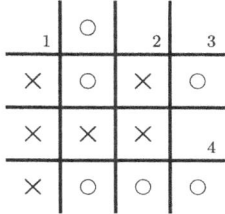 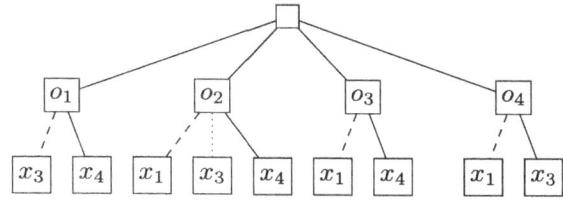

Fig. 1. Left: 4×4 Tic-Tac-Toe after 12 moves, with player $\bigcirc$ to go. Right: Winning strategies for player $\times$, depending on the move of player $\bigcirc$.

Example 1 (4×4 Tic-Tac-Toe). Consider a 4×4 Tic-Tac-Toe game after 12 moves have been played and it is now player $\bigcirc$'s turn. The current state of the board is visualized in the left part of Fig. 1. Our objective is to determine whether there exist one or more winning strategies for player $\times$ in their next move. If such strategies exist, we also aim to explicitly compute and enumerate all of them. This scenario can be encoded as the following QBF:

$$\forall O \exists X. \phi = \forall O \exists X. \text{valid-move}(O) \rightarrow (\text{valid-move}(X) \wedge \text{exclusive}(O, X) \wedge \text{win}(X)).$$

Hereby, the universal variables $O = \{o_1, o_2, o_3, o_4\}$ represent the possible moves available to player $\bigcirc$. In particular, the variable o_i encodes that player $\bigcirc$ puts their mark on empty field i as shown in Fig. 1. Analogously, we express the possible moves available to player $\times$ by the set of existential variables $X = \{x_1, x_2, x_3, x_4\}$. The predicate "valid-move" encodes that a player has to play precisely one move. The predicate "exclusive" ensures mutual exclusivity of the marks on the board, i.e., that at most one mark can be set on each position. Finally, the predicate "win(X)" represents the winning condition for player $\times$, specifying that their mark must be placed on either position 1,3, or 4 to win.

With the help of a QBF solver, one can check that the formula above is true. This confirms the existence of winning strategies for player $\times$. Moreover, from such a solver call, one can also extract a model of the QBF. This model, which we denote by F_1, encodes a winning strategy for player $\times$. For our example, say F_1 describes the strategy of picking the position with highest available index from the winning set $\{1, 3, 4\}$, excluding the position already marked by player $\bigcirc$. This strategy is depicted with solid lines in Fig. 1 (right).

To find further winning strategies, we exclude the strategy F_1 from our QBF search space, by adding it as a blocking set to the QBF. The updated formula $\forall O \exists X. (\phi \wedge \neg F_1)$ can be passed to a QBF solver again, returning a second strategy F_2. Say, strategy F_2 is defined by picking the position with lowest available index from the winning set $\{1, 3, 4\}$ (shown with dashed lines in Fig. 1), excluding the position previously marked by player $\bigcirc$. We have now identified all possible strategies to counter a move o_1, o_3, or o_4 by player $\bigcirc$. Hence, the QBF $\forall O \exists X. (\phi \wedge \neg F_1 \wedge \neg F_2)$ is now false. However, if player $\bigcirc$ puts their mark on position 2, there remains a third strategy, which involves selecting the middle index from the set $\{1, 3, 4\}$ (depicted with a dotted line in the right of Fig. 1), a strategy that has not been covered yet. We can enforce the QBF solver to identify this remaining strategy F_3 by excluding the other markings o_1, o_3, o_4 by disjoining them with the QBF obtaining $\forall O \exists X. ((\phi \wedge \neg F_1 \wedge \neg F_2) \vee o_1 \vee o_3 \vee o_4)$. Note that F_3 is only a "partial" winning strategy, as it relies on the assumption that player $\bigcirc$ makes a specific move. We will formally introduce and discuss such partial solutions in Sect. 5.

4   Disjoint Solutions for QBFs and Their Enumeration

In this section, we recall and summarize the results from [15] for enumerating *disjoint* solutions for QBFs and the notion of *blocking Skolem/Herbrand sets*.

Definition 1 (Blocking Skolem/Herbrand Set). *Let $\Phi = \Pi.\phi$ be a true QBF and let F be a Skolem set for Φ. Then $\neg\phi_F$ is a blocking Skolem set for Φ, where $\phi_F = \bigwedge_{f_y \in F}(y \leftrightarrow f_y)$. Dually, for a false QBF $\Phi = \Pi.\phi$ with Herbrand set H, ϕ_H is a blocking Herbrand set for Φ, where $\phi_H = \bigwedge_{h_x \in H}(x \leftrightarrow h_x)$.*

Note that blocking Skolem sets are negated, while blocking Herbrand sets are not. In [15], we showed that by incrementally adding blocking Skolem/Herbrand sets to a QBF until the formula changes its truth value, one can efficiently enumerate (counter-)models for a QBF. However, in this way, not all (counter-)models can be computed, but only all *disjoint* ones. For space reasons, we only state the following definition for models of true QBFs. By replacing Skolem with Herbrand sets and exchanging the roles of universal and existential variables, one obtains a dual version for counter-models of false QBFs.

Definition 2 (Disjoint Models). *Two Skolem sets F and F' of a true QBF are disjoint if there exists an existential variable y and $f_y \in F$, $f'_y \in F'$ such that f_y and f'_y are not logically equivalent.*

The notion of disjointness can also be stated in terms of the tree representation of Skolem/Herbrand sets: two Skolem/Herbrand sets are disjoint if and only if their tree representations do not share a common path, i.e., there is no full path from the root to a leaf that appears in both trees. We summarize some properties of disjoint models described in [15]. A dual version for disjoint counter-models for false QBFs can be obtained by replacing blocking Skolem sets by blocking Herbrand sets, which are added disjunctively to the formula.

Proposition 1. *Let $\Phi = \Pi.\phi$ be a true QBF. (1) If F is a Skolem set of Φ and F' is a Skolem set of $\Pi.(\phi \wedge \neg\phi_F)$, then F and F' are disjoint. (2) If $F_1, \ldots, F_m$ are pairwise disjoint Skolem sets for Φ and if $\Pi.(\phi \wedge \neg\phi_{F_1} \wedge \cdots \wedge \neg\phi_{F_m})$ is false, then m is the maximal number of pairwise disjoint Skolem sets for Φ.*

Proposition 1 suggests an iterative approach to enumerate all disjoint (counter-)models for a given QBF. Details of this algorithm are described in [15]. However, the somewhat restrictive notion of disjoint (counter-)models is not adequate to describe all interesting solutions of a QBF. Example 1 demonstrates that some solutions, such as the third strategy, cannot be discovered by enumerating only disjoint models.

5   Enumeration of All Solutions

When all disjoint models for a true QBF $\Phi = \Pi.\phi$ are computed, the corresponding Skolem functions cover all possibilities to turn the matrix ϕ into $\top$ for at least one assignment of the universal variables in Φ. However, assignments with additional possibilities might exist. For instance, in Example 1, the two disjoint models F_1 and F_2 cover all possible moves to counter a move of player $\bigcirc$ on positions 1, 3, or 4. However, there still exists a third possibility when player $\bigcirc$ puts their mark on position 2. To formally describe such partial solutions, we introduce the following notion.

Definition 3 (Restricted Models). *Let $\Phi = \Pi.\phi$ be a true QBF and let P be a propositional formula in the universal variables of Φ. If F is a Skolem set for $\Pi.(P \to \phi)$, then (F, P) is a* restricted Skolem set *(or* restricted model*) for Φ.*

In a restricted Skolem set (F, P) for Φ, F is a model for Φ only for those assignments of the universal variables for which the formula P evaluates to true. For assignments that do not satisfy P, the relation of F and Φ can be arbitrary. A restricted Skolem set is a classical Skolem set if and only if $P \equiv \top$. Restricted counter-models are defined dually.

Definition 4 (Restricted Counter-models). *Let $\Phi = \Pi.\phi$ be a false QBF and let P be a propositional formula in the existential variables of Φ. If H is a Herbrand set for $\Pi.(\phi \wedge P)$, then the pair (H, P) is a* restricted Herbrand set *(or* restricted counter-model*) for Φ.*

Example 2. Consider the QBF $\Phi = \forall x \exists y.(x \vee y)$. Then $(\{f_y = \neg x\}, \top)$ and $(\{f_y = \bot\}, x)$ are two restricted models for Φ, but $(\{f_y = \bot\}, \neg x)$ is not a restricted model for Φ.

Once an algorithm has computed all disjoint solutions for a QBF, there might still exist restricted (counter-)models. In this section, we discuss two methods to enumerate these remaining partial solutions. The algorithms presented in the following do not actually enumerate *all* possible solutions for a given QBF, but they compute a set of solutions that allows us to obtain all possible solutions by combining them. We call such a set a *basis*.

Definition 5 (Basis). *Let $\Phi = \Pi.\phi$ be a true QBF with universal variables X and existential variables Y. A set $\mathcal{F} = \{(F_1, P_1), \ldots, (F_m, P_m)\}$ of restricted Skolem sets for Φ is called a* basis *of Skolem sets for Φ if it satisfies the following condition: for any Skolem set F of Φ and any X-assignment σ, there exists exactly one partial Skolem set $(F', P') \in \mathcal{F}$ such that $P'(\sigma) \equiv \top$ and $f_y(\sigma) \equiv f'_y(\sigma)$ for all $y \in Y$, where $f_y \in F$ and $f'_y \in F'$.*

A basis of Herbrand sets for false QBFs is defined dually. The condition of being a basis of Skolem/Herbrand sets consists of two parts: For each Skolem set F and each X-assignment σ, there is *at least one* and *at most one* partial Skolem set mimicking the behavior of F under σ. The "at least one" condition guarantees that a basis can generate all possible Skolem sets for Φ, while the "at most one" condition ensures that there is no redundancy within a basis.

Example 3. Consider the QBF $\Phi = \forall x \exists y.(x \vee y)$. A basis of Skolem sets for Φ is given by $\{((\{f_y = \neg x\}, \top), (\{f_y = x\}, x)\}$. Another possible basis is $\{((\{f_y = \top\}, x), (\{f_y = \bot\}, x), (\{f_y = \top\}, \neg x)\}$.

Example 3 shows that a basis for a QBF is not unique and that different bases may contain different numbers of elements. The main reason for this variability is that any (nontrivial) basis element can be decomposed into mutually exclusive parts. Specifically, if (F, P) is an element of a basis $\mathcal{F}$ and P can be expressed as $P \equiv P_1 \vee P_2$, where P_1 and P_2 have no models in common, then (F, P) can be replaced by (F, P_1) and (F, P_2), increasing the number of elements in $\mathcal{F}$ by one.

Conversely, to reduce the number of elements in a basis, we can merge elements $(F_1, P_1), (F_2, P_2)$ into a single element $(F, P_1 \vee P_2)$, provided that P_1 and P_2 do not share a common model. The new Skolem functions in F are then given by $(P_1 \rightarrow f_{y,1}) \wedge (P_2 \rightarrow f_{y,2})$, where $f_{y,1} \in F_1$, $f_{y,2} \in F_2$. By repeatedly merging elements until no further reductions are possible, we can obtain a minimal basis. The minimality of a basis can, in fact, be characterized by a simple property of its restriction conditions P.

Definition 6 (Minimal Basis). *A basis $\mathcal{F}$ is minimal if there exists an assignment σ such that $P(\sigma) \equiv \top$ for all $(F, P) \in \mathcal{F}$.*

The first basis in Example 3 is minimal, while the second one is not. Minimal bases have a unique and minimal number of elements.

Proposition 2. *Let $\mathcal{F}$, $\mathcal{F}'$ be bases for a QBF Φ. If $\mathcal{F}$ is minimal, then $|\mathcal{F}| \leq |\mathcal{F}'|$. In particular, all minimal bases for Φ have the same number of elements.*

Proof. Let $\mathcal{F} = \{(F_1, P_1), \ldots, (F_m, P_m)\}$. Since $\mathcal{F}$ is minimal, there exists an assignment σ such that $P_i(\sigma) \equiv \top$ for all $i = 1, \ldots, m$. Since $\mathcal{F}$ is a basis, the evaluations of the F_i under σ are all pairwise different. For each of these m different evaluations, there has to exist a partial (counter-)model $(F_i', P_i') \in \mathcal{F}'$ with $P_i'(\sigma) \equiv \top$ and $f_y(\sigma) \equiv f_y'(\sigma)$ for all $y \in Y$, $f_y \in F_i$, $f_y' \in F_i'$. Since these elements must be pairwise distinct, it follows that $|\mathcal{F}'| \geq m$. The second claim follows from the first one.

For true QBFs of the form $\forall X \exists Y.\phi$ we can easily compute the total number of Skolem sets from a basis[1]. By replacing Skolem with Herbrand sets, one obtains an analogous result for false formulas with prefix $\exists X \forall Y \exists Z$.

Proposition 3. *Let $\Phi = \forall X \exists Y.\phi$ be a true QBF. Furthermore let $\mathcal{F} = \{(F_1, P_1), \ldots, (F_m, P_m)\}$ be a basis of Skolem sets for Φ. The total number of Skolem sets for Φ is given by*

$$\prod_{\substack{X\text{-assignment} \\ \sigma}} |\{i \in \{1, \ldots, m\} \mid P_i(\sigma) \equiv \top\}|.$$

---

[1] In fact, we could also consider true formulas with prefix $\forall X \exists Y \forall Z$, but with universal reduction [9] the rightmost universal quantifier can always be eliminated without changing the number of models.

Proof. Any Skolem set F for Φ is uniquely determined by the evaluations of all Skolem functions $f_y \in F$ under all X-assignments σ. Since these evaluations are independent for different assignments, it suffices to compute the number of possible evaluations for each σ and then multiply them to obtain the total number of Skolem sets.

For fixed σ, we claim that $|\{i \in \{1, \ldots, m\} \mid P_i(\sigma) \equiv \top\}|$ gives precisely the number of different possible evaluations of Skolem sets under σ. To see this, note that each partial Skolem set $(F_i, P_i) \in \mathcal{F}$ with $P_i(\sigma) \equiv \top$ gives exactly one possibility for the evaluations under σ, given by evaluating the partial Skolem functions in F_i under σ. Note that these evaluations all have to be different, because $\mathcal{F}$ is a basis. If there were different $(F_i, P_i), (F_j, P_j) \in \mathcal{F}$ with $P_i(\sigma) \equiv P_j(\sigma) \equiv \top$ and $f_{i,y}(\sigma) \equiv f_{j,y}(\sigma)$ for all $y \in Y$, then this would violate the "at most one"-part of being a basis. Thus, $|\{i \in \{1, \ldots, m\} \mid P_i(\sigma) \equiv \top\}|$ gives a lower bound for the number of different possible evaluations under σ. To see that it is also an upper bound, we have to show that the evaluation of every Skolem set F for Φ under σ can be obtained from one of the (F_i, P_i), but this follows directly from the "at least one"-part of the basis property.

Next, we present two methods for computing a basis of solutions for a given QBF. For a simpler presentation, we consider true QBFs with quantifier prefix $\forall X \exists Y$ and false QBFs with quantifier prefix $\exists X \forall Y \exists Z$.

5.1   SAT-Based Basis Computation

In [15], an approach was presented for computing the number of all models for a true QBF $\Phi = \forall X \exists Y.\phi$. We describe an adaptation of this method to compute a basis of Skolem sets for Φ. The total number of solutions follows from Proposition 3.

First, we compute all disjoint models for Φ using, for instance, [15, Alg. 1]. Then, in order to identify additional restricted models, we invoke a SAT solver on the propositional matrix ϕ. If there still exist restricted solutions, the solver returns assignments σ_X and σ_Y of the universal and existential variables, respectively, such that ϕ evaluates to true under the combination of σ_X and σ_Y. From these assignments, we can construct a partial Skolem set (F, P), where P a propositional formula with unique satisfying assignment σ_X, and $F = \{f_y = \sigma_Y(y) \mid y \in Y\}$. We then exclude this partial solution from the search space by conjunctively appending the formula $\neg(P \wedge \phi_F)$ to ϕ. This process is repeated iteratively until all satisfying assignments of the propositional matrix have been identified. This approach does not work for false formulas.

5.2   Refinement-Based Basis Computation

We now describe the refinement-based approach for computing a basis of solutions for arbitrary QBFs. The details of the method are described in Algorithm 1. For a simpler presentation, we state the algorithm for true QBFs of the form $\Phi = \forall X \exists Y.\phi$. The needed changes for false QBFs $\exists X \forall Y \exists Z.\phi$ are discussed later.

The core idea of the algorithm is to alternate between computing disjoint models and disjoint counter-models for iteratively refined formulas. For true formulas, we begin by computing all disjoint models and exclude them as blocking Skolem sets. The resulting formula becomes false, and we compute its disjoint counter-models. These counter-models indicate for which parts of the search space we have already identified all solutions. By excluding the counter-models as blocking Herbrand sets, we restrict our search to only those parts of the search space that still contain solutions. Thus, any newly identified models will be partial models of the original formula, restricted to the remaining parts of the search space. To keep track of these restrictions, we construct a formula P that encodes which parts of the search space are still under consideration. We then continue by computing disjoint models for the updated true formula, obtaining partial models that are restricted by P. This alternating process continues, refining the restrictions P of the constructed partial models in every iteration, until P becomes unsatisfiable, indicating that all partial solutions have been found.

Algorithm 1 works as follows. First, we initialize a propositional formula P. This formula represents those assignments of the universal variables X for which we have not yet identified all partial Skolem sets and is continuously updated as the algorithm progresses. Since initially all assignments lead to solutions, P is initialized as $\top$. Furthermore, the algorithm defines a propositional formula ψ, which is initially set to ϕ and will continuously be refined with found blocking Skolem and Herbrand sets. The stopping criterion of the algorithm is defined in line 2, where the loop terminates once all (partial) solutions for all assignments have been identified, which is the case if and only if P becomes unsatisfiable. Within the loop in line 3, first all disjoint solutions for the current QBF instance $\Pi.\psi$ are computed using a black-box algorithm computeDisjoint($\Pi.\psi$) (this could be, e.g., [15, Alg. 1]). By construction, this formula is always true and we obtain a set of all disjoint Skolem sets $\mathcal{F}'$ for $\Pi.\psi$. The formula ψ is constructed so that assignments that do not satisfy P are excluded from consideration. This allows us to ignore those parts of the search space for which all solutions have already been found. Therefore, the found Skolem sets for $\Pi.\psi$ are only partial models for $\Pi.\phi$, restricted to models of P. In line 4, we construct those restricted models and append them to the basis $\mathcal{F}$.

In line 5, the propositional formula ψ is enriched with blocking sets to exclude the disjoint solutions from $\mathcal{F}'$. Since $\Pi.\psi$ is now a false QBF, the next call to computeDisjoint($\Pi.\psi$) in line 6 yields a set $\mathcal{H}$ of all disjoint Herbrand sets for $\Pi.\psi$. As the universal variables appear in the first quantifier block, each of these Herbrand sets corresponds to precisely one assignment of the universal variables for which ψ evaluates to false. These assignments indicate new parts of the search space for which we have already identified all (partial) solutions for $\Pi.\phi$.

Thus, these assignments must be excluded in all subsequently identified partial solutions. To do this, the formula P is updated in line 7 by appending the negations of these assignments to P. Additionally, also the formula ψ is updated to exclude the exhausted parts of the search space by disjunctively appending

Algorithm 1. Refinement-Based Basis Computation – True Formula

Input: true QBF $\Phi = \Pi.\phi = \forall X \exists Y.\phi$

Output: A minimal basis $\mathcal{F}$ of Skolem sets for Φ

1: $\mathcal{F} \leftarrow \emptyset$, $P \leftarrow \top$, $\psi \leftarrow \phi$
2: **while** P is satisfiable **do**
3:    $\mathcal{F}' \leftarrow$ computeDisjoint$(\Pi.\psi)$
4:    $\mathcal{F} \leftarrow \mathcal{F} \cup \{(F, P) \mid F \in \mathcal{F}'\}$
5:    $\psi \leftarrow \psi \wedge \bigwedge_{F \in \mathcal{F}'} \neg \phi_F$
6:    $\mathcal{H} \leftarrow$ computeDisjoint$(\Pi.\psi)$
7:    $P \leftarrow P \wedge \bigwedge_{H \in \mathcal{H}} \neg \phi_H$
8:    $\psi \leftarrow \psi \vee \bigvee_{H \in \mathcal{H}} \phi_H$
9: **end while**
10: **return** $\mathcal{F}$

blocking Herbrand sets from $\mathcal{H}$ in line 8. This turns the QBF $\Pi.\psi$ back into a true formula and the next iteration begins.

Notably, the algorithm remains largely the same for false input formulas. The only differences occurs in line 5 and line 8, which must be replaced for false formulas by the following modified snippet.

5: $\psi \leftarrow \psi \vee \bigvee_{F \in \mathcal{F}'} \phi_F$
8: $\psi \leftarrow \psi \wedge \bigwedge_{H \in \mathcal{H}} \neg \phi_H$

The set $\mathcal{F}'$ now contains disjoint Herbrand sets and $\mathcal{H}$ disjoint Skolem sets. Consequently, we have adapted how blocking sets are appended to the formula ψ accordingly. The remainder of the algorithm remains unchanged.

We note that Algorithm 1 can be interrupted at any time to return all solutions that have been found until that point.

Theorem 1. *Algorithm 1 terminates and is correct.*

Proof. For termination, note that, because the universal variables appear in the first quantifier block, each Herbrand set $H \in \mathcal{H}$ computed in line 6 corresponds to precisely one assignment of the universal variables. Thus, by appending the negation of this Herbrand set $\neg \phi_H$ to P in line 7, this assignment gets excluded from the models of P. Since the Herbrand sets are also excluded from ψ in line 8, they cannot reoccur in subsequent iterations. Thus, in each iteration, we exclude at least one new assignment from the models of P. Consequently, after at most $2^{|X|}$ iterations P will become unsatisfiable and the algorithm will terminate.

For correctness, we show that the returned set $\mathcal{F}$ satisfies the property of Definition 5. The minimality of $\mathcal{F}$ follows directly from the construction. We split this proof into two parts: existence of a partial Skolem set with the desired property and uniqueness of it.

For existence, let F be an arbitrary Skolem set for Φ and let σ be an arbitrary X-assignment. At some point in the algorithm, a Herbrand set corresponding to σ is computed. Say this happens in the k-th iteration. Let $\mathcal{F}_k$ be the value of $\mathcal{F}$ at the beginning of the k-th iteration and let $\mathcal{F}'_k$ be the set of disjoint Skolem sets computed during the k-th iteration. If there exists a partial model in $\mathcal{F}_k$

satisfying the condition of Definition 5 for F and σ, we are done. So assume that this is not the case. We will show that such a partial model is then constructed from $\mathcal{F}'_k$ during the k-th iteration.

Any partial model (F', P) constructed in line 4 during the k-th iteration satisfies $P(\sigma) \equiv \top$, because, by assumption, the Herbrand set that excludes σ is only computed and appended to P afterwards. Moreover, this also implies that all remaining partial solutions for the assignment σ are contained in $\mathcal{F}'_k$. This means that the X-assignment σ can be extended to a full assignment τ on $X \cup Y$ such that $\psi(\tau) \equiv \top$ (there had been partial solutions before) and $(\psi \wedge \bigwedge_{F' \in \mathcal{F}'_k} \neg \phi_{F'})(\tau) \equiv \bot$ (there are no more partial solutions left). In particular, because F does not appear in $\mathcal{F}_k$ by assumption, we can choose τ so that $\tau(y) \equiv f_y(\sigma)$ for all $f_y \in F$. But this means that there exists $F' \in \mathcal{F}'_k$ with $f'_y \in F'$ such that $\phi_{F'}(\tau) = (\bigwedge_{y \in Y} y \leftrightarrow f'_y)(\tau) \equiv \top$, showing that $f_y(\sigma) \equiv \tau(y) \equiv f'_y(\tau) \equiv f'_y(\sigma)$ for all $y \in Y$ as required in Definition 5.

For uniqueness, let σ be an arbitrary X-assignment. We show that once a partial Skolem set (F, P) has been computed and F has been excluded from ψ in line 5, no subsequent partial model (F', P') will be computed such that $P'(\sigma) \equiv \top$ and $f_y(\sigma) \equiv f'_y(\sigma)$ for all $y \in Y$, $f_y \in F$, $f'_y \in F'$. This implies the uniqueness condition in Definition 5.

Let σ_F denote the extension of σ to the existential variables, defined by $\sigma_F(y) \equiv f_y(\sigma)$ for all $y \in Y$. By definition, we have $\phi_F(\sigma_F) \equiv \top$. Thus, once $\neg \phi_F$ is appended to ψ, σ_F no longer satisfies ψ. Disjunctively appending blocking Herbrand sets H to ψ in line 8 does not affect this as long as $\phi_H(\sigma) \equiv \bot$. Hence, another Skolem set F' with $f_y(\sigma) \equiv f'_y(\sigma)$ for all $y \in Y$ can only appear after a blocking Herbrand set with $\phi_H(\sigma) \equiv \top$ has been appended to ψ. However, in this case, P is also updated to exclude σ as a model, ensuring that from that point onward $P(\sigma) \equiv \bot$. Thus, we never compute another partial Skolem set (F', P') that satisfies both $P'(\sigma) \equiv \top$ and $f_y(\sigma) \equiv f'_y(\sigma)$ for all $y \in Y$.

Example 4. For $\Phi = \Pi.\phi = \forall x, y \exists a, b.(y \vee \neg a) \wedge (x \vee \neg y \vee \neg b) \wedge (\neg x \vee \neg y \vee \neg a \vee \neg b)$ the full assignment tree of Φ is depicted in Fig. 2a. We use Algorithm 1 to compute a basis of Skolem sets for Φ. To this end, we initialize $\mathcal{F}$ to the empty set, P to $\top$, and ψ to ϕ. Then we compute all disjoint models for Φ.

Disjoint models: Disjoint models for $\Pi.\psi$ are $F_1 = \{f_a(x, y) = \bot, f_b(x, y) = \bot\}$ and $F_2 = \{f_a(x, y) = y, f_b(x, y) = \neg y\}$. Since P is $\top$, we update $\mathcal{F}$ to $\mathcal{F} = \{(F_1, \top), (F_2, \top)\}$. Moreover, we exclude F_1 and F_2 from the search space by appending them as blocking Skolem sets. This updates ψ to $\psi' = \phi \wedge \neg \phi_{F_1} \wedge \neg \phi_{F_2}$. We have now identified all disjoint models for Φ. The resulting formula is now false, so we proceed by computing counter-models for $\Pi.\psi'$. The full assignment tree of the false QBF $\Pi.\psi'$ is depicted in Fig. 2b.

Disjoint counter-models: The disjoint counter-models for $\Pi.\psi'$ are $H_1 = \{h_x = \bot, h_y = \bot\}$, $H_2 = \{h_x = \bot, h_y = \top\}$, and $H_3 = \{h_x = \top, h_y = \bot\}$. Hence, there are no more partial solutions for both assignments that map x to $\bot$ as well as for the assignment $\sigma_3 = \{x \mapsto \top, y \mapsto \bot\}$. We update P to $P = \neg \phi_{H_1} \wedge \neg \phi_{H_2} \wedge \neg \phi_{H_3} \equiv x \wedge y$, in order to exclude these assignments from all future partial models. Moreover, also ψ' is updated to

$$\psi'' = \psi' \vee \phi_{H_1} \vee \phi_{H_2} \vee \phi_{H_3} = (\phi \wedge \neg\phi_{F_1} \wedge \neg\phi_{F_2}) \vee \phi_{H_1} \vee \phi_{H_2} \vee \phi_{H_3}.$$

By adding the counter-models H_1, H_2 and H_3 as blocking Herbrand sets, any extension of the assignments encoded in H_1, H_2, and H_3 to the existential variables a and b leads to a satisfying assignment for ψ'' (see Fig. 2c). As $\Pi.\psi''$ is a true QBF, we continue by computing models. All further models for $\Pi.\psi''$ are only partial models for Φ, restricted to models of $P = x \wedge y$.

Disjoint Models: The formula $\Pi.\psi''$ only has one model, namely $F_3 = \{f_a(x, y) = \bot, f_b(x, y) = \top\}$. Note that our construction only ensures that F_3 renders the original formula ϕ true for the assignment $\{x \mapsto \top, y \mapsto \top\}$. For all other assignments, we cannot make any guarantees. For instance, under the assignment $\{x \mapsto \bot, y \mapsto \top\}$ the Skolem functions in F_3 let ϕ evaluate to $\bot$. We update $\mathcal{F}$ to $\mathcal{F} = \{(F_1, \top), (F_2, \top), (F_3, x \wedge y)\}$ and append F_3 as a blocking Skolem set to ψ''. This yields $\psi''' = \psi'' \wedge \neg\phi_{F_3}$. As $\Pi.\psi'''$ is now a false formula again, we compute its counter-models. The full assignment tree of $\Pi.\psi'''$ is depicted in Fig. 2d.

Disjoint Counter-Models: The formula $\Pi.\psi'''$ only has one counter-model, given by $H_4 = \{h_x = \top, h_y = \top\}$. Hence, we have found all partial solutions for the last open assignment that maps both x and y to $\top$. We update P accordingly to $P = P \wedge \neg\phi_{H_4} \equiv \bot$. For completeness, we update ψ''' by appending H_4 as a blocking Herbrand set. Since P is now unsatisfiable, we can stop our computation and know that a minimal basis of Skolem sets is given by $\mathcal{F} = \{(F_1, \top), (F_2, \top), (F_3, x \wedge y)\}$. Using Proposition 3, we can also deduce that the total number of Skolem sets for Φ is $2 \cdot 2 \cdot 2 \cdot 3 = 24$.

6   Evaluation

We implemented the presented approach for solution enumeration in C++, using DepQBF 6.03 [12] as backend solver. In our tool QEnum[2], the resolution proofs for true and false QBFs produced by this solver are processed by the QBF certification framework QRPCert [14], extracting the Skolem and Herbrand functions in the AIGER format.[3] The Skolem (Herbrand) functions are appended conjunctively (disjunctively) using the incremental interface of DepQBF. For true QBFs, the propositional model-counter Ganak [17] is called, while OuterCount [19] is called for false QBFs. We note that our tool is the first to enumerate and count all solutions of false QBFs. Thus, for this use case, no comparison to other tools is possible. All experiments were performed on dual-socket AMD EPYC 7313 16 cores @ 3.7 GHz machines running Ubuntu 24.04 with a 32 GB memory limit.

---

[2] https://github.com/PlankAndreas/QEnum.
[3] http://fmv.jku.at/aiger/.

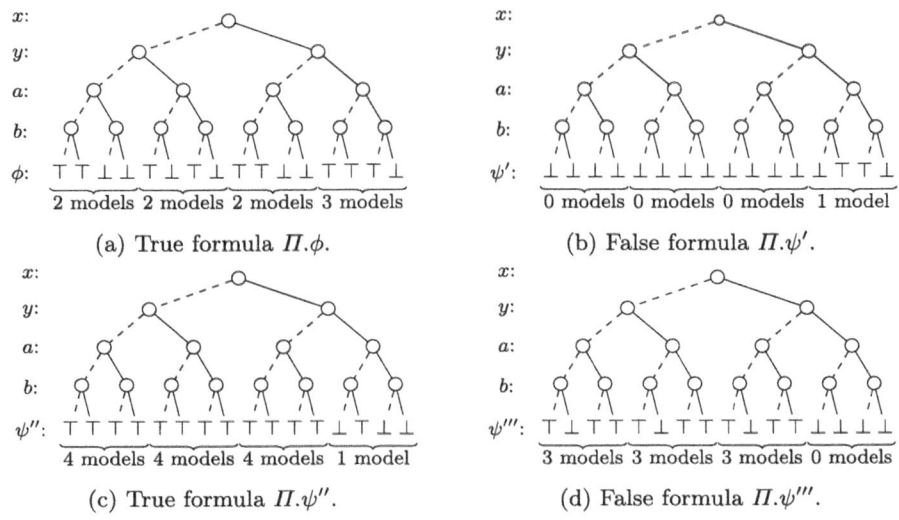

Fig. 2. Assignment tree of the formula from Example 4 as Algorithm 1 progresses. Dashed edges indicate assignments to ⊥ and solid edges to ⊤.

Table 1. Experiments with Tic-Tac-Toe encoding.

Tic-Tac-Toe		formula structure		#solutions		runtime [s]	
size	open positions	#vars	#clauses	#disjoint	#total	disjoint	total
4 × 4	3	5	31	1	4	0.23	0.42
	4	6	261	2	24	0.35	1.14
	5	8	3131	1	64	0.22	0.81
	6	9	46 663	1	64	0.44	1.17
5 × 5	7	10	823 551	1	64	56.35	63.72
	8	11	16 777 225	1	64	28 828.64	29 301.60

Case Study 1: Tic-Tac-Toe Encoding. In our first case study, we consider smaller encodings of the game Tic-Tac-Toe with boards of size 4 × 4 and 5 × 5, similar to the example discussed in Sect. 3. We evaluated how many solutions we could enumerate within a time limit of 12 h and a memory limit of 32 GB. This set is of interest because the enumerated solutions can be manually checked and evaluated. The results of these evaluations are presented in Table 1. All instances are true. Notably, we observe a rise in runtime for the formula with seven open positions, driven by a significant increase in the number of clauses. Interestingly, while computing all models requires some effort, the computation time is still significantly lower than that needed to compute the disjoint models. Although the runtime increases for the final formulas, the computed models remain small.

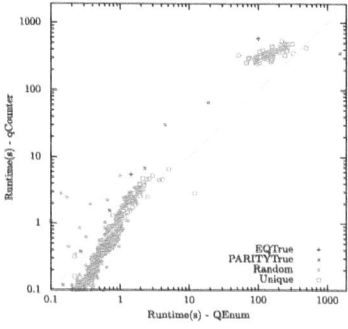 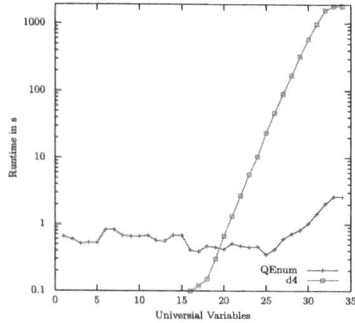

Fig. 3. QEnum vs qCounter (left) and d4 (right) for full model counting.

Case Study 2: Solution Enumeration of Benchmarks from QBF Evaluation. In the second case study, we evaluate how many solutions can be explicitly enumerated for benchmarks used in the 2QBF and PCNF tracks of QBFEval 2022 within a time frame of 300 s consisting of 950 formulas. This is possible, because our approach is based on an anytime algorithm, which returns a subset of the solutions if it is interrupted before termination. In total, we could find 292 solutions. One solution was found for 158 formulas. For 19 formulas between two and ten solutions were returned. Finally, more than ten solutions were found for ten formulas (with 42 being the highest model count that was computed within less than one minute). Note that these formulas are very hard and need to be simplified by preprocessors [8] which modify the solution space.

Case Study 3: Solution Counting. We compare the model counting capabilities of our tool with exact solution counters. We focus on crafted benchmarks, because the formulas considered in the second case study are beyond the scope of modern solution counters. Further, the exact and complete counters d4 [11] and qCounter [15] only work for true formulas. First, we compare the runtime of the SAT-based solution counter qCounter with QEnum. We consider crafted benchmark families as in [7], unique-SAT encodings, as well as randomly generated formulas for which the full model count is known by construction. These formulas were already considered in [11,15] for the evaluation of solution counters. The results are shown in the left part of Fig. 3. QEnum outperforms the comparable tool qCounter for the harder formulas. For both tools, the crafted formulas are hard by construction (as they rely on the Q-resolution based solver DepQBF). For the recursive model counter d4 all those formulas are easy. However, there are also cases where QEnum outperforms d4 as shown on the right of Fig. 3 for formulas $\Phi_i = \forall X \exists Y. \phi$ such that $|X| = i$, $|Y| = 35 - i$, and ϕ is a simple CNF formula over these variables. Obviously, the recursive search of d4 does not involve any advanced QBF reasoning techniques.

Conclusion. The case studies illustrate the practical feasibility of our enumeration-based approach and show that it is comparable to exact state-of-the-art model counters. In the future, we plan to extend our approach to QBFs with arbitrary quantifier structure, e.g., by combining the recursive search of d4 with the refinement-based approach of QEnum. We also plan to investigate the potential of preprocessing, which requires developing solution reconstruction techniques.

Acknowledgements. We thank the anonymous reviewers for their feedback. This research was funded by the Austrian Science Fund (FWF) [10.55776/COE12]. C.H. was supported by the LIT AI Lab funded by the state of Upper Austria.

References

1. Baluta, T., Shen, S., Shinde, S., Meel, K.S., Saxena, P.: Quantitative verification of neural networks and its security applications. In: Proc. of the 2019 ACM SIGSAC Conf. on Computer and Communications Security, pp. 1249–1264. ACM, New York (2019)
2. Becker, B., Ehlers, R., Lewis, M., Marin, P.: ALLQBF solving by computational learning. In: Automated Technology for Verification and Analysis, pp. 370–384. Springer Berlin Heidelberg, Berlin (2012)
3. Beyersdorff, O., Mikolás, J., Lonsing, F., Seidl, M.: Quantified Boolean formulas. In: Handbook of Satisfiability, vol. 336, pp. 1177–1221. IOS Press, Amsterdam (2021)
4. Biondi, F., Enescu, M.A., Heuser, A., Legay, A., Meel, K.S., Quilbeuf, J.: Scalable approximation of quantitative information flow in programs. Presented at the (2018). https://doi.org/10.1007/978-3-319-73721-8_4
5. Chakraborty, S., Meel, K.S., Vardi, M.Y.: Algorithmic improvements in approximate counting for probabilistic inference: from linear to logarithmic SAT calls. In: Proc. of Int. Joint Conf. on Artificial Intelligence, pp. 3569–3576. IJCAI/AAAI Press, USA (2016)
6. Gomes, C.P., Sabharwal, A., Selman, B.: Model counting. In: Handbook of Satisfiability, pp. 993–1014. IOS Press, Amsterdam (2021)
7. Heisinger, S., Seidl, M.: True crafted formula families for benchmarking quantified satisfiability solvers. In: Intelligent Computer Mathematics, pp. 291–296. Springer Nature Switzerland, Cham (2023)
8. Heule, M., Järvisalo, M., Lonsing, F., Seidl, M., Biere, A.: Clause elimination for SAT and QSAT. J. Artif. Intell. Res. **53**, 127–168 (2015)
9. Kleine Büning, H., Lettmann, T.: Propositional logic: deduction and algorithms. Cambridge Tracts in Theoretical Computer Science, vol. 48. Cambridge University Press, USA (1999)
10. Ladner, R.E.: Polynomial space counting problems. SIAM J. Comput. **18**(6), 1087–1097 (1989)
11. Lagniez, J.M., Capelli, F., Plank, A., Seidl, M.: A top-down tree model counter for quantified Boolean formulas. In: Proc. of the 33rd. Int. Conf. on International Joint Conference on Artificial Intelligence IJCAI (2024)
12. Lonsing, F., Egly, U.: DepQBF 6.0: a search-based QBF solver beyond traditional QCDCL. In: de Moura, L. (ed.) CADE 2017. LNCS (LNAI), vol. 10395, pp. 371–384. Springer, Cham (2017). https://doi.org/10.1007/978-3-319-63046-5_23

13. Narodytska, N., Shrotri, A., Meel, K.S., Ignatiev, A., Marques-Silva, J.: Assessing heuristic machine learning explanations with model counting. In: Janota, M., Lynce, I. (eds.) SAT 2019. LNCS, vol. 11628, pp. 267–278. Springer, Cham (2019). https://doi.org/10.1007/978-3-030-24258-9_19
14. Niemetz, A., Preiner, M., Lonsing, F., Seidl, M., Biere, A.: Resolution-based certificate extraction for QBF. In: Cimatti, A., Sebastiani, R. (eds.) SAT 2012. LNCS, vol. 7317, pp. 430–435. Springer, Heidelberg (2012). https://doi.org/10.1007/978-3-642-31612-8_33
15. Plank, A., Möhle, S., Seidl, M.: Counting QBF solutions at level two. Constraints **29**(1), 22–39 (2024)
16. Sang, T., Beame, P., Kautz, H.A.: Performing Bayesian inference by weighted model counting. In: Proc. of the 20th Nat. Conf. on Artificial Intelligence, pp. 475–482. AAAI Press / The MIT Press, Dagstuhl (2005)
17. Sharma, S., Roy, S., Soos, M., Meel, K.S.: GANAK: a scalable probabilistic exact model counter. In: Proc. of Int. Joint Conf. on Artificial Intelligence, pp. 1169–1176. Int. Joint Conf. on Artificial Intelligence Organization, Macao (2019)
18. Shaw, A., Juba, B., Meel, K.S.: An approximate Skolem function counter. In: Conf. on Artificial Intelligence, AAAI, pp. 8108–8116. AAAI Press, Vancouver (2024)
19. Shukla, A., Biere, A., Pulina, L., Seidl, M.: A survey on applications of quantified Boolean formulas. In: Proc. of the Int. Conf. on Tools with Artificial Intelligence, pp. 78–84. IEEE, USA (2019)
20. Zhou, Z., Qian, Z., Reiter, M.K., Zhang, Y.: Static evaluation of noninterference using approximate model counting. In: Proc. of IEEE Symposium on Security and Privacy, pp. 514–528. IEEE Computer Society, San Francisco (2018)

Interpolating Parametric Array Theories

Rodrigo Raya[1]([✉])[iD] and Christophe Ringeissen[2][iD]

[1] École Polytechnique Fédérale de Lausanne, Lausanne, Switzerland
`rodrigo.raya@epfl.ch`
[2] CNRS, Inria, LORIA, Université de Lorraine, 54000 Nancy, France
`christophe.ringeissen@loria.fr`

Abstract. Parametric array theories are extensions of the quantifier-free theory of arrays with relations that hold componentwise. We show that these theories retain rich (general and uniform) quantifier-free interpolation properties. Our results include the interpolation properties of the simple flat array fragment, which were left open in the literature.

1 Introduction

Array theories are quantifier-free relational languages used in program verification to model unbounded data structures and sets of processes [5]. Quantifier-free interpolation algorithms for array theories are of interest to prove safety properties of programs, since they help to discover program invariants based on the analysis of unsafe program traces [13]. Unfortunately, classical array theories, such as the array property fragment [2], do not have quantifier-free interpolation algorithms [12].

Despite these negative results, we identify expressive array theories with desirable interpolation properties. Our paper shows the (general and uniform) quantifier-free interpolation properties in array theories that generalise the extensionality axiom [16] to functions and relation symbols. For conciseness, we focus on the least expressive array fragment exhibiting each interpolation property. We give full proofs for the (general) quantifier-free interpolation property of combinatory array logic and the uniform interpolation property of the simple flat array fragment.

Our results close the open question in [8] about the quantifier-free interpolation property of the simple flat array fragment and relate to a number of interpolation results in the literature [8,11,13,17]. Unlike the results in [8,17], our results also cover the uniform interpolation property. Table 1 compares our results with those obtained for the array property fragment in [12], those obtained for the extensional theory of arrays in [3,7] and those obtained for arrays with length in [8].

Paper Organisation. Section 2 introduces basic notions of many-sorted logic, quantifier-free interpolation and parametric array theories. Section 3 describes the quantifier-free interpolation algorithm for combinatory array logic. The extension to general quantifier-free interpolation is treated in Sect. 4. Uniform

© The Author(s), under exclusive license to Springer Nature Switzerland AG 2026
G. Casini et al. (Eds.): JELIA 2025, LNAI 16094, pp. 182–189, 2026.
https://doi.org/10.1007/978-3-032-04590-4_13

Table 1. Summary of interpolation properties of fragments studied in the paper.

SMT Theory	QF	General	Uniform
Array Property Fragment	no [12]	no [12]	no [12]
Arrays with Extensionality	yes [3]	yes	no [7]
Combinatory Array Logic	yes	yes	no [7]
Contiguous Arrays with Maxdiff	yes [8]	yes [8]	?
Simple Flat Fragment	yes	yes	yes

interpolation for the simple flat array fragment is treated in Sect. 5. Section 6 concludes the paper.

2   Preliminaries

We use standard notions of many-sorted logic and define many-sorted theories, combination theories, quantifier-free interpolation properties and the array theories that we treat.

Many-Sorted Theories. We view a theory as the set of all interpretations satisfying a given set of sentences. Given a signature Σ, the theory of equality with uninterpreted function symbols is the set of all structures over Σ. The pure theory of equality is obtained from this one when the signature only contains the equality symbol. We use the usual notion in logic of truth of formulas. A formula φ is true with respect to a theory T, denoted by $T \models \varphi$, if φ is true in any model of T. To evaluate the truth of a formula with free variables, we consider these variables as universally quantified.

Combination Theories. Given two theories T_1 over signature Σ_1 and T_2 over signature Σ_2, their combination is given by the set of interpretations over the signature $\Sigma_1 \cup \Sigma_2$ such that the reduct of the interpretation to Σ_1 is a structure in T_1 and the reduct of the intepretation to Σ_2 is a structure in T_2. We say that the theories are disjoint if the set of function and predicate symbols over the signatures Σ_1 and Σ_2 are disjoint. We say that the theories are strongly disjoint if, furthermore, the sets of sorts in Σ_1 and Σ_2 are disjoint. This implies that each literal of a quantifier-free formula belongs to exactly one of the combined theories. Strongly disjoint theories admit simple interpolation procedures.

Quantifier-Free Interpolation. We use the definition from [8].

Definition 1 (Quantifier-free interpolation). *A theory T admits quantifier-free interpolation if and only if for every pair of quantifier-free formulas ϕ, ψ such that $\phi \wedge \psi$ is T-unsatisfiable, there exists a quantifier-free formula θ, called an interpolant, such that (i) $T \models \phi \rightarrow \theta$, (ii) $\theta \wedge \psi$ is T-unsatisfiable, and (iii) only the variables occurring in both ϕ and ψ occur in θ.*

The notion of general quantifier-free interpolation [4, Definition 2.2] captures the scenario where the semantics of certain relations and functions are irrelevant for the verification process.

Definition 2 (General quantifier-free interpolation). *Let T be a theory over signature Σ, T has the general quantifier-free interpolation property if and only if for every signature Σ' (disjoint from Σ) and for every pair of quantifier-free $\Sigma \cup \Sigma'$-formulas ϕ, ψ such that $\phi \wedge \psi$ is $T \cup EUF(\Sigma')$-unsatisfiable, there is a quantifier-free formula θ such that (i) $T \cup EUF(\Sigma') \models \phi \to \theta$, (ii) $\theta \wedge \psi$ is $T \cup EUF(\Sigma')$-unsatisfiable, and (iii) all variables, functions and relation symbols from Σ' occurring in θ also occur in ϕ and ψ.*

A notion of uniform interpolant or cover was introduced in [10].

Definition 3 (Uniform interpolation). *Let T be a theory and, given an existential formula $\exists \overline{e}.\phi(\overline{e}, \overline{y})$, the set of residues of $\exists \overline{e}.\phi(\overline{e}, \overline{y})$ is $\mathrm{Res}(\exists \overline{e}.\phi(\overline{e}, \overline{y})) = \{\theta(\overline{y}, \overline{z}) \mid T \models \exists \overline{e}.\phi(\overline{e}, \overline{y}) \to \theta(\overline{y}, \overline{z})$ and $\theta(\overline{y}, \overline{z})$ is quantifier-free$\}$. A formula $\psi(\overline{y})$ is a T-cover of $\exists \overline{e}.\phi(\overline{e}, \overline{y})$ if and only if $\psi(\overline{y}) \in \mathrm{Res}(\exists \overline{e}.\phi(\overline{e}, \overline{y}))$ and $\psi(\overline{y})$ implies (modulo T) all the other formulas in $\mathrm{Res}(\exists \overline{e}.\phi(\overline{e}, \overline{y}))$. The theory T has the uniform quantifier-free interpolation property if and only if every existential formula $\exists \overline{e}.\phi(\overline{e}, \overline{y})$ has a T-cover.*

Existential quantifier elimination yields uniform interpolants.

Proposition 1. *If a theory T eliminates existential quantifiers over its different sorts, then it has the uniform quantifier-free interpolation property.*

Diff Functions and Their Iterations diff functions were introduced in [3] to recover the interpolation property in the extensional theory of arrays. The term $\mathrm{diff}(x, y)$ returns an index where the arrays x and y are different or an arbitrary index if they are equal. Iterated diffs were introduced in [8] to have several witnesses of some formula. Iterated difss can either appear explicitly in the formula as distinct functional terms $\mathrm{diff}^1, \ldots, \mathrm{diff}^n, \ldots$ or be simulated using the theory's language with formulas of the form

$$\varphi(i, x, y) := \exists x', x''.x' = x \wedge x'' = write(x', \mathrm{diff}(x, y), y[\mathrm{diff}(x, y)]) \wedge i = \mathrm{diff}(x'', y)$$

which is used to define the properties that $i := \mathrm{diff}^2(x, y)$ satisfies.

$$F ::= A \mid F_1 \wedge F_2 \mid F_1 \vee F_2 \mid \neg F \mid \mathrm{map}_R(\overline{A}) \mid a[i] = e$$
$$A ::= a \mid write(A, i, E) \mid K(e) \mid \mathrm{map}_f(\overline{A})$$
$$E ::= A[i] \mid e$$

Fig. 1. T_{CAL}'s syntax.

Combinatory Array Logic [14], T_{CAL}, uses a quantifier-free many-sorted language, comprising an index sort, an element sort, and an array sort. In Fig. 1, we use instances of letter i to refer to variables of the index sort, letter e to refer to variables of sort element and letter a to refer to a variable of the array sort. Function symbol write takes as input an array, an index and an element and returns an array. Function read, $\_[\_]$, takes an array and an index and returns an element. Function K takes as input an element and returns an array which is constantly equal to that element. Function $\mathrm{map}_f(\overline{A})$ takes as input a tuple of arrays and returns an array where the i-th component is the result of applying function f to the i-th component of the input arrays. Relation $\mathrm{map}_R(\overline{A})$ takes as input a tuple of arrays and returns true if and only if relation R holds for each tuple of elements in the i-th component. Formally, the introduced symbols satisfy the following axioms.

$$\forall a, i, e.\, \mathrm{write}(a, i, e)[i] = e$$
$$\forall a, i, j, e.\, i = j \vee \mathrm{write}(a, i, e)[j] = a[j]$$
$$\forall e, i.\, K(e)[i] = e$$
$$\forall a_1, \ldots, a_k, i.\, \mathrm{map}_f\,(a_1, \ldots, a_k)\,[i] = f\,(a_1[i], \ldots, a_k[i])$$
$$\forall a_1, \ldots, a_k.\, \mathrm{map}_R(a_1, \ldots, a_k) \leftrightarrow \forall i.\, R(a_1[i], \ldots, a_k[i])$$

We use f for map_f and R for map_R when no ambiguity occurs.

Simple Flat Array Fragment [1,9,15], T_{F}, uses a quantifier-free many-sorted language, comprising a sort for indices, a sort for elements, a sort for integers, a sort for sets of indices, and a sort for arrays. In Fig. 2, we use (indexed) instances of letter i to refer to variables of the index sort, letter x to refer to variables of sort set, letter k to refer to a variable of the integer sort and letter a to refer to a variable of the array sort. The logic has as atoms set interpretations of the form $\{i \mid \varphi(\overline{a}[i])\}$ where $\overline{a}$ is a set of array variables, $\overline{a}[i]$ denotes the set of elements in the i-th component of the array variables and φ is a formula in the theory of elements. These set interpretations are combined with Boolean algebra expressions and cardinality constraints. The semantics of these symbols is the standard.

$$F ::= A \mid F_1 \wedge F_2 \mid F_1 \vee F_2 \mid \neg F$$
$$A ::= i_1 = i_2 \mid i \in B \mid B_1 \subseteq B_2 \mid T_1 \leq T_2$$
$$B ::= x \mid \emptyset \mid B_1 \cup B_2 \mid B_1 \cap B_2 \mid B^c \mid \{i \mid \varphi(\overline{a}[i])\}$$
$$T ::= k \mid K \mid T_1 + T_2 \mid K \cdot T \mid |B|$$
$$K ::= \ldots \mid -2 \mid -1 \mid 0 \mid 1 \mid 2 \mid \ldots$$

Fig. 2. T_{F}'s syntax.

3   Quantifier-Free Interpolation

We illustrate the quantifier-free interpolation properties of Table 1 on combinatory array logic extended with generalised diff terms.

Definition 4 (Generalised diff terms). *Given a relation $R(\bar{e}, \bar{c})$ over some element variables $\bar{e}$ and constants $\bar{c}$, the term $\mathrm{diff}_R^{\bar{c}}(\bar{a})$ is defined to yield an index of the arrays $\bar{a}$ where the relation $R(\bar{a}[i], \bar{c})$ does not hold if such an index exists or an arbitrary index if no such index exists.*

The interpolation procedure takes a pair of combinatory array logic formulas (ϕ, ψ) as input and performs the following steps.

1. Replace each atom $\neg R(\bar{a}, \bar{c})$ by an atom $\neg R(\bar{a}[\mathrm{diff}_R^{\bar{c}}(\bar{a})^i], \bar{c})$ where i is a natural number increased at each instantiation of this particular relation.
2. Each write operation $b = write(a, i, v)$ is supplemented with a term $b[i] = v$.
3. For each index j ranging over the set of indices formed by
   - the set of index variables used in formula ϕ or ψ and
   - the diff terms introduced in Step 1
   or alternatively, if the above set of indices is empty, the singleton set of indices $\{\mathrm{diff}_0\}$ with an index witnessing the non-emptiness of the index sort,
   - replace each write term $b = write(a, i, v)$ (previously supplemented) by a conjunction of terms of the form $i \neq j \to a[j] = b[j]$.
   - replace each atom $R(\bar{a}, \bar{c})$ by a conjunction of terms of the form $R(\bar{a}[j], \bar{c})$.
4. Replace each atom $a[j]$ by a variable a_j.
5. For each pair of variables j_1 and j_2 and for each array variable used in reads, introduce the formula $j_1 = j_2 \to a_{j_1} = a_{j_2}$.
6. Compute an interpolant I of the resulting pair of formulas.
7. Output I with each variable a_j rewritten into $a[j]$.

Theorem 1. *If the theory of elements has quantifier-free interpolation, then the above procedure computes quantifier-free interpolants for combinatory array logic with diffs.*

Proof. A key insight is that the formulas in Step 6 are expressed in a strongly disjoint theory combination. Thus, it is trivial to compute interpolants.

4   General Quantifier-Free Interpolation Properties

The main difference from Sect. 3 is that before applying Step 6, we need to eliminate array variables from uninterpreted relations or functions. We do this by rewriting relations of the form $R(\ldots, a, \ldots)$, where a is an array variable, into $R_{\ldots, a, \ldots}(\ldots, \ldots)$, while ensuring that the congruence axioms of R hold. For example, we need to ensure that if $a = b$ then $R_a(\ldots, \ldots) = R_b(\ldots, \ldots)$ for all instances of the parameters of R that appear in the formula. The equality $a = b$ can be encoded by enforcing the equality between element variables $a_i = b_i$ where i ranges over the set of indices in Step 3 of the quantifier-free interpolation algorithm. We eliminate index variables occurring under uninterpreted functions or relations using similar encoding methods. The resulting formulas are in a strongly disjoint combination of the theory of indices with equality and the theory of elements with additional uninterpreted functions and relation symbols. Interpolating over this theory then yields the following lemma.

Theorem 2. *If the theory of elements is general quantifier-free interpolating, then the theory of combinatory array logic is general quantifier-free interpolating.*
Proof. A key insight is that the formulas in Step 6 are again expressed in a strongly disjoint theory combination. Thus, it is trivial to compute interpolants from interpolants of the index theory and general interpolants of the element theory.

5 Uniform Interpolation Properties

Ghilardi [7] has shown the failure of uniform interpolation for the extensional theory of arrays with diff. His proof requires some set-theoretic assumptions.

Corollary 1. *Using standard set-theoretic assumptions, the formula*

$$G(c_1, c_2, d_1, d_2, i) := c_1[i] \neq c_2[i] \wedge d_1[i] = d_2[i]$$

cannot eliminate i uniformly in combinatory array logic with diff functions. Thus, combinatory array logic with diffs does not have the uniform interpolation property.

In contrast, we can show that the simple flat array fragment eliminates existential quantifiers. From Proposition 1, it follows that the simple flat array fragment is uniform interpolating.

Theorem 3. *The simple flat array fragment is uniform interpolating.*
Proof. The quantifier elimination routine reuses ideas from quantifier elimination algorithms in the literature [6].

6 Conclusion

We have investigated the quantifier-free interpolation properties for several theories of data structures introduced after the original paper of Kapur, Majumdar and Zarba [13]. We proved that the pointwise generalisation of relations introduced in the theory of combinatory array logic preserves the quantifier-free interpolation property of the quantifier-free array theory with diffs. Finally, we showed that while uniform interpolation fails for combinatory array logic, this property is recovered in the simple flat array fragment. The interpolation properties of the later fragment were open in [8]. These results are in contrast with those in [12] which show that strongly related array logics do not admit quantifier-free interpolation. Our results enable the use of interpolation algorithms for accelerating the discovery of invariants in the verification of programs manipulating data structures for a whole class of properties that hold componentwise. The implementation of this technique appears to be the most interesting research direction in connection with our work.

References

1. Alberti, F., Ghilardi, S., Pagani, E.: Cardinality constraints for arrays (decidability results and applications). Formal Methods Syst. Des. **51**(3), 545–574 (2017). https://doi.org/10.1007/s10703-017-0279-6

2. Bradley, A.R., Manna, Z., Sipma, H.B.: What's decidable about arrays? In: Emerson, E.A., Namjoshi, K.S. (eds.) VMCAI 2006. LNCS, vol. 3855, pp. 427–442. Springer, Heidelberg (2005). https://doi.org/10.1007/11609773_28

3. Bruttomesso, R., Ghilardi, S., Ranise, S.: Quantifier-free interpolation of a theory of arrays. Logical Methods Comput. Sci. (2012). https://doi.org/10.2168/LMCS-8(2:4)2012. publisher: Episciences.org

4. Bruttomesso, R., Ghilardi, S., Ranise, S.: Quantifier-free interpolation in combinations of equality interpolating theories. ACM Trans. Comput. Logic **15**(1), 1–34 (2014). https://doi.org/10.1145/2490253

5. Daca, P., Henzinger, T.A., Kupriyanov, A.: Array folds logic. In: Chaudhuri, S., Farzan, A. (eds.) CAV 2016. LNCS, vol. 9780, pp. 230–248. Springer, Cham (2016). https://doi.org/10.1007/978-3-319-41540-6_13

6. Feferman, S., Vaught, R.: The first order properties of products of algebraic systems. Fundam. Math. **47**(1), 57–103 (1959)

7. Ghilardi, S.: Interpolation properties for array theories: positive and negative results. In: CIBD 2024. Amsterdam (2024)

8. Ghilardi, S., Gianola, A., Kapur, D., Naso, C.: Interpolation results for arrays with length and MaxDiff. ACM Trans. Comput. Logic **24**(4), 1–33 (2023).https://doi.org/10.1145/3587161

9. Ghilardi, S., Pagani, E.: Higher-order quantifier elimination, counter simulations and fault-tolerant systems. J. Autom. Reason. **65**(3), 425–460 (2020). https://doi.org/10.1007/s10817-020-09578-5

10. Gulwani, S., Musuvathi, M.: Cover algorithms and their combination. In: Drossopoulou, S. (ed.) ESOP 2008. LNCS, vol. 4960, pp. 193–207. Springer, Heidelberg (2008). https://doi.org/10.1007/978-3-540-78739-6_16

11. Hoenicke, J., Schindler, T.: Efficient interpolation for the theory of arrays. In: Galmiche, D., Schulz, S., Sebastiani, R. (eds.) IJCAR 2018. LNCS (LNAI), vol. 10900, pp. 549–565. Springer, Cham (2018). https://doi.org/10.1007/978-3-319-94205-6_36

12. Hoenicke, J., Schindler, T.: Interpolation and the array property fragment (2019). arXiv:1904.11381 [cs]

13. Kapur, D., Majumdar, R., Zarba, C.G.: Interpolation for data structures. In: Proceedings of the 14th ACM SIGSOFT international symposium on Foundations of software engineering, pp. 105–116. ACM, Portland Oregon USA (2006).https://doi.org/10.1145/1181775.1181789

14. de Moura, L., Bjorner, N.: Generalized, efficient array decision procedures. In: 2009 Formal Methods in Computer-Aided Design, pp. 45–52. IEEE, Austin (2009). https://doi.org/10.1109/FMCAD.2009.5351142

15. Raya, R., Kunčak, V.: NP satisfiability for arrays as powers. In: Finkbeiner, B., Wies, T. (eds.) VMCAI 2022. LNCS, vol. 13182, pp. 301–318. Springer, Cham (2022). https://doi.org/10.1007/978-3-030-94583-1_15

16. Stump, A., Barrett, C., Dill, D., Levitt, J.: A decision procedure for an extensional theory of arrays. In: Proceedings 16th Annual IEEE Symposium on Logic in Computer Science, pp. 29–37. IEEE Comput. Soc, Boston, MA, USA (2001).https://doi.org/10.1109/LICS.2001.932480

17. Totla, N., Wies, T.: Complete instantiation-based interpolation. J. Autom. Reason. **57**(1), 37–65 (2016). https://doi.org/10.1007/s10817-016-9371-7

Maximum Satisfiability Formulations for Nonlinear Integer Programming

Zhifei Zheng⦿, Sami Cherif(✉)⦿, Rui Sá Shibasaki⦿, Chu-Min Li⦿,
and Jialu Zhang⦿

Laboratoire MIS UR 4290, Université de Picardie Jules Verne, Amiens, France
{zhifei.zheng,sami.cherif,rui.sa.shibasaki,chu-min.li,
jialu.zhang}@u-picardie.fr

Abstract. This paper introduces novel Maximum Satisfiability (MaxSAT) formulations for the Nonlinear Integer Programming (NLIP) problems with discrete polynomial functions. We develop a generic framework based on three established integer encoding techniques from the literature. Our approach treats each polynomial term as an atomic unit and demonstrates how it can be efficiently encoded through compact representations of integer assignments. Additionally, we present two distinct decomposition methods based on the degrees of polynomial terms. This work lays a foundation for future research and has the potential to extend the applicability of modern MaxSAT solvers to a wider range of optimization problems.

1 Introduction

Satisfiability (SAT) and Maximum Satisfiability (MaxSAT) are powerful formalisms with strong expressive ability under propositional logic. Given a propositional formula in Conjunctive Normal Form (CNF), SAT consists in deciding whether it is satisfiable [5]. MaxSAT is a natural optimization extension of SAT, in which the goal shifts to finding an assignment that maximizes the number of satisfied clausal constraints in the given formula (MinSAT is another optimization extension of SAT [22]). MaxSAT methodologies have been applied to solve problems in various domains, including hardware and software verification [15,28], planning and scheduling [7,30] and bio-informatics [13,14]. Empowered by pseudo-Boolean constraints, MaxSAT has been successfully applied to integer linear problems (ILP). However, existing literature has not extensively explored the capacity of MaxSAT to solve nonlinear integer programming problems (NLIP).

Like ILP, the NLIP problems are also frequently encountered in multiple domains, such as portfolio management, transportation, and network design [10, 17,26]. These problems are usually difficult to solve, due to the integer variables and the nonlinearity of constraints. In this sense, here we propose an encoding scheme for modeling NILP problems as MaxSAT instances, so that state-of-art MaxSAT solvers can serve as an alternative approach to solve such problems.

G. Casini et al. (Eds.): JELIA 2025, LNAI 16094, pp. 190–206, 2026.
https://doi.org/10.1007/978-3-032-04590-4_14

In this paper, we particularly focus on NLIP problems with polynomial functions, *i.e.*, exponential, logarithmic and other non-polynomial functions are not considered. Furthermore, we assume that the integer variables are bounded by an integer constant. It is worth noting that, even considering these assumptions the problem is already challenging, as shown by previous work in the literature. Indeed, in [24], it was proven that the optimization of a degree-4 polynomial function constrained to the set of integer lattice points of a convex polygon is NP-hard. Additionally, it was shown in [18] that, if the variables are not bounded, integer programming with quadratic constraints is *undecidable*, *i.e.*, there cannot exist a general algorithm to solve every instance of the problem.

Furthermore, in the literature, several works have proposed methods for transforming pseudo-Boolean constraints into clauses, e.g., [1,11,25]. More related to our work, in [2], the authors discuss how to transform linear problems with finite domains into equivalent SAT problems, and propose six different mapping methods. However, they do not consider the nonlinear case. Meanwhile, the nonlinear situations are also of interest to the community of Satisfiability Modulo Theories (SMT). Classical nonlinear integer arithmetic (NIA) problems are handled on a higher abstraction level, usually by simplifying problems into linear forms, then conducting typical bit-blasting into CNF [8,20]. To the best of our knowledge, there is no work presenting an end-to-end formulation from Nonlinear polynomial integer programming directly to MaxSAT. It is also worth noting that, as pointed out in [27], the pseudo-Boolean field has not been as developed as the satisfiability field, which is the reason why we develop our work through the lens of MaxSAT.

The contribution of this paper is twofold. First, an encoding of high-order nonlinear polynomial terms is formally described. Second, we propose a complete encoding of polynomial NLIP problems to MaxSAT formulations. The encoding of polynomial terms is based on well-known integer representations in the literature, namely the one-hot, unary, and binary representations. We first discuss how these representations can be generalized to encode nonlinear terms, then study the complexities of our models in terms of the number of variables and clauses derived for such formulations. A complete MaxSAT formulation for NILP can already be obtained by the conjunction of clauses encoding each term individually. Finally, we propose decomposition strategies that can reduce the complexity of the final MaxSAT formulation in terms of the number of variables and clauses.

The remainder of this paper is organized as follows. Section 2 introduces the fundamental definitions and notations of MaxSAT and NLIP. It also discusses related work and proposes the generic framework for transforming NLIP into MaxSAT formulations. Section 3 takes each polynomial term as an atomic unit, using the three different representations to encode any given polynomial term. Section 4 takes one step forward and decomposes the degree of the given polynomial terms, therefore decreasing the complexity of the encodings. Finally, we conclude and discuss future work in Sect. 5.

2   Preliminaries

2.1   Maximum Satisfiabilty

In this paper, we consider the most generic variant of MaxSAT, namely Weighted Partial MaxSAT [3,21]. This problem takes as input a bipartite weighted formula $\phi = H \cup S$, where H is the set of hard clauses that must be satisfied as in SAT, and S is the set of soft clauses, in which each clause C is associated with an integer weight C. The objective of Weighted Partial MaxSAT is to obtain an assignment α that maximizes (resp. minimizes) the sum of the weight of satisfied (resp. falsified) soft clauses while satisfying all the hard clauses. Formally, let $cost_\alpha(\phi)$ denote the sum of weights of soft clauses in ϕ falsified by the assignment α, Weighted Partial MaxSAT thus seeks for $optimum(\phi) = \min_\alpha cost_\alpha(\phi)$.

In the following sections, we simply use MaxSAT to refer to the most generic version defined above. Note that in classical MaxSAT, weights are positive integers. However, within this paper, we allow the weight to be negative, since a negative weight can always be normalized to a positive one. In the remainder of this paper, we use $SatW_\alpha(\phi)$ to denote the sum of weights of clauses in ϕ satisfied by α, which can be abbreviated as $SatW(\phi)$ when the context is clear. Additionally, we mention that previous literature introduces Pseudo-Boolean (PB) constraints [27], which can be formalized as $\sum_j w_j \cdot l_j \vartriangleright c$, where $w_j \in \mathbb{N}, c \in \mathbb{N}$, l_j is a literal and $\vartriangleright \in \{=, >, \geq, <, \leq\}$. When all the coefficients of literals are equal to one and can thus be omitted, we refer to such forms more commonly as cardinality constraints.

2.2   Nonlinear Integer Programming

In this section, we formally define NLIP and introduce the terminologies that will be used throughout this paper. Here, we consider the case where integer variables are bounded, i.e., the domain of variables is $\mathbf{V} = \{0, 1, \ldots ub\}$. Additionally, coefficients are also restricted to be integers, and the objective function and constraints are restricted to be polynomials.

Definition 1 (Polynomial Term and High-order Term). *A term $T(\mathbf{X})$ of variables $\mathbf{X} = (X_1, \ldots, X_n)$ is called a polynomial term if it can be written as:* $T(\mathbf{X}) = c \cdot \prod_{q \in Q} X_q^{k_q}$, *where $c \in \mathbb{Z}, k_q \in \mathbb{N}, \forall q \in Q$ and $Q \subseteq \{1, \ldots, n\}$.*

We refer to a term with only one variable (*e.g.*, X_1^2) as a *pure term*, and a term with different variables (*e.g.*, $X_1 X_2$) as a *cross term*. We call $k = \sum_{q \in Q} k_q$ the *order* of $T(\mathbf{X})$. In particular, when $k \geq 2$, we refer to this term as a *high-order term*. If the context is clear, we abbreviate $T(\mathbf{X})$ as T. Using this notation, we can now formalize discrete nonlinear polynomial functions as follows:

Definition 2 (Nonlinear Polynomial Function). *A discrete polynomial function $P(\mathbf{X})$ is nonlinear if it contains at least one high-order term.*

Definition 3 (Nonlinear Integer Programming). *A NLIP model with n integer variables and l constraints can be formalized as the following form [16,23]:*

$$\max \quad f(\mathbf{X}) \qquad\qquad\qquad\qquad\qquad\qquad \text{(NLIP)}$$
$$s.t. \quad g_i(\mathbf{X}) \le b_i \qquad i = 1, \dots, l \quad ; \mathbf{X} \in \mathbb{X}, \ \mathbb{X} \subseteq \{0, \dots, ub\}^n$$

where f and all g_i functions are polynomials and at least one of them is nonlinear, and ub is a global upper bound of all variables.

2.3   Integer Encodings with MaxSAT

In this subsection, we introduce Boolean-variable-based representations of integers. Given a bounded natural integer variable $X \in \mathbb{N}$ such that $X \le ub$, where ub is a constant upper bound, a series of Boolean variables x_i are used to represent X, with the following well-known methods: one-hot representation [12,19], unary representation [4,6], and binary representation [11,31]. Note that one-hot, unary, and binary representations correspond to Standard mapping (S), Full regular mapping (FR), and Full logarithmic mapping (FL) in [2], respectively.

Given a natural number $X \le ub$, the one-hot representation and the unary representation both use $ub + 1$ Boolean variables to represent X. In a one-hot formulation, the bit with the index corresponding to the value of X is assigned to 1, and the other bits are assigned to 0. In the unary representation, the bits with indexes smaller than or equal to the value of X are assigned to 1, and the other bits are assigned to 0. Note that, since $X \in \mathbb{N}$, 0 is an implicit lower bound for X, x_0 is therefore fixed to 1 in the unary representation. On the other hand, the binary representation uses $\lfloor \log_2 ub \rfloor + 1$ Boolean variables to represent X. The bits that are true in the binary encoding of X are assigned to 1, and the other bits are assigned to 0. In this context, when representing the integer variable $X_q \in \mathbf{X}$ ($q \in \{1, 2, .., n\}$), we denote the used Boolean variables as $x_r^{(q)}$,

Table 1. Summary of Notations

	Notation	Description
Sets and Numbers	$\mathbb{N}$	The set of natural numbers: $\{0, 1, 2, \dots\}$
	$\mathbb{Z}$	The set of integer numbers: $\{\dots, -2, -1, 0, 1, 2, \dots\}$
	ub	The upper bound for all original integer variables
	$\mathbf{V}_c$	The value set $\mathbf{V}_c = \{0, 1, \dots, \lfloor c \rfloor\}$, where c is a given constant
Variables and Functions	X	An integer variable, where $X \le ub$
	$\mathbf{X}$	A vector with all its components as integers
	$T(\mathbf{X})$	A polynomial term on $\mathbf{X}$ (abbreviated as T)
	$P(\mathbf{X})$	A nonlinear polynomial function on $\mathbf{X}$
	$x_r^{(q)}$	Boolean variables encoding X_q
Indices	q	Index for the integer variables in a term
	r	Index for Boolean variables encoding an integer variable

where r is the index of the encoding variables. We summarize the notations and indexes used within this paper in Table 1. Hereafter, log denotes the logarithm with base 2.

Based on the integer representations, we can transform the NLIP formulation into a MaxSAT formulation. The objective function of NLIP is modeled as weighted soft clauses, and the NLIP constraints are modeled as hard clauses. Regarding the objective function, if all soft clauses are unit clauses with only one literal (which can always be ensured by replacing all non-unit clauses with literals and adding hard constraints to ensure the relation), each of them can be regarded as one term in the objective function, with their weights as the coefficients. Given an NLIP instance, a MaxSAT formulation is obtained by transforming the objective and constraints from functions to clauses. Indeed, in the next section, we show how this can be done by using integer encodings to represent any given polynomial term.

3   Atomic Formulations for Nonlinear Terms

Without loss of generality, we focus on the formulation of a polynomial term, with m variables and the order of k, appearing in the objective function, formalized as $T(\mathbf{X}) = c \cdot \prod_{q=1}^{m} X_q^{k_q}$, where $\sum_{q=1}^{m} k_q = k$. All variables X in the discussion are bounded within the finite set $\mathbf{V}_{ub} = \{0, \dots, ub\}$. Although we develop the idea from the perspective of objective functions, the same procedure can be applied to transformations of constraint functions. Consequently, transforming the entire NILP reduces to encoding each polynomial term that appears in it. The one-hot, unary, and binary formulations are subsequently given in the following Subsects. 3.1, 3.2, and 3.3.

3.1   One-Hot Formulation

Given a polynomial term T, the one-hot formulation ensures a direct mapping between each possible value of the term and its corresponding encoding. Considering the one-hot encoding of integer variables X_q, we have that $X_q = \sum_{r_q=0}^{ub} r_q \cdot x_{r_q}^{(q)}$, and therefore the product of m integer variables produces the product of m encoding variables x for each possible permutation of values in $\mathbf{V}_{ub}$, corresponding to the auxiliary variables $z_{r_1 \dots r_m}$. We present below the MaxSAT formulation (OH) for the polynomial term in the objective function, and we prove its soundness in Theorem 1.

Soft Clauses

$$(z_{r_1 \dots r_m}, c \cdot \prod_{q=1}^{m} r_q^{k_q}) \qquad \forall (r_1, \dots, r_m) \in \mathbf{V}_{ub}^m : c \cdot \prod_{q=1}^{m} r_q^{k_q} \neq 0 \qquad \text{(OH-S)}$$

Hard Clauses

$$\overline{z}_{r_1 \dots r_m} \vee x_{r_q}^{(q)} \qquad \forall q \in \{1, \dots, m\}, \forall (r_1, \dots, r_m) \in \mathbf{V}_{ub}^m \qquad \text{(OH-H1)}$$

$$(\bigvee_{q=1}^{m} \overline{x}_{r_q}^{(q)}) \vee z_{r_1 \dots r_m} \qquad \forall (r_1, \dots, r_m) \in \mathbf{V}_{ub}^m \qquad \text{(OH-H2)}$$

$$\bigvee_{r \in \mathbf{V}_{ub}} x_r^{(q)} \qquad\qquad \forall q \in \{1, \ldots, m\} \qquad\qquad \text{(OH-H3)}$$

$$\overline{x}_r^{(q)} \vee \overline{x}_{r'}^{(q)} \qquad\qquad \forall q \in \{1, \ldots, m\}, \forall (r, r') \in \mathbf{V}_{ub}^2 : r < r' \qquad \text{(OH-H4)}$$

OH uses the hard clauses OH-H1 to OH-H4 to construct the auxiliary structure supporting the direct mapping of fixed point values of the polynomial term. The formulation first introduces a new series of auxiliary variables $z_{r_1 \ldots r_m}$ for any possible assignment $(r_1, \ldots, r_m) \in \mathbf{V}_{ub}^m$. Equation OH-H1 together with OH-H2 is equivalent to $z_{r_1 \ldots r_m} \leftrightarrow \bigwedge_{q=1}^m x_{r_q}^{(q)}$ $\forall (r_1, \ldots, r_m) \in \mathbf{V}_{ub}^m$. They link auxiliary variables z with the original indicator variables x, ensuring that $z_{r_1 \ldots r_m}$ corresponds to the combination of certain x, i.e., the one-hot representation of $(r_1, \ldots, r_m)$. Equations OH-H3 and OH-H4 guarantee the structure of one-hot, ensuring that exactly one value can be taken for each variable X_q. Based on the structure obtained by hard clauses, Eq. OH-S reformulates the polynomial term T as weighted soft clauses, considering the validity of equality $SatW(\text{OH} - \text{S})$ as proved in the following theorem.

Theorem 1. *The OH formulation is sound and requires $O(ub^m)$ auxiliary variables, $O(m \cdot ub^m)$ clauses, and $O(ub^k)$-valued soft weights.*

Proof. We prove the validity of the OH formulation by proving that $SatW_\alpha(\text{OH} - \text{S})$ is equal to the original polynomial term $T(\mathbf{X})$, for a fixed values vector X such that $X_q = \sum_{r_q=0}^{ub} r_q \cdot x_{r_q}^{(q)}$ where $q \in \{1, \ldots, |X|\}$, given by the assignment α.

$$
\begin{aligned}
SatW(\text{OH} - \text{S}) &= \sum_{r_1=0}^{ub} \cdots \sum_{r_m=0}^{ub} c \cdot \prod_{q=1}^m r_q^{k_q} \cdot z_{r_1 \ldots r_m} \\
&= \sum_{r_1=0}^{ub} \cdots \sum_{r_m=0}^{ub} c \cdot \prod_{q=1}^m (r_q^{k_q} \cdot x_{r_q}^{(q)}) && \text{(by OH-H1 and OH-H2)} \\
&= c \cdot \prod_{q=1}^m \sum_{r_q=0}^{ub} (r_q \cdot x_{r_q}^{(q)})^{k_q} && \text{(by Distributivity)} \\
&= c \cdot \prod_{q=1}^m (\sum_{r_q=0}^{ub} r_q \cdot x_{r_q}^{(q)})^{k_q} && \text{(by OH-H3 and OH-H4)} \\
&= c \cdot \prod_{q=1}^m X_q^{k_q} = T(\mathbf{X}) && \text{(since } \sum_{r_q=0}^{ub} r_q \cdot x_{r_q}^{(q)} = X_q)
\end{aligned}
$$

Therefore, $\max SatW(\text{OH} - \text{S}) \Leftrightarrow \max T(\mathbf{X})$ and the formulation is sound. The complexity of the number of auxiliary variables $z_{r_1 \ldots r_m}$ is $O(ub^m)$. There are $O(ub^m)$ soft clauses and $O(m \cdot ub^m + ub^m + m + m \cdot ub^2) = O(m \cdot ub^m)$ hard clauses, so the overall number of clauses is bounded by $O(m \cdot ub^m)$. Finally, the upper bound of soft weights $c \cdot \prod_{q=1}^m r_q^{k_q}$ is $O(ub^k)$. □

Note that, based on different situations of $T(\mathbf{X}) = c \cdot \prod_{q=1}^m X_q^{k_q}$, different special cases can occur. Indeed, when all $k_q = 1$, the complexity of auxiliary variables and clauses in the OH formulation decreases to $O(ub^k)$ and $O(k \cdot ub^k)$. Also, half-reification should be performed when applicable: When $m = 1$, $T(\mathbf{X})$ reduces to a pure power term $T_{pure} = c \cdot X^k$, in which case there is no necessity to introduce auxiliary variables z. In this case, Eqs. OH-H1 and OH-H2 are omitted, and we replace the z variables in OH-S by the original x variables. When $c > 0$, Eq. OH-H2 becomes redundant, whereas when $c < 0$, Eq. OH-H1 becomes redundant.

3.2   Unary Formulation

In this subsection, we develop the unary formulation. In this case, the encoding variables x serve as a counter for the encoded term. This allows us to decompose the value of a given polynomial term $T(\mathbf{X})$ as the sum of a series of increments, namely, the *difference* ($\widetilde{T}$).

The theory of differences can be traced back to the application of finite difference methods in numerical analysis [9,29]. Differences are to discrete functions what derivatives are to continuous functions, as well as prefix sums are to discrete functions what integrals are to continuous functions. Differences provide a natural framework for decomposing discrete functions into incremental contributions used in the unary representation. Therefore, we apply the idea of difference and prefix sum on the polynomial term T. The *difference* of T is defined as follows:

Definition 4 (Difference of a polynomial term).   *For a polynomial term* $T(\mathbf{X}) = c \cdot \prod_{q=1}^{m} X_q^{k_q}$, *its difference* $\widetilde{T}$ *at point* $\mathbf{X} = (r_1, \ldots, r_m)$ *is defined by:*

$$\widetilde{T}(r_1, \ldots, r_m) = \begin{cases} 0 & \text{if } \exists q \in \{1, \ldots, m\} : r_q = 0 \\ \sum_{S \subseteq \{1, \ldots, m\}} (-1)^{|S|} T(r_1', \ldots, r_m') & \text{otherwise} \end{cases}$$

where $r_q' = r_q - 1$ *if* $q \in S$, *and* $r_q' = r_q$ *if* $q \in \{1, \ldots, m\} \setminus S$.

Based on the definition of difference and the structure of polynomial terms, Proposition 1 describes the scale of $\widetilde{T}$ and Proposition 2 formally establishes an inductive form of the difference function for polynomial terms.

Proposition 1.   *Given* $T(\mathbf{X})$ *with the order of* k, *it holds that the order of* $\widetilde{T}(\mathbf{X})$ *is smaller than* k.

Proof. The set $\{1, \ldots, m\}$ has 2^m different subsets. It is known that 2^{m-1} of them have odd cardinality ($|S|$ is odd) and 2^{m-1} of them have even cardinality ($|S|$ is even), therefore the coefficients of the highest-order terms will cancel out in the summation.   □

Proposition 2.   *Given a polynomial term* $T(\mathbf{X}) = c \cdot \prod_{q=1}^{m} r_q^{k_q}$ *and a fixed point* $\mathbf{X} = (r_1, \ldots, r_m)$ *s.t.* $X_q \neq 0$, $\forall q \in \{1, \ldots, m\}$, *we have* $\widetilde{T}(r_1, \ldots, r_m) = (r_m^{k_m} - (r_m - 1)^{k_m}) \cdot \widetilde{T}(r_1, \ldots, r_{m-1})$, *where* $T(r_1, \ldots, r_{m-1})$ *is defined as* $c \cdot \prod_{q=1}^{m-1} r_q^{k_q}$.

Proof. This can be proven by reasoning on the cases where $m \in S$ or $m \notin S$ separately as follows:

$$\widetilde{T}(r_1, \ldots, r_m) = \sum_{S \subseteq \{1, \ldots, m\}} (-1)^{|S|} T(r_1', \ldots, r_m')$$

$$= \sum_{S \subseteq \{1, \ldots, m-1\}} (-1)^{|S|} T(r_1', \ldots, r_{m-1}') \cdot r_m^{k_m} + \sum_{S \subseteq \{1, \ldots, m-1\}} (-1)^{|S|+1} T(r_1', \ldots, r_{m-1}') \cdot (r_m - 1)^{k_m}$$

$$= \widetilde{T}(r_1, \ldots, r_{m-1}) \cdot r_m^{k_m} - \widetilde{T}(r_1, \ldots, r_{m-1}) \cdot (r_m - 1)^{k_m} = (r_m^{k_m} - (r_m - 1)^{k_m}) \cdot \widetilde{T}(r_1, \ldots, r_{m-1})$$

□

This recursive formula enables us to naturally compute the difference function for high-order terms and is also relevant in the later discussion. Knowing the definition of difference, we thus introduce the notion of its *prefix sum*.

Definition 5 (Prefix difference sum of a polynomial term). *The prefix difference sum of $T(\mathbf{X})$ at point $\mathbf{X} = (X_1, \ldots, X_m)$ is defined as:*

$$PreSum_T(\mathbf{X}) = \sum_{r_1=1}^{X_1} \sum_{r_2=1}^{X_2} \cdots \sum_{r_m=1}^{X_m} \widetilde{T}(r_1, \ldots, r_m)$$

The following proposition reveals that the relationship between the prefix sum and difference is analogous to the integral and derivative.

Proposition 3. *Let T be a polynomial term. Then, $PreSum_T(\mathbf{X}) = T(\mathbf{X})$.*

Proof. This result can be proven by induction on the dimension m of $\mathbf{X}$. When $m = 1$, $T(X) = T(X) - T(X - 1)$ and we have:

$$PreSum_T(X) = \sum_{r=1}^{X} (T(r) - T(r-1)) = T(X) - T(0) = T(X)$$

The proposition thus holds. We then prove that the case of $m + 1$ holds under the hypothesis that the case of m holds. Given $\mathbf{X} = (X_1, \ldots, X_{m+1})$, we have:

$$PreSum_T(\mathbf{X}) = \sum_{r_1=1}^{X_1} \cdots \sum_{r_m=1}^{X_m} \left(\sum_{r_{m+1}=1}^{X_{m+1}} \widetilde{T}(r_1, \ldots, r_{m+1}) \right) \quad \text{(by Definition 5)}$$

$$= \sum_{r_1=1}^{X_1} \cdots \sum_{r_m=1}^{X_m} \left(\sum_{r_{m+1}=1}^{X_{m+1}} (r_{m+1}^{k_{m+1}} - (r_{m+1} - 1)^{k_{m+1}}) \cdot \widetilde{T}(r_1, \ldots, r_m) \right) \quad \text{(by Proposition 2)}$$

$$= \sum_{r_1=1}^{X_1} \cdots \sum_{r_m=1}^{X_m} \left(\widetilde{T}(r_1, \ldots, r_m) \cdot \sum_{r_{m+1}=1}^{X_{m+1}} (r_{m+1}^{k_{m+1}} - (r_{m+1} - 1)^{k_{m+1}}) \right)$$

$$= \left(\sum_{r_1=1}^{X_1} \cdots \sum_{r_m=1}^{X_m} \widetilde{T}(r_1, \ldots, r_m) \right) \cdot X_{m+1}^{k_{m+1}}$$

$$= T(r_1, \ldots, r_m) \cdot X_{m+1}^{k_{m+1}} = T(r_1, \ldots, r_{m+1}) = T(\mathbf{X}) \quad \text{(by Inductive Hypothesis)}$$

□

Based on Proposition 3, we thus manage to construct the unary formulation (UNA) for any given $T = c \cdot \prod_{q=q_1}^{m} X_q^{k_q}$ as follows:

Soft Clauses

$$(z_{r_1 \ldots r_m}, \widetilde{T}(r_1, \ldots, r_m)) \qquad \forall (r_1, \ldots, r_m) \in \mathbf{V}_{ub}^m : \widetilde{T}(r_1, \ldots, r_m) \neq 0 \qquad \text{(UNA-S)}$$

Hard clauses

$$\overline{z}_{r_1 \ldots r_m} \vee x_{r_q}^{(q)} \qquad \forall q \in \{1, \ldots, m\}, \forall (r_1, \ldots, r_m) \in \mathbf{V}_{ub}^m \qquad \text{(UNA-H1)}$$

$$(\bigvee_{q=1}^{m} \overline{x}_{r_q}^{(q)}) \vee z_{r_1 \ldots r_m} \qquad \forall (r_1, \ldots, r_m) \in \mathbf{V}_{ub}^m \qquad \text{(UNA-H2)}$$

$$\overline{x}_r^{(q)} \vee x_{r-1}^{(q)} \qquad \forall q \in \{1, \ldots, m\}, \forall r \in \mathbf{V}_{ub} \qquad \text{(UNA-H3)}$$

Equations UNA-S to UNA-H3 make up the unary representation (UNA) for any polynomial term. The main structure remains similar to OH, with auxiliary variables $z_{r_1 \ldots r_m}$ added in the same situation describing the combination of co-appearance of $x_{r_q}^{(q)}$. Equations UNA-H1 and UNA-H2 align with OH-H1 and OH-H2, building the connection between auxiliary variables and original variables. UNA-H3 is equivalent to $x_r^{(q)} \to x_{r-1}^{(q)}$, ensuring the structure of unary representation. Finally, Eq. UNA-S builds upon the two previous equations, transforming $T(\mathbf{X})$ into weighted soft clause based on the following proposition.

Theorem 2. *The UNA formulation with Eqs. UNA-S to UNA-H3 is sound and requires $O(ub^m)$ auxiliary variables, $O(m \cdot ub^m)$ clauses, and $O(ub^{k-1})$-valued soft weights.*

Proof. We prove the validity of the UNA formulation by proving that $SatW(\text{UNA} - \text{S})$ is equal to the original polynomial term $T(\mathbf{X})$.

$$SatW(\text{UNA} - \text{S}) = \sum_{r_1=1}^{ub} \sum_{r_2=1}^{ub} \cdots \sum_{r_m=1}^{ub} \widetilde{T}(r_1, \ldots, r_m) z_{r_1 \ldots r_m}$$
$$= \sum_{r_1=1}^{ub} \sum_{r_2=1}^{ub} \cdots \sum_{r_m=1}^{ub} \widetilde{T}(r_1, \ldots, r_m) \prod_{q=1}^{m} x_{r_m}^{(q)} \quad \text{(by UNA-H1 and UNA-H2)}$$
$$= T(\mathbf{X}) \quad \text{(by UNA-S and Proposition 3)}$$

Therefore, $\max T(\mathbf{X}) \Leftrightarrow \max SatW(\text{UNA} - \text{S})$ and the formulation is sound. There are $O(ub^m)$ introduced auxiliary variables, and there are $O(ub^m)$ soft clauses and $O(m \cdot ub^m + ub^m + m \cdot ub^m) = O(m \cdot ub^m)$ hard clauses. Based on Proposition 1, the corresponding weight $\widetilde{T}(r_1, \ldots, r_m)$ is within the scale of $O(ub^{k-1})$. □

In MaxSAT solving, the soft weight scale of an instance is generally positively correlated to its difficulty. The most important benefit brought by the unary representation is the decrease of the scale of the soft weight. The unary representation ensures that the order of soft weight is always one less than the order of the term, i.e., reducing the soft weight scale from $O(ub^k)$ to $O(ub^{k-1})$. An interesting observation attached to this advantage is that for any separable quadratic function, e.g., $F = x_1^2 + x_2^2$, the soft weight would become a linear function of original variables, making the formulation much more tractable for applications.

3.3 Binary Formulation

Binary representation is the most compact encoding featuring the logarithmic projection of integer variables to Boolean bits. In this subsection, we expand the binary formulation at a term-level sense. Given any polynomial term $T(\mathbf{X}) = c \cdot \prod_{q=1}^{m} X_q^{k_q}$ where $\sum_{q=1}^{m} k_q = k$, the binary formulation reformulates this into $T(\mathbf{X}) = c \cdot \prod_{q=1}^{k} X_{\Omega(q)}$, where Ω is a mapping such that each original variable X_q appears exactly k_q times in the expanded product. This transforms a product with exponents into an equivalent product of

k individual variables. Based on this reformulation, we formulate T as the following equation, denoted by $SatW(\text{BIN} - \text{S})$ and proved by Theorem 3: $T(\mathbf{X}) = c \cdot \prod_{q=1}^{k} X_{\Omega(q)} = \sum_{(r_1,\ldots,r_k) \in \mathbf{X}_{\log ub}^k} c \cdot 2^{\sum_{q=1}^{k} r_q} \cdot z_{r_1 \ldots r_k}$, where $z_{r_1 \ldots r_k}$ is the auxiliary variable introduced to represent the combination of any possible permutation of $x^{(\Omega(q))}$ representing $X_{\Omega}(q)$ in the binary representation. The binary formulation (BIN) is thus formalized as follows:

Soft Clauses

$(z_{r_1 \ldots r_k}, c \cdot 2^{\sum_{q=1}^{k} r_q})$ $\hspace{3cm}$ $\forall (r_1, \ldots, r_k) \in \mathbf{V}_{\log ub}^k$ $\hspace{1cm}$ (BIN-S)

Hard Clauses

$\overline{z}_{r_1 \ldots r_k} \vee x_{r_q}^{(\Omega(q))}$ $\hspace{1.5cm}$ $\forall q \in \{1, \ldots, k\}, \forall (r_1, \ldots, r_k) \in \times \mathbf{V}_{\log ub}^k$ $\hspace{0.5cm}$ (BIN-H1)

$(\bigvee_{q=1}^{k} \overline{x}_{r_q}^{(\Omega(q))}) \vee z_{r_1 \ldots r_k}$ $\hspace{1.5cm}$ $\forall (r_1, \ldots, r_k) \in \mathbf{V}_{\log ub}^k$ $\hspace{0.5cm}$ (BIN-H2)

Equations BIN-S to BIN-H2 compose the binary formulation (BIN). The hard constraints BIN-H1 and BIN-H2 altogether are equivalent to $z_{r_1 \ldots r_k} \leftrightarrow \bigwedge_{q=1}^{k} x_{r_q}^{(\Omega(q))}$. Note that, after rewriting the original index set as Ω, duplicate $x_{r_q}^{(\Omega(q))}$ may appear within one clause of BIN-H2, and we only keep one of them. Based on the hard clauses, Eq. BIN-S reformulates $T(\mathbf{X})$ as soft clauses, as proposed in the following theorem.

Theorem 3. *The BIN formulation is sound and introduces auxiliary variables and clauses in the scale of $O((\log ub)^k)$ and $O(k \cdot (\log ub)^k)$, with the soft weight in the scale of $O(ub^k)$.*

Proof. We prove the validity of the UNA formulation by proving that $SatW(\text{UNA} - \text{S})$ is equal to the original polynomial term $T(\mathbf{X})$ as follows:

$$SatW(S) = \sum_{(r_1, \ldots, r_k) \in \mathbf{V}_{\log ub}^k} c \cdot 2^{\sum_{q=1}^{k} r_q} \cdot z_{r_1 \ldots r_k} = \sum_{r_1 = 0}^{\lfloor \log ub \rfloor} \cdots \sum_{r_k = 0}^{\lfloor \log ub \rfloor} c \cdot 2^{\sum_{q=1}^{k} r_q} \cdot z_{r_1 \ldots r_k}$$

$$= c \cdot \sum_{r_1 = 0}^{\lfloor \log ub \rfloor} \cdots \sum_{r_k = 0}^{\lfloor \log ub \rfloor} \prod_{q=1}^{k} 2^{r_q} x_{r_q}^{(\Omega(q))} \hspace{2cm} \text{(by BIN-H1 and BIN-H1)}$$

$$= c \cdot \prod_{q=1}^{k} (\sum_{r_q = 0}^{\lfloor \log ub \rfloor} 2^{r_q} x_{r_q}^{(\Omega(q))}) \hspace{2.5cm} \text{(by Distributivity)}$$

$$= c \cdot \prod_{q=1}^{k} X_{\Omega(q)} = T(\mathbf{X}) \hspace{1cm} (\text{since } \sum_{r_q = 0}^{\lfloor \log ub \rfloor} 2^{r_q} \cdot x_{r_q}^{(\Omega(q))} = X_{\Omega(q)})$$

Therefore, $\max T(\mathbf{X}) \Leftrightarrow \max SatW(\text{BIN} - \text{S})$ and the formulation is sound. There are $O((\log ub)^k)$ $z_{r_1 \ldots r_k}$ variables introduced as auxiliary variables, and there are $O((\log ub)^k)$ soft clauses and $O(k \cdot (\log ub)^k + (\log ub)^k) = O(k \cdot (\log ub)^k)$ hard clauses. The soft weight $c \cdot 2^{\sum_{q=1}^{k} r_q}$ is bounded within $O(ub^k)$. $\hspace{1cm}$ $\square$

The following example presents a polynomial term under the BIN.

Example 1. Suppose $T(\mathbf{X}) = X_1^2 X_2$ and $ub = 3$, we use Boolean variables $x^{(1)}$ to represent X_1 and $x^{(2)}$ to represent X_2 in the binary encoding. Since $\lfloor \log ub \rfloor = \lfloor \log 3 \rfloor = 1$, we need 2 Boolean variables for each integer variable, indexed by 0 and 1. Under binary representation, we rewrite $T(\mathbf{X}) = X_1 X_1 X_2$ and introduce auxiliary Boolean variables $z_{r_1 r_2 r_3}$ $\forall (r_1, r_2, r_3) \in \{0,1\}^3$. Following Eq. BIN-S, we thus obtain the soft clauses:

$$S = \{(z_{000}, 2^0), (z_{001}, 2^1), (z_{010}, 2^1), (z_{011}, 2^2), (z_{100}, 2^1), (z_{101}, 2^2), (z_{110}, 2^2), (z_{111}, 2^3)\}$$

and, from Eqs. BIN-H1 and BIN-H2, we obtain the following hard clauses:

$$\overline{z}_{r_1 r_2 r_3} \vee x_{r_1}^{(1)}, \quad \overline{z}_{r_1 r_2 r_3} \vee x_{r_2}^{(1)}, \quad \overline{z}_{r_1 r_2 r_3} \vee x_{r_3}^{(2)} \qquad \forall (r_1, r_2, r_3) \in \{0,1\}^3 \qquad \text{(From } BIN - H1\text{)}$$

$$\overline{x}_{r_1}^{(1)} \vee \overline{x}_{r_2}^{(1)} \vee \overline{x}_{r_3}^{(2)} \vee z_{r_1 r_2 r_3} \qquad \forall (r_1, r_2, r_3) \in \{0,1\}^3 \qquad \text{(From } BIN - H2\text{)}$$

Therefore, we can represent T as follows: $T(\mathbf{X}) = 2^0 \cdot z_{0,0,0} + 2^1 \cdot z_{0,0,1} + 2^1 \cdot z_{0,1,0} + 2^2 \cdot z_{0,1,1} + 2^1 \cdot z_{1,0,0} + 2^2 \cdot z_{1,0,1} + 2^2 \cdot z_{1,1,0} + 2^3 \cdot z_{1,1,1} = SatW(S)$

To verify the soundness of this representation, let's compute the value of T for specific values of X_1 and X_2. For example, suppose $X_1 = 3 = 2^1 + 2^0$ and $X_2 = 2 = 2^1$. In binary encoding, this corresponds to $x_1^{(1)} = 1$, $x_0^{(1)} = 1$ for X_1 and $x_1^{(2)} = 1$, $x_0^{(2)} = 0$ for X_2. With these values, the variables $z_{0,0,0}$, $z_{0,0,1}$, $z_{0,1,0}$, $z_{0,1,1}$, $z_{1,0,0}$, $z_{1,0,1}$, $z_{1,1,0}$, and $z_{1,1,1}$ can be determined. More specifically, since $x_0^{(1)} = 1$, $x_0^{(2)} = 0$, we have $z_{0,0,0} = 0$. Similarly, since $x_0^{(1)} = 1$, $x_1^{(2)} = 1$, we have $z_{0,0,1} = 1$. Following this logic, we determine that $z_{0,1,1} = 1$, $z_{1,0,1} = 1$, and $z_{1,1,1} = 1$, while all other z variables are 0. Therefore, we have: $T(X_1, X_2) = \sum_{r_1=0}^{1} \sum_{r_2=0}^{1} \sum_{r_3=0}^{1} 2^{r_1 + r_2 + r_3} \cdot z_{r_1 r_2 r_3} = 2 + 4 + 4 + 8 = 18$. This matches the actual value $X_1^2 X_2 = 3^2 \cdot 2 = 18$, confirming the soundness of BIN.

In Table 2, we summarize the complexities of the three presented representations. The three formulations offer different trade-offs in terms of advantages and disadvantages. The one-hot formulation provides a straightforward implementation but suffers from high complexity as the number of variables increases. The unary formulation's key advantage is its reduced soft weight scale, which generally improves the solvability of the resulting MaxSAT instance; however, it still maintains high complexity in terms of auxiliary variables and constraints. The binary formulation offers the most compact encoding with logarithmic scaling, but becomes more complex when dealing with high-order terms that contain only a few different variables. These characteristics guide the selection of appropriate encoding methods based on the specific structure of polynomial terms

Table 2. Complexity Analysis of Different Atomic Formulations, where m is the number of different variables in the term, $k \geq m$ is the order of the term and ub is the upper bound of the integer variables

Aspect	One-hot	Unary	Binary
Auxiliary Variables	$O(ub^m)$	$O(ub^m)$	$O((\log ub)^k)$
Constraints	$O(m \cdot ub^m)$	$O(m \cdot ub^m)$	$O(k \cdot (\log ub)^k)$
Highest Soft Weight	$O(ub^k)$	$O(ub^{k-1})$	$O(ub^k)$

in practical applications. Despite the quantified complexity, it is also an important factor that the formulation should be compatible with the original semantic information of the problem being formulated. Additionally, it may be beneficial to introduce a mixture of representations when multiple variables appear in the same polynomial term, each with different semantic properties. Different representation methods can be selected to match the specific contextual meaning of each variable.

4   Order Decomposition: Beyond Atomic Handling

In this section, we develop the idea of decomposing any given polynomial term $T(\mathbf{X}) = c \cdot \prod_{q=1}^{m} X_q^{k_q}$ from the perspective of its order $k = \sum_{q=1}^{m} k_q$. This idea is invoked by the following two limitations of the atomic formulation: (i) The atomic formulations are obtained with the complexity of an exponential level, which is even the case for the most compact BIN formulation, which requires $O((\log ub)^k)$ auxiliary variables and $O(k \cdot (\log ub)^k)$ clauses. (ii) The atomic formulations cannot take advantage of the similar structure of multiple terms within one NLIP. In this section, we present the idea of order-wise decomposition, which is based on the BIN formulation and manages to improve these limitations.

In Sect. 3.3, we presented the BIN formulation that can formulate any polynomial term under the form $T(\mathbf{X}) = c \prod_{i=1}^{k} X_{\Omega(i)}$. In the decomposition, we regard Ω as a set of indices, i.e., $T(\mathbf{X}) = c \prod_{q \in \Omega} X_q$. The essence of decomposition is to introduce auxiliary variables y to represent the intermediate products, therefore avoiding the exponential complexity produced by the combination of all k units. Algorithm 1 describes the whole process recursively. Its core idea is to partition the set of variables into two smaller subsets, then recursively process each subset, and finally combine their results. Specifically, when Ω contains only one element q, it directly returns the corresponding Boolean variable $x^{(q)}$; otherwise, it partitions Ω into two disjoint subsets Ω_1 and Ω_2, recursively calls Decompose to obtain encodings for each subset, and finally merges the intermediate results through the Mul operation, avoiding the exponential complexity that would arise from processing all possible variable combinations.

Algorithm 1: Decompose(Ω)

Input: A set of variable indices Ω
Output: Boolean encoding of the product of variables indexed by Ω

1 **if** $|\Omega| = 1$ *with* $\Omega = \{q\}$ **then**
2 $\quad$ **return** $x^{(q)}$; $\qquad\qquad\qquad\qquad\qquad\qquad\qquad$ // Base case
3 **else**
4 $\quad$ $(\Omega_1, \Omega_2) \leftarrow \text{Partition}(\Omega)$; $\qquad$ // Split Ω into two disjoint subsets
5 $\quad$ $y^{(\Omega_1)} \leftarrow \text{Decompose}(\Omega_1)$; $\qquad\quad$ // Recursively encode first part
6 $\quad$ $y^{(\Omega_2)} \leftarrow \text{Decompose}(\Omega_2)$; $\qquad$ // Recursively encode second part
7 $\quad$ **return** $\text{Mul}(y^{(\Omega_1)}, y^{(\Omega_2)})$; $\qquad\qquad$ // Combine using Mul operation
8 **end**

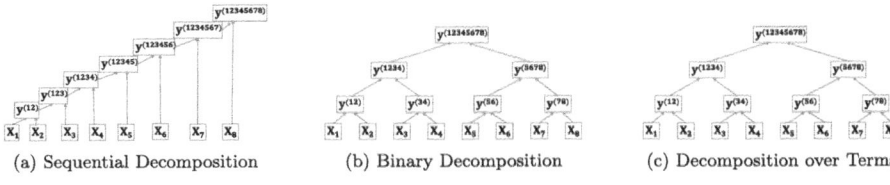

(a) Sequential Decomposition   (b) Binary Decomposition   (c) Decomposition over Terms

Fig. 1. Sequential decomposition (a) and binary decomposition (b) of polynomial term $T = X_1X_2X_3X_4X_5X_6X_7X_8$, and a decomposition plan (c) for the high-order polynomial function of $P(\mathbf{X}) = X_1X_2X_3X_4 + X_3X_4X_5X_6 + X_1X_2X_5X_6$.

We then introduce the operation of multiplication Mul based on the BIN formulation. Given two integers A bounded by ub_a and B bounded by ub_b, Mul is the operation obtaining the binary formulation of the product of the two integers. Suppose $x^{(a)}$ and $x^{(b)}$ are two series of binary variables representing A and B with the binary encoding, $Mul(x^{(a)}, x^{(b)})$ introduces a new series of Boolean variables $y_r^{(ab)}$ $\forall r \in \mathbf{V}_{\log(ub_a \cdot ub_b)}$ to encode the product $A \cdot B$ in binary representation. This operation is formalized through the following constraints.

Hard Constraints in $Mul(x^{(a)}, x^{(b)})$

$$z_{r_a r_b}^{(ab)} \leftrightarrow (x_{r_a}^{(a)} \wedge x_{r_b}^{(b)}) \qquad\qquad \forall (r_a, r_b) \in \mathbf{V}_{\log ub_a} \times \mathbf{V}_{\log ub_b} \text{ (Mul-1)}$$

$$\sum_{r=0}^{\lfloor \log(ub_a \cdot ub_b) \rfloor} 2^r y_r^{(ab)} = \sum_{r_a=0}^{\lfloor \log ub_a \rfloor} \sum_{r_b=0}^{\lfloor \log ub_b \rfloor} 2^{r_a + r_b} z_{r_a r_b}^{(ab)} \qquad\qquad \text{(Mul-2)}$$

Equation Mul-1 rewrites Eq. BIN-H1 and BIN-H2 in the constraint level, adding auxiliary variables $z_{r_a r_b}^{(ab)}$ and enforcing the link with original variables $x^{(a)}$ and $x^{(b)}$. Equation Mul-2 then aligns the value of variables $y^{(ab)}$ with the value embedded by $z^{(ab)}$. In the following context, we refer to Mul-1 and Mul-2 as $y^{(ab)} \leftarrow Mul(x^{(a)}, x^{(b)})$ and use this operation as a constraint in a higher level. The following proposition analyzes the complexity of $Mul(x^{(a)}, x^{(b)})$, where $PB(\#l, w_{max})$ is the scale of clauses number obtained through a PB encoding of $\sum_{i=1}^{\#l} w_i l_i \triangleright c$, with $\#l$ denoting the number of literals and $w_{max} = max_{1 \leq i \leq \#l} w_i$ representing the highest weight.

Proposition 4. *Given two integers $A \leq ub_a$ and $B \leq ub_b$ encoded using $x^{(a)}$ and $x^{(b)}$ variables, the $Mul(x^{(a)}, x^{(b)})$ operation introduces $O(PB(\log ub_a \cdot \log ub_b, ub_a \cdot ub_b))$ clauses.*

Proof. The two series of auxiliary variables, $z^{(ab)}$ and $y^{(ab)}$, are in the scale of $O(\log ub_a \cdot \log ub_b)$ and $O(\log(ub_a \cdot ub_b)) = O(\log ub_a + \log ub_b)$ respectively, yielding the overall complexity of $O(\log ub_a \cdot \log ub_b)$. There are $O(\log(ub_a) \cdot \log(ub_b))$ clauses in Eq. Mul-1. The scale of clauses in Mul-2 depends on the selection of Pseudo-Boolean encoding. The number of literals $\#l$ appearing in it is bounded by the numbers of $z^{(ab)}$ and $y^{(ab)}$, and the largest weight w_{max} is bounded by $ub_a \cdot ub_b$. $\qquad\square$

Based on the operation of Mul, Decompose(Ω) can be performed as show-cased in Algorithm 1, leaving the partition strategy (line 4) a degree of free-dom. Figure 1 illustrates two different partitioning strategies, namely Sequential Decomposition (1a) and Binary Decomposition(1b): Sequential Decomposition always isolates one variable at a time, while Binary Decomposition recursively divides the variable set into two roughly equal parts. Limited by space, here we only formalize Sequential Decomposition in the following formulation.

Soft Clauses

$$(y_r^{(1...k)}, c \cdot 2^r) \qquad\qquad \forall r \in \mathbf{V}_{k \cdot \log ub} \qquad\qquad \text{(SD-S)}$$

Hard Constraints

$$y^{(12)} \leftarrow Mul(x^{(1)}, x^{(2)}) \qquad\qquad\qquad \text{(SD-H1)}$$

$$y^{(1...\mathcal{K})} \leftarrow Mul(y^{(1,...,\mathcal{K}-1)}, x^{(\mathcal{K})}) \qquad \forall \mathcal{K} \in \{3, \ldots, k\} \qquad \text{(SD-H2)}$$

Equations SD-S to SD-H2 comprise the Sequential Decomposition. The hard constraints perform $k - 1$ times of Mul and subsequently encode $\prod_{q=1}^{\mathcal{K}} X_q$ by $y^{(1...\mathcal{K})}$. The soft clauses in SD-S are then built on the top level of variables $y_r^{(1...k)}$. The following theorem discusses the complexity of formulations for polynomial terms obtained under the idea of decomposition.

Theorem 4. *Given a polynomial term $T(\mathbf{X}) = c \prod_{q \in \Omega} X_q$, the decomposition-based formulation introduce clauses in the scale of $O(k \cdot PB(k^2(\log ub)^2, ub^k))$.*

Proof. There are always $k - 1$ times of Mul operations, within each of them the upper bounds of both ub_a and ub_b are ub^k, since all the intermediate products of $\prod_{q \in \Omega} X_q$ are bounded by ub^k. Follow Proposition 4, the theorem holds. □

Note that often in the complexity of PB constraints, a Logarithmic function is applied to the maximum weight w_{max}, leaving a non-exponential complexity of the formulation. Theorem 4 holds for all decomposition-based formulations, despite the selection of the partition strategy. Nevertheless, the flexibility left by the partition strategy benefits the potential of different polynomial terms sharing common structure, as an example given in Fig. 1c.

5   Conclusion

In this paper, we have explored different MaxSAT-based formulations for non-linear polynomial integer programs. We first dive into this topic through the perspectives of the variable-wise polynomial representations, with three distinct encoding plans favoring different real-life scenarios, therefore, three formulations are proposed with a thorough discussion on their complexity. Then, we focus on the order-wise decomposition of polynomial terms, based on which formulations with compact complexity are obtained.

As future work, it would be interesting to continue exploring the other three integer mapping ways proposed in [2], as well as refine the selection strategy of representation/decomposition methods. Practically, a thorough implementation of NLIP-MaxSAT formulations can be applied on different real-world problems, therefore broadening the scope of application of SAT and MaxSAT modern technologies. We also hope to develop an API enabling the use of our non-linear formulations, to be made available to the community.

Acknowlegement. This work is partially supported by the ANR-24-CE23-6126 project (BforSAT) and by the ANR-19-CHIA0013-01 chair (MASSAL'IA), co-funded by the French national research agency and the French electricity distribution network operator Enedis.

References

1. Abío, I., Nieuwenhuis, R., Oliveras, A., Rodríguez-Carbonell, E.: BDDs for pseudo-boolean constraints - revisited. In: Sakallah, K.A., Simon, L. (eds.) Theory and Applications of Satisfiability Testing - SAT 2011 - 14th International Conference, SAT 2011, Ann Arbor, MI, USA, June 19–22, 2011. Proceedings, volume 6695 of Lecture Notes in Computer Science, pp. 61–75. Springer (2011)
2. Ansótegui, C., Manyà, F.: Mapping problems with finite-domain variables into problems with Boolean variables. In: SAT 2004 - The Seventh International Conference on Theory and Applications of Satisfiability Testing, 10–13 May 2004, Vancouver, BC, Canada, Online Proceedings (2004)
3. Bacchus, F., Järvisalo, M., Martins, R.: Maximum satisfiabiliy. In: Handbook of Satisfiability, pp. 929–991. IOS Press (2021)
4. Barrett, C., Berezin, S.: A proof-producing Boolean search engine. In: Program Commitee, p. 25 (2003)
5. Biere, A., Heule, M., van Maaren, H., Walsh, T. (eds.) Handbook of Satisfiability - Second Edition, Volume 336 of Frontiers in Artificial Intelligence and Applications. IOS Press (2021)
6. Bofill, M., et al.: Constraint solving approaches to the business-to-business meeting scheduling problem. J. Artif. Intell. Res. **74**, 263–301 (2022)
7. Cherif, S., Sattoutah, H., Li, C.M., Lucet, C., Brisoux-Devendeville, L.: Minimizing working-group conflicts in conference session scheduling through maximum satisfiability (short paper). In: Shaw, P. (ed.) 30th International Conference on Principles and Practice of Constraint Programming, CP 2024, September 2–6, 2024, Girona, Spain, volume 307 of LIPIcs, pp. 1–11. Schloss Dagstuhl - Leibniz-Zentrum für Informatik (2024)
8. Cimatti, A., Griggio, A., Irfan, A., Roveri, M., Sebastiani, R.: Experimenting on solving nonlinear integer arithmetic with incremental linearization. In: Beyersdorff, O., Wintersteiger, C.M. (eds.) SAT 2018. LNCS, vol. 10929, pp. 383–398. Springer, Cham (2018). https://doi.org/10.1007/978-3-319-94144-8_23
9. Courant, R., Friedrichs, K., Lewy, H.: Über die partiellen differenzengleichungen der mathematischen physik. Math. Ann. **100**(1), 32–74 (1928)
10. Duran, M.A., Grossmann, I.E.: An outer-approximation algorithm for a class of mixed-integer nonlinear programs. Math. Program. **39**(3), 337 (1987)

11. Eén, N., Sörensson, N.: Translating pseudo-Boolean constraints into SAT. J. Satisf. Boolean Model. Comput. **2**(1–4), 1–26 (2006)
12. Van Gelder, A.: Another look at graph coloring via propositional satisfiability. Discret. Appl. Math. **156**(2), 230–243 (2008)
13. Graça, A., Lynce, I., Marques-Silva, J., Oliveira, A.L.: Efficient and accurate haplotype inference by combining parsimony and pedigree information. In: Horimoto, K., Nakatsui, M., Popov, N. (eds.) Algebraic and Numeric Biology - 4th International Conference, ANB 2010, Hagenberg, Austria, July 31- August 2, 2010, Revised Selected Papers, Volume 6479 of Lecture Notes in Computer Science, pp. 38–56. Springer (2010)
14. Guerra, J., Lynce, I.: Reasoning over biological networks using maximum satisfiability. In: Milano, M. (ed.) Principles and Practice of Constraint Programming - 18th International Conference, CP 2012, Québec City, QC, Canada, October 8– 12, 2012. Proceedings, Volume 7514 of Lecture Notes in Computer Science, pp. 941–956. Springer (2012)
15. Gupta, A., Ganai, M.K., Wang, C.: SAT-based verification methods and applications in hardware verification. In: Bernardo, M., Cimatti, A. (eds.) SFM 2006. LNCS, vol. 3965, pp. 108–143. Springer, Heidelberg (2006). https://doi.org/10. 1007/11757283_5
16. Hemmecke, R., Koppe, M., Lee, J., Weismantel, R.: Nonlinear integer programming. In: Jünger, M., et al. (eds.) 50 Years of Integer Programming 1958-2008 - From the Early Years to the State-of-the-Art, pp. 561–618. Springer (2010)
17. Markowitz, H.M.: Portfolio selection: efficient diversification of investments (1959)
18. Jeroslow, R.G.: There cannot be any algorithm for integer programming with quadratic constraints. Oper. Res. **21**(1), 221–224 (1973)
19. Klieber, W., Kwon, G.: Efficient CNF encoding for selecting 1 from n objects. In: Proc. International Workshop on Constraints in Formal Verification, p. 14 (2007)
20. Kremer, G., Reynolds, A., Barrett, C., Tinelli, C.: Cooperating techniques for solving nonlinear real arithmetic in the cvc5 SMT solver (system description). In: Blanchette, J., Kovács, L., Pattinson, D. (eds.) Automated Reasoning - 11th International Joint Conference, IJCAR 2022, Haifa, Israel, August 8–10, 2022, Proceedings, Volume 13385 of Lecture Notes in Computer Science, pp. 95–105. Springer (2022)
21. Li, C.M., Manyà, F.: MaxSAT, hard and soft constraints. In: Biere, A., Heule, M., van Maaren, H., Walsh, T. (eds.) Handbook of Satisfiability - Second Edition, Volume 336 of Frontiers in Artificial Intelligence and Applications, pp. 903–927. IOS Press (2021)
22. Li, C.M., Manyà, F., Quan, Z., Zhu, Z.: Exact MinSAT solving. In: Strichman, O., Szeider, S. (eds.) SAT 2010. LNCS, vol. 6175, pp. 363–368. Springer, Heidelberg (2010). https://doi.org/10.1007/978-3-642-14186-7_33
23. Li, D., et al.: Nonlinear Integer Programming, vol. 84. Springer (2006)
24. De Loera, J.A., Hemmecke, R., Köppe, M., Weismantel, R.: Integer polynomial optimization in fixed dimension. Math. Oper. Res. **31**(1), 147–153 (2006)
25. Manthey, N., Philipp, T., Steinke, P.: A more compact translation of pseudo-Boolean constraints into CNF such that generalized Arc consistency is maintained. In: Lutz, C., Thielscher, M. (eds.) KI 2014. LNCS (LNAI), vol. 8736, pp. 123–134. Springer, Cham (2014). https://doi.org/10.1007/978-3-319-11206-0_13
26. Pardalos, P.M., Rendl, F., Wolkowicz, H.: The quadratic assignment problem: A survey and recent developments. In: Pardalos, P.M., Wolkowicz, H. (eds.) Quadratic Assignment and Related Problems, Proceedings of a DIMACS Workshop, New Brunswick, New Jersey, USA, May 20–21, 1993, Volume 16 of DIMACS

Series in Discrete Mathematics and Theoretical Computer Science, pp. 1–42. DIMACS/AMS (1993)

27. Roussel, O., Manquinho, V.: Pseudo-boolean and cardinality constraints. In: Biere, A., Heule, M., van Maaren, H., Walsh, T. (eds.) Handbook of Satisfiability - Second Edition, Volume 336 of Frontiers in Artificial Intelligence and Applications, pp. 1087–1129. IOS Press (2021)

28. Safarpour, S., Mangassarian, H., Veneris, A., Liffiton, M.H., Sakallah, K.A.: Improved design debugging using maximum satisfiability. In: Formal Methods in Computer-Aided Design, 7th International Conference, FMCAD 2007, Austin, Texas, USA, November 11–14, 2007, Proceedings, pp. 13–19. IEEE Computer Society (2007)

29. Strikwerda, J.C.: Finite difference schemes and partial differential equations. In: SIAM (2004)

30. Surynek, P.: Lazy compilation of variants of multi-robot path planning with satisfiability modulo theory (SMT) approach. In: 2019 IEEE/RSJ International Conference on Intelligent Robots and Systems, IROS 2019, Macau, SAR, China, November 3–8, 2019, pp. 3282–3287. IEEE (2019)

31. Zheng, Z., Cherif, S., Shibasaki, R.S.: Optimizing power peaks in simple assembly line balancing through maximum satisfiability. In: 36th IEEE International Conference on Tools with Artificial Intelligence, ICTAI 2024, Herndon, VA, USA, October 28–30, 2024, pp. 363–370. IEEE (2024)

Exact Approaches for the Diverse Satisfiability Problem

Zhifei Zheng⬢, Sami Cherif$^{(\boxtimes)}$⬢, Rui Sá Shibasaki⬢, Chu-Min Li⬢,
and Jialu Zhang⬢

Laboratoire MIS UR 4290, Université de Picardie Jules Verne, Amiens, France
{zhifei.zheng,sami.cherif,rui.sa.shibasaki,chu-min.li,
jialu.zhang}@u-picardie.fr

Abstract. Given a Conjunctive Normal Form (CNF) formula ϕ and a positive integer k, the problem of Diversity Satisfiability (Diverse SAT) consists in finding k assignments satisfying ϕ while maximizing the sum of pairwise distances among them. Previous related works mainly focus on the design of heuristic algorithms, while this paper focuses on introducing exact methods. A quadratic integer programming (QIP) model is first proposed. Then, based on two novel weight functions, namely the direct weight (DW) and the incremental weight (IW), we reformulate the QIP models into two integer linear programming (ILP) models, which can also be adapted to Maximum Satisfiability (MaxSAT) instances. Extensive experiments were conducted to evaluate the efficiency of the proposed methods, showing that the proposed approaches are able to compute optimal solutions for the studied instances with linear models achieving superior performance.

1 Introduction

Propositional Satisfiability (SAT) is a decision problem that consists in determining whether a given CNF (Conjunctive Normal Form) formula can be satisfied by an assignment of the variables [6], also referred to as a model of the formula. SAT is the first problem proven to be NP-complete [8], and serves as a core engine in various real-life applications such as hardware and software verification [1,7], planning and scheduling [29,30] and bio-informatics [21,22], among many others. While the classical SAT problem requires finding a single model that satisfies a given CNF formula, many real-world applications demand multiple models with diverse heterogeneous structural characteristics. In such cases, relying on just one satisfying assignment may lead to incomplete analyses or missed insights.

One notable example arises in Bounded Model Checking (BMC) [1], where each SAT model represents a possible verification path. However, focusing on a single model increases the likelihood of overlooking corner-case bugs, as it may not capture the full spectrum of possible behaviors in the system under verification. This limitation highlights the need to generate multiple diverse solutions, thereby improving the robustness and completeness of debugging and verification processes. Building upon this observation, Nadel introduced the Diverse Satisfiability (Diverse SAT) problem in [24] which, given a CNF formula, seeks to

G. Casini et al. (Eds.): JELIA 2025, LNAI 16094, pp. 207–224, 2026.
https://doi.org/10.1007/978-3-032-04590-4_15

identify k satisfying models that are as distinct as possible. The degree of diversity is typically quantified by the sum of pairwise Hamming distances between selected models, ensuring that each solution contributes to maximizing structural variation. In the same paper, an incomplete method empowered by a dedicated variable decision heuristic is proposed. More recently, [20] presents an efficient local search algorithm for this problem.

Another closely related problem proposed in the literature is the Maximum Hamming Distance problem for Constraint Satisfaction Problems (CSPs), first introduced in [9] by Crescenzi and Rossi. This problem is restricted to finding only two distinct models. As such, when the variables are binary, the problem becomes essentially similar to Diverse SAT with $k = 2$. Since solving SAT with a single model is already NP-complete, the Diverse SAT problem, which requires identifying k diverse models, poses an even greater computational challenge. In particular, for a given parameter p, Misra et al. [23] prove that, even in the restricted case where $k = 2$, determining two models that differ in exactly (or at least) p variables remains NP-hard. In [2], Angelsmark and Thapper provide an upper bound of $\mathcal{O}(1.7338^n)$ for solving Max-Hamming Distance 2-SAT (i.e., Diverse SAT with $k = 2$ where the given instance contains only clauses of length 2). More generally, they show that, for Max-Hamming Distance l-SAT, where l is the maximum length of clauses in the given CNF formula, an upper bound of $\mathcal{O}((2a)^n)$ can be established, under the hypothesis that the underlying l-SAT instance can be solved within $\mathcal{O}(a^n)$ with a certain constant a.

In this paper, we focus on introducing exact approaches for Diverse Satisfiability which, to the best of our knowledge, have not been explored in the literature. We propose two generic approaches, based on Quadratic Integer Programming (QIP) and linear Pseudo-Boolean programming. The latter can be easily transformed to Maximum Satisfiability (MaxSAT) models. Our QIP approach formulates the objective function in a quadratic way, and the linear Pseudo-Boolean/MaxSAT approach reformulates the objective as a linear combination of Boolean variables. This linear combination is based on two weight functions, namely Direct Weight (DW) and Incremental Weight (IW). The efficiency of the proposed approaches is also thoroughly evaluated in numerical experiments.

The remainder of this paper is structured as follows. Section 2 establishes the formal definitions, notations, and theoretical foundations of Diverse SAT, along with the introduction of the standard Quadratic Integer Programming (QIP), linear programming and Maximum Satisfiability (MaxSAT) paradigms. Section 3 introduces our exact approaches, including the QIP formulation, the linear formulation, and the adapted MaxSAT formulation. Section 4 provides a comprehensive analysis of our experimental results. Finally, Sect. 5 summarizes our contributions and outlines directions for future research.

2   Preliminaries

2.1   (Diverse) Satisfiability

Let X be a set of Boolean variables taking values in $\{True, False\}$ (or $\{1,0\}$). A literal l is either a variable $x \in X$ or its negation $\overline{x}$. The positive literal $l = x$ is referred to as satisfied (falsified) when x is *True* (*False*), while the negative literal $l = \bar{x}$ is satisfied (falsified) when x is *False* (*True*). A clause C is a disjunction ($\vee$) of literals and can be represented as a set of literals. For convenience, we can write C as $C^+ \cup C^-$, where C^+ is the set of positive literals and C^- is the set of negative literals. C is satisfied if at least one of its literals is satisfied. A formula in Conjunctive Normal Form (CNF) is a conjunction ($\wedge$) of clauses. We often write a CNF ϕ with m clauses as a set of clauses, e.g., $\phi = \{C_1, \ldots, C_m\}$. It is satisfied if all of its clauses are satisfied. Given a CNF formula ϕ containing Boolean variables in X, the propositional Satisfiability (SAT) problem consists in determining whether there exists an assignment $\alpha : X \rightarrow \{True, False\}$ satisfying ϕ. When such an assignment exists, it is called a model of ϕ.

Hereafter, we formally introduce the notions of Hamming distance between two assignments, which equals the number of variables taking different values in the two assignments. Then, we formally define the notion of *diversity* for a set of assignments, which corresponds to the sum of pairwise Hamming distances among pairs of distinct assignments. This notion is necessary to the introduction of the diverse satisfiability problem.

Definition 1 (Hamming Distance of Assignments). *Given a set of Boolean variables X and two assignments α_1, α_2 of the variables in X, the Hamming distance between α_1 and α_2, denoted $Dis(\alpha_1, \alpha_2)$, is defined as follows:*

$$Dis(\alpha_1, \alpha_2) = |\{x \in X \mid \alpha_1(x) \neq \alpha_2(x)\}| = \sum_{x \in X} |\alpha_1(x) - \alpha_2(x)|$$

Definition 2 (Diversity of Assignments). *Given a set of Boolean variables X and a set $A = \{\alpha_1, \ldots, \alpha_k\}$ of k assignments of the variables in X, the diversity of A, denoted $Div(A)$ is defined as follows:*

$$Div(A) = \sum_{i=1}^{k-1} \sum_{j=i+1}^{k} Dis(\alpha_i, \alpha_j) \tag{1}$$

Given a CNF formula ϕ and an integer $k \geq 2$, the Diverse Satisfiability (Diverse SAT) problem thus consists in finding a set of k models of ϕ with maximal diversity. More formally, we seek :

$$A = \underset{\substack{\mathcal{A} \in \{0,1\}^{k \times |X|} \\ \forall \alpha \in A, \, \alpha \text{ model of } \phi}}{\arg\max} Div(\mathcal{A})$$

In [24], Nadel introduces the notion of *variable diversity*, i.e., the number of its *True* assignments times the number of its *False* assignments, as formally defined below. This notion served as an online criteria to evaluate the devotion of a single variable to the overall diversity quality, finally leading to the variable-based heuristic proposed by Nadel. We formalize the idea behind this design in Proposition 1 and present the corresponding formal proof, which was not explicitly described in [24].

Definition 3 (Variable Diversity). *Given a set of Boolean variables X and a set $A = \{\alpha_1, \ldots, \alpha_k\}$ of k assignments of the variables in X. The diversity of $x \in X$ in A, denoted $Div(x, A)$, is defined as follows:*

$$Div(x, A) = T(x, A) \cdot F(x, A)$$

where $T(x, A) = |\{\alpha \in A \mid \alpha(x) = 1\}|$, and $F(x, A) = |\{\alpha \in A \mid \alpha(x) = 0\}|$.

Proposition 1. *Given a set of Boolean variables X and a set $A = \{\alpha_1, \ldots, \alpha_k\}$ of k assignments of the variables in X, we have:*

$$Div(A) = \sum\nolimits_{x \in X} Div(x, A) \qquad (2)$$

Proof.

$$
\begin{aligned}
Div(A) &= \sum\nolimits_{i=1}^{k-1} \sum\nolimits_{j=i+1}^{k} Dis(\alpha_i, \alpha_j) \\
&= \sum\nolimits_{i=1}^{k-1} \sum\nolimits_{j=i+1}^{k} |\{x \in X \mid \alpha_i(x) \neq \alpha_j(x)\}| \\
&= \sum\nolimits_{i=1}^{k-1} \sum\nolimits_{j=i+1}^{k} \sum\nolimits_{\substack{x \in X: \\ \alpha_i(x) \neq \alpha_j(x)}} 1 \\
&= \sum\nolimits_{x \in X} \sum\nolimits_{i=1}^{k-1} \sum\nolimits_{\substack{j=i+1: \\ \alpha_i(x) \neq \alpha_j(x)}}^{k} 1 \\
&= \sum\nolimits_{x \in X} T(x, A) \cdot F(x, A) = \sum\nolimits_{x \in X} Div(x, A)
\end{aligned}
$$

2.2   Quadratic and Linear Integer Programming

Quadratic Integer Programming (QIP) enables to represent mathematical programming models with integer variables, a quadratic objective function and linear constraints. As defined in [27], below is the formal form of a QIP model:

$$(QIP) \qquad \max_x x^\top H x + c^\top x$$
$$\text{s.t. } x \in \mathcal{P} \qquad\qquad x \in \mathbb{Z}^n$$

where $H \in \mathbb{Q}^{n \times n}$ and is symmetric, $c \in \mathbb{Q}^n$, $\mathcal{P}$ is a polyhedron, represented as $\mathcal{P} = \{x : Ax \leq b\}$, $A \in \mathbb{Q}^{m \times n}$, $b \in \mathbb{Q}^m$. On the other hand, Integer Linear Programming is defined as a linear objective function and linear constraints over integer variables. When the variables are Boolean, it is commonly referred to as Linear Pseudo-Boolean (LPB) programming [12] and can be formalized as follows:

$$(LPB) \qquad \max f(x_1, \ldots, x_n)$$
$$\text{s.t. } f_j(x_1, \ldots, x_n) \geqq 0, \quad j \in \{1, \ldots, m\} \qquad x_i \in \{0, 1\}^n$$

where $f(x_1, \ldots, x_n) = \sum_{i=1}^{n} w_i \cdot x_i$ and $w_i \in \mathbb{Z}$ are integer weights.

2.3 Maximum Satisfiability

Maximum Satisfiability (MaxSAT) is a natural optimization extension of SAT (another optimization extension of SAT is MinSAT [18]). In this paper, we use its most generic version, namely Weighted Partial MaxSAT [4,17]. This problem takes as input a bipartite weighted formula $\phi = H \cup S$, where H is a set of hard clauses that must be satisfied as in SAT, and S is a set of weighted soft clauses of the form (C, W_C), in which W_C is a positive integer weight associated with the clause C. The objective of Weighted Partial MaxSAT is to obtain an assignment α that maximizes (resp. minimizes) the sum of the weight of satisfied (resp. falsified) soft clauses while satisfying all the hard clauses. Formally, let $cost_\alpha(\phi)$ denote the sum of weights of soft clauses in ϕ falsified by the assignment α satisfying all hard clauses in H, Weighted Partial MaxSAT seeks $optimum(\phi) = \min_\alpha cost_\alpha(\phi)$. In the rest of the paper, we use MaxSAT to refer to its Weighted Partial variant. Additionally, previous literature introduces Pseudo-Boolean (PB) constraints that can be efficiently encoded in CNF form [28]. These constraints take the following form:

$$\sum_j a_j \cdot l_j \rhd b \qquad \text{where } a_j \in \mathbb{N}, b \in \mathbb{N}, l_j \text{ is a literal and } \rhd \in \{=, \geq, \leq\}.$$

A special kind of Pseudo-Boolean constraint is referred to as a cardinality constraint when all the coefficients of literals are equal to one [28]. For the remainder of this paper, we distinguish between the cardinality constraints and Pseudo-Boolean constraints based on the presence of literal coefficients, i.e., formulations without coefficients are treated as cardinality constraints.

3 Formulations for Diverse Satisfiability

In this section, we present three distinct formulations for the Diverse SAT problem, namely the Quadratic Integer Programming formulation and two linear (Pseudo-Boolean) formulations. We start with a QIP formulation presented in Sect. 3.1, transforming the original optimization naturally into a quadratic objective function. In Sect. 3.2, we discuss the general idea of bridging the gap between the formulation with integer variables and quadratic objective, and the formulation with Boolean variables and linear objective, therefore leading to the two models proposed in Sect. 3.3. Finally, we showcase that the linear formulations can be adapted to MaxSAT in Sect. 3.4.

3.1 Quadratic Formulation for Diverse SAT

In this subsection, we present a QIP formulation for the Diverse SAT problem. This formulation is naturally based on Proposition 1, which expresses the diversity of a set of assignments as the sum of each variable's diversity. Based on this idea, we define a QIP model with the following two series of variables, where $K = \{1, \ldots, k\}$ corresponds to the k models and $N = \{1, \ldots, n\}$ corresponds to the n variables:

$$\max \sum\nolimits_{j \in N} O_j \cdot (k - O_j) \tag{QIP-0}$$

subject to

$$\sum\nolimits_{\overline{x}_j \in C_h^-} (1 - V_{i,j}) + \sum\nolimits_{x_j \in C_h^+} V_{i,j} \geq 1 \qquad \forall (i,h) \in K \times M \tag{QIP-1}$$

$$O_j = \sum\nolimits_{i=\{1,\dots,K\}} V_{i,j} \qquad \forall j \in N \tag{QIP-2}$$

$$O_j \in \mathbb{N}^+, V_{i,j} \in \{0,1\} \qquad \forall (i,j) \in K \times N \tag{QIP-3}$$

Fig. 1. The QIP model for Diverse SAT

- **Integer variables** O_j $\quad \forall j \in N$: the number of *True* assignments of the j-th variable among all the k models, i.e., $T(x_j, A)$.
- **Binary variables** $V_{i,j}$ $\quad \forall (i,j) \in K \times N$: the Boolean value for the j-th variable of the i-th model, i.e., $\alpha_i(x_j)$.

We obtain the formulation shown in Fig. 1, denoted QP, and where $M = \{1, \dots, m\}$ corresponds to the m clauses in the given CNF formula ϕ. Equation QIP-0 is a reformulation of Proposition 1, dictating that the maximization objective, diversity, equals the sum of all variable diversity. Equation QIP-1 ensures that all of the constructed k assignments in A are feasible models of ϕ. Equation QIP-2 links the Boolean variables V and the integer variables O. This QIP formulation requires $\mathcal{O}(k \cdot n)$ variables and $\mathcal{O}(k \cdot m + n)$ constraints.

3.2   Bridging Quadratic and Linear Formulations

In the last subsection, the proposed QIP formulation naturally relies on integer variables along with a quadratic objective function, which matches the original form of Proposition 1. However, the quadratic term in the objective function leaves a heavy burden on the solving procedure. Therefore, in this subsection, we propose an alternative plan that transforms the QIP formulation into a linear formulation. For each original Boolean variable $x_j \in X$ in the given CNF formula ϕ, we first introduce a series of auxiliary Boolean variables to represent the number of *True* assignments of x_j throughout the k models, i.e., $T(x_j, A)$. Note that the mapping relationship between the auxiliary Boolean variables and the integer $T(x_j, A)$ has to cooperate with the weight functions.

Next, we develop two distinct weight functions, namely *Direct Weight (DW)* and *Incremental Weight (IW)*, to reformulate the original quadratic objective term $Div(x_j, A) = T(x_j, A) \cdot (k - T(x_j, A))$. An illustration of the two weight functions for a scenario of $k = 10$ models is shown in Fig. 2. The first weight function DW directly associates each possible value of $T(x_j, A)$ with its corresponding contribution to diversity. The blue points distributed on the parabolic curve showcase that the diversity peak appears when the variables x_j are assigned *True* in exactly half of the models. The second weight function IW takes an incremental approach, expressing $Div(x_j, A)$ as a sum of marginal contributions. The red points in Fig. 2 represent the change in the diversity value when

Direct weight

$$\mathcal{D}_r = r \cdot (k - r)$$

Incremental weight

$$\mathcal{I}_r = -2r + k + 1$$

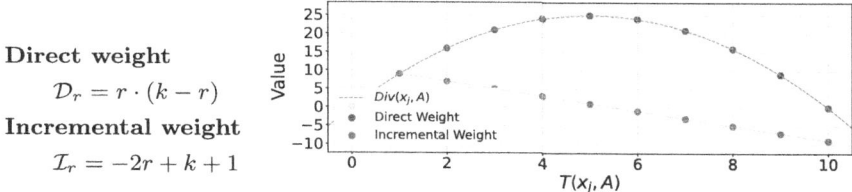

Fig. 2. The two weight functions DW and IW for a scenario with $k = 10$ Models

$T(x_j, A)$ increases by one. Note that these incremental values become negative after the midpoint, reflecting the diminishing returns of additional *True* assignments beyond balanced distribution. Formally, considering $r = T(x_j, A)$, we define the DW function as follows:

$$\mathcal{D}_r = r \cdot (k - r) \quad \forall r \in \{0, \ldots, k\}$$

and the IW function as:

$$\mathcal{I}_r = \mathcal{D}_r - \mathcal{D}_{r-1} = -2r + k + 1 \quad \forall r \in \{1, \ldots, k\}$$

Note that for any $r \in \{1, \ldots, k\}$, $\mathcal{D}_r = \sum_{r'=1}^{r} \mathcal{I}_{r'}$, which can be simply proven with a telescoping sum. These two distinct weight functions provide different but mathematically equivalent approaches to reformulate the original objective function, which is detailed in the following subsection.

3.3   Linear Formulations for Diverse SAT

Direct Weight Formulation. We first present the formulation for Diverse SAT with DW, which is built upon the following variables, where $K = \{1, \ldots, k\}$ and $N = \{1, \ldots, n\}$:

– **Binary variables** $U_{j,r} \quad \forall (r, j) \in (\{0\} \cup K) \times N$: $U_{j,r}$ is set to 1 when the number of *True* assignments of the j-th variable among all the K models equals to r, and to 0 otherwise.

$$\max \sum_{j=1}^{n} \sum_{r=0}^{k} \mathcal{D}_r \cdot U_{j,r} \tag{DW-0}$$

subject to

$$\sum_{\overline{x}_j \in C_h^-} (1 - V_{i,j}) + \sum_{x_j \in C_h^+} V_{i,j} \geq 1 \qquad \forall (i, h) \in K \times M \tag{DW-1}$$

$$\sum_{r \in (\{0\} \cup K)} U_{j,r} = 1 \qquad \forall j \in N \tag{DW-2}$$

$$\sum_{r \in (\{0\} \cup K)} r U_{j,r} = \sum_{i \in K} V_{i,j} \qquad \forall j \in N \tag{DW-3}$$

$$V_{i,j} \in \{0,1\}, U_{j,r} \in \{0,1\} \qquad \forall (i,j) \in K \times N, \forall (r, j) \in (\{0\} \cup K) \times N \tag{DW-4}$$

Fig. 3. Linear model for Diverse SAT with Direct Weight (DW).

$$\max \sum\nolimits_{j=1}^{n} \sum\nolimits_{r=0}^{k} \mathcal{I}_r \cdot U_{j,r} \tag{IW-0}$$

subject to

$$\sum\nolimits_{\overline{x}_j \in C_h^-} (1 - V_{i,j}) + \sum\nolimits_{x_j \in C_h^+} V_{i,j} \geq 1 \qquad \forall (i,h) \in K \times M \tag{IW-1}$$

$$U_{j,r} \leq U_{j,r-1} \qquad \forall (r,j) \in (K \setminus \{1\}) \times N \tag{IW-2}$$

$$\sum\nolimits_{r \in K} U_{j,r} = \sum\nolimits_{i \in K} V_{i,j} \qquad \forall j \in N \tag{IW-3}$$

$$V_{i,j} \in \{0,1\}, U_{j,r} \in \{0,1\} \qquad \forall (i,j) \in K \times N, \forall (r,j) \in K \times N \tag{IW-4}$$

Fig. 4. Linear model for Diverse SAT with Incremental Weight (IW).

- **Binary variables** $V_{i,j}$ $\forall (i,j) \in K \times N$: the Boolean value for the j-th variable of the i-th model, i.e., $\alpha_i(x_j)$.

Therefore, the formulation with the DW function $\mathcal{D}_r = r \cdot (k - r)$ can be obtained as in Fig. 3, where $M = \{1, \ldots, m\}$. Equation DW-0 formulates the objective function, where each term $D_r \cdot U_{j,r}$ indicates that there is a diversity contribution $D_r = r \cdot (k - r)$ when variable x_j is assigned to *True* in exactly r out of k models. Equation DW-1 ensures that each model α_i satisfies the original CNF formula ϕ, i.e., for each clause C_h in ϕ and each model α_i, at least one literal in the clause must be satisfied according to the variable assignments in α_i. Equation DW-2 enforces a single number of True assignments of the j-th variable among the k models. Equation DW-3 establishes the mapping relationship between the $U_{j,r}$ and the actual model assignments $V_{i,j}$. There are $\mathcal{O}(k \cdot n)$ variables and $\mathcal{O}(k \cdot m + n)$ constraints in the formulation of DW.

Incremental Weight Formulation. We develop another formulation for Diverse SAT using the IW function. The variables used in this formulation are:

- **Binary variables** $U_{j,r}$ $\forall (r,j) \in K \times N$: $U_{j,r}$ is set to 1 when the number of *True* assignments of the j-th variable among all the K models is larger than or equal to r, and to 0 otherwise.
- **Binary variables** $V_{i,j}$ $\forall (i,j) \in K \times N$: the Boolean value for the j-th variable of the i-th model, i.e., $\alpha_i(x_j)$.

The linear Pseudo-Boolean formulation with the IW function $\mathcal{I}_r = -2r + k + 1$ is obtained as shown in Fig 4. The structure of IW remains similar to DW. Equation IW-0 formulates the incremental contribution of the *True* assignments of the j-th variable x_j to the overall diversity. Equation IW-1 constrains the satisfiability of all obtained k models. Equation IW-2 ensures the order of the usage of $U_{j,r}$, which cooperates with IW-3 to establish the semantic information of $U_{j,r}$. The complexities in terms of the numbers of variables and constraints for IW are $\mathcal{O}(n \cdot k)$ and $\mathcal{O}(k \cdot (m + n))$, respectively.

Soft Clauses		Soft Clauses	
$(U_{j,r}, r \cdot (k-r))$	$\forall (r,j) \in (\{0\} \cup K) \times N$ (DW-0)	$(U_{j,r}, \mathcal{I}_r)$	$\forall (r,j) \in K \times N$ (IW-0*)
Hard Clauses		**Hard Clauses**	
$(\bigvee_{x_j \in C_h^-} \overline{V}_{i,j}) \vee (\bigvee_{x_j \in C_h^+} V_{i,j})$	$\forall (i,h) \in K \times M$	$(\bigvee_{x_j \in C_h^-} \overline{V}_{i,j}) \vee (\bigvee_{x_j \in C_h^+} V_{i,j})$	$\forall (i,h) \in K \times M$
(DW-1)		(IW-1)	
$\sum_{r \in (\{0\} \cup K)} U_{j,r} = 1$	$\forall j \in N$ (DW-2)	$U_{j,r} \rightarrow U_{j,r-1}$	$\forall (r,j) \in (K \setminus \{1\}) \times N$ (IW-2)
$\sum_{r \in (\{0\} \cup K)} r U_{j,r} = \sum_{i \in K} V_{i,j}$	$\forall j \in N$ (DW-3)	$\sum_{r \in K} U_{j,r} = \sum_{i \in K} V_{i,j}$	$\forall j \in N$ (IW-3)
(a) MaxSAT-DW		**(b) MaxSAT-IW**	

Fig. 5. The MaxSAT Formulation for Diverse SAT with DW (a) and IW (b).

3.4   MaxSAT Formulations

When focusing on the intrinsic requirement of Diverse SAT, one cannot omit the central task of obtaining Boolean satisfiability models - a task where MaxSAT might be intuitively better suited. In this subsection, we present the transformation from the previous linear formulations to MaxSAT. We reformulate the models in clause-like encodings along with PB/Cardinality constraints, as showcased in Fig. 5. Additionally, we note that Equation (IW-0*) in the MaxSAT-IW model may contain negative weights, which does not fit in the original standard of MaxSAT. Therefore, it is transformed through the following equation:

$$\begin{cases} (U_{j,i}, \mathcal{I}_r) & \mathcal{I}_r \geq 0, \\ (\overline{U}_{j,i}, -\mathcal{I}_r) & \mathcal{I}_r < 0, \end{cases} \quad \forall (r,j) \in K \times N \qquad \text{(IW-0)}$$

An illustrative example is showcased below. This normalization technique allows us to represent the incremental weight function properly within the standard MaxSAT framework, which requires non-negative weights for all soft clauses.

Example. *Suppose $k = 4$ and $n = 3$. According to the definition $\mathcal{I}_r = -2r + k + 1$, we have $\mathcal{I}_1 = 3$, $\mathcal{I}_2 = 1$, $\mathcal{I}_3 = -1$ and $\mathcal{I}_4 = -3$. For each variable x_j where $j \in \{1,2,3\}$. Before normalization, the soft clause set is $S = \{(U_{j,1}, 3), (U_{j,2}, 1), (U_{j,3}, -1), (U_{j,4}, -3)\}$. After applying the normalization rule, we obtain $S = \{(U_{j,1}, 3), (U_{j,2}, 1), (\overline{U}_{j,3}, 1), (\overline{U}_{j,4}, 3)\}$. We can remark that the contribution of x_j is formulated as $obj_{ini} = 3U_{j,1} + U_{j,2} - U_{j,3} - 3U_{j,4}$ before normalization, whereas it becomes $obj_{norm} = 3U_{j,1} + U_{j,2} + \overline{U}_{j,3} + 3\overline{U}_{j,4}$ after normalization. Since $\overline{U}_{j,r} = 1 - U_{j,r}$ for any Boolean variable, we can rewrite this as follows:*

$$obj_{norm} = 3U_{j,1} + U_{j,2} + (1 - U_{j,3}) + 3(1 - U_{j,4}) = 3U_{j,1} + U_{j,2} - U_{j,3} - 3U_{j,4} + 4 = obj_{ini} + 4$$

As adding a constant to all objective values does not change the optimal solution of a MaxSAT problem, the normalized formulation is equivalent to the original one in terms of finding the optimal diverse set of models.

4   Experimental Results

In this section, we present the experimental results of the proposed approaches. The experimental protocol, including the experimental environment, benchmarks, and solvers involved, is presented in Sect. 4.1. Section 4.2 reports the overall performance, and Sect. 4.3 compares the linear formulations empowered by the two distinct weight functions.

4.1 Experiment Protocol

All the experiments were conducted on the MatriCS platform[1], with a CentOS 8.6 system equipped with an Intel Xeon E5-2680 v4 processor operating at a base frequency of 2.40 GHz with Turbo Boost capability up to 3.30 GHz. The cutoff time set for all methodologies is 7200 seconds. Our experiments involve state-of-the-art solvers in each category. The QIP formulation proposed in 3.1 is solved by CPLEX [14]. The experiments of linear formulations proposed in 3.3 were conducted by both CPLEX and the dedicated Pseudo-Boolean solver RoundingSAT[2]. The two MaxSAT formulations proposed in 3.4 are tested on the three MaxSAT solvers CASHWMaxSAT-DisjCom [26], WMaxCDCL [19], and MaxHS [25]. We note that these three MaxSAT solvers are respectively SAT-based, Branch-and-Bound-based, and ILP-based solvers, and were the winners of the exact track in previous MaxSAT Evaluations[3] held respectively in 2024, 2023, 2021. To perform the CNF encoding, we used PySAT[4], with cardinality constraints encoded by Cardinality Networks [3], which is capable of encoding a constraint of $\mathcal{N}$-literal $\mathcal{K}$-cardinality in $\mathcal{O}(\mathcal{N} \log^2 \mathcal{K})$ clauses and auxiliary variables. For the PB constraints, we select the mode of "Best" available in PySAT. Additionally, we establish a naive enumeration approach based on state-of-the-art SAT solver CaDiCal [5]. The implementation logic of this approach is simple, with the SAT solver launched iteratively for k times and, after each iteration, a new clause is added to the formula to block the newly found satisfiable assignment. Once the k rounds are finished, we suspend the program and calculate the diversity based on the obtained k models.

The instances used in our experiment originate from three sources: there are 20 instances from the semiformal verification of hardware benchmark first proposed and used in [24], 88 instances from SATLIB[5] composing 5 families, and 181 instances from the Model Counting (MC) competition[6] held in 2024 [11], making up the 7 distinct families involved in the experiment. We omit instances with more than $100,000$ variables and instances where 10 models cannot be computed by CaDiCaL within the cutoff time, therefore all instances used guarantee that more than 10 distinct models exist. The scales of these instances vary from 39 variables and 66 clauses to 84914 variables and 7490695 clauses. In Table 1, for each family, we list out the original source, the number of instances $\#Ins$, the average number of variables $\#Var_{avg}$ and clauses $\#CL_{avg}$, and the average length of clauses Len_{avg}. Three different k values, $k = 2, 5, 10$ are tested.

---

[1] https://www.matrics.u-picardie.fr.
[2] https://gitlab.com/MIAOresearch/software/roundingsat.
[3] https://maxsat-evaluations.github.io/.
[4] https://pysathq.github.io/.
[5] https://www.cs.ubc.ca/~hoos/SATLIB/benchm.html.
[6] https://mccompetition.org/past_iterations.

4.2   Overall Performance

Figure 6 provides a comprehensive view of each approach's accumulated number of solved instances within the time limit under $k = 2, 5, 10$. We can observe that all of the proposed approaches manage to obtain optimal solutions for a considerable number of instances, especially for the smaller k value of 2. In particular, the linear formulations, empowered by both DW and IW weight functions, outperform QIP and achieve the best performances for all k values. The advantage is even enlarged as the k value increases, demonstrating good scalability of the linear approaches. Nevertheless, it is notable that in several cases, even though the QIP formulation with CPLEX manages to find the optimal value proven by some other solvers, it fails to prove its optimality, with 34, 31, and 19 instances, respectively, when $k = 2, 5, 10$. Despite the fact that CPLEX with QIP formulation falls behind the others, when cooperating with the linear formulations, CPLEX becomes the most powerful solver, obtaining the most optimal solutions in both the case of $k = 2$ and $k = 10$, whereas the solver CASHWMaxSAT achieves the best performance when $k = 5$.

Tables 2, 3, and 4 showcase the quality analysis of all the approaches tested for all the families within the benchmark, with $k = 2, 5, 10$, respectively. For each instance family, the diversity of the results obtained by the naive enumeration approach cooperating with CaDiCaL (CaDi.) is first reported. Consequently, the performances of the QIP approach empowered by CPLEX and

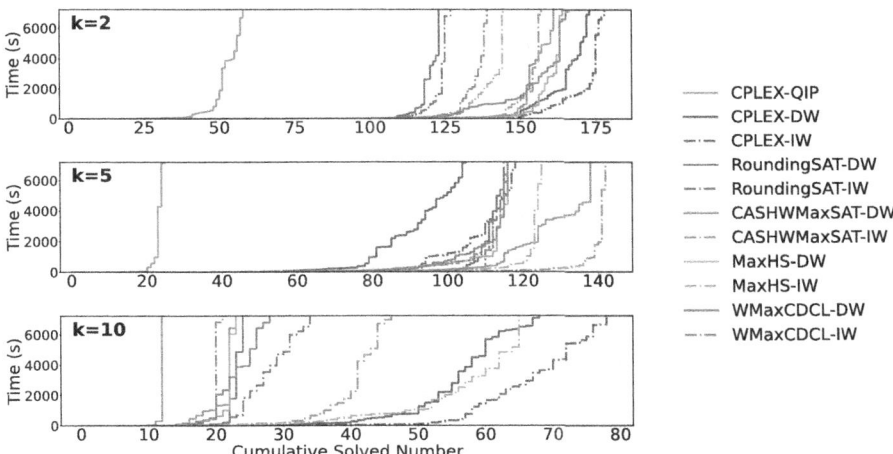

Fig. 6. Cumulative solved number of instances with respect to solving time in seconds for the proposed approaches.

the two linear models with two different weight functions (DW and IW) solved by CPLEX, RoundingSAT and the three MaxSAT solvers CASHW-MaxSAT (CASH.), MaxHS and WMaxCDCL, are reported under the format $\#OPT(tot\_time_{opt})[Div_{all}]$, where $\#OPT$ represents the number of optimally solved instances within the cutoff time, tot_time_{opt} is the corresponding average runtime of these optimally solved cases and Div_{all} the average diversity values obtained for all instances in each family. In the cases where there is no feasible solution computed within the cutoff time, the diversity is regarded as 0 for the corresponding instance. Among all our approaches, the one with the highest number of optimally solved instances within the shortest time is reported in bold. Furthermore, the highest overall diversity Div_{all} among all the approaches, including the naive enumeration cooperating with CaDiCaL, is underlined.

These tables present the performance in terms of the optimality solving capability of the approaches and their ability to compute more diverse solutions. Overall, these results demonstrate that the choice of solver and weight functions significantly impacts performance, with different combinations showing superior results depending on the given cases. In terms of diversity, for $k = 2, 5, 10$, the best diversity obtained by exact solvers is 3.70, 2.18, and 1.68 times better than the naive solution obtained by enumeration, when narrowing down the analysis scale to the cases with proven optimality, these data alter to 94, 57, and 9 times improvement. The substantial performance gap between the naive enumerator and the proposed exact approaches clearly demonstrates the inherent difficulty of the Diverse SAT, affirming the necessity of developing exact approaches for this challenging problem. We can also observe that with the increase of the value of k, for some instance families, the proposed exact approaches sometimes fail to obtain any feasible solutions within the cutoff time, which is especially the case for CPLEX-QIP and RoundingSAT. This might be owing to the fact that the internal goal of the exact solvers is to obtain the optimal solutions, so the incomplete intermediate result cannot fully reflect the solving process. For example, the IW empowered by CPLEX only manages to obtain 4 feasible results for the difficult family *hardware* when $k = 5$, but all of these results are optimal. Despite this perspective, the proposed approaches are still serving satisfying quality in the sub-optimal solutions, which showcases great robustness.

Table 1. Information of instances families.

Family	Source	#Ins	#Var_avg	#CL_avg	Len_avg
ais	SATLIB	4	155	2729	2.31
flat100+	SATLIB	30	425	1584	2.09
flat100-	SATLIB	30	155	561	2.09
hardware	[24]	20	49391	161547	2.41
logistics	SATLIB	4	1881	11682	2.55
mc2024	MC competition	181	6348	97255	3.00
morphed	SATLIB	20	500	3100	2.10
Total	–	289	7516	72727	2.69

4.3   Direct Vs Incremental Weight

To better understand the practical differences between the two proposed weight functions DW and IW, we conduct a detailed comparison of their performance across different instance families and solver configurations. Figure 7 showcases the runtime comparisons for the two different functions under $k = 2, 5, 10$. Each point in the illustrations corresponds to an instance, with its coordinates determined by the runtime using the two weight functions. When an instance cannot be solved within the cutoff time, the corresponding solving time is regarded as the cutoff time. Points below the diagonal indicate instances where IW performed better, while points above the diagonal are in favor of DW. We can observe that the distributions of points follow distinct trends when the value of k varies. When $k = 2$, DW is comparable with IW, with 76%, 45%, 34%, 47%, and 55% points lying under or on the diagonal line with the solvers CPLEX, RoundingSAT, CASHWMaxSAT, MaxHS, and WMaxCDCL, respectively. As k increases to 5 (10), we can find a trend where IW outperforms DW with the percentage of points of 70%, 64%, 63%, 71%, and 76% (67%, 54%, 73%, 61%, and 91%) lying under or on the diagonal line respectively. Based on the results throughout all values of k, we observe the advantage of IW over DW as k increases.

Table 2. Experimental results for $k = 2$.

Family	Enum.	CPLEX			RoundingSAT		MaxSAT (DW)			MaxSAT (IW)		
	CaDi.	QIP	DW	IW	DW	IW	CASH.	MaxHS	WMaxCDCL	CASH.	MaxHS	WMaxCDCL
ais	[18]	1(4)[6]	4(49)[34]	**4(15)[34]**	1(41)[8]	2(15)[13]	2(2)[34]	3(19)[34]	4(1656)[34]	2(2)[34]	3(23)[34]	3(73)[22]
flat100+	[2]	1(6685)[63]	30(35)[283]	30(24)[283]	**30(0)[283]**	30(0)[283]	30(1)[283]	30(16)[283]	30(4)[283]	30(1)[283]	30(3)[283]	30(6)[283]
flat100-	[2]	23(291)[73]	30(0)[103]	30(0)[103]	23(0)[82]	22(0)[74]	**30(0)[103]**	30(0)[103]	30(1)[103]	30(0)[103]	30(0)[103]	30(1)[103]
hardware	[5483]	0(-)[596]	4(62)[1177]	4(49)[1180]	0(-)[0]	4(194)[558]	**4(9)[19705]**	0(-)[18835]	0(-)[0]	4(11)[20556]	0(-)[18381]	0(-)[0]
logistics	[3]	1(5531)[216]	**3(19)[365]**	3(36)[368]	2(290)[136]	2(3643)[148]	2(57)[352]	3(95)[364]	2(166)[218]	2(22)[362]	2(152)[366]	1(19)[218]
mc2024	[579]	32(671)[587]	82(695)[845]	87(542)[832]	67(307)[464]	67(273)[436]	**89(364)[1965]**	79(379)[2223]	80(582)[493]	87(295)[1980]	79(426)[2177]	75(379)[441]
morphed	[2]	0(-)[0]	20(3)[200]	**20(1)[200]**	0(-)[0]	0(-)[0]	4(2739)[198]	19(9)[200]	20(1230)[200]	2(525)[200]	1(8)[200]	0(-)[0]
Total	[743]	58(696)[426]	173(339)[670]	**178(271)[662]**	123(172)[330]	127(208)[351]	161(270)[2654]	164(188)[2755]	166(472)[366]	157(171)[2722]	145(235)[2695]	139(208)[320]

Table 3. Experimental results for $k = 5$.

Family	Enum.	CPLEX			RoundingSAT		MaxSAT (DW)			MaxSAT (IW)		
	CaDi.	QIP	DW	IW	DW	IW	CASH.	MaxHS	WMaxCDCL	CASH.	MaxHS	WMaxCDCL
ais	[280]	0(-)[50]	1(5834)[119]	1(2348)[124]	0(-)[0]	0(-)[0]	1(1610)[323]	1(429)[314]	**1(337)[124]**	1(1952)[322]	1(500)[326]	1(379)[124]
flat100+	[32]	0(-)[59]	22(2578)[1493]	29(910)[2160]	**30(3)[2267]**	29(2)[2173]	30(63)[2267]	29(469)[2249]	28(452)[2173]	30(9)[2267]	30(99)[2267]	29(619)[2267]
flat100-	[50]	0(-)[595]	30(72)[827]	30(3)[827]	**30(1)[827]**	29(0)[787]	30(4)[827]	30(119)[827]	30(69)[827]	30(1)[827]	30(11)[827]	30(71)[827]
hardware	[42853]	0(-)[1919]	3(5664)[3850]	**4(1107)[3850]**	0(-)[0]	0(-)[0]	0(-)[89368]	0(-)[82752]	0(-)[0]	0(-)[8173]	0(-)[100673]	0(-)[0]
logistics	[38]	0(-)[0]	0(-)[995]	0(-)[1608]	0(-)[0]	0(-)[0]	0(-)[2622]	0(-)[2604]	0(-)[0]	0(-)[2836]	0(-)[2806]	0(-)[486]
mc2024	[5875]	25(544)[1477]	49(253)[2231]	51(402)[3012]	56(556)[1831]	57(268)[2477]	57(157)[11542]	56(205)[12568]	57(391)[1874]	61(149)[5063]	**61(140)[11308]**	56(240)[1892]
morphed	[30]	0(-)[87]	0(-)[1977]	3(3486)[1985]	0(-)[0]	0(-)[0]	20(3064)[2000]	0(-)[1855]	0(-)[0]	**20(272)[2000]**	3(2055)[2000]	0(-)[0]
Total	[6660]	25(544)[1132]	105(896)[2057]	118(544)[2624]	116(269)[1468]	115(134)[1859]	138(535)[13913]	116(250)[14086]	116(322)[1487]	**142(118)[4240]**	125(148)[14552]	116(292)[1514]

Table 4. Experimental results for $k = 10$.

Family	Enum.	CPLEX			RoundingSAT		MaxSAT (DW)			MaxSAT (IW)		
	CaDi.	QIP	DW	IW	DW	IW	CASH.	MaxHS	WMaxCDCL	CASH.	MaxHS	WMaxCDCL
ais	[1226]	0(-)[0]	0(-)[211]	0(-)[211]	0(-)[0]	0(-)[0]	0(-)[1348]	0(-)[1272]	0(-)[0]	0(-)[507]	0(-)[1366]	0(-)[0]
flat100+	[179]	0(-)[20]	5(3667)[1487]	**16(2714)[3905]**	0(-)[0]	4(3755)[1705]	0(-)[8956]	0(-)[8323]	0(-)[0]	0(-)[9350]	6(3420)[9350]	0(-)[0]
flat100-	[337]	0(-)[1501]	30(488)[3410]	**30(42)[3410]**	0(-)[0]	3(4821)[3410]	21(1015)[3410]	0(-)[3224]	7(4273)[594]	21(1343)[3410]	27(798)[3410]	0(-)[264]
hardware	[105280]	0(-)[0]	0(-)[14790]	0(-)[15886]	0(-)[0]	0(-)[0]	0(-)[7138]	0(-)[330172]	0(-)[0]	0(-)[15137]	0(-)[42646]	0(-)[0]
logistics	[208]	0(-)[0]	0(-)[0]	0(-)[1942]	0(-)[0]	0(-)[0]	0(-)[9496]	0(-)[9230]	0(-)[0]	0(-)[1892]	0(-)[9975]	0(-)[0]
mc2024	[28853]	12(34)[2719]	25(304)[6481]	25(52)[8808]	24(306)[1271]	27(539)[1900]	21(515)[8254]	23(389)[29240]	21(244)[925]	25(447)[13934]	**32(461)[31744]**	21(384)[703]
morphed	[168]	0(-)[0]	**8(5629)[7988]**	7(4466)[7993]	0(-)[0]	0(-)[0]	0(-)[7386]	0(-)[6548]	0(-)[0]	0(-)[6796]	0(-)[6371]	0(-)[0]
Total	[25504]	12(34)[1861]	68(1259)[6147]	**78(990)[7958]**	24(306)[1407]	34(1295)[1407]	42(558)[7608]	23(389)[429060]	28(1251)[641]	46(856)[11603]	65(874)[24755]	21(384)[468]

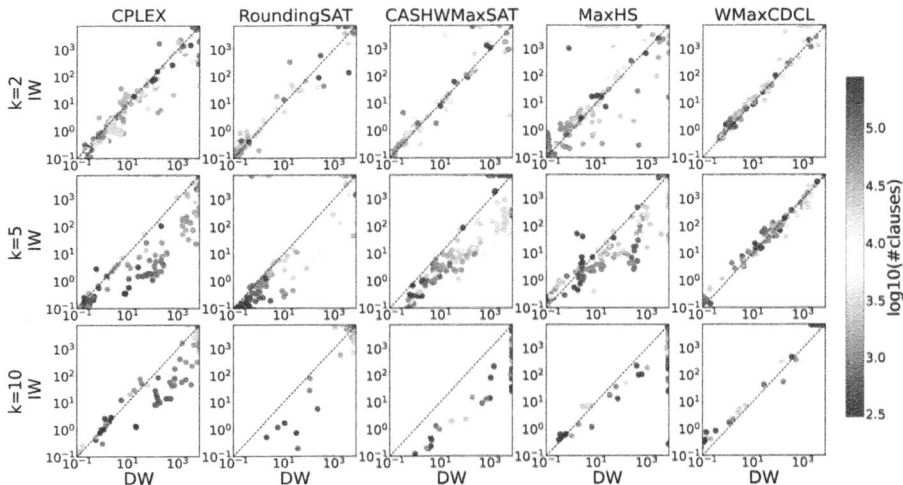

Fig. 7. Runtime comparison in logarithmic scale of the two weight functions IW and DW for $k = 2, 5, 10$. The color of each point corresponds to the scale (number of clauses) of the instance.

5   Conclusion

In this paper, we proposed exact approaches for the Diverse Satisfiability problem, based on Quadratic Integer Programming (QIP) and linear programming models, the latter of which was naturally adapted to Max-SAT formulations. Both approaches formulate the objective of Diverse SAT from a variable-wise diversity perspective. While the QIP model enables formulate the objective more naturally, the two linear approaches rely on two distinct, well-designed weight functions, namely direct weight and incremental weight, which manage to take advantage of both ILP and MaxSAT solvers' inherent capability for solving complex linear optimization problems. Extensive experiments across different values of the parameter number of models k demonstrate the efficiency of our proposed methodologies and particularly show the advantage of linear formulations over the QIP formulation, the incremental weight achieving the best performance as the instances' scale increases. As future work, we aim to explore the potential of designing dedicated algorithms for Diverse SAT that transcend the limitations of end-to-end solving schemes while preserving the structure and objective representation from our proposed approaches. Additionally, as we conduct experiments on an increasingly broader range of datasets, we anticipate establishing more optimal solutions for benchmarks to benefit researchers interested in this problem domain, which will also facilitate the design and evaluation of more efficient heuristic and approximation algorithms for Diverse SAT.

Acknowlegement. This work is partially supported by the ANR-24-CE23-6126 project (BforSAT) and by the ANR-19-CHIA0013-01 chair (MASSAL'IA), co-funded by the French national research agency and the French electricity distribution network operator Enedis. This work was also granted access to HPC resources of "Plateforme MatriCS" within University of Picardie Jules Verne. "Plateforme MatriCS" is co-financed by the European Union with the European Regional Development Fund (FEDER) and the Hauts-De-France Regional Council among others.

References

1. Agbaria, S., Carmi, D., Cohen, O., Korchemny, D., Lifshits, M., Nadel, A.: Sat-based semiformal verification of hardware. In: Bloem, R., Sharygina, N. (eds.), Proceedings of 10th International Conference on Formal Methods in Computer-Aided Design, FMCAD 2010, Lugano, Switzerland, 20–23 October, pp. 25–32. IEEE, 2010

2. Angelsmark, O., Thapper, J.: Algorithms for the maximum hamming distance problem. In: Faltings, B.V., Petcu, A., Fages, F., Rossi, F. (eds.) CSCLP 2004. LNCS (LNAI), vol. 3419, pp. 128–141. Springer, Heidelberg (2005). https://doi.org/10.1007/11402763_10

3. Asín, R., Nieuwenhuis, R., Oliveras, A., Rodríguez-Carbonell, E.: Cardinality networks and their applications. In: Kullmann, O. (ed.) SAT 2009. LNCS, vol. 5584, pp. 167–180. Springer, Heidelberg (2009). https://doi.org/10.1007/978-3-642-02777-2_18

4. Bacchus, F., Järvisalo, M., Martins, R.: Maximum satisfiabiliy. In: Handbook of Satisfiability, pp. 929–991. IOS Press, 2021

5. Fleury, A.B.K.F.M., Heisinger, M.: CaDiCaL, Kissat, Paracooba, Plingeling and treengeling entering the SAT competition 2020. In: Balyo, T., Froleyks, N., Heule, M.J., Iser, M., Järvisalo, M., Suda, M., (eds.), Proceedings of the SAT Competition 2020 – Solver and Benchmark Descriptions, volume B-2020-1 of Department of Computer Science Report Series B, pp. 51–53. University of Helsinki, 2020

6. Biere, A., Heule, M., van Maaren, H. (Eds.): Handbook of Satisfiability - Second Edition, volume 336 of Frontiers in Artificial Intelligence and Applications. IOS Press, 2021

7. Clarke, E., Kroening, D., Lerda, F.: A tool for checking ANSI-C programs. In: Jensen, K., Podelski, A. (eds.) TACAS 2004. LNCS, vol. 2988, pp. 168–176. Springer, Heidelberg (2004). https://doi.org/10.1007/978-3-540-24730-2_15

8. Cook, S.A.: The complexity of theorem-proving procedures. In: Harrison, M.A., Banerji, R.B., Ullman, J.D.(eds.), Proceedings of the 3rd Annual ACM Symposium on Theory of Computing, pp. 151–158. ACM, 1971

9. Crescenzi, P., Rossi, G.: On the hamming distance of constraint satisfaction problems. Theor. Comput. Sci. **288**(1), 85–100 (2002)

10. Elffers, J., Nordström, J.: Divide and conquer: towards faster pseudo-boolean solving. In: Lang, J. (ed.), Proceedings of the Twenty-Seventh International Joint Conference on Artificial Intelligence, IJCAI 2018, 13–19 July 2018, Stockholm, Sweden, pp. 1291–1299. ijcai.org, 2018

11. Fichte, J.K., Hecher, M., Shaw, A.: Model counting competition data format (version 1.1), 2024

12. Hammer Ivànescu, P.L., Rudeanu, S.: Boolean methods in operations research and related areas. Oekonometrie und Unternehmensforschung, no. 7, 1968

13. Hoos, H.H., Stützle, T.: Satlib: an online resource for research on sat. Sat **2000**, 283–292 (2000)
14. IBM Corporation. IBM ILOG CPLEX Optimization Studio, 2022
15. Ignatiev, A., Morgado, A., Marques-Silva, J.: PySAT: a python toolkit for prototyping with SAT oracles. In: SAT, pp. 428–437, 2018
16. Ignatiev, A., Tan, Z.L., Karamanos, C.: Towards universally accessible SAT technology. In: SAT, pp. 4:1–4:11, 2024
17. Argelich, J., Manya, F.: MaxSAT, Hard and Soft Constraints. In: Biere, A., Heule, M., van Maaren, H., Walsh, T. (eds.), Handbook of Satisfiability - Second Edition, volume 336 of Frontiers in Artificial Intelligence and Applications, pp. 903–927. IOS Press, 2021
18. Li, C.-M., Manya, F., Quan, Z., Zhu, Z.: Exact minsat solving. In: International Conference on Theory and Applications of Satisfiability Testing (SAT-2010), pp. 363–368, 2010
19. Li, S., Li, C.M., Coll, J., Habet, D., Manyà, F.: Wmaxcdcl in maxsat evaluation 2024. MaxSAT Evaluation 2024 Solver and Benchmark Descriptions, pp. 17–18, 2024
20. Liang, J., Zhou, J., Yin, M.: Diversat: a novel and effective local search algorithm for diverse SAT problem. In: Walsh, T., Shah, J., Kolter, Z. (eds.), AAAI-25, Sponsored by the Association for the Advancement of Artificial Intelligence, February 25–4 March 2025, Philadelphia, PA, USA, pp. 11290–11298. AAAI Press, 2025
21. Lynce, I., Marques-Silva, J.: SAT in bioinformatics: making the case with haplotype inference. In: Biere, A., Gomes, C.P. (eds.) SAT 2006. LNCS, vol. 4121, pp. 136–141. Springer, Heidelberg (2006). https://doi.org/10.1007/11814948_16
22. Manolios, P., Oms, M.G., Valls, S.O.: Checking pedigree consistency with PCS. In: Grumberg, O., Huth, M. (eds.) TACAS 2007. LNCS, vol. 4424, pp. 339–342. Springer, Heidelberg (2007). https://doi.org/10.1007/978-3-540-71209-1_26
23. Misra, N., Mittal, H., Rai, A.: On the parameterized complexity of diverse sat. *arXiv preprint* arXiv:2412.09717, 2024
24. Nadel, A.: Generating diverse solutions in SAT. In: Sakallah, K.A., Simon, L. (eds.) SAT 2011. LNCS, vol. 6695, pp. 287–301. Springer, Heidelberg (2011). https://doi.org/10.1007/978-3-642-21581-0_23
25. Niskanen, A., Berg, J., Järvisalo, M.: Maxhs in maxsat evaluation 2022. MaxSAT Evaluation 2022, p. 35, 2022
26. Pan, S., Wang, Y., Cai, S., Li, J., Zhu, W., Yin, M.: Cashwmaxsat-disjcad: solver description. MaxSAT Evaluation 2024 Solver and Benchmark Descriptions, p. 25, 2024
27. Pia, A.D., Dey, S.S., Molinaro, M.: Mixed-integer quadratic programming is in NP. Math. Program. **162**, 225–240 (2017)
28. Roussel, O., Manquinho, V.: Pseudo-Boolean and cardinality constraints. In: Biere, A., Heule, M., van Maaren, H., Walsh, T. (eds.), Handbook of Satisfiability - Second Edition, volume 336 of Frontiers in Artificial Intelligence and Applications, pp. 1087–1129. IOS Press, 2021
29. Surynek, P.: Lazy compilation of variants of multi-robot path planning with satisfiability modulo theory (SMT) approach. In: 2019 IEEE/RSJ International Conference on Intelligent Robots and Systems, IROS 2019, Macau, SAR, China, 3–8 November 2019, pp. 3282–3287. IEEE, 2019
30. Zheng, Z., Cherif, S., Shibasaki, R.S.: Optimizing power peaks in simple assembly line balancing through maximum satisfiability. In: 36th IEEE International Conference on Tools with Artificial Intelligence, ICTAI 2024, Herndon, VA, USA, 28–30 October 2024, pp. 363–370. IEEE, 2024

Temporal Reasoning

A Framework for Computing Upper Bounds in Passive Learning Settings

Benjamin Bordais[1,2]([envelope]) [iD] and Daniel Neider[1,2] [iD]

[1] TU Dortmund University, Dortmund, Germany
[2] Center for Trustworthy Data Science and Security, University Alliance Ruhr, Dortmund, Germany
benjamin.bordais@tu-dortmund.de

Abstract. The task of inferring logical formulas from examples has garnered significant attention as a means to assist engineers in creating formal specifications used in the design, synthesis, and verification of computing systems. Among various approaches, enumeration algorithms have emerged as some of the most effective techniques for this task. These algorithms employ advanced strategies to systematically enumerate candidate formulas while minimizing redundancies by avoiding the generation of syntactically different but semantically equivalent formulas. However, a notable drawback is that these algorithms typically do not provide guarantees of termination.

This paper develops an abstract framework to bound the size of possible solutions for a logic inference task, thereby providing a termination guarantee for enumeration algorithms through the introduction of a sufficient stopping criterion. The proposed framework is designed with flexibility in mind and is applicable to a broad spectrum of practically relevant logical formalisms, including Modal Logic, Linear Temporal Logic, Computation Tree Logic, Alternating-time Temporal Logic, Probabilistic Computation Tree Logic and even selected inference tasks for automata. In addition, our approach enabled us to develop a meta algorithm that enumerates over the semantics of formulas rather than their syntactic representations, offering new possibilities for reducing redundancy.

Keywords: Passive learning · stopping criterion · temporal logic

1   Introduction

The goal of formal verification is to provide strong guarantees on the behavior of various kinds of systems, including Artificial Intelligence systems which, despite being used everywhere, often lack safety guarantees. Formal verification techniques heavily rely on formal specifications, which describe the intended behavior of the system. However, constructing formal specifications is no easy task, and doing it manually often leads to errors, which makes the specifications unreliable. The lack of usable and trustworthy specifications is a large impediment on the effectiveness of formal methods [31].

G. Casini et al. (Eds.): JELIA 2025, LNAI 16094, pp. 227–243, 2026.
https://doi.org/10.1007/978-3-032-04590-4_16

To circumvent this issue, a recent research trend is targeted towards automatically generating (or learning) formal specifications, written as logical formulas, from examples. This approach has been explored in different settings, e.g., formal methods, artificial intelligence or software engineering, with many kinds of temporal logics, such as Linear Temporal Logic (LTL) [8,19,20,23,26,34], Computation Tree Logic (CTL) [7,11,25], Alternating-time Temporal Logic (ATL) [6,7], Signal Temporal Logic (STL) [4,22], Past Time LTL (PLTL) [2], the Property Specification Language (PSL) [29], Metric Temporal Logic (MTL) [27], etc. Note that learning from examples has also been studied in other context than temporal logics, see e.g. [1,15,30] for learning finite automata and regular expressions.

Learning logical formulas from examples is often done in a passive learning[1] setting where, given a finite set of positive and negative examples, the goal is to synthesize—or decide the existence of—a separating formula, i.e., a formula satisfied by all positive models, and rejected by all the negative ones. There are three main techniques used in the literature to solve the passive learning problem: (1) constraint-solving [7,9,14,18,23,28], which translates the learning problem into one or more constraint satisfaction problems and applies off-the-shelf solvers to find a solution; (2) neuro-symbolic techniques [20,35], which encode the learning problem into an input that (graph) neural networks can process to output a separating formula; and (3) enumerative search algorithms [22,26,34] which syntactically enumerate candidate formulas—possibly with the help of handcrafted templates [10,36]—until a separating formula is found.

While this latter enumeration technique is the most efficient in practice [22,26,34], many algorithms proposed in the literature lack theoretical groundings. Clever enumeration algorithms and correctness proofs are provided, but termination arguments are rarely given. The main goal of this paper is to provide a general framework from which one can derive upper bounds on the minimal size of separating formulas in various passive learning settings, which gives a termination condition for enumeration-based algorithms. A version of this theorem was established in [7, Theorem 2] with CTL- and ATL-formulas, we extend it here to a much wider class of logical formalisms.

There are several already-existing size-related results for passive learning, but they all focus on a specific setting, e.g., it is folklore that polynomial-size automata are sufficient to separate sets of positive and negative finite words (since any finite language is regular); in [21], a whole section is dedicated to LTL-fragments (evaluated on finite words) for which separating formulas may have polynomial size; in [16], the authors study the size of (temporal logic) formulas distinguishing non-bisimilar transition systems; in [13], the minimal size of separating concepts (which derive from description logic) is studied.

Our Contributions. In Sect. 2, we define an abstract logical framework that can be instantiated with many concrete logical formalisms. It is deliberately designed to be simple and easy to instantiate and consists of three sets of opera-

---

[1] As opposed to the active learning setting where a learner queries a teacher.

tors, of arity 0, 1, and 2. In our running example of Modal Logic (ML) formulas evaluated on Kripke structures, the operators (roughly) are $\neg, \wedge, \vee, [\cdot], \langle \cdot \rangle$.

In Sect. 3, we introduce the main result of this paper, which hinges on the notion of semantic values, to which logical formulas are mapped, that capture the semantics of the logics. Our main result Theorem 1 states that the minimal size of separating formulas, assuming one exists, is upper bounded by the total number of different semantic values. For our running example, the semantic values are the set of states of the Kripke structure from which a modal logic formula is satisfied.

In addition to the upper bounds that Theorem 1 provides, its proof suggests a promising semantic-based enumeration algorithm. Indeed, one of the common pitfalls of the enumeration algorithms of the literature, that clever techniques avoid as much as possible, is to generate syntactically different but semantically equivalent formulas. Following the proof of Theorem 1, we exhibit a meta algorithm—that can be instantiated with various concrete logics—which bypasses the above-mentioned issue by design since it enumerates semantic values instead of formulas. When instantiating this meta algorithm to modal logic, we obtain an exponential time algorithm, while formula-enumeration algorithms may have a doubly-exponential time complexity. This is discussed in Subsect. 3.3.

In Sect. 4, we demonstrate the applicability of Theorem 1 to a wide range of logical formalisms , including: our running example ML-formulas evaluated on Kripke structures, LTL-formulas evaluated on finite and infinite words, CTL-formulas evaluated on Kripke structures, ATL-formulas evaluated on concurrent game structures, PCTL-formulas evaluated on Markov chains (these last three cases are only very briefly discussed). Finally, we also apply Theorem 1 to establish upper bounds on the minimal size of words separating automata, thus showing that out framework does not only apply to logical formalisms.

For the case of ML-formulas evaluated on Kripke structures, we additionally exhibit fragments where the exponential upper bound that we derive from an application of Theorem 1 is (almost) tight.

An extended version of this paper with all the technical details can be found in [5]. Note that, in that extended version, we provide additional results, not present in the current paper. Most notably, we consider a more expressive abstract logical framework (with different formula types), which allows us to apply (a generalized version of) Theorem 1 to the case of LTL-formulas evaluated on Kripke structures.

2   Definitions

We let $\mathbb{N}$ (resp. $\mathbb{N}_1$) denote the set of (resp. positive) integers. For all $i \leq j \in \mathbb{N}$, we let $[\![i, j]\!] \subseteq \mathbb{N}$ denote the set $[\![i, j]\!] := \{k \in \mathbb{N} \mid i \leq k \leq j\}$.

For all non-empty sets Q, we let $2^Q := \{A \subseteq Q\}$ denote the set of subsets of Q. Furthermore, for all sets $(A_q)_{q \in Q}$ indexed by Q and tuples $\mathsf{S} \in \prod_{q \in Q} A_q$, for all $q \in Q$, we let $\mathsf{S}[q] \in A_q$ denote the element of S corresponding to $q \in Q$.

Modal Logic and Kripke Structures. In the following, we are going to use modal logic [3] as a running example to give the intuition behind the various notions that we will define. Thus, let us first introduce the syntax and semantics of modal logic formulas.

Definition 1. *Consider two non-empty sets of propositions* Prop *and of actions* Act. *(Graded) modal logic (*ML(Prop, Act)*-) formulas are constructed from the grammar:*

$$\varphi ::= p \mid \neg\varphi \mid \varphi \vee \varphi \mid \varphi \wedge \varphi \mid \langle a \rangle^{\geq k}\varphi \mid [a]\varphi$$

where $p \in$ Prop *is a proposition,* $a \in$ Act *is an action, and* $k \in \mathbb{N}_1$.

Modal logic formulas are usually evaluated on Kripke structures, i.e. graphs with proposition-labeled states and action-labeled transitions.

Definition 2. *A Kripke structure* K *is defined by a tuple* $(Q, I, A, \delta, P, \pi)$ *where* Q *is a non-empty set of states,* $I \subseteq Q$ *is the non-empty set of initial states,* A *is a non-empty set of actions,* $\delta : Q \times A \to 2^Q$ *is the transition function,* P *is a set of propositions, and* $\pi : Q \to 2^P$ *maps every state to the set of propositions satisfied at that state. Given a non-empty set of propositions* Prop *and a non-empty set of actions* Act, *we let* $\mathcal{K}(\mathsf{Prop}, \mathsf{Act})$ *denote the set of Kripke structures* $\mathcal{K}(\mathsf{Prop}, \mathsf{Act}) := \{K = (Q, I, A, \delta, \mathsf{Prop}, \pi) \mid \mathsf{Act} \subseteq A\}$.

Unless otherwise stated, a Kripke structure K *refers to the tuple* $(Q, I, A, \delta, P, \pi)$.

ML-formulas are evaluated on Kripke structures using the semantics below.

Definition 3. *Consider two non-empty sets of propositions* Prop *and of actions* Act, *and a Kripke structure* $K \in \mathcal{K}(\mathsf{Prop}, \mathsf{Act})$. *Given a state* $q \in Q$, *we inductively define when an* ML(Prop, Act)*-formula is satisfied in* q: $q \models p$ *iff* $p \in \pi(q)$; $q \models \neg\varphi$ *iff* $q \not\models \varphi$; $q \models \varphi_1 \vee \varphi_2$ *iff* $q \models \varphi_1$ *or* $q \models \varphi_2$; $q \models \varphi_1 \wedge \varphi_2$ *iff* $q \models \varphi_1$ *and* $q \models \varphi_2$; $q \models [a]\varphi$ *iff* $\delta(q, a) \subseteq \{q' \in Q \mid q' \models \varphi\}$; $q \models \langle a \rangle^{\geq k}\varphi$ *iff* $|\delta(q, a) \cap \{q' \in Q \mid q' \models \varphi\}| \geq k$. *Then, a Kripke structure* $K \in \mathcal{K}(\mathsf{Prop}, \mathsf{Act})$ *satisfies a formula* φ *(denoted* $K \models \varphi$*) if, for all* $q \in I$, *we have* $q \models \varphi$.

For all of the examples below on modal logic formulas, we fix two non-empty sets of propositions Prop and of actions Act.

Abstract Logical Formalism. The goal of this paper is to establish results that can be applied to a wide range of logics. Thus, we define an abstract logical formalism that can be instantiated with various concrete logical formalisms. Like the ML-syntax of Definition 1, the syntax of our abstract logical formalism is described by the operators that can be used (e.g., $\neg$, $\wedge$, etc.) along with their arity (e.g., one for $\neg$, two for $\wedge$, etc.)[2]. This abstract syntax is defined below.

---

[2] For simplicity in this paper, we only consider operators of arity 0, 1 or 2, but we would obtain (almost) identical results with operators of larger arities.

Definition 4. *The syntax of a logic* L *is described by a tuple of sets of operators* $\mathsf{Stx_L} = (\mathsf{Op_0}, \mathsf{Op_1}, \mathsf{Op_2})$ *where* $\mathsf{Op_0} \neq \emptyset$, *and for all* $i \neq j \in \{0, 1, 2\}$, $\mathsf{Op}_i \cap \mathsf{Op}_j = \emptyset$. *For all* $\mathsf{o} \in \mathsf{Op_0} \uplus \mathsf{Op_1} \uplus \mathsf{Op_2}$, *we let* $\mathsf{k_o} \in \{0, 1, 2\}$ *denote the arity of* o *satisfying* $\mathsf{o} \in \mathsf{Op_{k_o}}$. *The set* $\mathsf{Fm_L}$ *of* L-*formulas is then defined inductively as follows.*

- *For all* $\mathsf{o} \in \mathsf{Op_0}$, $\varphi := \mathsf{o}$ *is an* L-*formula:* $\varphi \in \mathsf{Fm_L}$.
- *For all* $\mathsf{o} \in \mathsf{Op_1}$ *and* $\varphi_1 \in \mathsf{Fm_L}$: $\mathsf{o}(\varphi_1) \in \mathsf{Fm_L}$.
- *For all* $\mathsf{o} \in \mathsf{Op_2}$, *and* $\varphi_1, \varphi_2 \in \mathsf{Fm_L}$: $\mathsf{o}(\varphi_1, \varphi_2) \in \mathsf{Fm_L}$[3].

Unless otherwise stated, whenever we consider a logic L, its syntax will be assumed to be given by the tuple of sets of operators $\mathsf{Stx_L} = (\mathsf{Op_0}, \mathsf{Op_1}, \mathsf{Op_2})$, and we will denote by $\mathsf{Op} := \mathsf{Op_0} \uplus \mathsf{Op_1} \uplus \mathsf{Op_2}$ the set of all operators.

Example 1. The ML(Prop, Act)-syntax of Definition 1 is equal to $\mathsf{Stx_{ML(Prop,Act)}} := (\{p \mid p \in \mathsf{Prop}\}, \{\neg, \langle a \rangle^{\geq k}, [a] \mid a \in \mathsf{Act}, k \in \mathbb{N}\}, \{\vee, \wedge\})$.

When removing operators from a logic, we obtain a fragment of that logic.

Definition 5. *A logic* L′ *with a syntax* $\mathsf{Stx_{L'}} = (\mathsf{Op_0'}, \mathsf{Op_1'}, \mathsf{Op_2'})$ *is a fragment of a logic* L *with a syntax* $\mathsf{Stx_L} = (\mathsf{Op_0}, \mathsf{Op_1}, \mathsf{Op_2})$ *if, for all* $i \in \{0, 1, 2\}$, *we have* $\mathsf{Op}_i' \subseteq \mathsf{Op}_i$. *In the following, when we refer to a fragment* L′ *of a logic* L, *we will denote by* Op′ *the set of operators of this fragment* L′.

In this paper we are particularly interested in the size of formulas. There are two natural ways to define the size $\mathsf{sz}(\varphi)$ of a formula φ: either as the size of its syntax tree; or as the size of its syntax DAG, i.e., the number of its sub-formulas . For instance, the syntax-tree size of the ML-formula $\varphi := \neg p \wedge \langle a \rangle^{\geq 2} p$ is five; its syntax-DAG size is four, since the set of sub-formulas of φ is $\mathsf{Sub}(\varphi) = \{p, \neg p, \langle a \rangle^{\geq 2} p, \varphi\}$. Here, we use the syntax-DAG size since it is very well-suited for the inductive arguments that we will use.

Definition 6. *We inductively define the set of sub-formulas* $\mathsf{Sub}(\psi)$ *of an* L-*formula* ψ: *for all* $\psi \in \mathsf{Op_0}$, $\mathsf{Sub}(\psi) := \{\psi\}$; *for all* $\psi = \mathsf{o}(\varphi)$, $\mathsf{Sub}(\psi) := \{\psi\} \cup \mathsf{Sub}(\varphi)$; *for all* $\psi = \mathsf{o}(\varphi_1, \varphi_2)$, $\mathsf{Sub}(\psi) := \{\psi\} \cup \mathsf{Sub}(\varphi_1) \cup \mathsf{Sub}(\varphi_2)$. *We then define the size of* φ: $\mathsf{sz}(\varphi) := |\mathsf{Sub}(\varphi)|$.

A model is a mathematical structure that gives meaning to the logic (i.e., semantics to formulas). As in any concrete setting, we assume that there is a satisfaction relation expressing when some model satisfies a formula. We will see later important properties that satisfaction relations may enjoy.

Definition 7. *Let* L *be a logic. A structure* M *is an* L-*model if there exists a satisfaction relation* $\models$ *between* M *and each* L-*formula: for all* $\varphi \in \mathsf{Fm_L}$, $M \models \varphi$ *means that the model* M *satisfies the formula* φ, *while* $M \not\models \varphi$ *means that it is not the case. A non-empty set* $\mathcal{C}$ *is a class of* L-*models if each structure* $M \in \mathcal{C}$ *is an* L-*model.*

---

[3] When writing concrete logical formulas, we will use the infix notation $\varphi_1 \circ \varphi_2$.

Example 2. The set of $\mathsf{ML}(\mathsf{Prop}, \mathsf{Act})$-models is equal to $\mathcal{K}(\mathsf{Prop}, \mathsf{Act})$, i.e. the set of Kripke structures $K = (Q, I, A, \delta, \mathsf{Prop}, \pi)$ such that $\mathsf{Act} \subseteq A$. The corresponding satisfaction relation $\models$ is given in Definition 3.

We can now define the passive learning problem.

Definition 8. *Consider a logic* L*, an* L*-fragment* L'*, and a class of* L*-models* $\mathcal{C}$*. A* $\mathcal{C}$*-sample* $\mathcal{S}$ *is a pair* $\mathcal{S} = (\mathcal{P}, \mathcal{N})$ *where* $\mathcal{P}, \mathcal{N} \subseteq \mathcal{C}$ *are two finite sets of* L*-models. This sample* $\mathcal{S}$ *is* L'*-separable if there is a* L'*-formula* $\varphi \in \mathsf{Fm}_{\mathsf{L}'}$ *such that: for all* $M \in \mathcal{P}$*, we have* $M \models \varphi$*; and for all* $M \in \mathcal{N}$*, we have* $M \not\models \varphi$*. In that case, the formula* φ *is called a* $\mathcal{S}$*-separating formula.*

We denote by $\mathsf{PvLn}(\mathsf{L}', \mathcal{C})$ *the decision problem that takes as input a* $\mathcal{C}$*-sample* $\mathcal{S}$*, and outputs yes if and only if the sample* $\mathcal{S}$ *is* L'*-separable.*

Unless otherwise stated, $\mathcal{C}$-samples $\mathcal{S}$ refer to the pair $\mathcal{S} = (\mathcal{P}, \mathcal{N})$. With an abuse of notation, we will also identify the sample $\mathcal{S} = (\mathcal{P}, \mathcal{N})$ with the set $\mathcal{P} \cup \mathcal{N}$.

3   Main Results

The main goal of this paper is to establish an upper bound on the minimal size of separating formulas, assuming they exist. Our approach does not work with every satisfaction relation, thus we need to assume that it satisfies some conditions. These conditions are met in various use-cases, several of which we detail in Sect. 4. In this section, we formally define the assumptions that we make on the satisfaction relation; we state the main theorem of this paper and we provide a detailed proof sketch. We then discuss a meta enumeration algorithm solving the passive learning problem derived from the proof of this theorem.

3.1   Assumptions on the Satisfaction Relation

Consider our running example of modal logic formulas evaluated on Kripke structures. Clearly, whether a ML-formula accepts a Kripke structure entirely depends on the set of states satisfying the formula. Hence, to find a separating ML-formula in a passive learning setting, we may not consider the exact syntactic shape of formulas, and instead focus on their semantic value, i.e. the set of states satisfying these formulas. We proceed similarly in our abstract logical formalism and consider a finite set SEM of semantic values and a semantic function $\mathsf{sem} : \mathsf{Fm}_{\mathsf{L}} \to \mathsf{SEM}$ mapping each L-formula to a semantic value.

Definition 9. *For a logic* L *and an* L*-model* M*, a pair* $\Theta_M = (\mathsf{SEM}_M, \mathsf{sem}_M)$ *is called an* (L, M)*-semantic pair (or simply an* (L, M)*-pair) if* SEM_M *is a finite non-empty set whose elements are called* semantic values *and* $\mathsf{sem}_M : \mathsf{Fm}_{\mathsf{L}} \to \mathsf{SEM}_M$ *is called a* semantic function*. Unless otherwise stated, an* (L, M)*-pair* Θ_M *refers to the pair* $\Theta_M = (\mathsf{SEM}_M, \mathsf{sem}_M)$*.*

Example 3. Consider a Kripke structure $K \in \mathcal{K}(\mathsf{Prop}, \mathsf{Act})$. We let $\Theta_K :=$ $(\mathsf{SEM}_K, \mathsf{sem}_K)$ be the $(\mathsf{ML}(\mathsf{Prop}, \mathsf{Act}), K)$-pair, such that $\mathsf{SEM}_K := 2^Q$ and $\mathsf{sem}_K : \mathsf{Fm}_{\mathsf{ML}(\mathsf{Prop},\mathsf{Act})} \to 2^Q$ maps each formula φ to the set of states satisfying it: $\mathsf{sem}_K(\varphi) := \{q \in Q \mid q \models \varphi\} \in \mathsf{SEM}_K$.

Consider the above $(\mathsf{ML}(\mathsf{Prop}, \mathsf{Act}), K)$-pair Θ_K. There are two crucial properties that this pair satisfies. The first one—which justifies the terminology "semantic value"—relates to capturing the behavior of $\mathsf{ML}(\mathsf{Prop}, \mathsf{Act})$-formulas w.r.t. the satisfaction relation $\models$ in K. Indeed, for any $\mathsf{ML}(\mathsf{Prop}, \mathsf{Act})$-formula φ, given $\mathsf{sem}_K(\varphi)$, one can decide if $K \models \varphi$: it holds if and only if $I \subseteq \mathsf{sem}_K(\varphi)$. In particular, this implies that if two $\mathsf{ML}(\mathsf{Prop}, \mathsf{Act})$-formulas are mapped to the same semantic value in SEM_K, then one is satisfied by K if and only if the other is. In such a case, we say that the pair Θ_K captures the $\mathsf{ML}(\mathsf{Prop}, \mathsf{Act})$-semantics .

Definition 10. *Consider a logic* L, *an* L-*model* M, *and an* (L, M)-*pair* Θ_M. *We say that* Θ_M *captures the* L-*semantics if, for all* $\varphi, \varphi' \in \mathsf{Fm}_\mathsf{L}$ *such that* $\mathsf{sem}_M(\varphi) = \mathsf{sem}_M(\varphi')$, *we have* $M \models \varphi$ *if and only if* $M \models \varphi'$.

Main theorem and proof sketch$\mathsf{SAT}_M := \{\mathsf{sem}_M(\varphi) \mid \varphi \in \mathsf{Fm}_\mathsf{L}, M \models \varphi\} \subseteq$ SEM_M *is such that, for all* $\varphi \in \mathsf{Fm}_\mathsf{L}$, *we have* $M \models \varphi$ *if and only if* $\mathsf{sem}_M(\varphi) \in$ SAT_M.

Example 4. For $K \in \mathcal{K}(\mathsf{Prop}, \mathsf{Act})$, we have $\mathsf{SAT}_K = \{S \subseteq Q \mid I \subseteq S\} \subseteq \mathsf{SEM}_K$.

Lemma 1. *For all* $K \in \mathcal{K}(\mathsf{Prop}, \mathsf{Act})$, *the* $(\mathsf{ML}(\mathsf{Prop}, \mathsf{Act}), K)$-*pair* Θ_K *from Example 3 captures the* $\mathsf{ML}(\mathsf{Prop}, \mathsf{Act})$-*semantics.*

The $(\mathsf{ML}(\mathsf{Prop}, \mathsf{Act}), K)$-pair Θ_K from Example 3 satisfies a second crucial property, which relates to how the semantic function sem_K can be computed. Consider for instance the $\mathsf{ML}(\mathsf{Prop}, \mathsf{Act})$-formula $\varphi := \varphi_1 \wedge \varphi_2$. The semantic value $\mathsf{sem}_K(\varphi) \in \mathsf{SEM}_K$ is equal to the set of states in K satisfying the formula φ, i.e., to the set of states in K that satisfy both formulas φ_1 and φ_2. Hence, $\mathsf{sem}_K(\varphi)$ can be computed from $\mathsf{sem}_K(\varphi_1)$ and $\mathsf{sem}_K(\varphi_2)$, regardless of what the formulas φ_1 and φ_2 actually are. In fact, this holds for all $\mathsf{ML}(\mathsf{Prop}, \mathsf{Act})$-operators, not only $\wedge$, e.g., the semantic value of the formula $\varphi := [a]\varphi'$ is the set of states whose a-successors are all in $\mathsf{sem}_K(\varphi')$. This second property that an (L, M)-pair Θ_M can satisfy is called the inductive property[4].

Definition 11. *For a logic* L *and an* L-*model* M, *an* (L, M)-*pair* Θ_M *satisfies the inductive property if the following holds. For all* $\mathsf{o} \in \mathsf{Op}_1$ *(resp.* $\mathsf{o} \in \mathsf{Op}_2$), *there is a* Θ_M-*compatible function* $\mathsf{sem}_M^\mathsf{o} : \mathsf{SEM}_M \to \mathsf{SEM}_M$ *(resp.* $\mathsf{sem}_M^\mathsf{o} : (\mathsf{SEM}_M)^2 \to \mathsf{SEM}_M$) *such that, for all* $\varphi_1 \in \mathsf{Fm}_\mathsf{L}$ *(resp.* $\varphi_1, \varphi_2 \in$ Fm_L), *we have* $\mathsf{sem}_M(\mathsf{o}(\varphi_1)) = \mathsf{sem}_M^\mathsf{o}(\mathsf{sem}_M(\varphi_1)$ *(resp.* $\mathsf{sem}_M(\mathsf{o}(\varphi_1, \varphi_2)) =$ $\mathsf{sem}_M^\mathsf{o}(\mathsf{sem}_M(\varphi_1), \mathsf{sem}_M(\varphi_2)))$.

Lemma 2. *For all* $K \in \mathcal{K}(\mathsf{Prop}, \mathsf{Act})$, *the* $(\mathsf{ML}(\mathsf{Prop}, \mathsf{Act}), K)$-*pair* Θ_K *from Example 3 satisfies the inductive property.*

---

[4] Note that this property has some links with the notion of compositionality.

In the following, we will focus on those classes of L-models $\mathcal{C}$ for which, for all models $M \in \mathcal{C}$, there are (L, M)-pairs satisfying the two above properties.

Definition 12. *Consider a logic* L *and an* L-*model* M. *An* (L, M)-*pair* Θ_M *inductively captures the* L-*semantics if it captures the* L-*semantics and satisfies the inductive property. Given a class of* L-*models* $\mathcal{C}$, *an* (L, $\mathcal{C}$)-*pair* Θ *is such that:* $\Theta = (\Theta_M)_{M \in \mathcal{C}}$ *where, for all* $M \in \mathcal{C}$, $\Theta_M = (\mathsf{SEM}_M, \mathsf{sem}_M)$ *is an* (L, M)-*pair that inductively captures the* L-*semantics.*

3.2   Main Theorem and Proof Sketch

We can now state the main theorem of this paper.

Theorem 1. *Consider a logic* L, *a class of* L-*models* $\mathcal{C}$ *and an* (L, $\mathcal{C}$)-*pair* Θ. *For all fragments* L$'$ *of the logic* L, *a* $\mathcal{C}$-*sample* $\mathcal{S}$ *is* L$'$-*separable if and only if there is a* $\mathcal{S}$-*separating* L$'$-*formula of size at most:* $n_\Theta^{\mathcal{S}} := \prod_{M \in \mathcal{S}} |\mathsf{SEM}_M|$.

Note that, in the extended version of this paper, we actually show that this bound $n_\Theta^{\mathcal{S}}$ holds for a setting more general than the passive learning problem. In that setting, we are given a set of models S and a set of subsets $\mathcal{R}_S \subseteq 2^Q$, and we are seeking formulas whose set of accepted S-models belongs to $\mathcal{R}_S$.

The core idea behind this theorem stems from a pigeonhole argument. Indeed, consider some $\mathcal{C}$-sample $\mathcal{S}$ and assume that an $\mathcal{S}$-separating L$'$-formula φ has two sub-formulas φ_1 and φ_2 that are mapped to the same semantic value in SEM_M by the function sem_M, for all $M \in \mathcal{S}$. Then the formula φ' obtained from φ by replacing φ_2 by φ_1 and the formula φ itself are mapped to the same semantic value in SEM_M, for all $M \in \mathcal{S}$. Thus, the formula φ' is also $\mathcal{S}$-separating. By repeating this process, we can obtain an $\mathcal{S}$-separating formula in which there are no two sub-formulas that are mapped to the same semantic value in SEM_M, for all $M \in \mathcal{S}$. The bound of Theorem 1 follows from the definition of formula size.

The proof sketch of Theorem 1 that we provide below actually ventures into a different direction than the one presented above. Although this proof (sketch) is slightly more complicated than the pigeonhole-argument-centered proof, it additionally allows to derive a semantic-based enumeration algorithm solving the passive learning problem.

Proof (sketch). Let L$'$ be fragment of the logic L and $\mathcal{S} = (\mathcal{P}, \mathcal{N})$ be a $\mathcal{C}$-sample. For simplicity, let us assume here that there is no arity-1 L$'$-operator: $\mathsf{Op}_1' = \emptyset$.

Let us first handle the case where there is a single (positive) L-model M in $\mathcal{S}$, i.e. $\mathcal{P} = \{M\}$ and $\mathcal{N} = \emptyset$. Our goal is to find an L$'$-formula satisfied by this model M. By assumption, the (L, M)-pair $\Theta_M = (\mathsf{SEM}_M, \mathsf{sem}_M)$ both a) captures the L-semantics and b) satisfies the inductive property. Property a) gives that any L$'$-formula $\varphi \in \mathsf{Fm}_{\mathsf{L}'}$ is satisfied by M if and only if $\mathsf{sem}_M(\varphi) \in \mathsf{SAT}_M$. Our goal is thus to find an L$'$-formula mapped in SAT_M by the function sem_M.

To find such a formula, we are going to compute the subset $\mathsf{sem}_M[\mathsf{Fm}_{\mathsf{L}'}] = \{\mathsf{sem}_M(\varphi) \mid \varphi \in \mathsf{Fm}_{\mathsf{L}'}\} \subseteq \mathsf{SEM}_M$ of all semantics values in SEM_M that L$'$-formulas can be mapped to by the function sem_M. Thanks to Property b), this set can actually be computed inductively. Initially, we set $\mathsf{SEM}^{\mathsf{L}'}_{M,0}$ to be the image, by the function sem_M, of the set of arity-0 L'-operators: $\mathsf{SEM}^{\mathsf{L}'}_{M,0} := \{\mathsf{sem}_M(\mathsf{o}) \mid \mathsf{o} \in \mathsf{Op}'_0\} \subseteq \mathsf{SEM}_M$. Then, at step $i \in \mathbb{N}$, for all arity-2 L'-operators $\mathsf{o} \in \mathsf{Op}'_2$ and for all pairs $(X_1, X_2) \in (\mathsf{SEM}^{\mathsf{L}'}_{M,i})^2$, we add the semantic value $\mathsf{sem}^{\mathsf{o}}_M(X_1, X_2) \in \mathsf{SEM}_M$ to $\mathsf{SEM}^{\mathsf{L}'}_{M,i+1} \supseteq \mathsf{SEM}^{\mathsf{L}'}_{M,i}$. The process then stops once we reach a fixed point, i.e. when $\mathsf{SEM}^{\mathsf{L}'}_{M,i+1} = \mathsf{SEM}^{\mathsf{L}'}_{M,i}$ for some $i \in \mathbb{N}$. Then, we let $\mathsf{SEM}^{\mathsf{L}'}_M := \mathsf{SEM}^{\mathsf{L}'}_{M,i}$, and we claim that $\mathsf{SEM}^{\mathsf{L}'}_M = \mathsf{sem}_M[\mathsf{Fm}_{\mathsf{L}'}]$. This equality can be proved by a double-inclusion: for the right-to-left inclusion, we show by induction on $\varphi \in \mathsf{Fm}_{\mathsf{L}'}$ that $\mathsf{sem}^{\mathsf{L}'}_M(\varphi) \in \mathsf{SEM}^{\mathsf{L}'}_M$. For the left-to-right inclusion, we show that, for all semantic values $X \in \mathsf{SEM}^{\mathsf{L}'}_M$, there is a L'-formula φ_X satisfying $\mathsf{sem}_M(\varphi_X) = X$ and such that the function $\mathsf{sem}_M : \mathsf{Sub}(\varphi_X) \to \mathsf{SEM}_M$ is injective. That way, we have $\mathsf{sz}(\varphi_X) = |\mathsf{Sub}(\varphi_X)| \leq |\mathsf{SEM}_M|$. Overall, if there is a $\mathcal{S}$-separating L'-formula, there is some $X \in \mathsf{SEM}^{\mathsf{L}'}_M \cap \mathsf{SAT}_M$. With a L'-formula φ_X satisfying the two above conditions, we obtain that: $\mathsf{sz}(\varphi_X) \leq |\mathsf{SEM}_M|$ and $\mathsf{sem}_M(\varphi_X) = X \in \mathsf{SAT}_M$, thus $M \models \varphi_X$.

Consider now the passive learning problem in its full generality where the sample $\mathcal{S}$ may contain arbitrarily many positive and negative models. We follow a similar procedure in this case, except that we manipulate subsets of tuples in $\prod_{M \in \mathcal{S}} \mathsf{SEM}_M$. As above, we use a fixed-point procedure to obtain the set $\mathsf{SEM}^{\mathsf{L}'}_{\mathcal{S}} \subseteq \prod_{M \in \mathcal{S}} \mathsf{SEM}_M$. Then, a L'-formula is $\mathcal{S}$-separating if and only if it is mapped by the function $(\mathsf{sem}_M)_{M \in \mathcal{S}}$ to a tuple $X \in \mathsf{SEM}^{\mathsf{L}'}_{\mathcal{S}}$ such that, for all $M \in \mathcal{P}$, we have $X[M] \in \mathsf{SAT}_M$ and for all $M \in \mathcal{N}$, we have $X[M] \in \mathsf{SEM}_M \setminus \mathsf{SAT}_M$. Furthermore, as above, we can show that, for all $X \in \mathsf{SEM}^{\mathsf{L}'}_{\mathcal{S}}$, there is a L'-formula φ_X such that, for all $M \in \mathcal{S}$ we have $\mathsf{sem}_M(\varphi_X) = X[M]$ and $(\mathsf{sem}_M)_{M \in \mathcal{S}} : \mathsf{Sub}(\varphi_X) \to \prod_{M \in \mathcal{S}} \mathsf{SEM}_M$ is injective. In turn, the size of such a formula is bounded from above by $|\prod_{M \in \mathcal{S}} \mathsf{SEM}_M| = \prod_{M \in \mathcal{S}} |\mathsf{SEM}_M|$.

3.3   A Semantic-Based Meta Algorithm

Many enumeration algorithms in the literature use sophisticated techniques to avoid generating syntactically different but semantically identical formulas. However, this proves to be a difficult task as deciding formula equivalence is hard. Thus, these algorithms often resort to using heuristics which do not entirely prevent enumerating semantically identical formulas.

The above proof sketch suggests a meta algorithm that circumvents this difficulty by not enumerating formulas syntactically, but semantically. It consists in enumerating over the possible semantic values of the formulas instead of the formulas themselves. This meta algorithm is described as Algorithm 1 in pseudo-code: in Lines 1–5, the set $\mathsf{SEM}^{\mathsf{L}}_{\mathsf{S}}$ is computed via a fixed point computation (S under approximates this set $\mathsf{SEM}^{\mathsf{L}}_{\mathsf{S}}$ until the while loop is exited, at which point we have $\mathsf{SEM}^{\mathsf{L}}_{\mathsf{S}} = S$); in Line 6, it is checked whether there is some $X \in \mathsf{SEM}^{\mathsf{L}}_{\mathsf{S}}$ such that for all $M \in \mathcal{P}$, we have $X[M] \in \mathsf{SAT}_M$ and for all $M \in \mathcal{N}$, we have

---

Algorithm 1. PassiveLearning$_{\mathsf{L},\Theta}$: Decides if an input $\mathcal{C}$-sample $\mathcal{S}$ is L-separable

---

Input: A $\mathcal{C}$-sample $\mathcal{S}$ of models
1: $\mathsf{S} \leftarrow \emptyset$, $\mathsf{S}' \leftarrow \{(\mathsf{sem}_M(\mathsf{o}))_{M \in \mathcal{S}} \mid \mathsf{o} \in \mathsf{Op}_0\}$
2: **while** $\mathsf{S} \neq \mathsf{S}'$ **do**
3:    $\mathsf{S} \leftarrow \mathsf{S}'$
4:    **for** $\mathsf{o} \in \mathsf{Op}_1$, $X \in \mathsf{S}$ **do** $\mathsf{S}' \leftarrow \mathsf{S}' \cup \{(\mathsf{sem}_M^{\mathsf{o}}(X[M]))_{M \in \mathcal{S}}\}$
5:    **for** $\mathsf{o} \in \mathsf{Op}_2$, $(X_1, X_2) \in \mathsf{S}^2$ **do** $\mathsf{S}' \leftarrow \mathsf{S}' \cup \{(\mathsf{sem}_M^{\mathsf{o}}(X_1[M], X_2[M]))_{M \in \mathcal{S}}\}$
6: **if** $\mathsf{S} \cap (\prod_{M \in \mathcal{P}} \mathsf{SAT}_M \times \prod_{M \in \mathcal{N}} (\mathsf{SEM}_M \setminus \mathsf{SAT}_M)) \neq \emptyset$ **then** Accept **else** Reject

---

$X[M] \in \mathsf{SEM}_M \setminus \mathsf{SAT}_M$. From the above proof (sketch), we immediately obtain the following result.

Theorem 2. *Consider a logic* L, *a class of* L-*models* $\mathcal{C}$ *and an* $(\mathsf{L}, \mathcal{C})$-*pair* Θ. *Algorithm 1 decides the passive learning problem* PvLn$(\mathsf{L}, \mathcal{C})$.

Complexity of Algorithm 1. This meta algorithm is described on an abstract logical framework which can be instantiated with concrete logics. The complexity of a concrete algorithm depends on the upper bound $n_\Theta^{\mathcal{S}}$, and on the complexity of a) computing the output of Θ_M-compatible functions $\mathsf{sem}_M^{\mathsf{o}}$; b) deciding if a semantic value in SEM_M is in SAT_M; and, if the set of operators Op is infinite, c) computing a finite subset of "relevant operators" that is sufficient to range over in Lines 1, 4, 5. For each individual logic, the bound $n_\Theta^{\mathcal{S}}$ is different and the operations a), b), and c) have different complexities. For our running example of modal logic formulas evaluated on Kripke structures, operations a), b), and c) can be done in polynomial time, while the bound $n_\Theta^{\mathcal{S}}$ is exponential. Thus, we obtain an exponential time algorithm (see Proposition 2).

Usefulness of Algorithm 1. This meta algorithm avoids generating syntactically different but semantically equivalent formulas by design as we shift paradigm from enumerating formulas to enumerating semantic values. This change of paradigm may induce a crucial difference complexity-wise. As mentioned above, for our running example, we have an exponential time algorithm. On the other hand, in Subsect. 4.1, we will exhibit modal logic fragments for which the minimal size of a separating formula is exponential. Thus, a formula-enumeration algorithm would have, in the worst case, a doubly-exponential complexity (as there are doubly exponentially many formulas of exponential size).

This semantic enumeration algorithm is not novel as some practical papers have implicitly used exactly this approach, even though they did not describe it as such, e.g., [33] with regular expressions, or [34] with LTL-formulas. We believe that this meta algorithm is best understood as a framework that can help the design of efficient enumeration algorithms for a wide range of logic learning problems, beyond the instantiations already present in the literature.

4   Use Cases

In this section, we instantiate our abstract logical framework on a zoo of concrete logical formalisms to demonstrate that it is widely applicable. We apply Theorem 1 in these different contexts to obtain (exponential) bounds on the minimal size of separating formulas. We also show that our formalism is applicable to non-logical settings with words separating automata.

4.1   Modal Logic

Let us start with modal logic. A direct application of Theorem 1, with what we have shown in Lemmas 1 and 2, is stated in the corollary below.

Corollary 1. *Consider a non-empty set of propositions* Prop, *a non-empty set of actions* Act, *and any fragment* L *of the modal logic* ML(Prop, Act). *For all* $\mathcal{K}$(Prop, Act)*-samples* $\mathcal{S}$, *if there is a* $\mathcal{S}$*-separating* L*-formula, there is one of size at most* 2^n, *with* $n := \sum_{K \in \mathcal{S}} |Q_K|$.

In fact, for some modal logic fragments, the upper bound established above is actually (almost) tight. To derive this lower bound, we use an already-existing result on the minimal size of words not accepted by a (non-deterministic) automaton.

Theorem 3 (Theorems 32 and 10 in [12]). *Let* $\Sigma := \{a, b, c, d, e\}$. *For all* $n \geq 3$, *there is an automaton* A_n *with* $25n + 111$ *states, a single initial state and such that a smallest word in* $\Sigma^* \setminus L(A_n)$ *is of size* $(2^n - 1) \cdot (n + 1) + 1$.

By turning automata into Kripke structures, we obtain the proposition below.

Proposition 1. *Let* Prop $:= \{p\}$, Act $:= \{a, b, c, d, e\}$, *and* $\mathsf{Op}_{[\cdot]} := \{[\alpha] \mid \alpha \in$ Act$\}$ *and* $\mathsf{Op}_{\langle \cdot \rangle} := \{\langle \alpha \rangle^{\geq 1} \mid \alpha \in$ Act$\}$. *Consider an* ML(Prop, Act)*-fragment* L' *satisfying the following:* $\{\neg, \langle \alpha \rangle^{\geq k} \mid \alpha \in \Sigma, \ k \geq 2\} \cap \mathsf{Op}' = \emptyset$, *and:*

-   *either* $\mathsf{Op}_{[\cdot]} \subseteq \mathsf{Op}'$ *and* $\vee \notin \mathsf{Op}'$;
-   *or* $\mathsf{Op}_{\langle \cdot \rangle} \subseteq \mathsf{Op}'$ *and* $\wedge \notin \mathsf{Op}'$.

Then, for all $n \in \mathbb{N}$, *there is a* $\mathcal{K}$(Prop, Act)*-sample* $\mathcal{S}$ *such that* $k := \sum_{K \in \mathcal{S}} |Q_K| \geq n$, *and the minimal size of an* $\mathcal{S}$*-separating* L*-formula is at least* $2^{\frac{k}{25}}$.

Furthermore, the instantiation of Algorithm 1 in this context of modal logic formulas evaluated on Kripke structures gives an exponential time algorithm.

Proposition 2. *Consider a non-empty set of propositions* Prop *and a non-empty set of actions* Act. *Algorithm 1 instantiated with* ML(Prop, Act)*-formulas and* $\mathcal{K}$(Prop, Act)*-samples has complexity* $2^{O(n)}$, *where* $n := \sum_{K \in \mathcal{S}} |Q_K|$.

We obtain an exponential-time algorithm, whereas, as mentioned in the previous section, the lower bound established in Proposition 1 shows that a simple formula-enumeration algorithm could have a doubly-exponential complexity.

4.2 Temporal Logics

Let us now turn to temporal logics and, more specifically, to Linear Temporal Logic (LTL) [24]. The LTL passive learning problem has been widely studied, as LTL-formulas feature a simple syntax and intuitive semantics, and thus constitute good interpretable models candidates, especially with artificial intelligence settings. See [9] for a more detailed discussion.

Before we present this logic, let us first introduce some notations. Consider a non-empty set Q. We let Q^*, Q^+ and Q^ω denote the set of finite, non-empty finite and infinite sequences of elements of Q, respectively. For all $\rho \in Q^* \cup Q^\omega$, we let $|\rho| \in \mathbb{N} \cup \infty$ denote the number of elements of ρ, and for all $i < |\rho|$, we let $\rho[i] \in Q$ denote the element at position i in ρ, and $\rho[i :] \in Q^* \cup Q^\omega$ denote the suffix of ρ starting at position i.

Linear Temporal Logic. LTL-formulas use different temporal operators $\mathbf{X} \in \mathsf{Op}_1$ (neXt), $\mathbf{F} \in \mathsf{Op}_1$ (Future), $\mathbf{G} \in \mathsf{Op}_1$ (Globally), $\mathbf{U} \in \mathsf{Op}_2$ (Until) to express properties about future events. We consider the case where these formulas are evaluated on finite or ultimately periodic words w (or "lasso")[5]. On such models, the semantics of the above operators can be informally described as follows: the formula $\mathbf{X}\varphi$ expresses the fact that the formula φ should hold in the next position, the formula $\mathbf{F}\varphi$ (resp. $\mathbf{G}\varphi$) means that the formula φ eventually (resp always) holds, while the formula $\varphi_1 \mathbf{U} \varphi_2$ means that the formula φ_2 eventually holds, and until then, the formula φ_1 holds. This is formally defined below.

Definition 13 (LTL syntax and semantics). *Consider a non-empty finite set of propositions* Prop. *The* LTL(Prop)-*syntax is as follows, with $p \in$* Prop:

$$\varphi ::= p \mid \neg\varphi \mid \varphi \vee \varphi \mid \varphi \wedge \varphi \mid \mathbf{X}\varphi \mid \mathbf{F}\varphi \mid \mathbf{G}\varphi \mid \varphi\mathbf{U}\varphi$$

The LTL(Prop)-*models* $\mathcal{W}(\mathsf{Prop})$ *are the finite (non-empty) and ultimately periodic words whose letters are subsets of propositions in* Prop. *Formally, we have:* $\mathcal{W}(\mathsf{Prop}) := \{u \cdot v^\omega \mid u, v \in (2^{\mathsf{Prop}})^*, \ u \cdot v \in (2^{\mathsf{Prop}})^+\}$. *Given a word* $w \in \mathcal{W}(\mathsf{Prop})$, *we define when* LTL(Prop)-*formulas are satisfied by w inductively as follows:* $w \models p$ *iff* $p \in w[0]$; $w \models \neg\varphi$ *iff* $w \not\models \varphi$; $w \models \varphi_1 \vee \varphi_2$ *iff* $w \models \varphi_1$ *or* $w \models \varphi_2$; $w \models \varphi_1 \wedge \varphi_2$ *iff* $w \models \varphi_1$ *and* $w \models \varphi_2$; $w \models \mathbf{X}\varphi$ *iff* $|w| \geq 2$ *and* $w[1 :] \models \varphi$; $w \models \mathbf{F}\varphi$ *iff* $\exists j < |w|, \ w[j :] \models \varphi$; $w \models \mathbf{G}\varphi$ *iff* $\forall j < |w|, \ w[j :] \models \varphi$; $w \models \varphi_1 \mathbf{U} \varphi_2$ *iff* $\exists j < |w|, \ w[j :] \models \varphi_2, \ \forall 0 \leq k \leq j - 1, \ w[k :] \models \varphi_1$.

With Theorem 1, we obtain an exponential bound on the minimal size of a separating formula in the passive learning problem, as formally stated below.

Corollary 2. *Consider a non-empty set of propositions* Prop, *and any* LTL-*fragment* L *of* LTL(Prop). *For all* $\mathcal{W}(\mathsf{Prop})$-*samples* $\mathcal{S}$, *if there is an $\mathcal{S}$-separating* L-*formula, there is one of size at most* 2^n, *with* $n := \sum_{w \in \mathcal{S}} ||w||$, *where for all* $w = u \cdot v \in \mathcal{W}(\mathsf{Prop})$, *we have* $||w|| := |u| + |v|$.

---

[5] Usually, LTL-formulas are evaluated either on finite words or on infinite words. We consider both cases at the same time as it does not change our underlying argument.

Remark 1. When considering the full logic LTL(Prop), there is actually a polynomial upper bound on the minimal size of separating formulas, as it is possible to succinctly describe the input. However, note that the above exponential upper bound holds for all fragments of LTL(Prop), not only the full logic. Furthermore, in the extended version of this paper, we provide a sub-exponential lower bound on the minimal size of a separating formula for some LTL-fragments (which is less tight than the one established in Proposition 1 with modal logic formulas).

Remark 2. As mentioned when discussing the meta algorithm in Sect. 3.3, in the practical paper [34] focusing on the passive learning problem of LTL-formulas evaluated on finite words, the search space is composed of a set of characteristic matrices representing the evaluation of LTL formulas at each word position. The enumeration of these characteristic matrices involves directly applying operators to them. For instance, propositional operators correspond to bitwise operations, the $\mathbf{X}$ operator shifts matrices one bit to the left, the $\mathbf{F}$ operator (eventually) performs a disjunction over leftward shifts, and so on. This corresponds to what we describe in the proof of Corollary 2 in [5].

The logics CTL, ATL, and PCTL. We quickly discuss three logical settings where the application of Theorem 1 is very similar to the case of modal logic.

The logic LTL is intrinsically linear as it only expresses properties in a single possible future, without branching operator. On the other hand, the Computation Tree Logic (CTL) uses all the temporal operators of the logic LTL and extends it with the use of path quantifiers (existential or universal) immediately followed by a temporal operator. Such CTL-formulas are evaluated on Kripke structures (without actions), e.g., the CTL-formula $\varphi = \exists \mathbf{G}\varphi'$ is satisfied by the states of a Kripke structure from which there exists an infinite path where all visited states satisfies the CTL-formula φ'. In fact, the CTL-semantics has an inductive behavior and Theorem 1 can be straightforwardly applied to this setting.

Corollary 3. *For all* CTL-*fragments* L *and samples* $\mathcal{S}$ *of Kripke structures (without actions and with a matching set of propositions), if there is a* $\mathcal{S}$-*separating* L-*formula, there is one of size at most* 2^n, *with* $n := \sum_{K \in \mathcal{S}} |Q_K|$.

In [5], we actually generalize Corollary 3 to Alternating-time Temporal Logic (ATL) formulas evaluated on concurrent multi-player game structures. The logic ATL extends the logic CTL by replacing the path quantifiers $\exists$ and $\forall$ with strategic operators $\langle\!\langle \cdot \rangle\!\rangle$. With this generalization, we recover the result proved in [7], and thus show that the abstract framework of this paper does capture and generalize the initial idea developed in [7].

The logic CTL uses existential and universal quantifiers overs paths. A probabilistic extension of this logic, called Probabilistic Computation Tree Logic (PCTL) [17], instead uses probabilistic quantification expressing properties about the likelihood that a temporal property is satisfied. Such PCTL-formulas are evaluated on Markov chains, e.g., the PCTL-formula $\varphi = \mathbb{P}_{\geq 1/2}(\mathbf{G}\varphi')$ is satisfied by the states of a Markov chain from which the probability of always seeing states satisfying φ' is at least $1/2$. As for CTL and ATL, the PCTL-semantics has an inductive behavior and Theorem 1 can be straightforwardly applied.

Corollary 4. *For all* PCTL-*fragments* L *and samples* S *of Markov chains (with matching set of propositions), if there is a* S-*separating* L-*formula, there is one of size at most* 2^n, *with* $n := \sum_{N \in S} |Q_N|$.

4.3 Minimal Size of Words Separating Automata

Let us now depart from logical formalisms and focus on automaton. What we establish here is not novel, but it shows that the abstract framework that we have introduced can be applied to various kinds of concrete formalisms .

The passive learning of automaton is a well-studied subject, dating back from the 70 s [15]. In this setting, the goal is, given a set of positive and negative finite words, to learn a finite automaton accepting the positive words, and rejecting the negative ones. Theorem 1 is useless in this setting. Indeed, it is folklore that if there exists a separating automaton, there is one whose number of states is at most linear in the size of the input, whereas an application of Theorem 1 would yield an exponential bound on the number of states. However, Theorem 1 can be applied in an interesting way in the reversed setting where the goal is to find words separating automata, i.e. we are given a set of positive and negative automata, and we want to exhibit a word accepted by the positive automata and rejected by the negative ones. In [5], we apply Theorem 1 to recover a well-known result on finite words separating finite automata. Below, we present the case of ultimately periodic words separating parity automata.

Definition 14. *A parity automaton* A *on an alphabet* Σ *is a tuple* $A = (Q, \Sigma, I, \delta, \pi)$ *where* Q *is a non-empty set,* $I \subseteq Q$, $\delta : Q \times \Sigma \to 2^\Sigma$, *and* $\pi : Q \to \mathbb{N}$. *An* A-*run* ρ *on a infinite word* $w \in \Sigma^\omega$ *is a infinite path* $\rho \in Q^\omega$ *such that* $\rho[0] \in I$, *and for all* $i \in \mathbb{N}$, *we have* $\rho[i + 1] \in \delta(\rho[i], u[i])$. *An infinite word* $w \in \Sigma^\omega$ *is accepted by* A *if there is an* A-*run* $\rho \in Q^\omega$ *on* w *such that* $\max\{n \in \mathbb{N} \mid \forall i \in \mathbb{N}, \exists j \geq i, \pi(\rho[j]) = n\}$ *is even.*

Corollary 5. *Consider a non-empty alphabet* Σ. *For all pairs* $(\mathcal{P}, \mathcal{N})$ *of finite sets of parity automata, if there is an ultimately periodic word* $w = u \cdot v^\omega \in \Sigma^\omega$ *accepted by all automata in* $\mathcal{P}$ *and rejected by all automata in* $\mathcal{N}$, *there there is one such word* w *of size at most* $2^n - 1 + 2^k$, *with* $n := \sum_{A \in \mathcal{P} \cup \mathcal{N}} |Q_A|$, *and* $k := \sum_{A \in \mathcal{P} \cup \mathcal{N}} |Q_A|^2 \cdot n_A$, *where, for all* $A \in \mathcal{P} \cup \mathcal{N}$, $n_A := |\{\pi(q) \mid q \in Q_A\}|$.

5   Conclusion and Future Work

The main contribution of this paper is Theorem 1. It provides theoretical groundings to enumeration algorithms as it exhibits a termination criterion. The simple abstract framework that we have considered enabled both straightforward applications of Theorem 1 in various logical settings and a less straightforward application of this theorem to an automaton setting.

We believe that one of the most promising future work is the study, both on the theoretical side and on the experimental side, of the meta algorithm discussed in Subsect. 3.3. (As mentioned before, it has already been successfully applied for learning regular expressions [33] and LTL formulas [34].) The main asset of this algorithm is that its nature prevents it from enumerating semantically-equivalent but syntactically-different formulas, which can be very significant in situations where the number of semantic values is (much) smaller than the number of candidate formulas.

Acknowledgements. This work was partially supported by the Deutsche Forschungs-gemeinschaft (grant number 434592664).

References

1. Angluin, D.: On the complexity of minimum inference of regular sets. Inf. Control **39**(3), 337–350 (1978). https://doi.org/10.1016/S0019-9958(78)90683-6
2. Arif, M.F., Larraz, D., Echeverria, M., Reynolds, A., Chowdhury, O., Tinelli, C.: SYSLITE: syntax-guided synthesis of PLTL formulas from finite traces. In: 2020 Formal Methods in Computer Aided Design, FMCAD 2020, Haifa, Israel, 21–24 September 2020, pp. 93–103. IEEE (2020). https://doi.org/10.34727/2020/ISBN. 978-3-85448-042-6_16
3. Blackburn, P., de Rijke, M., Venema, Y.: Modal Logic, Cambridge Tracts in Theoretical Computer Science, vol. 53. Cambridge University Press, Cambridge (2001). https://doi.org/10.1017/CBO9781107050884
4. Bombara, G., Vasile, C.I., Penedo, F., Yasuoka, H., Belta, C.: A decision tree approach to data classification using signal temporal logic. In: Proceedings of the 19th International Conference on Hybrid Systems: Computation and Control, pp. 1–10. HSCC '16, Association for Computing Machinery, New York, NY, USA (2016). https://doi.org/10.1145/2883817.2883843
5. Bordais, B., Neider, D.: A framework for computing upper bounds in passive learning settings. CoRR **abs/2504.03517** (2025). https://doi.org/10.48550/ARXIV. 2504.03517, https://doi.org/10.48550/arXiv.2504.03517
6. Bordais, B., Neider, D., Roy, R.: The complexity of learning temporal properties. CoRR **abs/2408.04486** (2024). https://doi.org/10.48550/ARXIV.2408. 04486, https://doi.org/10.48550/arXiv.2408.04486
7. Bordais, B., Neider, D., Roy, R.: Learning branching-time properties in CTL and ATL via constraint solving. In: Platzer, A., Rozier, K.Y., Pradella, M., Rossi, M. (eds.) Formal Methods. FM 2024. LNCS, vol. 14933, pp. 304–323. Springer, Cham (2024). https://doi.org/10.1007/978-3-031-71162-6_16
8. Camacho, A., Icarte, R.T., Klassen, T.Q., Valenzano, R.A., McIlraith, S.A.: LTL and beyond: formal languages for reward function specification in reinforcement learning. In: Kraus, S. (ed.) Proceedings of the Twenty-Eighth International Joint Conference on Artificial Intelligence, IJCAI 2019, Macao, China, 10–16 August 2019, pp. 6065–6073. ijcai.org (2019). https://doi.org/10.24963/IJCAI.2019/840, https://doi.org/10.24963/ijcai.2019/840

9. Camacho, A., McIlraith, S.A.: Learning interpretable models expressed in linear temporal logic. In: ICAPS, pp. 621–630. AAAI Press (2019)

10. Chan, W.: Temporal-logic queries. In: Emerson, E.A., Sistla, A.P. (eds.) Computer Aided Verification. CAV 2000. LNCS, vol. 1855, pp. 450–463. Springer, Berlin, Heidelberg (2000). https://doi.org/10.1007/10722167_34

11. Ehlers, R., Gavran, I., Neider, D.: Learning properties in LTL ∩ ACTL from positive examples only. In: 2020 Formal Methods in Computer Aided Design, FMCAD 2020, Haifa, Israel, 21–24 September 2020, pp. 104–112. IEEE (2020)

12. Ellul, K., Krawetz, B., Shallit, J.O., Wang, M.: Regular expressions: new results and open problems. J. Autom. Lang. Comb. **10**(4), 407–437 (2005). https://doi.org/10.25596/JALC-2005-407, https://doi.org/10.25596/jalc-2005-407

13. Funk, M.: Concept-by-example in el knowledge bases. Master's thesis, University of Bremen (2019)

14. Gaglione, J., Neider, D., Roy, R., Topcu, U., Xu, Z.: Maxsat-based temporal logic inference from noisy data. Innov. Syst. Softw. Eng. **18**(3), 427–442 (2022). https://doi.org/10.1007/S11334-022-00444-8

15. Gold, E.M.: Complexity of automaton identification from given data. Inf. Control **37**(3), 302–320 (1978)

16. Goranko, V., Kuijer, L.B.: On the length and depth of temporal formulae distinguishing non-bisimilar transition systems. In: Dyreson, C.E., Hansen, M.R., Hunsberger, L. (eds.) 23rd International Symposium on Temporal Representation and Reasoning, TIME 2016, Kongens Lyngby, Denmark, 17–19 October 2016, pp. 177–185. IEEE Computer Society (2016). https://doi.org/10.1109/TIME.2016.26, https://doi.org/10.1109/TIME.2016.26

17. Hansson, H., Jonsson, B.: A logic for reasoning about time and reliability. Form. Aspects Comput. **6**(5), 512–535 (1994). https://doi.org/10.1007/BF01211866, https://doi.org/10.1007/BF01211866

18. Ielo, A., Law, M., Fionda, V., Ricca, F., Giacomo, G.D., Russo, A.: Towards ilp-based LTL$_f$ passive learning. In: Bellodi, E., Lisi, F.A., Zese, R. (eds.) Inductive Logic Programming. ILP 2023. LNCS, vol. 14363, pp. 30–45. Springer, Cham (2023). https://doi.org/10.1007/978-3-031-49299-0_3

19. Kim, J., Muise, C., Shah, A., Agarwal, S., Shah, J.: Bayesian inference of linear temporal logic specifications for contrastive explanations. In: Kraus, S. (ed.) Proceedings of the Twenty-Eighth International Joint Conference on Artificial Intelligence, IJCAI 2019, Macao, China, 10–16 August 2019, pp. 5591–5598. ijcai.org (2019). https://doi.org/10.24963/IJCAI.2019/776

20. Luo, W., Liang, P., Du, J., Wan, H., Peng, B., Zhang, D.: Bridging ltlf inference to GNN inference for learning ltlf formulae. In: Thirty-Sixth AAAI Conference on Artificial Intelligence, AAAI 2022, Thirty-Fourth Conference on Innovative Applications of Artificial Intelligence, IAAI 2022, The Twelveth Symposium on Educational Advances in Artificial Intelligence, EAAI 2022 Virtual Event, February 22–1 March 2022, pp. 9849–9857. AAAI Press (2022). https://doi.org/10.1609/AAAI.V36I9.21221

21. Mascle, C., Fijalkow, N., Lagarde, G.: Learning temporal formulas from examples is hard. CoRR **abs/2312.16336** (2023). https://arxiv.org/pdf/2312.16336

22. Mohammadinejad, S., Deshmukh, J.V., Puranic, A.G., Vazquez-Chanlatte, M., Donzé, A.: Interpretable classification of time-series data using efficient enumerative techniques. In: HSCC '20: 23rd ACM International Conference on Hybrid Systems: Computation and Control, Sydney, New South Wales, Australia, 21–24 April 2020, pp. 9:1–9:10. ACM (2020). https://doi.org/10.1145/3365365.3382218

23. Neider, D., Gavran, I.: Learning linear temporal properties. In: Bjørner, N.S., Gurfinkel, A. (eds.) 2018 Formal Methods in Computer Aided Design, FMCAD 2018, Austin, TX, USA, October 30– 2 November 2018, pp. 1–10. IEEE (2018). https://doi.org/10.23919/FMCAD.2018.8603016

24. Pnueli, A.: The temporal logic of programs. In: 18th Annual Symposium on Foundations of Computer Science, Providence, Rhode Island, USA, 31 October–1 November 1977, pp. 46–57. IEEE Computer Society (1977). https://doi.org/10.1109/SFCS.1977.32

25. Pommellet, A., Stan, D., Scatton, S.: Sat-based learning of computation tree logic. In: Benzmüller, C., Heule, M.J., Schmidt, R.A. (eds.) Automated Reasoning. IJCAR 2024. LNCS, vol. 14739, pp. 366–385. Springer, Cham (2024). https://doi.org/10.1007/978-3-031-63498-7_22

26. Raha, R., Roy, R., Fijalkow, N., Neider, D.: Scalable anytime algorithms for learning fragments of linear temporal logic. In: TACAS 2022. LNCS, vol. 13243, pp. 263–280. Springer, Cham (2022). https://doi.org/10.1007/978-3-030-99524-9_14

27. Raha, R., Roy, R., Fijalkow, N., Neider, D., Pérez, G.A.: Synthesizing efficiently monitorable formulas in metric temporal logic. In: Dimitrova, R., Lahav, O., Wolff, S. (eds.) Verification, Model Checking, and Abstract Interpretation. VMCAI 2024. LNCS, vol. 14500, pp. 264–288. Springer, Cha (2024). https://doi.org/10.1007/978-3-031-50521-8_13

28. Riener, H.: Exact synthesis of LTL properties from traces. In: FDL, pp. 1–6. IEEE (2019)

29. Roy, R., Fisman, D., Neider, D.: Learning interpretable models in the property specification language. In: IJCAI, pp. 2213–2219. ijcai.org (2020)

30. Roy, R., Gaglione, J., Baharisangari, N., Neider, D., Xu, Z., Topcu, U.: Learning interpretable temporal properties from positive examples only. In: Williams, B., Chen, Y., Neville, J. (eds.) Thirty-Seventh AAAI Conference on Artificial Intelligence, AAAI 2023, Thirty-Fifth Conference on Innovative Applications of Artificial Intelligence, IAAI 2023, Thirteenth Symposium on Educational Advances in Artificial Intelligence, EAAI 2023, Washington, DC, USA, 7–14 February 2023, pp. 6507–6515. AAAI Press (2023). https://doi.org/10.1609/AAAI.V37I5.25800

31. Rozier, K.Y.: Specification: the biggest bottleneck in formal methods and autonomy. In: Blazy, S., Chechik, M. (eds.) VSTTE 2016. LNCS, vol. 9971, pp. 8–26. Springer, Cham (2016). https://doi.org/10.1007/978-3-319-48869-1_2

32. Sandor, J.: Handbook of Number Theory, II. Kluwer Academic Publishers, Dordrecht (2004)

33. Valizadeh, M., Berger, M.: Search-based regular expression inference on a GPU. Proc. ACM Program. Lang. **7**(PLDI), 1317–1339 (2023). https://doi.org/10.1145/3591274

34. Valizadeh, M., Fijalkow, N., Berger, M.: LTL learning on gpus. In: Gurfinkel, A., Ganesh, V. (eds.) Computer Aided Verification. CAV 2024. LNCS, vol. 14683, pp. 209–231. Springer, Cham (2024). https://doi.org/10.1007/978-3-031-65633-0_10

35. Wan, H., Liang, P., Du, J., Luo, W., Ye, R., Peng, B.: End-to-end learning of ltlf formulae by faithful ltlf encoding. In: AAAI, pp. 9071–9079. AAAI Press (2024)

36. Wasylkowski, A., Zeller, A.: Mining temporal specifications from object usage. Autom. Softw. Eng. **18**(3–4), 263–292 (2011)

On Temporal References via Definite Descriptions in First-Order Monadic Logic of Order

Andrzej Indrzejczak[1], Przemysław Andrzej Wałęga[1,2],
and Michał Zawidzki[1(✉)]

[1] University of Łódź, Łódź, Poland
{andrzej.indrzejczak,przemyslaw.walega,michal.zawidzki}@filhist.ini.lodz.pl
[2] Queen Mary University of London, London, UK

Abstract. Temporal reference, understood as the capability of referring to particular points of time, is an essential aspect of temporal reasoning. In this paper we model it with the definite description (iota) operator added to first-order monadic logic of order—a standard formalism for reasoning about time. This allows us to express temporal reference directly and with dedicated tools, which is of particular importance from the point of view of proof systems for automated reasoning. We construct a sound and complete tableau system, as well as provide complexity results for the satisfiability problem of the obtained logic.

Keywords: Temporal reference · Definite descriptions · Temporal referring expressions · Tableaux system

1 Introduction

The ability to refer to specific points in time is essential to everyday communication. We often do this using *referring expressions* such as 'the last time I read *On Denoting*' or 'the time when the system was upgraded to version 2.0'.

Research on temporal reference has a long tradition, driven both by formal analyses of natural language [46,49,58,65,68] and by applications in computer science, including temporal knowledge modelling [21,44], temporal query answering [1,17,21], and temporal information extraction [20]. This work has given rise to various logical frameworks [6,8,9,32,35] and automated reasoning techniques [9,22,23,31].

Temporal references can be *definite*, referring to a unique time point, or *indefinite*, lacking such specificity. This distinction parallels that between definite and indefinite articles [24,56,62] and reflects a deeper linguistic phenomenon. Present perfect sentences often employ indefinite reference, as they leave the number and timing of events unspecified [56], while simple past sentences typically involve definite reference to a specific time [68], though exceptions exist.

A widely studied approach to referentiality in temporal logic introduces new language elements to uniquely label time points. These labels have been known

G. Casini et al. (Eds.): JELIA 2025, LNAI 16094, pp. 244–262, 2026.
https://doi.org/10.1007/978-3-032-04590-4_17

as *clock-variables* [18,65], *nominals* in hybrid logics [6], or simply *names* [30]. Hybrid operators such as the satisfaction operator @ and existential binders are added to exploit these labels, substantially increasing the logic's expressive power and complexity [6,9,13,14,28,32].

These operators enable the expression of indexicals like 'now', which refers to the time of utterance [9,11]. Crucially, 'now' is not eliminable within the scope of temporal modifiers [46,76], and supports expressions like 'yesterday' or 'a year ago.' Deductive systems for hybrid temporal logics include tableaux [45,79], Hilbert-style systems [31,32], sequent calculi [22,37], and display calculi [23]. Hybrid logics also relate closely to *labelled deduction* [29,36], where there occur meta-language labels, which, however, can be internalised within the object language thanks to the presence of nominals and satisfaction operators [7,74].

However, hybrid logics lack dedicated mechanisms for referring to time points *via the properties they satisfy*. While some temporal logics permit this form of reference, it is usually incidental—emerging from the structure of time—rather than the result of an explicit mechanism.

In contrast, *definite descriptions* (DDs) have been extensively studied as a way to refer to objects based on their unique properties, exemplified by expressions like 'the present king of France' [71]. A standard formalisation uses Peano's term-forming operator ι [63], where $\iota x\varphi(x)$ denotes the unique x satisfying φ. Incorporating such operators into logic improves proof theory—yielding more concise formalisations and proofs, and avoiding infinite countermodels in invalid cases [43]. DDs can also outperform functional terms in several respects [43].

DD theories have been developed by Frege [64], Hilbert and Bernays [34], Rosser [70], Scott [73], Lambert [55], and others [4]. Recent years have seen the development of proof systems for DDs, including tableau systems [42,43], sequent calculi, and natural deduction [38–41,50–54,61]. These have been implemented in systems such as *KeYmaera X* [16], *PROVER9* [60], and in proof assistants like *Isabelle/HOL* [5,15].

Applications of DDs include *knowledge representation and reasoning* [2,59], *system verification* [16], and *formal ontology* [60]. However, their role in temporal contexts—where complex terms denote time points via descriptions—has not been thoroughly explored. To illustrate that DDs are a valuable tool in temporal settings—where commonly used constructs such as functional symbols or constants (when used in isolation) fall short—consider the following example:

Example 1. Let *last* be a unary functional symbol such that $last(x)$ denotes 'the final time point of the day on which time point x occurs'. Consider the sentence $\varphi := \forall x\,(last(x) = 23\!:\!59)$, which can be interpreted as: 'Every time point occurs on a day that ends at 23:59.'

When constructing an inference tree for φ, we obtain an infinite sequence of equalities:

$$last(23\!:\!59) = 23\!:\!59,$$
$$last(last(23\!:\!59)) = 23\!:\!59,$$
$$last(last(last(23\!:\!59))) = 23\!:\!59,$$

$$\vdots$$

This leads to the construction of an infinite Herbrand model that satisfies φ. Avoiding such infinite derivations typically requires additional loop-checking mechanisms.

By contrast, if we replace *last* with a corresponding DD, such that $last(x) \rightsquigarrow \iota y \, Last(x,y)$, and accordingly rewrite φ as $\forall x \, (\iota y \, Last(x,y) = 23:59)$, then, using standard tableau rules [42]—and without resorting to any external mechanisms—the derivation reduces to a pair of equalities:

$$\iota y(23\!:\!59, y) = 23\!:\!59, \qquad 23\!:\!59 = 23\!:\!59.$$

This yields a model with a singleton domain that satisfies the formula.

We aim to develop an automated reasoning tool for formal languages designed to express temporal reference. The main contributions of the paper are:

1. Providing a formal logic capable of expressing complex temporal references and indexicals by means of the iota-operator (Sect. 2).
2. Developing a sound and complete tableaux system for our logic, with well-behaving rules for temporal references (Sect. 3).
3. Showing computational complexity results of the satisfiability problem for well-behaving fragments of the logic (Sect. 4).
4. Extending the logic with the successor relation and with the λ-operator; the former is a standard relation studied in temporal logics and the latter allows us to overcome scoping difficulties of DDs (Sect. 5).

To construct a formal language appropriate for achieving our goal, we extend first-order monadic logic of order, denoted as FO($<$), by introducing the constant *now* and the ι-operator. FO($<$) is a standard logic for reasoning about time [47] and its terms correspond to points of time; the latter allow us to express temporal reference by means of a unique characterisation of a time point (using ι) and the time of utterance (using *now*), which is a crucial component of context for temporal references [46,66]. The obtained language can express a variety of temporal references, for example 'the last time I met Mary', as the complex term

$$\iota x \Big(MeetM(x) \wedge x < now \wedge \forall y \big(x < y < now \rightarrow (\neg MeetM(y)) \big) \Big). \qquad (1)$$

To define the semantics of this logic, we apply the Russell's theory of DDs [71,78], according to which stating that a term $\iota x\varphi(x)$ satisfies ψ, coincides with stating

$\exists x (\forall y (\varphi(y) \leftrightarrow x = y) \wedge \psi(x))$, namely that there exists a unique x s.t. $\varphi(x)$ and moreover $\psi(x)$. Although this approach has some deficiencies, it is a standard point of reference of almost all works devoted to the analysis of DDs. Moreover, Russell's theory has strong affinities to logics such as the logic of the existence predicate by Scott [73] or the definedness logic (or the logic of partial terms) of Beeson [3] and Feferman [26]. Finally, it appears that the Russellian approach to DDs fits better the context of temporal reference than the theories developed in the setting of free logics, since we assume that all variables denote some time points and only DDs can fail to denote uniquely (they can be improper).

To provide a well-behaving tableau system for the logic, we introduce a block of specific rules capturing the meaning of the ι-operator in our setting. In particular, our rules encode that DDs occurring in atomic formulas need to denote, that is, correspond to some variables. Moreover, we introduce rules capturing the fact that a time point denoted by a DD satisfies this description and that no other time point satisfies this description. Furthermore, we introduce a specific form of restricted analytic cut rule which allows for comparing DDs. We show that this calculus is sound and complete w.r.t. the semantics of our logic.

Regarding the computational complexity analysis, we show that each formula of $FO(<, \iota, now)$ can be translated in polynomial time to an equisatisfiable formula of $FO(<)$. A careful design of the translation makes the number of variables mentioned in a formula preserved. This, in turn, allows us to exploit results on the two-variable fragment of $FO(<)$ and show NExpTime-complete and NP-complete fragments of our logic.

Finally, we discuss how to extend the logic with additional expressions, namely the successor relation *succ* and the λ-operator. We observe that, in general, expressing *succ* requires three variables, so our complexity bounds for the two-variable fragments do not apply if we use such a translation. Instead, we discuss how to introduce *succ* as a primitive element of the language and how to extend the tableau calculus. Then, we observe that to overcome the scoping difficulties of DDs and to allow distinguishing between expressions like 'the present king of France is not bald' and 'it is not the case that the present king of France is bald', we can exploit predicate abstracts using the additional λ-operator. In particular, $\lambda x \varphi(x)$ means 'the property of being φ' [27,43,72] and, as we show, our calculus can be extended to capture this kind of constructs.

In Sect. 6 we conclude the paper and discuss directions of future work.

2   A Logic for Temporal References

In this section, aiming for a convenient representation and reasoning mechanism for complex temporal references, we introduce the logic $FO(<, \iota, now)$. For this, we use the standard temporal language $FO(<)$ of first-order logic with monadic predicates, identity ($=$), and the binary relation *earlier-later* ($<$) [25,47,67], and extend it with Peano's ι-operator for expressing DDs [63], as well as with Prior's constant *now* for capturing the temporal context of utterance [66]. This will allow us to naturally express various temporal references.

Syntax. The vocabulary of $FO(<, \iota, now)$ consists of a countable set Σ of unary predicates $P, Q, R, \ldots$, a denumerable set VAR of first-order variables $x, y, z, \ldots$, the *earlier-later* relation $<$, Boolean connectives $\neg$ and $\vee$, the existential quantifier $\exists$, the DD operator ι, and the constant now. Terms s and formulas φ are defined simultaneously by the following grammars:

$$s ::= x \mid now \mid \iota x \varphi(x), \tag{2}$$

$$\varphi ::= P(s) \mid s_1 = s_2 \mid s_1 < s_2 \mid \neg \varphi \mid \varphi_1 \vee \varphi_2 \mid \exists x \varphi, \tag{3}$$

where x ranges over variables, P over predicates, and s, s_1, s_2 over terms. Moreover, $\varphi(x)$ is a formula with a free variable x, where variables are bound in our language not only by quantifiers, but also by the ι-operator; we will call terms of the form $\iota x \varphi(x)$ *definite descriptions* (DDs). We will also sometimes write $s_1 > s_2$ instead of $s_2 < s_1$ and use other Boolean connectives as well as the universal quantifier, which are treated as the standard abbreviations.

We also consider the fragment of $FO(<, \iota, now)$ in which formulas use at most two variables, denoted $FO^2(<, \iota, now)$. Despite this restriction, $FO^2(<, \iota, now)$ can still express a range of complex temporal references. For example, the expression 'the last time I met Mary' can be captured using just two variables, as shown in Expression (1).

While standard formulations of the temporal operators *since* and *until* typically require three variables, they become definable with only two when the constant now is used to represent the initial or reference time point. For instance, 'I have not met John since I met Mary' can be formalised as:

$$\exists x \Big(x < now \wedge MeetM(x) \wedge \forall y \, (x < y < now \rightarrow \neg MeetJ(y)) \Big).$$

Here, the constant now introduces a contextual dimension to the language, serving as a temporal anchor that distinguishes past from future relative to the utterance time.

Semantics. We interpret $FO(<, \iota, now)$ over linear orders—a standard way of modelling the time line. To interpret now we adopt the *designated time semantics* [19] which consists in extending a model with a single time point t_0 standing for the 'utterance time of the context associated with the model' [10][1]. For the ι-operator, we introduce semantic conditions in the style of Russell's theory of DDs, namely to satisfy an atomic formula with a DD we require existence and uniqueness of a time point satisfying this description.

Formally, we let a *model* be a tuple of the form $\mathcal{M} = (\mathcal{T}, <, \mathcal{I}, t_0)$, where $\mathcal{T}$ is a non-empty set of time points (strictly) linearly ordered by $<$, whereas $\mathcal{I}$ is an interpretation function which assigns a subset of $\mathcal{T}$ to each predicate from Σ, and

---

[1] Designated time semantics is also used to interpret the 'actually' operator [12,33]; alternative semantics for *now* is provided by Kamp who uses two-dimensional models, where formulas are evaluated over pairs of time points with the second time point representing the time of utterance [46].

$t_0 \in \mathcal{T}$ is a time of utterance. *Satisfaction* of a formula φ in a model $\mathcal{M}$ under an assignment $v : \mathsf{VAR} \longrightarrow \mathcal{T}$, written as $\mathcal{M}, v \models \varphi$, is defined as usual for formulas without ι-operators. For ι-operators we use the following conditions, where $\lessgtr$ stands for one of the symbols in $\{=, <, >\}$, whereas s is a term not mentioning ι-operators (i.e., $s \in \mathsf{VAR} \cup \{now\}$) and $v[x \mapsto t]$ is an assignment which agrees with v on all elements of VAR except that it maps x to t—other symbols are standard i.e., $x, y \in \mathsf{VAR}$, $P \in \Sigma$, and φ, ψ are FO($<, \iota, now$)-formulas:

$$\mathcal{M}, v \models P(\iota x \varphi(x)) \quad \text{iff} \quad \text{there exists a unique } t \in \mathcal{T} \text{ s.t.}$$
$$\mathcal{M}, v[x \mapsto t] \models \varphi(x), \text{ and } t \in \mathcal{I}(P) \text{ for this } t$$

$$\mathcal{M}, v \models s \lessgtr \iota x \varphi(x) \quad \text{iff} \quad \text{there exists a unique } t \in \mathcal{T} \text{ s.t.}$$
$$\mathcal{M}, v[x \mapsto t] \models \varphi(x), \text{ and } v(s) \lessgtr t \text{ for this } t$$

$$\mathcal{M}, v \models \iota x \varphi(x) \lessgtr \iota y \psi(y) \quad \text{iff} \quad \text{there exist unique } t_1, t_2 \in \mathcal{T} \text{ s.t.}$$
$$\mathcal{M}, v[x \mapsto t_1] \models \varphi(x) \text{ and } \mathcal{M}, v[y \mapsto t_2] \models \psi(y),$$
$$\text{and moreover } t_1 \lessgtr t_2 \text{ for these } t_1, t_2$$

Observe that our semantics for ι-operators corresponds to the Russellian understanding of $\exists x (\forall y (\varphi(y) \leftrightarrow x = y) \wedge \psi(x))$ as expressing $\psi(\iota x \varphi(x))$, but restricted to atomic ψ only; the restriction to atomic formulas allows us to escape inconsistency resulted from applying the Russell's translation to arbitrary contexts. Note also that adopting such semantics has some important consequences, for example, the standard abbreviation of $=$ with $<$ is not applicable. In particular, $s_1 = s_2$ is not equivalent to $\neg(s_1 < s_2) \wedge \neg(s_1 > s_2)$; indeed, if one of s_1 or s_2 is a DD which is not proper, then $s_1 = s_2$ is not satisfied (in any model and valuation making one of the two an improper DD), but the formula $\neg(s_1 < s_2) \wedge \neg(s_1 > s_2)$ is always satisfied.

As usual, we say that an FO($<, \iota, now$)-formula φ is (logically) *satisfiable* if $\mathcal{M}, v \models \varphi$ for some $\mathcal{M}$ and v, whereas φ is (logically) *valid* if $\mathcal{M}, v \models \varphi$ for all $\mathcal{M}$ and v. This notions naturally extend to sets of formulas, treated as their conjunctions. Furthermore, we say that a formula $\varphi(x)$ with a single free variable x is *contextually satisfiable* if $\mathcal{M}, v[x \mapsto t_0] \models \varphi(x)$, for some $\mathcal{M}$ and v, whereas $\varphi(x)$ is *contextually valid*[2] if $\mathcal{M}, v[x \mapsto t_0] \models \varphi(x)$, for every $\mathcal{M}$ and v. Clearly, each logically valid formula is also contextually valid, but not vice versa [11, 46,48,66]. Observe that $\varphi(x)$ is contextually satisfiable iff $\varphi(now)$ is logically satisfiable, and $\varphi(x)$ is contextually valid iff $\neg\varphi(now)$ is not logically satisfiable. As all these problems reduce to (logical) satisfiability checking, we will focus on this problem when studying decidability and computational complexity.

As an example consider the sentence 'I was studying 'On Denoting' the last time I met Mary; therefore, I have not met her since I was studying 'On Denoting'', which can be expressed in FO($<, \iota, now$) with the formula

$$Study(s_M) \to \exists x \Big(x < now \wedge Study(x) \wedge \forall y (x < y < now \to \neg MeetM(y)) \Big), \quad (4)$$

---

[2] Kaplan called such formulas *valid* [49], but we support the idea of Blackburn and Jørgensen [9] to call them contextually valid, as it clearly marks the difference from the standard notion of validity.

where s_M stands for 'the last time I met Mary' which is expressed by Term (1). It can be checked that Formula (4) is logically valid in $FO(<, \iota, now)$, which coincides with our intuitions that it express a correct way of reasoning.

3   Tableau System

In this section, we present a tableau calculus for $FO(<, \iota, now)$ and prove its soundness as well as completeness w.r.t. the semantics from Sect. 2.

Timeline rules

$$(\text{NE})^* \ \frac{}{a = a} \qquad (\text{tran}) \ \frac{b_1 < b_2, b_2 < b_3}{b_1 < b_3} \qquad (\text{irref}) \ \frac{b < b}{\bot} \qquad (\text{tot}) \ \frac{}{b_1 < b_2 \mid b_1 = b_2 \mid b_2 < b_1}$$

Basic first-order rules

$$(\neg\neg) \ \frac{\neg\neg\varphi}{\varphi} \qquad (\vee) \ \frac{\varphi \vee \psi}{\varphi \mid \psi} \qquad (\neg\vee) \ \frac{\neg(\varphi \vee \psi)}{\substack{\neg\varphi \\ \neg\psi}} \qquad (\exists) \ \frac{\exists x \varphi}{\varphi[x/a]} \qquad (\neg\exists) \ \frac{\neg\exists x \varphi}{\neg\varphi[x/b]}$$

$$(\text{sym}) \ \frac{s_1 = s_2}{s_2 = s_1} \qquad (\text{rep}) \ \frac{s_1 = s_2, \varphi(s_1)}{\varphi[s_1/s_2]} \qquad (\text{clash}) \ \frac{\varphi, \neg\varphi}{\bot}$$

Definite description rules

$$(\text{cut}) \ \frac{}{b = d \mid b \neq d} \qquad (\iota S_1) \ \frac{P(d)}{a = d} \qquad (\iota S_2) \ \frac{d < s}{a = d} \qquad (\iota S_3) \ \frac{s < d}{a = d} \qquad (\iota S_4) \ \frac{d_1 = d_2}{a = d_1}$$

$$(\iota E_1) \ \frac{b = \iota x \varphi(x)}{\varphi[x/b]} \qquad (\iota E_2) \ \frac{b_1 = \iota x \varphi(x)}{\neg\varphi[x/b_2] \mid b_1 = b_2} \qquad (\neg\iota E) \ \frac{b \neq \iota x \varphi(x)}{\substack{\neg\varphi[x/b] \mid a \neq b \\ \varphi[x/a]}}$$

* The rule (NE) can be applied only if there are no free variables or *now* on the branch and no other rules are applicable.

Fig. 1. Tableau calculus for $FO(<, \iota, now)$

We use standard notions for tableaux. A *tableau* is a tree whose nodes are labelled with $FO(<, \iota, now)$-formulas. A *branch* is any path from the root to a leaf; we identify each node with its formula and each branch with the set of formulas along it. *Rules* take the form: $\frac{\Phi}{\Psi_1 \mid \ldots \mid \Psi_n}$, where the *premise* Φ and the *conclusions* $\Psi_1, \ldots, \Psi_n$ are (possibly empty) sets of $FO(<, \iota, now)$-formulas, and | indicates branching. A conclusion may also be the special symbol $\bot$. A rule is *applicable* to a branch if its premise is present and none of its conclusions is. Applying the rule extends the branch by adding one of its conclusions. If this conclusion is $\bot$, the branch is *closed*—no further rules apply. Otherwise, it remains *open*. A tableau is closed if all branches are closed; otherwise, it is open. A branch is *fully expanded* if no rules apply; a tableau is fully expanded if all its branches are. A *tableau-proof* of a formula φ is a closed tableau whose root is labelled with $\{\neg\varphi\}$. A calculus is *sound* if every $FO(<, \iota, now)$-formula with a tableau-proof is valid, and *complete* if every valid formula has a tableau-proof. The rules of our tableau calculus are shown in Fig. 1, where: $x, a, a_1, a_2 \in \mathsf{VAR}$ are variables amongst which a, a_1, a_2 are free and freshly introduced by the rule, $b, b_1, b_2, b_3 \in \mathsf{VAR} \cup now$ are free variables, or now, that must already occur on the branch, s, s_1, s_2 are terms, and d, d_1, d_2 are definite descriptions. We assume that bound and free variables are disjoint within any tableau, and derivations are defined up to renaming of bound variables. The expression $s_1 \neq s_2$ abbreviates $\neg(s_1 = s_2)$, and $\varphi[s_1/s_2]$ denotes the formula obtained by substituting every occurrence of s_1 with s_2 in φ.

The rule (NE) ensures that only non-empty timelines are considered, while (tran), (irref), and (tot) enforce that $<$ forms a strict linear order, capturing transitivity, irreflexivity, and trichotomy, respectively. All basic first-order rules are standard, except for the replacement rule (rep), which permits substitution of identical terms (including DDs) within formulas. The calculus-specific rules address definite descriptions (DDs). Rules $(\iota\mathsf{S}_1)$–$(\iota\mathsf{S}_4)$ ensure that DDs in atomic formulas denote: for each such formula, a free variable equal to the DD must exist on the branch. Rule $(\iota\mathsf{E}_1)$ asserts that the formula defining a DD holds of the denoted time point, while $(\iota\mathsf{E}_2)$ ensures it holds of no other. Rule $(\neg\iota\mathsf{E})$ guarantees that if a DD does not refer to a given point, then either its defining formula fails at that point or holds at a different one. The (cut) rule is a restricted form of cut that compares DDs on the branch with all free variables. This rule is essential for completeness—without it, we cannot guarantee the uniqueness of DD denotations. For example, consider the set $\Psi = \neg P(\iota x Q(x)), \neg Q(\iota x P(x)), R(\iota x (P(x) \vee Q(x)))$. Ψ is unsatisfiable: the last formula enforces a unique witness for $P(x) \vee Q(x)$, while the first two require at least two. Yet, without (cut), a tableau rooted in Ψ cannot be closed. To illustrate the calculus in action, Fig. 2 presents a tableau-proof of Formula (4). In this proof, we apply standard rules derivable from basic first-order logic:

$$(\neg \rightarrow) \ \frac{\neg(\varphi \rightarrow \psi)}{\begin{array}{c}\varphi \\ \neg\psi\end{array}} \quad (\wedge) \ \frac{\varphi \wedge \psi}{\begin{array}{c}\varphi \\ \psi\end{array}} \quad (\neg\wedge) \ \frac{\neg(\varphi \wedge \psi)}{\neg\varphi \mid \neg\psi} \quad (\forall) \ \frac{\forall x \varphi}{\varphi[x/b]} \quad (\neg\forall) \ \frac{\neg\forall x \varphi}{\neg\varphi[x/a]}.$$

In the remainder of this section, we show that the tableau calculus from Fig. 1 is sound and complete. To this end we will use the following two lemmas, which can be proved similarly as in the case of the standard first-order logic.

Lemma 1 (Coincidence Lemma). *Let φ be an $\mathrm{FO}(<, \iota, now)$-formula, $\mathcal{M}$ be an $\mathrm{FO}(<, \iota, now)$-model, and v_1, v_2 be assignments. If $v_1(x) = v_2(x)$ for each free variable x in φ, then $\mathcal{M}, v_1 \models \varphi$ iff $\mathcal{M}, v_2 \models \varphi$.*

Lemma 2 (Substitution Lemma). *Let φ be an $\mathrm{FO}(<, \iota, now)$-formula, $\mathcal{M}$ be an $\mathrm{FO}(<, \iota, now)$-model, x and a be free variables in φ, and v be an assignment. Then $\mathcal{M}, v \models \varphi[x/a]$ iff $\mathcal{M}, v[x \mapsto v(a)] \models \varphi$.*

Using these lemmas we can show that each rule of the calculus preserves satisfiability, which implies soundness of the calculus.

Theorem 1. *The tableau calculus from Fig. 1 is sound w.r.t. the semantics of* FO($<, \iota, now$).

Proof (Sketch). It suffices to show that for each rule $\frac{\Phi}{\Psi_1|\ldots|\Psi_n}$, if Φ is satsifiable, then so is Ψ_i for some $i \in \{1, \ldots, n\}$. By way of example, we will consider the rule ($\neg\iota$E). Throughout the proof we will use symbols a, b, b_1, b_2 in line with the notation adopted in the rules of our calculus.

($\neg\iota$E)   Assume that $b \neq \iota x\varphi(x)$ is satisfiable, so $\mathcal{M}, v \not\models b = \iota x\varphi$, for some $\mathcal{M}$ and v. Therefore, there exists no unique time point t s.t. $\mathcal{M}, v[x \mapsto t] \models \varphi(x)$ and moreover $v(b) = t$ for this time point. Two cases may occur: either $\mathcal{M}, v \not\models \varphi[x/b]$ or $\mathcal{M}, v \models \varphi[x/b]$. In the former one, $\mathcal{M}, v \models \neg\varphi[x/b]$, and hence, the left conclusion of the rule is satisfiable. In the latter case, since, by the assumption, $v(b) = t$ is not the unique time point s.t. $\mathcal{M}, v[x \mapsto t] \models \varphi(x)$, there must exist a time point $t' \neq t$ s.t. $\mathcal{M}, v[x \mapsto t'] \models \varphi(x)$. Without loss of generality

1. $\neg\big(Study(s_M) \rightarrow \exists x(x < now \wedge Study(x) \wedge \forall y(x < y \wedge y < now \rightarrow \neg MeetM(y))) \big)$

$\downarrow (\neg\rightarrow) : 1$

2. $Study(s_M)$

3. $\neg\exists x(x < now \wedge Study(x) \wedge \forall y(x < y \wedge y < now \rightarrow \neg MeetM(y)))$

$\downarrow (\iota S_1) : 2$

4. $a = s_M$

$\downarrow (rep) : 4, 2$

5. $Study(a)$

$\downarrow (\neg\exists) : 3$

6. $\neg(a < now \wedge Study(a) \wedge \forall y(a < y \wedge y < now \rightarrow \neg MeetM(y)))$

$\downarrow (\iota E_1) : 4$

7. $MeetM(a) \wedge a < now \wedge \forall y(a < y \wedge y < now \rightarrow \neg MeetM(y))$

$\downarrow (\wedge) : 7$

8. $MeetM(a)$

9. $a < now$

10. $\forall y(a < y \wedge y < now \rightarrow \neg MeetM(y))$

$(\neg\wedge) : 6$

11. $\neg a < now$ $\neg(Study(a) \wedge \forall y(a < y \wedge y < now \rightarrow \neg MeetM(y)))$

(clash) : 9, 11 $\downarrow$ $(\neg\wedge) : 11$

12. $\bot$

13. $\neg Study(a)$ $\neg\forall y(a < y \wedge y < now \rightarrow \neg MeetM(y))$

(clash) : 5, 13 $\downarrow$ $\downarrow (\neg\forall) : 13$

14. $\bot$ $\neg(a < a' \wedge a' < now \rightarrow \neg MeetM(a'))$

$\downarrow (\forall) : 10$

15. $a < a' \wedge a' < now \rightarrow \neg MeetM(a')$

$\downarrow (clash) : 14, 15$

16. $\bot$

Fig. 2. Tableau-proof of Formula (4); recall that s_M stands for Term (1), that is $\iota x\Big(MeetM(x) \wedge x < now \wedge \forall y\big(x < y < now \rightarrow (\neg MeetM(y))\big)\Big)$

let's assume that $a \in \mathsf{VAR}$ is s.t. $v(a) = t'$. Then, by the Substitution Lemma, we obtain that $\mathcal{M}, v \models \varphi[x/a]$. Moreover, since $v(b) = t \neq t' = v(a)$ we get $\mathcal{M}, v \models a \neq b$, as required.   ⊣

To prove that our calculus is complete, we will show that whenever an $\mathrm{FO}(<, \iota, now)$-formula φ does not have a tableau-proof, it is falsifiable, that is, there exist a model $\mathcal{M}$ and a valuation v s.t. $\mathcal{M}, v \not\models \varphi$. To that end, let's assume that $\mathcal{B}$ is an open and fully expanded branch of a tableau with φ at the root. We will show that using $\mathcal{B}$ we can construct a model $\mathcal{M}$ and a valuation v s.t. $\mathcal{M}, v \models \varphi$. First, let TERM be the set of all free variables occurring on $\mathcal{B}$ (and now if it occurs on $\mathcal{B}$). We define a relation $\approx$ over TERM s.t. $b_1 \approx b_2$ iff $b_1 = b_2$ occurs on $\mathcal{B}$. Note that, thanks to the expandedness of $\mathcal{B}$ and the of rules (sym), (tot), (irref) and (rep), we obtain that $\approx$ is an equivalence relation. Moreover, since $\mathcal{B}$ is fully expanded, due to the rule (rep) we have:

$$\text{If } b_1 \approx b_2, \text{ then } \varphi(b_1) \in \mathcal{B} \text{ iff } \varphi[b_1/b_2] \in \mathcal{B}. \tag{5}$$

Now we construct $\mathcal{M} = (\mathcal{T}, <, \mathcal{I}, t_0)$ and $v : \mathsf{VAR} \longrightarrow \mathcal{T}$ as follows:

$$\mathcal{T} = \{[b]_\approx \mid b \in \mathsf{TERM}\}, \qquad < = \{([b_1]_\approx, [b_2]_\approx) \in \mathcal{T} \times \mathcal{T} \mid b_1 < b_2 \in \mathcal{B}\},$$
$$\mathcal{I}(P) = \{[s]_\approx \in \mathcal{T} \mid P(s) \in \mathcal{B}\}, \qquad \mathcal{I}(now) = t_0,$$
$$t_0 = \begin{cases} [now]_\approx & \text{if } now \text{ occurs on } \mathcal{B}, \\ [b_0]_\approx & \text{otherwise,} \end{cases} \qquad v(x) = \begin{cases} [x]_\approx & \text{if } x \text{ is free on } \mathcal{B}, \\ t_0 & \text{otherwise,} \end{cases}$$

where b_0 is an arbitrary element of TERM. We can observe that $\mathcal{M}$ is well defined. First, we note that $<$ is a non-empty, strict, linear order. Indeed, the rule (NE) guarantees that $\mathcal{T} \neq \emptyset$. The rule (tot), the openness of $\mathcal{B}$, and the definition of $\approx$ ensure that, for any $[b_1]_\approx, [b_2]_\approx \in \mathcal{T}$, if $[b_1]_\approx \neq [b_2]_\approx$, then either $[b_1]_\approx < [b_2]_\approx$ or $[b_1]_\approx > [b_2]_\approx$. Moreover, there cannot be $[b]_\approx \in \mathcal{T}$ s.t. $[b]_\approx < [b]_\approx$, for if that were the case, by Cond. (5) we would need to have $(b < b) \in \mathcal{B}$, thus contradicting the openness of $\mathcal{B}$. Moreover, $\mathcal{I}$ is a well-defined function thanks to Cond. (5). Finally, v is well defined by the fact that $\approx$ is an equivalence relation.

To finish the completeness proof for the calculus, we need to show that φ is satisfied by $\mathcal{M}$ and v, but this is a direct consequence of the following lemma whose proof is conducted by induction on the complexity of ψ:

Lemma 3. *For every* $\mathrm{FO}(<, \iota, now)$*-formula* ψ, *if* $\psi \in \mathcal{B}$, *then* $\mathcal{M}, v \models \psi$.

Proof (Sketch). We proceed the proof by induction on the structure of ψ. By way of example, below we consider the case where $\psi := \neg P(\iota x \theta(x))$.

$\psi := \neg P(\iota x \theta(x))$ For the sake of contradiction, let us assume that $\mathcal{M}, v \not\models \neg P(\iota x \theta(x))$, and so, $\mathcal{M}, v \models P(\iota x \theta(x))$. By the respective satisfaction condition there exists a unique $b \in \mathsf{TERM}$ s.t. $\mathcal{M}, v[x \mapsto [b]_\approx] \models \theta$ and moreover $\mathcal{M}, v[x \mapsto [b]_\approx] \models P(x)$ for this b. By the expandedness of $\mathcal{B}$ and the presence of (cut), we get $b = \iota x \theta(x) \in \mathcal{B}$ or $b \neq \iota x \theta(x) \in \mathcal{B}$. In the former case, by the assumption, the expandedness of $\mathcal{B}$, and the definition of $\mathcal{I}$, we get $P(b) \in \mathcal{B}$, and further, thanks to the presence of (rep) amongst the rules, $P(\iota x \theta(x))$. But this contradicts the openness of $\mathcal{B}$. In the latter case, due to the application of $(\neg\iota\mathsf{E})$ to $b \neq \iota x\theta(x)$ we either obtain $\neg\theta[x/b] \in \mathcal{B}$ or $a \neq b, \theta[x/a] \in \mathcal{B}$. In the first case, by the induction hypothesis, we get $\mathcal{M}, v \models \neg\varphi[x/b]$, but by the Substitution Lemma, this yields $\mathcal{M}, v[x \mapsto [b]_{\approx}] \models \neg\varphi$ and contradicts the assumption we made about b. In the second case, the induction hypothesis gives us $\mathcal{M}, v \models \varphi[x/a]$, and by the Substitution Lemma, $\mathcal{M}, v[x \mapsto [a]_{\approx}] \models \varphi$. By the openness of $\mathcal{B}$, $[b]_{\approx} \neq [a]_{\approx}$, which, again, contradicts the assumption we made about b. Thus, $\mathcal{M}, v \not\models P(\iota x\theta(x))$, and so, $\mathcal{M}, v \models \neg P(\iota x\theta(x))$. $\dashv$

We have shown that for every $\mathrm{FO}(<, \iota, now)$-formula φ which generates an open tableau when put at the root, there exists an $\mathrm{FO}(<, \iota, now)$-model satisfying φ. This immediately yields the following result concluding the section:

Theorem 2. *The tableau calculus from Fig. 1 is complete w.r.t. the semantics of* $\mathrm{FO}(<, \iota, now)$. $\dashv$

4   Computational Complexity

In this section, we analyse the complexity of reasoning in $\mathrm{FO}(<, \iota, now)$. We begin by showing that the addition of temporal reference mechanisms—the ι-operator and the constant *now*—does not increase complexity. Specifically, reasoning in $\mathrm{FO}(<, \iota, now)$ can be reduced to reasoning in $\mathrm{FO}(<)$ in polynomial time. Crucially, the reduction does not introduce new variables (provided the input formula uses at least two), allowing known complexity results for $\mathrm{FO}(<)$ fragments to carry over to corresponding fragments of $\mathrm{FO}(<, \iota, now)$.

Let the size $|\varphi|$ of a formula φ denote the number of symbols it contains, excluding variables, the constant *now*, and brackets. Define $qdp(\varphi)$ and $\iota dp(\varphi)$ as the nesting depths of quantifiers and ι-operators, respectively, and let $\iota(\varphi)$ and $now(\varphi)$ be the number of occurrences of ι and *now* in φ.

Theorem 3. *Each* $\mathrm{FO}(<, \iota, now)$-formula φ can be translated, in polynomial time, to an equisatisfiable $\mathrm{FO}(<)$-formula φ' such that:

- $|\varphi'| \leq |\varphi| + 5 \cdot \iota(\varphi) + 3 \cdot now(\varphi)$,
- $qdp(\varphi') \leq qdp(\varphi) + 2 \cdot \iota dp(\varphi) + now(\varphi)$,
- *if* φ *mentions at least 2 variables, then* φ' *mentions the same variables as* φ.

Proof (Sketch). To remove *now* from φ, we introduce a fresh unary predicate *Now* and guarantee that its extension is a single time point; then we use *Now* to rewrite formulas mentioning *now*. To remove ι, in turn, we proceed inductively on ιdp. Our construction exploits a Russell-style translation of DDs [71,78] and reuses already quantified variables, which, as we show below, allows us to obtain φ' enjoying the properties stated in the theorem.

We define φ' as follows, where τ is a translation defined next and the second conjunct of φ' guarantees that *Now* holds at a single time point: $\varphi' = \tau(\varphi) \wedge$

$\exists z(Now(z) \land \forall z'(z \neq z' \rightarrow \neg Now(z')))$. To define τ we proceed inductively on the structure of φ. We perform two inductions; the external induction is on sets F_k, with $k \in \mathbb{N}$, consisting of formulas whose maximal nesting depth of ι-operators is k. The internal induction is over the structure of formulas in a given set F_k.

First we define τ for atomic formulas in F_0 as follows, where x and y are any variables, whereas $\lessgtr$ is one of the symbols in $\{=, <, >\}$: $\tau(P(x)) = P(x)$, $\tau(x \lessgtr y) = x \lessgtr y$, $\tau(now \lessgtr now) = \bot$, $\tau(P(now)) = \exists z(Now(z) \land P(z))$, $\tau(x \lessgtr now) = \exists z(Now(z) \land x \lessgtr z)$. Then, for any formulas ψ, ψ_1, and ψ_2 in F_0 we define τ as follows: $\tau(\neg\psi) = \neg\tau(\psi)$, $\tau(\psi_1 \land \psi_2) = \tau(\psi_1) \land \tau(\psi_2)$, $\tau(\exists x \psi) = \exists x \tau(\psi)$. Next, to translate formulas in F_{k+1}, it suffices to extend the translation for F_k with conditions for atomic formulas mentioning $\iota x \psi(x)$ s.t. $\psi(x) \in F_k$. To this end, we observe that x in $\iota x \psi(x)$ is not free, and so we can rewrite it using any other variable. We give one example of such a translation, as the remaining one are similar: $\tau(P(\iota x \psi(x))) = \exists z(P(z) \land \forall x(\tau(\psi(x)) \leftrightarrow x = z))$.

Each occurrence of now in φ extends $|\varphi'|$ by 3 and $qdp(\varphi')$ by 1, and each ι-operator extends $|\varphi'|$ by 5 and $qdp(\varphi')$ by 2, hence the required bounds. ⊣

Now, we can use the reduction from Theorem 3 and complexity results known for $\mathrm{FO}(<)$ over $\mathbb{N}$ [25,57,69,75,77] to determine the complexity of $\mathrm{FO}(<, \iota, now)$; recall that $\mathrm{FO}^2(<, \iota, now)$ stands for the two-variable fragment of $\mathrm{FO}(<, \iota, now)$.

Theorem 4. *The satisfiability checking problem over* $\mathbb{N}$ *is:*

- *decidable, but not elementary recursive in* $\mathrm{FO}(<, \iota, now)$,
- $\mathrm{NExpTime}$-*complete in* $\mathrm{FO}^2(<, \iota, now)$,
- NP-*complete in* $\mathrm{FO}^2(<, \iota, now)$ *with bounded number of predicates.* ⊣

In particular, the first item of the theorem holds by the results of Stockmayer [75], the second item by the results of Etessami et al. [25], and the third item by the results of Weis and Immerman [77]. It is also known that each formula φ of $\mathrm{FO}^2(<)$ can be translated (exponentially) to a formula φ' of unary tense logic (with operators 'eventually' and 'sometime in the past') s.t. the operator depth of φ' is no larger than $2 \cdot qdp(\varphi)$ [25]. Thus we can also exponentially translate $\mathrm{FO}^2(<, \iota, now)$ to unary tense logic and the second item of Theorem 3 provides us with a bound on the operator depth of the resulting formula.

It is important to note that the significant improvement in the complexity of the satisfiability problem—achieved by reducing the number of variables to two—comes at the cost of diminished expressive power. For example, it is well known that $\mathrm{FO}^2(<)$ has the same expressive power as the unary fragment of linear temporal logic, so it cannot express such operators as 'since' or 'until' [25] except for contexts in which now serves as a 'starting point', mentioned in Sect. 2.

5   Extensions of the Logic

In this section we will present two extensions of the logic. First, by introducing the successor operator to the language and second, by introducing λ-operator.

Successor Operator. In previous sections, we considered arbitrary strict linear orders. In some contexts, however, it is useful to restrict attention to *discrete* flows of time. For instance, if we take the *day* as the basic time unit, we may wish to express notions such as 'yesterday,' 'tomorrow,' or 'ten days from now.' This requires a binary *successor* operator *succ*, indicating that one point is the direct successor of another. In FO($<$), *succ* can be defined as: $succ(x, y) := x < y \land \neg \exists z(x < z \land z < y)$. However, this definition uses three variables and is thus not expressible in the two-variable fragment we focus on in this paper. Moreover, it also fails in FO($<, \iota, now$) due to the semantics of definite descriptions, as with the earlier issue that $=$ cannot be defined purely in terms of $<$ (see Sect. 2). Therefore, we introduce *succ* as a primitive relational constant in the language. This requires an extension of the tableau calculus, for which we provide new rules. These rules allow us to handle the extended logic FO($<, succ, \iota, now$), which augments FO($<, \iota, now$) with the successor relation:

$$\text{(order)} \ \frac{succ(s_1, s_2)}{s_1 < s_2} \qquad \text{(dis)} \ \frac{succ(b_1, b_2)}{\neg b_3 < b_2 \mid \neg b_1 < b_3} \qquad \text{(chain)} \ \frac{b_1 < b_2, \neg succ(b_1, b_2)}{\begin{array}{c} b_1 < a \\ a < b_2 \end{array}}$$

$$\text{(cut}_{succ}) \ \frac{b_1 < b_2}{succ(b_1, b_2) \mid \neg succ(b_1, b_2)}$$

The rule (order) ensures that *succ* is subsumed by $<$. The rule (dis) guarantees that there are no intermediate time points between a time point and its successor, whereas (chain) introduces an intermediate time point whenever two time points are not in the *succ* relation. Finally, (cut$_{succ}$) checks, for every pair of distinct time points, if they are in the *succ* relation.

Adapting the completeness proof of the calculus from Fig. 1 to the extended calculus accommodating *succ* is straightforward. In the definition of $\mathcal{M}$ it only requires adding the following clause: $succ = \{([b_1]_\approx, [b_2]_\approx) \mid succ(b_1, b_2) \in \mathcal{B}\}$ and including two inductive cases: $\psi := succ(b_1, b_2)$ and $\psi := \neg succ(b_1, b_2)$ in the proof of Lemma 3. The extended calculus is complete w.r.t. the family of linear, strict orders in which the *succ* relation is defined, that is, which are discrete. In this class there are not only structures of well-known order types such as $\mathbb{N}$ or $\mathbb{Z}$, but also more deviated ones such as $\omega \cdot \omega$ which is a structure in which ω structures of order type ω are 'appended' one after another.

λ-operator. As we mentioned in the introduction, originally, Russell treated descriptions as a kind of incomplete signs and showed how to get rid of them by means of contextual definitions of the form: $\psi[x/\iota y \varphi] := \exists x(\forall y(\varphi \leftrightarrow y = x) \land \psi)$. This leads to scoping difficulties and even to contradictions resulting therefrom if ψ is not atomic. To overcome these shortcomings in adopting Russell's approach to temporal reference, we followed the solution based on the idea of Indrzejczak [41]. However, one can avoid the scoping difficulties in a more direct way, by augmenting the language of FO($<, \iota, now$) (or FO($<, succ, \iota, now$)) with the extra operator λ allowing us to construct predicate abstracts. In the extended language terms are generated in the same way as in FO($<, \iota, now$) and formulas are given by the following grammar:

$$\varphi ::= P(u) \mid u_1 = u_2 \mid u_1 < u_2 \mid \neg \varphi \mid \varphi_1 \lor \varphi_2 \mid \exists x \varphi(x) \mid (\lambda x \varphi(x))(s),$$

where u, u_1, u_2 are variables or *now* and s is any term (e.g., a DD). The presence of λ in the language makes it possible to easily distinguish between the internal and external reading of negation. The former is encoded by $(\lambda x \neg \varphi(x))(s)$ whereas the latter is formalised as $\neg(\lambda x \varphi(x))(s)$. Extending the logic $FO(<, \iota, now)$ to $FO(<, \iota, \lambda, now)$ requires appropriate changes in the conditions defining the satisfaction relation:

$$\mathcal{M}, v \models (\lambda x \psi(x))(u) \quad \text{iff} \quad \text{there is } t \in \mathcal{T} \text{ s.t. } \mathcal{M}, v[x \mapsto t] \models \psi(x)$$
$$\text{and } v(u) = t \text{ or } \mathcal{I}(u) = t$$

$$\mathcal{M}, v \models (\lambda x \psi(x))(\iota y \varphi(y)) \quad \text{iff} \quad \text{there is a unique } t \in \mathcal{T} \text{ s.t. } \mathcal{M}, v[y \mapsto t] \models \varphi(y)$$
$$\text{and moreover } \mathcal{M}, v[x \mapsto t] \models \psi(x) \text{ for this } t$$

Also, for the tableau calculus we need a new set of rules involving both ι and λ. Thus, in the calculus for $FO(<, \iota, \lambda, now)$ the DD rules from Fig. 1 need to be replaced with the ones displayed below:

ι-rules

$$(\iota_1) \quad \frac{(\lambda x \psi(x))(\iota y \varphi(y))}{\begin{array}{c} \varphi[y/a] \\ \psi[x/a] \end{array}}$$

$$(\iota_2) \quad \frac{(\lambda x \psi(x))(\iota y \varphi(y)), \varphi[y/b_1], \varphi[y/b_2]}{b_1 = b_2}$$

$$(\neg \iota) \quad \frac{\neg(\lambda x \psi(x))(\iota y \varphi(y))}{\neg \psi[x/b] \mid \neg \varphi[y/b] \mid \varphi[y/a]}$$
$$a \neq b$$

λ-rules

$$(\lambda) \quad \frac{(\lambda x \psi(x))(b)}{\psi[x/b]}$$

$$(\neg \lambda) \quad \frac{\neg(\lambda x \psi(x))(b)}{\neg \psi[x/b]}$$

The proofs of the $FO(<, \iota, \lambda, now)$-calculus' soundness and completeness w.r.t. the class of strict linear orders are analogous to the ones from Sect. 3 and only require slight alterations in the inductive cases from the proof of Lemma 3.

6   Conclusions and Future Work

We have presented a logic for expressing and reasoning about temporal references by extending $FO(<)$ with the ι-operator, enabling DDs of time points, and a constant *now*, representing the time of utterance. The semantics follow a Russell-style theory of DDs, where satisfaction of an atomic formula containing a DD implies the description is proper. We introduced a sound and complete tableau system for the logic, incorporating specific rules to capture the semantics of DDs. Additionally, we provided a polynomial translation from our logic to $FO(<)$, which enabled complexity analysis: we identified fragments with NExpTime- and NP-complete satisfiability. The logic was further extended with a successor relation and the λ-operator, addressing scoping issues related to DDs.

For future work, we plan to extend the presented tableau system with a loop-checking mechanism that ensures termination and, ideally, achieves complexity-optimality for the decision procedure for the considered languages. We also aim to implement the tableau system and evaluate its performance empirically.

Another direction involves the development of a propositional tense logic that incorporates DDs via dedicated modal operators—serving as a counterpart to $FO(<, \iota, now)$, in the same way that $FO(<)$ corresponds to unary tense logic.

A further extension concerns two-dimensional first-order logics, where one dimension models time and the other models objects. Since such logics often exhibit poor computational properties, identifying well-behaved fragments constitutes an intriguing and worthwhile challenge.

Acknowledgements. Funded by the European Union (ERC, ExtenDD, project number: 101054714). Views and opinions expressed are however those of the author(s) only and do not necessarily reflect those of the European Union or the European Research Council. Neither the European Union nor the granting authority can be held responsible for them.

References

1. Artale, A., Kontchakov, R., Kovtunova, A., Ryzhikov, V., Wolter, F., Zakharyaschev, M.: Ontology-mediated query answering over temporal data: a survey. In: Schewe, S., Schneider, T., Wijsen, J. (eds.) 24th International Symposium on Temporal Representation and Reasoning (TIME 2017). Leibniz International Proceedings in Informatics (LIPIcs), vol. 90, pp. 1:1–1:37. Schloss Dagstuhl – Leibniz-Zentrum für Informatik, Dagstuhl, Germany (2017). https://doi.org/10.4230/LIPIcs.TIME.2017.1
2. Artale, A., Mazzullo, A., Ozaki, A., Wolter, F.: On free description logics with definite descriptions. In: Proceedings of the 18th International Conference on Principles of Knowledge Representation and Reasoning – Full Papers – Main Track, pp. 63–73 (2021). https://doi.org/10.24963/kr.2021/7
3. Beeson, M.J.: Foundations of Constructive Mathematics, Ergebnisse der Mathematik und ihrer Grenzgebiete, vol. 6. Springer, Berlin, Heidelberg (1985). https://doi.org/10.1007/978-3-642-68952-9
4. Bencivenga, E.: Free logics. In: Gabbay, D.M., Guenthner, F. (eds.) Handbook of Philosophical Logic, pp. 147–196. Springer Netherlands, Dordrecht (2002). https://doi.org/10.1007/978-94-017-0458-8_3
5. Benzmüller, C., Scott, D.S.: Automating free logic in HOL, with an experimental application in category theory. J. Autom. Reason. **64**(1), 53–72 (2020)
6. Blackburn, P.: Nominal tense logic. Notre Dame J. Form. Log. **34**(1), 56–83 (1993)
7. Blackburn, P.: Internalizing labelled deduction. J. Log. Comput. **10**(1), 137–168 (2000)
8. Blackburn, P.: Arthur prior and hybrid logic. Synthese **150**(3), 329–372 (2006)
9. Blackburn, P., Jørgensen, K.F.: Indexical hybrid tense logic. In: Bolander, T., Braüner, T., Ghilardi, S., Moss, L. (eds.) Advances in Modal Logic 9, pp. 144–60. College Publications, London (2012)
10. Blackburn, P., Jørgensen, K.F.: contextual validity in hybrid logic. In: Brézillon, P., Blackburn, P., Dapoigny, R. (eds.) Modeling and Using Context. CONTEXT 2013. LNCS, vol. 8175. pp. 185–198. Springer, Berlin, Heidelberg (2013). https://doi.org/10.1007/978-3-642-40972-1_14
11. Blackburn, P., Jørgensen, K.F.: Arthur prior and 'now'. Synthese **193**, 3665–3676 (2016)

12. Blackburn, P., Marx, M.: Remarks on Gregory's "actually" operator. J. Philos. Log. **31**, 281–288 (2002)
13. Blackburn, P., Tzakova, M.: Hybrid languages and temporal logic. Log. J. IGPL **7**(1), 27–54 (1999)
14. Blackburn, P.R.: Nominal tense logic and other sorted intensional frameworks. Ph.D. thesis, The University of Edinburgh (1990)
15. Blumson, B.: Anselm's God in Isabelle/HOL (2020)
16. Blackburn, P., Jørgensen, K.F.: Contextual validity in hybrid logic. In: Brézillon, P., Blackburn, P., Dapoigny, R. (eds.) CONTEXT 2013. LNCS (LNAI), vol. 8175, pp. 185–198. Springer, Heidelberg (2013). https://doi.org/10.1007/978-3-642-40972-1_14
17. Borgwardt, S., Lippmann, M., Thost, V.: Temporal query answering in the description logic DL-lite. In: Fontaine, P., Ringeissen, C., Schmidt, R.A. (eds.) FroCoS 2013. LNCS (LNAI), vol. 8152, pp. 165–180. Springer, Heidelberg (2013). https://doi.org/10.1007/978-3-642-40885-4_11
18. Bull, R.: An approach to tense logic1. Theoria **36**(3), 282–300 (1970)
19. Burgess, J.P.: Basic tense logic. Handbook of Philosophical Logic: Volume II: Extensions of Classical Logic, pp. 89–133 (1984)
20. Chang, A.X., Manning, C.D.: Sutime: a library for recognizing and normalizing time expressions. In: Lrec. vol. 3735, p. 3740 (2012)
21. Chomicki, J.: Temporal query languages: a survey. In: Gabbay, D.M., Ohlbach, H.J. (eds.) Temporal Logic. ICTL 1994. LNCS, vol. 827, pp. 506–534. Springer, Berlin, Heidelberg (2005). https://doi.org/10.1007/bfb0014006
22. Demri, S.: Sequent calculi for nominal tense logics: a step towards mechanization? In: Murray, N.V. (ed.) TABLEAUX 1999. LNCS (LNAI), vol. 1617, pp. 140–155. Springer, Heidelberg (1999). https://doi.org/10.1007/3-540-48754-9_15
23. Demri, S., Goré, R.: Cut-free display calculi for nominal tense logics. In: Murray, N.V. (ed.) TABLEAUX 1999. LNCS (LNAI), vol. 1617, pp. 155–170. Springer, Heidelberg (1999). https://doi.org/10.1007/3-540-48754-9_16
24. Dowty, D.R.: Tenses, time adverbs, and compositional semantic theory. Linguist. Philos. **5**, 23–55 (1982)
25. Etessami, K., Vardi, M.Y., Wilke, T.: First-order logic with two variables and unary temporal logic. Inf. Comput. **179**(2), 279–295 (2002)
26. Feferman, S.: Definedness. Erkenntniss **43**, 295–320 (1995)
27. Fitting, M., Mendelsohn, R.L.: First-Order Modal Logic, Synthese Library, vol. 277. Springer, Dordrecht (1998). https://doi.org/10.1007/978-3-031-40714-7
28. Franceschet, M., de Rijke, M., Schlingloff, B.H.: Hybrid logics on linear structures: expressivity and complexity. In: 10th International Symposium on Temporal Representation and Reasoning, 2003 and Fourth International Conference on Temporal Logic. Proceedings, pp. 166–173. IEEE (2003)
29. Gabbay, D.M.: Labelled Deductive Systems: Volume 1. Oxford University Press, Oxford (1996)
30. Gargov, G., Goranko, V.: Modal logic with names. J. Philos. Log. 607–636 (1993)
31. Goranko, V.: Hierarchies of modal and temporal logics with reference pointers. J. Log. Lang. Inform. **5**, 1–24 (1996)
32. Goranko, V.: Temporal logic with reference pointers. In: Gabbay, D.M., Ohlbach, H.J. (eds.) ICTL 1994. LNCS, vol. 827, pp. 133–148. Springer, Heidelberg (1994). https://doi.org/10.1007/BFb0013985
33. Gregory, D.: Completeness and decidability results for some propositional modal logics containing "actually" operators. J. Philos. Log. **30**, 57–78 (2001)

34. Hilbert, D., Bernays, P.: Grundlagen der Mathematik I, Die Grundlehren der mathematischen Wissenschaften, vol. 40. Springer, Berlin, Heidelberg (1968). https://doi.org/10.1007/978-3-642-86894-8

35. Hodkinson, I., Reynolds, M.: 11 temporal logic. In: Studies in Logic and Practical Reasoning, vol. 3, pp. 655–720. Elsevier (2007)

36. Indrzejczak, A.: Natural Deduction, Hybrid Systems and Modal Logics, Trends in Logic, vol. 30. Springer, Berlin, Heidelberg (2010). https://doi.org/10.1007/978-90-481-8785-0

37. Indrzejczak, A.: Simple cut elimination proof for hybrid logic. Log. Log. Philos. **16**, 129–141 (2016)

38. Indrzejczak, A.: Cut-free modal theory of definite descriptions. In: Bezhanishvili, N., D'Agostino, M., Studer, T. (eds.) Advances in Modal Logic 12, pp. 359–378. College Publications, Rickmansworth (2018)

39. Indrzejczak, A.: Fregean description theory in proof-theoretic setting. Log. Log. Philos. **28**(1), 137–155 (2019)

40. Indrzejczak, A.: Free definite description theory - sequent calculi and cut elimination. Log. Log. Philos. **29**(4), 505–539 (2020)

41. Indrzejczak, A.: Russellian definite description theory–A proof-theoretic approach. Rev. Symb. Log. **16**(2), 624–649 (2023)

42. Indrzejczak, A., Zawidzki, M.: Tableaux for free logics with descriptions. In: Das, A., Negri, S. (eds.) Automated Reasoning with Analytic Tableaux and Related Methods. TABLEAUX 2021. LNCS, vol. 12842, pp. 56–73. Springer, Cham (2021). https://doi.org/10.1007/978-3-030-86059-2_4

43. Indrzejczak, A., Zawidzki, M.: When iota meets lambda. Synthese **201**(2), 1–33 (2023)

44. Ji, S., Pan, S., Cambria, E., Marttinen, P., Philip, S.Y.: A survey on knowledge graphs: representation, acquisition, and applications. IEEE Trans. Neural Netw. Learn. Syst. **33**(2), 494–514 (2021)

45. Kaminski, M., Smolka, G.: Terminating tableaux for hybrid logic with eventualities. In: Giesl, J., Hähnle, R. (eds.) IJCAR 2010. LNCS (LNAI), vol. 6173, pp. 240–254. Springer, Heidelberg (2010). https://doi.org/10.1007/978-3-642-14203-1_21

46. Kamp, H.: Formal properties of 'now'. In: Meaning and the Dynamics of Interpretation, pp. 11–51. Brill (2013)

47. Kamp, J.A.W.: Tense logic and the theory of linear order. University of California, Los Angeles (1968)

48. Kaplan, D.: On the logic of demonstratives. J. Philos. Log. **8**, 81–98 (1979)

49. Kaplan, D.: Demonstratives: an essay on the semantics, logic, metaphysics, and epistemology of. Themes from kaplan, p. 481 (1989)

50. Kürbis, N.: A binary quantifier for definite descriptions in intuitionist negative free logic: natural deduction and normalization. Bull. Sect. Log. **48**(2), 81–97 (2019)

51. Kürbis, N.: Two treatments of definite descriptions in intuitionist negative free logic. Bull. Sect. Log. **48**(4), 299–317 (2019)

52. Kürbis, N.: A binary quantifier for definite descriptions for cut free free logics. Studia Logica (2021). **online first**

53. Kürbis, N.: Definite descriptions in intuitionist positive free logic. Log. Log. Philos. **30**(2), 327–358 (2021)

54. Kürbis, N.: Proof-theory and semantics for a theory of definite descriptions. In: Das, A., Negri, S. (eds.) TABLEAUX 2021. LNCS (LNAI), vol. 12842, pp. 95–111. Springer, Cham (2021). https://doi.org/10.1007/978-3-030-86059-2_6

55. Lambert, K.: Free logic and definite descriptions. In: Lambert, K. (ed.) New Essays in Free Logic, Applied Logic Series, vol. 23, pp. 37–48. Springer, Dordrecht (2001). https://doi.org/10.1007/978-94-015-9761-6_2

56. Leech, G.N.: Meaning and the English Verb. Pearson Education, Chennai (2004)

57. Meyer, A.R.: Weak monadic second order theory of succesor is not elementary-recursive. In: Parikh, R. (eds.) Logic Colloquium. Lecture Notes in Mathematics, vol. 453, pp. 132–154. Springer, Berlin, Heidelberg (2006). https://doi.org/10.1007/BFb0064872

58. Montague, R.: Universal grammar. Theoria **36**(3), 373–398 (1970)

59. Neuhaus, F., Kutz, O., Righetti, G.: Free description logic for ontologists. In: Hammar, K., et al. (eds.) Proceedings of the Joint Ontology Workshops co-located with the Bolzano Summer of Knowledge (BOSK 2020), Virtual & Bozen-Bolzano, Italy, August 31st to October 7th, 2020. CEUR Workshop Proceedings, vol. 2708. CEUR-WS.org, Bozen-Bolzano (2020)

60. Oppenheimer, P.E., Zalta, E.N.: A computationally-discovered simplification of the ontological argument. Australas. J. Philos. **89**(2), 333–349 (2011)

61. Orlandelli, E.: Labelled calculi for quantified modal logics with definite descriptions. J. Log. Comput. **31**(3), 923–946 (2021)

62. Partee, B.H.: Some structural analogies between tenses and pronouns in English. J. Philos. **70**(18), 601–609 (1973)

63. Peano, G.: Studii di logica matematica. Carlo Clausen (1897)

64. Pelletier, F.J., Linsky, B.: What is Frege's theory of descriptions. In: Linsky, B., Imaguire, G. (eds.) On Denoting: 1905–2005, pp. 195–250. Philosophia Verlag, Munich (2005)

65. Prior, A.: Past, Present and Future. Oxford University Press, Oxford (1967)

66. Prior, A.N., Hasle, P.F.: Papers on Time and Tense. Oxford University Press on Demand, Oxford (2003)

67. Rabinovich, A.: A proof of Kamp's theorem. Log. Methods Comput. Sci. **10** (2014)

68. Reichenbach, H.: Elements of Symbolic Logic. The MacMillan Company, New York (1947)

69. Robertson, E.L.: Structure of complexity in the weak monadic second-order theories of the natural numbers. In: Proceedings of the Sixth Annual ACM Symposium on Theory of Computing, pp. 161–171 (1974)

70. Rosser, J.B.: Logic for Mathematicians. Dover Publications, Mineola, New York (1978)

71. Russell, B.: On denoting. Mind **14**(56), 479–493 (1905)

72. Scales, R.: Attribution and Existence. Ph.D. thesis, University of California, Irvine (1969)

73. Scott, D.: Existence and description in formal logic. In: B. Russell, Philosopher of the Century, pp. 181–200. George Allen and Unwin Ltd., London (1967)

74. Seligman, J.: Internalization: the case of hybrid logics. J. Log. Comput. **11**(5), 671–689 (2001)

75. Stockmeyer, L.J.: The complexity of decision problems in automata theory and logic. Ph.D. thesis, Massachusetts Institute of Technology (1974)

76. Stojnić, U., Altshuler, D.: Formal properties of now revisited. Semant. Pragmat. **14**, 3–EA (2021)

77. Weis, P., Immerman, N.: Structure theorem and strict alternation hierarchy for FO^2 on words. In: Duparc, J., Henzinger, T.A. (eds.) CSL 2007. LNCS, vol. 4646, pp. 343–357. Springer, Heidelberg (2007). https://doi.org/10.1007/978-3-540-74915-8_27

78. Whitehead, A.N., Russell, B.: Principia Mathematica, vol. I. Cambridge University Press, Cambridge (1910)
79. Zawidzki, M.: Deductive Systems and the Decidability Problem for Hybrid Logics. Lodz University Press/Jagiellonian University Press, Łódź, Kraków (2014)

Alternating-Time Temporal Logic
with Default Actions

Jakub Michaliszyn[(✉)]

University of Wrocław, Wrocław, Poland
jmi@cs.uni.wroc.pl

Abstract. We introduce an extension of Alternating-Time Temporal Logic (ATL) that incorporates default actions to model communication failures in multi-agent systems. Our framework, ATL-kD, allows for a limited number of communication failures during which agents' intended strategies may not be delivered. In the event of such a communication failure, a predefined default action is played. We analyse the computational complexity of model checking in this setting, showing NP-hardness and coNP-hardness in general, but polynomial-time solvability when default actions are restricted to a fixed subset of agents. We also study a variant with default preferences, which better handles cases where the default action might be unavailable in some states due to protocol constraints. Additionally, we introduce default action updates, allowing the default action to be revised during system execution. Together, these results provide a formal foundation for robust verification under unreliable communication.

Keywords: multiagent logic · robust strategies · model checking

1   Introduction

The increased adoption of multi-agent systems (MAS) in safety-critical domains necessitates rigorous verification methods to ensure their correctness prior to deployment [15]. Recent advancements in model checking techniques address this challenge through various innovations, including integration of symbolic reasoning with probabilistic analysis [10,13,20], verification frameworks for parametrised systems with variable agent populations [5,14], and enhanced usability of verification tools through compositional approaches [7,8].

A fundamental limitation of these approaches is that they typically assume perfect communication and immediate execution of strategic decisions within the system [4]. In real-world scenarios, however, strategic decisions made by agents or coalitions may face transmission delays or failures, resulting in default actions being executed instead of optimal ones [9]. This aspect of multi-agent systems remains largely unexplored in the formal verification literature, despite its significant practical implications for critical systems operating under time constraints or unreliable communication channels.

© The Author(s), under exclusive license to Springer Nature Switzerland AG 2026
G. Casini et al. (Eds.): JELIA 2025, LNAI 16094, pp. 263–278, 2026.
https://doi.org/10.1007/978-3-032-04590-4_18

In many practical MAS applications such as air traffic control, autonomous vehicle coordination, or distributed sensor networks, communication delays or failures may prevent strategic decisions from reaching their executors in time. In such circumstances, systems must resort to predetermined default actions to maintain basic functionality. These default actions, while ensuring minimum safety requirements, may be suboptimal with respect to the system's global objectives and can significantly alter the strategic capabilities of agents or coalitions within the system.

Alternating-time Temporal Logic (ATL) [1,18] has emerged as a powerful formalism for reasoning about strategic behaviours in multi-agent systems. Recent advances in verification techniques have significantly expanded ATL's practical applications. For handling complex infinite domains, researchers have developed frameworks for reasoning about strategic behaviour in infinite-state reactive modules [2,12]. Three-valued abstractions have proven effective for verifying multi-agent systems, offering tractable model checking procedures with polynomial time bounds [16,17]. For systems with imperfect information, specialized agent-based abstractions have been developed to handle the epistemic dimension of strategic reasoning [3,19,21]. These advances collectively enhance ATL's applicability to increasingly complex systems, maintaining mathematical rigour.

In all these works, ATL implicitly assumes that agents can seamlessly implement their chosen strategies. In our approach, we extend these models to account for potential delays in strategy transmission and the subsequent execution of default actions. This realistic modelling approach requires a non-standard interpretation of ATL operators that acknowledges the possibility of strategy implementation failures.

1.1 Contribution

In this paper, we analyse the computational complexity of model checking ATL in an extended setting where strategic decisions may not be delivered on time.

Our first contribution is the introduction of a variant of the ATL logic with *default actions*. In this scenario, agents associate each strategy with a default action to be executed in the event of communication loss. In the simplest variant, which we call ATL-∞D, there is no bound on how often these defaults may be applied-connection failures can occur at any time. Under these conditions, ensuring a goal requires choosing default actions that guarantee its achievement, since the communication loss may be permanent. As a result, the strategy itself becomes irrelevant.

To avoid such an edge case, we introduce a bound on communication losses, obtaining the logic ATL-kD, where k is a natural number. We study the complexity of the model checking of this logic, showing that it is NP-hard and coNP-hard, and it is a member of Δ_2^P.

In ATL-kD, the communication loss and playing default actions may happen to all the agents. Next, we propose ATL-kD[s], a variant where the communication loss may only happen to s agents, and the other agents are immune to such problems. We prove that when s is fixed, the model checking can be solved in polynomial time.

We work with the standard definition of interpreted systems, where at each state, agents have their protocol that lists available actions. This means that in some states, agents' default action may not be available, in which case the system can play any action. We discuss that this issue can be solved by replacing a single default action by action preferences, i.e., a permutation of actions starting from the most desired one. While this alteration does not influence the complexity of ATL-kD, the model checking problem for ATL-kD[s] for fixed s is unlikely to have a polynomial-time algorithm as we prove that it is NP-hard.

Finally, we explore mutable default actions, allowing agents to revise their default actions whenever communication works. We show that this variant has the same computational complexity as the immutable default-action variant.

While robustness in multi-agent systems has been recently studied [6,11], this is, up to our knowledge, the first paper on default actions in the context of ATL logic.

2   Preliminaries

We here introduce the technical set-up for ATL. We assume a finite set of agents $Ag = \{1, \ldots, m\}$ and a finite set of propositional variables $\mathcal{V}$. For a tuple $t = (t_1, \ldots, t_m)$, by $t.i$ we denote its ith element t_i, with $i \leq m$. We are interested in the following structures.

Definition 1 (Interpreted system and its model). *An interpreted system is a tuple $IS = (\{L_i, Act_i, P_i, t_i\}_{i \in Ag}, s_I, \Pi)$ such that for each agent i:*

- *L_i is a finite set of possible local states;*
- *Act_i is a finite set of possible local actions;*
- *$P_i : L_i \to 2^{Act_i} \setminus \{\emptyset\}$ is a local protocol;*
- *$t_i : L_i \times Act_1 \times \cdots \times Act_m \to L_i$ is a (partial) local transition function;*
- *$s_I \in L_1 \times \cdots \times L_m$ is a global initial state;*
- *$\Pi : L_1 \times \cdots \times L_m \to 2^{\mathcal{V}}$ is a labelling function.*

Given an interpreted system $IS = (\{L_i, Act_i, P_i, t_i\}_{i \in Ag}, s_I, \Pi)$, its associated model $M_{IS} = (S, ACT, T, s_I, \Pi)$ is a tuple such that:

- *$S \subseteq L_1 \times \cdots \times L_m$ is the set of global states reachable via T from the initial state s_I;*
- *$ACT = Act_1 \times \cdots \times Act_m$ is the set of joint actions,*
- *$T : S \times ACT \to S$ is a (partial) global transition function such that $T(s, a)$ is defined if for all $i \in Ag$, $a.i \in P_i(s.i)$ and $t_i(s.i, a)$ is defined; in such a case, we have $T(s, a) = (t_1(s.1, a), \ldots, t_m(s.m, a))$;*
- *s_I and Π are the same as in IS.*

In the following we assume that all locally enabled joint actions can be executed, i.e., that for all global states $s \in S$ and joint actions $a \in ACT$ such that $a.i \in P_i(s.i)$ for all $i \in Ag$, $T(s, a)$ is defined.

When IS is clear from the context we write M for M_{IS}.

2.1   Alternating-Time Temporal Logic

Alternating-Time Temporal Logic (ATL) was introduced to reason about agents and their strategies [1].

The syntax of ATL is given by the following BNF:

$$\varphi ::= \ q \mid \top \mid \neg\varphi \mid \varphi \wedge \varphi \mid \langle\!\langle\Gamma\rangle\!\rangle X\varphi \mid \langle\!\langle\Gamma\rangle\!\rangle(\varphi U\varphi) \mid \langle\!\langle\Gamma\rangle\!\rangle G\varphi$$

where q is a propositional variable and $\Gamma \subseteq Ag$. We abbreviate $\langle\!\langle\Gamma\rangle\!\rangle(\top U\varphi)$ by $\langle\!\langle\Gamma\rangle\!\rangle\ F\varphi$ and we shorten other Boolean connectives ($\vee, \Rightarrow$) in the usual way.

We study ATL in the context of perfect information and perfect recall, so agents' strategies depend on the current global state of the system and on the history of global states visited while realising a current goal. In ATL, the formula $\langle\!\langle\Gamma\rangle\!\rangle X\varphi$ means "$\langle\!\langle\Gamma\rangle\!\rangle$ has a strategy to enforce φ in the next state (irrespective of the actions of the agents in $Ag \setminus \Gamma$)"; $\langle\!\langle\Gamma\rangle\!\rangle G\varphi$ means "$\langle\!\langle\Gamma\rangle\!\rangle$ has a strategy to enforce φ forever in the future"; and $\langle\!\langle\Gamma\rangle\!\rangle\varphi_1 U\varphi_2$ means "$\langle\!\langle\Gamma\rangle\!\rangle$ has a strategy to enforce that φ_2 holds at some point in the future and can ensure that φ_1 holds until then."

3   Requirements Analysis

We focus on the following settings. For a given interpreted system, we assume that there is some independent entity (*a server*) that applies agents actions and informs them about the outcomes of every action. We assume that the server knows agents' protocols and states, but does not know their strategies (or even goals). The agents are *clients* that are connected to the server via a connection with a limited reliability, therefore some of their actions may be not delivered in time. In such a case, the server applies the agent's default action.

Setting Default Actions. Different goals and different coalitions may require different default actions. Consider the formula $\varphi = \langle\!\langle\{1,2\}\rangle\!\rangle Gq \wedge \langle\!\langle\{1,3\}\rangle\!\rangle Gr$ ("Agents 1 and 2 can jointly guarantee staying in states satisfying q and Agents 1 and 3 can jointly guarantee staying in states satisfying r"). This formula expresses a conjunction of two different properties requires two different coalitions and (possibly) two different strategies of Agent 1. Requiring Agent 1 to have an identical default action for both conjuncts would be too restrictive and counter-intuitive. Therefore, we will assume that the default actions are defined per strategy. Consequently, in this paper the strategic operators are interpreted as the theoretical existence of a strategy with a default action and does not account for the possibility that delivering the default action may fail due to communication loss.

Then, there are two interesting cases: *immutable* and *mutable* default actions. In this paper, we focus on immutable default actions, which means that the default action is set whenever a strategy is set. This can also be seen as the robustness of the strategy itself. The mutable default actions variant is where default actions are set when strategies are set, but can be updated every time when an agent's action is successfully delivered. This variant is also interesting and we will discuss it later on (Sect. 7).

Single Default Actions Versus Default Action Preferences. One of the assumptions we make is that the default behaviour consists of a single default action. However, one of the fundamental parts of interpreted systems are protocols, which state that not all actions are allowed at all times (e.g., it is not possible to apply a break when it is already applied). If the default action is to be played by the server but is not allowed by the protocol, the server will take any allowed action instead.

Such "randomness" might be undesirable. One could also consider a case when instead of a single action, each agent chooses a *preference*, which is a permutation of its actions. In such a case, in any state, the server plays the first action from agent's permutation that is allowed by the protocol. This scenario is more complicated and leads to slightly worse complexity, as we will discuss later on.

Bounds on Communication Loss. If the communication loss is permanent, then agents' strategies are meaningless. We will consider this scenario, but we will also restrict the number of communication losses. This can be done in several ways: by restricting the total number of default actions in the system, consider a case where that default actions can happen at a given frequency, e.g., at most one failure in every 10 transitions. Here, our goal is to find *robust* strategies, and therefore we focus on the last variant. In such a case, in the formula $\langle\!\langle\{1\}\rangle\!\rangle F(q \wedge \langle\!\langle\{2\}\rangle\!\rangle Fr)$, the number of default action to be considered by Agent 2 does not depend on the number of default actions that were used for Agent 1 to get to the state satisfying q. Nevertheless, our hardness results can be adapted for the other variants—for example, for the frequency variant, one can insert additional dummy states to avoid this restriction.

Agents Awareness of Defaults. When the communication between the server and an agent is broken, the agent is not able to send its actions, but also is not able to update its state. We assume, however, that once the connection is restored, the agent gets full information on what actions were played during its blackout, so it can update its local state accordingly.

The standard definition of strategy for ATL only takes into account past states, not actions. One could argue that in the context of a limited number of default actions, this definition could also take a number of default actions left as an input. However, it makes no difference: for example, if agent i has different strategies for the case when there are 5 default actions left and when there are 3 default actions left, it can replace the latter by the former, because the strategy for 5 default actions has to account for the case when only up to 3 are played. This will not change the outcome of a formula. Therefore, we will keep the definition of strategy in the standard way.

4   Alternating-Time Temporal Logic with Default Actions

In this section, we introduce a novel semantics for ATL (with perfect information and perfect recall) that accounts for default actions.

Let $IS = (\{L_i, Act_i, P_i, t_i\}_{i \in Ag}, s_I, \Pi)$ be an interpreted system and $M_{IS} = (S, ACT, T, s_I, \Pi)$ be its model.

Definition 2 (Strategy with defaults). *A strategy with defaults for an agent* $i \in \Gamma$ *is a pair* (f_i, a_i) *consisting of:*

1. *a strategy, which is a function* $f_i : S^+ \to Act_i$ *such that for each sequence of global states* $s_1 \ldots s_k$ *we have* $f_i(s_1 \ldots s_k) \in P_i(s_k.i)$,
2. *a default action* a_i, *which is an action from* Act_i.

The default actions should be interpreted as follows. If the agents' action, following its strategy, is delivered, it is played. Otherwise, if the agent's default action is permitted in the current state, the default action is played, else an arbitrary allowed action is played by the server, beyond the control of the agent.

Given a set of agents Γ and an indexed set of strategies with defaults $F_\Gamma = \{(f_i, a_i) \mid i \in \Gamma\}$, we define $out_0(s, F_\Gamma)$ to be the set of infinite paths $s_0 s_1 \ldots$ such that $s_0 = s$ and for all $j \in \mathbb{N}$ there exists an action a such that $s_{j+1} = T(s_j, a)$ and for all $i \in \Gamma$, $a.i = f_i(s_0 \ldots s_j)$. This is a standard ATL definition; it does not consider any default actions.

Given $k \in \mathbb{N} \cup \{\infty\}$, a set of agents Γ and an indexed set of strategies with defaults $F_\Gamma = \{(f_i, a_i) \mid i \in \Gamma\}$, we define $out_k(s, F_\Gamma)$ to be the set of infinite paths $s_0 s_1 \ldots$ such that $s_0 = s$ and there is a set $D \subset \mathbb{N}$ of k natural numbers such that for each $j \in \mathbb{N}$, there is an action a_j such that $s_{j+1} = T(s_j, a_j)$ and

1. if $j \notin D$, then for all $i \in \Gamma$, $a.i = f_i(s_0 \ldots s_j)$.
2. if $j \in D$, then for all $i \in \Gamma$
   - $a.i = f_i(s_0 \ldots s_j)$ (the action following the strategy is played), or
   - $a_i \in P_i(s_j)$ and $a.i = a_i$ (the default action is played), or
   - $a_i \notin P_i(s_j)$ and $a.i \in P_i(s_j)$ (if the default action is not allowed by the protocol, any action is allowed).

The second condition refers to the connection loss, in which case some agents may still be able to deliver the actions from their strategy, some play their default action, and if the default action is not allowed by the protocol, any allowed action may be played.

We now define, for each $k \in \mathbb{N} \cup \{\infty\}$, the logic ATL with k defaults, denoted as ATL-kD. The syntax of ATL-kD is the same as the syntax with ATL.

For a path $p = s_1 \ldots$, by $p.i$ we denote s_i, the i-th element of p.

Definition 3 (Semantics of ATL-kD). *Given an interpreted system* $IS = (\{L_i, Act_i, P_i, t_i\}_{i \in Ag}, s_I, \Pi)$, *its associated model* M *and a global state* $s \in S$, *the k-defaults satisfaction relation $\models_{\overline{k}}$ is inductively defined as follows.*

$M, s \models_{\overline{k}} q$ *iff $q \in \Pi(s)$*

$M, s \models_{\overline{k}} \top$ *always holds*

$M, s \models_{\overline{k}} \neg\varphi$ *iff $M, s \models_{\overline{k}} \varphi$ does not hold*

$M, s \models_{\overline{k}} \varphi_1 \wedge \varphi_2$ *iff $M, s \models_{\overline{k}} \varphi_1$ and $M, s \models_{\overline{k}} \varphi_2$*

$M, s \models_{\overline{k}} \langle\!\langle \Gamma \rangle\!\rangle X\varphi$ *iff there is a set of strategies F_Γ for agents in Γ such that for all $p \in out_k(s, F_\Gamma)$ we have $M, p.2 \models_{\overline{k}} \varphi$*

$M, s \models_{\overline{k}} \langle\!\langle \Gamma \rangle\!\rangle \varphi_1 U \varphi_2$ *iff there is a set of strategies F_Γ for agents in Γ such that for all $p \in out_k(s, F_\Gamma)$, there is $j \geq 1$ such that we have $M, p.j \models_{\overline{k}} \varphi_2$ and for all $1 \leq i < j, M, p.i \models_{\overline{k}} \varphi_1$*

$M, s \models_{\overline{k}} \langle\!\langle \Gamma \rangle\!\rangle G\varphi$ *iff there is a set of strategies F_Γ for agents in Γ such that for all $p \in out_k(s, F_\Gamma)$ and all $i \geq 1$ we have $M, p.i \models_{\overline{k}} \varphi$*

Example 1. Consider the interpreted system IS with two agents $Ag = \{1, 2\}$ that models a system with a shared resource. Both agents want to access the resource, but the access is granted only if exactly one requires the resource at a time. More precisely, each agent has two actions R (request) and S (skip). Each agent also has two local states: the initial state l_W and the state l_A for when the agent already accessed the resource. The protocol functions allow all actions, and the transition functions are as follows: $t_1(l_W, (R, S)) = l_A$, $t_2(l_W, (S, R)) = l_A$, and for all other cases $t_i(s, a) = s$.

Assume that $s_I = (l_W, l_W)$ is the initial state and Π is the labelling function such that $\Pi((l_A, l_A)) = \{q\}$ and $\Pi(s) = \emptyset$ for other states s. The model M_{IS} of this interpreted system is depicted in Fig. 1.

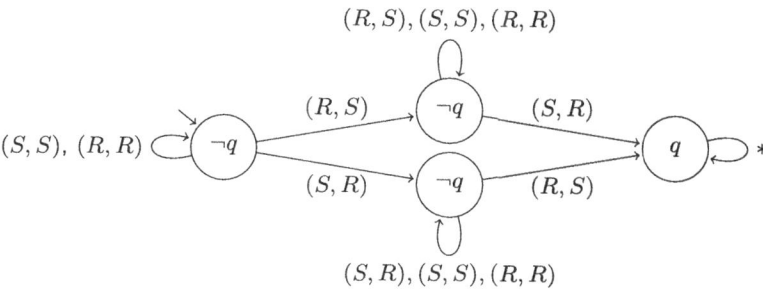

Fig. 1. Example of a model.

Observe that $M_{IS}, s_I \models_{\overline{0}} \langle\!\langle \{1, 2\} \rangle\!\rangle Fq$ but not $M_{IS}, s_I \models_{\overline{\infty}} \langle\!\langle \{1, 2\} \rangle\!\rangle Fq$. Indeed, the only state labelled by q (the state (l_A, l_A)) is reachable, but only if the agents switch their actions—if they pick any actions as defaults and then the connection is lost forever, they will never reach q.

Now assume $k \in \mathbb{N}_+$. In this case, the agents have a strategy to reach q, i.e., $M_{IS}, s_I \vDash_{\overline{k}} \langle\langle\{1,2\}\rangle\rangle Fq$ holds. For example, they can set (S, R) as the default action and play it in the first step and then keep playing (R, S). More precisely, their strategies with defaults are (f_1, S) and (f_2, R), where $f_1(p) = S$ if $p = (l_W, l_W)$ and $f_1(p) = R$ otherwise, and $f_2(p) = R$ if $p = (l_W, l_W)$ and $f_2(p) = S$ otherwise. This guarantees that after the first step, they will be in the state (l_A, l_W). Then, if the default action is played, they stay in this state. But since the default action can only be played a bounded number of times, they will eventually move on to (l_A, l_A).

Notice that in the case of $\langle\langle\Gamma\rangle\rangle X\varphi$, out_k can be replaced by out_0, because if there are strategies with defaults for the next operator, one can consider strategies where the default action is the same as the action following from the strategy.

The *model checking problem* for ATL-kD is defined as follows: given a model M_{IS} with the initial state s and an ATL-kD formula φ, decide whether $M, s \vDash_{\overline{k}} \varphi$.

5   Model Checking ATL with Default Actions

We start the complexity analysis with the proof that the model checking problem for ATL-kD is NP-hard for any $k \in \mathbb{N} \cup \{\infty\}$. The hardness holds even if we only consider ATL-kD properties "all the agents want to eventually satisfy a given atomic goal" (i.e., formulas $\langle\langle Ag\rangle\rangle Fq$).

Theorem 1. *For $k \in \mathbb{N}_+ \cup \{\infty\}$, model checking ATL-$k$D is NP-hard.*

Proof. We reduce the 3SAT problem, which asks for a given propositional formula, which is a conjunction of disjunctions of three literals, if there is a valuation that satisfies the formula.

Assume a formula $C_1 \wedge \cdots \wedge C_n$ over variables $x_1, \ldots, x_m$. We define an interpreted system IS with agents $Ag = \{1, \ldots, m\}$ (one for every variable). Each agent i has two actions $\top$ and $\bot$ and $n + 2$ states: $s_1^i, \ldots, s_{n+1}^i$ and s_-^i.

The protocol P_i is defined as follows: $P_i(s_j^i) = \{\top, \bot\}$ if $j \leq n$ and x_i is in C_j, otherwise $P_i(s_j^i) = \{\bot\}$. The transitions function is as follows:

- $t_i(s_j^i, (a_1, \ldots, a_m)) = s_{j+1}^i$ if $j \leq n$ and the valuation $[x_1 \leftarrow a_1, \ldots, x_m \leftarrow a_m]$ satisfies C_j.
- $t_i(s_j^i, (a_1, \ldots, a_m)) = s_-^i$ if $j \leq n$ and the valuation $[x_1 \leftarrow a_1, \ldots, x_m \leftarrow a_m]$ does not satisfy C_j.
- $t_i(s_-^i, (\bot, \ldots, \bot)) = t_i(s_{n+1}^i, (\bot, \ldots, \bot)) = s_-^i$.

The initial state is $(s_1^1, \ldots, s_1^m)$. We have one propositional value q such that $\Pi((s_{n+1}^1, \ldots, s_{n+1}^n)) = \{q\}$ and for all other tuples of states s, $\Pi(s) = \emptyset$.

The model of this system M_{IS} contains $n + 2$ global states, and from each state, there are at most 8 possible joint actions (see Fig. 2 for an example). Therefore, the size of the model is polynomial in the size of the formula.

Now, we claim that $M_{IS}, s_i \models_\infty \langle\!\langle Ag \rangle\!\rangle Fq$ if and only if the formula $C_1 \wedge \cdots \wedge C_m$ is satisfiable. Indeed, if there is a valuation $[x_1 \leftarrow a_1, \ldots, x_n \leftarrow a_n]$ that makes $C_1 \wedge \cdots \wedge C_m$ satisfied, then for each agent i, we can define the strategy with defaults (f_i, a_i) such that for each sequence $s_1 \ldots s_n$, $f_i(s_1 \ldots s_n) = a_i$ if $a_i \in P_i(s_n)$, and otherwise $f_i(s_1 \ldots s_n) = \bot$. This is defined so that at any state, the action following from the strategy is the same as the default action. A quick check shows that these strategies prove that $\langle\!\langle Ag \rangle\!\rangle Fq$ holds.

On the other hand, assume that $\langle\!\langle Ag \rangle\!\rangle Fq$ holds. Then, there is a set of strategies with defaults $F = \{(f_i, a_i) \mid i \in Ag\}$ that makes the formula true. Consider a valuation $\sigma = [x_1 \leftarrow a_1, \ldots, x_m \leftarrow a_m]$. Consider any clause C_i and the path in $out_k((s_1^1, \ldots, s_1^m), F)$ where all the agents use their default action in step i. Since the formula holds, this path leads to a state satisfying q, and therefore the default actions correspond to the valuation that makes this clause true. Since i was arbitrary, the valuation σ satisfies $C_1 \wedge \cdots \wedge C_n$, thus the formula is satisfiable.

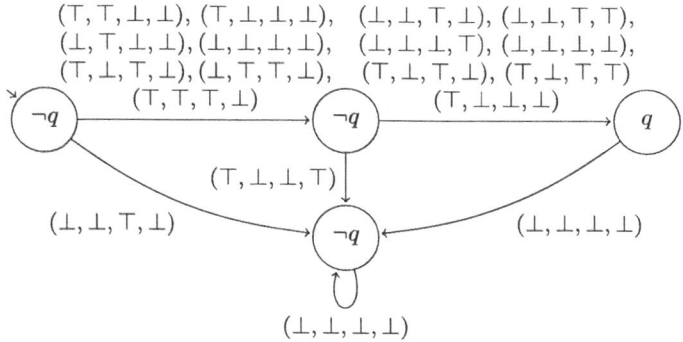

Fig. 2. The model for the formula $(x_1 \vee x_2 \vee \neg x_3) \wedge (\neg x_1 \vee x_3 \vee \neg x_4)$

Since we can reduce model checking ATL-kD to its complement by merely negating the formula, we obtain the following.

Corollary 1. *For* $k \in \mathbb{N}_+ \cup \{\infty\}$, *model checking ATL-$k$D is coNP-hard.*

We prove that the model-checking problem for ATL-kD can be solved in the complexity class $\Delta_2^P = P^{NP}$.

Theorem 2. *For* $k \in \mathbb{N} \cup \{\infty\}$, *model checking ATL-$k$D is in* Δ_2^P.

To prove the above, we employ the labelling algorithm, which for each subformula computes the set of states that satisfy this subformula. The steps for propositional variables and Boolean connectives are straightforward. The case of a formula of the form $\langle\!\langle \Gamma \rangle\!\rangle Xq$ can be done in the standard manner, as in this case the default action may be the action of the agents' strategy in the current state. For the remaining strategic operators, we employ the following lemma.

Lemma 1. *For any $k \in \mathbb{N} \cup \{\infty\}$, the problem: "given a model M_{IS}, a global state s, a set of agents Γ and an ATL-kD formula $\varphi \in \{\langle\!\langle\Gamma\rangle\!\rangle(qUr), \langle\!\langle\Gamma\rangle\!\rangle Gq\}$ decide whether $M_{IS}, s \models_{\overline{k}} \varphi$ " is in NP.*

Having this lemma, the proof of the theorem follows from the fact that we can compute a set of states satisfying $\varphi = \langle\!\langle\Gamma\rangle\!\rangle G\varphi$, in the following way. First, compute recursively the set of states satisfying φ. Add a fresh propositional variable q that is true where φ holds. Then, employ the NP oracle for the formula $\langle\!\langle\Gamma\rangle\!\rangle Gq$ (as the problem is in NP thanks to the lemma) for each state, eventually computing the set of states satisfying φ. For $\langle\!\langle\Gamma\rangle\!\rangle(\varphi_1 U\varphi_2)$, we perform in a similar manner. It remains to prove the lemma.

Proof (of Lemma 1). We consider three cases.

Case of $\varphi = \langle\!\langle\Gamma\rangle\!\rangle(qUr)$ **and** $k \in \mathbb{N}_+$. We first guess the defaults a_i for each $i \in \Gamma$. Then, we compute the set of states $S_0, S_1, \ldots S_k$ such that S_j satisfies φ with *at most* j default actions. First, we put $S_0 = \ldots = S_k$ as the set of states satisfying r. Then, we repeat the following procedure as long as possible, i.e., until the least fix point is reached.

1. For any global state $s \notin S_0$, if s is labelled by q and there are actions a_i' for $i \in \Gamma$, such that playing those actions in s guarantees reaching a state in S_0 (regardless of actions of agents not in Γ), then we add s to S_0.
2. For $j \in \{1, \ldots, k\}$ and any global state $s \notin S_j$, we **add** s to S_j if s is labelled by q and there are actions a_i' for $i \in \Gamma$, such that
   – playing actions a_i' in s guarantees reaching a state in S_j (regardless of actions of agents not in Γ), and
   – if every agent among Γ plays a_i', plays a_i, or a_i is not allowed by the local protocol and the agent plays any allowed action, then it is guaranteed that a state from S_{j-1} is reached.

The above algorithm is correct and works in polynomial time as adding a state can be done at most $|S|^{k+1}$ times and k is fixed.

Case of $\langle\!\langle\Gamma\rangle\!\rangle Gq$ **and** $k \in \mathbb{N}_+$. We first guess the defaults a_i for each $i \in \Gamma$. Then, we compute the set of states $S_0, S_1, \ldots S_k$ as in the previous case. This time, we initially put $S_0 = \ldots = S_k$ be the set of states satisfying q. Then, we repeat the following procedure as long as possible, i.e., until the greatest fixed point is reached.

1. For any global state $s \in S_0$, if there are no actions a_i' for $i \in \Gamma$, such that playing those actions in s guarantees reaching a state in S_0 (regardless on actions of agents not in Γ), then we remove s from S_0.
2. For $j \in \{1, \ldots, k\}$ and any global state $s \in S_j$, we **remove** s from S_j if there are no actions a_i' for $i \in \Gamma$, such that
   – playing actions a_i' in s guarantees reaching a state in S_j (regardless of actions of agents not in Γ), and

- if every agent among Γ plays a_i', plays a_i, or a_i is not allowed by the local protocol and the agent plays any allowed action, then it is guaranteed that a state from S_{j-1} is reached.

As above, the above algorithm is correct and works in polynomial time (the loop will be performed at most $|S|^{k+1}$ times).

Case of $k = \infty$. In this case strategies are meaningless: if there is a strategy with defaults, then there is one where in each state, the default action is played (if possible). Therefore, in this case, one has to guess default actions for Γ and then compute the set of states satisfying φ in a straightforward way.

5.1 Default Actions only for Selected Agents

In ATL-kD, any agent can be a subject to playing default actions. The case when only selected agents may have to play the default actions is also interesting. For example, in a client-server scenario, the agents on the client side may lose the communication with the server, but the agents on the server side are safe.

We consider ATL-kD[s], which is defined similarly to ATL-kD except that now only agents $1, \ldots, s$ may need to use their default actions, and the remaining agents always play their strategy. If s is a part of the input, one can set $s = |Ag|$, therefore the hardness results for ATL-kD transfer to ATL-kD[s]. Interestingly, when s is fixed, then instead of employing an NP oracle for a strategy operator, one can check all possible default actions. There are $|Act_1 \times \cdots \times Act_s|$ such actions, which for a fixed s is polynomial. This proves the following.

Theorem 3. *For each $k, s \in \mathbb{N}$, model checking ATL-kD[s] can be solved in polynomial time.*

6 Agents with Default Preferences

We now discuss the alternative semantics for ATL-kD, where instead of default actions, agents have default preferences. Recall that the default preference is a permutation of agent's actions, and when a default action is to be played, the first action in agent's permutation that is allowed by the protocol is chosen.

Model checking ATL-kD with preferences is in Δ_2^P, as preferences are polynomial objects and can be guessed in polynomial time. Therefore, one can prove counterparts of Lemma 1 and Theorem 2 in a straightforward way.

On the other hand, for any $k > 2$ and $s \geq 1$, we show that model checking ATL-kD[s] is NP-hard. This is in contrast to the case of default actions semantics, where this problem was solvable in polynomial time.

Theorem 4. *Model checking ATL-kD[s] with preferences is NP-hard for $k > 2$ (including $k = \infty$) and $s \geq 1$.*

We only sketch the proof.

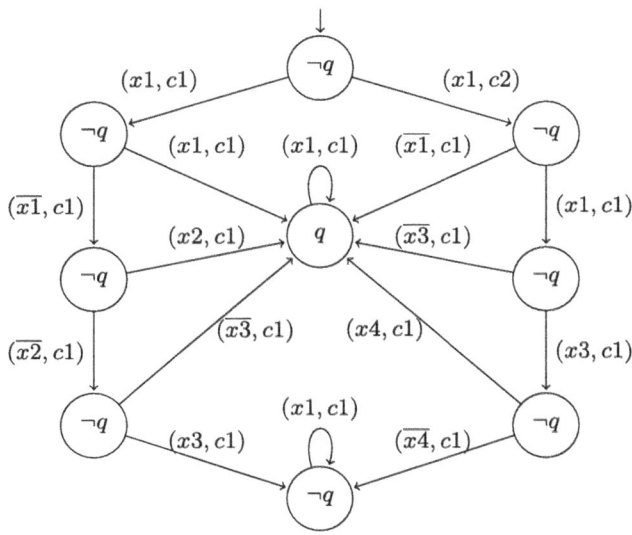

Fig. 3. Example of the model from the reduction for ATL with preferences for the formula $\psi = (x_1 \vee x_2 \vee \neg x_3) \wedge (\neg x_1 \vee \neg x_3 \vee x_4)$.

Proof (Sketch). We show the result for ATL-3D[1]. The proof works also for greater k; for greater s, one can add dummy agents.

We reduce 3SAT. Assume a formula $\psi = C_1 \wedge \cdots \wedge C_n$ over variables $x_1, \ldots, x_m$, where each C_i is a disjunction of exactly three literals. We define an interpreted system with 2 agents.

Agent 1 has $3n + 3$ states, the initial state l_I, states l_A and l_F, and three states for each clause. The actions of Agent 1 are $x1, \overline{x1}, \ldots, xm, \overline{xm}$.

Agent 2 has two states: l'_I, where it can play actions $c1, \ldots, cn$, and a state l'_F, where it can only play $c1$. All transitions of Agent 2 are to l'_F.

The only state labelled by q will be (l_A, l'_F). The intended model of this interpreted system is depicted in Fig. 3.

The formula will be $\langle\!\langle \{1\} \rangle\!\rangle Fq$. The idea is as follows. In the first state of the model, Agent 1 has to select default preference, which is a permutation of actions. For such a permutation, we consider a valuation σ defined as follows. For each i, if xi is before $\overline{xi}$, then $\sigma(x_i) = \top$, otherwise $\sigma(x_i) = \bot$.

Then, Agent 2 can play any action among $c1, \ldots, cn$, which means that the Agents move to a 3 state gadget for the corresponding clause. Those gadget work as follows: for each literal, we have one state with two allowed actions: one corresponding to this literal and one to the complementing one. E.g., for $\neg x_i$, the allowed actions are $\overline{xi}$ and xi. The action for this literal leads to the state l_A (the clause is satisfied), and the other one leads to the following literal in this clause or l_F, if there are no more literals.

The only interesting paths are the ones where the default actions are played by Agent 1 in steps 2, 3 and 4. If, regardless on the choice of Agent 2 in the first step, the default preference guarantees reaching l_A, this means that corresponding valuation σ was satisfying, therefore the formula is satisfiable. The other direction is similar.

7   Mutable Default Actions

Here we discuss the case when the default action is set for every strategic operator, but can be updated every time when an action is successfully performed by an agent. To formalise this, we will now consider a different notion of strategy with defaults, which is a pair consisting of a strategy and a *default update function*, which takes a sequence of global states and returns a new default action. The result of the function for the empty sequence is the initial default action.

Example 2. Consider a model with one agent presented in Fig. 4. Consider a formula $\langle\!\langle 1 \rangle\!\rangle Fq$ and the case with 1 default action. Under the semantics with default actions, the default action is either B, and the agent fails to satisfy the formula if it is applied in the first step, or A and the agent fails to satisfy the formula when its applied in the second step. In case of strategy updates, the default update function will return A as the initial default action, and for non-empty input it will return B. Therefore, the agent can send in the first step action A and a new default action B. If there are no communication issues, this action is played and the agent moves to the state in the middle, when it plays B, which is also its default action. In case of the communication issues, the default action A is played and the default action remains B. However, we assumed the limit 1 for default actions, so in the next step the agent can play B and will move to the state labelled by q.

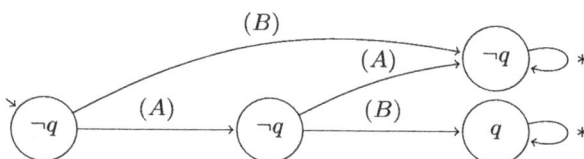

Fig. 4. Example for the strategy with updates with a single agent.

The proof of Theorem 2 can be easily adjusted for strategy updates, by guessing new default actions at appropriate places. On the other hand, the lower bound proof (Theorem 1) does not work in this case. Nevertheless, the model checking problem is NP-hard (and coNP-hard) as we can combine the ideas of Theorems 1 and 4.

Theorem 5. *For any* $k \in \mathbb{N} \cup \{\infty\}$, *the model checking problem for ATL-kD with strategy updates is in* Δ_2^P *and is both NP-hard and coNP-hard.*

Proof. We combine the ideas of Theorems 1 and 4. To do so, for a 3SAT formula $\psi = C_1 \wedge C_2 \wedge \cdots \wedge C_n$ over variables $x_1, \ldots, x_m$, where each C_i is a disjunction of three literals, we use $m + 1$ agents. Agents $1, \ldots, m$ have two actions $\bot, \top$, while the agent $m + 1$ has n actions $c1, \ldots, cn$. All agents have the same $n + 3$ states and transitions, as depicted in Fig. 5. The protocol allows agent $m + 1$ to play any action in l_I and only $c1$ in the remaining states. For an agent j with $j \in \{1, \ldots, m\}$, the protocol allows to play $\bot$ and $\top$ if states l_k such that the variable x_j is in the clause l_k and only $\bot$ in the remaining states. The transition function is as depicted in Fig. 5, and for each $k \in \{1, \ldots, n\}$ the transition from l_k to l_F is over the only joint action that corresponds to the valuation that makes this clause false, and the remaining actions lead to l_A (similarly to the proof of Theorem 1). Observe that the model of this interpreted system has also $n + 3$ states and at most $9n + 2$ actions, so is polynomial in the size of the input.

We assume that l_A is the only state labelled by q and consider the formula $\langle\!\langle\{1, \ldots, m\}\rangle\!\rangle q$. The idea is as follows: in the state l_I, the agents have to send a default action that will work in every state among $l_1, \ldots, l_n$ in case a default action is played there. Such a combined action exists iff the formula is satisfiable.

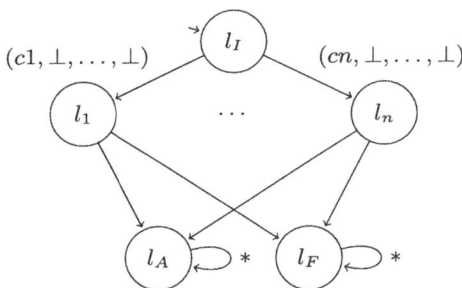

Fig. 5. Agents for the hardness of strategy updates. Actions for the transitions from l_1 to l_A are those corresponding to valuations satisfying C_1, and there is a single action that leads from l_1 to l_F that corresponds to a valuation not satisfying l_F (in both cases, the actions of agents corresponding to variables not in l_1 are $\bot$, as required by the protocol). Similarly for l_n.

8   Conclusions

We introduced default actions for ATL, which are meant to prove properties of the agents' strategy taking into account occasional communication loss. We proved that such actions, in the context of perfect information and perfect recall ATL, result in Δ_P^2 complexity, with a notable exception of a polynomial-time algorithm for the fixed number of agents.

Future work should include extending this research to ATL without perfect information. Here we assumed that the server knows agents states, and therefore can precisely apply their actions in the case of communication loss. Without perfect information, this assumption may be too far-fetched. Extending the results to ATL* is also interesting and introduces significant challenges due to ATL* inherent complexity and expressive power.

Acknowledgments. This work was supported by the National Science Centre (NCN), Poland under grant 2020/39/B/ST6/00521.

References

1. Alur, R., Henzinger, T.A., Kupferman, O.: Alternating-time temporal logic. J. ACM (JACM) **49**(5), 672–713 (2002)
2. Belardinelli, F., Lomuscio, A.: Abstraction-based verification of infinite-state reactive modules. In: ECAI 2016, pp. 725–733. IOS Press (2016)
3. Belardinelli, F., Lomuscio, A.: Agent-based abstractions for verifying alternating-time temporal logic with imperfect information. In: Proceedings of the 16th Conference on Autonomous Agents and MultiAgent Systems, pp. 1259–1267 (2017)
4. Bentahar, J., Meyer, J.J.C., Wan, W.: Model checking agent communication. In: Dastani, M., Hindriks, K., Meyer, J.J. (eds.) Specification and Verification of Multiagent Systems, LNCS, pp. 67–102. Springer, Boston, MA (2010). https://doi.org/10.1007/978-1-4419-6984-2_3
5. Conchon, S., Declerck, D., Zaïdi, F.: Parameterized model checking on the tso weak memory model. J. Autom. Reason. **64**(7), 1307–1330 (2020)
6. Di Cosmo, F., Mal, S., Prince, T.: Deciding reachability and coverability in lossy eos. In: Proceedings of the International Workshop on Petri Nets and Software Engineering, pp. 24–25 (2024)
7. Ferrando, A., Malvone, V.: Towards a compositional and user-friendly tool for multi-agent systems verification (2024)
8. Ferrando, A., Malvone, V.: Vitamin: a compositional framework for model checking of multi-agent systems. arXiv preprint arXiv:2403.02170 (2024)
9. Karabag, M.O., Neary, C., Topcu, U.: Planning not to talk: multiagent systems that are robust to communication loss. arXiv preprint arXiv:2201.06619 (2022)
10. Klein, J., et al.: Advances in symbolic probabilistic model checking with PRISM. In: Chechik, M., Raskin, J.-F. (eds.) TACAS 2016. LNCS, vol. 9636, pp. 349–366. Springer, Heidelberg (2016). https://doi.org/10.1007/978-3-662-49674-9_20
11. Kohler-Bussmeier, M., Capra, L., et al.: Robustness: a natural definition based on nets-within-nets. In: CEUR Workshop Proceedings, vol. 3430, pp. 70–87. CEUR Workshop Proceedings (2023)
12. Köster, M., Lohmann, P.: Abstraction for model checking modular interpreted systems over ATL. In: Dennis, L., Boissier, O., Bordini, R.H. (eds.) ProMAS 2011. LNCS (LNAI), vol. 7217, pp. 95–113. Springer, Heidelberg (2012). https://doi.org/10.1007/978-3-642-31915-0_6
13. Kouvaros, P., Botoeva, E., De Bonis-Campbell, C.: Formal verification of parameterised neural-symbolic multi-agent systems. In: Proceedings of the Thirty-Third International Joint Conference on Artificial Intelligence, pp. 103–110 (2024)

14. Kouvaros, P., Lomuscio, A., Pirovano, E., Punchihewa, H.: Formal verification of open multi-agent systems. In: Proceedings of the 18th International Conference on Autonomous Agents and Multiagent Systems, pp. 179–187 (2019)
15. Kupferman, O., Vardi, M.Y., Wolper, P.: Module checking. Inf. Comput. **164**(2), 322–344 (2001)
16. Lomuscio, A., Michaliszyn, J.: An abstraction technique for the verification of multi-agent systems against atl specifications. KR **14**, 428–437 (2014)
17. Lomuscio, A., Michaliszyn, J.: Verifying multi-agent systems by model checking three-valued abstractions. In: Proceedings of the 2015 International Conference on Autonomous Agents and Multiagent Systems, pp. 189–198 (2015)
18. Mogavero, F., Murano, A., Perelli, G., Vardi, M.Y.: Reasoning about strategies: on the model-checking problem. ACM Trans. Comput. Log. (TOCL) **15**(4), 1–47 (2014)
19. Niewiadomski, A., Kacprzak, M., Kurpiewski, D., Knapik, M., Penczek, W., Jamroga, W.: MsATL: a tool for SAT-based ATL satisfiability checking. arXiv preprint arXiv:2310.16519 (2023)
20. Parker, D.: Multi-agent Verification and Control with Probabilistic Model Checking. In: Jansen, N., Tribastone, M. (eds.) Quantitative Evaluation of Systems. QEST 2023. LNCS, vol. 14287, pp. 1–9. Springer, Cham (2023). https://doi.org/10.1007/978-3-031-43835-6_1
21. Tabatabaei, M., Jamroga, W.: Playing to learn, or to keep secret: alternating-time logic meets information theory. In: Agmon, N., An, B., Ricci, A., Yeoh, W. (eds.) AAMAS 2023, pp. 766–774. ACM (2023)

Theorem Proving

Deciding Non-fregean Identities: A Dual Tableau Approach

Joanna Golińska-Pilarek[1], Taneli Huuskonen[1], and Michał Zawidzki[2](✉)

[1] Faculty of Philosophy, University of Warsaw, 3 Krakowskie Przedmieście St.,
00-927 Warsaw, Poland
j.golinska@uw.edu.pl, taneli@poczta.onet.pl
[2] Department of Logic, University of Lodz, 3 Lindleya St., 91-131 Łódź, Poland
michal.zawidzki@filhist.uni.lodz.pl

Abstract. Non-Fregean logics reject Frege's Principle according to which sentences are names of their truth values. Instead, the non-Fregean framework assumes the existence of a universe of semantic correlates of sentences in the semantics and introduces into the language a non-truth-functional propositional connective of non-Fregean equivalence, $\equiv$, which enables referring to and reasoning about the denotations of sentences. It turns out that many non-classical logics – including modal, many-valued, intuitionistic, relevant, and paraconsistent logics – can be represented as non-Fregean systems. Thus, the non-Fregean approach offers a unified and inclusive framework for studying the nature of logical connectives and the principles underlying reasoning about the interplay between sentence meanings. Sentential Calculus with Identity (SCI) is a paradigmatic example of a classical non-Fregean logic. In the paper, we present a new, non-labelled dual tableau calculus for SCI, $\mathsf{DT_{SCI}}$ for which we prove soundness, completeness, and termination with an exponential bound on branch length. We compare $\mathsf{DT_{SCI}}$ with the already existing complexity-optimal labelled tableau calculus $\mathsf{T_{SCI}}$. We show that even though these systems use very different methodologies, which manifests itself not only in the presence of labels in one of them and the lack thereof in the other, but also in disparate sets of rules handling the identity connective and dissimilar techniques used throughout the completeness proofs, both offer a satisfactory solution to the problem of satisfiability/validity of SCI-formulas.

Keywords: sentential calculus with identity · dual tableaux · analytic tableaux · decision procedure · completeness · termination.

1 Introduction

Non-Fregean logics (NFL) constitute a broad and diverse class of logical systems alternative to classical logic, rejecting the so-called *Fregean axiom*, which identifies the denotations of sentences with their truth values [24]. In contrast, in the NFL approach, the denotations of sentences and their truth values are considered

© The Author(s), under exclusive license to Springer Nature Switzerland AG 2026
G. Casini et al. (Eds.): JELIA 2025, LNAI 16094, pp. 281–297, 2026.
https://doi.org/10.1007/978-3-032-04590-4_19

to be separate 'entities'. This allows one to capture more intricate phenomena than pure logical (in)equivalence, such as 'meaning the same' or 'referring to the same thing'. By enriching the semantic framework with a universe of sentence denotations and introducing a non-truth-functional connective of non-Fregean equivalence, the NFL-framework enables reasoning not only about truth, but also about semantic content. As shown by Golińska-Pilarek [10], NFL provides a unified and inclusive framework for analyzing and comparing a wide spectrum of logical systems, as it turned out that many non-classical logics (e.g., modal, many-valued, intuitionistic, relevant, paraconsistent) are non-Fregean or can be naturally extended to non-Fregean systems of greater expressive power (for details see Golińska-Pilarek [10]). The non-Fregean paradigm offers not only a unified framework for studying the nature of logical connectives, but also a powerful tool well suited for modelling inferential structures in natural language processing that require fine-grained semantic analysis, capturing context-sensitive meaning in knowledge representation, and formalizing principles underlying reasoning about the interplay between sentence meanings, areas in which classical truth-functional approaches often fall short.

SCI. The sentential calculus with identity (SCI), the first and paradigmatic example of a classical non-Fregean logic, was introduced by Suszko [22] and was further developed in numerous works [3–5, 23–25]. It is built upon classical propositional logic (CPL), augmented with an additional non-truth-functional connective of sentential identity $\equiv$, intended to represent a congruence over the domain of semantic correlates of sentences. SCI is the weakest NFL-logic that contains CPL. However, the class of non-equivalent propositional non-Fregean logics stronger than SCI and weaker than CPL is uncountable [11], and includes non-Fregean logics equivalent to some well-known modal logics (e.g., S4 and S5).

At the model-theoretic level, the key distinction between CPL and SCI lies in the structure of their domains: while the domain of a CPL model consists of two fixed truth values that every formula is mapped to, SCI models allow for arbitrarily many (but at least two) elements that sentences may denote (depending on the semantic interpretation, they might be states of affairs, meanings, situations, etc.). For example, under suitable assumptions, if a theory T extends Robinson arithmetic Q ($T1$), then the sentences 'T proves its own consistency' ($T2$) and 'T is inconsistent' ($T3$)[1] are logically equivalent, yet they can still be regarded as referring to different mathematical entities and differing in meaning or mathematical content. Thus, ($T1$) $\rightarrow$ (($T2$) $\leftrightarrow$ ($T3$)) does not entail ($T1$) $\rightarrow$ (($T2$) $\equiv$ ($T3$)) in SCI.

Deduction Systems for SCI. It is known that SCI is decidable; in particular, the problem of SCI-satisfiability is NP-complete [5]. Several deduction systems for SCI are present on the market: sequent calculi [6, 18, 26, 27], dual tableau systems [9, 14, 19] and a labelled tableau system, $\mathsf{T_{SCI}}$, introduced by Golińska-Pilarek et al. [12]. What demarcates $\mathsf{T_{SCI}}$ from the remaining systems is that the

---

[1] Although $T1$–$T3$ are not strictly propositional formulas, due to the absence of quantifiers, they can nonetheless be treated as such.

former enjoys the termination property and is therefore a decision procedure, whereas for the latter, termination is not intended or the corresponding proofs of termination are unconvincing due to substantive gaps or inaccuracies. The culprit of this fact is that the language of sequent and dual tableau systems coincides with the language of the logic—no external linguistic machinery is employed. Combined with the non-truth-functional nature of $\equiv$, this leads to the problem of how to handle formulas in which $\equiv$ is the main connective. While a standard rule for $\leftrightarrow$ suffices to reduce the equivalence to both arguments having the same logical value, an $\equiv$-formula requires more: sameness of references. Thus, to handle a formula that features $\equiv$ as the main connective, a substitution rule like $\frac{\varphi(\psi),\,\psi\equiv\vartheta}{\varphi(\psi/\vartheta)}$ is needed. However, it violates the subformula property and may produce infinite derivations. The labelled tableau system $\mathsf{T_{SCI}}$ avoids this by shifting the reasoning about the identity between formulas to the level of labels, thereby reducing the validity problem to a simple equality calculus.

Contents of the Paper. We introduce a dual tableau decision procedure $\mathsf{DT_{SCI}}$ for the logic SCI and compare it to $\mathsf{T_{SCI}}$, the decision procedure for SCI based on labelled tableaux. The main contribution of this paper is twofold. $\mathsf{DT_{SCI}}$ is the first non-labelled deduction system for SCI which enjoys the termination property. To address the usual failure of termination in non-labelled systems for SCI due to the lack of the subformula property, our dual tableau system imposes a non-obvious restriction on substitution in the specific rules for $\equiv$. This allows us to establish termination, but makes the completeness proof a highly non-trivial task. We compare $\mathsf{DT_{SCI}}$ and $\mathsf{T_{SCI}}$ with respect to both their theoretical foundations and their performance in implementation. Due to the considerable differences between both systems, this paves the way for a more extensive future analysis of the factors that affect the most the efficiency of deciding the validity of SCI-formulas.

In Sect. 2 we formally characterise the logic SCI. Sect. 3 contains a presentation of the dual tableau system $\mathsf{DT_{SCI}}$. Sect. 4 comprises the proofs of soundness and completeness of $\mathsf{DT_{SCI}}$ and in Sect. 5 we establish the termination and complexity results. In Sect. 6 we compare $\mathsf{T_{SCI}}$ and $\mathsf{DT_{SCI}}$ w.r.t. various criteria and discuss their implementations. The paper is concluded in Sect. 7.

2   SCI

Syntax. Let $\mathsf{AF} = \{p, q, \ldots\}$ be a countably infinite set of *atomic formulas*. Then, the following context-free grammar defines the set FOR of SCI-*formulas*:

$$\mathsf{FOR} \ni \varphi =:: p \mid \neg\varphi \mid \varphi \to \varphi \mid \varphi \equiv \varphi.$$

An expression $\varphi \not\equiv \psi$ abbreviates $\neg(\varphi \equiv \psi)$. For any $\varphi, \psi \in \mathsf{FOR}$, if we write $\varphi(\psi)$ to denote φ, it means that ψ is a proper subformula of φ. Now, if $\varphi, \psi \in \mathsf{FOR}$ are such that $\varphi(\psi)$, then by $\varphi(\psi/\vartheta)$ we denote the result of substituting all the occurrences of ψ in φ with ϑ. We impose a well-order $<_\ell$ on the countable set AF (which exists, as ensured by ZF) and extend it to SCI-connectives and parentheses by setting $\neg <_\ell \rightarrow <_\ell \equiv <_\ell$ ($<_\ell$) and $p <_\ell \neg$, for all $p \in \mathsf{AF}$. This induces the usual lexicographical order on the set FOR of all SCI-formulas, considered as strings over $\mathsf{AF} \cup \{\neg, \rightarrow, \equiv, (,)\}$. In addition, we define *complexity of a formula* φ, $|\varphi|$, as the number of symbols occurrences in φ. Finally, we define an ordering relation $\prec$ on FOR as follows: for any $\varphi, \psi \in \mathsf{FOR}$, $\varphi \prec \psi$ if and only if $|\varphi| < |\psi|$ or ($|\varphi| = |\psi|$ and $\varphi <_\ell \psi$). By the well-foundedness of $<_\ell$ it follows that $\prec$ is a well-order[2]. For example, assume that $p <_\ell q <_\ell r$. Then, for $\varphi := p \wedge (q \equiv r)$ and $\psi := p \wedge (r \leftrightarrow r)$, we have $|\varphi| = |\psi| = 7$ and $\varphi \prec \psi$.

Axioms. A set of Hilbert-style axiom schemes for SCI consists of schemes for CPL, which characterise the classical meaning of connectives $\neg$ and $\rightarrow$, and the following schemes for the identity connective $\equiv$ (we assume that $\equiv$ binds stronger than $\rightarrow$):

(Ax.1) $\varphi \equiv \varphi$
(Ax.2) $\varphi \equiv \psi \rightarrow \neg\varphi \equiv \neg\psi$
(Ax.3) $\varphi \equiv \psi \rightarrow (\chi \equiv \theta \rightarrow (\varphi \# \chi) \equiv (\psi \# \theta))$, for $\# \in \{\rightarrow, \equiv\}$
(Ax.4) $\varphi \equiv \psi \rightarrow (\varphi \rightarrow \psi)$.

Semantics. An SCI-*model* is a structure $\mathcal{M} = \langle U, D, \tilde{\neg}, \tilde{\rightarrow}, \tilde{\equiv} \rangle$, where: (1) $U \neq \emptyset$ is called the *universe* of $\mathcal{M}$, (2) $\emptyset \neq D \subsetneq U$ is the *set of designated values*, (3) $\tilde{\neg} : U \longrightarrow U$, $\tilde{\rightarrow} : U \times U \longrightarrow U$, $\tilde{\equiv} : U \times U \longrightarrow U$ are algebraic counterparts of the connectives: $\neg$, $\rightarrow$, and $\equiv$, respectively, which satisfy the following conditions, for all $a, b \in U$: (i) $\tilde{\neg}a \in D$ iff $a \notin D$, (ii) $a \tilde{\rightarrow} b \in D$ iff $a \notin D$ or $b \in D$, (iii) $a \tilde{\equiv} b \in D$ iff $a = b$. We define a *valuation* in an SCI-model $\mathcal{M} = \langle U, D, \tilde{\neg}, \tilde{\rightarrow}, \tilde{\equiv} \rangle$ as a function $V : \mathsf{FOR} \longrightarrow U$ such that for all $\varphi, \psi \in \mathsf{FOR}$: (a) $V(\neg\varphi) = \tilde{\neg}V(\varphi)$, (b) $V(\varphi \# \psi) = V(\varphi) \tilde{\#} V(\psi)$, for $\# \in \{\rightarrow, \equiv\}$.

An element $a \in U$, such that $a = V(\varphi)$, is called the *denotation of* φ. A formula φ is *satisfied* in an SCI-model $\mathcal{M} = \langle U, D, \tilde{\neg}, \tilde{\rightarrow}, \tilde{\equiv} \rangle$ and by a valuation V in $\mathcal{M}$, in symbols $\mathcal{M}, V \models \varphi$, if $V(\varphi) \in D$, that is, the denotation of φ in $\mathcal{M}$ is a designated value. A formula φ is *satisfiable* if there exist an SCI-model $\mathcal{M}$ and a valuation V which satisfy φ; it is *true* in a model $\mathcal{M} = \langle U, D, \tilde{\neg}, \tilde{\rightarrow}, \tilde{\equiv} \rangle$, in symbols $\mathcal{M} \models \varphi$, if it is satisfied in $\mathcal{M}$ by all the valuations in $\mathcal{M}$; it is *valid*, in symbols $\models \varphi$, if it is true in all SCI-models. A finite set of SCI-formulas $\{\varphi_1, \ldots, \varphi_n\}$ is valid if and only if the disjunction of all elements in $\{\varphi_1, \ldots, \varphi_n\}$ is valid[3]. It is worth noting that SCI is extensional in the sense that any subformula ψ of φ can be replaced with a formula ϑ denoting the same object as ψ without affecting the denotation of φ, as proved by Orłowska and Golińska-Pilarek [19].

---

[2] In the remainder of the paper, we assume that the ordering relation $<_\ell$, and thus also $\prec$, is pre-defined.

[3] Although this definition may appear counterintuitive, it follows from the convention that a set of formulas $\{\varphi_1, \ldots, \varphi_n\}$ is considered satisfiable if the conjunction $\bigwedge_{i=1}^{n} \varphi_i$ is satisfiable. Consequently, if $\bigwedge_{i=1}^{n} \varphi_i$ is not satisfiable, then its negation, $\neg \bigwedge_{i=1}^{n} \varphi_i = \bigvee_{i=1}^{n} \neg\varphi_i$, is valid. Therefore, the set $\{\neg\varphi_1, \ldots, \neg\varphi_n\}$ is valid as well.

SCI and Classical Propositional Logic. In SCI, the logical equivalence between a formula and its standard abbreviation is not sufficient for them to necessarily have the same denotation. Thus, identities such as $\neg(\varphi \to \neg\psi) \equiv \varphi \wedge \psi$ are not valid in SCI. For the sake of brevity, we confine ourselves to a language with $\neg$ and $\to$ as the only boolean connectives. Extending our framework to include additional boolean connectives as separate operators is a matter of routine.

It is well known that among all SCI-identities, only trivial identities are SCI-valid. Thus, SCI reveals non-trivial interrelations between $\equiv$ and boolean connectives. For example, formulas such as $\neg((\neg p \equiv \neg q) \to (p \equiv q))$ are SCI-satisfiable. In models where D and $U \setminus D$ are singletons, SCI collapses to CPL and $\equiv$ coincides with the classical logical equivalence. However, this does not hold for arbitrary models.

Example 1. The formula $(p \to (q \to r)) \leftrightarrow (q \to (p \to r))$ is SCI-valid, whereas the formula $(p \to (q \to r)) \equiv (q \to (p \to r))$ can be falsified already in a three-element SCI-model. Let $\mathcal{M} = \langle U, D, \tilde{\neg}, \tilde{\to}, \tilde{\equiv} \rangle$, where $U = \{a, b, c\}$, $D = \{a, b\}$, for $\tilde{\neg}$ we set $\tilde{\neg}a = c$, $\tilde{\neg}b = c$, and $\tilde{\neg}c = a$, the operation $\tilde{\to}$ is given by the table:

$\tilde{\to}$	a	b	c
a	a	a	c
b	b	b	c
c	b	a	a

For a valuation V in $\mathcal{M}$ such that $V(p) = a$, $V(q) = c$, and $V(r) = b$, we obtain $V(p \to (q \to r)) = a$, yet $V(q \to (p \to r)) = b$, which leads to the conclusion that $V((p \to (q \to r)) \equiv (q \to (p \to r))) \notin D$.

3   Dual Tableau System $\mathsf{DT_{SCI}}$

Modern tableau systems originate from Smullyan's analytic tableaux for classical logic [21], which refine earlier ideas of Beth's semantic tableaux [1,2] and Hintikka's model sets [16]. Their dual counterparts are based on Rasiowa-Sikorski diagrams for first-order logic without identity [20], a simplification of Kanger's formalisms [17]. Both offer cut-free, tree-based alternatives to Gentzen's sequent calculus. As the names suggest, tableaux and dual tableaux form dual classes of deduction systems: the former serve as unsatisfiability checkers (to prove φ, one refutes $\neg\varphi$), while the latter are validity checkers (to prove φ, one constructs a direct proof of φ). Although the two are intertranslatable [8,13], in specific contexts certain factors speak in favour of one or another. Over time, both have been developed for a wide range of logics. More detailed surveys can be found in d'Agostino et al.'s and Orłowska and Golińska-Pilarek's works [7,19].

Dual tableaux are top-down systems determined by the rules of inference and axioms. *Axioms* are distinguished sets of formulas, also referred to as *axiomatic sets.* Rules have the following form: (dtrule) $\frac{\Phi}{\Phi_1 \mid ... \mid \Phi_n}$, $n \geq 1$, where Φ, Φ_1, ..., Φ_n are finite sets of formulas. The set Φ is called the *premise* of the rule. The sets Φ_1, ..., Φ_n are said to be *conclusions*. The rules are supposed to preserve validity upward, where the validity of a finite set of formulas is the validity of the disjunction of its elements. Thus, in a set $\Phi_i = \{\varphi_1, ..., \varphi_m\}$ a comma can be interpreted as a disjunction, while branching '|' occurring in a rule (dtrule) as a conjunction. A rule (dtrule) *is applicable* to a finite set X if X is not an axiomatic set, $\Phi \subseteq X$, and there is $i \in \{1, ..., n\}$ such that $\Phi_i \not\subseteq X$.

The set of $\mathsf{DT_{SCI}}$ rules consists of the decomposition and specific rules presented in Fig. 1. It is assumed that φ, ψ, ϑ are arbitrary SCI-formulas with the proviso that in the specific rules $\vartheta \prec \psi$. A $\mathsf{DT_{SCI}}$-axiom is a finite set of SCI-formulas containing $\varphi \equiv \varphi$ or both φ and $\neg\varphi$, for some formula φ. A $\mathsf{DT_{SCI}}$-*proof tree* for an SCI-formula φ is a tree whose root is assigned the set $\{\varphi\}$ and each node of the tree, except the root, is obtained by an application of a $\mathsf{DT_{SCI}}$-rule to its predecessor node. A branch of a $\mathsf{DT_{SCI}}$-proof tree is *closed* if it contains a node with a $\mathsf{DT_{SCI}}$-axiomatic set of formulas. A $\mathsf{DT_{SCI}}$-proof tree is *closed* whenever all of its branches are closed. A formula φ is DT-*provable* if there is a closed $\mathsf{DT_{SCI}}$-proof tree for φ, which is then called a $\mathsf{DT_{SCI}}$-*proof* of φ.

The applicability of specific rules depends solely on whether negated identities, rather than identities, are present on a branch. Thus, no rule applies to a non-trivial identity, that is, an identity $\varphi \equiv \psi$ such that $\varphi \neq \psi$, and its corresponding proof tree remains open—which reflects the fact that such identities are not provable in SCI. To control the growth of formulas and ensure termination, we restrict rule application: a rule may be applied only if one non-identity side (which one exactly depends on the rule) is strictly smaller than the other. The rule *(sym)* reflects the symmetry of $\equiv$, that is, the fact that if two formulas have the same denotation, their order in an identity formula is irrelevant. The rule $(\equiv_1)$ reflects the fact that identical formulas must have the same truth value. The rule $(\equiv_2)$ encodes the extensionality of SCI, that is, it allows to replace a subformula ψ in φ with an identical formula ϑ, that is, a formula which has the same denotation as ψ, without affecting the denotation of φ. Axiomatic sets with trivial identities encode the reflexivity of $\equiv$, that is, the fact that $\varphi \equiv \varphi$ is valid for any formula φ. No separate rule is needed for transitivity.

Example 2. The formula $p \equiv \neg\neg p$, which expresses the identity of a formula and its double negation, is not SCI-valid and its $\mathsf{DT_{SCI}}$-proof tree consists of one node, namely $\{p \equiv \neg\neg p\}$. It becomes apparent that no formula of the form $\varphi \equiv \psi$ will yield a closed $\mathsf{DT_{SCI}}$-tree unless $\varphi = \psi$.

On the other hand, the formula $p \equiv \neg q \rightarrow (q \equiv \neg r \rightarrow p \equiv \neg\neg r)$ expresses an intricate relation between transitivity and congruency of the connective $\equiv$ w.r.t. $\neg$. If we apply $\mathsf{DT_{SCI}}$ to φ, we obtain the following proof tree which shows that the formula at the root is SCI-valid.

Decomposition rules

$$(\neg)\ \frac{X \cup \{\neg\neg\varphi\}}{X \cup \{\varphi\}} \qquad (\rightarrow)\ \frac{X \cup \{\varphi \rightarrow \psi\}}{X \cup \{\neg\varphi, \psi\}} \qquad (\neg \rightarrow)\ \frac{X \cup \{\neg(\varphi \rightarrow \psi)\}}{X \cup \{\varphi\} \mid X \cup \{\neg\psi\}}$$

Specific rules (applicable only if $\vartheta \prec \psi$)

$$(sym)\ \frac{X \cup \{\vartheta \not\equiv \psi\}}{X \cup \{\psi \not\equiv \vartheta, \vartheta \not\equiv \psi\}} \qquad (\equiv_1)\ \frac{X \cup \{\psi \not\equiv \vartheta\}}{X \cup \{\psi, \vartheta, \psi \not\equiv \vartheta\} \mid X \cup \{\neg\psi, \neg\vartheta, \psi \not\equiv \vartheta\}}$$

$$(\equiv_2)^*\ \frac{X \cup \{\varphi(\psi), \psi \not\equiv \vartheta\}}{X \cup \{\varphi(\psi/\vartheta), \varphi(\psi), \psi \not\equiv \vartheta\}}$$

$^*\varphi(\psi)$ may be of the form $\psi \not\equiv \vartheta$. In such a case the premise is of the form $X \cup \{\psi \not\equiv \vartheta\}$.

Fig. 1. Dual tableau system $\mathsf{DT_{SCI}}$

$$
\begin{array}{lll}
1. & \{p \equiv \neg q \rightarrow (q \equiv \neg r \rightarrow p \equiv \neg\neg r)\} & \\
2. & \{p \not\equiv \neg q,\ q \equiv \neg r \rightarrow p \equiv \neg\neg r\} & (\rightarrow) \\
3. & \{p \not\equiv \neg q,\ q \not\equiv \neg r,\ p \equiv \neg\neg r\} & (\rightarrow) \\
4. & \{p \not\equiv \neg q,\ q \not\equiv \neg r,\ p \equiv \neg\neg r,\ \neg r \not\equiv q\} & (sym) \\
5. & \{\underline{p \not\equiv \neg q},\ q \not\equiv \neg r,\ p \equiv \neg\neg r,\ \neg r \not\equiv q,\ \underline{p \equiv \neg q}\} & (\equiv_2) \\
6. & \qquad\qquad\qquad \otimes & \\
\end{array}
$$

Finally, an invalid formula $\neg q \equiv \neg p \rightarrow (r \equiv q \rightarrow r \equiv p)$ illustrates the fact that $\equiv$ does not act 'downwards', that is, the identity of two complex formulas does not need to imply the identity of their constituents.

$$
\begin{array}{lll}
1. & \{\neg q \equiv \neg p \rightarrow (r \equiv q \rightarrow r \equiv p)\} & \\
2. & \{\neg q \not\equiv \neg p,\ (r \equiv q \rightarrow r \equiv p)\} & (\rightarrow) \\
3. & \{\neg q \not\equiv \neg p,\ r \not\equiv q,\ r \equiv p\} & (\rightarrow) \\
4. & \{\neg q \not\equiv \neg p,\ r \not\equiv q,\ r \equiv p,\ q \equiv p\} & (\equiv_2),\ q \prec r \\
5. & \{\neg q \not\equiv \neg p,\ r \not\equiv q,\ r \equiv p,\ q \equiv p,\ \neg p \not\equiv \neg p\} & (\equiv_2),\ p \prec q \\
6. & \{\neg q \not\equiv \neg p,\ r \not\equiv q,\ r \equiv p,\ q \equiv p,\ \neg p \not\equiv \neg p,\ q \not\equiv q\} & (\equiv_2),\ q \prec r \\
& \qquad\qquad\qquad\qquad \text{open} & \\
\end{array}
$$

4 Soundness and Completeness

Soundness. Dual tableau systems are validity checkers, that is, in order to prove the validity of a formula, we build a proof tree with that formula at the root and try to close all branches with valid leaves. Thus, to prove the soundness of $\mathsf{DT_{SCI}}$ it suffices to show that all $\mathsf{DT_{SCI}}$-axioms are valid and all $\mathsf{DT_{SCI}}$-rules preserve validity upward. A rule (dtrule) is $\mathsf{DT_{SCI}}$-*correct* whenever it holds that, if all $\Phi_1, \ldots, \Phi_n$ are SCI-valid, then Φ is SCI-valid. A rule (dtrule) is $\mathsf{DT_{SCI}}$-*invertible* whenever it holds that, if Φ is SCI-valid, then all $\Phi_1, \ldots, \Phi_n$ are SCI-valid.

Proposition 3. $\mathsf{DT_{SCI}}$-*axioms are* SCI-*valid and the* $\mathsf{DT_{SCI}}$-*rules are* $\mathsf{DT_{SCI}}$-*correct.*

Proof (Sketch). The proof of SCI-validity of $\mathsf{DT_{SCI}}$-axiomatic sets is straightforward. Let X be a finite set of SCI-formulas and let $\varphi, \psi, \theta \in \mathsf{FOR}$ be such that

$\theta \prec \psi$. $\mathsf{DT_{SCI}}$-correctness of decomposition rules easily follows from the classical semantics of the operations $\tilde{\neg}$ and $\tilde{\rightarrow}$ in SCI-models. By way of example, we will prove the proposition for the rule $(\equiv_2)$.

Assume that $X \cup \{\varphi(\psi/\vartheta), \varphi(\psi), \psi \not\equiv \vartheta\}$ is SCI-valid. Suppose that $X \cup \{\varphi(\psi), \psi \not\equiv \vartheta\}$ is not SCI-valid. Then, there exist an SCI-model $\mathcal{M} = \langle U, D, \tilde{\neg}, \tilde{\rightarrow}, \tilde{\equiv} \rangle$ and an SCI-valuation V in $\mathcal{M}$ such that $\mathcal{M}, V \not\models \varphi(\psi)$, $\mathcal{M}, V \not\models \psi \not\equiv \vartheta$, and, for every $\chi \in X$, it holds that $\mathcal{M}, V \not\models \chi$. Thus, the following hold: (1) $\mathcal{M}, V \not\models \varphi(\psi)$, (2) $\mathcal{M}, V \models \psi \equiv \vartheta$. By the assumption, we obtain that (3) $\mathcal{M}, V \models \varphi(\psi/\vartheta)$. The condition (2) and the extensionality property imply that $\mathcal{M}, V \models \varphi(\psi) \equiv \varphi(\psi/\vartheta)$, and so, $V(\varphi(\psi)) = V(\varphi(\psi/\vartheta))$. Thus, $V(\varphi(\psi)) \in D$ iff $V(\varphi(\psi/\vartheta)) \in D$. By (3) we get $V(\varphi(\psi/\vartheta)) \in D$, so $V(\varphi(\psi))$ is also in D. Hence, $\mathcal{M}, V \models \varphi(\psi)$, which contradicts (1). $\qquad \square$

The proof of Proposition 3 exhibits that all rules of $\mathsf{DT_{SCI}}$ are not only $\mathsf{DT_{SCI}}$-correct, but also $\mathsf{DT_{SCI}}$-invertible. Therefore, due to the results proved by Hähnle and Beckert [15], $\mathsf{DT_{SCI}}$ is *confluent*, that is, every partial proof tree of a valid formula φ can be expanded into a full proof of φ. Now, Proposition 3 allow us to formulate:

Theorem 4 (Soundness of $\mathsf{DT_{SCI}}$). *The system $\mathsf{DT_{SCI}}$ is sound, that is, if there exists a $\mathsf{DT_{SCI}}$-proof of an SCI-formula φ, then φ is valid.*

Proof. Let $\varphi \in \mathsf{FOR}$ have a $\mathsf{DT_{SCI}}$-proof. Then, there exists a closed $\mathsf{DT_{SCI}}$-proof tree with the formula φ at the root and each of its branches ends with a $\mathsf{DT_{SCI}}$-axiomatic set of formulas. By Proposition 3, all $\mathsf{DT_{SCI}}$-axiomatic sets are valid and each application of $\mathsf{DT_{SCI}}$-rules reflect SCI-validity, that is, if all conclusions of a rule that has been applied are SCI-valid, then so is the premise to which the rule has been applied. Therefore, going from the bottom to the top of the $\mathsf{DT_{SCI}}$-proof tree, at each step of the construction we get sets which are valid. In particular the set $\{\varphi\}$ at the root of the tree is also valid, whence the validity of φ follows. $\qquad \square$

Completeness. To prove the completeness of $\mathsf{DT_{SCI}}$, we must show that if a formula φ lacks a closed $\mathsf{DT_{SCI}}$-proof tree, then it is not valid–that is, it is falsified by some SCI-model and valuation. As usual, this requires constructing a countermodel that falsifies all formulas on an open branch. However, the standard stepwise decomposition method is insufficient here, as no rule applies to non-negated identities. For instance, in the case of $\varphi \equiv \psi$ with $\varphi \neq \psi$, the proof tree may reduce to a single root node. Hence, we must also account for formulas not explicitly present on the open branch.

The proof proceeds in two main stages. First, we focus on the inequalities occurring on an open branch $\mathcal{B}$. Rather than following the actual sequence of $(\equiv_2)$ rule applications, we begin with an arbitrary formula φ_1. If $\mathcal{B}$ contains an inequality $\psi_1 \not\equiv \vartheta_1$ such that $\vartheta_1 \prec \psi_1$ and ψ_1 is a subformula of φ_1, then applying $(\equiv_2)$ yields a new formula $\varphi_2 = \varphi_1(\psi_1/\vartheta_1)$. This process can be repeated: for example, $\varphi_3 = \varphi_2(\psi_2/\vartheta_2)$, and so on. Since $\prec$ is a well-ordering and each transformation satisfies $\varphi_{n+1} \prec \varphi_n$, this sequence must eventually terminate. That is, there exists a finite n such that no inequality on $\mathcal{B}$ justifies a further application of $(\equiv_2)$ to φ_n.

The main goal of this first stage is to establish the existence of a function $h\colon \mathsf{FOR} \to \mathsf{FOR}$ such that, starting from any formula φ and applying $(\equiv_2)$ exhaustively, we always arrive at $h(\varphi)$—independent of the order of substitutions.

In the second stage, we define the countermodel based on the function h and show that it satisfies the properties required to complete the proof.

For formulas ψ, ϑ, let $r_{\psi, \vartheta}$ be the function on formulas that replaces every occurrence of ψ in its argument with ϑ. More formally,

$$r_{\psi,\vartheta}(\varphi) = \begin{cases} \vartheta & \text{if } \varphi = \psi, \\ \varphi & \text{if } \psi \neq \varphi \in \mathsf{AF}, \\ \neg r_{\psi,\vartheta}(\eta) & \text{if } \psi \neq \varphi = \neg\eta, \\ r_{\psi,\vartheta}(\eta) \mathbin{\#} r_{\psi,\vartheta}(\zeta) & \text{if } \psi \neq \varphi = \eta \mathbin{\#} \zeta, \quad \# \in \{\to, \equiv\}. \end{cases}$$

Note that $r_{\psi,\vartheta}(\varphi) = \varphi$ whenever ψ is not a subformula of φ, in particular when $\varphi \prec \psi$. Moreover, if $\vartheta \preceq \psi$, then $r_{\psi,\vartheta}(\varphi) \preceq \varphi$ for all φ.

For the remainder of this section, let $\mathcal{B}$ be an open branch of a $\mathsf{DT_{SCI}}$-proof tree where all rules have been applied exhaustively, and let λ be the union of all nodes on $\mathcal{B}$. Define $\Lambda = \{r_{\psi,\vartheta} \mid \psi \not\equiv \vartheta \in \lambda, \ \vartheta \prec \psi\}$, and let Λ^* be the set of all finite compositions of elements of Λ, including the identity. We define relations R and R^* on formulas as follows: for $\varphi, \psi \in \mathsf{FOR}$, $\varphi \, R \, \psi$ if $\psi = s(\varphi)$ for some $s \in \Lambda$, and $\varphi \, R^* \, \psi$ if $\psi = s(\varphi)$ for some $s \in \Lambda^*$. Thus, R^* is the reflexive transitive closure of R. Furthermore, if $\varphi \, R \, \psi$ (and hence if $\varphi \, R^* \, \psi$), then $\varphi \preceq \psi$.

For any formula φ, define $h(\varphi)$ as the $\prec$-least element of the set $\{s(\varphi) \mid s \in \Lambda^*\}$. It follows that $s(h(\varphi)) = h(\varphi)$ for all $s \in \Lambda^*$, and in particular, $h(h(\varphi)) = h(\varphi)$. This holds because for any ψ and $t \in \Lambda^*$, we have $t(\psi) \preceq \psi$, so the minimality of $h(\varphi)$ ensures it is fixed under all $s \in \Lambda^*$. We say that a function $f\colon \mathsf{FOR} \to \mathsf{FOR}$ is *transparent* on φ if, for every formula ψ and $\# \in \{\to, \equiv\}$, the following hold: (1) $f(\neg\varphi) = \neg f(\varphi)$, (2) $f(\varphi \mathbin{\#} \psi) = f(\varphi) \mathbin{\#} f(\psi)$, (3) $f(\psi \mathbin{\#} \varphi) = f(\psi) \mathbin{\#} f(\varphi)$.

Propositions 5–7, presented below, are essential for the completeness theorem but are technically involved. For clarity of exposition, we omit their proofs here

.

Proposition 5. *The following hold for all formulas φ, ψ: (1) $h(h(\varphi)) = h(\varphi)$, (2) $h(\varphi \to \psi) = h(h(\varphi) \to h(\psi))$, (3) $h(\varphi \equiv \psi) = h(h(\varphi) \equiv h(\psi))$.*

We define a function $t\colon \mathsf{FOR} \to \{T, F\}$ inductively as follows.

$$t(p) = \begin{cases} T & \text{if } \neg p \in \lambda, \\ F & \text{otherwise.} \end{cases} \qquad t(\varphi \equiv \psi) = \begin{cases} T & \text{if } h(\varphi) = h(\psi), \\ F & \text{otherwise.} \end{cases}$$

$$t(\neg\varphi) = \begin{cases} T & \text{if } t(\varphi) = F, \\ F & \text{otherwise.} \end{cases} \qquad t(\varphi \to \psi) = \begin{cases} T & \text{if } t(\varphi) = F \text{ or } t(\psi) = T, \\ F & \text{otherwise.} \end{cases}$$

The following properties of λ follow directly from the assumptions that $\mathcal{B}$ is open and the rules of $\mathsf{DT_{SCI}}$ have been applied exhaustively thereon.

Fact 1. The following hold for all formulas φ, ψ: (1) If $\neg\neg\varphi \in \lambda$, then $\varphi \in \lambda$. (2) If $\varphi \to \psi \in \lambda$, then $\neg\varphi \in \lambda$ and $\psi \in \lambda$. (3) If $\neg(\varphi \to \psi) \in \lambda$, then $\varphi \in \lambda$ or $\neg\psi \in \lambda$. (4) If $\varphi \not\equiv \psi \in \lambda$ and $\varphi \prec \psi$, then $\psi \not\equiv \varphi \in \lambda$. (5) If $\varphi \not\equiv \psi \in \lambda$, then $\{\varphi, \psi\} \subseteq \lambda$ or $\{\neg\varphi, \neg\psi\} \subseteq \lambda$. (6) If $\varphi \in \mathsf{AF}$, then $\{\varphi, \neg\varphi\} \not\subseteq \lambda$. (7) $\varphi \equiv \varphi \notin \lambda$.

Proposition 6. *Let* $\varphi \in \lambda$. *Then* $t(\varphi) = F$.

Proposition 7. *For every formula* φ, *we have* $t(\varphi) = t(h(\varphi))$.

Let us now define a structure $\mathcal{M}_\mathcal{B} = (U_\mathcal{B}, \tilde{\neg}_\mathcal{B}, \tilde{\to}_\mathcal{B}, \tilde{\equiv}_\mathcal{B}, D_\mathcal{B})$ as follows:
(1) $U_\mathcal{B} = \{\varphi \in \mathsf{FOR} \mid \varphi = h(\varphi)\}$, (2) $\tilde{\neg}_\mathcal{B}\varphi = h(\neg\varphi)$, (3) $\varphi \tilde{\to}_\mathcal{B} \psi = h(\varphi \to \psi)$, (4) $\varphi \tilde{\equiv}_\mathcal{B} \psi = h(\varphi \equiv \psi)$, (5) $D_\mathcal{B} = \{\varphi \in U \mid t(\varphi) = T\}$.

Proposition 8. *The structure* $\mathcal{M}_\mathcal{B}$ *is an* SCI-*model.*

Proof (Sketch). Let first p be an atomic formula such that $\neg p \notin \lambda$. Then $p \in U \setminus D$ and $\neg p \in D$, so $D_\mathcal{B}$ is a non-empty proper subset of $U_\mathcal{B}$. Moreover, $U_\mathcal{B}$ is closed under the operations $\tilde{\neg}_\mathcal{B}$, $\tilde{\to}_\mathcal{B}$, and $\tilde{\equiv}_\mathcal{B}$, because h is idempotent by Proposition 5.

Let $\varphi, \psi \in U_\mathcal{B}$. Using Proposition 7 and the definition of $\mathcal{M}_\mathcal{B}$, we get the following: (1) $t(\tilde{\neg}_\mathcal{B}\varphi) = t(\neg\varphi)$, which implies $\tilde{\neg}_\mathcal{B}\varphi \in D_\mathcal{B}$ iff $\varphi \notin D_\mathcal{B}$, (2) $t(\varphi \tilde{\to}_\mathcal{B} \psi) = t(\varphi \to \psi)$, which implies $\varphi \tilde{\to}_\mathcal{B} \psi \in D_\mathcal{B}$ iff $\varphi \notin D_\mathcal{B}$ or $\psi \in D_\mathcal{B}$ (3) $t(\varphi \tilde{\equiv}_\mathcal{B} \psi) = t(\varphi \equiv \psi)$, which implies $\varphi \tilde{\equiv}_\mathcal{B} \psi \in D_\mathcal{B}$ iff $\varphi = \psi$. □

Proposition 9. *The function* h *is a valuation in* $\mathcal{M}_\mathcal{B}$.

Proof. Let $\varphi, \psi \in \mathsf{FOR}$. Then: (1) $h(\neg\varphi) = h(\neg h(\varphi)) = \tilde{\neg}_\mathcal{B} h(\varphi)$, (2) $h(\varphi \to \psi) = h(h(\varphi) \to h(\psi)) = h(\varphi) \tilde{\to}_\mathcal{B} h(\psi)$ (3) $h(\varphi \equiv \psi) = h(h(\varphi) \equiv h(\psi)) = h(\varphi) \tilde{\equiv}_\mathcal{B} h(\psi)$. □

Proposition 10. *For every formula* $\varphi \in \lambda$, *it holds that* $\mathcal{M}_\mathcal{B}, h \not\models \varphi$.

Proof. Let $\varphi \in \lambda$. Then $t(h(\varphi)) = t(\varphi) = F$ by Proposition 7 and 6, and therefore, $h(\varphi) \notin D_\mathcal{B}$. Hence, $\mathcal{M}_\mathcal{B}, h \not\models \varphi$ □

Theorem 11 (Completeness of $\mathsf{DT_{SCI}}$). *For every* SCI-*formula* φ, *if* φ *is valid, then there is a closed* $\mathsf{DT_{SCI}}$-*proof tree for* φ.

Proof. Let φ be a valid SCI-formula. Suppose that a closed $\mathsf{DT_{SCI}}$-proof tree for φ does not exist. We will prove the contraposition of the statement of the theorem. Let $\mathcal{B}$ be an open branch of a $\mathsf{DT_{SCI}}$-proof tree for φ where all the rules of $\mathsf{DT_{SCI}}$ have been exhaustively applied and let λ be the union of all the nodes that occur on $\mathcal{B}$. Clearly, $\varphi \in \lambda$, so by Proposition 10, $\mathcal{M}_\mathcal{B}, h \not\models \varphi$. Since, by Proposition 8, $\mathcal{M}_\mathcal{B}$, is an SCI-model, and, by Proposition 9, h is a valuation in $\mathcal{M}_\mathcal{B}$, φ is not true in some SCI-model, and hence φ is not valid. □

Example 12. Let us consider a formula $\varphi = \neg q \equiv \neg p \to (r \equiv q \to r \equiv p)$, where we assume that $p \prec q \prec r$. A derivation tree for φ looks as follows:

1.	$\{\neg q \equiv \neg p \to (r \equiv q \to r \equiv p)\}$	
2.	$\{\neg q \not\equiv \neg p, r \equiv q \to r \equiv p\}$	$(\to)$: 1
3.	$\{\neg q \not\equiv \neg p, r \not\equiv q, r \equiv p\}$	$(\to)$: 2
4.	$\{\neg q \not\equiv \neg p, r \not\equiv q, r \equiv p, \neg p \not\equiv \neg p\}$	$(\equiv_2)$, $p \prec q$: 3
5.	$\{\neg q \not\equiv \neg p, r \not\equiv q, r \equiv p, \neg p \not\equiv \neg p, q \not\equiv q\}$	$(\equiv_2)$, $q \prec r$: 4
6.	$\{\neg q \not\equiv \neg p, r \not\equiv q, r \equiv p, \neg p \not\equiv \neg p, q \not\equiv q, q \equiv p\}$	$(\equiv_2)$, $q \prec r$: 5

$$
\begin{array}{c}
\overline{\qquad\qquad\qquad} \\
\{\dots\} \quad \{\neg q \not\equiv \neg p, r \not\equiv q, r \equiv p,
\end{array}
$$

7.	$\{\dots\}$ $\{\neg q \not\equiv \neg p, r \not\equiv q, r \equiv p,$ $\neg p \not\equiv \neg p, q \not\equiv q, q \equiv p, \neg\neg q, \neg\neg p\}$	$(\equiv_1)$: 6
8.	$\{\neg q \not\equiv \neg p, r \not\equiv q, r \equiv p,$ $\neg p \not\equiv \neg p, q \not\equiv q, q \equiv p, q, p\}$	$2 \times (\neg)$: 7

9.	$\{\dots\}$ $\{\neg q \not\equiv \neg p, r \not\equiv q, r \equiv p,$ $\neg p \not\equiv \neg p, q \not\equiv q, q \equiv p, q, p, r\}$	$(\equiv_1)$: 8

open

For the open branch $\mathcal{B}$ of the above derivation tree, the set λ contains the following formulas: (1) $\neg q \not\equiv \neg p$, $\neg p \not\equiv \neg p$, $r \not\equiv q$, $q \not\equiv q$, (2) p, q, r, $\neg\neg p$, $\neg\neg q$, (3) $r \equiv p$, $q \equiv p$ (4) $\neg q \equiv \neg p \to (r \equiv q \to r \equiv p)$, $r \equiv q \to r \equiv p$. Based on (1), we can determine Λ in the following way: $\Lambda = \{r_{\neg p, \neg q}, r_{q, r}\}$, and further define Λ^* as the set of all finite compositions of elements of Λ.

We also get: (1) $h(\neg q \not\equiv \neg p) = h(\neg p \not\equiv \neg p) = \neg p \not\equiv \neg p$, (2) $h(r \not\equiv q) = h(q \not\equiv q) = q \not\equiv q$, (3) $h(p) = p$, (4) $h(q) = h(r) = q$, (5) $h(\neg\neg p) = h(\neg\neg q) = \neg\neg p$, (6) $h(r \equiv p) = h(q \equiv p) = q \equiv p$, (7) $h(\neg q \equiv \neg p \to (r \equiv q \to r \equiv p)) = \neg p \equiv \neg p \to (q \equiv q \to q \equiv p)$, (8) $h(r \equiv q \to r \equiv p) = q \equiv q \to q \equiv p$. Thus, the set $U_{\mathcal{B}}$ contains the following elements: $\neg p \not\equiv \neg p$, $q \not\equiv q$, p, q, $\neg\neg p$, $q \equiv p$, $\neg p \equiv \neg p \to (q \equiv q \to q \equiv p)$, $q \equiv q \to q \equiv p$, neither of which belongs to $D_{\mathcal{B}}$ (which stays in line with Proposition 6).

5 Termination

As it turns out, the restriction that we impose on applications of the specific rules for $\equiv$ suffices to establish termination of the system.

Proposition 13. *Let φ be a formula that occurs at the root of a $\mathsf{DT_{SCI}}$-tree T. Then, for each formula ψ occurring in T, it holds that $|\psi| \leq |\varphi|$.*

Proof (Idea). We prove the proposition by showing that, for each rule (r) of $\mathsf{DT_{SCI}}$, if (r) was applied to a node v introducing ψ to a branch, then there must exist ϑ in v such that $|\psi| \leq |\vartheta|$. $\square$

Together with the fact that no rule of $\mathsf{DT_{SCI}}$ introduces new atomic formulas to the branch, Proposition 13 gives us the following:

Theorem 14. *The length of every branch of a tree with a formula φ occurring at the root has an exponential upper bound.*

Proof (Sketch). Let φ be a formula that occurs at the root of a $\mathsf{DT_{SCI}}$-proof tree and let $n = |\varphi|$. Hence, there are at most n occurrences of atomic formulas and connectives in φ. Therefore, by Proposition 13, every formula occurring on a branch is a string consisting of at most $3n$ symbols chosen from at most $n + 3$ possibilities. So, there are at most $\sum_{i=1}^{n}(n + 3)^{3i}$ different formulas in any node on the branch. It follows that since any rule in $\mathsf{DT_{SCI}}$ has at most 2 active formulas in its premise, it can be applied no more than $\left(\sum_{i=1}^{n}(n + 3)^{3i}\right)^{2}$ times on the same branch. Hence, the length of the branch is in $O(n^{f(n)})$, for some linear function f, as there is a fixed finite set of rules.   □

$\mathsf{DT_{SCI}}$-rules are finitely branching, so the confluence of $\mathsf{DT_{SCI}}$ and Theorem 14 yield:

Corollary 15. *Any derivation conducted with the rules of $\mathsf{DT_{SCI}}$ applied in any order is terminating.*

It turns out that in the worst-case scenario we cannot go below the exponential branch length when deciding the validity of φ with $\mathsf{DT_{SCI}}$.

Example 16. Consider the formula $\varphi = (p_1 \equiv q_1 \wedge \ldots \wedge p_n \equiv q_n) \rightarrow ((q_1 \wedge \ldots \wedge q_n) \equiv r)$. We use the conjunction connective $\wedge$ for clarity of presentation, where $\varphi \wedge \psi$ is an abbreviation of $\neg(\varphi \rightarrow \neg\psi)$. If we run $\mathsf{DT_{SCI}}$ on φ, a single application of the rules $(\rightarrow)$ and $(\neg)$, followed by n applications of $(\rightarrow)$, results in $(p_1 \not\equiv q_1), \ldots, (p_n \not\equiv q_n)$ and $(q_1 \wedge \ldots \wedge q_n) \equiv r$ being introduced to the branch. The last identity formula is not decomposable and the former n negated identities, together with the fact that $p_i \prec q_i$, for $i \in \{1, \ldots, n\}$, pave the way to applying $(\equiv_2)$ 2^n times and producing 2^n variants of the identity formula. In particular, each formula of the form $(x_1 \wedge \ldots \wedge x_n) \equiv r$, where $x_i \in \{q_i, p_i\}$, for $i \in \{1, \ldots, n\}$, is introduced to the branch by a single application of $(\equiv_2)$.

6 Related Work

$\mathsf{T_{SCI}}$ The system $\mathsf{T_{SCI}}$, introduced by Golińska-Pilarek et al. [12], is a labelled tableau whose language of deduction includes two disjoint countably infinite sets of labels $\mathsf{L^-}$ and $\mathsf{L^+}$, as well as the auxiliary symbol ':' and the equality symbol $=$. Labels represent denotations of formulas: elements of $\mathsf{L^+}$ stand for elements of D, while elements of $\mathsf{L^-}$ act as elements of $U \setminus D$. $\mathsf{T_{SCI}}$ is sound and complete w.r.t. the semantics presented in Sect. 2.

Example 17. Consider the two formulas from Example 2: $p \equiv \neg\neg p$ and $p \equiv \neg q \rightarrow (q \equiv \neg r \rightarrow p \equiv \neg\neg r)$. The $\mathsf{T_{SCI}}$-proof tree for the first one consists of 4 branches and 25 nodes, whereas in the latter case we have 12 branches and 81 nodes. In both cases, these numbers considerably exceed the corresponding values in $\mathsf{DT_{SCI}}$ (1 branch, 1 node and 1 branch, 6 nodes, respectively).

Comparison. The system $\mathsf{T_{SCI}}$ is a *labelled* tableau, while $\mathsf{DT_{SCI}}$, introduced in this paper, is the first *non-labelled* deduction system for SCI that guarantees termination. Both are sound and complete decision procedures for SCI, but they differ significantly in design and performance.

In $\mathsf{DT_{SCI}}$, the deduction language coincides with that of SCI, whereas in $\mathsf{T_{SCI}}$ it is reduced to a simple equality calculus. The two systems also differ in the number and branching of rules, as detailed in the table below. In $\mathsf{T_{SCI}}$, an open and fully expanded branch retains all subformulas of the input formula along with their denotations, making model reconstruction relatively straightforward. In contrast, $\mathsf{DT_{SCI}}$ does not always fully decompose the input formula, and an open proof tree does not necessarily yield a model satisfying it, even if it exists, which is not always the case—since $\mathsf{DT_{SCI}}$ checks validity, an open tree indicates non-validity, which may or may not imply unsatisfiability.

Reasoning in $\mathsf{T_{SCI}}$ tends to be simpler due to its more information-preserving rules. This is reflected in their complexity: $\mathsf{T_{SCI}}$ is complexity-optimal, while $\mathsf{DT_{SCI}}$ has an exponential worst-case bound on branch length. Nonetheless, our empirical tests using implementations of both systems show that efficiency varies with the input formula. For instance, a $\mathsf{DT_{SCI}}$-proof tree for $\varphi \equiv \psi$ with $\varphi \neq \psi$ consists of a single node, whereas $\mathsf{T_{SCI}}$ may produce many branches before terminating. While $\mathsf{DT_{SCI}}$ performs particularly well on SCI-identities, it also often yields smaller proof trees for a wide range of complex formulas (see Example 17). However, in some cases, $\mathsf{T_{SCI}}$ proves more efficient.

number of	$\mathsf{T_{SCI}}$	$\mathsf{DT_{SCI}}$
rules for $\neg$ and $\rightarrow$	4	3
specific rules for $\equiv$	8	3
closure rules or axioms	2	2
2-branching rules	2	2
4-branching rules	1	0

Implementations. We developed proof-of-concept implementations of theorem provers based on the labelled tableau system $\mathsf{T_{SCI}}$ and the non-labelled system $\mathsf{DT_{SCI}}$. Both are written in Haskell using similar, non-optimized programming techniques and were not subjected to extensive testing, as they serve as temporary tools for ongoing research[4]. We focused on the depth and size of the proof trees rather than on the processing time. One factor that biased the test results is the set of connectives handled natively by the back end. The $\mathsf{DT_{SCI}}$ prover, developed earlier, incorporates rules for all standard connectives ($\neg$, $\wedge$, $\vee$, $\rightarrow$, $\leftrightarrow$, and $\equiv$). The prover for $\mathsf{T_{SCI}}$ internally translates a formula into a form using only $\neg$, $\rightarrow$, and $\equiv$ before trying to prove it. This translation slightly increases the output size for the $\mathsf{T_{SCI}}$ prover. However, external pre-processing

---

[4] The code is available at https://github.com/tanelihuuskonen/tableaux-2021.

effectively removes this difference for formulas without $\equiv$, as the classical connectives are treated nearly identically. The $\mathsf{DT_{SCI}}$-based prover exhibits exponential tree depth in the worst case, and a theoretical argument suggests that formulas with a large number of identities could be particularly challenging for it. Testing provided additional support for this conjecture. Specifically, transforming formulas into a simplified Horn clause-like normal form using the translation function T ([12, Appendix]) consistently worsened the performance of the $\mathsf{DT_{SCI}}$ prover. On the other hand, the $\mathsf{T_{SCI}}$-based prover behaved in unpredictable ways, usually performing worse in the normal form but occasionally showing significant improvement. In general, the $\mathsf{DT_{SCI}}$-based prover turned out to handle most formulas better than the one based on $\mathsf{T_{SCI}}$ provided that the number of identities was not excessive. The inferior worst-case behaviour of the former did not manifest in typical test cases.

Test Cases. We found interesting test cases which reveal that no prover performs best on all inputs. Below we present a formula φ and its translation $T(\varphi)$. We use $\wedge$ for convenience of presentation:

$$\varphi =: (((p_1 \equiv q_1) \wedge (p_2 \equiv q_2)) \wedge (p_3 \equiv q_3)) \rightarrow (((q_1 \equiv q_2) \equiv q_3) \equiv r)$$
$$T(\varphi) =: ((v_6 \equiv (p_1 \equiv q_1)) \rightarrow ((v_7 \equiv (p_2 \equiv q_2)) \rightarrow ((v_2 \equiv (v_6 \wedge v_7))$$
$$\rightarrow ((v_3 \equiv (p_3 \equiv q_3)) \rightarrow ((v_0 \equiv (v_2 \wedge v_3)) \rightarrow ((v_8 \equiv (q_1 \equiv q_2))$$
$$\rightarrow ((v_9 \equiv q_3) \rightarrow ((v_4 \equiv (v_8 \equiv v_9)) \rightarrow ((v_5 \equiv r) \rightarrow ((v_1 \equiv (v_4 \equiv v_5))$$
$$\rightarrow ((v \equiv (v_0 \rightarrow v_1)) \rightarrow v)))))))))))).$$

The results display the maximal branch length and the size of the entire tree:

Formula	$\mathsf{DT_{SCI}}$		$\mathsf{T_{SCI}}$	
	depth	**size**	**depth**	**size**
$T(\varphi)$	114	977841	153	235988

Other systems for SCI. Apart from $\mathsf{T_{SCI}}$ and $\mathsf{DT_{SCI}}$, several other proof systems for SCI have been proposed. However, with the exception of these two, none guarantees termination—even though SCI is decidable and, in fact, belongs to NP [5, Thm. 2.3]. Below, we focus on alternative dual-tableau systems for SCI.

The first such system, proposed by Golińska-Pilarek [9], includes only one rule for handling $\equiv$:

$$\frac{\{\varphi(\psi)\}}{\{\psi \equiv \vartheta, \varphi(\psi)\} \mid \{\varphi(\psi/\vartheta), \varphi(\psi)\}}.$$

This rule encodes the extensionality of $\equiv$ and corresponds to the analogous rule for standard identity ($=$) in a dual tableau calculus for first-order logic. Despite its conceptual simplicity and elegance, the system lacks termination. Since no constraints are imposed on ϑ, the rule for $\equiv$ can be applied indefinitely, introducing formulas of unbounded length.

Several years later, Golińska-Pilarek and Welle introduced a revised system, $\mathsf{DT^*_{SCI}}$ [14], which preserved the original decomposition rules for Boolean connectives but replaced the single $\equiv$ rule with the following set:

$$(\textit{ref})\ \frac{X}{X \cup \{\varphi \not\equiv \varphi\}} \quad (\textit{sym})\ \frac{X \cup \{\varphi \not\equiv \psi\}}{X \cup \{\varphi \not\equiv \psi, \psi \not\equiv \varphi\}} \quad (\textit{tran})\ \frac{X \cup \{\varphi \not\equiv \psi, \psi \not\equiv \vartheta\}}{X \cup \{\varphi \not\equiv \psi, \psi \not\equiv \vartheta, \varphi \not\equiv \vartheta\}}$$

$$(\equiv_\neg)\ \frac{X \cup \{\varphi \not\equiv \psi\}}{X \cup \{\varphi \not\equiv \psi, \neg\varphi \not\equiv \neg\psi\}} \quad (\equiv_\rightarrow)\ \frac{X \cup \{\varphi \not\equiv \psi, \vartheta \not\equiv \chi\}}{X \cup \{\varphi \not\equiv \psi, \vartheta \not\equiv \chi, (\varphi \rightarrow \vartheta) \not\equiv (\psi \rightarrow \chi)\}}$$

$$(\equiv_\equiv)\ \frac{X \cup \{\varphi \not\equiv \psi, \vartheta \not\equiv \chi\}}{X \cup \{\varphi \not\equiv \psi, \vartheta \not\equiv \chi, (\varphi \equiv \vartheta) \not\equiv (\psi \equiv \chi)\}}.$$

While $\mathsf{DT}^*_{\mathsf{SCI}}$ and $\mathsf{T}_{\mathsf{SCI}}$ handle the $\equiv$ connective similarly, they differ in one crucial respect. $\mathsf{T}_{\mathsf{SCI}}$, being fully analytic and labelled, introduces identity-based formulas only when relevant compound formulas are already present on the branch. In contrast, $\mathsf{DT}^*_{\mathsf{SCI}}$ may introduce such formulas even if absent, allowing rules like $(\equiv_\neg)$, $(\equiv_\rightarrow)$, and $(\equiv_\equiv)$ to be applied repeatedly—potentially leading to infinite branch expansion and non-termination.

7 Conclusions

In this paper, we introduced a novel dual tableau decision procedure $\mathsf{DT}_{\mathsf{SCI}}$ for the logic SCI. $\mathsf{DT}_{\mathsf{SCI}}$, as opposed to $\mathsf{T}_{\mathsf{SCI}}$ – the only alternative decision procedure for SCI present on the market – does not involve labels that are external to the language of SCI. In $\mathsf{T}_{\mathsf{SCI}}$, labels are essential to ensure termination, as they allow us to reduce the identity of formulas to the equality of labels. In contrast, $\mathsf{DT}_{\mathsf{SCI}}$ achieves termination by restricting applications of $\equiv$-rules to cases where newly introduced formulas are not greater (with respect to a well-ordering) than those already present on the branch. This prevents unbounded formula growth – one of the main causes of non-termination in earlier dual tableau systems for SCI. Remarkably, this restriction preserves completeness, though it requires a non-standard proof strategy. Despite its non-optimal worst-case complexity, $\mathsf{DT}_{\mathsf{SCI}}$ often exhibits considerably better performance compared to the complexity-optimal $\mathsf{T}_{\mathsf{SCI}}$, as evidenced by preliminary tests. A natural avenue for future research is to build large benchmark sets of SCI-formulas to empirically identify classes for which each procedure yields more efficient derivations in terms of size and runtime.

Acknowledgements.. Research reported in this paper was supported by the National Science Centre, Poland (grant number: UMO-2017/25/B/HS1/00503).

References

1. Beth, E.W.: Semantic entailment and formal derivability. Mededeelingen der Koninklijke Nederlandsche Akademie van Wetenschappen, Afd. Letterkunde **18**, 309–342 (1955)
2. Beth, E.W.: The Foundations of Mathematics: A Study in the Philosophy of Science. North-Holland Publishing Company, Amsterdam (1959)

3. Bloom, S.L.: On generalized logics. Stud. Log. **33**(1), 65–68 (1974). https://doi.org/10.1007/BF02120867
4. Bloom, S.L., Suszko, R.: Semantics for the sentential calculus with identity. Stud. Log. **28**(1), 77–81 (1971). https://doi.org/10.1007/BF02124265
5. Bloom, S.L., Suszko, R.: Investigations into the sentential calculus with identity. Notre Dame J. Form. Log. **13**(3), 289–308 (1972). https://doi.org/10.1305/ndjfl/1093890617
6. Chlebowski, S.: Sequent Calculi for SCI. Stud. Log. **106**(3), 541–563 (2017). https://doi.org/10.1007/s11225-017-9754-8
7. D'Agostino, M., Gabbay, D.M., Hähnle, R., Posegga, J. (eds.): Handbook of Tableau Methods. Springer, Dordrecht (1999). https://doi.org/10.1007/978-94-017-1754-0
8. Fitting, M.: Tableaus and dual tableaus. In: Golińska-Pilarek, J., Zawidzki, M. (eds.) Ewa Orłowska on Relational Methods in Logic and Computer Science. OCL, vol. 17, pp. 105–128. Springer, Cham (2018). https://doi.org/10.1007/978-3-319-97879-6_5
9. Golińska-Pilarek, J.: Rasiowa-Sikorski proof system for the non-Fregean sentential logic SCI. J. Appl. Non-Classical Log. **17**(4), 511–519 (2007). https://doi.org/10.3166/jancl.17.511-519
10. Golińska-Pilarek, J.: Non-fregean world of logics. J. Philos. Log. **54**, 575–620 (2025). https://doi.org/10.1007/s10992-025-09795-6
11. Golińska-Pilarek, J., Huuskonen, T.: Number of extensions of non-Fregean logics. J. Philos. Log. **34**(2), 193–206 (2005). https://doi.org/10.1007/s10992-004-6366-3
12. Golińska-Pilarek, J., Huuskonen, T., Zawidzki, M.: Tableau-based decision procedure for non-Fregean logic of sentential identity. In: Platzer, A., Sutcliffe, G. (eds.) Automated Deduction – CADE 28, LNCS, vol. 12699, pp. 41–57. Springer, Cham (2021). https://doi.org/10.1007/978-3-030-79876-5_3, all omitted proofs can be found at https://arxiv.org/abs/2104.14697
13. Golińska-Pilarek, J., Orłowska, E.: Tableaux and dual tableaux: transformation of proofs. Stud. Logica. **85**(3), 291–310 (2007). https://doi.org/10.1007/s11225-007-9055-8
14. Golińska-Pilarek, J., Welle, M.: Deduction in non-Fregean propositional logic SCI. Axioms **8**, 115 (2019). https://doi.org/10.3390/axioms8040115
15. Hähnle, R., Beckert, B.: Proof confluent tableau calculi. In: Murray, N.V. (ed.) TABLEAUX 1999. LNCS (LNAI), vol. 1617, pp. 34–35. Springer, Heidelberg (1999). https://doi.org/10.1007/3-540-48754-9_7
16. Hintikka, J.: Two Papers on Symbolic Logic: Form and Content in Quantification Theory and Reductions in the Theory of Types. Acta philosophica Fennica, Societas Philosophica, Helsinki (1955)
17. Kanger, S.: Provability in Logic. Acta Universitatis Stockholmiensis. Stockholm Studies in Philosophy 1, Almqvist and Wiksell, Stockholm (1957)
18. Michaels, A.: A uniform proof procedure for SCI tautologies. Stud. Log. **33**(3), 299–310 (1974). https://doi.org/10.1007/BF02123284
19. Orłowska, E., Golińska-Pilarek, J.: Dual Tableaux: Foundations, Methodology, Case Studies, Trends in Logic, vol. 33. Springer, Dordrecht (2011). https://doi.org/10.1007/978-94-007-0005-5
20. Rasiowa, H., Sikorski, R.: On the Gentzen theorem. Fundam. Math. **48**, 57–69 (1960). http://matwbn.icm.edu.pl/ksiazki/fm/fm48/fm4814.pdf
21. Smullyan, R.: First-Order Logic, Ergebnisse der Mathematik und ihrer Grenzgebiete. 2. Folge, vol. 43. Springer Verlag, Berlin, Heidelberg (1968). https://doi.org/10.1007/978-3-642-86718-7

22. Suszko, R.: Non-Fregean logic and theories. Analele Universității București, Acta Logica **11**, 105–125 (1968)
23. Suszko, R.: Identity connective and modality. Stud. Log. **27**(1), 7–39 (1971). https://doi.org/10.1007/BF02282541
24. Suszko, R.: Abolition of the Fregean axiom. In: Parikh, R. (ed.) Logic Colloquium. Lecture Notes in Mathematics, vol. 453, pp. 169–239 (1975). https://doi.org/10.1007/BFb0064874
25. Suszko, R.: The Fregean axiom and Polish mathematical logic in the 1920s. Stud. Log. **36**(4), 377–380 (1977). https://doi.org/10.1007/BF02120672
26. Wasilewska, A.: A sequence formalization for SCI. Stud. Log. **35**(3), 213–217 (1976). https://doi.org/10.1007/BF02282483
27. Wasilewska, A.: DFC-algorithms for Suszko logic and one-to-one Gentzen type formalizations. Stud. Log. **43**(4), 395–404 (1984). https://doi.org/10.1007/BF00370509

Exposure and Hiding: Approaching the Objective Probability and Hiding the Secret in Zero-Knowledge Proof

Yini Huang[ID], Beishui Liao[ID], and Xingchi Su[(✉)][ID]

Zhejiang University, Hangzhou, China
x.su1993@gmail.com

Abstract. Zero-knowledge proofs (ZKPs) allow a prover to convince a verifier that they possess a secret without revealing any information about that secret. This paper formalizes a widely-used ZKP protocol, specifically the Schnorr protocol, using Probabilistic Hoare Logic (PHL) and Product Probabilistic Relational Hoare Logic ($\times$PRHL). The deterministic states are defined based on the set-extension style, which captures the information change of the participants in the protocol. In particular, PHL demonstrates that the probability of a prover consistently passing the challenges posed by the verifier asymptotically approaches 1 if the prover actually holds the secret. Furthermore, we explore the Schnorr protocol within a generalized framework where the initial probabilistic state assigns a probability p for holding the secret (instead of strictly 1 or 0) and a probability $1 - p$ for not holding it (instead of strictly 0 or 1). This characterization shows that the ZKP protocol can be considered a method to "expose" the probability p of a prover holding a secret, even when p is initially unknown to anyone. $\times$PRHL constructs a coupled product program to prove computational indistinguishability between the real protocol and a simulator, thereby proving the zero-knowledge property. Our work provides a novel formal framework for analyzing and understanding ZKPs and highlights the advantages of probabilistic reasoning in cryptographic verification.

Keywords: Zero Knowledge Proof · Probabilistic Hoare Logic · formal verification

1 Introduction

A zero-knowledge proof (ZKP) is an interactive proof between a prover and a verifier, where the prover convinces the verifier that a particular statement is true without revealing any additional information beyond that truth value itself [5]. This process must satisfy the following three properties:

1. **Completeness**: If the statement is true, then an honest verifier (that is, one following the protocol properly) will be convinced of this fact by an honest prover.

© The Author(s), under exclusive license to Springer Nature Switzerland AG 2026
G. Casini et al. (Eds.): JELIA 2025, LNAI 16094, pp. 298–312, 2026.
https://doi.org/10.1007/978-3-032-04590-4_20

2. **Soundness**: If the statement is false, then no cheating prover can convince an honest verifier that it is true, except with some small probability.
3. **Zero-knowledge**: If the statement is true, then no verifier learns anything other than the fact that the statement is true.

We take the Schnorr protocol [12] as a running example of a zero-knowledge proof in this paper: Given an integer y, a large prime p, and a generator g of a cyclic group, Uma wants to prove to Bob that she knows a value x such that g^x mod p $= y$, without revealing x. In each round, Uma generates a random r where $r \in [0, \mathrm{p} - 2]$, computes the *commitment* $C = g^r$ mod p, and sends C to Bob. Bob then randomly issues a *challenge* e, where $e \in \{0, 1\}$. If $e = 0$, Bob requests r as the *response*; if $e = 1$, Bob requests $(x + r)$ mod $(\mathrm{p} - 1)$ as the *response*. If $e = 0$, Bob verifies that g^r mod p $= C$. If $e = 1$, Bob verifies that $g^{(x+r) \mod (\mathrm{p}-1)}$ mod p $= (C \cdot y)$ mod p. We suppose that it repeats for n rounds. If the protocol runs properly, as n increases, the probability that a dishonest prover can pass all challenges decreases exponentially. Specifically, if the prover does not know x, under the Discrete Logarithm Assumption, the verifier's best strategy is to guess randomly, succeeding with a probability of $\frac{1}{2}$ each round. After n rounds, the probability of her successfully guessing all challenges would become negligible. On the other hand, if the prover actually knows x, she can always provide the correct response, ensuring that she passes all challenges with probability 1. This mechanism, therefore, ensures that the verifier can be confident that the prover indeed knows the secret x after sufficient rounds of challenges.

From Modal Logic to Hoare Logic. Zero-knowledge proofs (ZKPs) are extensively used in modern cryptographic applications. Cryptographers have provided computational verification on whether the classical ZKP protocols meet the three properties. Logicians aim to establish a formal framework for analyzing ZKPs more rigorously. Halpern et al. [6] used epistemic logic to characterize the zero-knowledge property, proving that the verifier gains no knowledge beyond the truth of the statement. Jaramillo [10] integrated cryptographic probability logic into dynamic epistemic logic to model interactions in ZKPs. Lehnherr et al. [11] further advanced the approach by using justification logic with probabilistic additionals to analyze interactive proof systems, capturing confidence dynamics with accumulating justifications.

However, these epistemic-logic-based approaches rooted in the modal logic face two inherent limitations:

1. Possible-world semantics to characterize *asymptotic probability convergence* (e.g., verifier's confidence increase/decrease rate) requires extra construction of probabilities;
2. The combinatorial complexity of modal operators with probabilistic extensions impedes automated verification.

To overcome these limitations, we employ *Probabilistic Hoare Logic* (PHL) [3] and *Product Probabilistic Relation Hoare Logic* (×PRHL) [9]. Hoare Logic [7,8] expresses program correctness with Hoare triples of the form $\{P\}C\{Q\}$. If the precondition P holds initially, the postcondition Q is satisfied after successfully executing the program C. As an extension of standard Hoare Logic, probabilistic Hoare logic introduces:

- Probabilistic commands for modeling randomization in the command C;
- Probabilistic description in the precondition P and the postcondition Q.

This framework is straightforward to capture the probability convergence properties emphasized in our generalized ZKP setting.

Generalization of Completeness and Soundness. The completeness and soundness of Zero-Knowledge Proofs (ZKPs) assume that the initial state is either that the prover possesses the secret or does not. This initial state can be represented by bipolar probabilistic distributions over two conflicting situations: holding the secret or not holding the secret. In this scenario, holding the secret has a probability of 1, while not holding it has a probability of 0 (and vice versa). Thus, completeness and soundness ensure that a proper ZKP protocol results in the probability of the prover always succeeding being close to 1 or 0.

However, what if we consider more general probabilistic distributions for the initial states? For instance, let's denote p as the probability of holding the secret and $1 - p$ as the probability of not holding it. We would expect a complete and sound ZKP protocol to result in the probability of the prover successfully passing the challenges being close to p, which consequently means the probability of failure in passing would be close to $1 - p$. Based on this observation, we can understand the concept of ZKPs in two aspects:

1. A ZKP protocol **exposes** the objective probability that a prover has the secret (also does not have the secret).
2. A ZKP protocol **hides** the information on the secret from anyone except the prover herself.

We call them the exposure-hiding feature of ZKPs. In this paper, we give a new definition of the deterministic states in a partial way, in contrast to the classical Hoare logic. The probabilistic states adapt to the new deterministic states. The syntax of our PHL does not vary from the classical setting.

Our work makes two key contributions: First, we use PHL and $\times$PRHL to formalize ZKPs, providing a more verification-friendly framework than previous approaches. This enables rigorous analysis of the completeness, soundness, and zero-knowledge properties of the Schnorr protocol. Second, we generalize the initial probabilistic state, moving beyond the traditional bipolar distribution to an arbitrary probability p of the prover holding the secret. This offers a deeper understanding of their functionality. These contributions advance the formal analysis of ZKPs, highlighting the advantages of probabilistic reasoning in cryptographic verification.

2 Probabilistic Hoare Logic for ZKP

2.1 Syntax and Semantics of Deterministic Formulas

Let $\mathbb{PV} = \{X, r_1, \ldots, r_n, c_1, \ldots, c_n, e_1, \ldots, e_n, s_1, \ldots, s_n\}$ be a set of program variables. Here, X represents the secret value x in the example. For each integer $i \in [1, n]$ which denotes the number of rounds, the variables r_i, c_i, e_i, and s_i correspond to the random number generated by the prover, the commitment sent by the prover to the verifier, the challenge issued by the verifier, and the response provided by the prover after receiving the challenge, respectively, in the i-th round. The arithmetic operator set is defined as $\{+, -, \times, \mathrm{mod}, \ldots\} \subseteq \mathbb{Z} \times \mathbb{Z} \to \mathbb{Z}$.

Definition 1 (Arithmetic expressions). *Given a set of program variables* $\mathbb{PV}$, *we define the arithmetic expression E as follows:*

$$E := n \mid x \mid (E \ aop \ E)$$

This syntax allows an arithmetic expression (E) to be either an integer constant (n), a program variable (x), or a composition of two arithmetic expressions (E aop E) built by an arithmetic operation (aop).

Given an instantiation of the Schnorr protocol, the generator g and the module p are fixed as integer constants. The set of Boolean constants is defined as $\mathbb{B} = \{\top, \bot\}$. We define relational operators (rop) on arithmetic expressions, including $>, <, \geq, =, \leq, \ldots$, as functions in $\mathbb{Z} \times \mathbb{Z} \to \mathbb{B}$. Logical operators (lop), such as $\land, \lor, \neg, \to, \ldots$, can be applied to any Boolean expressions.

Definition 2 (Boolean expressions). *The Boolean expression B is defined as follows:*

$$B := \top \mid \bot \mid (E \ rop \ E) \mid \neg B \mid (B \ lop \ B).$$

A Boolean expression represents truth values, true or false. The expression $(E \ rop \ E)$ represents that the truth value is determined by the binary relation rop between two integers.

The semantics of deterministic expressions is defined on deterministic states $S = (KP, KV)$ where KP and KV represent the knowledge bases of the prover and the verifier, respectively, and satisfy the following conditions:

1. KP is a *partial function* $\mathbb{PV} \rightharpoonup \mathbb{Z}$ such that
$$KP(x) = \begin{cases} z \in \mathbb{Z}, & x \in \{r_1, \ldots, r_n, c_1, \ldots, c_n, s_1, \ldots, s_n\} \\ 0 \ or \ 1, & x \in \{X, e_1, \ldots, e_n\} \end{cases};$$
2. KV is a *partial function* $\mathbb{PV} \backslash \{X, r_1, \ldots, r_n\} \rightharpoonup \mathbb{Z}$ such that
$$KV(x) = \begin{cases} z \in \mathbb{Z} & x \in \{c_1, \ldots, c_n, s_1, \ldots, s_n\} \\ 0 \ or \ 1 & x \in \{e_1, \ldots, e_n\} \end{cases};$$
3. $KP(x) = KV(x)$ if $x \in Dom(KP) \cap Dom(KV)$.

It is worth noting that the deterministic states are defined differently from those in the classical Hoare logic. We require S to be a partial function, which means that S can describe just a subset of program variables and leave others undecided. For each $S = (KP, KV)$, let $Dom(KP)$ be the subset of $\mathbb{PV}$ that KP assigns values. Similar to $Dom(KV)$. Let $\mathbb{S}$ be the set of all deterministic states.

Deterministic expressions consist of arithmetic expressions and Boolean expressions. The semantics of them shows how a deterministic state assigns values to these expressions.

Definition 3 (Semantics of deterministic expressions). *The semantics of deterministic expressions are defined on $S = (KP, KV)$ inductively as follows:*

$$[\![x]\!]S = \begin{cases} KP(x) & \text{if } x \in Dom(KP) \\ KV(x) & \text{if } x \in Dom(KV) \\ \texttt{undecided} & \text{otherwise} \end{cases}$$

$$[\![n]\!]S = n$$
$$[\![E_1 \ aop \ E_2]\!]S = [\![E_1]\!]S \ aop \ [\![E_2]\!]S$$
$$[\![\top]\!]S = \text{TRUE}$$
$$[\![\bot]\!]S = \text{FALSE}$$
$$[\![E_1 \ rop \ E_2]\!]S = [\![E_1]\!]S \ rop \ [\![E_2]\!]S$$
$$[\![\neg B]\!]S = \neg[\![B]\!]S$$
$$[\![B_1 \ lop \ B_2]\!]S = [\![B_1]\!]S \ lop \ [\![B_2]\!]S$$

$[\![x]\!]S$ is well-defined since $KP(x) = KV(x)$ if $x \in Dom(KP) \cap Dom(KV)$. Then, we give the syntax of deterministic formulas, which are defined based on two special propositions: PKX and PASS. PKX represents that the prover knows the secret x and PASS means that on some deterministic state, the prover passes the challenge proposed by the verifier.

Definition 4 (Syntax of deterministic formulas). *The deterministic formulas are defined as follows:*

$$\varphi := PKX \mid \text{PASS} \mid \neg\varphi \mid (\varphi \wedge \varphi)$$

The syntax of deterministic formulas is much simpler than the classical one since, in the Schnorr protocol, we merely need to capture the properties involving these two propositions and their logical combinations. For example, $(\neg\text{PASS})$ represents the prover does not pass the challenge and $(\neg PKX \wedge \text{PASS})$ means that the prover cheats successfully. The syntax and semantics of deterministic expressions are used when we define the semantics of deterministic formulas.

Definition 5 (Semantics of deterministic formulas). *The semantics of deterministic formulas is defined inductively as follows:*

- $S \vDash PKX$ *iff* $KP(\mathtt{X}) = 1$.
- $S \vDash \mathsf{PASS}$ *iff* $[\![g]\!]S^{[\![s_i]\!]S}$ mod $[\![p]\!]S = [\![c_i]\!]S \cdot [\![g]\!]S^{[\![\mathtt{X}]\!]S \cdot [\![e_i]\!]S}$ mod $[\![p]\!]S$ *for every integer* $i \in [1, n]$ *such that* $\{c_i, e_i, s_i\} \subset Dom(KV)$.
- $S \vDash \neg\varphi$ *and* $S \vDash (\varphi \wedge \varphi)$ *are defined in the normal way.*

To remark, $KP(\mathtt{X}) = 1$ represents that the prover has the secret $\mathtt{X}$. The truth value of PASS is determined by whether the equations hold: the equations hold when g^{s_i} mod p $= c_i \cdot g^{\mathtt{X} \cdot e_i}$ mod p for all i. Note this naturally handles both cases that $e_i = 0$ and $e_i = 1$. When $e_i = 0$, the right side simplifies to c_i mod p, representing cases where the verifier's challenge is r_i. When $e_i = 1$, the right side is $c_i \cdot g^{\mathtt{X}}$ mod p, representing cases where the verifier's challenge is $(\mathtt{X} + r_i)$ mod $(\mathrm{p} - 1)$.

2.2 Probabilistic Expressions and Formulas

As the Schnorr protocol indicates, the probability that the prover passes the challenges continues to rise as the game rounds increase if the prover indeed has the secret. We must capture this observation using probabilistic formulas and model it through probabilistic states.

Definition 6 (Probabilistic expressions). *Let* $\mathbb{RV}$ *be a set of real variables. The real expression* r *is defined as follows:*

$$r := a \mid \delta \mid \mathbb{P}(\varphi) \mid r \ aop \ r$$

Here $a \in \mathbb{R}$ is a real number and $\delta \in \mathbb{RV}$ is a real variable. $\mathbb{P}(\varphi)$ is the probability of a deterministic assertion φ being true.

Definition 7 (Semantics of probabilistic expressions). *Given an interpretation* I *mapping real variables to real numbers and a probabilistic state* μ, $\mu : \Gamma \to [0, 1]$, *such that: (1)* Γ *is a set of deterministic states i.e.,* $\Gamma \subseteq \mathbb{S}$, *and (2)* $\sum_{S \in \Gamma} \mu(S) \leq 1$. *The semantics of real expressions is defined inductively as follows.*

$$[\![a]\!]_\mu^I = a$$
$$[\![\delta]\!]_\mu^I = I(\delta)$$
$$[\![\mathbb{P}(\varphi)]\!]_\mu^I = \sum_{S \vDash \varphi} \mu(S)$$
$$[\![r_1 \ aop \ r_2]\!]_\mu^I = [\![r_1]\!]_\mu^I \ aop \ [\![r_2]\!]_\mu^I$$

Here, $\mathbb{P}(\varphi)$ represents the probability that φ holds. It equals the sum of probabilities of all deterministic states where φ holds. Let $D(\mathbb{S})$ denote the set of all probabilistic states. Let μ_S denote the pointed distribution on a deterministic state S, which means that $\mu(S) = 1$.

Definition 8 (Syntax of probabilistic formulas). *Probabilistic formulas are defined as follows.*

$$\Phi = (r \ rop \ r) \mid \neg\Phi \mid (\Phi \wedge \Phi)$$

where r is a real expression.

For example, the formula $(\mathbb{P}(\text{PASS}) = \frac{1}{2})$ represents that the probability of passing the challenge equals $\frac{1}{2}$. We can express the properties of probabilities by probabilistic formulas.

Definition 9 (Semantics of probabilistic formulas). *Given an interpretation I, the semantics of probabilistic assertion is defined on probabilistic states μ as follows:*

- *$\mu \vDash^I r_1 \ rop \ r_2$ iff $[\![r_1]\!]_\mu^I \ rop \ [\![r_2]\!]_\mu^I$*
- *$\mu \vDash^I \neg\Phi$ iff not $\mu \vDash^I \Phi$*
- *$\mu \vDash^I (\Phi_1 \wedge \Phi_2)$ iff $\mu \vDash^I \Phi_1$ and $\mu \vDash^I \Phi_2$*

2.3   Commands

Each program consists of commands which can change the deterministic and probabilistic states. To model the randomized behaviors in ZKPs, we introduce the probabilistic assignment and the randomized choice. Additionally, to represent the exchange of information between the prover and the verifier, we also define a send command. Intuitively, each command may change the knowledge base of the prover KP or that of the verifier KV.

Definition 10 (Syntax of command expressions). *The commands are defined inductively as follows:*

$$C := \mathtt{skip} \mid x \leftarrow_A E \mid x \xleftarrow{\$}_A \mathbb{D} \mid C_1 \oplus_\rho C_2 \mid C_1; C_2 \mid \mathtt{if} \ B \ \mathtt{then} \ C_1 \ \mathtt{else} \ C_2 \mid \mathtt{Send}_{A \to B} x$$

where $A, B \in \{P, V\}$ and $A \neq B$.

We use the index A, B to denote who is performing the command. $\mathtt{Send}_{A \to B} x$ means that A sends the information x to B. In various systems of classical probabilistic Hoare logic, either probabilistic assignment or randomized choice are used since they are equivalent in most cases. However, we introduce both since we divide randomized behaviors into two types. The first is an assignment from a given probabilistic distribution $x \xleftarrow{\$}_A \mathbb{D}$. We will not interpret it in the normal way. Rather, we treat it similarly to a normal assignment since, in the ZKP protocol, we only use it to generate a value for an undecided variable *w.r.t.* some distribution. The value itself does not affect the upcoming executions. Moreover, the deterministic and probabilistic formulas that we investigated in this paper are not directly related to these values. So, a probabilistic assignment does not 'split' the execution into different branches. The second type of randomized behavior is the probabilistic choice between two programs $C_1 \oplus_\rho C_2$. It, in effect, splits the execution into two branches with probability ρ and $(1 - \rho)$.

Definition 11 (Semantics of command expressions). *The semantics of commands is a function* $[\![C]\!] \in D(\mathbb{S}) \to D(\mathbb{S})$. *For each* $\mu \in D(\mathbb{S})$ *where* $\mu : \Gamma \to [0,1] \in D(\mathbb{S})$,

- $[\![\texttt{skip}]\!](\mu) = \mu$
- $[\![x \leftarrow_P E]\!](\mu) = \sum_{S \in \Gamma} \mu(S) \cdot \mu_{S'}$, *where* $S = (KP, KV)$, $S' = (KP', KV')$, $KV' = KV$, $Dom(KP') = Dom(KP) \cup \{x\}$ *and* $KP'(x') = \begin{cases} [\![E]\!]S & \text{if } x' = x; \\ KP(x') & \text{otherwise.} \end{cases}$
- $[\![x \leftarrow_V E]\!](\mu)$ *is defined respectively.*
- $[\![x \stackrel{\$}{\leftarrow}_A \mathbb{D}]\!](\mu) = [\![x \leftarrow_A n]\!](\mu)$ *for some* $n \in \mathbb{D}$.
- $[\![C_1 \oplus_\rho C_2]\!](\mu) = \rho [\![C_1]\!](\mu) + (1 - \rho)[\![C_2]\!](\mu)$
- $[\![C_1; C_2]\!](\mu) = [\![C_2]\!]([\![C_1]\!](\mu))$
- $[\![\texttt{if } B \texttt{ then } C_1 \texttt{ else } C_2]\!](\mu) = [\![C_1]\!](\downarrow_B(\mu)) + [\![C_2]\!](\downarrow_{\neg B}(\mu))$, *where* $\downarrow_B(\mu)$ *denotes the distribution* μ *restricted to those states where* B *is true.*
- $[\![\texttt{Send}_{V \to P} x]\!](\mu) = \sum_{S \in \Gamma} \mu(S) \cdot \mu_{S'}$, *where* $S = (KP, KV)$, $S' = (KP', KV')$, $KV' = KV$, $Dom(KP') = Dom(KP) \cup \{x\}$ *and* $KP'(x') = \begin{cases} KV(x') & \text{if } x' = x; \\ KP(x') & \text{otherwise.} \end{cases}$
- $[\![\texttt{Send}_{P \to V} x]\!](\mu)$ *is defined respectively.*

We write $x \leftarrow_P E$ to denote assigning x the value of expression E in the prover's knowledge base while retaining the verifier's knowledge. Similarly to $x \leftarrow_V E$.

3   Formal Verification of the Schnorr Protocol

We present a formalization of the Schnorr protocol with our proposed probabilistic Hoare logic. We aim to give a semantic analysis of its execution process, verify its soundness and completeness, and prove the zero-knowledge property syntactically. We follow the tradition of Hoare logic to check if a Hoare triple $\{\phi\}C\{\psi\}$ holds, which means that starting from any initial state that satisfies ϕ and executing any program specification C, to check if the consequence state satisfies ψ.

3.1   Soundness and Completeness

We assume an initial state in a highly generalized scenario where the probability that the prover has the private X is given by $\mathbb{P}(PKX) = p$, while the probability that the prover does not have X is $1 - p$. Here, the parameter p represents an objective probability rather than a subjective probability since it does not represent the degree of belief of any agent. Thus, we can understand the initial state to be a mixed state as the quantum mechanism. We do not have any information on the exact probability distribution within the mixed state. This initial state satisfies the precondition $\{\mathbb{P}(PKX) = p \land \mathbb{P}(\neg PKX) = 1 - p\}$.

The Schnorr protocol can be expressed as a sequence of commands: $C_1; C_2 \oplus_{\frac{1}{2}} C_3; C_4 \oplus_{\frac{1}{2}} C_5; C_6$, where

- $C_1 : r_1 \xleftarrow{\$}_P \mathbb{D}$ (a discrete distribution over $[0, \mathrm{p} - 2]$). (The prover generates a random integer.)
- $C_2 : c_1 \leftarrow_P g^{r_1} \mod \mathrm{p}$; $\mathrm{Send}_{P \rightarrow V} c_1$. (The prover honestly computes the commitment and sends it to the verifier.)
- $C_3 : c_1 \leftarrow_P g^{r_1 - \mathrm{X}} \mod \mathrm{p}$; $\mathrm{Send}_{P \rightarrow V} c_1$. (The prover computes the commitment for cheating and sends it to the verifier.)
- $C_4 : e_1 \leftarrow_V 0$; $\mathrm{Send}_{V \rightarrow P} e_1$. (The verifier chooses the challenge 0 and sends it to the prover.)
- $C_5 : e_1 \leftarrow_V 1$, $\mathrm{Send}_{V \rightarrow P} e_1$. (The verifier chooses the challenge 1 and sends it to the prover.)
- C_6 : if $e_1 = 0$ then $(s_1 \leftarrow_P r_1; \mathrm{Send}_{P \rightarrow V} s_1)$ else $(s_1 \leftarrow_P (\mathrm{X} + r_1)$ $\mod (\mathrm{p} - 1); \mathrm{Send}_{P \rightarrow V} s_1)$. (The prover responds to the verifier according to the challenge.)

Note that the prover's action $C_2 \oplus_{\frac{1}{2}} C_3$ captures that, if the prover does not know X, the prover can only guess the verifier's challenges between r and $(\mathrm{X} + r) \mod (\mathrm{p} - 1)$ with fifty-fifty chance; if the prover knows X, he can also randomly generate a commitment c_1 and can always pass the final challenge. This randomization is necessary since any deterministic choice would fail half the time.

We strictly follow the semantics of commands to model how information propagates within each execution paths and ultimately influences the verification outcome of the protocol. The execution diagram of the first round is shown in a tree structure as Fig. 1. It begins with the initial probabilistic state, where the prover knows the secret X with probability p and does not know it with probability $1 - p$. The knowledge base of two participants are denoted as $Dom(KP)$ and $Dom(KV)$. Then, the prover generates the random number r_1, which does not split the execution into branches. Next, computing the commitment c_1 is shown as a randomized choice to capture the possible cheating performed by the prover. So, the execution is branched. The verifier will also randomly choose a challenge e_1, which brings about new branches. At last, The prover responds with s_1 based on the challenge.

After a successful execution of the first round, the postcondition to verify over the final probabilistic state is $\{\mathbb{P}(PKX \land \mathrm{PASS}) = p \land \mathbb{P}(\neg PKX \land \mathrm{PASS}) = \frac{1-p}{2} \land \mathbb{P}(\neg PKX \land \neg \mathrm{PASS}) = \frac{1-p}{2}\}$.

Every layer of the diagram represents a probabilistic state, denoted by μ_i. Each μ_i is a probabilistic distribution over some deterministic states. For example, μ_2 is a distribution over four different deterministic states. Their corresponding probabilities are marked beside. $Dom(KP_i^j)$ and $Dom(KV_i^j)$ show the information change in the knowledge base of the prover and the verifier.

The last layer μ_4 is a probability distribution over eight deterministic states. We can check that $\mu_4 \models \mathbb{P}(PKX \land \mathrm{PASS}) = \frac{1}{2}$ (prover has the secret and

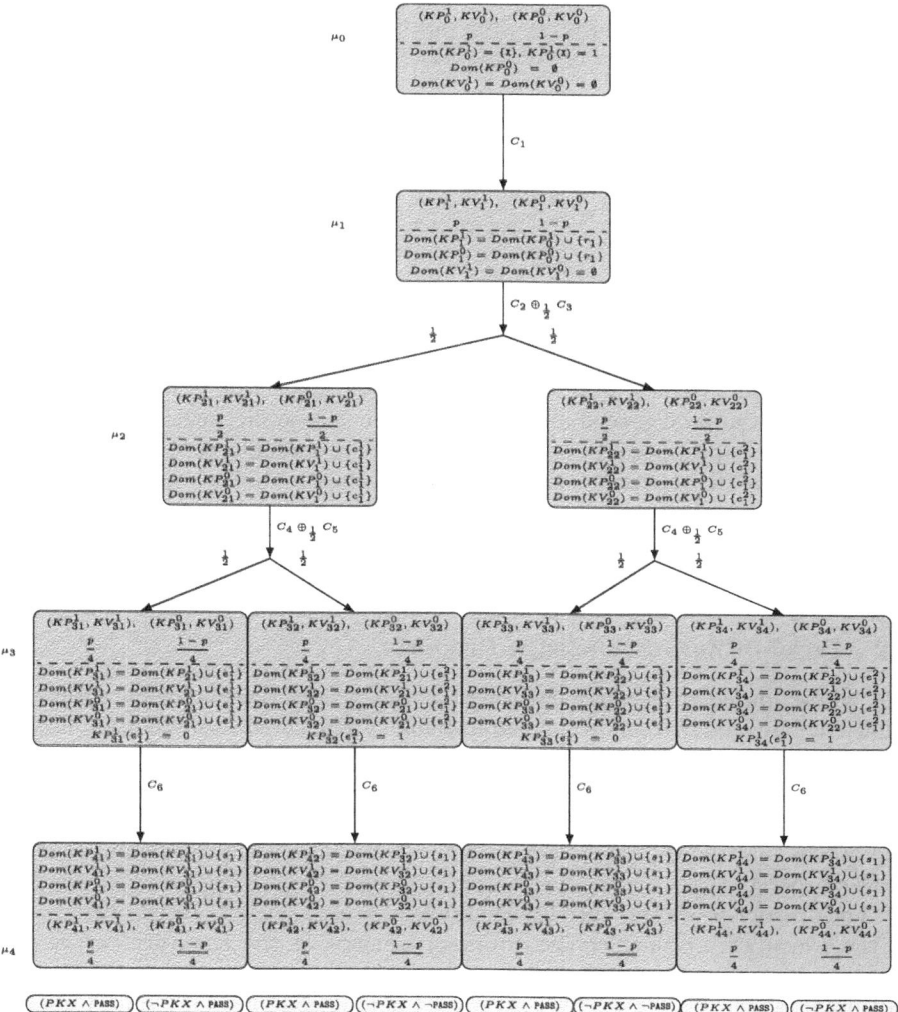

Fig. 1. The execution diagram of the Schnorr protocol in the 1st round

passes the challenge), $\mu_4 \models \mathbb{P}(\neg PKX \wedge \neg \text{PASS}) = \frac{1}{4}$ (prover has no the secret and fails the challenge), and $\mu_4 \models \mathbb{P}(\neg PKX \wedge \text{PASS}) = \frac{1}{4}$ (prover has no the secret but cheats successfully).

Therefore, we verify the Hoare triple $\{\mathbb{P}(PKX) = p \wedge \mathbb{P}(\neg PKX) = 1 - p\}$ $C\{\mathbb{P}(PKX \wedge \text{PASS}) = p \wedge \mathbb{P}(\neg PKX \wedge \text{PASS}) = \frac{1-p}{2} \wedge \iota(\neg PKX \wedge \neg \text{PASS}) = \frac{1-p}{2}\}$. Interested readers can check the diagram according to the semantics of commands and probabilistic formulas.

Theorem 1. *For any integer $n \geq 1$, the probability of passing, denoted as $\mathbb{P}(\mathsf{PASS})$, and the probability of not passing, denoted as $\mathbb{P}(\neg\mathsf{PASS})$, after n rounds are given by:*

$$\mathbb{P}(\mathsf{PASS}) = p + \frac{1-p}{2^n}, \quad \mathbb{P}(\neg\mathsf{PASS}) = (1-p)\left(1 - \frac{1}{2^n}\right).$$

The proof is omitted.

Corollary 1. *After sufficiently many rounds, the probability that the prover passes challenges $\mathbb{P}(\mathsf{PASS})$ asymptotically approaches the objective probability that the prover possesses the secret $\mathbb{P}(PKX)$.*

In particular, when $p = 0$, i.e., the prover does not actually have X, $\mathbb{P}(\mathsf{PASS})$ equals $\frac{1}{2^n}$ in the final probabilistic state. When n is sufficiently large, $\mathbb{P}(\mathsf{PASS})$ asymptotically approaches 0, indicating that the probability of the verifier being convinced that the prover has the secret approaches 0. On the other hand, when $p = 1$, i.e., the prover actually has the secret X, the probability $\mathbb{P}(\mathsf{PASS})$ almost equals 1, meaning that the prover convinces the verifier. This validates the soundness and completeness of the Schnorr protocol.

3.2 Proof of Zero-Knowledge Property

The zero-knowledge property ensures that the verifier does not gain additional knowledge beyond the validity of the statement. The classical method to disclose the property is constructing a 'simulator', which is also a piece of program and is able to construct a computationally indistinguishable transcript from that of a real protocol between the prover and the verifier [4]. This indistinguishability guarantees that the verifier cannot extract any meaningful information about the prover's secret.

The transcript of the verifier, denoted as a pair (c_1, s_1), in the first round of the execution of the Schnorr protocol consists of the commitment c_1 and the response s_1 received from the prover. A simulator is a program which aims to 'simulate' the real protocol, but it does not involve any information on the secret x. The transcripts (c_1', s_1') that the simulator generates have the same probability distribution as the real protocol generates. To prove this, we need to compare two programs, which cannot be done within the framework of the PHL. Thus, we first construct the simulator program and then show that it generates the same distribution as the real protocol on the transcript (c_1, s_1) using Product Probabilistic Relational Hoare Logic ($\times$PRHL) [9]. Unlike the standard Probabilistic Relational Hoare Logic [1,2] which compares two programs by paralleling them and describes their relationships, $\times$PRHL combines two programs into one program and treats it as the PHL. It explicitly constructs a coupled product program that generates the coupling distribution as its output to show some relationships between programs. In this way, we can reason about the distribution over the pairs and show why randomness is similar between the real protocol and the simulator.

×PRHL reasons about the judgements involving precondition, postcondition, two independent programs and one product program, which have the form:

$$\{\phi\} \begin{array}{c} c_1 \\ c_2 \end{array} \{\psi\} \blacktriangleright c_\times$$

ϕ and ψ are probabilistic formulas about pairs of probabilistic states. c_1 and c_2 are probabilistic programs to be compared in parallel. $c_\times$ is the product program, which simulates two correlated executions of c_1 and c_2.

The core inference rule in ×PRHL is [SAMPLE] shown as follows:

$$\text{SAMPLE} \;\; \frac{f : \mathbb{D}_1 \to \mathbb{D}_2 \text{ bijection}}{\{\forall v \in \mathbb{D}_1, \psi\{v, f(v)/x_1\langle 1\rangle, x_2\langle 2\rangle\}\} \begin{array}{c} x_1 \xleftarrow{\$} \mathbb{D}_1 \\ x_2 \xleftarrow{\$} \mathbb{D}_2 \end{array} \{\psi\} \blacktriangleright \begin{array}{c} x_1\langle 1\rangle \xleftarrow{\$} \mathbb{D}_1; \\ x_2\langle 2\rangle \leftarrow f(x_1\langle 1\rangle) \end{array}}$$

This rule intuitively represents that if we can construct a bijection between two probabilistic distributions, two independent probabilistic assignments can be 'coupled' by the bijection. The product program generates a random pair $(x_1\langle 1\rangle, x_2\langle 2\rangle)$ where $x_2\langle 2\rangle$ is deterministically assigned by $f(x_1\langle 1\rangle)$. More details on the notion of coupling and ×PRHL can be found in [9].

Now, we prove the zero-knowledge property of the Schnorr protocol. We first give the fragment of the real program P_1 and the simulator S_1:

$$\text{Program } P_1: \begin{array}{c} r \xleftarrow{\$} \mathbb{D} \\ c \leftarrow g^r \bmod p \end{array}, \text{Program } S_1: \begin{array}{c} r' \xleftarrow{\$} \mathbb{D} \\ c' \leftarrow (g^{r'} \cdot y^{-e}) \bmod p \end{array}.$$

First, we prove that the output distributions over commitments are equivalent. We sketch the proof by coupling. In the case of $e = 0$, we select the identity function to be the bijection $f = \text{Id}$ in the rule [SAMPLE], apply the assignment rule [ASSN], the sequence rule [SEQ] and the case analysis rule [CASE] in order.

$$\text{SAMPLE} \;\; \frac{f : \text{Id}}{\vdash \{e = 0\} \begin{array}{c} r \xleftarrow{\$} \mathbb{D} \\ r' \xleftarrow{\$} \mathbb{D} \end{array} \{r = r' \wedge e = 0\} \blacktriangleright \begin{array}{c} r \xleftarrow{\$} \mathbb{D}; \\ r' \leftarrow r \end{array}}$$

$$\text{ASSN} \;\; \frac{}{\vdash \{r = r' \wedge e = 0\} \begin{array}{c} c \leftarrow g^r \bmod p \\ c' \leftarrow (g^{r'} \cdot y^{-e}) \bmod p \end{array} \{c = c'\} \blacktriangleright \begin{array}{c} c \leftarrow g^r \bmod p \\ c' \leftarrow (g^{r'} \cdot y^{-e}) \bmod p \end{array}}$$

$$\text{SEQ} \;\; \frac{\vdash \{e = 0\} \begin{array}{c} r \xleftarrow{\$} \mathbb{D} \\ r' \xleftarrow{\$} \mathbb{D} \end{array} \{r = r' \wedge e = 0\} \blacktriangleright \begin{array}{c} r \xleftarrow{\$} \mathbb{D}; \\ r' \leftarrow r \end{array} \qquad \vdash \{r = r' \wedge e = 0\} \begin{array}{c} c \leftarrow g^r \bmod p \\ c' \leftarrow (g^{r'} \cdot y^{-e}) \bmod p \end{array} \{c = c'\} \blacktriangleright \begin{array}{c} c \leftarrow g^r \bmod p \\ c' \leftarrow (g^{r'} \cdot y^{-e}) \bmod p \end{array}}{\vdash \{e = 0\} \begin{array}{c} r \xleftarrow{\$} \mathbb{D}; c \leftarrow g^r \bmod p \\ r' \xleftarrow{\$} \mathbb{D}; c' \leftarrow (g^{r'} \cdot y^{-e}) \bmod p \end{array} \{c = c'\} \blacktriangleright \begin{array}{c} r \xleftarrow{\$} \mathbb{D}; c \leftarrow g^r \bmod p; \\ r' \leftarrow r; c' \leftarrow (g^{r'} \cdot y^{-e}) \bmod p \end{array}}$$

In the case of $e = 1$, we give the same proof except f is set to be a 'Plus k' function, *i.e.*, $f(r) = r + k$:

$$\text{SAMPLE} \ \frac{f : +k}{\vdash \{e = 1\} \ \begin{array}{c} r \xleftarrow{\$} \mathbb{D} \\ r' \xleftarrow{\$} \mathbb{D} \end{array} \ \{r' = r + k \wedge e = 1\} \ \blacktriangleright \ \begin{array}{c} r \xleftarrow{\$} \mathbb{D}; \\ r' \leftarrow r + k \end{array}}$$

$$\text{ASSN} \ \frac{}{\vdash \{r = r' + k \wedge e = 1\} \ \begin{array}{c} c \leftarrow g^r \ \text{mod p} \\ c' \leftarrow (g^{r'} \cdot y^{-e}) \ \text{mod p} \end{array} \ \{c = c'\} \ \blacktriangleright \ \begin{array}{c} c \leftarrow g^r \ \text{mod p} \\ c' \leftarrow (g^{r'} \cdot y^{-e}) \ \text{mod p} \end{array}}$$

$$\text{SEQ} \ \frac{\begin{array}{c} \vdash \{e = 1\} \ \begin{array}{c} r \xleftarrow{\$} \mathbb{D} \\ r' \xleftarrow{\$} \mathbb{D} \end{array} \ \{r' = r + k \wedge e = 1\} \ \blacktriangleright \ \begin{array}{c} r \xleftarrow{\$} \mathbb{D}; \\ r' \leftarrow r + k \end{array} \\ \vdash \{r = r' + k \wedge e = 1\} \ \begin{array}{c} c \leftarrow g^r \ \text{mod p} \\ c' \leftarrow (g^{r'} \cdot y^{-e}) \ \text{mod p} \end{array} \ \{c = c'\} \ \blacktriangleright \ \begin{array}{c} c \leftarrow g^r \ \text{mod p} \\ c' \leftarrow (g^{r'} \cdot y^{-e}) \ \text{mod p} \end{array} \end{array}}{\vdash \{e = 1\} \ \begin{array}{c} r \xleftarrow{\$} \mathbb{D}; c \leftarrow g^r \ \text{mod p} \\ r' \xleftarrow{\$} \mathbb{D}; c' \leftarrow (g^{r'} \cdot y^{-e}) \ \text{mod p} \end{array} \ \{c = c'\} \blacktriangleright \ \begin{array}{c} r \xleftarrow{\$} \mathbb{D}; \quad c \leftarrow g^r \ \text{mod p}; \\ r' \leftarrow r + k; c' \leftarrow (g^{r'} \cdot y^{-e}) \ \text{mod p} \end{array}}$$

Combining the conclusions, we have:

$$\text{CASE} \ \frac{\begin{array}{c} \vdash \{e = 0\} \ \begin{array}{c} r \xleftarrow{\$} \mathbb{D}; c \leftarrow g^r \ \text{mod p} \\ r' \xleftarrow{\$} \mathbb{D}; c' \leftarrow (g^{r'} \cdot y^{-e}) \ \text{mod p} \end{array} \ \{c = c'\} \blacktriangleright \ \begin{array}{c} r \xleftarrow{\$} \mathbb{D}; \ c \leftarrow g^r \ \text{mod p}; \\ r' \leftarrow r; \ c' \leftarrow (g^{r'} \cdot y^{-e}) \ \text{mod p} \end{array} \\ \vdash \{e = 1\} \ \begin{array}{c} r \xleftarrow{\$} \mathbb{D}; c \leftarrow g^r \ \text{mod p} \\ r' \xleftarrow{\$} \mathbb{D}; c' \leftarrow (g^{r'} \cdot y^{-e}) \ \text{mod p} \end{array} \ \{c = c'\} \blacktriangleright \ \begin{array}{c} r \xleftarrow{\$} \mathbb{D}; \ c \leftarrow g^r \ \text{mod p}; \\ r' \leftarrow r + k; c' \leftarrow (g^{r'} \cdot y^{-e}) \ \text{mod p} \end{array} \end{array}}{\vdash \{\top\} \ \begin{array}{c} r \xleftarrow{\$} \mathbb{D}; c \leftarrow g^r \ \text{mod p} \\ r' \xleftarrow{\$} \mathbb{D}; c' \leftarrow (g^{r'} \cdot y^{-e}) \ \text{mod p} \end{array} \ \{c = c'\} \blacktriangleright \ \begin{array}{l} \text{if } e = 0 \text{ then} \ \begin{array}{c} r \xleftarrow{\$} \mathbb{D}; \ c \leftarrow g^r \ \text{mod p}; \\ r' \leftarrow r; \ c' \leftarrow (g^{r'} \cdot y^{-e}) \ \text{mod p} \end{array} \\ \text{else} \ \begin{array}{c} r \xleftarrow{\$} \mathbb{D}; \ c \leftarrow g^r \ \text{mod p}; \\ r' \leftarrow r + k; c' \leftarrow (g^{r'} \cdot y^{-e}) \ \text{mod p} \end{array} \end{array}}$$

Note that $c = c'$ as the postcondition implies that the commitment c generated by the prover and the commitment c' generated by the simulator are probabilistically equivalent, which means that they follow the same probability distribution.

The postcondition $c = c'$ holds because the product program couples the randomness of the real prover's execution and the simulator through a bijection, ensuring that for every possible output, the distributions of c and c' are equivalent. Since the bijection guarantees a one-to-one correspondence between the random choices in both programs, the resulting distributions over c and c' are probabilistically indistinguishable, even though the simulator runs without knowing the secret X.

Similarly, to prove the output distribution over responses s_1 are equivalent, we consider the real program P_2 and the simulator S_2: Program P_2:

$$r \xleftarrow{\$} \mathbb{D}$$
$$s \leftarrow (e \cdot x + r) \mod (p-1)$$
, Program S_2:
$$r' \xleftarrow{\$} \mathbb{D}$$
$$s' \leftarrow r' \mod (p-1)$$
.

The proof is similar. The key difference lies in the case where $e = 1$. The bijection f to be constructed should be replaced by an additive coupling $f(r) = r + a$, with $a \in \mathbb{Z}$. This ensures that the response distribution remains under modular arithmetic. The full proof is omitted.

4   Conclusion

In this paper, we formally verified the soundness and completeness of a zero-knowledge protocol, the Schnorr protocol, using a refined probabilistic Hoare logic. By semantic analysis on the execution tree of the protocol and syntactic reasoning by ×PRHL, we demonstrated that a ZKP protocol can be treated as a method to expose the unknown objective probability that the prover holds the secret, without disclosing any extra information. Unlike methods based on epistemic logic, our approach sacrifices strong expressiveness in knowledge to support simpler probabilistic reasoning. We chose this trade-off because completeness and soundness can be established through probabilistic reasoning. Moreover, we aim to prove the zero-knowledge property via computational indistinguishability rather than perfect indistinguishability. Our method enhances the feasibility of formal verification for existing software.

In future work, we plan to relax the constraints of zero-knowledge and explore interactive proofs. This direction could be particularly intriguing if we consider scenarios where the verifier can gain more information about the secret by issuing additional challenges. The interplay between revealing and concealing the secret suggests more sophisticated aspects of communication and information exchange.

References

1. Barthe, G., Grégoire, B., Zanella Béguelin, S.: Formal certification of code-based cryptographic proofs. In: Proceedings of the 36th annual ACM SIGPLAN-SIGACT symposium on Principles of programming languages. pp. 90–101 (2009)
2. Barthe, G., Katoen, J.P., Silva, A.: Foundations of probabilistic programming. Cambridge University Press (2020)
3. Den Hartog, J., de Vink, E.P.: Verifying probabilistic programs using a hoare like logic. Int. J. Found. Comput. Sci. **13**(03), 315–340 (2002)
4. Fiege, U., Fiat, A., Shamir, A.: Zero knowledge proofs of identity. In: Proceedings of the nineteenth annual ACM symposium on Theory of computing. pp. 210–217 (1987)
5. Goldwasser, S., Micali, S., Rackoff, C.: The knowledge complexity of interactive proof systems. SIAM J. Comput. **18**(1), 186–208 (1989). https://doi.org/10.1137/0218012
6. Halpern, J.Y., Pass, R., Raman, V.: An epistemic characterization of zero knowledge. In: Proceedings of the 12th Conference on Theoretical Aspects of Rationality and Knowledge. pp. 156–165 (2009)

7. Hoare, C.A.R.: An axiomatic basis for computer programming. Commun. ACM **12**(10), 576–580 (1969)
8. Hoare, C.A.R.: Procedures and parameters: An axiomatic approach. In: Symposium on semantics of algorithmic languages. pp. 102–116. Springer (2006)
9. Hsu, J.: Probabilistic couplings for probabilistic reasoning. University of Pennsylvania (2017)
10. Jaramillo, M.C.: Epistemic logics for cryptographic protocols and zero-knowledge proofs (2021)
11. Lehnherr, D., Ognjanović, Z., Studer, T.: A logic of interactive proofs. J. Log. Comput. **32**(8), 1645–1658 (2022)
12. Schnorr, C.P.: Efficient identification and signatures for smart cards. In: Advances in Cryptology–CRYPTO'89 Proceedings 9. pp. 239–252. Springer (1990)

On a Second-Order Version of Russellian Theory of Definite Descriptions

Yaroslav Petrukhin$^{(\boxtimes)}$

University of Łódź, Lindleya 3/5, 90-131 Łódź, Poland
yaroslav.petrukhin@gmail.com

Abstract. Definite descriptions are first-order expressions that denote unique objects. In this paper, we propose a second-order counterpart, designed to refer to unique relations between objects. We investigate this notion within the framework of Russell's theory of definite descriptions. While full second-order logic is incomplete, its fragment defined by Henkin's general models admits completeness. We develop our theory within this fragment and formalize it using a cut-free sequent calculus.

Keywords: Definite descriptions · Second order logic · Proof theory · Lambda-abstraction · Sequent calculi · Cut admissibility

1 Introduction

Definite descriptions are usually expressed as first-order constructs in the form $\iota x \varphi$, where ι is a term-forming operator, x is an individual variable, and φ is a formula. The core idea behind definite descriptions is to denote the unique object x that satisfies the formula φ. In this work, we propose a second-order extension of this concept: $\iota X \varphi$, where X is a relational variable. Such expressions are meant to signify the unique *relation* for which the formula φ holds true.

First-order quantifiers deal with objects, whereas second-order quantifiers concern the properties of objects or relations between objects. We utilize this relationship between first-order and second-order quantifiers when introducing second-order definite descriptions. It is noteworthy that prior efforts have been made to examine definite descriptions in the realm of second- or higher-order logics, as conducted by Makarenko and Benzmüller [18]. Nonetheless, in their analysis, definite descriptions continue to function as first-order expressions pertaining to objects.

Let us present several examples of the second-order definite descriptions. The first example is the transitive closure of a graph: ιR TransitiveClosure(R, G). This describes the unique binary relation R that forms the transitive closure of the edge relation in graph G. The expression

$$\iota P \; (\mathsf{Path}(P, a, b, G) \land \forall P' \, (\mathsf{Path}(P', a, b, G) \rightarrow \mathsf{Length}(P) \leq \mathsf{Length}(P')))$$

represents 'the shortest path relation between two nodes a and b in graph G', where P is a path (represented as a relation), and the description denotes the

G. Casini et al. (Eds.): JELIA 2025, LNAI 16094, pp. 313–326, 2026.
https://doi.org/10.1007/978-3-032-04590-4_21

unique shortest path from node a to node b in graph G. The connectivity relation in a graph can be formalized as $\iota R \ (\forall x \forall y \ (R(x, y) \leftrightarrow \exists P \ \mathsf{Path}(P, x, y, \ G)))$. Finally, the expression $\iota R \ (\mathsf{TotalOrder}(R) \wedge \forall x \forall y \ (P(x, y) \rightarrow R(x, y)))$ denotes the total order extending a given partial order P, assuming such an extension is unique.

Russellian theory of definite descriptions [23,32] is arguably one of the most recognized and frequently accepted, notwithstanding the criticism it has received. It possesses several disadvantages; nevertheless, there are methods to mitigate at least some of them. We follow the presentation of Russellian theory as articulated by Indrzejczak and Zawidzki [14] and Indrzejczak and Kürbis [13]. In Russellian theory, definite descriptions are characterized by the following formula, where ψ must be limited to atomic formulas, unless additional mechanisms are introduced to mark scope distinctions:

$$\psi(\iota y \varphi) \leftrightarrow \exists x(\forall y(\varphi \leftrightarrow y = x) \wedge \psi)$$

Indrzejczak, Zawidzki, and Kürbis' approach characterize them with the help of λ-operator as follows:

$$(\lambda x \psi)\iota y \varphi \leftrightarrow \exists x(\forall y(\varphi \leftrightarrow y = x) \wedge \psi)$$

This approach allows both complex and primitive predicates to be applied to definite descriptions while avoiding scope-related issues. In particular, it helps us answer the question: in the negated expression $\neg \psi(\iota y, \varphi)$, does the negation apply to the entire expression, or solely to ψ? Whitehead and Russell, seeing the issue, proposed the method of scope distinctions [32]. Nonetheless, it is recognized for its clumsiness. One may attempt to circumvent the issue by limiting the formulas to atomic ones; however, this considerably diminishes the expressive capacity of Russellian theory. Nonetheless, this methodology has been employed by Kalish, Montague, and Mar [15] as well as Francez and Więckowski [3] in their natural deduction systems, and Indrzejczak [12] in his cut-free sequent calculus. Another concept has been proposed by Kürbis [16]. He implements a binary quantifier represented as $Ix[\varphi, \psi]$. This resolves the issues; but, if one wants to consider definite descriptions as terms, an alternative approach is required. This inspired Indrzejczak, Zawidzki, and Kürbis [13,14] to apply predicate abstracts of the form $\lambda x \varphi$ ('the property of being φ') to terms, including definite descriptions, to obtain formulas called lambda atoms. They observe that predicate abstracts built by means of the lambda-operator have been previously utilized by Stalnaker and Thomason [25], Bressan [2], Fitting [4], Scales [24], Fitting and Mendelsohn [5], and Indrzejczak [9].

Another source for motivation for the introduction of λ is that if ψ is complex in the Russelian formula characterizing definite descriptions, one may readily encounter a contradiction. The application of λ addresses this problem, while a similar outcome could be attained through the adoption of free logic (rendering the entire theory deductively weaker and incapable of inferring contradictions; see, e.g. [10]) or the utilization of paraconsistent logic [20].

This study adheres to the framework established by Indrzejczak and Kürbis [13] in presenting the semantics and employs their cut-free sequent calculus, which is adequate with respect to this semantics. We extend their approach by incorporating second-order quantifiers, a second-order variant of identity, and ultimately a second-order interpretation of lambda terms and definite descriptions. Unlike them, we do not provide a constructive proof of the cut admissibility theorem, as we believe this subject, due to its complexity, requires a separate paper.[1] However, we provide a semantic proof of this statement obtained as a consequence of a Hintikka-style completeness proof in the spirit of [1,17].

The structure of the paper is as follows. Section 2 introduces the languages and semantics of the logics under consideration. In Sect. 3, we present the corresponding sequent calculi and prove soundness, completeness, and cut admissibility. Section 4 concludes the paper.

2 Languages and Semantics

We start with a description of the logic **RL** from [13,14], which corresponds to the formulation of the Russellian theory involving λ discussed above.

The language $\mathcal{L}$ of **RL** is a standard first-order language with identity and without function symbols, but supplied with λ and ι. The language is built from two disjoint sets of symbols: VAR, representing variables, and PAR, representing parameters. In the proof-theoretic framework of **RL**, elements of VAR are used exclusively as bound variables, while PAR provides the symbols for free variables. The language contains the set CON of constant symbols as well. In contrast, the semantic framework does not enforce this distinction. The basic terms of the language consist of variables, parameters, and constants. Additionally, we allow expressions formed using the definite description operator ι applied to predicate abstracts. These are referred to as quasi-terms. "We mention only the following formation rules for the more general notion of a formula used in the semantics" [13, p. 115]:

- If P^n is an n-ary predicate symbol (including $=$) and $t_1,\ldots,t_n \in VAR \cup PAR \cup CON$, then $P^n(t_1,\ldots,t_n)$ is a formula (atomic formula).
- If φ is a formula and $x \in VAR$, then $(\lambda x\varphi)$ is a predicate abstract.
- If φ is a formula and $x \in VAR$, then $\iota x\varphi$ is a quasi-term.
- If φ is a predicate abstract and t a term or quasi-term, then φt is a formula (lambda atom).

We write $\mathcal{F}$ for the set of all formulas of $\mathcal{L}$, $x, y, z, x_1, \ldots$ for the members of VAR, $a, b, c, a_1, \ldots$ for the elements of PAR, $k, k_1, k_2, \ldots$ for the elements of

---

[1] The cut admissibility theorem for second- and higher-order logics has remained an unresolved issue in proof theory for an extended duration, referred to as Takeuti's conjecture [28]. Various scholars, utilizing distinct methodologies, reached a positive resolution: Tait [26], Prawitz [21], Takahashi [29], Girard [6]. See also Takeuti [27] and Rathjen and Sieg [22] on this issue. Developing a syntactic constructive proof remains an open problem.

CON, φ_t^x for the result of replacing x by t in φ, and, similarly, $\varphi_{t_1,\ldots,t_n}^{x_1,\ldots,x_n}$ for the result of a simultaneous replacing $x_1,\ldots,x_n$ by $t_1,\ldots,t_n$ in φ. When t is a variable y, we assume that y is free for x in φ, meaning that the substitution does not cause any formerly free occurrence of y to become bound within φ. We presume a similar condition for $\varphi_{t_1,\ldots,t_n}^{x_1,\ldots,x_n}$.

The semantics of **RL**. We define the notion of a model, following [13, p. 115f]. A *model* is a structure $M = \langle D, I \rangle$, where for each n-argument predicate P^n, $I(P^n) \subseteq D^n$. An *assignment* v is a function $v : VAR \cup PAR \to D$. An *x-variant* v' of v agrees with v on all arguments, save possibly x. We write v_o^x to denote the x-variant of v with $v_o^x(x) = o$. The notion of *satisfaction* of a formula φ *with* v, in symbols $M, v \models \varphi$, is defined as follows, where $t \in VAR \cup PAR \cup CON$:

$$M, v \models P^n(t_1,\ldots,t_n) \text{ iff } \langle v(t_1),\ldots,v(t_n)\rangle \in I(P^n)$$
$$M, v \models t_1 = t_2 \text{ iff } v(t_1) = v(t_2)$$
$$M, v \models (\lambda x \psi)t \text{ iff } M, v_o^x \models \psi, \text{ where } o = v(t)$$
$$M, v \models (\lambda x \psi)\iota y \varphi \text{ iff there is an } o \in D \text{ such that } M, v_o^x \models \psi,$$
$$M, v_o^x \models \varphi_x^y, \text{ and for any } y\text{-variant } v' \text{ of } v_o^x,$$
$$\text{if } M, v' \models \varphi, \text{ then } v'(y) = o$$
$$M, v \models \neg\varphi \text{ iff } M, v \not\models \varphi$$
$$M, v \models \varphi \wedge \psi \text{ iff } M, v \models \varphi \text{ and } M, v \models \psi$$
$$M, v \models \forall x \varphi \text{ iff } M, v_o^x \models \varphi, \text{ for all } o \in D.$$

The truth conditions for $\vee$, $\to$, $\leftrightarrow$, and $\exists$ are standard. As for the constants, we postulate that $I(k) \in D$, for each constant k. The notions of satisfiable and valid formulas are defined in a standard way. The consequence relation is understood as follows, for all $\Gamma \subseteq \mathcal{F}$ and $A \in \mathcal{F}$: $\Gamma \models_{\mathbf{RL}} \varphi$ iff in every model M and every assignment v, if $M, v \models \psi$, for all $\psi \in \Gamma$, then $M, v \models \varphi$.

Let us now describe the logic $\mathbf{RL}^2$, a second-order generalization of $\mathbf{RL}$.

The language $\mathscr{L}$ of $\mathbf{RL}^2$ is a second-order extension of $\mathcal{L}$. In addition to individual variables and parameters, we have the sets $VAR^2 = \{X, Y, Z, X_1, \ldots\}$ and $PAR^2 = \{A, B, C, A_1, \ldots\}$ of n-ary relational variables and parameters, respectively (unary ones might be called property variables and parameters). As in the first-order case, this distinction is important for proof theory, but might be relaxed in the case of semantics. In addition to individual constants, we have the set $CON^2 = \{K, K_1, K_2, \ldots\}$ of relational constants. They represent fixed n-ary relations over individual constants. The terms are constants and individual variables/parameters. Notice that relational variables/parameter are not terms. Atomic formulas are as follows: $t_1 = t_2$, $P(t_1,\ldots,t_n)$, $X = Y$, and $X(t_1,\ldots,t_n)$, if $t_1,\ldots,t_n$ are terms, P is an n-ary relation symbol, and X and Y are n-ary relational variables/parameters.[2] In addition to the above described atomic and first-order formulas, we define the following ones:

---

[2] The formula $X = Y$ is understood as $\forall x_1 \ldots \forall x_n (X(x_1,\ldots,x_n) \leftrightarrow Y(x_1,\ldots,x_n))$. The formula $t_1 = t_2$ might be defined as $\forall X(X(t_1) \leftrightarrow X(t_2))$.

- If φ is a formula and $X \in VAR^2$, then $\forall X \varphi$ and $\exists X \varphi$ are formulas.
- If φ is a formula and $X \in VAR^2$, then $(\lambda X \varphi)$ is a *relational* abstract.
- If φ is a formula and $X \in VAR^2$, then $\iota X \varphi$ is a *pseudo*-term.
- If φ is a relational abstract and t is a pseudo-term, then φt is a formula.

We write $\mathscr{F}$ for the set of all formulas of $\mathscr{L}$, φ_P^X for the result of replacing X by a predicate symbol P in φ.

The first version of the semantics (without a complete calculus). In a model $M = \langle D, I \rangle$, an assignment v should be redefined as follows[3]: $v(x) \in D$, for $x \in VAR \cup PAR$, and $v(X) \subseteq D^n$, for $X \in VAR^2 \cup PAR^2$, an X-*variant* v' of v agrees with v on all arguments, save possibly X. We write v_O^X to denote the X-variant of v with $v_O^X(X) = O$, where $O \subseteq D^n$. The definition of the notion of satisfaction of a formula φ with v is extended by the following cases, where $t \in VAR \cup PAR$:

$$M, v \models X(t_1, \ldots, t_n) \text{ iff } \langle v(t_1), \ldots, v(t_n) \rangle \in v(X), \text{ if } X \text{ is } n\text{-ary,}$$

$$M, v \models X = Y \text{ iff } v(X) = v(Y),$$

$$M, v \models (\lambda X \psi)\iota Y \varphi \text{ iff there is an } O \subseteq D^n \text{ such that } M, v_O^X \models \psi,$$
$$M, v_O^X \models \varphi_X^Y, \text{ and for any } Y\text{-variant } v' \text{ of } v_O^X,$$
$$\text{if } M, v' \models \varphi, \text{ then } v'(Y) = O$$

$$M, v \models \forall X \varphi \text{ iff } M, v_O^X \models \varphi, \text{ for all } O \subseteq D^n,$$

$$M, v \models \exists X \varphi \text{ iff } M, v_O^X \models \varphi, \text{ for some } O \subseteq D^n.$$

This semantics lacks the completeness theorem. In order to obtain this theorem, we need to deal with a fragment of the second-order logic: we should restrict the interpretations of the relational variables/parameters. Henkin's [7] concept of a general model will help us with this issue.

The second version of the semantics (with a complete calculus). The semantics of $\mathbf{RL^2}$. Although second-order logic is known to be incomplete, there exists a fragment that is complete with respect to general models [7] (see [31] for more details). A *general model* is a pair $\mathfrak{M} = \langle M, G \rangle$, where $M = \langle D, I \rangle$ is a model and G is a set of relations on D, each of which is a subset of D^n for some $n \geq 1$; that is, $G \subseteq \bigcup_{n \geq 1} \mathcal{P}(D^n)$. Notice that $v(X) \in G \subseteq \mathcal{P}(D^n)$. We define the notion of satisfaction of a formula φ with v in a general model, symbolically $\mathfrak{M}, v \models \varphi$, for second-order formulas as follows:

$$\mathfrak{M}, v \models X(t_1, \ldots, t_n) \text{ iff } \langle v(t_1), \ldots, v(t_n) \rangle \in v(X), \quad \text{if } X \text{ is } n\text{-ary,}$$

$$\mathfrak{M}, v \models X = Y \text{ iff } v(X) = v(Y),$$

$$\mathfrak{M}, v \models (\lambda X \psi)\iota Y \varphi \text{ iff there is an } O \in G \text{ such that } \mathfrak{M}, v_O^X \models \psi,$$
$$\mathfrak{M}, v_O^X \models \varphi_X^Y, \text{ and for any } Y\text{-variant } v' \text{ of } v_O^X,$$
$$\text{if } \mathfrak{M}, v' \models \varphi, \text{ then } v'(Y) = O$$

$$\mathfrak{M}, v \models \forall X \varphi \text{ iff } \mathfrak{M}, v_O^X \models \varphi, \text{ for all } O \in G,$$

$$\mathfrak{M}, v \models \exists X \varphi \text{ iff } \mathfrak{M}, v_O^X \models \varphi, \text{ for some } O \in G.$$

---

[3] Formally, this makes v a function with a dependent domain.

Notice that each relational constant K^n corresponds to a set of n-tuples of individual constants, and is interpreted as an element of the general model domain $G \subseteq \mathcal{P}(D^n)$. By this concept, we understand the elements of G to be syntactically named via relational constants, allowing us to treat them as concrete surrogates for second-order values during the construction of canonical models.

The notions of a satisfiable formula and a valid formula are defined in a standard way. The consequence relation is defined as follows, for all $\Gamma \subseteq \mathscr{F}$ and $\varphi \in \mathscr{F}$: $\Gamma \models_{\mathbf{RL^2}} \varphi$ iff in every general model $\mathfrak{M}$ and every assignment v, if $\mathfrak{M}, v \models \psi$, for all $\psi \in \Gamma$, then $\mathfrak{M}, v \models \varphi$. This can be extended to the multiple-conclusion consequence relation: for all $\Gamma, \Delta \subseteq \mathscr{F}$, $\Gamma \models_{\mathbf{RL^2}} \Delta$ iff in every general model $\mathfrak{M}$ and every assignment v, if $\mathfrak{M}, v \models \psi$, for all $\psi \in \Gamma$, then $\mathfrak{M}, v \models \chi$, for some $\chi \in \Delta$. A sequent is an ordered pair written as $\Gamma \Rightarrow \Delta$, where Γ and Δ are finite multisets of formulas. We write $\models_{\mathbf{RL^2}} \Gamma \Rightarrow \Delta$ iff $\Gamma \models_{\mathbf{RL^2}} \Delta$. If $\mathcal{S}$ is a set of sequents and H is a sequent, we write $\mathcal{S} \models_{\mathbf{RL^2}} H$ iff $\models_{\mathbf{RL^2}} S$, for all $S \in \mathcal{S}$, implies $\models_{\mathbf{RL^2}} H$.

3   Sequent Calculi. Soundness, Completeness, and Cut Admissibility

On Figs. 1 and 2, we present sequent calculi for $\mathbf{RL}$ and $\mathbf{RL^2}$, respectively. The sequent calculus for $\mathbf{RL}$ is due to Indrzejczak and Kürbis [13]; it is an extension of the calculus G1c of Troelstra and Schwichtenberg [30] by rules for identity and lambda atoms.

If $\mathcal{S}$ is a set of sequents and H is a sequent, we write $\mathcal{S} \vdash_{\mathbf{RL^2}} H$ iff there is a proof of H from $\mathcal{S}$ in $\mathbf{RL^2}$, i.e. there exists a tree whose nodes are sequents such that the leaves are either axioms or members of $\mathcal{S}$, the root is H, and each node is obtained from its immediate predecessors by an application of a rule from the calculus. If $\mathcal{S}$ is a set of sequents and H is a sequent, then we write $\mathcal{S} \vdash_{\mathbf{RL^2}}^{cf} H$ iff $\mathcal{S} \vdash_{\mathbf{RL^2}} H$ and each cut is on a formula that belongs to $\mathcal{S}$. Two examples of proofs in $\mathbf{RL^2}$ are presented in the proof of the subsequent proposition.

Proposition 1. *The following rules are derivable (with the help of the cut rule) in the sequent calculus for* $\mathbf{RL^2}$, *where* $\mathscr{A}$ *is an atomic formula:*

$$(=^2 +)\ \frac{X = X, \Gamma \Rightarrow \Delta}{\Gamma \Rightarrow \Delta} \qquad (=^2 -)\ \frac{\mathscr{A}_C^X, \Gamma \Rightarrow \Delta}{B = C, \mathscr{A}_B^X, \Gamma \Rightarrow \Delta}$$

Proof. Consider the following proofs in $\mathbf{RL^2}$.

$$\frac{\dfrac{X_{a_1,\dots,a_n}^{x_1,\dots,x_n} \Rightarrow X_{a_1,\dots,a_n}^{x_1,\dots,x_n} \qquad X_{a_1,\dots,a_n}^{x_1,\dots,x_n} \Rightarrow X_{a_1,\dots,a_n}^{x_1,\dots,x_n}}{(\text{Cut})\ \dfrac{}{\Rightarrow X = X}} (\Rightarrow =^2) }{\Gamma \Rightarrow \Delta} \qquad X = X, \Gamma \Rightarrow \Delta$$

$$\frac{\dfrac{\dfrac{\mathscr{A}_B^X \Rightarrow \mathscr{A}_B^X}{\mathscr{A}_B^X \Rightarrow \mathscr{A}_B^X, \mathscr{A}_C^X} (\Rightarrow W) \qquad \dfrac{\dfrac{\mathscr{A}_C^X \Rightarrow \mathscr{A}_C^X}{\mathscr{A}_C^X, \mathscr{A}_B^X \Rightarrow \mathscr{A}_C^X} (W \Rightarrow)}{B = C, \mathscr{A}_B^X \Rightarrow \mathscr{A}_C^X} (=^2 \Rightarrow)}{(\text{Cut})\ \dfrac{}{B = C, \mathscr{A}_B^X, \Gamma \Rightarrow \Delta}} \qquad \mathscr{A}_C^X, \Gamma \Rightarrow \Delta$$

$$(\text{Cut}) \ \frac{\Gamma \Rightarrow \Delta, \varphi \quad \varphi, \Pi \Rightarrow \Sigma}{\Gamma, \Pi \Rightarrow \Delta, \Sigma} \qquad (\text{AX}) \ \varphi \Rightarrow \varphi \qquad (\text{W}\Rightarrow) \ \frac{\Gamma \Rightarrow \Delta}{\varphi, \Gamma \Rightarrow \Delta}$$

$$(\Rightarrow \text{W}) \ \frac{\Gamma \Rightarrow \Delta}{\Gamma \Rightarrow \Delta, \varphi} \qquad (\text{C}\Rightarrow) \ \frac{\varphi, \varphi, \Gamma \Rightarrow \Delta}{\varphi, \Gamma \Rightarrow \Delta} \qquad (\Rightarrow \text{C}) \ \frac{\Gamma \Rightarrow \Delta, \varphi, \varphi}{\Gamma \Rightarrow \Delta, \varphi}$$

$$(\wedge \Rightarrow) \ \frac{\varphi, \psi, \Gamma \Rightarrow \Delta}{\varphi \wedge \psi, \Gamma \Rightarrow \Delta} \qquad (\Rightarrow \wedge) \ \frac{\Gamma \Rightarrow \Delta, \varphi \quad \Gamma \Rightarrow \Delta, \psi}{\Gamma \Rightarrow \Delta, \varphi \wedge \psi} \qquad (\neg \Rightarrow) \ \frac{\Gamma \Rightarrow \Delta, \varphi}{\neg\varphi, \Gamma \Rightarrow \Delta}$$

$$(\vee \Rightarrow) \ \frac{\varphi, \Gamma \Rightarrow \Delta \quad \psi, \Gamma \Rightarrow \Delta}{\varphi \vee \psi, \Gamma \Rightarrow \Delta} \qquad (\Rightarrow \vee) \ \frac{\Gamma \Rightarrow \Delta, \varphi, \psi}{\Gamma \Rightarrow \Delta, \varphi \vee \psi} \qquad (\Rightarrow \neg) \ \frac{\varphi, \Gamma \Rightarrow \Delta}{\Gamma \Rightarrow \Delta, \neg\varphi}$$

$$(\rightarrow \Rightarrow) \ \frac{\Gamma \Rightarrow \Delta, \varphi \quad \psi, \Gamma \Rightarrow \Delta}{\varphi \rightarrow \psi, \Gamma \Rightarrow \Delta} \qquad (\Rightarrow \rightarrow) \ \frac{\varphi, \Gamma \Rightarrow \Delta, \psi}{\Gamma \Rightarrow \Delta, \varphi \rightarrow \psi} \qquad (\forall \Rightarrow) \ \frac{\varphi_b^x, \Gamma \Rightarrow \Delta}{\forall x \varphi, \Gamma \Rightarrow \Delta}$$

$$(\leftrightarrow \Rightarrow) \ \frac{\Gamma \Rightarrow \Delta, \varphi, \psi \quad \varphi, \psi, \Gamma \Rightarrow \Delta}{\varphi \leftrightarrow \psi, \Gamma \Rightarrow \Delta} \qquad (\Rightarrow \forall) \ \frac{\Gamma \Rightarrow \Delta, \varphi_a^x}{\Gamma \Rightarrow \Delta, \forall x \varphi} \qquad (\Rightarrow \exists) \ \frac{\Gamma \Rightarrow \Delta, \varphi_b^x}{\Gamma \Rightarrow \Delta, \exists x \varphi}$$

$$(\Rightarrow \leftrightarrow) \ \frac{\varphi, \Gamma \Rightarrow \Delta, \psi \quad \psi, \Gamma \Rightarrow \Delta, \varphi}{\Gamma \Rightarrow \Delta, \varphi \leftrightarrow \psi} \qquad (\exists \Rightarrow) \ \frac{\varphi_a^x, \Gamma \Rightarrow \Delta}{\exists x \varphi, \Gamma \Rightarrow \Delta} \qquad (= +) \ \frac{b = b, \Gamma \Rightarrow \Delta}{\Gamma \Rightarrow \Delta}$$

$$(= -) \ \frac{\mathscr{A}_c^x, \Gamma \Rightarrow \Delta}{b = c, \mathscr{A}_b^x, \Gamma \Rightarrow \Delta} \qquad (\lambda \Rightarrow) \ \frac{\psi_b^x, \Gamma \Rightarrow \Delta}{(\lambda x \psi)b, \Gamma \Rightarrow \Delta} \qquad (\Rightarrow \lambda) \ \frac{\Gamma \Rightarrow \Delta, \psi_b^x}{\Gamma \Rightarrow \Delta, (\lambda x \psi)b}$$

$$(\iota_1 \Rightarrow) \ \frac{\varphi_a^y, \psi_a^x, \Gamma \Rightarrow \Delta}{(\lambda x \psi)\iota y \varphi, \Gamma \Rightarrow \Delta} \qquad (\iota_2 \Rightarrow) \ \frac{\Gamma \Rightarrow \Delta, \varphi_b^y \quad \Gamma \Rightarrow \Delta, \varphi_c^y \quad b = c, \Gamma \Rightarrow \Delta}{(\lambda x \psi)\iota y \varphi, \Gamma \Rightarrow \Delta}$$

$$(\Rightarrow \iota) \ \frac{\Gamma \Rightarrow \Delta, \varphi_b^y \quad \Gamma \Rightarrow \Delta, \psi_b^x \quad \varphi_a^y, \Gamma \Rightarrow \Delta, a = b}{\Gamma \Rightarrow \Delta, (\lambda x \psi)\iota y \varphi}$$

where a is a fresh parameter (*Eigenvariable*), not present in Γ, Δ and φ, whereas b, c are arbitrary parameters. $\mathscr{A}$ in $(= -)$ is an atomic formula.

Fig. 1. Sequent calculus for **RL**

$\square$

Proposition 2 *([13], Lemma 1). The following two statements hold in* **RL**:

- $\vdash_{\mathbf{RL}} b_1 = b_2, \varphi_{b_1}^x \Rightarrow \varphi_{b_2}^x$, *for any formula* φ,
- *if* $\vdash_{\mathbf{RL}}^n \Gamma \Rightarrow \Delta$, *then* $\vdash_{\mathbf{RL}}^n \Gamma_{b_2}^{b_1} \Rightarrow \Delta_{b_2}^{b_1}$, *where n is the height of a proof.*

Proposition 3. *The following two statements hold in* **RL²**:

- $\vdash_{\mathbf{RL^2}} B_1 = B_2, \varphi_{B_1}^X \Rightarrow \varphi_{B_2}^X$, *for any formula* φ,
- *if* $\vdash_{\mathbf{RL^2}}^n \Gamma \Rightarrow \Delta$, *then* $\vdash_{\mathbf{RL^2}}^n \Gamma_{B_2}^{B_1} \Rightarrow \Delta_{B_2}^{B_1}$, *where n is the height of a proof.*

Proof. Similarly to [13, Lemma 1].

$$(=^2\Rightarrow)\ \frac{\Gamma\Rightarrow\Delta,X^{x_1,\ldots,x_n}_{b_1,\ldots,b_n},Y^{x_1,\ldots,x_n}_{b_1,\ldots,b_n}\quad X^{x_1,\ldots,x_n}_{b_1,\ldots,b_n},Y^{x_1,\ldots,x_n}_{b_1,\ldots,b_n},\Gamma\Rightarrow\Delta}{X=Y,\Gamma\Rightarrow\Delta}$$

$$(\Rightarrow=^2)\ \frac{X^{x_1,\ldots,x_n}_{a_1,\ldots,a_n},\Gamma\Rightarrow\Delta,Y^{x_1,\ldots,x_n}_{a_1,\ldots,a_n}\quad Y^{x_1,\ldots,x_n}_{a_1,\ldots,a_n},\Gamma\Rightarrow\Delta,X^{x_1,\ldots,x_n}_{a_1,\ldots,a_n}}{\Gamma\Rightarrow\Delta,X=Y}$$

$$(\exists^2\Rightarrow)\ \frac{\varphi^X_A,\Gamma\Rightarrow\Delta}{\exists X\varphi,\Gamma\Rightarrow\Delta}\qquad(\Rightarrow\exists^2)\ \frac{\Gamma\Rightarrow\Delta,\varphi^X_B}{\Gamma\Rightarrow\Delta,\exists X\varphi}\qquad(\iota^2_1\Rightarrow)\ \frac{\varphi^Y_A,\psi^X_A,\Gamma\Rightarrow\Delta}{(\lambda X\psi)\iota Y\varphi,\Gamma\Rightarrow\Delta}$$

$$(\forall^2\Rightarrow)\ \frac{\varphi^X_B,\Gamma\Rightarrow\Delta}{\forall X\varphi,\Gamma\Rightarrow\Delta}\qquad(\iota^2_2\Rightarrow)\ \frac{\Gamma\Rightarrow\Delta,\varphi^Y_B\quad\Gamma\Rightarrow\Delta,\varphi^Y_C\quad B=C,\Gamma\Rightarrow\Delta}{(\lambda X\psi)\iota Y\varphi,\Gamma\Rightarrow\Delta}$$

$$(\Rightarrow\forall^2)\ \frac{\Gamma\Rightarrow\Delta,\varphi^X_A}{\Gamma\Rightarrow\Delta,\forall X\varphi}\qquad(\Rightarrow\iota^2)\ \frac{\Gamma\Rightarrow\Delta,\varphi^Y_B\quad\Gamma\Rightarrow\Delta,\psi^X_B\quad\varphi^Y_A,\Gamma\Rightarrow\Delta,A=B}{\Gamma\Rightarrow\Delta,(\lambda X\psi)\iota Y\varphi}$$

where $a_1,\ldots,a_n$ are fresh individual parameters, not present in Γ and Δ; $b_1,\ldots,b_n$ are arbitrary individual parameters; A is a fresh relational parameter, not present in Γ,Δ and φ; B and C are arbitrary relational parameters.

Fig. 2. RL^2 extends **RL** by the following second-order rules.

Theorem 1. *All the rules of* **RL^2** *are sound.*

Proof. By a routine check. For the case of **RL** see [13]. $\qquad\blacksquare$

As for our completeness proof, we follow the Hintikka-style strategy originally described in [1,17] for hypersequent calculi for some non-classical first-order logics. We adapt this proof for the second-order case. Readers interested in further details on the Hintikka-style approach to completeness proofs may consult [8,11]. Notice that the Henkin-style completness proof for **RL** is given in [13].

Definition 1 *([1], Definition 4.9). An* extended sequent *is an ordered pair of (possibly infinite) sets of formulas. Given two extended sequents $S_1=\Gamma_1\Rightarrow\Delta_1$ and $S_2=\Gamma_2\Rightarrow\Delta_2$, we write $S_1\sqsubseteq S_2$ if $\Gamma_1\subseteq\Gamma_2$ and $\Delta_1\subseteq\Delta_2$. An extended sequent is called* finite *if it consists of finite sets of formulas.*

Definition 2 *([1], Definition 4.11; extended for the second-order quantifiers and $=$, ι, and λ). An extended sequent $\Gamma\Rightarrow\Delta$ admits the* witness property *if the following hold (recall that parameters play the role of free variables):*

(1) If $\forall x\varphi\in\Delta$, then $\varphi^x_k\in\Delta$, for some individual constant k.
(2) If $\exists x\varphi\in\Gamma$, then $\varphi^x_k\in\Gamma$, for some individual constant k.
(3) If $\forall X\varphi\in\Delta$, then $\varphi^X_K\in\Delta$, for some relational constant K.
(4) If $\exists X\varphi\in\Gamma$, then $\varphi^X_K\in\Gamma$, for some relational constant K.
(5) If $(\lambda x\psi)\iota y\varphi\in\Gamma$, then $\varphi^y_k\in\Gamma$ and $\psi^x_k\in\Gamma$, for some individual constant k.
(6) If $(\lambda x\psi)\iota y\varphi\in\Delta$, then for each individual parameter b, $\varphi^y_b\in\Delta$, or $\psi^x_b,\in\Delta$, or for some individual constant k, $k=b\in\Delta$ and $\varphi^y_k\in\Gamma$.

(7) If $(\lambda X\psi)\iota Y\varphi \in \Gamma$, then $\varphi_K^Y, \psi_K^X \in \Gamma$, for some relational constant K.
(8) If $(\lambda X\psi)\iota Y\varphi \in \Delta$, then for each relational parameter B, $\varphi_B^Y \in \Delta$, or $\psi_B^X \in \Delta$, or for some relational constant K, $K = B \in \Delta$ and $\varphi_K^Y \in \Gamma$.
(9) If $X = Y \in \Delta$, then either $(X^n(k_1, \ldots, k_n) \in \Gamma$ and $Y^n(k_1, \ldots, k_n) \in \Delta)$ or $(Y^n(k_1, \ldots, k_n) \in \Gamma$ and $X^n(k_1, \ldots, k_n) \in \Delta)$, for some individual constants $k_1, \ldots, k_n$.

Definition 3 *([1], Definition 4.12; adapted for the case of ordinary sequents). Let $\Gamma \Rightarrow \Delta$ be an extended sequent and S be a set of sequents.*

(1) $\Gamma \Rightarrow \Delta$ is called S-consistent if $S \nvdash_{\mathbf{RL^2}}^{cf} H$, for every sequent $H \sqsubseteq \Gamma \Rightarrow \Delta$.
(2) $\Gamma \Rightarrow \Delta$ is internally S-maximal with respect to an $\mathscr{L}$-formula φ iff:
    (a) If $\varphi \notin \Gamma$, then $\Gamma, \varphi \Rightarrow \Delta$ is not S-consistent.
    (b) If $\varphi \notin \Delta$, then $\Gamma \Rightarrow \Delta, \varphi$ is not S-consistent.
(3) $\Gamma \Rightarrow \Delta$ is called internally S-maximal if it is internally S-maximal with respect to any $\mathscr{L}$-formula.
(4) $\Gamma \Rightarrow \Delta$ is called S-maximal if it is S-consistent, internally S-maximal, and it admits the witness property.

Lemma 1 *[1, Lemma 4.13][17, Proposition 41]. Let $\Gamma \Rightarrow \Delta$ be an extended sequent that is internally S-maximal with respect to an $\mathscr{L}$-formula φ. Then:*

(1) If $\varphi \notin \Gamma$, then $S \vdash_{\mathbf{RL^2}}^{cf} \Theta, \varphi \Rightarrow \Lambda$ for some sequent $\Theta \Rightarrow \Lambda \sqsubseteq \Gamma \Rightarrow \Delta$.
(2) If $\varphi \notin \Delta$, then $S \vdash_{\mathbf{RL^2}}^{cf} \Theta \Rightarrow \Lambda, \varphi$ for some sequent $\Theta \Rightarrow \Lambda \sqsubseteq \Gamma \Rightarrow \Delta$.

Proof. By an adaptation of the proof of Proposition 41 from [17]. □

Lemma 2 *[1, Lemma 4.15][17, Lemma 43]. Let S be a set of sequents and let $\Gamma \Rightarrow \Delta$ be a S-consistent finite extended sequent. Then, there exists a S-consistent finite extended sequent $\Gamma' \Rightarrow \Delta'$ such that $\Gamma \subseteq \Gamma'$ and $\Delta \subseteq \Delta'$ and $\Gamma' \Rightarrow \Delta'$, and $\Gamma' \Rightarrow \Delta'$ admits the witness property.*

Proof. Similarly to [17, Lemma 43]. If $\forall x\varphi \in \Delta$, we take a fresh individual constant k and add the formula φ_k^x to Δ. If $\exists x\varphi \in \Gamma$, we again take a fresh constant k and add the formula φ_k^x to Γ. Similarly, we proceed for the second-order quantification, $=$, ι, and λ. We continue this procedure until the obtained extended sequent admits the witness property. Since the set of formulas in the sequent $\Gamma \Rightarrow \Delta$ is finite, and at each step the added formula is either a subformula or a witness-instantiated variant of an existing formula – where witness instantiations are limited to a finite set of constants and predicate names – the number of possible new formulas is finite as well. Furthermore, formulas are added only once. Therefore, the saturation procedure must terminate after a finite number of steps. The finite extended sequent $\Gamma' \Rightarrow \Delta'$ is produced from $\Gamma \Rightarrow \Delta$ through this method. We will demonstrate that each such extension preserves the S-consistency of the extended sequent.

Suppose that $(\lambda X\psi)\iota Y\varphi \in \Delta$. Let $\Gamma' \Rightarrow \Delta'$ be the extended sequent obtained from $\Gamma \Rightarrow \Delta$ by adding φ_B^Y, ψ_B^X, and $K = B$ to Δ and φ_K^Y to Γ, where K is a relational constant that does not occur in $\Gamma \Rightarrow \Delta$. Assume for the contradiction that $\Gamma' \Rightarrow \Delta'$ is not S-consistent. By Lemma 1, there are sequents $\Theta \Rightarrow \Lambda, \Pi \Rightarrow \Sigma, \Upsilon \Rightarrow \Phi, \Psi \Rightarrow \Omega \sqsubseteq \Gamma \Rightarrow \Delta$ such that $S \vdash^{cf}_{\mathbf{RL^2}} \Theta \Rightarrow \Lambda, \varphi^Y_B, S \vdash^{cf}_{\mathbf{RL^2}} \Pi \Rightarrow \Sigma, \psi^X_B,$ $S \vdash^{cf}_{\mathbf{RL^2}} \varphi^Y_K, \Upsilon \Rightarrow \Phi,$ and $S \vdash^{cf}_{\mathbf{RL^2}} \Psi \Rightarrow \Omega, K = B$. By weakening, we get $S \vdash^{cf}_{\mathbf{RL^2}}$ $\varphi^Y_K, \Upsilon \Rightarrow \Phi, K = B$ (or one could get $S \vdash^{cf}_{\mathbf{RL^2}} \varphi^Y_K, \Psi \Rightarrow \Omega, K = B$). Applying weakening and $(\Rightarrow \iota^2)$, we obtain $S \vdash^{cf}_{\mathbf{RL^2}} \Theta, \Pi, \Upsilon \Rightarrow \Lambda, \Sigma, \Phi, (\lambda X \psi) \iota Y \varphi$. This contradicts the fact that $\Gamma \Rightarrow \Delta$ is S-consistent.

The other cases are considered similarly.   □

Lemma 3 *[1, Lemma 4.16][17, Lemma 44].* *Let S be a set of sequents and H be a S-consistent finite extended sequent. Let φ be an $\mathcal{L}$-formula. Then, there exists a S-consistent finite extended sequent H' such that:*

  – $H \subseteq H'$,
  – H' *is internally S-maximal with respect to* φ,
  – H' *admits the witness property.*

Proof. Similarly to the proof of Lemma 44 from [17].   □

Lemma 4 *[1, Lemma 4.17][17, Lemma 45].* *Let S be a set of sequents. Every S-consistent sequent can be extended to a S-maximal extended sequent $\Gamma \Rightarrow \Delta$.*

Proof. Similarly to the proof of Lemma 45 from [17].   □

Theorem 2 (strong completeness of $\mathbf{RL^2}$). *Let S be a set of sequents and H be a sequent. If $S \models_{\mathbf{RL^2}} H$, then $S \vdash^{cf}_{\mathbf{RL^2}} H$.*

Proof. Suppose that $S \nvdash^{cf}_{\mathbf{RL^2}} H$. By Lemma 4, there exists a S-maximal extended sequent $\Gamma \Rightarrow \Delta$ such that $H \sqsubseteq \Gamma \Rightarrow \Delta$. Using $\Gamma \Rightarrow \Delta$, we construct a structure $M = \langle D, I \rangle$. D is the set of equivalence classes of terms. We denote the equivalence class to which a term t belongs by $[t]$. For all individual variables $v(x) = [x]$, for all individual parameters $v(a) = [a]$, for all individual constants, $I(k) = [k]$. For all predicate letters (including $=$), $\langle [t_1], \ldots, [t_n] \rangle \in I(P^n)$ iff $P^n(t_1, \ldots, t_n) \in \Gamma$. We construct a general structure $\mathfrak{M} = \langle M, G \rangle$ as follows: M is defined above and G is a set of subsets on D. As for relational variables, parameters, and constants, we postulate that $v(X) \in G$, $v(A) \in G$, and $I(K) \in G$. For all relational variables, $\langle [t_1], \ldots, [t_n] \rangle \in v(X^n)$ iff $X^n(t_1, \ldots, t_n) \in \Gamma$. We prove the following two statements together by induction on the complexity of χ:

(a) If $\chi \in \Gamma$ then $\mathfrak{M}, v \models \chi$.
(b) If $\chi \in \Delta$ then $\mathfrak{M}, v \nvDash \chi$.

  χ is $t_1 = t_2$. (a) $\mathfrak{M}, v \models t_1 = t_2$ iff $v(t_1) = v(t_2)$ iff $[t_1] = [t_2]$ and as these are equivalence classes, iff $t_1 = t_2 \in \Gamma$. (b) If $t_1 = t_2 \in \Delta$, $t_1 = t_2 \notin \Gamma$, since $S \nvdash^{cf}_{\mathbf{RL^2}} H$. Then $[t_1] \neq [t_2]$. Hence, $v(t_1) \neq v(t_2)$. Thus, $\mathfrak{M}, v \models t_1 \neq t_2$.
  χ is $X^n(t_1, \ldots, t_n)$. (a) $\mathfrak{M}, v \models X^n(t_1, \ldots, t_n)$ iff $\langle [t_1], \ldots, [t_n] \rangle \in v(X^n)$ iff $X^n(t_1, \ldots, t_n) \in \Gamma$. (b) If $X^n(t_1, \ldots, t_n) \in \Delta$, then $X^n(t_1, \ldots, t_n) \notin \Gamma$, since $S \nvdash^{cf}_{\mathbf{RL^2}} H$. Then $\langle [t_1], \ldots, [t_n] \rangle \notin v(X^n)$. Hence, $\mathfrak{M}, v \nvDash X^n(t_1, \ldots, t_n)$.

χ is $\varphi \leftrightarrow \psi$. (a) Assume that $\varphi \leftrightarrow \psi \in \Gamma$. Suppose that ($\varphi \notin \Gamma$ or $\psi \notin \Gamma$) and ($\varphi \notin \Delta$ or $\psi \notin \Delta$). By Lemma 1, there are sequents $\Theta \Rightarrow \Lambda$ and $\Pi \Rightarrow \Sigma$ such that $\Theta \Rightarrow \Lambda, \Pi \Rightarrow \Sigma \sqsubseteq \Gamma \Rightarrow \Delta$ as well as $\mathcal{S} \vdash_{\mathbf{RL^2}}^{cf} \varphi, \psi, \Theta \Rightarrow \Lambda$ and $\mathcal{S} \vdash_{\mathbf{RL^2}}^{cf} \Pi \Rightarrow \Sigma, \varphi, \psi$. By weakening and ($\leftrightarrow\Rightarrow$), $\mathcal{S} \vdash_{\mathbf{RL^2}}^{cf} \varphi \leftrightarrow \psi, \Theta, \Pi \Rightarrow \Lambda, \Sigma$. This contradicts the $\mathcal{S}$-consistency of $\Gamma \Rightarrow \Delta$. Hence, either $\varphi, \psi \in \Gamma$ or $\varphi, \psi \in \Delta$. Thus, by the induction hypothesis, either ($\mathfrak{M}, v \models \varphi$ and $\mathfrak{M}, v \models \psi$) or ($\mathfrak{M}$, v $\not\models \varphi$ and $\mathfrak{M}, v \not\models \psi$). Therefore, $\mathfrak{M}, v \models \varphi \leftrightarrow \psi$.

(b) Assume that $\varphi \leftrightarrow \psi \in \Delta$. Suppose that ($\varphi \notin \Gamma$ or $\psi \notin \Delta$) and ($\psi \notin \Gamma$ or $\varphi \notin \Delta$). By Lemma 1, there are sequents $\Theta \Rightarrow \Lambda$ and $\Pi \Rightarrow \Sigma$ such that $\Theta \Rightarrow \Lambda, \Pi \Rightarrow \Sigma \sqsubseteq \Gamma \Rightarrow \Delta$ as well as $\mathcal{S} \vdash_{\mathbf{RL^2}}^{cf} \varphi, \Theta \Rightarrow \Lambda, \psi$ and $\mathcal{S} \vdash_{\mathbf{RL^2}}^{cf} \psi, \Pi \Rightarrow \Sigma, \varphi$. By weakening and ($\Rightarrow\leftrightarrow$), $\mathcal{S} \vdash_{\mathbf{RL^2}}^{cf} \Theta, \Pi \Rightarrow \Lambda, \Sigma, \varphi \leftrightarrow \psi$. This contradicts the $\mathcal{S}$-consistency of $\Gamma \Rightarrow \Delta$. Hence, either ($\varphi \in \Gamma$ and $\psi \in \Delta$) or ($\psi \in \Gamma$ and $\varphi \in \Delta$). Thus, by the induction hypothesis, either ($\mathfrak{M}, v \models \varphi$ and $\mathfrak{M}, v \not\models \psi$) or ($\mathfrak{M}, v \not\models \varphi$ and $\mathfrak{M}, v \models \psi$). Therefore, $\mathfrak{M}, v \not\models \varphi \leftrightarrow \psi$.

χ is $\exists X\varphi$. (a) Assume that $\exists X\varphi \in \Gamma$. By the witness property of $\Gamma \Rightarrow \Delta$, there exists a relational constant K such that $\varphi_K^X \in \Gamma$. By the induction hypothesis, $\mathfrak{M}, v \models \varphi_K^X$. Since $K \in G$, it holds that $\mathfrak{M}, v \models \exists X\varphi$.

(b) Assume that $\mathfrak{M}, v \models \exists X\varphi$. We show that $\exists X\varphi \notin \Delta$. By definition, there exists some $O \in G$ such that $\mathfrak{M}, v \models \varphi_O^X$. By the induction hypothesis, $\varphi_O^X \notin \Delta$. By Lemma 1, there exist a sequent $\Theta \Rightarrow \Lambda \sqsubseteq \Gamma \Rightarrow \Delta$ such that $\mathcal{S} \vdash_{\mathbf{RL^2}}^{cf} \Theta \Rightarrow \Lambda, \varphi_O^X$. By the rule ($\Rightarrow \exists^2$), $\mathcal{S} \vdash_{\mathbf{RL^2}}^{cf} \Theta \Rightarrow \Lambda, \exists X\varphi$. Since $\Gamma \Rightarrow \Delta$ is $\mathcal{S}$-consistent, $\exists X\varphi \notin \Delta$.

χ is $X = Y$. (a) Assume that $X = Y \in \Gamma$. Suppose that there are $o_1, \dots, o_n \in D$ such that ($X^n(o_1, \dots, o_n) \notin \Gamma$ or $Y^n(o_1, \dots, o_n) \notin \Gamma$) and ($X^n(o_1, \dots, o_n) \notin \Delta$ or $Y^n(o_1, \dots, o_n) \notin \Delta$). By Lemma 1, there are sequents $\Theta \Rightarrow \Lambda, \Pi \Rightarrow \Sigma \sqsubseteq \Gamma \Rightarrow \Delta$ such that $\mathcal{S} \vdash_{\mathbf{RL^2}}^{cf} X^n(o_1, \dots, o_n), Y^n(o_1, \dots, o_n), \Theta \Rightarrow \Lambda$ and $\mathcal{S} \vdash_{\mathbf{RL^2}}^{cf} \Pi \Rightarrow \Sigma, X^n(o_1, \dots, o_n), Y^n(o_1, \dots, o_n)$. By the rules of weakening and ($=^2\Rightarrow$), $\mathcal{S} \vdash_{\mathbf{RL^2}}^{cf} X = Y, \Theta, \Pi \Rightarrow \Lambda, \Sigma$. This contradicts the $\mathcal{S}$-consistency of $\Gamma \Rightarrow \Delta$. Therefore, for all $o_1, \dots, o_n \in D$, either ($X^n(o_1, \dots, o_n) \in \Gamma$ and $Y^n(o_1, \dots, o_n) \in \Gamma$) or ($X^n(o_1, \dots, o_n) \in \Delta$ and $Y^n(o_1, \dots, o_n) \in \Delta$). Thus, by the induction hypothesis, either ($\mathfrak{M}, v \models X^n(o_1, \dots, o_n)$ and $\mathfrak{M}, v \models Y^n(o_1, \dots, o_n)$) or ($\mathfrak{M}, v \not\models X^n(o_1, \dots, o_n)$ and $\mathfrak{M}, v \not\models Y^n(o_1, \dots, o_n)$). Therefore, it holds that either ($\langle [o_1], \dots, [o_n] \rangle \in v(X^n)$ and $\langle [o_1], \dots, [o_n] \rangle \in v(Y^n)$) or ($\langle [o_1], \dots, [o_n] \rangle \notin v(X^n)$ and $\langle [o_1], \dots, [o_n] \rangle \notin v(Y^n)$). Hence, $v(X) = v(Y)$. Thus, $\mathfrak{M}, v \models X = Y$.

(b) Assume that $X = Y \in \Delta$. By the witness property of $\Gamma \Rightarrow \Delta$, there are individual constants $k_1, \dots, k_n \in D$ such that either ($X^n(k_1, \dots, k_n) \in \Gamma$ and $Y^n(k_1, \dots, k_n) \in \Delta$) or ($Y^n(k_1, \dots, k_n) \in \Gamma$ and $X^n(k_1, \dots, k_n) \in \Delta$). Thus, by the induction hypothesis, either ($\mathfrak{M}, v \models X^n(k_1, \dots, k_n)$ and $\mathfrak{M}, v \not\models Y^n(k_1, \dots, k_n)$) or ($\mathfrak{M}, v \models Y^n(k_1, \dots, k_n)$ and $\mathfrak{M}, v \not\models X^n(k_1, \dots, k_n)$). Hence, ($\langle [k_1], \dots, [k_n] \rangle \in v(X^n)$ and $\langle [k_1], \dots, [k_n] \rangle \notin v(Y^n)$) or ($\langle [k_1], \dots, [k_n] \rangle \in v(Y^n)$ and $\langle [k_1], \dots, [k_n] \rangle \notin v(X^n)$). Therefore, $v(X) \neq v(Y)$. Hence, $\mathfrak{M}, v \not\models X = Y$.

χ is $\lambda X\psi(\iota Y\varphi)$. (a) Assume that $\lambda X\psi(\iota Y\varphi) \in \Gamma$. By the witness property of $\Gamma \Rightarrow \Delta$, there exists a relational constant K such that $\varphi_K^Y, \psi_K^X \in \Gamma$.

By the induction hypothesis, $\mathfrak{M}, v \models \varphi_K^Y$ and $\mathfrak{M}, v \models \psi_K^X$. Suppose that for some $O_1, O_2 \in G$, $\varphi_{O_1}^Y, \varphi_{O_2}^Y \notin \Delta$ and $O_1 = O_2 \notin \Gamma$. By Lemma 1, there are sequents $\Theta \Rightarrow \Lambda, \Pi \Rightarrow \Sigma, \Upsilon \Rightarrow \Phi \sqsubseteq \Gamma \Rightarrow \Delta$ such that $\mathcal{S} \vdash_{\mathbf{RL^2}}^{cf} \Theta \Rightarrow \Lambda, \varphi_{O_1}^Y$, $\mathcal{S} \vdash_{\mathbf{RL^2}}^{cf} \Pi \Rightarrow \Sigma, \varphi_{O_2}^Y$, and $\mathcal{S} \vdash_{\mathbf{RL^2}}^{cf} O_1 = O_2, \Upsilon \Rightarrow \Phi$. By weakening and the rule $(\iota_2^2 \Rightarrow)$, $\mathcal{S} \vdash_{\mathbf{RL^2}}^{cf} \lambda X \psi(\iota\, Y\varphi), \Theta, \Pi, \Upsilon \Rightarrow \Lambda, \Sigma, \Phi$. This contradicts the $\mathcal{S}$-consistency of $\Gamma \Rightarrow \Delta$. Therefore, for all $O_1, O_2 \in G$, $\varphi_{O_1}^Y \in \Delta$, or $\varphi_{O_2}^Y \in \Delta$, or $O_1 = O_2 \in \Gamma$. Hence, by the induction hypothesis, either, for all $O_1, O_2 \in G$, $\mathfrak{M}, v \not\models \varphi_{O_1}^Y$, or $\mathfrak{M}, v \not\models \varphi_{O_2}^Y$, or $\mathfrak{M}, v \models O_1 = O_2$. Consequently, for all $O_1, O_2 \in G$, if $\mathfrak{M}, v \models \varphi_{O_1}^Y$ and $\mathfrak{M}, v \models \varphi_{O_2}^Y$, then $\mathfrak{M}, v \models O_1 = O_2$. Thus, for any Y-variant v' of v_K^X, if $\mathfrak{M}, v' \models \varphi$, then $v'(Y) = K$. Since $\mathfrak{M}, v \models \varphi_K^Y$ and $\mathfrak{M}, v \models \psi_K^X$, we obtain $\mathfrak{M}, v_K^X \models \psi$ and $\mathfrak{M}, v_K^X \models \varphi_X$. So there is $K \in G$ such that $\mathfrak{M}, v_K^X \models \psi$, $\mathfrak{M}, v_K^X \models \varphi_X$, and for any Y-variant v' of v_K^X, if $\mathfrak{M}, v' \models \varphi$, then $v'(Y) = K$. Hence, $\mathfrak{M}, v \models \lambda X \psi(\iota\, Y\varphi)$.

(b) Assume that $\lambda X \psi(\iota Y \varphi) \in \Delta$. By the witness property of $\Gamma \Rightarrow \Delta$, for each each relational parameter B, $\varphi_B^Y \in \Delta$, or $\psi_B^X \in \Delta$, or for some relational constant K, $\left(K = B \in \Delta \text{ and } \varphi_K^Y \in \Gamma \right)$. By the induction hypothesis, for each relational parameter B, $\mathfrak{M}, v \not\models \varphi_B^Y$, or $\mathfrak{M}, v \not\models \psi_B^X$, or for some relational constant K, $\left(\mathfrak{M}, v \not\models K = B \text{ and } \mathfrak{M}, v \models \varphi_K^Y \right)$. Therefore, $\mathfrak{M}, v \not\models \lambda X \psi(\iota Y \varphi)$.

The other cases are treated similarly.

Then one needs to show that $\mathfrak{M}$ is a model of $\mathcal{S}$ but not of H. This can be done by the same technique as in [17, Theorem 48].   □

Theorem 3. *For every sequent* $\Gamma \Rightarrow \Delta$, $\vdash_{\mathbf{RL^2}} \Gamma \Rightarrow \Delta$ *implies that there exists a cut-free derivation of* $\Gamma \Rightarrow \Delta$ *in* $\mathbf{RL^2}$.

Proof. Follows from Theorem 2.   □

4   Conclusion. Subjects for Future Research

The most apparent avenue for further research is the development of second-order variants of other theories of definite descriptions. This approach could be further generalized to examine higher-order theories of definite descriptions. Another route is to consider the modifications of Russellian theory of DD with a non-classical foundation. For example, in [20], a version of Russellian theory based on Nelson's paraconsistent logic was introduced. One could try to develop its second- or higher-order version. Rather than adopting alternative theories, one can consider remaining within $\mathbf{RL^2}$ and conducting additional investigation: for example, one could try to find a constructive proof of cut admissibility for this logic, building upon the existing proof for $\mathbf{RL}$ as presented in [13].

Acknowledgments. I would like to express my sincere gratitude and appreciation to Olena Dubchak for the everlasting inspiration. I am grateful to the anonymous reviewers for their insightful and constructive comments, which helped to improve the presentation of the paper. Funded by the European Union (ERC, ExtenDD, project number: 101054714). Views and opinions expressed are however those of the author(s) only and do not necessarily reflect those of the European Union or the European Research Council. Neither the European Union nor the granting authority can be held responsible for them.

References

1. Avron, A., Lahav, O.: A simple cut-free system for a paraconsistent logic equivalent to S5. In: Advances in Modal Logic, vol. 12, pp. 29–42. College Publications (2018)
2. Bressan, A.: A General Interpreted Modal Calculus. Yale University Press, Yale (1972)
3. Francez, N., Więckowski, B.: A proof-theoretic semantics for contextual definiteness. In: Moriconi, E., Tesconi, L. (eds.) Proceedings of the Second Pisa Colloquium in Logic, Language and Epistemology, pp. 181–212. Edizioni ETS, Pisa (2014)
4. Fitting, M.: A modal logic epsilon-calculus. Notre Dame J. Form. Log. **16**(1), 1–16 (1975)
5. Fitting, M., Mendelsohn, R.L.: First-Order Modal Logic. Synthese Library, vol. 277. Springer, Dordrecht (1998). https://doi.org/10.1007/978-3-031-40714-7
6. Girard, J.-Y.: Une extension de l'interprétation de Gödel à l'analyse et son application à l'élimination des coupures dans l'analyse et la théorie des types. In: Fenstad, J.E. (ed.) Proceedings of the Second Scandinavian Logic Symposium. Studies in Logic and the Foundations of Mathematics, vol. 63, pp. 63–92. North-Holland, Amsterdam (1971)
7. Henkin, L.: Completeness in the theory of types. J. Symb. Log. **15**(2), 81–91 (1950)
8. Indrzejczak, A.: Linear time in hypersequent framework. Bull. Symb. Log. **22**(1), 121–144 (2016)
9. Indrzejczak, A.: Existence, definedness and definite descriptions in hybrid modal logic. In: Olivetti, N., Verbrugge, R., Negri, S., Sandu, G. (eds.) Advances in Modal Logic, vol. 13. College Publications (2020)
10. Indrzejczak, A.: Free definite description theory - sequent calculi and cut elimination. Log. Log. Philos. **29**(4), 505–539 (2020)
11. Indrzejczak, A.: Sequents and Trees. An Introduction to the Theory and Applications of Propositional Sequent Calculi. Birkhäuser, Cham (2021)
12. Indrzejczak, A.: Russellian definite description theory – a proof-theoretic approach. Rev. Symb. Log. **16**(2), 624–649 (2023)
13. Indrzejczak, A., Kürbis, N.: A cut-free, sound and complete Russellian theory of definite descriptions. In: Ramanayake, R., Urban, J. (eds.) Automated Reasoning with Analytic Tableaux and Related Methods. TABLEAUX 2023, LNCS, vol. 14278, pp. 112–130. Springer, Cham (2023). https://doi.org/10.1007/978-3-031-43513-3_7
14. Indrzejczak, A., Zawidzki, M.: When iota meets lambda. Synthese **201**(2), 1–33 (2023)
15. Kalish, D., Montague, R., Mar, G.: Logic. Techniques of Formal Reasoning, 2nd edn. Oxford University Press, New York, Oxford (1980)

16. Kürbis, N.: A binary quantifier for definite descriptions in intuitionist negative free logic: natural deduction and normalization. Bull. Sect. Log. **48**(2), 81–97 (2019)
17. Lahav, O., Avron, A.: A semantic proof of strong cut-admissibility for first-order Gödel logic. J. Log. Comput. **23**(1), 59–86 (2013)
18. Makarenko, I., Benzmüller, C.: Positive free higher-order logic and its automation via a semantical embedding. In: Schmid, U., Klügl, F., Wolter, D. (eds.) KI 2020. LNCS (LNAI), vol. 12325, pp. 116–131. Springer, Cham (2020). https://doi.org/10.1007/978-3-030-58285-2_9
19. Manzano, M.: Extensions of First Order Logic. Cambridge Tracts in Theoretical Computer Science, vol. 19. Cambridge University Press, Cambridge (1996)
20. Petrukhin, Y.: A binary quantifier for definite descriptions in Nelsonian free logic. In: Indrzejczak, A., Zawidzki, M. (eds.) Proceedings Eleventh International Conference on Non-Classical Logics. Theory and Applications, EPTCS, vol. 415, pp. 5–15 (2024)
21. Prawitz, D.: Hauptsatz for higher order logic. J. Symb. Log. **33**, 452–457 (1968)
22. Rathjen, M., Sieg, S.: Proof theory. In: Stanford Encyclopedia of Philosophy. https://plato.stanford.edu/entries/proof-theory/#Bib. Accessed 10 Feb 2025
23. Russell, B.: On denoting. Mind **14**, 479–493 (1905)
24. Scales, R.: Attribution and Existence. Ph.D. Dissertation. University of California, Irvine (1969)
25. Stalnaker, R.C., Thomason, R.H.: Abstraction in first-order modal logic. Theoria **34**(3), 203–207 (1968)
26. Tait, W.W.: A nonconstructive proof of Gentzen's Hauptsatz for second order predicate logic. Bull. Am. Math. Soc. **72**, 980–983 (1966)
27. Takeuti, G.: Proof Theory. North-Holland, Amsterdam, American Elsevier, New York (1975)
28. Takeuti, G.: On a generalized logic calculus. Jpn. J. Math. **23**, 39–96 (1953). An erratum was published in Jpn. J. Math. **24**, 149–156 (1954)
29. Takahashi, M.: A proof of cut-elimination in simple type theory. J. Math. Soc. Jpn. **19**(4) (1967)
30. Troelstra, A.S., Schwichtenberg, H.: Basic Proof Theory. Oxford University Press, Oxford (1996)
31. Väänänen, J.: Second-order and Higher-order logic. In: Stanford Encyclopedia of Philosophy. https://plato.stanford.edu/entries/logic-higher-order/. Accessed 29 Jan 2025
32. Whitehead, A.N., Russell, B.: Principia Mathematica, vol. I. Cambridge University Press, Cambridge (1910)

Author Index

© The Editor(s) (if applicable) and The Author(s), under exclusive license to Springer Nature Switzerland AG 2026
G. Casini et al. (Eds.): JELIA 2025, LNAI 16094, pp. 327–328, 2026.
https://doi.org/10.1007/978-3-032-04590-4

The manufacturer's authorised representative in the EU is Springer
Nature Customer Service Centre GmbH, Europaplatz 3, 69115 Heidelberg,
Germany. If you have any concerns regarding our products, please
contact ProductSafety@springernature.com

Printed and bound by CPI Group (UK) Ltd, Croydon, CR0 4YY

28/04/2026

02098518-0007